The Hindu H

The Hindu History

A.K. Mazumdar

Introduction by T.N. Chaturvedi

RUPA

Published by
Rupa Publications India Pvt. Ltd 2008
7/16, Ansari Road, Daryaganj
New Delhi 110002

Sales centres:
Allahabad Bengaluru Chennai
Hyderabad Jaipur Kathmandu
Kolkata Mumbai

ISBN: 978-81-291-1576-8

Twelfth impression 2022

15 14 13 12

Typeset by Mindways Design, New Delhi

Printed in India

CONTENTS

THREE

PREFACE TO THE FIRST EDITION

The title of this book is my own. It is, perhaps, a more dignified title than the work properly deserves. I should tell my readers, at the very outset, that I am not appearing before the public as a rival to my illustrious countryman, the late Mr Romesh Chand Dutt whose *Ancient India* is a highly admirable book; nor, to Mr VA Smith whose *Early History of India* is an inimitable work. In 1891, my headmaster, the late Sri Raj Sahen Ratnamani Gupta of the Dacca Collegiate School desired me to write a history of our nation. Following his wish, I have worked so long, alone in a lonely field, groping my way in the dark ages of the past. If my chronology is satisfactory, a great puzzle will be solved and the reconstruction will become easier. Mine is an attempt at reconstruction and a very poor one, indeed. Yet, I believe, with a certain measure of confidence that whoever will work in the same field, will arrive at almost similar conclusions.

In preparing this book, I have received valuable suggestions and encouragement from many generous persons, both Indian and foreign. In the initial stage of my labours and Indian travels, I was helped by Baby Harendralal Roy, Zamindar of Bhagyakul; Babu Dharanikant Lahiri, Zamindar of Kalipur; Raja Jagat Kisore Acharya of Muktagacha; Rai Bahadur Banamali Roy, Zamindar of Pabna; and Kumar Sri Harabhamji Raoji, of Morvi (Kathiawar). Immense is my debt to my professor and patron, Mr SC Hill, who was ever alive to my interests. He brought me to the notice of his friend the late Viceroy Lord Curzon whose encouraging words cheered me at a time when my spirits were low. To Col. Sir Richard Temple, editor, *Indian Antiquary*, belongs the real credit of this work, as he gave me the 'searchlight of true criticism'. (*Ind. Antiquary, vol. XXXI, 1902.*) Sir Asutosh Mukherji, Vice-Chancellor, the Syndicate and Dr G Thibaut, Registrar, Calcutta University, gave me indirect encouragement (1910). My thanks are also due to many scholars, authors, and writers of Bengal and abroad. This edition of the book is brought out with many imperfections. It is certain to have a second impression, which I trust will be brought out in due form and fashion.

Dacca
25 December 1917 *AK Mazumdar*

PREFACE TO THE SECOND EDITION

The first edition having run out, I venture to publish the second, thoroughly revised and enlarged. The demand for the book is largely an indication of the readers' indulgence due to a pioneering work, rather than its intrinsic merit.

'Old India' said Professor Weber, 'is still full of riddles'. Mr RC Dutt was the first pioneer in this field. I add the political outlines, which present the whole Hindu history in a readable form. In reconstructing it, I have closely followed Hindu traditions in their rational forms. I have included all that I could carefully gather from the numerous sources, along with my own discoveries. The readers, however, would be wrong to expect an authoritative work on the subject; that is reserved for a doughty scholar.

A regular Hindu history has long been a great desideratum in the world. I tried to meet it to some extent. But great was my apprehension when I first published my work, lest it should be doomed to utter failure. To my great relief and joy, I soon found the result otherwise. From the Magistrate, Dacca, to the authorities of the India Office Library, London and the Secretary to the President, United States of America—all heartily welcomed my little work. Government of India, Foreign Department, has encouraged my humble labours. The Curator, Bureau of Education, Simla Secretariat, the governments of the Central Provinces and the Punjab have purchased a few copies. Dr ME Sadler, Vice-Chancellor, Leeds University and President, Calcutta University Commission, Mr GF Shirras, Director-General, Department of Statistics, India, Dr John Marshall, Director-General of Archaeology in India and others have encouraged me with friendly notes of appreciation. Kumar Devendra Prasad Jain, of the All-India Jain Community, Arrah Branch, was equally enthusiastic.

My special thanks are due to Lt. Col. SF Bayley, Resident in Nepal and to Major CH Gabriel, First Assistant to the Resident in Kashmir, for their interest in my humble work.

Like an Indian sage of old traditions to whose clan I belong, I cannot but sing the praise of three eminent, noble and true Hindu princes whose sympathy and appreciation have urged me to bring out this edition in a comprehensive form. My debt is not so much to their gold, as to their golden hearts, noble instincts, and genuine pleasure at the sight of a history of their remote ancestors! Blessed be the names and lines of His Highness Chandra Singh Shumsher Jung Bahadur, Maharaja–Rana of Nepal, His Highness Virendra Kisore Manikya Bahadur, Maharaja of Tripura; and His Highness Sir Bhavani Singh, Maharaja–Rana of Jhalawar in Rajputana.

I have spent my time, money and energy on the work for some thirty years. I have constantly thought of the Indian people and have written for their benefit. Recently, two gentlemen have joined me in this stupendous work. My friend Babu Indramohan Das of Dacca and Babu Nagendra Kumar Roy, a young and enterprising publisher of this town, have come forward to promote the interests of the nation, by publishing this edition at great cost.

To the generous British government is due the recovery of a considerable portion of our past history. The Archaeological Department of India has been working wonders. Still, the results of researches are not yet brought home to the people in their vernaculars.

Only the learned few possess a correct knowledge of ancient India. The masses still revel in marvels, delight in dreams and soar with hyperboles. To them, ancient India is a dreamland—a veritable paradise on earth! Judging the present by those imaginary notions, they harbour grave discontents that know no remedy, because they never study the past. In Europe and America, all classes of people love history, for history makes man wise, history makes man practical. In India, it is generally neglected. Even in the universities, it is reserved for the intellectual parrots who require no brain, but the efforts of memory to learn it! This neglect of history was one of the causes that led to the downfall of the

Hindu nation. To be prosperous again, Hindus must study history carefully, remembering the wise remark of Professor Max Müeller, 'A people that feels no pride in the past, in its history and literature, loses its mainstay of national character'.

Dacca
30 March 1920 ***AK Mazumdar***

INTRODUCTION

Old India is still full of riddles

—Max Weber

History is a discipline where nothing is frozen in time. Every generation interprets and rewrites history in line with its new understanding of the past, based upon new evidence, unearthed through various means—archaeological or literary, which alter its understanding of the past. However, in this process of continuous renewal, one fact never changes—the new is always built upon the foundations of the old.

Thus, when every generation creates its own version of history, it does so on the basis of the history that has been written earlier. The image of the past may alter radically, it may become clearer on some previously obscure issue or event; sometimes, it may so prove that what had previously been thought to be true did not actually occur or exist. But, by and large, the historian of the present builds upon the work of the historians who came before him. It is the rare pioneer-historian who is ignored by his successors in the field. In fact, it usually turns out that his pioneering scholarship is the beginning point for the modern historian. Take, for instance, the case of the great nineteenth century historian Jacob Burckhardt. Burckhardt revolutionised the study of the Renaissance in Europe, through the methodology that he applied and the interpretation that he arrived at. The striking fact is that today, over a century after Burckhardt wrote his magisterial tome, every serious scholar of the Renaissance, especially those specialising in the Italian variant, have to genuflect before the master. It is not that Burckhardt was right or wrong, it is that history is, really speaking, a continuing dialogue between generations of historians on their favourite subject. Thus, Burckhardt is the lodestar for historians of the Renaissance.

This holds true for A.K. Mazumdar, whose book, *The Hindu History*, is as relevant to the scholar of ancient India today as when it was first published in the early twentieth century. Remember, this is the time when the ancient history of our country was slowly but surely coming out of the shadows into the clear light of the historian's lamp. Today, much of what we take as a known about our past, was actually unknown. The close probings into the literature of our people, and scrutinising it in a scientific manner, thus eliciting from it historical data of the greatest import, combined with the evidence being unearthed across the country through archaeological digs, brought forward an India that even the fantasist could not have imagined.

It is hard for us to imagine that people were ignorant of a figure such as the Buddha, but the fact of the matter is that as late as the mid-nineteenth century, he was a mere shadow. The chronology of dynasties which ruled small and large kingdoms and empires in ancient times was either totally unknown, or pure conjecture, for which there was no proof at all. The doors to our past were sealed so fast that we had forgotten the existence of a ruler such as Ashoka, who stands tall among monarchs. And even as revelation after revelation was made, knowledge of it was confined to the lucky few. For, archaeological data was not easily accessible, as it took a long time to be properly assessed, compiled, and made available to scholars. To the vast majority of people, the exciting new knowledge of the past was not easily ascertained.

The principal writings on the history of ancient India were also being done by European scholars. This is not to deny their importance, or to denigrate them. What they did was something for which we have to be grateful. For, after all, if history was being largely ignored by Indians, it was their fault, not that of the Europeans. It is the supreme irony that the people from whom we were trying to free our country, were actually letting us know about our past, whatever be their motive. Indian scholars were few and far between, who were ready to take on the onerous task of examining our past—and making it our own. One of those hardy few was Mazumdar. The first edition of Mazumdar's book was published in 1917, and a corrected edition came out in 1920.

Some will look askance at the title itself, but it must be noted that division of Indian history into the tripartite Hindu, Muslim, and British periods was the norm for the time. It was in no way a reflection of prejudice for or against any particular community. It was, quite simply, the way people approached the study of history in India, where modern tools were only just making their presence felt.

It is necessary to remember also that at this time, it was often said that Indians did not really have any sense of history, or even interest in it, and were satisfied by fantasies posing as history. As Mazumdar himself laments, 'Only the learned few possess a correct knowledge of ancient India. The masses still revel in marvels, delight in dreams and soar with hyperboles. To them, ancient India is a dreamland—a veritable paradise on earth!' But historians, Mazumdar among them, had begun to realise that our ancient epics and other writings were a key to an understanding and knowledge of the past, and should not be dismissed out of hand. It was important to ally a reading of textual evidence with the new evidence of archaeology, to distill the core of ancient India's history. This is exactly what Mazumdar has done. We can see this method at its best in his careful reading of the Vedas and the Puranas to describe the social and economic condition of the people, and the manner in which Mazumdar creates a chronology for the Solar and Lunar dynasties.

It must also be noted that Mazumdar was—quite naturally—a child of his time. It is interesting to note how matters as since then have acquired a certain measure of controversy. For instance, Mazumdar, as was the norm in his day, has read the epics as indicating an invasion of India by the Aryans, who came into conflict with the original inhabitants of the land. Today, there is less surety that there was an invasion, and that it may actually have been a series of migrations. There is today, of course, even a school of thought with an interpretation of its own, which believes that the Aryans in fact, originated in India. These are of course, inevitable in a book such as this, rooted in its time.

Mazumdar's work is a pioneering work by a pioneering historian of ancient India. Based on extensive and intensive research in extant sources as the bibliography shows, and meticulous in its approach, this volume continues to provide a roadmap for researchers and scholars in our time for a fruitful exploration of our past.

What comes across forcefully, even after the passage of eighty years, is Mazumdar's scholarly zeal and enthusiasm, and his desire to recreate the history of ancient India. And recreate it not just as a scholastic exercise, but as an attempt to bring within the sphere of knowledge of his countrymen, a clear and authentic history of India, based not on wishes and dreams, but rooted in evidence. It is this element which justifies any reading of this book today. Our dialogue continues with Mazumdar, this historian of ancient India, in our never-ending quest for knowledge. I congratulate the publishers, Rupa & Co, for making available once again this classic work of Indian history.

T. N. Chaturvedi
December 2007

ONE

1

HINDUS—THEIR CLASSICAL ANTIQUITY AND GREATNESS

The researches of the last fifty years have thrown much light on the so-called 'dim ages' of the past. We are now able to say, quite independently of Hindu authorities that in the most ancient world, at least four different peoples lived in the 'noon-day glare of civilisation.' Egypt, Chaldea, India, and China had been the earliest seats of civilisation. Except India, the other three countries have yielded extensive remains of their ancient glories hitherto concealed in the bosom of the earth. In the case of India, no such tangible proofs have as yet been found. The most ancient Indians seldom used stone for building purposes. They had wooden superstructures, sometimes overlaid with thin gold leaves, on brickbuilt plinths. The use of stone as a building material was perhaps, learnt by the Hindus from the Persians and the Greeks much later. Of the four peoples, the Aryans were the most advanced. The Aryans have always been supreme in the world. Their civilisation was spiritualistic, while that of the other three less so. And, the Aryan civilisation had a strong influence on the other three. There was full and free commercial intercourse between them. And, more than once was India invaded by Egypt and Assyria!

Like the ancient Egyptians, the Greeks and the Japanese, we are known to the world by a name not our own. I-Tsing, the Chinese traveller in India (AD 671 to 95) says that foreigners called the Indians Hindus.

The word Hindu owes its origin to the Vedic *Sapta Sindhavas*, Zend *Hapta Hendu*, the land of the seven branches of the Indus. Eastern Afghanistan, Kashmir and the Punjab then formed the home of the first Hindus who, however, called themselves *Arya*—excellent, noble. The Jews called us *Hondu*; the Parsis *Hindus* or *Hindus*. Hindu then meant the people of the region watered by the seven branches of the Indus. The word Hindu has now a different meaning—a mixed people of the Aryans and the Aryanised non-Aryans, with a peculiar religion. It was the Muhammadan rulers of India who made the name *Hindu* so general and prominent in the soil.

With the possible exception of the Chinese, Hindus are the oldest nation in the world. Their national existence and civilisation date from the dawn of human history. The Egyptians, Assyrians, Greeks, Romans, and Persians now are part of history. It is the Hindus alone who have survived the test of time; with but slight changes, they are still the same people as they were thousands of years back. The following, amongst others, will show the classical antiquity and greatness of the Indians:

- 'Ere yet the pyramids looked down upon the valley of the Nile; when Greece and Italy—those cradles of European civilisation—nursed only the tenants of the wilderness, India was the seat of wealth and grandeur.' (Thorton's *History of the British Empire in India, vol. I, p. 3*).
- 'India is the source from which not only the rest of Asia but the whole western world derive their knowledge and their religion.' (Professor Heeren's *Historical Researches*).
- Even in the much more ancient Vedic age, the civilisation of the North-Western Indians was so far advanced that Professor Wilson could describe it as 'differing little, if at all, from that in which they were found by the Greeks at Alexander's invasion.'
- 'It is remarkable that the inhabitants of India at that date were nearly the same as now. The descriptions of the people, as given by those who accompanied Alexander—their religion, laws, government and character—would suit the present generation of Hindus with little variation.' (Peter Parley's *Tales About Greece, p. 94*).

The longest national life of the Hindus has not been without its practical contribution. Their sixty-four *kalas* (branches of learning) show

how scientific, how perfect their turn of minds have been! The verdicts of eminent scholars are fully in favour of their greatness. The following, amongst others, may be cited in illustration of the point:

- 'Hindus have made a language, a literature and religion of rare stateliness.' (Dr WW Hunter).
- 'A great people of the Orient, who had attained the highest stage of culture, had developed an extraordinary literature and achieved the height of an amazing practical philosophy (at least 800 years before Christ) are not to be treated with contempt, because their conception of religion and their estimate of the right ideals of practical civilisation differ from our own.' (*Editor's Note, H.H.W. vol. 2*).
- 'No nation on earth can vie with the Hindus in respect of the antiquity of their civilisation and the antiquity of their religion.' (*Theogony of the Hindus*).
- 'If I were to look over the whole world to find out the country most richly endowed with all wealth, power and beauty that nature can bestow—in some parts a very paradise on earth—I should point to India.' (Max Müeller's *India: What Can It Teach Us*).
- 'To the Indians from whom, perhaps, all the cultivation of the human race has been derived, plays were known long before they could have experienced any foreign influence.' (AW von Schlegel).
- 'India must have been one of the earliest centres of human civilisation.' (HR Hall, *British Museum*).

Alberuni came to India in the train of Sultan Mahmud (AD 1030). He was a learned man and interested in the history of India. The pundits tried to satisfy his curiosity with their legendary lore. Needless to say that the learned enquirer was highly disappointed and commented unfavourably on the absence of a regular Hindu history.

It is but natural for an Alberuni to expect the history of a nation as old and great as India. We cannot deny that we do not possess a regular history of our gloried past. Of the so-called legendary tales, there is no lack in India. The *Vansavalis* of Orissa, Nepal and Mysore, the *Pattavalis* of the Jain pontiffs, and the historical romances generally pass for good histories. But a close examination of these has proved that they are works more of fancy than of facts and figures. The only possible exception to these is the *Rajatarangini*—the versified history of Kashmir, written in AD 1148. But this too, is not altogether free from faults. Moreover, it is chiefly a work of local interest, with only occasional references to the general history of India. Some of its errors are:

(i) It gives the date of Ashoka the Great as 1200 BC, while the real dates are known to be 264 to 227 BC.
(ii) It gives the date of Mihirakula as 704 to 634 BC, while the real date is about AD 530.
(iii) Toramana is placed seven centuries after Mihirakula, while it is well known that he was the father of Mihirakula.
(iv) Three centuries are given to the reign of Ranaditya (AD 222 to 522).

Of course, there is no gainsaying the fact that our ancestors have not bequeathed to us any rich and reliable historical work on the early period. But we cannot so readily admit the charge often brought against them of their entire incapacity for writing history. Col. Tod writes: 'Who would believe that the Hindus who carried so many sciences to perfection, knew not the simple art of writing history?' RC Dutt writes: 'Who would believe in the absence of a true historical sense in the ancient Hindus whose earliest works are the Vedas?'

Dr Fleet's favourable views are reflected below:

(i) They (the ancient Hindus) could write short historical compositions, concise and to the point, but limited in extent (*I.G.I.*).
(ii) The historical chapters of the Puranas do certainly indicate a desire on the part of the ancient Hindus not to ignore general history altogether and are clearly based on ancient archives which had survived in a more or less complete shape and were somehow or other accessible to the composers of those works or upon some prototype which had been so based (*I.G.I., New Edn., vol. 2 p. 17*).

The point here seems to be only partly true. We are told at several places that formerly, *Itihasa* (history) and *Purana* (theogony) were two distinct subjects. In the fourteenth century BC, the great writer Vyasa put them in a coherent shape. His compilation of the Puranas, current in his time, was called the *Purana-Samhita*. He taught Romaharshana history and the Puranas. In time, the Purana ramified into eighteen principal branches. This is why the Hindus still attribute all the Puranas to the pen of Vyasa. One condition that a proper Purana should satisfy is that it should note the principal dynasties and the dynastic achievements. Here is the origin of the historical chapters of the Puranas. History gradually disappeared as the Puranas grew in popularity, leaving 'genuine materials in abundance'.

(iii) An attempt on the part of the Hindus to put together anything in the shape of a general history is the *Rajatarangini*, written in AD 1148 to 49.
To the same twelfth century, perhaps, belongs Chand's *Prithviraj Raso*, every inch of which is a noble history. But no mention is made of it.

(iv) With this instance (the Bower manuscript) before us, it is not unreasonable to hope that an exploration of some buried city or even of one or other of the numerous private collections of ancient manuscripts, that still remain to be examined, may some day result in the discovery of some of the early and authentic *Vansavalis (I.G.I., vol. 2, p. 10)*.

Perhaps, the best judgement on the point has come from J Kennedy, who rightly observes:

'The true history of India is hidden under a thick veil of Brahmanical or bardic fiction.' *(I.G.I., vol. 2, p. 309)*.

We trust, Kennedy means to say here that a considerable part of the ancient Hindu history lies in buried cities also.

THE OBSCURITY OF ANCIENT HINDU HISTORY: ITS CAUSES

India, like China and Egypt, has been called 'a land of evasive mystery'. We cannot say how far this assertion can be maintained. India is rather a land of 'open secret'. Modern scholarship has lifted the mantle of mystery to a visible extent and now many things, once legendary, mist-wreathen, have become pure and settled facts. There are reasons why the ancient Hindu history had eluded the grasp of even veteran foreign scholars. Their imperfect knowledge of the language and their alien approach to Hindu religion and race were perhaps, a great bar to their clear understanding of the subject. Col. Tod says: 'Much would reward him who would make a better digest of the historical and geographical matter in the Puranas. But we must discard the idea that the histories of Rama and Krishna are mere allegories, an idea supported by some, although their races, their cities and their coins still exist.'

The chief causes of the obscurity of ancient Hindu history are noted below:

(i) *Paucity of plain facts and sober chronology*

Of historical facts, there is no lack; but they are not pure and plain and are often found mixed up with a good deal of spiritualistic fables. Fact and fiction cannot sometimes be distinguished; sometimes even a grain of truth cannot be salvaged from a bushel of legends. The Hindu regard for a general history perhaps, continued up to AD 700 after which the nation's general desire for truth also got vitiated. During the great Rajput revival (AD 800 to 1200), history became of provincial or local interest, polluted by panegyrics, encomiums, hyperboles. The *yugas*, the regnal years of the kings in the Sanskrit epics and the Puranas are given in stellar, not in solar years. Hence, they appear so grand and improbable.

(ii) *Deification of historic persons*

Ever since the introduction of medium-worship in Hinduism, notable historic characters have been made the object of popular worship. To translate men into divine beings, many superhuman powers and deeds are ascribed to them. Facts and fiction are so cleverly interwoven that the whole assumes an aspect of some mystic grandeur. Thus, the Devas (not gods)—a superior branch of the Aryans who dwelt near the tableland of Pamir—have been brought into popular worship by later thinkers as 'gods'—Brahma, Shiva, Indra, Vishnu, Durga, Kumara, Ganesa, Kuvera—the whole lot of the Deva-Aryans are now the objects of Hindu worship. These Deva-Aryans should not be confounded with the Vedic gods of similar names, who are pure divine spirits and not men. By superior qualifications, extraordinary merits, the Deva-Aryans rose to an enviable and inimitable position; yet they were but mortals. They had power, pelf, pedigree, pride; they had wars, commerce and colonies. But since they are worshipped, they are declared immortal. Such spiritualistic evolution meant loss to our history.

(iii) *Spiritual interpretation*

It appears that the ancient Hindus, like some other nations, represented everything in the world spiritually. Hence, we find them calling the less advanced people by such names as monkeys, cows, bulls, rams, bees, bears, snakes, and horses. The great Sanskrit epics and the Puranas, originally meant to be genuine histories, have long been transformed into theological works with suitable additions and subtractions.

(iv) *Confusion of terms*

The original meaning of words and expressions have changed. For instance, Vivaswan, the father of Manu, was a historic personage. The word also means the sun. In later times, his dynasty has invariably been called or described as the solar dynasty.

Valmiki, however, spoke of it as Ikshvaku's line or Kakustha or Raghu's line. Similarly, *Soma Vansa* now means the lunar dynasty, though Soma the man had nothing to do with Soma the moon. The word *Parvata-raj* originally meant the 'Hill King' of Simla in the Himalayas but afterwards 'king of the mountains'—the Himalaya. Thus, Parvati now means 'daughter of the Himalaya mountain'. Hastinapura meant 'the city of King Hasti', but later it was made to mean 'the city of elephant (*hasti*)'. In fact, the town is known by words, all meaning an elephant; thus we hear of Hastipura, Karipura, Gajapura, Gajahwayapura, and so on. Another source of confusion is in the likeness of names of persons living at different times: such as Manu, Kapila, Vasista, Narada, Patanjali, Vyasa, Katyayana, Vikramaditya, Varahamihira, and Chanakya. These should be carefully distinguished.

(v) *Attempts at suppression of history*

Perhaps, to suit the needs of some age, the Hindus suppressed history and invented legends instead. Such an age could most possibly be the century from AD 650 that marked the end of the imperial dynasties of north India and general disorder and revival of the non-Aryans. It was during this period that the astronomer Brahmagupta (b. AD 598) published the new monstrous chronology. There was another reason for suppression. The Buddhists, jealous of Hindu revival, often attacked the morally weak points of Hindu history. The Brahmans, therefore, cautiously amended the vulnerable parts.

Some examples will do well here. The term *Kumbha-yoni* refers to the noted sages Agastya and Vasista, because they were born of a prostitute, from *Kumbha*—a harlot. But to hide the disgrace and ensure regard for such people, the meaning of the word *Kumbha* was shifted to mean a pot or pitcher. Similarly, the five Pandava brothers are said to have had divine origin. Still, the great epic contains Vyasa's true account. The *Agni Purana* declares the Pandavas as Sakas—Scythians—as they were begotten by sages in the northern mountains. Such examples abound in the epics and the Puranas. But luckily these books are not hopelessly spoiled. One epic or Purana gives a legend, while another gives the fact. In the *Vishnu Purana* and elsewhere is given the legend of Yayati's premature old age and rejuvenation. But the true history is found in the *Mahabharata* where it is stated that the eldest son, Jadu, revolted against his father and so was set aside from the throne. The legend of Trisanku, a solar king, is well known. But the *Harivansa* gives his correct history.

(vi) *Hinduisation of the masses*

The Indo-Aryans clung long to their Vedas, Upanishadas and the Darshanas; but these books were not intelligible to women and Sudras in general. So, it is said that Vyasa wrote his great epic and compiled the Puranas. Gradually, the high-caste people declined and the low-caste people advanced till both came on the same level to form a new nation called the Hindus on the plain of the Ganges. Pure Brahmanism, a very ancient faith, now gave place to Hinduism. History was bruised and mutilated to make didactic legends and fables that still prevail in the country.

(vii) *Foreign invasions*

Foreign invasions, especially the plundering raids of some, have done much harm to our Indian lore. Temples were looted and demolished, libraries were sacked and burnt. Lahore, Delhi, Kanauj, Mathura, Ujjaini, Chitor, Somnath were all centres of the then great Hindu learning and religion. All of them fell under the evil genius of Sultan Mahmud, Iltutmish and Alauddin.

(viii) *Decline and fall of the Hindus*

The Indo-Aryans of India found themselves in a large country. They were then only one people, having one law, one religion and one tongue.

Distinct provinces were not yet formed. Then there was a regular need of history and there were Xenophons also. The Brahmans, the court-bards and the encomiasts were the usual recorders of events. Genuine historical fragments are still discernible in the later Puranas and elsewhere. In time, India split up; the country India became a continent India. Different provinces arose. The Brahmans divided themselves into ten distinct sects. Vernaculars arose and so did religious sects, manners, and customs. With these, national history also assumed a provincial character. Gradually, national unity broke up into jarring units.

Mutual feuds brought the country gradually to death's door. Occasionally, someone would rise and seize the suzerainty for a period, but the country would again come to grief under its weak successors. Naturally enough, the historian (if we may call him so) of the time would sing his master's praise profusely like a poet and not write a sober account of the whole. No doubt, on many occasions, the Hindus of the different parts of the country assembled and stood shoulder to shoulder to oppose a foreign foe, but in their gallant stand they were rather egged on by a strong sense of religion than by a noble sense of national union. Thus, India ceased to be an organic whole.

(ix) *Want of archaeological knowledge of the ancient Hindus*

(x) *Decline of Hindu intellect*

(xi) *Peculiarity of India as a country*
- (a) Its entire exclusiveness from the rest of the world.
- (b) Its vastness—it being really a world in miniature.
- (c) Its unhappy gifts of beauty.

(xii) *Over-spiritualistic tendency of the later Hindu mind*

(xiii) *Classic antiquity of the Hindu nation*

Different tastes and subjects prevailed in different ages.

(xiv) *Want of critical acumen of the later Hindus*

Critical history is quite a modern subject even in Europe.

(xv) *Lack of inscriptional and architectural evidence before 600* BC

For a detailed information of the topic, the curious reader should read Tod's masterly introduction to his classical work, *Annals and Antiquities of Rajasthan.*

HINDU HISTORY LIES CONCEALED

It has already been noted that the later Brahmans and the bards bruised and mutilated history for the sake of adaptation. So, a good deal of our history lies covered in bardic ballads and legends. Perhaps, more than this lies concealed in the buried cities of old, exploration of which brings to light every year many important facts. Every find, each discovery, contributes a mite to our knowledge of past history; for instance, the discovery of the Piprawah Vase and the Bower Manuscript has made known two great new discoveries. Recent excavations in the North-West Frontier Province have confirmed the description of Yuan Chwang about Kanishka's erection of a huge statue of Buddha with Buddhistic gods and angels. The excavations now carried on under Dr Spooner at Bankipore (ancient Pataliputra) bring to light many facts regarding Ashoka's capital and palace. Recent finds of two silver coins near Pandua (Bengal) of AD 317 and AD 514, in which Bengali letters are engraved, show that the vernacular alphabets came into being at the beginning of the Christian era or even earlier. Unfortunately, our ancestors were not archaeologists. They could not decipher ancient inscriptions on coins. Hence in some cases, tradition has been distorted; in others, overlaid with false gilding. Take for instance, the iron pillar of Delhi in the Qutab Square. Many still believe that it is the same iron pillar of the Pandavas, who had erected it after their victory over the Kauravas. But its inscription, deciphered, revealed otherwise.

Tireless toils and constant vigorous researches of eminent scholars, mostly European, have cleared the Augean stable of our history in the last fifty years. We trust many points of our history hitherto unknown, will be brought to light.

ATTEMPTS AT RECONSTRUCTION

The eminent scholars who came to India in the service of the East India Company did not fail to turn their genius to the exploration of the Indian lore. Results were great, though not in the line of general history. The discovery of Sanskrit (AD 1780) gave a great impetus. Missionary views or Christian contempt for things heathenish could not deter the movement. The then scholarship soon found, chiefly from the labours of Sir William Jones, that their belief that 'everything except the blind forces of Nature owes its origin to the genius of the Greeks', was wrong. In Christendom, Usher's famed chronology melted before the new critical school of research and the Egyptologists and the Assyriologists have revealed things of several thousand years past. Of course, in the case of Egypt and Assyria, the scholars could take their secure stand on architectural remains and other tangible proofs. On the other hand, in the case of ancient India, scholars could depend on no such materials. So, any sound chronological measure of our history before the time of the *Ramayana* is not fully possible.

Insuperable difficulties lie in the way of a clear interpretation of our ancient history; yet many attempts have been made in Europe for its reconstruction, but without satisfactory results. The western mind has been roused. Schlosser's classical *Weltgeschichte* contained only a condensed summary on ancient India. In the most recent German *Weltgeschichte*, however, ancient India is given almost as much space as Rome and Greece. In the *Historians' History of the World* published by the *Times of London*, some hundred pages only are allotted to ancient India.

In the current school history syllabuses of India, the sixth or seventh century BC is the starting point (Elphinstone). Some even begin from 1400 BC, showing their limited faith in Hindu chronology. Some others begin from 2000 BC but the period antecedent to the Great War is shown almost void of political history, with some descriptions of the Vedas and the Vedic civilisation being the only relieving points. Tod tried to add flesh and blood to the skeletal king-lists incorrect. Sir William Jones counted back to 3500 BC with no better results. A truly noble attempt has been made of late by VA Smith who in his *Early History of India* has reconstructed old material in an excellent way. But even here, he has left the most ancient period unnoticed. He appears to have had a mind to reconstruct the whole history, but has left it untouched, saying, 'Many attempts, all alike unsuccessful, have been made in Europe to reconstruct ancient Hindu history, even by distilling old legends. Modern criticism, however, is of the opinion that bardic lays cannot be made the basis of sober history.'

OPPOSITION TO RECONSTRUCTION

Many great men frankly admit that the world's debt to India is immense; for she has been the light-giver to all. Yet, to how many is she known abroad? To the Orientalists and specialists, India may be a favourite or familiar country, but even to the average Englishman, she is nothing but a name of five letters! To what is the world's apathy due? Is it due to the absence of a regular Hindu history? Or, is it due to the world's indifference to India? We know and believe that the Hindus have a history of their own to tell if the world be not found wanting in its listening ears. There was a time when Europe looked to Greece as the sole land of all inspiration. But the vigorous researches of a noble band of scholars have swept away that once-prevalent idea of the Graeco–Romanic foundation of European civilisation and have satisfactorily established the fact that 'the languages, literature, art, and philosophy of the West are connected by innumerable bonds with those of ancient India.' We know not why the poet still sings: East is East and West is West.

As regards the feasibility of reconstruction, scholars appear to be divided: some favour it, while others are opposed to it. The views are indicated below:

(i) The researches of a multitude of scholars working in various fields during the past forty years have disclosed an unexpected wealth of material for the reconstruction of ancient Indian history (VA Smith).

(ii) The attempt to write a connected relation of the national transactions of India before the Muslim conquest is now justified by an adequate supply of material facts and sufficient determination of essential chronological data (*ibid*).

(iii) The Chinese, Indian and Egyptian antiquities are never more than curiosities (*The Maxims and Reflections of Goethe, No.* 325, in B Saunder's translation).

(iv) It would be a very extraordinary and imperfect history of India that should put together from such references and from the Puranas, the *Rajatarangini*, the historical romances, the general body of the literature, such *Vansavalis* as have been obtained from Orissa and

Nepal and the few items of alleged history incidentally given in the *Pattavalis* (Dr Fleet's Paper on *Epigraphy, I.G.I. vol. 2, p. 21*).

To show the incapacity of the ancient Hindus to write history properly, Dr Fleet says: 'Though genuine material once abounded in India, yet we find no national history of the Hindus.'

Now again, when attempts are being made at reconstruction, he says: 'It would be a very extraordinary and imperfect history.'

We fail to account for the learned doctor's views. Does he mean to say that the once-abundant genuine material are now rare? We rather think that the reconstruction of our history in an entire form is long overdue. The vigorous researches of great scholars—mostly English—in India, Burma, Ceylon, China, Tibet, Turkistan, and Afghanistan have added much to the already existing material fit for a coherent shape. The most valuable point of modern scholarship is the excellent critical method of Ranke, Goethe and others, as opposed to Voltaire's definition of history as *fable convenue*. In this book, I shall follow the principle of 'Conservation and Reform'. It will best serve us as a clue to the labyrinth of our ancient history. Here again, we are between Scylla and Charybdis. Wordsworth's line, 'We murder to dissect,' suggests to us that the European mind is a little too over-critical, while the Hindu mind is over-credulous. We cannot say how far this work will commend itself at home and abroad.

SOURCES OF RECONSTRUCTION

A nation is known by its actions and its actions are known from its history. We Hindus often boast of our glorious past, but we possess no regular history. We cannot reasonably blame or abuse a foreigner if he occasionally expresses a good-natured contempt for this want of our national history.

With most of us, history is still a bundle of legends, tales, fables, and folklore that have really made us an 'artificially-fed people'. We still revel in marvels, delight in dreams and soar with hyperboles. The living nations of the world like love and culture, history and geography the most. But we Hindus have lost a true sense and appreciation of even these subjects. We care little for history. Our Indian universities also do not give a wider recognition to ancient Indian history. Europe, America and our generous British government here are spending lots of money for the recovery of our past history from obscurity. Political history up to 600 BC is now fairly well established, but the earlier parts still await reconstruction. Scholars do not grudge 'scientific facts' as much as they do chronology which still hangs about as a great puzzle. Let me state an example, which I believe to be true. Some give the initial point as 5000 BC on astronomical but imaginary grounds. Next, I turn to find and examine the sources that may supply us with genuine materials for reconstruction.

These are broadly four, as indicated below:

I. Tradition

It is enshrined in our secular and sacred writings. Though the value of tradition is inferior to contemporary evidence, yet it may be regarded with a high degree of probability. For the period from the earliest times to 327 BC we have mainly to depend on literary tradition alone. Later, tradition has been proved correct by inscriptions and other evidence. Dr Fleet also, in his paper on epigraphy, in the *Imperial Gazetteer of India, vol. 2*, has attached great importance to tradition and observes further that it would not be proper or safe to advance theories in direct opposition to the settled convictions and time-honoured traditions of the soil.

II. Archaeological evidence

These are:

(a) Epigraphic
(b) Monumental and
(c) Numismatic.

III. Contemporary and other works dealing with historical topics

IV. Foreign accounts

Let us next examine these sources.

I. TRADITION

(i) The Vedas and the Vedangas

They tell us much about the direct political history of the earliest period; further, they shed much light upon the civilisation of a period extending over 1,800 years.

(ii) The Samhitas

They are over twenty in number. Like the Vedas, they do not contribute much to the political history of India. The *Manu-Samhita*—the chief of these—tells us much about laws, duties, religious observances, manners, customs of kings and the people.

(iii) The Sanskrit epics

The original epics are lost. In their present shape they are merely historical romances. Yet, they are great storehouses of history, of many scientific facts. Their historical value is considerable for the earliest period of Indian history. The historic elements lie concealed and scattered. They now rank almost as the Hindu scriptures but originally they were not so.

Professor Max Müeller holds that the whole of the *Ramayana* and the *Mahabharata* are recast in modern Sanskrit. There is probably considerable truth in the assertion. By modern Sanskrit we mean the form of Sanskrit used for the last two thousand years. The northerners used a free, irregular and archaic tongue called *Brahma Bhasha* or *Balhika Bhasha* (the ancient Bactrian tongue).

The grammars of Indra, Chandra and Mahesa first perfected, polished and reformed that northern tongue, which was now called *Sanskrita* or *Deva Bhasha* (*R.V. VI, 89–II;* also *Sanskrit Rhetoricas—Bagbhata, Kavya-Chandrika, Kavyadarsha*). The probable date of the origin of this new polished tongue is about 2800 BC. Roughly speaking, this Sanskrit falls into three classes—Old (2800 to 1300 BC), Middle (1300 to 200 BC) and Modern (200 BC to up till now). Sanskrit was generally used, no doubt, in secular writings, human compositions but the so-called revealed literature—the Vedas, the Brahmanas and the Upanishadas—were mostly written in India in their old northern tongue.

The Vedic priests and other learned men thought it rather heretical to deviate from the old school. Valmiki and Vyasa wrote their epics in Old Sanskrit. The subject-matter of the Sanskrit epics in the present shape consists of old genuine material and later additions and interpolations. The language also betrays old and later specimens of Sanskrit.

The Ramayana

It contains less historical material than the *Mahabharata*. The shape and size of the original epic have been doubled by additions. Valmiki's first book has been mostly replaced by a new one. The last book is admittedly of a second hand. Besides, there are many interpolations throughout the book. Side by side with Valmiki's sober language, elegant ideas and correct chronology, there appear the monstrous, the improbable and the ludicrous. However, with patient and careful toil, we can glean from it some facts that help the sound framework of dynastic annals.

(b) *The Mahabharata*

Like the *Ramayana*, it is, in its present form, quite a new book altogether. It is rightly called the 'Encyclopaedia of Hinduism'. The original poem called the *Bharata-Sambita* in 8,000 shlokas, lengthened to 24,000 shlokas afterwards, was mainly historical. This historic portion is still available in the present grand epic. The incidental mention of mighty kings and their deeds, here and there throughout the epic, enables us to correct and corroborate the bare king-lists of ancient dynasties. The *Shanti-Parva* (Peace-Book) abounds in historical allusions relating to the most ancient and other periods of our history. Besides, the epics are valuable as traditional pictures of social life in the Heroic Age.

(iv) Historical works

- (a) The *Rajatarangini* (the Kashmir Chronicle): A cautious use of its confused mass of ancient tradition is advised.
- (b) *The Kumarapala Charitra*
- (c) *The Khoman Raesa*
- (d) *Prithviraj Raso*
- (e) *Rajavali*
- (f) The Pali histories of Ceylon. The *Dipavansa* and *Mahavansa* of the fourth and fifth centuries AD mainly relate to the incidents of the Maurya dynasty.
- (g) The *Jataka* stories occasionally give the political history of India in the fifth and sixth centuries BC.
- (h) Several Jain books, especially the *Satrunjaya Mahatmya* of the fifth century AD, give numerous historical allusions of no mean value.

(i) The Puranas. They may be classed under three groups: *Hindu Puranas, Jain Puranas* and *Buddhist Puranas*. Most of the principal Puranas of these three contribute much to our ancient history. Their historical chapters contain the most authentic accounts of our historical traditions. Some of them give king-lists and facts from the earliest times down to the Gupta period in the fifth century AD.

Before 1200 BC *Itihasa* (history) and Purana (theogony) were two distinct subjects. Gradually, the professional puranists divided the *Purana-Samhita* of Vyasa into eighteen principal branches, adding new material age after age. The Purana was in existence long, long before 1200 BC. The eighteen chief Puranas and the numerous minor Puranas all turn to history. The dynastic lists appear in many: the *Vayu Purana* (composed perhaps in AD 300), the *Matsya Purana* (perhaps in AD 400), the *Vishnu Purana* (composed perhaps in AD 450), *Brahmanda Purana* and the *Bhagavata Purana* (composed much later). The king-lists of the last two are incorrect. But those of *Vayu Purana, Matsya Purana* and *Vishnu Purana* are complete and more or less authentic. The *Bhabishya Purana* also gives many facts.

In some cases, the evidence of the *Vishnu Purana* has been found inferior to that of the *Vayu Purana* and *Matsya Purana*.

On the authority of the Puranas, the well-informed English scholar, VA Smith, observes as follows:

> Modern European writers have been inclined to disparage unduly the authority of the *Puranic* lists, but closer study finds in them much genuine and valuable historical tradition. For instance, the *Vishnu Purana* gives the outline of the history of the Maurya dynasty with a near approach to accuracy and the Radcliffe manuscript of the *Matsya Purana* is equally trustworthy for the Andhra dynasty. Proof of the surprising extent to which coins and inscriptions confirm the *Matsya Purana* list of the Andhra line has been recently published.

Tod, Dr Fleet and several eminent scholars have expressed a similar view on the Puranas.

(j) Tantras. Their historical notices and geographical elements furnish good material occasionally.

(k) General literature and semi-historical romances. These are incidental historic items only.

II ARCHAEOLOGICAL EVIDENCE

(a) *Epigraphic*

This is the most secure source. It gives the correct knowledge of many periods. It is obtainable from Ashoka's edicts, record on tablets of stone and copper plates and towers. The oldest inscription is said to be the dedication of the relics of Buddha (a few bits of bones) by his Sakya relatives in the Piprahwah stupa about 493 BC (Dr Hoernle gives this date, but others suggest 450 BC).

However, recent adverse criticism has discredited this theory. So, the next oldest known inscription is that of 250 BC.

(b) *Numismatic*

Here is another secure and fruitful source of our history. All traditions point to the general currency of a gold coin called *nishka* in ancient India, for commercial and donative purposes. Future explorations of Taxila, Oudh, Delhi, Mathura will no doubt bring to light many of those coins to the delight and wonder of the literary world. From 327 BC various kinds of coins abound which furnish bare facts and aid the research scholars. They form the sole evidence for the Indo-Greek and the Indo-Parthian dynasties of Indian rulers.

III. CONTEMPORARY AND OTHER SIMILAR WORKS

(i) The *Kalpa Sutras*.

(ii) Sanskrit grammars.
Linguistic specialists have extracted from Sanskrit grammars and similar works many incidental references to ancient tradition, which collectively amount to a considerable addition to historical knowledge.

(iii) Architectural remains.

(iv) Astronomical and geographical works.

(v) The *Ramayana*, Sanskrit Rhetorics, *Harivansa*, *Raghuvansa*, and other poems; Biographies such as *Salivahana Charitam*,

Sriharsha Charitam, Vikramanka Charitam, Rama Charitam (a poem on the Pala dynasty of Bengal); *Prabandhakosham, Kathasaritsagara*, and other tales and novels.

(vi) The local annals of Nepal, Orissa, Assam, Mysore, Rajputana, Gujarat.

(vii) Other works in Sanskrit, Prakrit and Tamil.

(viii) Jain works in general, especially the Jain accounts of the Chalukya dynasty of the west.

(ix) Geological researches of India.

(x) Pedigrees and successions.

(xi) Official records.

(xii) Ancient paintings, sculptures and brass-reliefs.

(xiii) Dynastic archives and chronicles.

(xiv) Introductions and colophons of literary works.

(xv) Medals, grants and manuscripts.

(xvi) Sanskrit dictionaries.

IV. FOREIGN ACCOUNTS

This embraces the accounts of foreign travellers and writers and also the references in books and monuments of other nations.

A. Western intercourse with India before the Christian era

(a) *The Egyptians*

The mythological accounts of Osiris and Isis, having political connection with ancient India, apparently deserve no special notice but still may be believed to have a strong background of facts. They were the first to import the 'wondrous products of Arabia and India.'

(i) Under King Saukh-ka-Ra, the first Ophir Voyage to Punt (Somaliland) and Ophir (Sanskrit *Sauvira*, lying on the eastern shore of the Gulf of Kutch, western India) was accomplished, its leader and guide being Hannu, 2500 BC (*H.H.W., vol. I, pp. 108–09*).

(ii) Dr Royle has shown some points of similarity between ancient Egypt and ancient India and has microscopically traced indigo (an Indian product) in the blue stripes of some Egyptian mummy clothes. (*Dr Royle's Essay on the Antiquity of Hindu Medicine, pp. 129–37*).

(iii) The *Old Testament, Book of Genesis (XXXVII, 25)* tells us that 'the Ishmeelites coming from Gilead with their camels bearing spices and balm and myrrh, wee going to carry them down to Egypt'—1927 BC.

(iv) Greek historians have made the Pharaoh Ramses II (Sesostris) penetrate and subdue the countries of Media, Persia, Bactriana, and India, as far as the ocean and even claim he penetrated Europe as far as Thrace, where his course was only checked by want of supplies. (*H.H.W., vol. I, p. 146, circa 1300* BC).

Dr Robertson has discredited it as 'an invention of the Egyptian priests.' However, the editor of *H.H.W.* says: 'Such vague traditions probably represent a racial memory of actual historical events, distorted of course as to all details.'

(b) The Assyrians

(i) Tradition affirms that the Deva-Aryans of the north were notorious for drinking *sura* (wine). Hence, they were called suras. Another clan refrained from liquor and differed in their form of worship, eating, drinking. They were, therefore, ridiculed as asuras—people without wine, teetotalers. On political grounds, hostilities ensued between the two tribes known as the 'Deva-Asura War' lasting thirty-two years, off and on. A section of the asuras, defeated in the conflict, were forced to leave the north and take shelter in Persia and Turkey. Vritra and his brother Bala founded kingdoms in Persia and Turkey. Their defeat and exodus are clearly shown in the *Rig Veda* (*R.V.I., 80. 2: III, pp. 33–37;* Dr KM Banerji's *Aryan-Witness, p. 62*). It is not to be supposed that the Assyrians were Aryans. The leaders Vritra and Vala (Bala or Bel) no doubt took small Aryan bands with them. Hostilities renewed with the Deva-king, Indra: a treaty followed. Sometime later, Indra treacherously broke the terms of the treaty, killed Vritra in an unjust battle and assumed the glorious title of *Vritraghna*—killer of Vritra (*Mahabharata*). This is dated about a little before 2800 BC. The Assyrians burned with revenge and never forgave the Aryans. Vague traces of Assyrian attacks on the sea coasts of western India are found in the *Rig Veda* and elsewhere.

(ii) Zonaras says that when hostilities broke out between the Assyrians and the Median King, Kykius, about 620 BC, a Hindu king agreed to arbitrate between them and wrote a letter to the King of Media. Babylon occupied a favourable position for peaceful commerce. Mesopotamia occupied the very centre of the world of ancient civilisation. It was the connecting link between Persia and India on one hand, and Lybia, Syria and Egypt on the other. Even Chinese ideas were to some extent accessible through the mediation of India. (*H.H.W., vol. I, p. 472*).

(iii) The pictures on the black obelisk of Shalmanaser II show us such beasts as apes and elephants, being brought as tribute to the conqueror, confirming in the most unequivocal way the belief based on Ctesias and Strabo that the Assyrians held commercial relations with India. (*H.H.W., vol. I, p. 484*).

(iv) The Muslins of Dacca were famous in the Roman and even Assyrian time. (Lee-Warner's *Citizen of India, p. 11*).

(v) The Babylonians imported the following commodities from India: precious stones, onyx, dogs, dyes, finest wool, and spices. (*H.H.W., vol. I, pp. 487–90*).

(vi) Ctesias tells us that the Assyrian Queen Semiramis invaded India in 2001 BC and fought with a Hindu king on the right bank of the Indus, whose name is not known but whose title was *Sthavarapati* (Greek *Stabrobates*). We shall discuss this later on.

(c) The Phoenicians

The Phoenicians (Latin Poeni, Rig-Vedic Sanskrit *Pani* or traders)—most probably Aryans—had established their colony on the Levant Sea as early as 2800 BC. The *Panis* were a section of the Asura-Aryans. They were traders, from the root *pan* which means to trade (cf. English *Company*, Com = Skr. Sam = together, and *pan* means to trade, so it means a 'body of men trading together'). They are abused in the *Rig Veda* as faithless, treacherous and deceitful—an idea maintained also by the classical authors of Europe (*R.V. 133, 5; VI, 51, 14; VII, 6, 3*). Tyre was built in 2750 BC.

Their trade-empire extended from Great Britain in the north-west to India and Ceylon in the south-east. They came to India around the fourteenth or the thirteenth century. Long, long before 561 BC when the Persians conquered Babylon, the Phoenicians had settled on the Bahrein Islands in the Persian Gulf for pearl fishery and the Indian trade (*Dr Royle's Essay, pp. 122*). They carried on their trade by the Red Sea along the caravan road from the shores of the Persian Gulf to the Mediterranean coast. They imported diamond, pearls, gold, tin, various spices, onyx and agate, ebony and ivory, rich carpets, garments and embroidery from India.

Some scholars have hunted out from the poems of Homer (eleventh century BC) Sanskrit names of things transmitted to Greek by the Phoenicians. For instance, Homer's use of *kassiteros* is the Sanskrit *kastira* (tin). Again, at several places, Homer referred to the skill of the 'Sidonian artists' when he mentioned the 'Silver vase', costly carpets and garments. But Sir George Birdwood says that 'these articles of luxury, though latterly produced in Sidon itself, came originally from India'. (*Ind. Arts of India, pp. 263–64*).

(d) The Jews

We have no proof of any Jewish trade with India before 1050 BC. However, there are allusions to extensive caravan routes in several passages of the *Old Testament*.

(i) The Jewish king, Solomon, was the first to give an impetus to trade. He even founded a seaport at Ezion-Gaber (992 BC).

(ii) The ships of Solomon sailed from Ezion-Gaber under the guidance of the mariners of Hiram and returned home after three years, laden with the gold of Ophir (Sanskrit *sauvira*—Coptic *Sophir* or *Sofir*). Its *almug* wood (red sandalwood), apes (Sanskrit *kapi*, Hebrew *kof*), peacocks (Hebrew *tukkim*, Malayalam *tokei*, Tamil *siki*, Sanskrit *Sikhi*), and (ivory *shenhabbim*, Sanskrit *ibhu*, an elephant) were also imported.

There appears to be some discrepancy among the scholars regarding the identification of Ophier. Various countries have been proposed such as India, Ceylon, Peru, and Rhodesia. The form of the word suggests that *Ophir* or *Sophira* or *Sophara* was Sanskrit; *Sauvira*—a sea-board tract between Sindh and Gujarat. The mention of *Berygaza* (modern Broach, Sanskrit *Bhrigu-kachchha*) in the same commercial period suggests that these western parts of India were in direct commercial contact with the West.

(iii) The Jewish commercial spirit did not survive Solomon even a hundred years. So, we no more hear of them.

(e) The Greek notice of India

(i) According to mythological accounts, Bacchus and Heracles are said to have come to India, lived here and left children (McCrindle, *Strabo, XV, 7–8*). The followers of Alexander and even Megasthenes believed these, though generally they are supposed to be quite false. We think the tradition is not void of truth altogether, though distorted, magnified and wrongly identified sometimes.

(ii) Reference in Homer (eleventh century BC). Dr Schwanbeck holds that the Greeks of Homer's time knew India. Homer's 'righteous Ethiopians of the east' meant the Indians. In *Odyssey, Book I*, Homer refers to India in a very general way. Homer in his *Iliad* (*p. 230*) speaks of the Eden fountain thus: 'Finally identifying the place beyond all question, we have the Eden fountain whose waters part into four streams following each in opposite direction.' Oxus (Sanskrit *Wankshus* or *Chakshus*), Obei (Vedic *Yavyavati*), Hsito (Sanskrit Sita or Sira), now Yarmond and the Ganges. Homer's use of *Kassiteros* (tin) is Sanskrit *Kastira* (tin). Sir G Birdwood gives a number of Homeric passages descrbing costly garments—originally going to Sidon from India (*Indus Arts of India, pp. 263–64*). For references in Homer, see *Iliad, XXIII, lines 865–70; Pope, Iliad, VI, lines 358–67; Pope, Iliad, XXIV, lines 281–84*.

(iii) Anaximander (610–547 BC). The first Greek geographer, he prepared an abstract of the world. It is not yet known if he ever mentioned India. But his preceptor, the philosopher Thales, derived the origin of the world from 'primal waters'—a clear Hindu theory of old. Empedocles, Anaxagoras, and Domeoritus came to India to study philosophy.

(iv) Pythagoras (sixth century BC). His theories and ideas throw much light on the prevailing ideas of the Hindus of that age.
(v) Skylax and his followers (541–40 BC).
(vi) Herodotus (450 BC) gives full and valuable facts regarding the relations between India and the Persian Empire. (*Book III, Chapters 98–106*).
(vii) The accounts of Ctesias are of little worth as they only narrate the travellers' tales about the wonders of India (401 BC).
(viii) The accounts of the historians of Alexander (327 BC) and of the ambassadors Megasthenes and Deimachus (close of the fourth century BC).
(ix) The following six useful books about the Greek and the Roman notices of India by McCrindle; (1) *Ktesias;* (2) *Indika of Megasthenes and Arrian;* (3) *Periplus of the Erythraean Sea* (Guide to the Red Sea. This Red Sea means the one between Arabia and Africa and also the eastern-most part of the Arabian Sea, close to the west of Gujarat); (4) *Ptolemy's Geography;* (5) *Alexander's Invasion* and (6) *Ancient India* (as described by other classical authors).

(f) The Persian notice

(i) The Indian invasion of Cyrus happened in 541–40 BC. A Hindu king sent envoys and coins to Cyrus.
(ii) The first Persian notice of India appears from the two inscriptions of the Persian king Darius, son of Hystaspes, at Persepolis and Nakashi-Rustam. The latter is dated about 486 BC (Rawlinson, *Herodotus, vol. 2, p. 403, IV, 207*).
(iii) Hindu soldiers shared defeat with the Persians under Mardonius at Plataea (480 BC) in Greece when Xerxes attacked Greece.
(iv) The Persian occupation of the Indus Valley. Hindu soldiers fought with Alexander on the side of the Persian monarch Darius (fourth century BC). Besides soldiers, many Indian men of learning and art lived in the Persian court. Indian wisdom spread to the West through Persia. Striking resemblance between Indian and Greek philosophy and drama is perhaps due to that.
(v) Persian influence on India. Dr Spooner speaks of the Zoroastrian period of Indian history—*J.R.A.S.* 1915. The

architecture of Persepolis bears a resemblance to that of Pataliputra.

B. Eastern intercourse of India

(a) The Chinese historians. The two encyclopaedias of China give descriptions of the intercourse and trade by sea with China from the seventh century BC to the seventeenth century AD. *Wi-lio*, written between AD 239–65, gives us the valued information of the Kushan occupation of Magadha in the third century AD.

(b) Chinese travellers in India. Some forty-five are known.

(i) Ssu-ma-ch'ien, the Chinese 'father of history' wrote his work in about 100 BC. He tells us much about the early annals of India.

(ii) Fa-Hien in India (AD 399 to AD 414) during the Gupta rulers, notices the Gangetic Valley.

(iii) Yuan Chwang (AD 629–645). His book is entitled *A Treasure-house of Accurate Information.*

(iv) I-Tsing and others give full accounts of India.

(c) Inscriptions from the Hindu colonies of the Malayan peninsula and the Malayan archipelago furnish some facts.

(d) The *Brahmanda Purana* and the Jain Sanskrit work, the *Satrunjaya Mahatmya*, written about AD 420 corroborate many points of Hindu intercourse with the East.

(e) The great maritime activity of the Cholas of the eleventh century AD is shown by many points of Eastern reference.

C. The Muslim notice of India

The first Muslim invasion of India was in AD 636. Muslim conquest of north India happened by AD 1200. As yet, seven of the Muhammadan writers on ancient India in the intermediate period are known: (1) Sulaiman; (2) Ebn Khurdatba; (3) El Masudi; (4) El Ist-khiri; (5) Ibn Haukal; (6) El Edrisi and (7) Alberuni.

Their accounts (except Alberuni's) tell us much about our political history. Alberuni (AD 1030) came to India in the train of Sultan Mahmud of Gazni. He was a learned mathematician and astronomer. After having studied Sanskrit in India most diligently he wrote his famous work entitled *The Tahkik-i-Hind* (An Enquiry into India) which furnishes a very good account of Hindu manners, science and literature, though little of political history.

D. Modern research

India owes a deep debt to the patient research of both Indian and foreign scholars for the gradual recovery of our lost and forgotten history. No living person can describe even a part of the great services done to India by the first great English scholar Sir William Jones. Sir William was a great master of Latin and Greek. In India he soon became proficient in Sanskrit. He discovered that the Hindu king Chandragupta was no other than the Sandra Coptos of Alexander's historians. The discovery of this synchronism proved to be a key element in the understanding of Hindu chronology. His English translation of Kalidasa's *Abhigyan Shakuntalam* was greeted with excitement in England and elsewhere. Perhaps, the establishment of the Asiatic Society of Bengal at Calcutta in AD 1784 and a journal connected therewith was his greatest monument. Jones aimed at a reconstruction of the Hindu history, but being busy with modern Sanskrit literature, he could not recover the facts of that history. He was followed by Colebrooke, a gigantic figure whose genius illumined every branch of Hindu learning. He left India in AD 1815. Col. Wilford was another great scholar. His learned papers are preserved in *Asiatic Researches, Vol. X*. His wonderful array of facts overwhelms the readers with a deep sense of his vast erudition and the accuracy of his references. The correctness of his data cannot be doubted. Colebrooke was followed by Professor HH Wilson. He translated the *Vishnu Purana* and from the ancient king-lists and other material wrote a history of the Hindus but it was rejected by the scholars. We next find Dr Miller in the field.

After the establishment of the Royal Asiatic Society in London in AD 1823, the attention of Europe was directed to the Indian antiquities regarding religion, society, philosophy, politics, architecture, and the arts.

Justic Pargiter's *Dynasties of the Kaliyuga* provides a solution to many a knotty problem.

James Prinsep occupies a seat of reverence in the field of Indian research. His first decipherment of the Ashokan inscriptions illuminated a considerable portion of the Buddhist history of India. His discovery of many new truths from his collection of coins of western India cleared the history of the post-Buddhist dynasties. His proposal for an epigraphic arrangement was not carried out owing to his death at the early age of forty.

E. Other pioneering works

- Dr Burnell's discussion of the palaeography of the Deccan; decipherment of coins and inscriptions of the South; General Sir Alexander Cunningham's publication of Ashoka's Edicts (1877).
- The Bombay civilian, Dr Fleet's *Catalogue of Gupta Inscriptions* and his solution of Gupta chronology.
- Professor Keilhorn's *Epigraphy of North India*, published in parts.
- Luther's *Epigraphy of Brahmi Inscriptions.* Louis Rice's *Epigraphy* containing over a thousand inscriptions of south India, helps the reconstruction of Southern history.

(i) Numismatologists

(1) Rapson, *Indian Coins.* (2) Cunningham, *Coins of Ancient India and Medieval India.* (3) Von Solett and P Gardener, *The Coins of Greek and Scythian Kings of Bactria and India in the British Museum.* (4) VA Smith, *The Gupta Coinage, The Andhra History and Coinage, Catalogue of Coins in the Indian Museum.* (5) Allen, *Catalogue of Gupta Coins.* Besides, the labours of J Fergusson, M Kitto, Edward Thomas in north India; of Sir W Elliot in south India; of Col. M Taylor and Dr Stevenson's works in western India deserve grateful acknowledgement.

(ii) German scholars

- Dr Fryankie, Professor Leggie, M Fowcher and Professor Grunwadell's researches on the Saka dynasties.
- Professor Rapson's labours on the Kshatrapa rulers, i.e. Scythian viceroys of Gujarat, give detailed accounts. Col. Tod's *Rajasthan* gives a systematic account of the Rajputs and their remote ancestors.
- AK Forbes gives a history of Gujarat.
- VA Smith's *Early History of India.*

(iii) Indian scholars

(1) Dr Rajendra Lal Mitra's labours on the Pala, Sena, Ganga and the Kesari dynasties of east India. (2) Dr DR Bhandarkar's *Early History*

of the Deccan. (3) Dr Bhou Daji's *History of Western India* and especially his labours on Vikramaditya. (4) Haraprasad Sastri. (5) Dr Bhagwanlal Indraji. (6) Dr A Coomaraswami, *Ancient India.*

Scholars in Europe and America and the British government of India are spending vast amounts of money for the recovery of ancient Indian history. Our Indian chiefs and other rich men take little or no interest in the matter. Recently, the Tara brothers of Bombay have been contributing twenty thousand rupees or more a year for the excavations of ancient Pataliputra. May not other wealthy Indians follow the example of these noble Parsee brothers? But we must remember with a sigh that the noble example of Kalhana's attempt at historiography was followed by no Indian of the plains!

Elphinstone justly observed: 'As the rudest nations are seldom destitute of some account of the transactions of their ancestors, it is a natural subject of surprise that the Hindus should have attained to a high pitch of civilisation without any work that at all approaches to the character of a history.' Though things have improved in these eighty years, though liberal education, research libraries, museums, first-rate journals, improved communication with Europe and America have offered a good many opportunities, yet, has the world heard of a regular history from any Indian?

2

HINDU ART OF WRITING

The edicts and inscriptions of Ashoka the Great had long baffled the early scholars. In 1795, Col. Wilford thought them to be of Pandava origin. In 1809, Sir William Jones tried to decipher them but in vain. He, however, concluded that the Indian alphabets were children of the Semitic alphabets. In 1821, Cope and others supported Jones. Lapsius wrote a paper endorsing Jones' views (1834). Sterling in 1834 visited Khandagiri in Orissa, examined the letters inscribed there and thought they were an imitation of the Greek alphabet.

It was the genius of J Prinsep whose efforts first deciphered the Ashokan edicts. His first detection of the words *danam* and *piyadasi* led to the following discoveries in 1837–38:

(a) Facsimiles of *Ancient Inscriptions* lithographed by J Prinsep, *J.A.S.B. vol. VII 1837.*
(b) Alphabets from the fifth century BC up to their present state, *J.A.S.B. vol. VII 1837.*
(c) *The Delhi Pillar Explained,* ibid.
(d) In Ashoka's time, in the third century BC, two quite distinct alphabets were in use, viz., Indo-Bactrain (Kharosthi, Sanskrit, Kharostri) in the North-West Frontiers and Indo-Pali in India.

THEORIES AS TO THE ORIGIN OF THE INDIAN ALPHABETS

(i) Prinsep gives it a Greek origin. A Muller, M Senart and M Joseph support it.

(ii) Professor Wilson: 'The Indian alphabets were made after the Greek or Phoenician model.'

(iii) Sir William Jones gives it the Semitic origin.

(iv) Weber, Benfey, Pot, Westergird, Buhler, Max Müeller, F Muller, Sayce, Whitney, and Lennermot believe in the Semitic origin.

(v) Dr Dickie: 'The Cuneiform Assyrian alphabet, with the aid of the South Semitic alphabet has fathered the Indian alphabets.'

(vi) Dr Burnell: 'The Indian alphabet is originated by the Aramaean alphabet. That alphabet was once current in Persia and Babylonia.'

(vii) Benfey speaks of the Phoenician origin. Dr Taylor objects to that, for, the Phoenician trade ceased with India by 800 BC. If the Phoenician alphabet had come to India in Solomon's time, then in 700 years (from 1000 BC to 264 BC) there would have arisen a good many alphabets in India before Ashoka. But in Ashoka's time, we find only one alphabet in western India. Research has brought to light no alphabet in India before the sixth century BC. Further, there is no resemblance between the Phoenician and the Indian alphabets (Dr Taylor's *History of the Alphabet, vol. II.* Dr Taylor also contradicts Burnell's theory).

(viii) Dr Taylor's theory: 'The Indian alphabet owed its origin to the Sebian alphabet which was an off spring of the Phoenician alphabet. Through the connection of India with the western world by both land and sea, the Indo-Bactrian alphabet had entered north-west India by the Khyber Pass. The alphabet of western India had come from the West by sea. Yemen of Arabia was a great centre of trade from 1000 BC. There was the exchange of all commodities. Egypt brought cloth, glass and papyrus. Syria brought wine, oil, brass. Phoenicia brought arms. India sent ivory, gold, precious stones and other articles. At first the Sebians were the leaders and immensely rich. Trade of Yemen with Egypt was in full swing till 2500 BC and with India till 1000 BC. Even under the Ptolemies, the Egyptians never traded with India direct. The large Sebian ships used to visit the Red Sea, the Persian Gulf, the African Coast and

> the mouth of the Indus. The *Periplus* also states that Aden was the centre of trade. In the beginning of the second century AD, Indian goods were exchanged at Diocoridus Islands near the Somali coast. Thus, the Sebian alphabet—itself a branch of the Phoenician—had an ample opportunity to come to India.'

The point is briefly this: The Indians before the sixth century BC knew not the art of writing. The merchants of western India brought an alphabet from the West, in the seventh or the eight century BC, for their commercial purposes. The Brahmans soon borrowed it from the merchants and made it all their own, of course, in a quite altered form, called the *Brahmi Lipi*, which afterwards became the parent of the various Indian alphabets. The other alphabet used by Ashoka in the North-West Provinces soon fell into disuse, as it did not suit the Indian tongues.

Two reasons mainly led to such an inference: (a) absence of any archaeological evidence to show that writing did exist in India before 600 BC; (b) presence of several Sanskrit texts to show that knowledge in ancient India was mainly transmitted by means of a highly trained memory.

Almost all have ignored the originality of the Indian alphabet. We, however, find two great figures holding a contrary view:

(1) 'The peculiarities of the Indian alphabet demonstrate its independence of all foreign origin and it may be confidently urged that all probabilities and inferences are in favour of an independent invention'. (Professor J Dowson, *J.R.A.S. New Series, vol. XIII*).
(2) 'It (the Indian alphabet) must have been a local invention of the people themselves for the simple reason that there were no people from whom they could have obtained it.' (Cunningham's *Corp. Ins. Indicarum*).
(3) 'Formerly, there was hieroglyphic writing in India and Ashoka's letters were fashioned in imitation of that.' (*ibid*).

Unlike ancient Egypt and Assyria, India is rich in tradition—secure tradition, I may say. Of course, the evidence of tradition is rather inferior, yet it has undoubtedly a high degree of probability. All traditions point to the fact that our remote ancestors were not ignorant of the art of writing. The following will bear out its truth to a great extent:

THE VEDAS

(a) R.V.X., 71. *1–4*

'Children first know the names of objects; that is their first step towards learning a language; their inner thoughts and language gradually develop through the grace of the Goddess of Learning.'

'As they cleanse *saktu* (powdered grain) with a sieve, so have the wise purified language by their intellect. That refined tongue gives them many benefits. In the composition lies fortune.'

'The wise find their way to language by means of sacrifice; thus they got the language which the seers had in their minds. Having got that, they spread it everywhere. The seven metres utter prayers in that language.'

'Some see the words, and yet cannot make out the sense; some hear words, but fail to understand their meanings! As a loving wife, dressed in her gayest, reveals her person to her own lord, so does the Goddess of Speech reveal herself only to her chosen few.'

(b) Ibid., 71.7

'Those who had eyes and ears, i.e. wisdom, attained extraordinary power in expressing their ideas.' Besides, there are other riks in the Rig Veda that show the existence of writing.

(c) The *Kaushitaki Brahmana*

(i) The *Kaushitaki Brahmana* (VII, 6) has it—'Pathyasvasti (a goddess), knows the 'northern region'. Now, Pathyasvasti is *Vach* (the Goddess of Speech). Hence, in the northern region speech is better known and better spoken: and it is to the north that men go to learn speech. It is said that men listen to the instruction of any one who comes from that quarter. For, this is renowned as the region of speech'. (Muir's *Org. Sanskrit Texts, p. 338*).

(Formerly, Aryans from India used to go to *Uttara Kuru* to study science, language. *Pathyasvasti*—an Aryan woman of ancient Afghanistan went to the north, studied there and obtained the title of *Vak*, i.e. Sarasvati.)

(ii) The *Gopatha Brahmana* of the *Sama-Veda* describes and discusses alphabet and letters.
(iii) The *Tandya Brahmana* also hints at alphabet and letters.

THE VEDANGAS

(a) Siksha, (i.e. training of articulation)

All early grammarians insisted on the distinct and correct articulation of letters and sounds as otherwise the gods would be displeased. Even Panini—the last of the Vedic grammarians (about 800 BC) says in his work on Siksha: 'The letters should be so uttered that they are neither indistinct nor eaten.' He further states in the same work that according to Mahesa, there are sixty-three or sixty-four letters. Brahma also confirms it.

(b) Kalpa, i.e. the treatise on rites and rituals

Geometry (Sanskrit, *Sulva Sastra*) forms a part of it. In medieval Sanskrit, it is called *rekha ganita*, i.e. lineal measurement of plane surface. The words *rekha* (line) and *lekha* (writing) are basically the same. The former applies to geometry, while the latter to the lineal representation of ideas or thoughts, i.e. writing. These two are kindred. The existence of the former shows the existence of the latter. These 'Rules of the Cord' form a part of the *Taittiriya Samhita* of the '*White Yajur Veda*' of the fourteenth century BC.

(c) Vyakarana (Grammar)

Formerly, the people of Central Asia spoke a free tongue, called *Balhika Bhasha* or *Brahma Bhasha*. At the request of the learned Aryans, Indra, Chandra and Mahesa wrote the first scientific grammars. From that time, the chaste tongue *Sanskrita* came to be used. These grammarians invented letters. *Brahma*, the first Aryan Pope, perfected and introduced the alphabet, afterwards known as the *Brahmi Lipi*—father of the alphabets, *Sarada, Sriharsha* and *Kutila* and grandfather of the later Indian alphabets. The *Brahmi-Lipi* was the alphabet of the Aryans and Mahesa their grammar. Panini has quoted the alphabet of Mahesa. As the great English poet Spenser tried in his poem to preserve the old school, so Valmiki, Vyasa and his disciples tried to preserve the old Vedic School. Vedic

Sanskrit prevailed till 1000 BC. From 1000 BC to 700 BC sacred Sanskrit and secular Sanskrit flourished alike. From 700 BC, Pali reigned supreme for at least five hundred years. Panini flourished about 800 BC and compiled his *Grammar in Eight Lectures* to serve both secular and sacred writings. The main points are as follows:

(i) Panini's grammar contains the words *libi* and *lipi* (alphabet), *Nishka* and *Rupya* (coins).

(ii) The fourteen rules of Mahesa quoted by Panini in the beginning of his grammar, show the divisions of the alphabet.

(iii) Panini frankly admitted his debt to his predecessors like Yaska, Paraskara, Sakatayana, Vyasa and his disciples whose works he had consulted and whose rules he had quoted in his grammar.

(iv) Panini has used the word *grantha* (a written book) four times in his grammar.

(v) He has used the word *Yavanani* (alphabet of the Greeks?) which shows that other alphabets were then in use in India.

(d) The Nirukta (philology) of Yaska and Prosody also refer to the existence of an alphabet.

THE UPANISHADAS

The *Taittiriya, Siksha-valli* section, mentions *Varna* (letters) and *Swara* (vowels).

The *Chhandogya Upanishad* (*p.* 132) states that Indra invented the fourteen vowels; Chandra invented the four aspirant S', Sh, S, H, and Mahesa invented the twenty-nine letters from *ka* to *wa*.

THE SAMHITAS (CODES)

Manu Samhita, Chapter VIII, sl. 47, 51–52: 'If a creditor applies to the king for the recovery of money from the debtor, then the king must first prove from the evidence of witness and document, the debt and then cause the amount to be paid to the creditor and if it appears that the debtor denies the debt altogether then he must punish the debtor in a suitable way.'

Ibid sl. 168: 'Anything done under compulsion regarding gift, possession, evidence, writing must be set down as invalid.'

Vishnu Samhita, VII, lays down thirteen sutras on the writing of documents.

Narada: 'In a law-suit, he whose case is proved to be true by the evidence of witness or written document or possession or by swearing is certainly the winner; otherwise, he is defeated.'

Manu, Narada, Yajnavalkya, Katyayana, Gautama, Vrihaspati, Baudhayana—all ancient law-givers—hold that written evidence is the strongest of all.

Yajnavalkya Chapter 1, sl. 318–30; Chapter II, sl. 5–7 refer to writing, to be used in plaints, documents with definite dates.

Vyasa: 'A draft should be first drawn on a piece of wood, or clay; then after necessary correction, it should be set down in some writing material.'

(The writing material were wood, rock, clay, metallic plates, barks and leaves of trees, bricks, and paper. Yajnavalkya speaks of paper made of cotton and other material).

Parasara (in his *Code, Chapter X*) speaks of the Kayasthas as professional writers.

Vrihaspati says: 'Since men are apt to forget things even in six months, Brahma made a regular alphabet to be used in writing of various kinds, long, long ago.'

THE SANSKRIT EPICS

It appears from the *Ramayana* that it was written by Valmiki.

Rama, Sundara Book, canto 36: Hanuman speaking to Sita, says, 'I have come as a spy of Rama. Just see the ring bearing his name. The end of your sorrows is near, rest assured.'

The same epic tells us that Rama was well-versed in the poems and the plays of his times, containing various Prakrit elements.

The *Mahabharata*, discoursing on the Golden Age, states that there was no sale of the Vedas then.

The same epic, *Shanti Parva* mentions the Brahmi alphabet and the matter of the Vedas being written in it.

Elsewhere, in the same epic, it is said that the sellers, blamers and the writers of the Vedas (for sale) shall go to hell.

Yuan Chwang also speaks of the *Brahmi Lipi* as being of Brahma.

Here, it may be argued by some that the references to the art of writing in ancient India as given in the *Codes*, are really later interpolations. But scholars generally believe that the present metrical codes are based on the old prose, the Dharma *Sutras*.

THE PURANAS

- The *Padma Purana, Patalakhanda, Chapter 63* describes at length the *Brahmi* or *Deva Lipi*.
- The *Garuda Purana, Part I, Chapters 209–16* deals with alphabet and grammar.
- The glory of the *Bharmi* or *Deva* alphabet has been recorded in different Puranas.

OTHER NOTICES

The *Bhava-Prakasa* (a medical work) states that Brahma wrote in simple language a great work on medicine called the *Brahma Samhita* in a lakh (1,00,000) of shlokas.

Trade concerns and state affairs required writing. A state could not but keep records. Dr Fleet also speaks of our 'ancient archives'. (*Imp. Gaz. of Ind., vol. 2, Epigraphy, p. 4*).

The Sanskrit epics and the Puranas testify that the horse of a sacrifice had to be let loose with a letter of challenge on the forehead of the beast. The victor usually erected pillars of victory on the conquered tracts. They had to issue invitation letters to the conquered chiefs under imperial seal and signature to attend a sacrifice. Holy grounds were marked with sacrificial posts of metal. These were meant to proclaim their glories in written descriptions to posterity.

All grants of lands, tributary engagements, contracts, treaties required writing. The gold coins called *nishka* and other articles of gift often bore a description of the royal donors. Shafts, swords, rings, chariots often bore inscriptions of their distinguished owners. Letters passed between kings, private persons, merchants, lovers.

The early *Rig Veda* of over a lakh of hymns, the *Rik Pratisakhyas* and the *Anukramanikas*—all very voluminous—were divided into books, cantos, chapters, sections, and subsections. We cannot say if mortal memory, however trained, could remember those delicate details.

The largest number in the Hindu arithmetic is of eighteen digits. Without writing, how could such highly complex calculations be made?

The earliest alphabetists are said to have been the Egyptians, the Babylonians, the Phoenicians, and the Chinese. These peoples were known to one another. Scholars hold that from China to Egypt, there was once one domain of great Aryan influence. They also hold that the people of Egypt, Chaldea and China were perhaps a fusion of the natives and the Aryan intruders from Central Asia. The Phoenicians also were no other than Aryan colonists in Asia Minor. Their name in the *Rig Veda* was *Pani* merchants (Latin *Poeni*).

Findings of some inscriptions in Asia Minor of the fourteenth century BC shows the invocation to the Vedic gods Varuna and Nasatya. The most probable fact is that the Aryan *Panis* first traded with the West; afterwards a colony of them settled in Asia Minor.

Speaking of the Phoenician influence on history, the editor of *Historians' History of the World* observes that their position was more due to their circulation of the cultures of the eastern lands to western countries than to their own creations (*H.H.W., vol. 2. p. 353*); that 'Even Chinese ideas were to some extent accessible through the mediation of India' (*ibid. vol. 1, p. 472*); Yajnavalkya (circa 1350 BC) speaks of paper made of cotton and other material. Nearchus also (fourth century BC) refers to the Hindu manufacturing of paper from cotton.

The ancient Hindus knew the approximate shape and size of their own land (Cunningham's *Anc. Geo. Of India*). They knew the distances of places all over India. The waysides were marked with *krosankas* (i.e. milestones).

3

HINDU CHRONOLOGY

'Chronology,' says Professor Petrie, 'is the backbone of history.' Judged by this, we Hindus have strong muscles but a weak backbone; more material for reconstruction, but less secure chronology. Looking into our own chronology we meet with two forms of it—one historical and the other monstrous, meant to magnify things and thereby attract 'lightless mass' towards Hinduisation. Needless to say that we have nothing to do with the *yugas*, the monstrous chronology and the legends. Though based on astronomical calculations, yet for historical purposes, the said monstrous chronology may be safely rejected.

In ancient India, five different kinds of years were current. Of them, the solar years of 365 and a quarter days and the lunar year of 354 days were most prominent. In all secular matters, the lunar year has been in common use. Bhaskara in his *Siddhanta Siromani* also states: 'The measurement of months, days and year is regulated by the course of the moon.'

We shall now consider the principal years of ancient India and see which of them furnishes us with the sound chronological backbone of our history.

(i) The *Gavam-Ayana*, i.e. the Cows' Era (solar), used by the Vedic seers who reckoned such 460 cycles, four years made a *cow* or cycle. Therefore, they counted 1,840 years in all. As the initial or the final point of it is not known, we better abandon it.

(ii) The *Kaliyuga Era* (lunar) begins in 3102 BC, i.e. 2950 BC (solar).
(iii) *Saptarshi Era* of Kashmir (lunar) begins in 3076 BC, i.e. 2925 BC (solar).
(iv) The *Yudhisthira Era* (1388 BC) is long dead.
(v) The *Maurya Era* (312 BC), is now obsolete.
(vi) The *Samvat Era* begins in 58 BC (lunar), i.e. 56 BC (solar).
(vii) The *Sakavda* (solar) begins in AD 78.
(viii) The *Gupta Era* begins in AD 319.
(ix) The *Harsha Era* begins in AD 605–6.

We find three *Kaliyugas* in our Hindu writings—the Aryan *Kaliyuga*, the war *Kaliyuga* and the astronomical but imaginary *Kaliyuga* of Brahmagupta (b. AD 598). Of these, the first is historical and genuine; the second is a clever invention of the later Brahmans to magnify Krishna and to popularise his worship. The third is to last 4,32,000 years and is an imaginary period and as such falls beyond the domain of history. The *Mahabharata* and the *Bhagavata Purana* are foremost in preaching the war of *Kaliyuga*. Hence, the *Kaliyuga* epoch, 3102 BC is usually identified with the era of Yudhisthira and the date of the *Mahabharata War*. This wrong notion has seriously disturbed the balance of our Hindu chronology.

Then, what is the Aryan *Kaliyuga* epoch? What is its historical origin? The answer is clearly hinted in the *Mahabharata, Shanti Parva*, Chapter 59. The facts in full are: the moral fall of the Aryans, then living in and around the Kashmir valley was rapid. The seers and the sages lived apart from the mass; they seldom married and were mostly given to religious contemplation. The mass of the Aryans, without a proper leader soon became vicious, indulging in rape, adultery and theft. Aryan nature ran quite wild. Brahma, the greatest Aryan sage, came to know of this. To reform and regenerate the Aryans he held a council, to ask the chief sages and seers to marry and be in touch with the people. Many, however, refused to marry, but some thirty sages agreed. Brahma himself married. The sages now became known as *prajapatis*, i.e. progenitors. Of these, there were seven wise brothers known in history as *Saptarishi*, i.e. the seven seers. From them have come the high-caste Hindus of India. The national character of the Aryans was soon essentially reformed by the vigorous efforts of Brahma who is further said to have drawn up a long penal code for the regulation of society. This work, condensed over the years, gave rise to the *Niti-sastras* of Vrihaspati, Sukra, Kamandaka, Chanakya and others.

To mark the epoch of this Aryan downfall, the *Kaliyuga* era was established. It began from 2950 BC (solar) and continues to this day. The *Saptarishi* era was founded in honour of the seven wise seers already referred to. It has ever been confined to its native place, Kashmir. The difference of the two years is 26 years lunar or 25 years solar. Therefore, 2925 BC was the starting point of the *Saptarishi* era. Doubtless, these two eras are historical. Here is the beginning of our Hindu history. We may place the rule of Manu VII, the first king of the solar dynasty, approximately in the year 2800 BC or a little later.

Having fixed this outer limit of our chronology, we next proceed to determine the other important periods and points. According to some, Chandragupta ascended the throne in 321 BC. This is incredible. Alexander died in 323 BC. How could Chandragupta, then a helpless fugitive, win north India and Afghanistan in two years? We are, therefore, inclined to think that he was crowned in 312 BC, having fought and worked hard for ten years (323 BC to 313 BC) to build his empire. This also appears from the following:

'Sthulabhadra—the nineth successor of Mahavira and a minister of the nineth and the last Nanda, died either 215 or 219 years after the death of Mahavira—the same year in which the last Nanda was slain by Chandragupta' (*J.R.A.S. XI, 246*). Mahavira died about 531 BC or 528–27 BC. Therefore, 531–219 = 312 or 527–215 = 312 BC. The Maurya era in which King Kharavela of Kalinga dated his inscription also proves the initial point of it as 312 BC.

Most of the Puranas assign to the Nanda Dynasty a regnal length of hundred years (lunar). The *Vayu Purana* gives ninety-six years. Taking this minimum, we have ninety-six lunar years = ninety-three solar. Therefore 312+93 = 405. So, Nanda the Rich was crowned in 405 BC. Nanda ruled for forty years and his eight sons for fifty-three years.

The *Sisunaga Dynasty*. The Puranic figures of 362 years (*Vishnu Purana*), 360 years (*Bhagavata*) and 332 years (*Vayu Purana*) for only ten kings, though not altogether impossible do not seem to be credible. Taking twenty-five years to a reign we can allow 250 years at most for the ten Sisunaga rulers, 405+250 = 655. Therefore, the year 655 BC is the date when Sisunaga, the first king, ascended to the throne. The date of Buddha, the great Hindu reformer, deserves here a passing notice. All traditions affirm that he died at the advanced age of eighty. As this was according to the lunar measure, Buddha therefore lived seventy-seven solar years. The date of Buddha's death has not yet been finally settled. It was formerly believed to be sometime about the middle of the sixth century BC. Later research of Fleet, Buhler, Takakusu (*J.R.A.S. 1905, p. 51*) and Sarat Chandra Das, (*J.R.A.S. Part I, 1886, pp. 193–203*) proves it to be 487–86 BC (487 + 77 = 564). Therefore, Buddha was born in April or early May 564 BC and died in April or early May 487 BC.

The *Pradyota Dynasty.* The Puranas assign to the five rulers of the line, a period of 138 years. But Pandit Kaliprasanna Vidyaratna in his translation of the *Vishnu Purana* adopted 128 years, perhaps on good authority. This would be a minimum of 128 lunar = 124 solar years. Therefore, 655 + 124 = 779 BC witnessed the end of the Varhadratha dynasty and the beginning of the Pradyota.

The *Mahabharata War.* The *Vishnu Purana* (*IV, 24–32*) states that from the birth of Parikshit, grandson to Arjuna, to the coronation of Nanda the Rich, there elapsed 1015 years (lunar). Three other Puranas make it 1050 years; i.e. a minimum 1015 = about 983 solar years or 405 + 983 = 1388. Hence, it is highly probable that the Great War took place in November and December 1389 BC. Again, 1389–779 = 610 years during which 23 or 22 kings ruled. *The Bhagavata Purana* gives the distance from the Great War to Nanda as 1,000 years lunar = 969 years solar or 405 + 969 = 1374. Therefore, the date of the War falls on 1374 BC. Needless to say that we prefer this latter date.

The Date of the Ramayana. Rama preceded the Pandavas by some sixty years only. Satananda, son to Gautama, author of the *Hindu Logic*, was the priest to the marriage of Rama and Sita. Kripa and Kripi, grandchildren of Satananda, were afterwards fostered by King Santanu of Hastinapur. Kripi was married to Drona, the military preceptor to the Kauravas and the Pandavas. Yudhisthira ascended the throne in 1388 BC; Rama began to rule around 1450 BC. Bibhishana, ally of Rama and king of Sinhala tendered his submission to the Pandava general on the eve of the conquest of southern India. Of course, he was then in his old age. The *Ramayana* was composed no later than 1435 BC.

The Solar Dynasty. It is already noted that Manu began to rule around 2800 BC and the *Mahabharata War* started around 1389 BC. Therefore, 2800–1389 = 1411 years: sixty-one kings of the solar line from Manu and Nala, great-grandson of Rama gives an average of 23.2 years to a reign.

Coming of the Aryans. The Aryans had entered India long before the rise of the so-called solar and the lunar dynasties of north India. Scholars disagree as to the earliest date of the Aryan invasion of India. Their views are noted below:

(i) 'It is purely conjectural'—Professor AA Macdonell.
(ii) Professor Jacobi and others give the date as 'at least 4000 BC'.
(iii) General surmise is 2000 BC or a little earlier.
(iv) 'The beginning of this invasion ... dates from a vaguely-determined period which can hardly be more recent than 2000 BC.' (*The Historians' History of the World, vol. 2, p. 483*).

Nobody can say exactly when the Aryans first came to India. Within historic times, the first Aryan occupation of India appears to have occurred about 3000 BC or earlier. Owing to great political disturbances in Central Asia many Aryans came out and settled in West Asia, Babylonia, Afghanistan, and India during 2825 BC or a little later. Manu began to rule in north India around 2800 BC. The *Panis*, i.e. Phoenicians founded their colony in Asia Minor in 2800. The date of Manu is warranted by all traditions and as such may pass for historical date. The Egyptologists vary as to the initial point of their chronology; some give it as 6000 BC and some, as 3000 BC. *The Historians' History of the World* has adopted the mean, i.e. 4500 BC. An eminent English scholar has given it as about 2800 BC. These earliest dates of Egypt, Babylonia and China are conjectural, and yet entitled to a 'certain measure of confidence'. Whatever be the exact date of the first Aryan invasion of India, it is almost certain that the *Kaliyuga* era (2950 BC) and the *Saptarishi* era (2925 BC) of Kashmir are historical.

The *Sisunaga Dynasty*. The Puranic figures of 362 years (*Vishnu Purana*), 360 years (*Bhagavata*) and 332 years (*Vayu Purana*) for only ten kings,

The Samvat and the Sakavda. In direct opposition to Hindu tradition, some scholars have sported curious theories as to the origin of these two eras. According to Professor Keilhorn, Kanishka was the founder of the *Samvat* in 58 BC. Dr Buhler thinks that the former 'Era of Malwa', afterwards became known as the *Vikrama Samvat* owing to its possible connection with Yasodharman of Ujjain.

Again, three different theories are advanced as to the origin of the *Sakavda* (AD 78): (i) It marks the foundation of the Saka Kushan Empire by Kadphises I (AD 45 to 85); (ii) Kanishka founded it; and (iii) It was established by the Sake Satraps of Gujarat when they freed themselves from the yoke of the Indo-Parthian kings.

The basis of these inferences appears to be very weak. Kanishka, according to Dr Stein and others, belonged to the second century AD. Besides, he was not a Saka (Scythian). The Chinese historian Pankuo states that the Sakas were sworn enemies of the Kushans. So, Kanishka could not be the founder of the *Samvat* or the *Sakavda*. Again, if *Sakavda* means a Scythian era (which it is not), the Kushan emperor Kadphises, cannot be its founder. The Satraps of Gujarat were local governors and Scythians the enemies of the Hindus. How could then Hindus of India at large adopt their enemy's era as their own? It is not reasonable nor likely that the Hindus, even to this day, should use the era of their foe, while they have forgotten the era of Yudhisthira, Chandragupta and Harshavardhan!

Hindu tradition connects these two eras with their two great national heroes—Vikramaditya of Ujjain and Salivahana of *Pratisthana*, afterwards *Paithan* (on the Godavari—capital of the Andhra empire of Maharashtra). The first is reckoned from the birth of Vikrama in 56 BC and the second from the death or coronation of Salivahana in AD 78 (see *Savda-Kalpa-Druma*).

Tradition affirms that the first great Vikramaditya lived at Ujjain from 56 BC to perhaps AD 20 or 25 (his father was Gandarbha Sena, brother of the noted poet Bhartrihari; and son, Prince Madhava Sena), that he saved the nation and Hinduism by signally defeating the Scythians whose political importance and outlandish manners had appalled the Indians; that he was just, truthful, mighty, magnanimous, a partron of learning and a staunch supporter of Hinduism; that his very name Vikrama Sena began to be called *Vikramaditya* and his city *Avanti* began to be called *Ujjayini* (the victorious city).

The people most probably started an era after his name but he modestly declined the honours, maintaining that success against the Sakas was largely due to the people of Malwa. So, the era began as *Malavabda*, i.e. the era of Malwa. By it, Vikrama perhaps, showed both compliment and appreciation. However, it continued for several centuries unaltered. Then, fresh successes of new Vikramadityas converted that running era into its later name of *Vikrama Samvat.*

The following points regarding Vikrama's time and historic character will show that he was not a mere 'wandering shadow' from the first century BC to the sixth century AD.

(i) Dr WW Hunter once took from the pandits of Ujjain a list of her rulers which convinced him that the first Vikrama lived there in the first century BC and AD.

(ii) It is said that Vikrama was defeated or killed by the mighty Andhra prince Salivahana. This Salivahana was no other than Sala, native Hala (VA Smith), a king of the Andhra list, ruling from AD 69 to AD 74. Vikrama came to the throne at forty. Therefore, he ruled from 14 or 15 BC to perhaps AD 20.

(iii) The glorious title of *Vikramaditya* (the very sun in prowess) was borne by eight different kings, all noted in history and all fit to assume it. The first one must have been the greatest. Otherwise, the title would not be so enviable.

(iv) *The Satrunjaya Mahatmya, Chapter XIV*, the oldest Sanskrti Jain work composed in AD 420 or AD 598 (Weber) says that 'Javada, a merchant of Saurashtra (Kathiawar) sent a fleet to China and the Eastern Archipelago, which returned after twelve years with a burden of gold. The father of Javada lived in the time of Vikrama who was born 470 years after the death of Mahavira.' Now, Mahavira died in 527 BC. Therefore, Vikrama was born in 527–470 = 57 BC.

(v) The parentage of this first Vikrama differs from that of any other known as Vikramaditya.

(vi) The *Agni Purana* declares him of Scythian origin. This is only possible for the first Vikramaditya.

(vii) Bhartrihari's ideas and language, used in the *Centuries*, differ a good deal from those of the later authors.

(viii) In the *Kumara Sambhava*, Kalidasa refers to the evil influences of a great comet. This seems to show that Kalidasa had witnessed the rise of a great comet and its serious after-effects. India, Central Asia and Eastern Europe were then being convulsed by the Scythian invasions. The great comet was seen in India in AD 1910. It completes a cycle in seventy-six years. Twenty-five revolutions take us back to AD 10. Vikrama assumed the reins of government in 14 or 15 BC. Kalidasa, therefore, may have written his poem sometime between AD 15 and 20.

(ix) *The History of Oudh* tells us that the Mauryas, the Greeks and the Mitras ruled there; then came Vikrama who with his son, held it for eighty years. Then, it was long under the Guptas of Magadha. To revive Hinduism, Vikrama built 360 temples there. Sravasti also was under Vikrama and his son for fourteen years only. It is said that he occupied Sravasti 500 years (485 solar) after the death of Buddha. Therefore, 487–485 = 2 BC. He was an avowed enemy of the Buddhists.

(x) Kashmir was under the Guptas in the fourth century AD. The Vikramaditya (not of *Samvat*) of the Gupta family set up Pratapaditya, a near relation, on the Kashmir throne. AD 343 (*Rajatarangini*).

(xi) Yasodharman Vikramaditya placed Maitrigupta—a poet of his court—on the Kashmir throne (about AD 558).

(xii) Kalidasa's work on astronomy, the *Jyotirvid-Abharana* shows that he wrote it sometime between 35 and 30 BC. Both Vikrama and Salivahana were called *Sakari*, i.e. foe of the Scythians. Vikrama was called Vikramaditya and Salivahana—Sakaditya. The latter is also called Sala Sakendra or Sakanarapati, etc. The name Salivahana probably originated from Sala-Satavahana. The classical Sala corrupted into local Hala is mentioned on the Andhra list. VA Smith's descriptions of Hala tally entirely with the Hindu descriptions of Sala or 'Salivahana'. Hala ruled from AD 78. The Saka era is counted from his coronation (the cave inscription of Badami AD 578) in AD 78. The *Historians' History of the World* also has admitted this origin of the Saka era, that began with the Andhras who brought it to their Magadhan Empire.

(xiii) Pankuo wrote his history of the *Han* dynasty of China about AD 80 or 90. He used the present tense in speaking of Kadphises I's subjugation of the four other Yue-chi tribes. Dr Marshall in his paper on Kanishka's time in *J.R.A.S.April, 1915*, shows Kanishka as subsequent to Kadphises I. So, Kanishka could not be living in 57 BC to be the founder of *Samvat*.

(xiv) Vikrama's *Amara Sinha* was not the same as the one who built the temple of Bodh Gaya in AD 500. Again, we hear of five Varahamihiras—the first, author of the *Vrihad Samhita*, lived in 58 BC; the second, author of a revised edition of *Brahma Siddhanta* lived in AD 80 (see *Jyotishi* p. 62); the third, author of the present *Vrihat Samhita*, lived in AD 285 (see, *Vr. Samhita, Chapter I, Sl. 2;* also *Chapter III Sl.* 22); the fourth, author of the *Panćha Siddhantika* lived in the sixth century AD; and the fifth lived in AD 1600 (see *Visvakosha*).

4

THE PREHISTORIC ARYANS

ANTIQUITY OF HUMAN CIVILISATION

Human civilisation is old, very old. There is no definite way of knowing through how many stages it has passed. We of today cannot form a clear idea of it from the sketchy accounts preserved. Our own historians, if we may call them so, desire us to accept 80,000 BC as the date of the dawn of human civilisation. It is already stated that the grand period of one Manu called a Manvantara lasts 12,000 years (lunar). Six such Manvantaras are said to have already gone. And, a considerable period of Manu VII, son of Vivasvan, has also already run. The notions of other ancient nations far surpass those of the Hindus as regards the length of periods. The Jewish and the Christian world alone long remained fettered within an imagined limit of time. The following excerpts from *The Historians' History of the World* will show what a great change has come upon them regarding their idea of the past:

'Prior to 1859, the people of Christendom rested secure in the supposition that the chronology of man's history was fully known from the very year of his creation. One has but to look to the first chapter of Genesis to find in the margin the date 4004 BC recorded with all confidence, as the year of man's first appearance on the globe. But half a century ago, research, chiefly of a geological nature, revealed new and important facts as to the antiquity of man. Now the historian can speak of dates anterior to 4004 BC. The Egyptologist is disposed to date the building of the Pyramids, a full thousand years earlier than that. And, the Assyriologist is learning to speak of the state of civilisation in Chaldea some 6000 or 7000 BC with a certain measure of confidence. But he no longer thinks of these dates as standing anywhere near the beginning of history. He knows that man in that age, in the centres of progress, had attained a high state of civilisation and he feels sure that there were some thousands of centuries of earlier time during which man was slowly emerging through savagery and barbarism of which we have only the most fragmentary record.

'He does not claim to know anything of the dawn of civilisation. Wherever he turns—in China, Egypt, Chaldea, India—he finds, at best a period of only 8,000 to 10,000 years, giving proof of a civilisation already far advanced. Of the exact origin we know nothing absolutely. The creation of man with its fixed date is a chapter that has vanished from modern histories.' (*H.H.W., vol. I, Introduction*)

Again, it says elsewhere:

'Until the crypts by the Nile and the earth-mounds by the Tigris and Euphrates gave up their secrets, absolutely nothing was known to scholarship of the main sweep of civilisation more ancient than about the sixth century BC. Beyond that, all was myth fable, unauthenticated tradition. Now, the indubitable monuments of civilisation carry us back over a period at least three times as great. Archbishop Usher's famed chronology which so long dominated the ideas of men, is swept away. In the year 4004 BC, the so-called year of creation, vast communities of people, in widely separated portions of the earth, had attained a high degree of civilisation. The more recent excavations by the Americans at the site of Nippar have carried the evidence back to 6000 even 7000 BC. But note how these new figures disturb the balance of history. If our forerunners of eight or nine thousand years ago were in noon-day glare of civilisation, where shall we look for the much talked of "dawnings of history"? By this new standard, the Romans seem our contemporaries in latter-day civilisation; the "golden age" of Greece is but of yesterday; the Pyramid builders are only relatively remote'. (*H.H.W., vol. I, pp. 625–26*).

It is manifest from these that 'the fabled glory of ancient India, Assyria, and Egypt, was no myth, but a very tangible reality'. In the case of India, the architectural remains of the most ancient period are very few. Yet, scholars assign to them a very high and venerable position. The same view of India was expressed by Thornton in 850, several years before these scholars published the wonderful results of their new research. The following points indicate the great antiquity of India.

(i) Her commercial intercourse with Ancient Egypt, Assyria and Assyrio-Babylonia.
(ii) Her ethnological similarities with the most ancient people of these countries.
(iii) Her age-old traditions, often garbed in mythological dress. There is still a class of scholars in Europe who cannot bring themselves to believe the secure Hindu tradition. But eminent authorities are not wanting to hold that:

    (a) 'there is no myth without its background of fact'. (*H.H.W., vol. II, p. 368*).
    (b) 'there is no smoke without some fire is a maxim which the historian should never overlook'. (*ibid.*)
    (c) 'Under the embellishments of the story, and although the facts are clothed in concrete, fabulous and symbolic forms, one can find serious information scarcely affected by the myths, traits of a striking reality which are not due to popular imagination nor to the romantic verve of historians, but which bear the impress of a far-off origin and an incontestable authenticity'. (*H.H.W., vol. II, p. 426*).

Research, mainly English, has lifted the mantle of ages so visibly that the historian may now peep far into the dim ages of the past. Today, men believe things that they would not or did not yesterday. We believe things that the Anglo-Indians do not. Again, the things which the latter see in India and believe, are not often believed in Europe. Europe has, only half a century ago, burst forth from the shell of an imaginary chronology. Hindus always believed in their antiquity. The thousands of centuries before 4004 BC, during which man was slowly climbing towards civilisation is not a new truth to the Hindus who always believed in the existence of six former Manus whose periods cover 72,000 years (lunar). Even then, civilisation was perhaps somewhat advanced. But nobody can give the exact date of the dawn of human civilisation. However, according to Hindus, human history began about 80,000 (lunar) years ago, when Manu I was the ruler. He is also called the *Adima* (the First Patriarch) cf. *Adam*. It is said that he was a very mighty king. Satarupa was his wife. He had seven very worthy and heroic sons who occupied lands in the seven continents of the world, where their children continued to rule. We do not know where Manu I ruled. But there are strong reasons to think that his capital and kingdom were somewhere in the north-west of Europe.

It is now a point of general acceptance that India within the Indus was not the cradle of the most important branch of the East Aryans whose descendants are now represented by the high-caste Hindus. The *Rig Veda* and the Puranas generally agree in pointing to the northern home of the Aryans. The *Bhavishya Purana* and a *Tantra* give a very clear and definite account of the early Aryans. They state that the Aryans at first lived in *Uttara Kuru*, i.e. Siberia, from where they gradually marched towards the south, sending off bands in different directions (*R.V.I. 22–16; I. 64–14; I. 80–51*). They stopped long at selected places till they came to the *Madhya Bhumi*, i.e. Midland of Asia where they finally settled. It is from here that the Aryans entered India. Unmistakable traces of an Arctic home of the Aryans were found in the Vedas (*R.V.I.*, 30–9; I 64–14; *V. 54–15; VI. 19–7*). Thus far, we have broad, settled facts. Beyond this, all traces are lost. No doubt, northern Asia furnished a home to the Aryans but we cannot believe that the physical conditions were such as might create the first Aryans. Many reasons incline us to admit North-West Europe to have been the 'wet nurse' for the first Aryan children. The *Rig Veda* mentions the existence of large Aryan kingdoms in *Roosam* (Russia) and *Hariyupia* (East Europe) before 3000 BC.

Our ancient geography tells us that the Indo-Aryans divided the globe into three principal land-masses—*Aswa-kranta* (Eurasia), the 'horse-shaped'; *Rathakranta* (Africa), the 'car-shaped' and *Vishnu-kranta* (the two Americas), 'Vishnu mounted on his eagle'. Such pictorial representations were common with the early Hindus. The initial *Aswa* is the origin of 'Asia'. The next important information we have, is *saptadvipa prithivi:* the earth has seven continents—*Saka,* Europe, (continent of power); *Jambu* (Asia), so-called from the abundance of *Jambu* trees in ancient times; *Plaksha*, probably the submerged Indo-African continent; *Pushkara*, North America, from Sanskrit *Pushkaras*·

or lakes; *Kusa*, South America, from Sanskrit *Kusa* or grass, Llanos, prairies; *Krauncha* or Oceania, so-called perhaps from the abundance of cranes Sanskrit *Crauncha* or gulls, skua-gulls; and *Salmali*, perhaps Africa, from the abundance of *Salmali*, i.e. silk-cotton trees. We cannot say how far this identity can be maintained. What is certain is that *Jambu* was Asia and *Saka*, Europe. The *Mahabharata* calls it *Saka* or *Sakala Dwipa* ('powerful continent'). In Sanskrit *Ishu-kranta*, or perhaps *Ishurupa* (land of skilled archery) is also a name of Europe. Europe perhaps came from 'Hariyupia' (*R.V.*)

Beyond doubt, Europe is the most powerful of the continents by way of its position, climate, advantage of long coastline, and natural resources. (For full particulars, *vide:* (i) Longmans' *Geography of the World, p. 187* (ii) George Grove's *Geography, pp. 55–59*).

Again, Europe is geographically a part of Asia and as such it forms the largest and the greatest peninsula of Asia. Peninsulas enjoy special boons of nature. So, Europe was and will always be, first in the civilisation and influence of the people. The North-West Europe again is an excellent peninsula. Hence, there is every likelihood that human civilisation first dawned there. Geologists prove the existence of a highly civilised continent in North-West Europe. Another was in Higher Asia. Increase in number, volcanic eruptions and occasional floods forced the primitive Aryans to move eastward in different bands. Some may have settled at the mouth of the Volga (Sanskrit *Variga*, a larger river). Others, taking the most northerly route, gradually reached higher Asia whence they came down to settle in the Central Asiatic tableland. From this central home, the Aryans dispersed in different directions. The following also supports our gleaning from the Puranas and other works:

'Turning then to the Hindus, the eastern-most branch of the great Indo-Germanic or Aryan race, we find as was to be expected, the same utter obscurity as to the origin that we have seen encompassing all questions of racial beginnings elsewhere. One, however, is justified in feeling that in the case of the Hindus, secure traditions carry us one stage further back than is the case, for example, with such races as the Egyptians and the Chinese. For, it is accepted as a clear historic fact that the Aryan race who came to be at a very early date—at least 1000 BC—the absolutely dominant race practically throughout the vast territory of India, had invaded this territory from the north-west. In short, they had come from that Central Asiatic centre of distribution which we have just spoken of as the long-accepted traditional cradle of the Aryan races. Whether at a still earlier period, this migration had its source in more distant lands, including ultimately the Atlantic borders of Europe is altogether problematical, but that the immediate source of invasion was Central Asia, is not to be doubted'. (*H.H.W., vol. 2, p. 482*).

By *Saka-dwipa*, the Indo-Aryans meant Europe. It should be noted here that *Saka-dwipa* and *Jambu-dwipa* did not always mean the same lands. The former at first meant Europe, afterwards East Europe, more specifically the Black Sea and the north of Europe; then the country to the east of the Caspian Sea. Later, Hindu writers meant by *Saka-dwipa* the Central Asiatic region.

Saka-dwipa (Greek, *Sakataj*) and the Scythians appear to have been closely connected with our early history.

It is said that Buddha, the first king of the lunar dynasty was a *Saka*. According to the *Agni Purana*, the five Pandava brothers, the first Vikramaditya of Malwa, the Andhras of the South were Scythians. King Samva, a son of Krishna brought a colony of the Sakali Brahmans to the Punjab and established them there near *Mitra-sthana* or *Mula-sthana* (now, Mooltan) to conduct worship there in the famous Sun Temple, founded by the king in that city. Yuan Chwang visited the temple. The Sun God, worshipped there, was of pure gold. He called the place *Mul-Sambura*, a corruption of ancient *Mulasthana Sambapura*. From there, the Sakali Brahmans scattered all over India. The astronomers Aryabhatta and Varahamihira were of the same clan. These brahmans are still gurus (spiritual guides) to many native chiefs of India. After dispersion some Aryans still continued to live on the tableland, their descendants long, long after, partly mixed with the Mongols and known as the Scythians, invaded Europe and India where they held great political sway for several centuries before and after the Christian era. It was a band of these Sakas who became known in some parts of Europe as the Saxons (Sanskrit *Saka-sunu*).

It is notable here that the early Scythians were essentially the same people as the Hindus. So, they were easily accepted into the Hindu society. The later Scythians were generally notorious for their corrupt, and outlandish manners. However, their political importance, long stay in India, and gradual adoption of Hindu manners smoothed their way to Hindu recognition. Thus, the Hunas, the Kushans, the Mongoloids became absorbed in the Hindu population. Even some of the Moghul emperors were half-Hinduised.

5

THE ARYANS

The history of India would be incomplete and less interesting unless told in reference to other lands of interests. For this reason, we give here a brief sketch of the Aryans. The Accadians lived north of them, the Yellow People lived in the east, the Dravidians in the south, the Semitic and the Coptic peoples in the west. Of the Aryans themselves, we do not know much. Ethnologists believe that they were a fair tall race, with acquiline nose, strong muscular frame and very high brain power. Beyond doubt, these Aryans excelled the other advanced nations of the time by their spiritualistic civilisation. From various Puranas we glean the following meagre sketch about the Aryans.

They lived in good caves and in wooden or leafed houses. They were very fond of fire, as it gave them warmth and comforts in their cold homes. Their food was chiefly milk, butter, honey, flower, leaves, grains, roots, fruits, juice of the milk-tree. 'Honest water' no longer allayed their thirst; so they used beverage of several kinds such as *gauri, baruni* and *soma-rasa*.

Sincere prayer and profound meditation were their only forms of worship. They knew neither temple nor image. Flower, leaves, incense or other offerings were not used in worship. The most learned of them sought nature's God. But the mass worshipped Him through the medium of various beneficent spirits of nature. Some of their women were very learned. The Aryans were noted for their general plain living and high thinking. They knew the use of some metals and cattle formed their chief wealth. In their constant effort to pierce through the mysteries of the universe they early conceived the idea of the existence of God and perhaps, of one God. Their scientific turn of mind first discovered the grand order of nature and conceived a lofty idea of purity. Their moral ideal also was very lofty. Their regard for truth, promise, and hospitality was great. They were conscious of sin and believed that God, sincerely prayed to, might take away all sins. They knew the soul, the law of karma (action), and immortality of the soul. They had no towns or cities in the modern sense. They lived in *gramas* (villages); different families of the same stock often living together in clans. At times they would fight with their enemies. Their great thinkers called rishis (seers) conceived by deep meditation some lofty ideas about God and universe which they composed in metres afterwards called *riks* (hymns) and were sung by different families in a sort of choir, at daybreak, midday and at sundown. Some scholars hold that these *riks* began to be compiled from 4500 BC. Their language was an older form of classical Sanskrit. This was what may be called the old Rig Vedic period. The Aryans sang the hymns from memory and perhaps, did not have any sort of alphabet till then.

Commerce is the grand instrument of civilisation in the world. The Aryans under review had high commercial spirits. They were very bold and adventurous. They travelled much and visited foreign lands and brought home all necessary information. We know that gold, the excellent metal, was in high request with the 'excellent people'. At first, an overland caravan trade was carried on especially with the West, diffusing Aryan knowledge and civilisation everywhere. Gradually, the Aryans felt inclined to colonise the West. Before long, they entered Babylonia, Assyria and Egypt. The Aryan merchants called *Panis* in the *Rig Veda*, afterwards settled in Asia Minor, in a sea board tract—150 to 200 miles long and 50 to 60 miles broad—around 2800 BC (*H.H.W.*). Before 3000 BC the Aryans adopted navigation. The *Sataritra Nau* (a ship of 100 oars) and other reference to sea abound in the *Rig Veda*. Modern research gives us still more wonderful facts—as will appear from the following:

'It is coming to be a common agreement among the Assyriologists that the original peoples of Babylon were of a race that was not Semitic. Just what it was, these scholars are not prepared to say although the inclination of belief is that it was an Indo-European race and most likely of the Turanian family.

'It has been often observed that Southern Babylonia was originally the proper home of the Sumerians before 4000 BC. Northern Babylonia was peopled by the Semitic people whom Prof Hommel thinks immigrants from some parts of Central Asia and not Arabic Bedouins.' (*H.H.W., vol. I. p. 352*).

Archælogical research tends to show that colonists from ancient India in remote ages settled in Mesopotamia. The Mesopotamian culture displayed by the ancient Babylonians and Assyrians, was derived from the Sumerians who were no other than the Indian emigrants into Mesopotamia. '*Meso-potamia*' is Sanskrit *Madhya-Vedi* (a doab). Sanskrit=*madhya*, Prakrit=*majjho*, Bengali=*mejo*, English=*mizzen*. HR Hall of the British Museum, London, speaks thus on the origin of the Sumerians:

'The Sumerian culture springs into our view readymade as it were, which is what we should expect if it was as seems on their grounds probable, brought into Mesopotamia from abroad.... The earliest scenes of their culture-development had, perhaps, not been played upon the Babylonian stage at all, but in a different country, away across the Persian mountains to the eastward.... The ethnic type of the Sumerians, so strongly marked in their statues and relief, was as different from those of the races which surround them as was their language from those of the Semites ... or others; they were decidedly Indian in type. The face-type of the average Indian of today is, no doubt, much the same as that of his race ancestors thousands of years ago. And, it is by no means improbable that the Sumerians were an Indian race which passed certainly by land, perhaps, also by sea, through Persia to the valley of the two rivers. It was in the Indian home (perhaps the Indus valley) that we suppose for them that their culture developed. There, their writing may have been invented and progressed from a purely pictorial to a simplified and abbreviated form which afterwards in Babylonia took on its peculiar *cuneiform* appearance owing to its being written with a square ended stylus on soft-clay. There is little doubt that India must have been one of he earliest centres of human civilisation and it seems natural to suppose that the strange un-Semitic people who came from the East to civilise the West, were of Indian origin, especially when we see with our eyes how very Indian the Sumerians were in type.'

Another class of archæologists hold that there were trade relations between west India and Sumer, about 6000 BC, and there is the linguistic and ethnic resemblance between the Sumerians and the Dravidians. Besides, from their statues, we see them with shaven heads and wearing long garments. Their physiognomy and dress bear such close resemblance to the Dravidians that their common origin is not improbable, as such striking similarity cannot be merely accidental.

We think, these Sumerians were neither Indo-Aryans nor Dravidians. We have shown elsewhere, from the *Rig Veda* and the *Mahabharata* that in the great Deva-Asura War (twenty-nineth century BC) fought, off and on, for thirty-two years, the Devas had driven out other opponent Aryan tribes from Central Asia. The Sumerians were people of the Sumeru (the *Good Hill* of the North). Rudra had driven some to the shores of the western sea. The two brothers Vritra and Bala, with their Aryan followers settled in Persia and Mesopotamia, respectively. The *Panis,* though traders, were however, allies of the Asuras, shared defeat with them and were ousted from the North. They planted their colony on the Levant Sea about 2800 BC. Their capital Tyre was built in 2750 BC. For a like fault, these *Panis* of the West, were almost exterminated by Alexander the Great in the fourth century BC (Vide also Dr Banerji's *Aryan Witness p. 62*).

The new name of *Assyria* is perhaps, an imitation of Sanskrit A'suriya. Failing to cope with the Asuras at first, Indra led the Northern colonists and settled them somewhere in A'pa, i.e. Afghanistan and some in India. Then, he turned towards the north, gathered strength and defeated the Asuras, and regained their lost states. Vritra concluded a treaty with Indra and founded a new capital at Babylon. But the infamous Indra wilfully broke the terms of the treaty and treacherously killed Vritra in an unjust battle. Summoned by Prince Abhyavarti, son to king Chayamana and an ally of Indra, the latter went to East Europe and killed several sons of Varasikha of the Vrichivat clan (*R.V. VI. 27. 5*). Probably, the Greeks also shot off from the central home towards the west about this time. Thus Russia, East Europe, Greece, West Asia, Mesopotamia, Persia, Afghanistan, and India were filled by the Aryan Colonists sometime before and after 2800 BC.

Again, authorities are not willing to show that the early Aryans were also very closely connected with the ancient Egyptians by blood, or at least by bone. We quote from the same *H.H.W.*, texts in illustration of the above:

(1) 'Among the earlier students of the subject, Heeren was prominent in pointing out an alleged analogy between the form of skull of the Egyptian and that of the Indian races. He believed in the Indian origin of the Egyptians.'

The Editor of *The Historians' History of the World*, however says,

> Heeren believed, the skulls of the Egyptians and of the Indian races of antiquity, as preserved in the tombs of the respective countries, bear a close resemblance to one another. What after all, does it prove? Presumably, it implies that these two widely separated nations have perhaps had a common origin. But it might mean that the Egyptians had one day been emigrants from India or conversely; or that the forefathers of both nations had, at a remoter epoch, occupied some other region, perhaps in an utterly different part of the globe from either India or Egypt.

This too, is open to doubt for, unity of origin from a seeming similarity of skulls alone is not sufficient.

(2) 'The Egyptians were essentially orientals.' (*H.H.W., vol. I. p. 198*).
(3) The Egyptians are said to have been divided into castes, similar to those of India. (*ibid, p. 200*)
(This certainly alludes to a much later Hindu influence on Egypt).

The Egyptians themselves called their country *Kamit*, i.e. Black Country. The Semìtic people called Egypt *Mior* or *Musr*, Hebrew *Misraim*, Arabic *Masr*—all being corruptions of Hindu *Misra Desa* (country of mixed people; so called because people from different parts of the globe repaired there for trade). But the early Aryan name for Egypt was *Ekantina*—a country of people devoted to one Supreme Being. Hindus still call Egypt *Misar*. Modern scholars also believe that 'the Egyptians of history are a fusion of an indigenous white race of N.E. Africa and an intruding people of Asiatic origin.' (*H.H.W., vol. I, p. 66*).

(4) Dr Royle also held similar views in his comparison between ancient Egypt and ancient India.

(5) Tod says, 'Ancient writers assert that from ancient Ethiopia (now, 'Nubia') Egypt had her civilised institutions and that the Ethiopians were of Indian origin. Cuvier quoting Syncellus, even assigns the reign of Amenophis as the epoch of the colonisation of Ethiopia from India.' (*Rajasthan, vol. II, p. 180*).

From these, it is highly probable that the Aryans formed a most important part of the early peoples of Egypt and Assyria. Below is given an estimate of the civilisation of these latter, which, no doubt, indirectly proves the greatness of the Aryans:

'Even under the Old Kingdom, Egypt is a country in a high state of civilisation: a centralised government, a high level of technical skill, a religion in exuberant development, an art that has reached its zenith, a literature that strives upward to its culminating point—we see displayed in its monuments. In ancient Babylonia alone, the nation of the Sumerians reached a similar height.' (*H.H.W., Vol. I, p. 59*).

(6) Homer called the Indians 'eastern Ethiopians'. This seems to show that the Greeks believed in the racial affinity of the Hindus and the Egyptians.

Thus we see, the sphere of early Aryan domination and influence was very large. The Aryan merchants called *Panis* spread the Aryan civilisation everywhere. Their trade was at first an overland one, carried on camels. But before 3000 BC, they took to navigation for sea-borne trade. At first, it was, doubtless, a mere coasting-trade, carried on with the countries of the west.

Towards India, the Aryans did not advance far. Their occupation of Kashmir took place perhaps not later than 3000 BC. The Aryans loved and praised their own *Madhya Bhumi* (Central Region) as a *Land of Promise*, while they hated and called India as a *Land of Vice*. Certainly, they knew her great physical defects such as intense heat and enervating climate. India now appears as a smiling garden of Nature. Successive civilisations have filled her with many good things of other lands. Most of our garden, flowers, fruits, good-stuffs, and spices are not the true natives of the soil. When the Aryan world, indicated above, enjoyed the 'noon-day glare of civilisation'. India was mostly a tree-clad land, full of birds, beasts and reptiles. There were dark-skinned aborigines and

Nagas and Kols who lived almost in the buff. Only the Dravidians knew the elements of civilised culture such as clothing and housing, use of fire, implements of peace and war, domestication of animals, agriculture, government, and the arts of paining.

Neither the Aryans nor the Non-Aryans appear to have entered India through choice. External compulsion made them seek a refuge here. Perhaps about 4000 BC, some political disturbance happened in parts of Central Asia, which drove the Nagas (Tibeto-Burmans) to enter India through her north-eastern gate.

Their muscular frame, yellowish complexion, flat nose, small eyes, high cheek-bones, and scanty beard show that they originally belonged to the Mongoloid stock. At one time, they spread over a considerable part of north India, but pressed by later invaders, they have long settled in the sub-Himalayan countries, extending from north-east Assam to the Laddakh district in Kashmir. The Akas, Duflas, Missimis, Maurees, Lepchas, Bhutias, Sikkimese, Gurkhas, Garos, Kukis, and the Nagas are their descendants. In the initial stage of their Indian life, of course, they depended on hunting and the wild products of the land. They knew not the use of metals and used implements of sharpened stone and fish-bone only. As they continued to live in the country, they gradually took to a settled course of life. In later times, the Aryan sages improved them much by teaching them various peaceful arts. The Puranas say these Aryan sages even raised up issue in their women to turn the Nagas into a finer race!

The *Rig Veda* I, 92, 7–8; IV, 56.4; V, 18.5; VI, 19.10; VII, 86.7; and VIII, 56.3 makes mention of a class of men called *Dasyus* or *Dàsas* who were *adeva* (without gods) and *avrata* (without worship). Western scholars think that they, being defeated by the Aryans, became *Sudras*. This conclusion is open to some objection. For, the *Sudras* originally were not a distinct class, but slaves, composed of both Aryans and the *Dasyus;* the *Sudras* were mostly Dravidian converts. Even to this day, some seventy per cent of the Hindus form the so-called depressed classes whose water is not acceptable and who are generally regarded as the untouchables. The later Vedas mention a class of men called the *Nishada jati*, i.e. the hunter class. (vide, *Yajur* Veda, Chapter on *Rudra*). They are dark, short in stature, snub-nosed, eat wild food, and drink water from earthen pots. We think the early Rig Vedic *Dasyus* were the later

Nishadas or the pre-Dravidan races. At present, some of them speak the Munda tongue, some the Dravidian tongues; the Bhils speak an Aryan tongue. Their relations with the Veddas of Ceylon and with the aborigines of the Malayan Archipelago, the Andaman and the Nicobar Islands, and Australia have led some to call them an Austro-Asiatic race. Some hold that they came originally from Australia. Smith thinks that they scattered from India, their primitive homes. Sir HH Risley classifies the wild people of the Central Provinces and the Deccan along with the Dravidian type. No other western scholar has done so before.

In the Vedic Age, the *Nishadas* lived under their own chiefs, not very far from the Aryan settlements. They would set trap, catch birds and beasts and fed mainly on that. It is said that Aryans served as priests to the *Rudra* sacrifices celebrated by the *Nishada* chiefs. Of course, the priests would get some fees and other gifts. The term *Dasyu* (robber) seems to have been applied to the Dravidians also; yet these Dravidians were not barbarous robbers. They were navigators, civilised and brave. They had 'hundred cities'. Why did the Dravidians bear Aryan names? Many rishis had lived in north India and taught the natives before the rise of the Aryan kingdoms there. The rishis may have given them Aryan names. The Puranas assert that the so-called non-Aryans of India also came from the North and were half-caste Aryans. For Aryan fathers begot them on the native women of the North. So, they were called *Deva-yoni-s*. If we accept this view, then we face one difficulty. All the Northerners were white or yellow; but the Indian nōn-Aryans are called *'dark-skinned'*. Hence, we are bound to admit that the non-Aryans had entered India long, long before the Aryans.

It is possible that different bands of the Tibeto-Burmans had entered India at different times. One group of them came to India as late as the thirteenth century AD. These, called *Ahoms*, gradually conquered the province of Assam, called after them. They became Hinduised and ruled the country till it became a British province. The *Ahoms* possess a correct history of their own.

Probably, to these Tibeto-Burmans (Sanskrit *Nagas*) we owe the importation of *orange* from China or thereabout. The etymology of the word seems to confirm the belief of the people. Orange is a corruption of *naranga*, contracted from Sanskrit *nagaranga* (i.e. delighter of the Nagas). In the *Mahabharata* time, Chittagong Division, and the Tipperas (now, Bangladesh and Tripura) were known as the *Nagaloka* (i.e. land of the Nagas). The third Pandava, Arjuna had married the Naga princess Ulupi. The royal families of Manipur and Tippera had become Aryan before the fourteenth century BC. The word remains only in the Naga Hill and the Naga people. In these Naga tracts, they tried orange plantations long, as they do tea now. But the orange has been found to thrive most in Sylhet and other neighbouring districts. In India, Nagpur turns out the best oranges. But we are not sure, if the Naga of Nagpur has anything to do with the Tibeto-Burmans.

To them succeeded in later times, the Kolarians (Sanskrit *Kola*)—another non-Aryan people from Central Asia or North Asia—through perhaps the same north-east passes. The word *coolie* probably comes from the name. They were the ancestors of the Mundas, the Santhals, the Bhils, the Andaman Islanders, and the Veddas of Ceylon. In course of time, they spread throughout India and to Ceylon. They now mostly live in the north-eastern edge of the Deccan plateau. They did not know how to tame cattle, but knew how to use iron implements.

Lastly, came the Dravidians with a still higher civilisation. In point of materialistic civilisation, they were no mean rivals of the Aryans. They are now found chiefly in south India and north Ceylon. Scholars differ as to their original home. Some think that they came from upper Asia and entered India through the north-western passes. From the existence of the *Brahuis*, a Dravidian colony in Baluchistan, they infer that these people came from the North. If so, they were perhaps an Acadian or a Turanian offshoot. Others regard them as the remnants of the people of Lemuria—the submerged Indo-African continent—known to the early Aryans by the name of *Plaksha Dwipa*. Dr Hærnle holds that these people once filled the whole of India, Ceylon, the Andaman, the Nicobar Islands, Australia, and other islands in the east. Some make them of Egyptian origin. Whatever be their origin, it is certain that they were a better people following agriculture and trade, using implements of copper, clearing the jungles, wearing ornaments of gold, building forts and cities, and having a monarchical form of government. They were dark in complexion, bold in spirits, tillers of the soil and worshippers of Mother Earth under the symbols of serpent. They drove their predecessors to the hills and forests and occupied the northern plains. But in time they also had to face a new invader in the Aryans whom they fought desperately for centuries; but at last failing to cope with the newcomers, they retreated to the Deccan where their children still form the largest part of the people.

There is very little room to doubt that the non-Aryans became disposed of in two different ways. The spirited and freedom-loving Nagas and Kolas went to the hills, and the bold Dravidians went beyond the Vindhyas. A large body of them surrendered to the Aryans, adopted the victors' manners, and gradually became Hinduised. Thus, it is that the middle-caste Hindus were formed of the sub-caste Aryans and the Dravidian converts; the low-caste Hindus were formed of sub-caste low Aryans and the Naga and Kola converts.

Though yet far backward, the non-Aryans are found brave, truthful, honest, and loyal. It was mainly the Dravidian army that helped Rama to defeat Ravana, the Tamil king of Ceylon and southern most peninsula. The Dravidian sepoys lent material aid to the success of the English at Plassey (AD 1756). And, it is well known that the Dogras and the Gurkhas—the Indian highlanders are second to none in bravery and sturdiness.

6

ARYAN INVASION OF INDIA

Many of our countrymen think that we are an autochthonous people and not immigrants.

This view appears to be held also by Muir:

'They (the Aryans) could not have entered from the West, because it is clear that the people who lived in that direction, were descended from those very Aryans of India; nor could the Aryans have entered India from the north-west, because we have no proof from history of philosophy that there existed any civilised nation with a language and religion resembling theirs which could have issued from either of those quarts at that early period and have created Indo-Aryan civilisation.' (Muir's *Original Sanskrit Texts*).

But scholars generally hold that the Aryans lived somewhere in Central Asia and thence spread gradually everywhere. They further hold that from the eastern shores of the Caspian Sea, the Aryans colonised the north-west parts of the Himalayas and from there they spread over the northern plains of India. The reasons shown for this are three:

(i) The rivers, towns and countries mentioned in the *Rig Veda* are found in Central Asia. For example, *Yakshu* is the country on the Oxus river. *Aja, Arjika* are certainly not in India. *Gandhar*—Candahar; *Roosam*—Russia; *Saradia Sigra? Hari-yupia*—East Europe; *Indralaya*—north of the Hindukush mountain, marked in W & AK Johnston's map as Inder Alaya!

(ii) *Rivers Yavya-vati*—Ob or Obei, *Arjukia* Araxes or Jaxartes, *Sita* or *Sira*—(Hsito) now yarmond, *Yakshu*—Oxus, Sindhu—(Indus) with its seven branches—*Satadru* (Sutlej), *Parushni*—Ravi, *Asikni*—Chandrabhaga (Chenab), *Marutbridha*—confluence of Chenab and Beas, *Vitasta*—Beas, *Susoma*—Indus, *Arjikia*—Vipasa, *Rasa*—Rahma Araxes. *Kramu*—Kurum, *Gomati*—Gomal, *Kubbha*—Cophes, River cabul, *Suvastu*—Swat in East Afghanistan, Lake *Arar*—Aral.

2. *Complexion and religion.* The Aryans were white and fair but their enemies in India were dark. Central Asia was the mother of white people and India, of black people. The names of gods and the languages of the Aryan peoples of the Old World point to a common origin in some spot in Central Asia. cf.

   (i) *Rig Veda*—Vayu, Soma, Yama, Mitra, Asura, *Zend Avesta*—Vayu, Homa, Yima, Mithra, Ahura.

   (ii) *Rig Veda*—Axiwan, Arusa, Gandharwa, Ahana. Greek—lxion, Eros, Kentaurus, Daphoni.

   (iii) Sanskrit, Persian and the languages of Europe have been proved by philologists and linguists to be of common origin.

3. VG Tilak, following Dr Warren, Gilbert, Mr Winchel, Prof Spencer, Prof Geiki, Mallard Reed, M Jeraffe (Norway) and others, has tried to prove, in his *Orion*, the Arctic home of the Aryans. His arguments are:

   (i) The *Rig Veda* mentions longest days and nights, and excessive cold.

   (ii) Astronomical calculations prove that the Arctic region was once fit for human habitation.

   (iii) There was six months' day and six months' night. The sun rises there in the south. The stars do not rise and set there.
   This description tallies with several hymns of the *Rig Veda*.

   (iv) Calculation of the year from *winter*. (*R.V.I, 80.5; I, 64.14; V, 54,15; VI, 10.7*).
   Their prayer was 'May we live a hundred years in winter's bliss with our sons and grandsons'.

(v) Going to the Indo-Aryans to the 'Northern Land of Promise' for studying language (*Kaushitaki Brahmana*).

(vi) The discourse of the *deluge* in the *Satapatha Brahmana*.

(vii) The countries *Yaksu, Rusam* and *Hariyupia*—of the *Rig Veda* are Oxus (Bactria), Russia and East Europe.

(viii) From *Rig Veda* I. 22. 16 it appears that *Uttara-Kuru* (Siberia) was the *pratnauka*, i.e. primitive home of the Aryans. There they lived from 10,000 BC to 8000 BC. The reason for leaving this Arctic home is mentioned in the *Zend Avesta* thus:

'The paradise of the Aryans was in the Arctic region; there the sun was seen only once in the year. But snow once fell so heavily that the country became ruined. Owing to excessive cold, the Aryans left it and started for the South.'

From *Rig Veda*, I, 22. 16–21 appears the southward migration of the Aryans under their leader Vishnu. Gradually, they colonised a country called *Indralaya*—modern 'Inder Alaya' shown on Johnston's map of Asia. The 'Inder Alaya' seems to be some 400 miles south of its ancient site. It was a cold place. The Aryans therefore used meat, wine and very warm clothing. Fire was an object of their constant worship. The later manners and customs of the Indo-Aryans were evidently of cold countries. In 'Indralaya', they lived from 8000 to 5000 BC. Here, they lived in seven families or tribes ('Sapta-dhama') which perhaps were—

The Indo-Aryans, the Iranians, the Teutons, the Slavonians, the Celts, the Pelasgii, and the Romance people (Italians).

From 'Indralaya' the Aryans dispersed in different directions after 5000 BC. Here, the Aryan ancestors lived together, worshipped the same gods, and spoke the same tongue. *Dyaus pitri* in time became the Greek *Zeus Pater*, and Roman *Jupiter*. Their tongue at 'Indralaya' was *Brahma-Bhasha* often mentioned in the Upanishadas. That tongue, gradually refined by the Devas, became *Sanskrita*, i.e. perfected and polished.

The Vedic hymns, according to Tilak, were composed not later than 4500 BC and they show the reminiscences of their Arctic home.

Bailly believed in the common origin of the Egyptians, Chaldeans, Indians, and the Chinese. He further held that the ancestors of these peoples once lived in a place called Sibir or Simir (i.e. Sanskrit Sumer = Sumeru—the reputed cradle-home of the Aryans in Central Asia) north of Tatar, i.e. Tartary, about 49° or 50° north latitude. (*Universal History, Vol. VI, Chap. 25*).

We cannot go so far as to believe Bailly's idea of the common origin of those peoples. There never was, nor is, nor shall ever be a country of pure Aryans. Even in their northern home, the Aryans certainly lived amidst the Mongolian people. The most probable fact is that in all countries of the world where Aryan civilisation is now found, there were natives, advanced or less so, to whom in later ages succeeded the Aryans in small bands to be afterwards supreme in every respect. This is the case in India where people of pure Aryan descent are not over ten percent.

That a senior branch of the Aryans of Central Asia came down to India to be afterwards known as the *Hindus* from river Sindhu perhaps requires no fresh proof here. The *Uttara Madra*, Balk, Kamboja, Gandhar (East Afghanistan) had become Aryan colonies before they reached India proper.

No definite date can be assigned to this first Aryan invasion of India. That it happened before 3000 BC cannot be doubted. Professor Jacobi and others have supposed it to be at least 4000 BC. If we carefully consider several other points of reference, we reasonably arrive at that date. We have already seen that scholars generally agree to say that the Aryans had colonised Chaldea and Egypt before 2800 BC. The *Panis*, (Rigvedic '*Panis*' merchants) perhaps colonised the shores of the Levant as early as 2800 BC. From these we may infer that the Aryans of Central Asia felt inclined to found colonies abroad at some time between 3000 BC to 2800 BC. Colonisation usually follows commerce and the early Aryans loved commerce from their heart of hearts as the Aryan children of Europe do in modern times. Their acquaintance with river Sindhu (Indus) gave a fresh impetus to their natural bent on trade.

Whatever be the exact date of the Aryan invasion of India, it is certain that East Afghanistan, Kashmir and the Punjab became a thoroughly Aryan province by 2800 BC. The *Rig Veda* bears testimony to it. Of course, the country was not had easily and so on. Centuries of struggle went on between the 'fair-coloured' Aryans and the dark-skinned *Dasyus* before peace and order could be established in the soil.

7

RISE OF KINGDOMS

THE VAIRAJA DYNASTY

We have seen that by 3000 BC the Aryans lived in numerous colonies now known as East Afghanistan, the Punjab, Kashmir, West Tibet, Balkh and Russian Turkestan (RV *Yakshu*, Puranic *Wankshu* or Bankshu or Bakshu, Greek Bactria). In the northern colonies, the Aryans, divided into tribes, clans or families, lived under themselves, free from any political restraints. Of course, on occasions, they would fight between themselves, and would combine to repel an enemy. In the south, the Aryan settlements were new and constantly exposed to grave dangers from the non-Aryans. Hence, the necessity of powerful monarchs was painfully felt by the new Aryan settlers of the south. All tradition points to Brahmavarta (now) Bithoor as the seat of a powerful dynasty. Under powerful and patronising rulers, it soon became an ideal kingdom in all respects. Politics, religion, learning, trade, and art equally flourished in this early Aryan kingdom. The *Sarasvati* (Sarsuti) praised and held sacred in the *Rig Veda*, watered this land. So great was Manu's admiration for it that he in his *Code* (Book II) has desired all to learn religion and manners from the Brahmans of this holy and happy abode. With noble pride, we look back over some five thousand years to that 'land of promise'! Mind loses itself in the thoughts of those glories of yore! Here happened the first political outburst of the Indo-Aryans! Here originated the caste-system of the Hindus. Here was the first centre of Indo-Aryan culture. Here were born Princess Devahuti—female writer of some Rig Vedic hymns: Kapila and Patanjali—the authors of the *Sankhya* and *Yoga* philosophy; Rishabhadeva—the founder of *Jainism*; Dhruva of happy memory; Bharata—after whom we call our land *Bharata-Varsha* and the great poet Valmiki. Some say that the Vairaja dynasty ruled in Bhramavarta in Central Asia; that the Indian Brahmavarta was of later origin.

Below are given the authorities that treat of the Vairaja dynasty: *Vishnu Purana*, Book I, Chap VII; Book II, Chap I and 13: *Narasimha Purana*, Chap 30; *Agni Purana*, Chap 18; *Brahma Purana*, Chap 2 and 5; *Harivansa*, Chap 7; *Bhagavata*, Book IV, Chap 52; *Siva Purana*, *Dharma Samhita*, Chap 23; *Varaha Purana, Chap 2;* *Brahmanda Purana*, Chap 10; *Devi Bhagavata*, Chap VIII. 4. Genealogy of the Vairaja Dynasty

Virata — Manu — Priyavrata — Uttanapada — Princess Devahuti.

Line of Priyavrata according to *Vishnu Purana.*

Priyavrata — Agnidhra and 9 others — 5 Nabhi — Rishabha Deva — Bharata — Sumati — Indra-dyumna — 10 Paramesthi — Pratihara — Pratiharta — Bhuva — Udgitha — 15 Prastara — Prithu — Nakta — Gaya — Nara — 20 Virata — Dhiman — Mahanta — Manasyu — Twasta — 25 Biraja — Raja — Satajit — 28 Visvagjyoti.

Line of Uttanapada according to *Vishnu Purana.*

Uttanapada → Dhruva, Uttama (killed by Yakshas) — 5 Sishti and another called Bhavya — Ripu and 4 others — Chakshusha — Manu (II) — Uru and 9 others — 10 Anga (Youngest of the 6 brothers) — Vena — Prithu — Antardhi-Pali — Havirdhana — 15 Prachinavarhi and 4 others.

Prachetas (10 brothers: had a common wife.) End of the line.

VIRATA (2950–2930 BC)

Virata appears to have been the first great king of the dynasty. The line bifurcates with his two grandsons Priyavrata and Uttanapada. In the first branch—from Virata to Visvagjyoti—there were twenty-eight rulers who probably ruled for 700 years from 2950 BC onwards. Tradition asserts that Brahmavarta lay between the rivers Sarasvati and Drishadvati. That tract was about a hundred miles to the north-west of Delhi and in extent, about sixty-five miles long and from twenty to forty miles broad. The Sarasvati, then a mighty river, is now lost in the desert and still survives in a tiny stream named Sarsuti. Brahmavarta was not his sole kingdom. He probably exercised paramount sway over other tribal lords. It is certain that he had fought out all foes, organised a mighty state, encouraged learning, trade and arts and filled Brahmavarta with the best learned men available. With the aid of these sages and seers, he remodelled society so perfectly that Manu described it as divine and urged all to imitate the moral manners and customs of Brahmavarta. The Sarasvata Brahmans long remained the best of the five Gaurian Brahmans of north India. We have reasons to believe further that Virata maintained a strong navy to keep off sea-pirates from ravaging the country or looting merchantmen, and to explore and conquer new lands, tales about which the merchants had brought home from abroad. We have already noted that the Aryans were bold navigators. We shall prove it from the *Rig Veda* and other works later on. After his death, his son and successor Manu ascended the throne around 2930 BC.

MANU (2930–2900 BC)

Hindu tradition describes him as 'a great progenitor, an illustrious emperor, a benefactor and a great conqueror.' He was more ambitious than his father. He found the treasury full, army and navy strong, and the people willing. So, he made preparations for conquests. In the following years, he conquered the greater part of *Jambu-dwipa* (Asia) excluding West Asia and South-East Asia.

Manu's whole life was heroic. After subjugating North Asia, he turned his victorious army to other lands. He is credited with having conquered countries in other continents of the globe as well. The point is startling, but not too impossible to be true. It is said that he ruled this empire composed of distant parts from his capital in Brahmavarta (*Bhagavata, Book III, Chapter 21*). His was a wise and beneficent rule. These commercial and political relations of the Aryans helped the diffusion of civilisation over the globe. This point in particular, Manu, the law-giver, had in mind when he said that the people of the earth should learn good manners, customs, religion, and morals from Brahmavarta (*Manu Samhita, II 17–24, Shlokas:* also, Wilson's *Preface to Vishnu Purana, p. LXVII*).

To distinguish him from Vaivaswat Manu, he is often called Svayambhuva Manu. This Manu is perhaps the Menes of Egypt.

Manu had two sons and one daughter. The eldest, Priyavrata, was heroic and helped his father much in his conquests. Manu's daughter, Devahuti, was an accomplished princess. So great was her fondness for learning that she chose, over many worthy and princely suitors, the poor but learned sage Kardama as her lord. Manu gave her a large estate, wealth, ornaments, cattle, and carts. Her thirst for knowledge was fully satisfied in her new home. To her we owe several hymns of the *Rig Veda*. But she is more reputed as the mother of our first and great philosopher—Kapila.

PRIYAVRATA (2900–2875 BC)

Priyavrata succeeded his father around 2900 BC. He is said to have been the greatest monarch of the line. According to *Bhagavata*, he married Princess Varhishmati, a daughter of Visvakarman, the great deva architect. But according to *Vishnu Purana*, Priyavrata married a daughter of Kardama and had by her ten sons and two daughters. If Kardama be thè same whom Priyavrata's sister Devahuti had married, the said marriage becomes almost impossible. The names of the ten sons of Priyavrata appear to be somewhat different in different Puranas. Only *Vishnu* and *Garuda Puranas* agree. We will adopt their names. Three of his sons refused royalty. Priyavrata partitioned his empire and sent the seven sons to seven different continents as Viceroys. The eldest, Prince Agnidhra got *Jambu-dwipa* (Asia), Medhatithi got *Plaksha* (now, submerged Indo-African continent), Vapushman got *Salmali* (Africa: is Somali land a corruption of ancient *Salmali-dwipa*?), Dyutiman got some land in *Krauncha-dwipa* (perhaps, Australasia), Bhavya got *Saka-dwipa* (Europe), Savana or Savala got *Pushkara-dwipa* (continent of good lakes, i.e. North America), Jyotishman got *Kusa-dwipa* (continent of Llanos, i.e. South America, *Vishnu Purana II. 1; Bhagavata V.I.; Devi-Bhagavat, VIII. 4*).

Priyavrata was a great man. His special fame rests on his conquests. It is said that one half of his empire was lighted by the sun, while the other half remained in darkness. This simply means that his dominions lay widely scattered over the globe like our worldwide British Empire. Puranists called him 'Priyavrata the Great.' In his old age, he took to religion, leaving his kingdom to his eldest son, Agnidhra. The bold maritime activities and the conquests of these early Hindus may be regarded by some as nothing more than curiosities. In defence, it may be said that all the traditions of India point to them as facts; modern research also finds those ancients living in a 'noon-day glare of civilisation'. The Aryans, whether of the past or of modern times, have displayed extraordinary strength of mind and body. Moreover, what is impossible with the early Indo-Aryans whose *Rig Veda*, grammar and philosophy are still extant and excite the wonder of the world?

Priyavrata is said to have introduced the worship of the goddess Shashthi who bears one-sixth of the power of the Creator. In Bengal, she is still worshipped by the womenfolk in June for a son. Priyavrata for long had no child. On the instruction of a seer, he worshipped the goddess and obtained a son.

AGNIDHRA (2875–2850 BC)

Priyavrata was succeeded by his eldest son Agnidhra, formerly a Viceroy under his father in North Asia. We are told that he ruled the people like his father. He assumed the reins of government in Brahmavarta around 2875 BC. The empire of Priyavrata split up under his sons who ruled their own kingdoms, large or small, without any connection with the central government. The system of a central government with subordinate parts was almost absent then. Agnidhra's reign was not an eventful one. In his old age, he divided his Asiatic possessions amongst his nine sons, as follows:

(1) Nabhi got *Himavarsha* or *Nabhivarsa* which is now the tract between the north-west Himalaya and the Arabian Sea.
(2) Hari got *Naishadhavarsha* or *Harivarsha* between the mountains *Nishadha* (Nyssa) and *Hemakuta* (Karakorum). This tract is now covered by Karakorum region and the Russian Turkestan.

(3) Ilavrita got *Ilavarsha* between the mountains *Nila* and *Nyssa* now known as the tableland of Pamir (Sanskrit *Parvata Meru* or *Sumeru*).
(4) Ramyaka got what is now called Chinese Tartary, between mountains *Sveta* (Sofed Koh) and *Nila*.
(5) Hiranmaya got what is now known as Mongolia between the mountains Sringavan and Sofed Koh.
(6) Kuru got *Kuruvarsha* now Siberia, between *Uttara Samudra* (North Sea) and Mount Sringavan.
(7) Kimpurusha got what is now North China northward to the sea.
(8) Bhadrasva got the southern half of the Chinese Empire.
(9) Ketuman got *Ketumalvarsha* between the Caspian Sea and the Malyavan mountain. This is now *Russiatic Turkestan* on the eastern shores of the Caspian Sea.

(This partition of Asia into nine parts is mentioned by (i) *Vishnu Purana II. 2,* (ii) *Bhagavata, V. 16,* (iii) *Devi Bhagavata VIII, Chapters 4 and 8,* (iv) *Garuda Purana I Chapter 54,* (v) *Brahma Purana, Chapter 18,* (vi) *Varaha Purana, Chapter* 38, and (vii) *Brahmanda Purana, Chapter 75*).

NABHI AND RISHABHA DEVA (2850–2825 BC)

Agnidhra was succeeded by his eldest son Nabhi around 2850 BC. He appears to have had an eventless reign. The military spirit of his ancestors had gone. Other new Aryan dynasties were rising into prominence in the north and the east. Nabhi's power was mainly confined to the south of north-west Himalayas. Perhaps, he thought more of peace and religion than of politics. His son Rishabha Deva succeeded him in about 2840 BC. Like his father, he also thought little of polities. Moreover, he was of a religious turn of mind. He had numerous wives, chief of whom was Jayanti, the daughter of Indra, king of the Deva Aryans of the north. He begot a hundred sons, the eldest of whom was Bharata. He tried his utmost to make his sons pious and meritorious. He ruled his subjects based on righteous principles and wise counsels given by sages and seers. It is said that his kingdom was so prosperous that greed and theft were unknown. On a festive occasion, he went with his queen, Jayanti, to his father-in-law's house. There, while seeing the dance of a prostitute named

Nilanjasa, he suddenly grew sick of the world and its pleasures. Before long, he returned home and installed Bharata on the throne and then renounced the world in 2825 BC. He retired to the Kailas mountain and there built himself a cottage in which he passed some years in religious contemplation. He discovered the first principles of Jainism. The Jains call him *Adinath* or first Tirthankara, i.e. spiritual conqueror. The Jain merchants of western India have dedicated splendid buildings and temples to Rishabha Deva on Mount Abu (Rajputana). The tenets of Rishabha Deva were mainly these: salvation is possible without the idea of God; creation is self-done and eternal; extreme regard for life in any form; moral self-culture; living in a state of nature.

These, said he, lead to *kevala jnana*, i.e. pure wisdom which finally leads to *mukti* (salvation). Yatis alone are entitled to have the enviable 'pure wisdom'—a step to salvation.

He thought of no God and gave no idea of God. Creation, according to him, is eternal. He admitted the authority of the Vedas partially, for he could not approve animal slaughter. His religion was pure, sublime and natural and as such it was at first meant for the wise alone, though afterwards it was introduced amongst laymen in suitable forms by the later Jains.

BHARATA (2825 BC)

Prince Bharata came to the throne around 2825 BC. He was pious but warlike. He is credited with having conquered eight islands of the sea. What led to these foreign conquests is not known. We believe that at the entreaty of the Aryan merchants oppressed by the natives of those places, Bharata conquered and annexed those islands to his kingdom. Bharata's kingdom, called *Bharatavarsha* and composed of nine parts, is mentioned in *Vishnu Purana, II, Chapter 2; Matsya Purana, Chapter 113; Vayu Purana, Chapter 34; Varaha Purana Chapter 75; Bhagavata V, Chapter 16; Garuda Purana, Part I, Chapter 54; Brahma Purana, Chapter 18; Mahabharata, Bhishma Book, Chapter 6; Harivansa, Kurma Purana, Chapter 45; Markandeya Purana, Chapter 54; Agni Purana, Chapter 119; Siva Purana, Dharma Samhita, Chapter 33; Devi Bhagavata, Chapter 4;* and *Padma Purana, Swarga Part, Chapter 2.*

These works simply mention the nine parts. Except perhaps one, the others give no definite position of them. Astronomers Varahamihira (d AD 587) and Bhaskara (AD 1114) are wrong in their supposed identifications of those parts in India itself. Cunningham also appears to have been misled by them. The correct meaning is that *Bharatavarsha*, i.e. Bharata's kingdom (not India) included eight islands and India proper. The *Vayu Purana* alone, better informed, gives a somewhat clearer idea: 'The kingdom of Bharata consists of nine islands that are separated from one another by sea; so they are not easy of access.' They are: *Indra-dwipa*, then perhaps an island in the mouth of the Indus, and now a part of Sind; *Kaseru*, Cutch; *Tamravarna*, Ceylon; *Gobhastiman*, Andaman; *Naga or Nagavara*, Nicobar; *Saumya*, Sumatra; *Gandharva*, Java; *Baruna*, Borneo; India proper (most probably, the north-west part of it).

In time India alone was called Bharatavarsha. Bharata was pious, affectionate to his people and hospitable to strangers and guests. He is called one of the five great emperors of ancient India. He performed an imperial sacrifice. He had three sons by his queen, Panchajani, who were often at war with one another. He devised various means to bring order into his house but in vain. The princes grew more wild day by day. Annoyed, Bharata was going to leave home when the queen and the princes fell at his feet, begged his pardon and pressed him to stay, solemnly promising to behave. Bharata had no faith in their words; so he left home and went to the hermitage of Pulastya to practise yoga there. At first he improved much in the spiritual sphere. But soon an incident happened which quite arrested his progress. They said the king had left his palace and pleasures but not his attachment which caused his fall. One day when Bharata was performing some ablutions in a river, a deer, far gone in pregnancy, came to the opposite bank to drink. Suddenly terrified by the roar of a lion, she leaped into the stream for fear of her life. She had almost crossed the river when she dropped her young in the water and died. The poor fawn came floating near the king. Bharata was moved and out of pity took it home and began to pet it with great care. Other sages warned him but to no avail. He looked on that exercise of mercy as a wary to heaven. For a year or two Bharata entirely forgot his God and reared the fawn, with care and affection. One day, when Bharata was out and the fawn, now a grown deer, was at large, a wild herd of deer came near the hermitage. The pet deer at once forgot his benefactor, joined the herd and went away. Bharata, on his return, found the deer missing and felt the loss most keenly. His thoughts were now after the pet and he died before long, thinking of the deer.

After Bharata, the dynasty fast declined. Though it ran to the twenty-eighth generation, we find no kings worthy of historic note.

The line of Uttanapada, the second son of Manu deserves mention here.

Uttanapada's line was a short one of fourteen kings and was extinct by 2500 BC or earlier.

UTTANAPADA (2900 BC)

Manu gave his second son a kingdom, we know not where. This Uttanapada was a weak king and an uxorious person. He had two queens—Suruchi and Suniti. The queens had a son each. The king was particularly fond of Suruchi who had him tied to her apron strings. As a consequence, Suniti and her son Dhruva were always slighted. One day, during the absence of Suruchi, the king took Dhruva, then aged only six, on his lap and fondled him. Queen Suruchi, incensed at this, suddenly stepped in, rebuked the king and forced him to put Dhruva down at once from his lap. This slight from the stepmother cut Dhruva to the quick. He went to his mother and complained. Suniti calmed the grieving prince, saying, 'My son, pray to God, who alone can make man happy and great.' The young prince caught the idea and thenceforward learnt to pray to God for better days for the kingdom. When he grew up to be a lad, he stole away from his mother to live in a wood like an ascetic and to pray to God with thorough concentration of mind. The devotion of Dhruva is still a favourite subject among the Hindus all over India. Dhruva asked for a kingdom and by the grace of God, he gained it. The proud queen, Suruchi, and her son Uttama passed time merrily for several years. Then, bad times came upon them. Once Prince Uttama, with a large retinue, went for hunting. In the course of his prolonged hunting excursions, Uttama reached the country of the *Yakshas*, north of the Himalayas. There, a fight ensued between the two parties and Uttama was killed by the *Yakshas*. The king, under the influence of queen Suruchi, had banished the innocent queen, Suniti, and her son. Now, he grew penitent and recalled Suniti and Dhruva. Having crowned Dhruva on the throne, the old king took religious retirement.

DHRUVA (2865 BC)

Dhruva began to rule around 2865 BC. To avenge his brother's death, he led an army against the *Yakshas* and after a sharp conflict, defeated them. He was an exceedingly popular ruler. After a long, peaceful and happy reign, he attained *Bramha jnana* (a true knowledge of the Supreme Being) and left the raj to his eldest son Sisti (*Vis. P. 1, 11–12*).

Dhruva was followed by five kings of whom not much is known. The tenth, Anga, is said to have been important. To show his supremacy, he performed a horse sacrifice. He was a vigorous and good ruler. But unhappily, so terribly did his son Vena oppress him that he was compelled to abdicate. Bhrigu and other sages then placed Vena on the throne.

VENA (2825 BC)

Even when young, Vena was turbulent and cruel. It is said that, in his boyhood, he often killed his playmates most frivolously. Now, royalty made him blind and insolent. His tyranny knew no bounds. He embraced Jainism and was initiated by Rishabha Deva himself. He was a sworn enemy of the Brahmans. He forced even the rishis (seers) to pay him tribute. He forced the Brahmans to carry his palanquins. He stopped all religious performance in the state. The whole kingdom was filled with consternation. To save the country, people saw no other alternative but to kill the wicked king. Ere long Vena was done to death.

Anarchy followed. Life and property were at the mercy of the robbers. The Brahmans became alarmed and decided to place Vena's young son Prithu on the throne.

PRITHU (2815 BC)

Prithu made an excellent king; soon his full authority was established over the entire kingdom. There were new villages, towns, ports, castles, and camps. The country became highly prosperous under him. They say he was like Manu in parental affection towards his people, like Brahma in authority, like Vrihaspati in Vedic lore, and like Vishnu in self-possession. He was modest, meek and of winning manners. In doing good to others, he was unrivalled. His praise was on everybody's lips.

From his time, court encomiasts called the *Suta* and *Magadha* first came in vogue. He died after a very long and glorious reign of forty or fifty years. His queen, Archi, became a sati and immolated herself on her husband's funeral pyre. His capital was called *Prithudaka* (now, Pehoa). The caste system first began around his time.

Prithu was succeeded by his eldest son, Antardhi, who, when crowned was called Bijitaswa. Out of affection, he appointed his three other brothers to three parts of the kingdom. Prithu had left a large hoard in the treasury, which his pious son utilised in long expensive sacrifices and charities. His grandson Prachinavarhi's reign is reputed for numerous grand sacrifices. It is said that the earth for many miles was filled with his sacrificial altars. He was succeeded by his ten sons whose common name was Pracheta. We here meet with an instance of polyandry. The ten Pracheta brothers had one common wife. With them the line of Uttanapada comes to an end. Pracheta were very pious; they refused royalty for Brahmanhood. Their successors passed for sages, and enjoyed a high reputation as model Brahmans.

8

ARYAN REGENERATION

We have already said the northern Aryans lived in numerous clans, tribes or families, all free in their thinking, living and actions. Around 3000 BC the Aryan society took a new turn. The Aryans lived apart from the masses. Many seldom married. The result was that in half a century, the Aryan mass of the north became rotten to the core. This moral downfall of the Aryans has been clearly depicted in the *Mahabharata, Peace Book, Chapter 59*. In order to distinctly mark this downfall of the Aryans, an epoch called the *Kaliyuga* (Iron Age) was started by the sages. The initial point of it is 3102 BC lunar or 2950 BC solar. That *Kaliyuga* era runs even to this day. The sages, alarmed at the anarchical state of society, informed Brahma, the greatest Aryan seer. What Pope was to early Christendom, Brahma was to the Aryans. He held an assembly of the sages and seers whom he addressed thus: 'Seers and sages, to allow society to go on without the best thinkers to guide the masses, is to leave the body without the head. True wisdom—the path to salvation—is attainable in the world and not in aloofness from it. So, I desire those of you who are still young, to marry and beget virtuous children for the benefit of the society. For better government, I further propose to introduce monarchies in the various clans.' All modestly bowed to his reasonable command, but many declined to marry for fear of the loss of penance. Only twenty-one of the most distinguished seers, including Brahma himself, married. They are known as *Prajapati* rishis, i.e. progenitors. Brahma married the fair Savitri, reputed for her chastity. She bore him two daughters but no son. So, he took a second wife from the Indian side, born of a milkman family. Still he had no male issue. The progenitors were mostly representatives of clans that owned principalities in different localities. They begot many children, some of whom became seers and some warriors. The great sage Bhrigu begot fourteen sons. Of them only two—Chyavana and Apnuvan—became seers and twelve became *devatas*, i.e. warriors. Of the latter, Daksha, the youngest, founded a small kingdom near the source of the Ganges, with his capital at Kanakhala, two miles south of Haridwar. The seven seers, known in history as *Saptarshi*, are said to have been the ancestors of the high-caste Hindus of India.

An era called the *Saptarshi*, of which the initial point is 3076 BC lunar or 2925 BC solar was started in Kashmir in honour of them. The era is still current there.

Below is a genealogy that indicates the sources of all future dynasties of India:

A. The lines of the Seven Seers (*Saptarshi*).

1. Marichi—Kasyapa—Vivasvan—(from him originates the solar dynasty). 2. Atri—Soma (from him comes the lunar dynasty). 3. Angira begot seven seers and ten warrior sons, Vrihaspati and others. 4. Pulastya—Visravas—Kuvera. 5. Pulaha or Gati-Kardama, Variman and Sahishnu. Kapila and nine daughters (*Harivansa* and *Vishnu Purana*). 6. Kratu or Sannati—The *Valakhilya* sages said to be pigmies in stature. 7. Vasista.

B. Two out of the fourteen sons of the great sage Bhrigu became seers and twelve kings. Daksha, the youngest of these, founded a small kingdom near the source of the Ganges.

The Brahmans and the Kshatriyas of ancient dynasties were descendants of these seven or eight seers. Other lines originated from other progenitors. The *Rig Veda*, the Sanskrit epics and the Puranas have mentioned many distinguished kings who belonged neither to the solar nor to the lunar dynasty, but to other less important dynasties, no longer represented or recognised.

Brahma, Vishnu, and Siva make the Hindu Trinity. Brahma is the Creator, Vishnu the Preserver and Siva the Destroyer and Reproducer. Needless to say, this later spiritual evolution was based on historical data (see also, AA Macdonell's *Sanskrit Literature*). Historically, Brahma, the greatest Aryan sage, regenerated the Aryans, by asking the seers to raise sons. (*Mahabharata*, and *Brahma Vaivarta Purana, Brahma Khanda*, Chapter 8 also *Srikrishna Khanda,* Chapter 32).

Marichi's son was Kasyapa, so-called from *kasya*, a special preparation of *Soma* juice, which was his favourite drink. He was a great warrior. Tradition has it (*Rajatarangini*) that he had wrested the flowery vale, now called Kashmir (*Kasyapa Meru* or *Mir*), from a Daitya king called Jalodbhava. Kasyapa married several daughters of Daksha, King of Kanakhala. By his first wife Diti, he had begot two powerful sons, namely Hiranyaksha and Hiranyakasipu. Their children became known as the Daityas. They soon multiplied and attained great political importance. From his second wife Aditi, Kasyapa begot twelve sons, called Adityas, after their mother, Aditi.

These new Aryans occupied all tracts north of the Himalayas. About 2860 BC the Daitya and the Danava Aryans grew to be very powerful. It is said that they built a small empire.

The excellent people that the world has perhaps, yet produced were the Devas, a section of the new Aryans. Many of the prominent Devas have long passed for gods, and have lost their original historic characters. Yet, doubtless they were men—excellent men—the 'Shining Ones'. We give below proof of the human side of the Deva Aryans, though the Sanskrit epics, the Puranas and other works have been highly saturated with their deification:

(i) Yudhisthira, speaking on death, observes: 'Nobody can escape death. Death kills the Devas, the Danavas, the Gandharvas and all'. (*Mahabharata,* Drona Book, Chapter 50).
(ii) Again, Narada, also speaking on death, says: 'The Devas, with Indra at their head, also die like men. The Devas also have mortal names and frames'. (*Mahabharata,* Drona Book, Chapter 55).
(iii) In reply to the taunt of Indra, the King of the Devas, the Daitya Emperor Bali said: 'I, you and all others, who will in time, obtain the Indraship, will go the same way as hundreds of Indras have already gone. This Indraship is not held by anybody for ever. Many others will gain the Indraship in future'. (*Mahabharata,* Peace Book, Chapter 227).

The Devas belonged to many families—the most important being the Aditya, the Visvadeva, the Basu, the Tushita, the Abhasvara, the Marut, the Maharajika, the Sadhya and the Rudra. Thirty-three of the Devas attained special excellence. These thirty-three Devas afterwards became magnified in popular legend into thirty-three crores of Devas as if one Deva is equal to a crore of ordinary mortals!

The *Matsya Purana,* Chapter 95, gives the homes of the different people of that time.

(i) The Daityas and the Danavas lived on the *Sweta Parvata* (Sofed Koh) to the far north.
(ii) The Devas lived on the Sumeru, now perhaps known as Pamir tableland.
(iii) The Rakshasas, Pisachas and Yakshas lived on the Himalayas (perhaps, ancestors of the Dravidians).
(iv) The Gandharvas and Apsaras (Ancestors of the Afghans) lived on the Hemakuta (Karakoram).
(v) The Nagas and Takshakas (ancestors of the Turks) lived on the Nishadha (Mt. Nyssa).
(vi) The great seers lived on the Mt. Nila to the far north.
(vii) The Pitris lived on the Sringawan hills to the west of Mt. Sumeru, i.e. on the eastern shores of the Caspian Sea. Other accounts are found elsewhere.

The kings of the Vairaja dynasty of Bithoor gradually lost all hold on the north. Around 2860 BC, Daityas grew so powerful that several of them are called by the Puranists as emperors. The Devas also gradually rose to great eminence by 2850 BC. Their rise and excellent progress was watched with extreme jealously by the Daityas. The brotherly and friendly relations between the Daityas and the Devas were now strained.

Before long, an incident happened that drove both to bitter hostilities for thirty-two long years, off and on. This is known as the First Great Civil War or the Dev-Asura War. Somadeva, the chief of the Atri clan and founder of the future lunar dynasty of north India, intending to perform an imperial sacrifice, summoned amongst others the Daityas who, however, indignant at this presumptuous audacity of the Devas, refused to attend. Instead, they declared war on the Devas and soon invaded the Deva territory. We do not know the strength of each army nor the details of the battles fought. The conflict was very sharp and the loss of lives on both sides considerable. The war began in 2850 BC or a little after and ended in 2818 BC. The Devas were unrivalled in religion, learning, arts, and industries; but perhaps inferior to the Daityas in military operations. So, they sustained great losses at first. Then, a Deva General, Purandara by name, took charge. His successes in the war led the Devas to declare him their king with the title of Indra (literally, the most exalted king). Defeat quickened the Daitya spirit and after some time they fell on the Devas with such terrible force that the Devas failed to hold their ground. The Deva cause was going to be lost when Siva, the mighty chief of the Rudras, took the field at the entreaty of the Devas and turned the tide of the battle. He inflicted a signal defeat on the Daityas and drove the enemies to the shores of *Paschima Samudra* (western sea: Arabian or Caspian Sea). When the Daityas were consolidating their power in the north, some migrated to the south, and founded kingdoms in several parts of India. One powerful kingdom was to the south of the Vindhyas; several were on the eastern Vindhyas, one was in Kikata (Gaya province). When the northern Daityas weakened a little, the southern Daityas came forward against the Devas. The south now became the centre of the battle field. Rudra (Siva) again led an army and after a hard struggle killed Tripura, the Daitya king of the Central Province. The services of Rudra to the Deva cause have been thankfully sung by the seers:

(i) 'Able-bodied, possessed of many forms, terrible Rudra is wearing bright gold ornaments. He is the lord of the universe and preserver of all.'
(ii) 'O worshipful Rudra! You are the holder of bow and arrow. You have many forms and have worn the ornaments called *nishka*. You preserve the whole wide world. Who is stronger than you?'
(iii) 'Let us pray to the fierce Rudra seated in the car, youthful, terrible like a beast, destroyer of foes. May his army kill our enemies.'
(iv) 'As the son bends to his blessing father, so do we bend before you, O great Rudra!'
(v) 'Be propitious: be not angry with us; do not destroy us. We shall all—sons, grandsons together—pray to Thee much in this Sacrifice.' (*R.V. II. 33. 5–9*).

To the heroic Rudra family, the debt of the Devas appears to have been immense. Tradition bears the bright record of the deeds of one female warrior, Uma, wife of Rudra. In terrible battles she killed the Daitya chiefs—Mahisha, Sumbha and Nishumbha (grandson of Prahlada) and their generals—Dhumraksha, Chanda, Munda and Raktabija, on the Vindhya hills. Alarmed at these reverses, one great Daitya king, Durg by name, collected a very strong and large army. The Devas feared that their fate now hung by a slender thread. So, they were filled with dismay. But Uma again took the field with a lion ramp. Still no heart cherished the least hope of her success against such enormous odds. Before the battle, she inspired her soldiers with her martial spirit, so much so that her soldiers saw her as the very goddess of Victory incarnate. The battle was the fiercest — Uma won the day after all. Later, her son Kartika became the general of the Deva army. He killed the last great Daitya, Taraka by name (a somewhat detailed description is given of the wife and sons of Rudra in the *R.V. VI. 66. 3; VI 66; II and VI, 66. 64*).

The worship and image of Siva of the later ages originated from the descriptions given in the *Rig Veda* already quoted. The Devas gave Uma the title of 'Durga' for having slain the most formidable foe Durg. Her worship first began a century later, about 2700 BC. It is said that Suratha first started her puja. To clear the point, we quote a portion of the early genealogy: Soma (the founder of the lunar dynasty)—Buddha—Chaitra — Adhiratha—Suratha. Again, Uttanapada—Dhruva—Utkala—Nandi. Suratha, being defeated by Nandi, lost his kingdom and went to the woods, grief-stricken. A Vaisya king ruled Kalinga then. His grandson, Prince Samadhi, was turned out of the house for his extreme liberality. Samadhi met Suratha and both became friends. Once, they saw a great sage named Medhasa. At his instance, they followed him to Pushkara, seven miles from Ajmer, and there they long prayed to Durga for better times. In their worship, they became *siddha*, i.e. successful. It is said that Suratha fought again and regained his kingdom, as did Samadhi to regain Kalinga. That Durga puja now forms the greatest festival in Bengal with the difference that formerly her worship was without form and in the spring season, but now her image is worshipped in autumn.

The war was a defensive one for the Devas. The Daitya power continued in the North and in India. The hostilities stopped for sometime. But we shall hear of fresh outbreak hereafter. The Devas gradually secured great political importance. A few of the most distinguished Devas deserve special notice here:

(i) Brahma, son to the sage Niranjana, was the Pope of the Aryans; he lived on the Pamir plateau of which the eastern boundary was Mt. Thian-san (Chinese Thian-san = abode of Brahma cf. also San-Po = Brahmaputra). Hindu tradition points to this greatest seer as the first source of all knowledge, secular and sacred. It was he who had first compiled the Vedic hymns, drawn up a penal code, compiled an alphabet which afterwards became parent of the *Sarada, Sriharsha* and *Kutila* alphabets, wrote the first great medical work, was the first great astronomer, reformer, regenerator, and coloniser. He was the very angel of peace and progress and knew little or no about fighting. No pope in the early Christendom commanded a greater respect and confidence as did Brahma in the then Aryan world. He was the supreme authority on all matters. It is said that Ujjain, the house of Brahma on the Sumeru (Pamir) and Siddhapuri —now *Sid-rov* (see *Johnston's Map of Asia*) in Siberi—were on the 0° meridian of the Hindus. Four great rivers flowed down the tableland: the Bhadra or Subhadra (Ob or Obei; *R.V.*), *Yavyavati* flowed to the north; the Sita (Hsi-to) now *Yarmond* and Subahini (Hwang Ho) flowed eastward to the Chinese Sea. The Wankshu (*R.V., Yakshu,* river Oxus) flowed to the west; and the Alaknanda (the Ganges) flowed southward. Later, when spiritual ideas were evolved out of these historical data, Brahma came to be known as the Creator—an idea still prevalent in all Hindu writings! We have mentioned Brahma as a coloniser. He was perhaps, the first to discover the home of philosophy in India and Burma where he lived for penitential purposes, performed sacrifices and then filled them with sages, who afterwards planted extensive penance-groves and created hermitages there. Modern Burma—Sanskrit Brahmadesa—owed its name to Brahma who had lived there for several years on the Iravati (*Sabdakalpa Druma, Brahma*). From Brahma's first astronomical observations made in Assam, the country received the name of *Prag-Jyotisha.*

(ii) Rudra was the chief of the Rudra family of eleven brothers. He lived on the Kailasa mountain. He was a great hero, physican, law-giver, and the greatest grammarian that the world has ever produced. His first wife Sati probably lent the word Sati to a self-immolating Hindu widow. In the Puranas, he is known as Siva (the great benefactor). Heroic Uma, his second wife already noted, was daughter to a king of Simla.

(iii) Indra was the title of the Deva-king, Purandara or Sakra. He had killed ninety-nine powerful Daityas and performed hundred sacrifices. For his valour he was elected the first Indra. He married Sachi Devi, daughter of a Daitya chief named Puloma. He had three sons and one daughter. This Princess, Jayanti, was married to Rishabha Deva, the well-known founder of Jainism.

Indra lived at his capital Amaravati — in the tract called Indralaya— now shown as *Inder Alaya* in *Johnston's Map*, to the north of the Hindukush mountain. Most probably, the original Indralaya was some 400 miles more northerly than it is now. In the *Rig Veda*, we find Indra in two capacities—as the rain god and as the Deva king and the greatest protector of the Aryans. Of the gods of the *Rig Veda*, Indra is the most prominent and is invoked with some 250 hymns. We quote a few for illustration:

(a) Visvamitra, invoking Indra, says: 'O Indra! Killing the *Dasyus*, save the Aryans'. (*R.V. III, 34*).

(b) 'One day, in one single engagement, Indra killed 50,000 of the enemies'. (*R.V. IV, 28*).

(c) 'The powerful non-Aryan chiefs Ku-yava and Ayu lived in forest tracts and would fall on the Aryan villages and towns, with their men, whenever an opportunity occurred'. (*R.V. I, 104*).

(d) 'The most powerful was Krishna who lived on the river Ansumati. His army was 10,000 strong. Very great was his oppression. So, Indra killed him'. (*R.V. VII, 96*).

(e) 'Indra also punished even refractory and wicked Aryan kings. Two Aryan kings, Arna and Chitra-ratha, were killed by Indra in a battle on the river Sarayu'. (*ibid*).

(f) 'Indra gave a realm to King Duryoni after killing the non-Aryan chief Kujavacha'. (*R.V. I, 174*).

(g) 'Indra killed the non-Aryan kings Nava Vastwa and Vrihadratha and placed Aryan kings on their thrones'. (*R.V. X, 49*).

The Indras, one after another, continued to rule in the north till sometime after the *Mahabharata War*. Then we hear of them no more.

Some sages first introduced the worship of Indra into the Aryan society. It, however, met with a storm of opposition from other sages. The praise and dispraise of Indra are recorded in the numerous hymns of the *Rig Veda*. The worship consisted mostly in Bacchanalian feats. This religious difference led the Iranians to separate from the Indo-Aryans. The Iranians were strict moralists. Even the majority of the Indo-Aryans were opposed to the worship of Indra.

(iv) Vishnu was the youngest of the Adityas, but the greatest of them all in merit. He was a warrior and had killed several powerful Daityas. It is said that he had built Lanka in Ceylon for the summer residence of Indra.

(v) Daksha, son of Bhrigu, ruled at Kanakhala near Haridwar. He was father-in-law to most of the elderly Devas. He had married his princess, Dakshayani, to Rudra. She was very chaste. So, they called her Sati. Once, Daksha was present in Deva assembly where all but Rudra rose to him. Daksha felt hurt. After some time Daksha performed a sacrifice to which he invited all the Devas but Rudra and Sati. Sati was aggrieved and came down from Kailas to her father's house. Daksha chastised Rudra so mercilessly in her presence that she was cut to the quick and died soon after. Sati already enjoyed a great reputation for her virtue. Her relics were distributed and interred all over India. That has given rise to fifty-one sacred places of the Hindus.

(vi) Vrihaspati was priest and guru to the Devas, and Sukra, a poet, was priest to the Daityas and the Danavas. Both were well-versed in the Vedic lore, wrote about law, medicine, astronomy, and the art of government. Vrihaspati is said to have first formulated atheism as a political precepte.

9

THE GREAT RENAISSANCE

THE 29TH CENTURY BC

The Aryans of the north were chiefly of two classes—the Suras and the Asuras. The former were so-called from their excessive drinking of Sura (wine), while the latter were ridiculed as Asuras, i.e. teetotalers or people without wine. The Asuras were puritans and small in number; while the Suras were a large set of chartered libertines. We have noticed their moral fall. We have also noticed the reformation and regeneration of the Aryans, by the greatest seer Brahma. The new children of the rishis, now called themselves Devas, 'godly men or shining people.' These Deva Aryans were certainly men like us—mortal beings—historic persons. Later on, spiritual ideas were evolved out of the pure historical data. Even in this new creation of their divinity, their semi-historical character is clearly visible. It is already noted that the Aryans were composed of many tribes, clans and families. The countries of Central Asia were mostly under the influence of the Deva Aryans. The word Asura has become opprobrious in India: it now means a demon, or an evil genius. The rishis were the best specimens of the Aryans. Brahma, the most versatile genius, was the acknowledged chief of the time. It is said that under his instructions, eight *Surendras*, i.e. chiefs of the Devas, conducted the administration of the Aryan state of the north.

By the middle of the thirtieth century BC, the downfall of the Aryans was almost complete. The 88,000 seers never married; even many females took to religion and never married. The time is marked by the *Kaliyuga* epoch, beginning in 3102 BC (lunar) = 2950 BC (solar).

About 2900 BC or later, Brahma set about to regenerate the Aryans. His reformation brought about the great renaissance of the twenty-nineth century BC, not yet known in human history.

Scholars are eloquent in their praises of Hindu wisdom, arts, and tongue; but they do not know the rich store of lore of the renaissance. In comparison, all later Hindu wisdom appears as mere commentaries.

Below is given a brief history of the Deva renaissance which forms the fountainhead of all our later knowledge and art. The history of no nation, ancient or modern, gives us a people like the Devas. Each of the thirty-three principal Devas was a versatile genius. Of the most distinguished Romans, Caesar alone excelled. Some of the courtiers of Philip II of Spain were experts in pen, sword and altar. But they are nothing when compared to the Devas.

RELIGION

The method of worship took a new turn with the Devas. Our rishis had followed a simple natural course. But the Devas introduced magnificent sacrifices, often connected with their conquests. Brick-built altars of various shapes were devised. Several priests were employed. Beasts were killed. Grand feasts followed, along with gifts to sages and the poor, music, song and dance.

LITERATURE

It is a general belief that the four Vedas, except the oldest parts of the *Rig Veda*, were composed and compiled in India. No doubt, there is much truth in it. We, however, believe that all the Vedas originated in parts in the north. It is said that Brahma had sent men to collect the earliest hymns of the *Rig Veda*. These amounted to a huge mass, numbering about a lakh (1,00,000) of hymns. Evidently, a very small number of them came to India.

With the beginning of grand sacrifices and other rites and rituals, the *Yajur Veda* (the Black one) also began in the north. Surya Deva, the youngest brother of Brahma, had compiled the *Samans* (*Chhandogya* Upanishad; *Black Yajur Veda, p.* 477 and *Manu Samhita, IV,* 124).

The *Sama Veda* was composed in *Devaloka*, i.e. in the north and brought to India afterwards. Manu's adjective *pitrya* is wrongly explained as 'sacred to the manes'. Dr Buhler and Professor Max Müeller have also followed the wrong meaning and said, '*Sama Veda* is sacred to the names'; though this Veda knows nothing of a *sraddha* ceremony. The great sage Atharva, born of the Angira clan, (some identify him with the great sage Bhrigu) and a disciple of Brahma, wrote a Veda of his own, full of charms, spells, incantations, domestic rites, and medicines. It was intended for the common people of the north. In its present form of twenty books, this Veda is said to have been composed by other sages of the Angira clan. Its chapter on Brahma-Vidya (theosophy) is a novel feature. Yet, it long remained non-canonical. The *Mundakopanishad* states in the beginning that Brahma taught Atharva theosophy. The spirit of the time had even inspired some women to compose a good number of hymns which are still extant.

The word Bible, originally a book, afterwards came to mean 'the holy book', or the scripture. So, the word Veda originally meant 'knowledge' (of the Aryans) but afterwards, 'sacred knowledge.' Tradition asserts that Atharva's first collection and arrangement of the Rig, Yajur and Sama hymns became known as the *trayi* of the north. They are our modern poetry, prose and songs chanted on different occasions. Agni Deva collected the later Rig Vedic hymns in India. The seer Vayu collected the *Black Yajur Veda* in India (*Manu I. 23*); also *Satapatha Brahmana, XI. 4*. The *White Yajur Veda* was composed by Yajnavalkya in the fourteenth century BC.

The study of the Vedas now became important with all the Aryans who followed the Vedic religion. To facilitate the Vedic study, six supplementary subjects were cultivated at the same time. These were the *siksha* (orthography and correct articulation) and *kalpa* rites and rituals. Different sacrifices, their method of performance, altars, effects, and priests were explained in it. Here lies the origin of the rudiments of Hindu geometry and *Vyakarana* (grammar). Before 2900 BC, the Aryans spoke a free tongue called the *Brahma bhasha* or *Balhika bhasha*. This was a free, irregular and rugged language. Dr Macdonell calls it an older form of classical Sanskrit. Most of the Rig Vedic hymns are composed in it. The authors of the Indian *Brahmanas* and the Upanishadas also used that rugged tongue, more or less. The Aryans now requested the

Devas to refine that tongue. There was thus a need for writing a regular grammar. Several Devas took up language and gave it the most scientific treatment. Indra invented the fourteen vowels. Mahesa invented the twenty-nine letters (twenty-five consonants *Ka* to *ma* + four semi-vowels—Y, R, L and W). Chandra invented the four aspirants S', Sh, S, H. Brahma made up the remaining sixteen or seventeen letters. This new alphabet called the *Brahmi lipi* contained sixty-three or sixty-four letters representing all the varieties of sounds. Indra, Chandra, Mahesa and Kumara wrote a grammar each. The first two—the *Aindra* and the *Chandra* grammars are now forgotten. The *Mahesa* grammar is still extant, though rare. A portion of the grammar of Kumara, a son of Mahesa, is preserved in the *Garuda Purana*. The grammar of Mahesa, the first scientific grammar in the world, now became standard with the Aryans. The *Brahma bhasha*, now refined by the rules of the new grammars, became known as *Sanskrita* or Deva *bhasha* (tongue of the Deva Aryans).

Some of the views of eminent scholars on Sanskrit, its use and its relation to other ancient languages of the world are given below:

(1) 'Sanskrit is the greatest language in the world. As mathematics is the foundation of astronomy, so is Sanskrit the basis of philology'. (Professor Max Müeller's *Science of Language*).
(2) 'Sanskrit is more perfect and copious than Greek and Latin and more exquisite and eloquent than either'. (Professor Bopp in *Edinburg Review*).
(3) 'Sanskrit was at one time the only language of the world'. (Professor Bopp).
(4) 'Justly it is called *Sanskrit*, i.e. perfected or finished'. (Schlegel's *History of Literature*).
(5) 'The modern philology dates from the study of Sanskrit by the Europeans'. (Dr Hunter).
(6) 'In point of fact, the *Zend* is derived from Sanskrit'. (Professor Heeren's *Historical Researchs*).
(7) 'Sanskrit is the origin of the modern languages of Europe'. (M Dubois).
(8) 'All the languages of the Indo-European family are derived from Sanskrit'. (Dr Ballantyne).

(9) 'It is only of late years that any relationship was allowed between Hebrew and Sanskrit, but Furst and Delitzach have abundantly proved it and it is now universally acknowledge'. (Pococke's, *India in Greece*).

It is wrong to suppose that Sanskrit is the mother of those tongues. Sanskrit is, in fact, one of the numerous tongues that sprang up from the Aryan tongue of Central Asia, known to us perhaps as *Brahma* or *Balhika bhasha*. Sanskrit was made by the Deva Aryans: hence it is often called Deva *bhasha*.

Valmiki and Vyasa followed the Mahesa grammar. The so-called 'arsha prayogas' of Valmiki and Vyasa are wrongly explained as poetic licence. They are correct according to the Mahesa or other Vedic grammars, but wrong according to Panini and others. Panini is now universally admired for his 'shortest and the fullest grammar in the world.' In the history of Sanskrit literature, two persons appear to be singularly fortunate: the grammarian Panini and the annotator Mallinatha. From compilers, both now pass for excellent authors. All science, all secrets of the perfect language lie in Mahesa's arrangement of the alphabet in fourteen rules, adopted and explained by Panini. Mahesa wrote his grammar for Vedic use, but Panini meant his work for both secular and sacred compositions. A critic defending an apparently erroneous expression of Vyasa in the *Mahabharata* says that Panini is to Mahesa, what a drop of water is to the ocean.

The following is his observation: 'Vyasa has derived many excellent gems from the sea of Mahesa grammar. Are they possible in the grammar of Panini which is no better than a little water accumulated in the footprint of a cow?'

In the branch of *Nirukta*, i.e. Vedic glossary, the names of the first Indra, Soma, Kasa-Kritsna stand prominent. Their works have long disappeared. So, we cannot say what improvements they made in that study.

Chhandas (prosody) also received some attention. The Rig Vedic hymns were composed in seven different metres. Dr Macdonell says 'The metrical skill is considerable'. (*Imp. Gaz. India, vol. II, p. 210*).

It is well known that Indo-Iran, West Asia and Europe bear a striking resemblance in language and other matters. Scholars, after careful enquiry and examination, have found that those languages, though akin, do not yet prove a racial unity. They trace all the tongues to an Aryan tongue of Central Asia. I think this Aryan tongue was the *Brahma bhasha* or the *Balhika bhasha*. Both Brahma tongue and Sanskrit were brought to India.

The renaissance is noticeable in the field of astronomical research also. It does not appear that our astronomy had made much progress before 3000 BC. Only a few passages of the *Rig Veda* describe the motions of the celestial hemisphere or of the stars therein. The earlier rishis knew the *rikshas*, the great and little bears (*R.V. I, 24. 10*). They knew of a day and night of six months each in the Arctic region. Long dawns are mentioned in some twenty or twenty-five hymns. Short dawns are also mentioned (*R.V. 92. I; I. 92. 10; I. 48. 6*). The sunless north and the Aurora Borealis are hinted at. The celestial pole was in the zenith and the revolutions of the stars were round a perpendicular axis. The great antiquity of the Hindu astronomy has been discussed by some of the greatest astronomers in Europe and is still unresolved. Cassini, Bailly and Play fair maintain that observations noted before 3000 BC are still extant and prove a considerable degree of progress made at that period. Their opponents like La Place and De Lambre and others have doubted the authenticity of the observations and the validity of the conclusions. We, however, are not disposed to brush aside the point so easily. Tradition preserved in the *Mahabharata, Peace Book* and elsewhere, states that at least nine astronomers flourished in the twenty-ninth century BC. It is already noted that Brahma and Vrihaspati excelled in the *Vedangas* of which astronomy is a part. So, it is likely that some progress was made in the subject before 2900 BC by Brahma, Vivaswan, Soma, Vrihaspati, Garga (not of the first century BC), Narada, Parasara (not father of Vyasa), Pulastya and Vasista. The last two were two of the seven seers known as *Saptarishi*. These names alone have come down to us; but their observations and works lie concealed in priestly obfuscation.

Brahma made certain observations in Kamarupa in Assam. To commemorate this earliest observation in India, Kamarupa was called the *Prag-Jyotisha Desa*. The work of Vivaswan, now known as the *Surya Siddhanta* received its final reduction, perhaps in the fifth or the sixth century after Christ. The book, though a learned one, suffers greatly from obscurity. The work of Brahma, called the *Brahma Siddhanta*, was revised by Varahamihira around AD 80.

It is often alleged that the early Rig Vedic seers knew not the planets for, the *Rig Veda* makes no distinct mention of them. We think those early rishis had no occasion to speak of them. Moreover, the rishis watched the course of the moon through the circles of steady groups of stars, to ascertain the auspicious hours for sacrifice. The planets were wandering luminaries. The sun they certainly knew and called it the upholder of the earth (*RV*). The *Rig Veda* makes indirect reference to a planet called *Brahmanaspati*, perhaps, later *Vrihaspati* (Jupiter). Some give the date of the discovery of Jupiter as 4500 BC; an eminent English astronomer, as 4000 BC. Hindus recognise numberless planets, chief of which are: *Ravi* (Sun), Soma (Moon), *Mangala* (Mars), *Boodha* (Mercury), *Vrihaspati* (Jupiter), *Sukra* (Venus), *Sanaischara* (Saturn), *Rahu* (Node), and *Ketu* (Apside). For some reason, I am inclined to believe that some of the astronomers mentioned above, had discovered some of the planets in the twenty-ninth century BC. Thus, Vivaswan was perhaps the discoverer of the sun; hence he is often spoken of as the sun and his dynasty as solar. Soma discovered the moon; so, he is often called Chandra (moon) and his dynasty as lunar. Mars was perhaps discovered by Skanda or Kartikeya, son to Siva. This is clear from the legend connected with the birth of Skanda, the Deva General (*Mahabharata, Wood Book*). Kumara is a name of Skanda. So, it seems probably that the second part of his name, *Mara,* is what *Mars* comes from.

Boodha, properly *Wudha* (Woden), son to Soma, was perhaps the discoverer of Mercury. Vrihaspati, priest to the Devas and the seers, discovered Jupiter, called in Sanskrit Vrihaspati or Jiva, Latin Giovdi. Its name of *Sthula graha* (the largest planet) is perhaps connected with Thor. Usanas, priest to the *Danavas* and the Daitya Aryans, perhaps discovered Venus (Sanskrit *Sukra* = the bright planet). Hence, he is often called Sukracharya. Its other name, Bhrigu, is found in ancient Sanskrit, *Frigga* and English, *Fri*. Usanas was son to the great sage Bhrigu. Saturn, (Sanskrit *Sanais-chara*; Zend, *Sani-char, 'slow mover'*) was perhaps, discovered by Sani, a son to Vivaswan by his queen Chhaya. A curious legend, illustrative of the evil eye of Sani, is connected with the birth of the elephant-headed Hindu god Ganesa. Ganesa was the second son of Mahesa by Durga, princess of the hill kingdom of Simla. It is said that all the Devas except Sani came to see Ganesa. Under pressure, Sani did come at last. Just as he saw Ganesa, the child's head was found missing. Soon, however, a young elephant's head was brought and set in its place. It is difficult to assess the astronomical significance of this legend. As a god, Ganesa is the first to be worshipped as his calm figure, besmeared with vermilion, is to be met with at the entrance of temples everywhere in India. He is the reputed giver of success in all undertakings.

At first, they knew only five planets; to these they added two—the sun and the moon, making seven in all. Rahu and Ketu are not stars, but two opposite points where the sun's ecliptic cuts the orbit of the moon. As the influence of these two (node and apsis) was found equal to that of a regular planet, they included them also as planets. The regular seven planets move forward, but Rahu and Ketu move in an ultra course, i.e. in an opposite direction from the sun. Hindus exclude the earth, but include the moon, as a planet. The moon has been long regarded in the West as a satellite or secondary planet, moving round the earth. Recently, however, it s found as a joint-star or joint-planet with the earth. This joint relation was perhaps long known to the early rishis who, therefore, ignored the earth as a planet.

It also deserves notice here that several words in Sanskrit meaning the earth come from roots meaning to move. The Rig-Vedic *gau* (earth), *Zend, gou* and Greek, *goia* are all from the root *ga*, to go, to move. Ancient Sanskrit *cu* perhaps means the same. English *earth* Greek *era*, Sanskrit *ira* comes from Sanskrit *ri* to go, to move. Hence, *gau* (earth) means a moving body.

A planet in Sanskrit is called a *graha* from root *grah*, to receive. Does it then mean a star that receives light or motion, say, from the sun? *Graha* means a burden, a dependant, a meaning quite irrelevant here. *Graha* formerly meant a cup to hold *soma* juice for libation; then, the consecrated *soma* juice itself. In the soma sacrifice, the two *grahas* used were called Sukra and Manthis, perhaps, the evening and the morning stars. Soma, moon, passes through the twenty-eight steady constellations, with its mild beams. This is figuratively spoken of as the moon's feeding the stars with its *sudha*, i.e. mild nectarine rays or juice. The moon, therefore, at first came to be called a *graha* (a cup or vessel of juice); from that, the meaning shifted to a moving or wandering star.

It seems that those early rishis knew the different classes of stars such as the fixed stars, the steady constellations, the moving stars, the comets and the meteors. They had carefully observed and examined the nature and character of these different classes of stars. From experience, they no doubt, found that the steady groups of stars were most convenient for their calculating the auspicious hours for sacrifice. Thus, they gradually discovered twenty-eight constellations, fourteen to the north of the equator and fourteen to the south. Of these the twenty-eight, *Abhijit*, is often ignored. The moon makes a cycle through these once in 27 1/3 days. They knew the Milky Way and the two Dog-Stars, Canis Major and the Canis Minor (*Dvau Cwanau, Syama Savalau*). *The Satapatha Brahmana, XI. 4*, mentions *Jyotinshi*, i.e. resplendent planets.

Colebrooke speaks of a *Jyotisha* of the *Rig Veda* with a commentary. Professor Max Müeller believes the work to have been composed after the Sutra period, although the doctrines and the rules propounded therein, belong to the earliest stage of Hindu astronomy. Its practical object is to convey a knowledge of the heavenly bodies necessary for fixing the time for sacrifices and to establish a sacred calendar.

The improvements and discoveries of the renaissance are noted below:

1. They knew the solar and the lunar year.
2. The words *Savitri* and *Sunu* (English sun), both from the root *su* to beget, show that they knew the sun as the source of all life, animation, and health. The *quickening* power of the sun-god was acknowledged and worshipped as Mitra Deva, in the north, in India, Persia, West Asia and Europe before Christ. The car of the sun drawn by seven ponies shows their knowledge of the seven colours of the sunbeam, also expressed in *sapta-didhiti*. The *Rig Veda* mentions the sun as 'the upholder of the earth.' This seems to imply a knowledge of the universal attraction and gravity. The word *martanda* (sun) from *mrita* (dead) and *anda* (egg, ball) shows that they knew the solar ball was dead, i.e. motionless. This seems to prove indirectly that the earth moves round the sun. This is further apparent from the Rig Vedic *gau* applied to the earth, meaning a moving body. This shows the motions of the earth.
3. The word *chandramas* (moon) derived from *chandra* (cheery light) and *mas* (measure) seems to show that they knew the moon is lighted by the sun.

4. The word *Brahmanda*, mundane egg or ball, shows that they knew the earth to be round. The sun, moon and the stars all appear round. So, it is easy for any intelligent observer to regard the earth also as round. The word *prithvi* (earth) from *prithu* (broad, vast) suggests that they knew the earth to be very large.
5. Their discovery of the *nakshatra chraka*, i.e. circle of the twenty-eight constellations through which the moon passes once in 27⅓ days is really a great wonder. It is already said that they used the solar year of 365¼ days and the lunar year of 354 days. The solar year afterwards fell into disuse and was brought to India perhaps by the Buddhist missionaries from Egypt or Greece about the Christian era. The *samvat* is a lunar era, while the *sakavada* is solar. A month then had 27 days and the year began from the month of *Agrahayana*, i.e. 16 November. They determined the mean motions of the sun and the moon.
6. They knew the equator (*vishuvat*). The two points where the equator cuts the *ravi-marga*, i.e. the orbit of the sun, are called *sankrantis*, i.e. equinoxes, both autumnal and vernal, now falling on 23 September and 23 March. Thirteen hundred years ago, the equinoxes fell on the 30 *Chaitra* or 15 April and 30 *Asvin* (15 October). By careful observation and fine calculation, they discovered that the sun proceeds or recedes one day in about 66 years or 54 *bikālas* a year. (*the surya siddhanta*). They also knew the two solstices and the solstitial points. For this motion, the sun was probably called by them *surya*. They could explain an eclipse (*grahana*, seizure of one planet by another). The discovery of the solar zodiac is not a point of great merit, at least to those who had discovered the circle of twenty-eight constellations. It is often alleged that the Hindus borrowed it from the Greeks. This is possibly wrong for the Greek Cleostratus added only the ram and the archer in the sixth century BC. Gradually, they added the rest and made up twelve. The *Ramayana* and the *Mahabharata* know some of them. But we can explain them as interpolations or later insertions. Colebrooke, however, has hunted out the earliest mention of the zodiacal signs in a passage in the *Code of Baudhayana* who flourished not later than 600 BC. Be that as it may, it is certain that the *Rig Veda* knows not even a single sign of the zodiac. It is probable that the Hindus

and the Greeks, both had it from the Assyrians who excelled all other ancient nations in astronomy.

Professor Bipin Behari Sen of Calcutta tries to indicate the indistinct mention of some of the signs of the Zodiac in the *Rig Veda* thus: 'Siva is the bull-bannered god. Formerly, his conveyance was a dog, which was later replaced by a bull. The sign Taurus is the bull. By its side, is Sirius called *Rudra* (a star). This perhaps supplied the clue. Again, the Milky Way rises from the Pole, passes through the constellation Cepheus and Cygnus and then bifurcates. Again, from Cepheus, it crosses Cassiopeia and Perseus and falls into Auriga where the bright star Capella was once the *Agni-taraka*. Modern astronomers give the name of a small star near that. In the stream of the Ganges was born Skanda (Hindu Mars). Pleiades (our *Krittikas*) were there and tended Skanda. Sirius took him for his son. I think this Skanda is no other than the planet Mars. Skanda Deva is still worshipped as the presiding planet Mars. Hymns to both are the same. The tale of the birth of both is alike in the Puranas. Hence, it may be said that the birth of Skanda is the discovery of the planet Mars. The *Mahabharata, Wood Book, Birth of Skanda*, also confirms the idea. A legend has it that the Ganga, rising from heaven, stayed for a while in the water pitcher of Brahma; thence issuing out, it fell on the matted hair of Siva and thence turning south, it flowed towards the region of Yama. In plain words, the Milky Way coming from the Pole, enters Orion; thence it falls on the white Sirius; then it turns southward and enters the southern part of the solar ecliptic, Sirius (Rudra) riding on the bright Taurus (bull) is on the march, brightening the sky. The stars (gods) also are going in clusters. Kalidasa in his *Kumara Sambhava* (Birth of Mars) describes the marriage procession of Siva in the same way. The *Mahimna-stotra* also gives a similar description of Siva.

The images of Mitra Deva have been dug out from many parts of Europe. In some, the god or the goddess is found killing bulls. Many suppose that Mitra's killing bulls is really the sun's going into Taurus.

We know nothing about their observations or of the instruments used. Certainly, they possessed a *Dura-Vikshana* (telescope), at least of a rude kind, which was used in astronomical observations and navigation.

The Deva-Aryans also made considerable progress in medicine. Later Hindu medicine is much indebted to astronomy. We do not know how early astronomy gave help to our medical science. It seems probable that the Devas did not fail to turn their knowledge of astronomy to medical discoveries as well. Of the nine astronomers, Brahma and Vivaswan appear as the first great medical experts. Their search for 'auspicious hours', soon gave them a knowledge of the good or bad influence of the planets. Some diseases are specially caused by some planets under certain situations. Some stones, metals, cereals, plants, roots, animals are found congenial or propitiatory to some planets. A correct knowledge of their close relationship much aided the discoveries of medicines.

In connection with the Vedangas, the remark of Dr Thibaut is worth quoting here.

'The want of some rule by which to fix the right time for the sacrifices gave the first impulse to astronomical observations; urged by this want, the priest remained watching, night after night, the advance of the moon through the circle of the *nakshatras* (stars), and day after day the alternate progress of the sun towards the north and the south. The laws of phonetics were investigated because the wrath of the gods followed the wrong pronunciation of a single letter of the sacrificial formulas; grammar and etymology had the task of secring the right understanding of the holy texts. The connection of philosophy and theology is so close that it is often impossible to decide where the one ends and the other begins and is too well known to require any comment. Whatever science is closely connected with the ancient Indian religion must be considered as having sprung up among the Indians themselves'. (*J.A.S.B,* 1875, p. 227).

Dr Thibaut was the first to publish to the world the fact that geometry was first discovered in India, in eighth century BC.

M Bailly in his *History of Astronomy* says, 'Indians attained great distinction in Geometry and Astronomy, 3000 BC'.

THE UPA-VEDAS (MINOR VEDAS)

Medicine

Modern research has revealed that the ancient Assyrians excelled in astronomy but were far less advanced in medicine. In this connection, the following quotation is interesting: 'They (the Assyrians) indeed used, as did the Vedic Indians, external and internal remedies; but they probably regarded them as charms. Whatever progress they may have made in the science of medicine, the records of it in the ancient inscriptions prove that it was somewhat less than what we know of the Vedic physicians and their cures.' (*H.H.W., vol. I, p. 538*).

The Devas carried the science of medicine to a high degree of perfection. Brahma, Rudra, Indra, Dhanvantari, and the two Asvin brothers were medical experts. Besides, as is clear from the following, there were other great physicians:

(i) Brahma

He wrote a medical work in plain Sanskrit in a lakh of shlokas, divided into a thousand chapters. His work entitled *The Brahma-Samhita* is divided into eight parts; hence it is called *Ashtanga*. Brahma gave it to Vivaswan who again gave it to his disciples in an abridged form (*Bhavaprakasa* and *Brahma Vaivarta Purana*).

(ii) Rudra

He is called *Vaidyanatha*, i.e. Lord of the Physicians, or father of the Hindu medical science. Brahma had carefully compiled his great medical work from the Vedas, but Rudra was a great practical physician. Four hymns of the *Rig Veda* clearly show this: The seer Grit-Samada says: 'O Rudra, remove our diseases: make our sons strong and healthy with thy medicinal drugs. I have heard thou art the greatest of the physicians. O Rudra, let thy medicines cure us and make us happy. O giver of our desires, cure all my evils and pardon my faults. I utter a sincere hymn in praise of thee—O great white god. We worship thee, O bright Rudra! We sing of thy bright name.' (*R.V. II 33. 1–4*).

(iii) Dhanvantari

He was another noted physician. Like Vikramaditya, his name has become a title assumed by all medical experts of after ages. He was the author of the *Chikitsya-tatva-bijnanam*. He discovered, among other things: (a) *Amrita*—the 'immortal drink,' a special preparation of the *soma* juice that saved men from premature decay and death; (b) the use of many wonderful drugs and metals; (c) the art of reviving creatures killed; and (d) the medicines for beasts, birds and plants.

(iv) Asvin brothers

Sons to Vivaswan. These twin brothers studied medicine with their father and Daksha and became highly proficient in the science. Yama, another son of Vivaswan, also became a physician. They wrote *Chikitsya-sara-Tantram* and *Bhramaghnam*, respectively. Yama on his part wrote *Jnanarnavam*.

The medical skill and success of the Asvins will appear from the following:

(i) Like Dhanvantari and Sukra, (priests to the Daityas and *Danavas*) they could restore life to beings done to death. They had cured all soldiers wounded in the Devasura war. Indra had cut off the head of sage Dadhichi. It is said that the Asvins reset the head soon and brought him back to life. They also reset the head of Brahma, cut off by an angry Rudra.

(ii) Rejuvenation of the great sage Chyavana and Bhargava is also credited to the Asvins. Chyavana, son to Bhrigu and brother of Sukra, lived in a garden where Princess Sukanya went to cull flowers with her friends. Playfully she pricked the eye of Chyavana, then absorbed in divine thoughts. The eye bled profusely. Sukanya went home and told her father. King Saryati came to Chyavana to beg his pardon. But Chyavana demanded the princess' hand. The king hesitated, as the sage was old. Sukanya, however, married him willingly and began to serve him with extreme devotion. Sukanya was a relation of the Asvins who, pleased with her fidelity, gave Chyavana a medicine called *Chyavana Prasa* which rejuvenated the old sage.

(iii) King Rijraswa regained his impaired eyesight.

(iv) Bisapla, queen of king Khela, had lost a leg in battle. The Asvins made an excellent iron leg for her which enabled her to walk with great ease.

They cured the paralysed arm of Indra; made a new set of artificial teeth for Pusha, son to Daksha, and restored vision to the two blinded eyes of Bhaga.

(v) Princess Ghosha, daughter of king Kakshivan, suffered from leprosy for which none would marry her. Asvins cured her of it. Then she was married.

(vi) When sage Kanva became blind, the Asvins cured his blindness.
(vii) The son of a hunter was deaf. Through the treatment of the Asvins, he regained his power of hearing. (*R.V. I, 116 to 118*).
(viii) The husband of Badhrimati was impotent. The Asvins cured him of the disease.

The *Rig Veda* and the Puranas abound in such examples.

Military Science (*Dhanur*-Veda)

Brahma knew no fighting. Rudra, Indra, Vishnu and others were great fighters. The great sage Bharadvaja is credited with having excelled in archery (*Mahabharata, Peace Book, Chapter 210*).

The following points are noteworthy:

(i) Even in those days, kings personally went to battle, equipped with elephants and horses, and followed by their officers and army.
(ii) Armour, helmet and swords were in use, as were war music, bugles and flags.
(iii) *Bajra* (thunder) and other arms and weapons were also used. *Bajra* was perhaps a king of modern cannon-ball. The two kinds of *nalika astra* mentioned by Sukra in his *Art of Government*, were perhaps cannon and muskets. The Devas knew how to temper steel and make sword. The *Mahabharata* states that Brahma had tempered steel in his sacrificial fire and made a good sword which came down to the Pandavas through a series of most distinguished heroes. 'The steel of India ... is celebrated in the oldest Persian poem. It is mentioned in the Talmud (*Avodah Zarah*) as 'parzela Hinduah' (Elphinstone's *History, p. 10,* 9th *edition*).
(iv) Various types of arrows were used: some would emit fire, some poisons; the end of some arrows had whetted iron, others had sharpened deer-horn to pierce the enemy. (*R.V. IV., 3 and 4*).
(v) Horses attained great distinction.
(vi) Battles were often very fierce. Air fight, use of gas are also mentioned.
(vii) One day, in one single engagement, Indra had killed 50,000 of the enemies. (*R.V. IV., 28*).

The *Rig Veda* records many such terrible battles. The object of war then was the defence of country, religion and people generally. The Aryan war with the non-Aryans has been compared with the extermination of the native Americans by the Spaniards.

MUSIC (GANDHARVA VEDA)

The Aryans were very fond of music. So, the subject received its due share of attention from the seers. Narada was an expert in music, whose skill in harp is well known. Hindu tradition points to the sage Bharata as being the inventor of the seven notes and the creator of music and drama. The seven notes—*sa, re, ga, ma, pa, dha,* and *ni* were evolved out of the three Vedic notes—*Udatta, Anudatta,* and *Svarita*, now known as *Udara, Mudara* and *Tarà. Udatta* (gravely accented tune) gave rise to *nishada* and *gandhara. Anudatta* (lowly accented tune) gave rise to *rishaba* and *dhaivata. Svarita* (prolate) gave rise to *sharja, madhyama* and *panchama*. Vedic *Siksha* (laws of phonetics) shows how the Vedic seers excelled in music. The Vedic hymns were sung in choir in different families. Indra's court often resounded with music and dancing. The *Rig Veda* mentions that feasts were accompanied by religious or social singing, dancing, musical instruments and sonorous prayers. Seer Madhuchchanda, son of Visvamitra (not son of Gadhi of Kanouj but the famous composer of the holy verse *Gayatri*), mentions these in the *Rig Veda*. There was a paucity of musical instruments in the earliest Vedic period.

A harp called *ksheni* was in use (*R.V.* II, 30.13) *and karkari* (a drum) was the musical instrument (*R.V.* II, 40.3 prevalent during the time). Scenic representation of plays began at this time, dancing being the chief element. Then drama in Sanskrit came to be called *nataka*, from the root *nat*, to dance. It is said that Bharata caused the first play entitled *Lakshmi-Svayamvaram* (choice of Vishnu by Lakshmi) to be acted before the Devas. Music was played by the Aryans in sacrifices, marriages, coronations, feasts, and evening parties.

It is said that *Indra-dhvaja* or the *Jarjara puja* festival gave rise to our earliest drama. The Indra puja festival is still celebrated in Nepal. During this festival, the common people of the north would drink their fill, sing, and amuse themselves with rude performances of some popular themes. It attracted the attention of Brahma, who, for the sake of instruction and entertainment, created a new subject called the *Natya-Veda* (drama). He gave his first lessons on it to a sage called Bharata, who gathered together some smart young men and trained them in the regular dramatic art. At the suggestion of Mahesa, dancing was adopted. So, the elements of a regular play were dialogues, songs, dance, performance, and sentiments (Bharata's *Natya Sastra Book I, 16–17*). The original *Natya-Veda* of Bharata is lost. The one we have now was compiled from the earlier works towards the close of the third century or in the beginning of the second century BC. Abhinava Gupta wrote a commentary on it in the nineth century AD (H P Sastri, *J.A.S.B., October 1909;* see also, Bharata's *Natya Sastra, BK VI, 32*).

Bharata says that he performed his plays in heaven. The Devas, *vidyadharas, apsaras* and others acted in them. In time, those actors, gradually skilled, composed plays themselves. They composed such excellent plays that the seers felt insulted and in anger, cursed the drama (*Natya Sastra, Book XXXVI 23–24*). The first play enacted in heaven (i.e. the north) was *The Defeat of the Asuras*. There, the Asuras, highly enraged, disturbed the performance. So, Visvakarman, at the instance of Brahma, constructed a theatre hall, and placed it under guard. It had a regular stage, galleries and a dressing room. Several other plays were enacted to the great delight of all. The lunar king Nahusha was raised to Indraship by the Devas for some time, who witnessed the performance in the north and brought it to his Indian court afterwards. Bharata's disciples named Kolahala, Vatsa, Sandilya and Dhurtita enacted plays in India.

ARTS AND ARCHITECTURE (STHAPATYA-SILPA)

In this field, the name of Twashta, honoured with the glorious title of Visvakarman (Latin Vulcan, Master of Arts), stands foremost. He was the son of Prabhasa, of the Basu family of the Deva-Aryans. Vrihaspati was his maternal uncle. He brought about a revolution in the Aryan arts. He was the inventor of ornaments, of *bimanas* (aerial cars, like modern balloons, aeroplanes). He was the first to make fine palaces, houses, gardens, images, ornaments of various excellent designs, tanks, pleasure gardens, and wells. The various arts now current among the Hindus are said to have been invented by him. He is still worshipped by the Hindu artists and artisans. He improved ship-building. Stone and bricks as building material came in use, though infrequently. Palaces and houses were generally built of wood on brick plinths, with engravings and floral frescoes. In the houses of the rich, wooden work was often plated with gold which was then in great demand among the Aryans; use of precius stones in the buildings was not rare. (*Matsya Purana, Book 5; Garuda Purana, Book VI; Vishnu Purana, Book I, Chapter 15*).

There are many proofs of the excellence of Hindu art in those early times. The *Rig Veda* and other works mention golden ornaments, turbans, precious clothes, and ornaments set with precious stones.

It is highly probable that there were, before 2800 BC steam or electric cars, ships, aeroplanes, balloons. The Vedas and the Puranas give many examples of them (*cf. R.V. I. 37. 1*).

In architecture also, progress of ancient India was like that of modern Europe. The buildings of the most ancient India have now disappeared or lie deeply buried. The *Rig Veda* mentions a large building of thousand doors and thousand pillars (*R.V. II, 41.5* and *VII, 88.5*); an iron town (*R.V. VII, 3* and *95*); a stone-built town (*R.V. IV, 30*). Now, no trace is found of the Vedic towns, villages and palaces.

The most useful art was that of writing invented by Brahma; hence it was called *Brahmi lipi*. It is highly probable and also believed by General Cunningham and others that the Aryans, like the Egyptians, first used some pictorial or nature alphabet. As natural phenomena supplied the data for their religious thoughts, so natural objects suggested their first letters. With the renaissance, Brahma invented the new alphabet. Most of the scholars have ignored the originality of the Indian alphabet. We have discussed the point at some length in our chapter on *Hindu Art of Writing*. If the Hindus had borrowed their alphabet from the Egyptian, Phoenician, Sebian, Semitic or Aramean scripts, then they would have thankfully acknowledged their debt, as they did to the Greeks and the Romans in astronomy. But we know nothing of the kind. From the time of the Vedas till modern times, all books mention the art of writing.

LAW

Here again, Brahma was the first great law-giver. Manu's Code, first drawn up around 2770 or 2760 BC, quotes the views of Atri, Gautama and two others. Hence, it is clear that in the twenty-nineth century BC, four or five great seers gave laws for the reformation of the Aryan society.

We have already spoken of the *Kaliyuga* in connection with the downfall of the Aryans. Bhishma, speaking to Yudhisthira observes:

> Formerly, there was neither a king nor a kingdom. People were pious and protected themselves. In time, they fell from religion. Wisdom gradually disappeared. Greed entered their lives. Theft, indulgence, carnal desires became rife. Conscience was dulled, purity of thought and speech was a mere word. The Vedas were disregarded. Sacrifices were discontinued. The thoughtful Aryans, then alarmed, related to Brahma the sad state of society and asked him for a remedy. This marks the *Kaliyuga* (Iron Age) of the northern Aryans and the following regeneration and renaissance form the *Satyayuga* (Golden Age) of the Hindus.
>
> It is manifest from these that the Aryan society then was composed of two sets of men—the pick of the Aryans lived aloof and were exclusively given to religious contemplation; most of them were unmarried. On the other hand, the masses were rotten to the core. So, Brahma began to reform society. He asked the leading sages and seers to marry and he himself married. For better government of the masses, he drew up a penal code (*Danda Niti*) in a lakh of chapters. Rudra condensed it in 10,000 chapters, then further condensed it in 5,000 chapters, entitled *Bahudantaka*. Vrihaspati abridged it in 3,000 chapters and Sukra in 1,000. In time, the sages further condensed it. These have survived in the works of Kamandaka and others'. (*Mahabharata, Peace Book, Chapter 59*).

RELIGION

In the same twenty-nineth century BC, religion also took a new turn. We now notice the rise of three new religions among the Aryans who appear to have been very bold and free in their religious thoughts:

(i) Rise of Brahmanism

Opposition of the atheists led the later Brahmans to declare the Vedas to be of divine origin. Thus, the Vedas are talked of as the Hindu

Scriptures. In reality, the religion of the early Rig Vedic hymns composed before 3000 BC was not very high. Monotheism of the Vedas perhaps belongs to the Upanishadic period of Vedic composition. The early Rig Vedic religion was simply a sort of thought-idolatry. The early seers had earnestly asked Nature to explain the mystery of the universe, but had got no satisfactory answer. Then, they turned back from external query and looked within. Now, imperial self supplied them with all clear information regarding creation, universe, soul and God. The great sage Narayana—related to Brahma—pioneer of the wisdom-seekers, was the first to discover, '*Ekam sat, bipra bahudha badanti*'.

There is but one God, but the learned call Him many. (see also *R.V. X. 83–3:* He is one, though He bears the name of many.)

The following will corroborate our inference:

(a) 'The *Rig Veda* gives three things—ceremonial religion, earthly prosperity and enjoyment, but no salvation, no true bliss'. (*Mahabharata, Peace Book, Chapter 270*).

(b) 'Spiritual truth is described in the Vedas in a highly abstruse form'. (*Mahabharata, Peace Book, Chapter 210*).

(c) The Vedic seers say, in the Veda, 'The nature of Brahma lies so concealed that even the profoundest seers do not know it'. (*Mahabharata, Peace Book, Chapter 237*).

(d) 'Neither the Devas nor the seers knew what Brahma is. The great sage Narayana (who lived at the Vadarika hermitage in Kashmir) first discovered it. From him the seers, sages, devas, kings and others gradually knew of Brahma'. (*ibid., Chapter 210*).

The nature and idea of Brahma were fully discussed in the Upanishadas and finally and finely wrought out in Vyas's *Brahma Sutra* or Vedanta philosophy, composed some time about 1400 BC or after.

So long the word *rishi* (seer) commanded the highest respect. But now those who became proficient in the knowledge of Brahma, came to be known by the new glorious epithet of *Brahmana*. The 88,000 *Urdha-retas* first ranked as the foremost Brahmans, as did other meritorious rishis. Before long, all good Aryans became Brahmans. The discovery of Brahma led to the rise of Brahmanism. It was a highly philosophical religion, with puritanic rigidity. In mild and modified form, it partially exists even now. Brahmanism in time gave rise to Hinduism.

(ii) Rise of Jainism

Like Brahmanism, Jainism is an ancient religion of India (see *Jain Harivansa, Aristanemi Purana*). *Mahabharata* mentions it thus: 'Owing to the diversity of religions such as Aryan, Jaina and *Mlechchch*, people become doubtful' (*Mahabharata, Peace Book, Chapter 258*).

Jina is a spiritual conqueror. Rishabha Deva of the Vairaja dynasty was king of Bithoor and married Jayanti, daughter of Indra. After a long and prosperous rule, he left the raj to his eldest son Bharata and turned anchorite. After profound penance, he became a *siddha*, i.e. a spiritual conqueror. His religion Jainism consisted mainly of moral self-culture, perfect preservation of all life, eternity of matter, and the belief that salvation is obtainable without admitting a God. His disciples became known as *Yatis*. The Vedas allowed slaughter of animals only for sacrificial purposes, but Jainism allowed no sacrifice, no harm to any living thing. The Jains lived on hills or in forests far away from human dwellings, almost in a state of nature. They would eat only those ripe fruits that fell from trees by themselves; they would make fire with dry logs. It is evident that their religion was not meant for the masses. Soul, karma, rebirth, moksha were the same as in the Hindu religion. The *Bhagavata* has recognised Rishabha Deva as an incarnation. The Jains call him *Adinatha* or the first Prophet. In truth, Jainism was not a new religion but the first ethical exposition of Vedic truths. Twenty-three other reformers rose in different times, to remodel Jainism, the latest being Parsvanatha (eighth century BC) and Vardhamana Mahavira (sixth century BC).

(iii) Rise of Materialism

Some tribes of the Aryans seem to have been quite antagonistic to the Vedas. They were atheists and did not believe in God, soul, and the next world. With them, attainment of materialistic happiness was the *summum bonum* of life. Of the Daityas, Hiranyakasipu, the first great Daitya monarch and asvagriva were staunch materialists. Hiranyakasipu is notorious for the persecution of his pious son Prahlada. Asvagriva, the sworn enemy of the Vedic religion, tried to efface all Vedic trace from the world. It is said that he once stole the Vedas, and often harassed the performance of sacrifices. From this time, memorisation of the Vedic hymns became a necessity. Later, Vrihaspati formulated these atheistic views into something like a philosophy. (*Vishnu Purana, Mat. P., Lunar Dynasty, Chapter 24.*)

10

CONDITION OF THE PEOPLE AS DESCRIBED IN THE EARLY VEDAS

Religion dominated society. Most of the people were pious, truthful and moderate. From nature-worship rose thought-idolatry; then henotheism, monotheism, perfect toleration, catholoic ideas.

The seers prayed for the prosperity and progress of the country and people; they prayed for a good crop (*R.V. IV.* and *X.*). Agriculture flourished; excessive rain, drought, premature decay, famine, and death were rare. Irrigation was resorted to. Even horses were employed in ploughing. Wheat, barley, pulses, sesamum, various roots and fruits were the chief products.

Trade, both inland and foreign, was undisturbed and good. There was sea borne trade (*R.V. I.,* and *IV., 55*).

There was joint family system (*R.V. I., 114*). Father was the provider and protector; mother was the mistress of the home, daughter would do the household chores and so forth. Sons were known by the name of their fathers. The head of the family was the authority in all respects. In rites, festivals and sacrifices, the wife was the inseparable partner (*R.V. I.* and *V.*). Adultery of both male and female was equally blameworthy.

Ordinarily, the son would inherit the property; in default of a son, the daughter's son was the heir (*R.V. III.* and *VII*).

There was marriage of daughters with worthy bridegrooms. Ornaments and wealth had to be given as dowry (*R.V. X.*). In marriage, there were sports, amusements, song, dance, music, and feasts and fancy dresses of bride and bridegroom, as there is now. A bridegroom also used ornaments and perfumes (*R.V. V. 60.4*). Marriage-fee (modern *pana*), and rich dowry were in use. King Svanaya married his daughters to Kakshivan and gave him much as dowry (*R.V. V., 125, I.*). The great sage Richika married Satyavati, daughter of Gadhi, king of Canouj and obtained much wealth from the father-in-law (*Vishnu Purana* and *Bhagavata Purana*). Daughters were married with fine dresses and ornaments. (*R.V. IX., 46.2* and *X., 39.14*).

Women even then wore a veil, and participated in all ceremonies with their husbands; princesses married by self-choice. Female chastity was a matter of great glory. Women excelled in housekeeping, cooking, training their children, and were devoted to learning (cf. Devahuti, Aditi, Apala). They wore bright dresses and ornaments. They could prepare excellent sweetmeats with ghee and milk.

Sati (self-immolation of a widow) was known, though the practice was most probably rare. Professor AA Macdonell thinks that it was an old custom and was at first confined to the military castes only and afterwards imitated by others. The following instances show its antiquity.

(i) Archi, qeen of Prithu, a king of the Vairaja dynasty became a sati.
(ii) Sankusuka, a seer, is shown as inducing a sati, to stay from the resolve. (*R.V. X., 18.8*).
(iii) Manu does not mention it but emphasises the leading of a pure life. Daksha, Vishnu and Parasara suggest it as an inferior alternative.
(iv) Kausalya's desire to commit sati after Dasaratha's death.
(v) Sagara's mother was about to be a sati, but was prevented by the sage Aurva, as she was pregnant.
(vi) Sita, in the Asoka garden wished to die, upon hearing a false report of Rama's death.
(vii) The mother of Vedavati died a sati.
(viii) The eight chief queens of Krishna died with him.
(ix) Madri died a sati.
(x) A wife of Kansa became a sati.
(xi) Mandodari, queen of Ravana, became a sati.

(The practice of sati was considered as an inferior alternative open to the widows. A pure life was generally subscribed by the law-givers).

Bigamy and polygamy were general in kings; polyandry was rare. Mention is made of Raja, *Nagarapati* (a district chief) and of *gramapati* (a village chief). There were proper arrangements for good rule, collection of revenue and warfare. Even in those days there were towns, villages, palaces, rest-houses, roads, carriages, arms and weapons, soldiers, sports, trade, hospitality to strangesrs. The Aryans knew earthwork and architecture. (*R.V., II.* and *V.*)

The Aryans knew the use of various metals such as gold, silver and iron. There were blacksmiths, potters, carpenters, sawyers, barbers, sailors, physicians, priests, goldsmiths, and weavers. The currency was chiefly of gold. (*R.V., IV* and *V*). There were beautiful villages and towns, some brick and stone-built houses, broad streets and roads, fine steps for ascent on hills, fine cars drawn by ponies, boats, sea-going vessels, and other good conveyances for land, water and sky. Fine clothes, turbans, jewels, and ornaments were in common use.

There were libations of *soma* juice, invocation of gods with earnest, sincere and simple prayers. Some animals were killed in sacrifice. The Aryans partook of the offered meat.

The learned Aryans spoke and composed hymns in almost classical Sanskrit. The masses perhaps, used a loose Sanskrit.

There was no caste; of course, there were merit-classes such as rishis, devas, *Panis*, Aryans and Anaryhas. Women and Sudras could compose Vedic hymns and other works. For example, Kavasa of *Rig Veda* and Mahidasa of *Aitareya Aranyaka*.

Music, song, dance, feast and lighting became national in India from the earliest Vedic period. The festivities helped political organisation, development of literature (later epics, drama, opera, and yatra were born of those), culture of religion, reformation and progress of society, development of arts and industries, and excellence in weaving.

Vedic feasts were of several kinds—religious, harvesting, ceremonial, and evening party. On the village common, the villagers, mostly of the same *gotra* or clan, would get together during an auspicious hour, make an altar, light a holy fire, spread the *kusa* grass for various deities to sit thereon, invoking them by name, singing hymns in their praise for health, wealth, peace, and progeny. After offering the produce of their field and *soma* juice the villagers would sit together to dine and drink their fill. At night, by light, they would chant Vedic hymns to please the gods and would dance together—both men and women. Often, distant relations were invited to dine with them. The wife of Indra regrets the absence of a relative in a feast thus:

> All others are come: but what wonder, my father-in-law is not come! Should he come, he could eat fried barley and *drink soma* juice. After an excellent dinner, he could go home again. (*R.V. X., 28., 1*).

11

INDIA ABROAD

HINDU GEOGRAPHY

Elphinstone makes the following remarks on Hindu geography:

> The Hindus have made less progress in this than in any other science. India, and some other countries nearest to it, appear to be the only part of the earth at all known to the Hindus. Within India, their ancient books furnish geographical divisions that can be recognised. But all beyond India is plunged in a darkness from which the boldest speculations of modern geographers have failed to rescue it.
>
> The name of places beyond the Indus, do not coincide with those of Alexander's historians, though many on the Indian side do. It would seem, therefore, as if the Hindus had, in early times, been as averse to travelling as most of them are still; and that they would have remained for even unconnected with the rest of the world if all mankind have been as exempt from restlessness and curiosity as themselves. (*History of India, Book III, Chapter II, pp. 145–46.*)

Doubtless, our geography, like several other subjects, has suffered terribly from mythological fables and priestly obfuscation. Yet, a good deal may be rescued and reconstructed from the Vedas, the *Brahmanas*, the Upanishadas, the Sanskrit epics, the Puraṇas, the Tantras and the astronomical works.

Hindu geography is of two kinds, viz., *Kha-gola*—mathematical and astronomical geography and *Bhu-gola*—political geography.

They knew the following points regarding the earth:

(i) It originated from the gradual condensation of the 'primal waters,' (*ambhah apraketah* of the *Rig Veda*).

(ii) It is very large in extent (cf. *Prithivi*).

(iii) It is over 80,000 years (lunar) old since the dawn of human civilisation.

(iv) It is round (cf. Brahmanda—the mundane-egg or ball). The rotundity of the earth appears from the circular shadow cast on the moon (*Mahabharata*). Bhaskaracharya (twelfth century AD) compares the earth to a *kadamva* flower—a very apt simile.

(v) The sun is the upholder of the earth (*Rig Veda*); self-poised, it rests in the sky (Bhaskara).

(vi) The earth moves, though it appears still (Aryabhatta). Modern geography speaks of the two motions of the earth. Hindu geography admits its daily motion and states that the yearly motion is only a product of the first and not a separate motion.

(vii) It draws all objects towards its centre (Aryabhatta).

(viii) *Vishuvat* (equator) is the middle part of it. It is spoken of as a *Vritta* (circle). The equator passes through Lanka, where days and nights are equal all the year round. There is no shadow on the equator. Hindus knew of the unequal lengths of the days and nights. Valmiki in his *Ramayana* speaks of the sunless north and refers to the Northern Streamers. The *Rig Veda* also states similar phenomena in the Arctic region. Bhaskara says, 'When it is morning at Lanka, it is midnight at Roma'. They knew the equinoxes and the solstices. They knew of the alternate progress of the sun towards north and south. They knew of the precession of the equinoxes, being fifty-four *bikalas* a year, or one day in about sixty-six years. They could explain an eclipse. They recognised six seasons and knew their cause. They knew the ocean currents, the tides and their cause. They knew *badavanala* (submarine volcanoes).

(ix) North Pole was their *Sumeru* (not to be confounded with the *Sumeru* mountain of Central Asia); South Pole was their *Kumeru*. Longitude was reckoned from Ujjain in Malwa.

(x) The earth was formerly uneven.

The *Mahabharata* speaks of the earth as composed of numberless islands of which forty-nine are the main ones.

In a Hindu's daily prayer occurs the following: 'O mother Earth, composed of the three land-masses—Aswa Kanta, Ratha Kanta and Vishnu Kanta—take away all the sins from me.' We have already said that Aswa Kanta—the car-shaped land—is perhaps Africa, and the Vishnu Kanta is perhaps the two Americas.

In the *Mahabharata* the minister Sanjaya describes the earth at some length to the blind Raja Dhritarastra. There the earth is described as having seven continents. We think *Jambu* is Asia. *Saka* (the Powerful Continent) is Europe. *Salmali* is Africa. *Plaksha* is the Indo-African continent now submerged. *Pushkara* is North America. *Kusa* is South America. *Krauncha* is Australia.

Hindus speak of *seven* seas as surrounding the earth. They are all of salt water.

Hindu knowledge of Asia—*Jambu Dwipa*—appears extensive. It is surrounded by salt seas. In shape, it looks like a large lotus-leaf.

ASIA (JAMBU-DWIPA)

The attached islands are: *Svarna-prastha, Chandra Sakta, Abartana, Ramanaka, Manda-harina, Panchajanya* (Papuan?), *Sinhala* (Ceylon), and *Lanka* (a small is land, now a part of Ceylon). The last two only are now recognised.

Lakes

The *Mahabharata*, describing the conquests of Arjuna in the north speaks of the Caspian Sea as *Kshiroda Sagara*. The *Kaushitaki Upanishad* (pages 146–47) mentions the lake Aral as *Arar*. The *Manasa Sarovara* is our modern Mansarowar. The other small lakes of Central Asia are called *rishi-kulyas*.

Rivers

The Vedic *Wakshus* is our Oxus. Sita (Hsito = Sira) is now Yarmond. *Yei-nei-sei* is Hiranwati (*Mahabharata*). Ob or Obei is our Vedic *Yavyawati. Su wahini* is modern Huang-ho.

Mountains

Himavat is Himalaya; Suktiman is Sulaiman; Hemakuta, Hindu Kush; Gandha madan, Belurtag; Kailasa is Kailas; Nishadha, Nyssa; Sveta (White Mt.) is Sofed Koh; Malyavan, Insan and Khanghan.

Countries

Asia was divided into nine principal divisions called *Varshas:* Bharata Varsha (India); Ketumala Varsha (Afghanistan, Persia and Turkey); Bhadraswa Varsha (China); Kimpurusha (Tibet); Hari Varsha (Tartary); Ila Varsha (Mongolia); Ramyaka (South Siberia); Hiranmaya (Central Siberia); and Uttar Kuru (North Siberia).

The countries of India according to the *Sakti-sangama Tantra* (*Chapter* 7) are Anga (Fast Bibar, now Bhagalpur division); Banga (Bengal); Kalinga (between Orissa and the river Krishna); Kalinga (Kalinga and up to 104 miles to its south); Kerala; Kashmir; Kamarupa (north of Garo Hills); Maharashtra (British Bombay Presidency down to Kolhapur); Andhra (south-west of Orissa); Saurashtra (Kathiawar); Gujarat; Tailanga; Malayala (Malabar Coast); Karnataka (between Ramanatha and Seringapatam); Avanti (a part of Malwa); Bidarbha (Berar and a part of Hyderabad); Maru (Marwar); Abhira (on the river Tapti, near the Vindhya Range); Malwa (east of Ujjain and north of river Godavari); Chola (between Dravira and Tailanga); Panchala (west of Kárnal and north of Delhi); Kamboja (noted for its horses; in north-west India); Virata (Jaipur); Pandya (south of Kamboja and west of Delhi, perhaps a part of the Punjab); Videha (north Bihar); Balhika (Bulkh); Kirata (a small country in the Vindhya range); Multan (between river Karatoa and Hinglez: said to be full of *mlechchhas*, i.e. unclean beings); Khorasan (Persia—between Hinglez and Makkesa); Airaka (north of Persia); Bhotanta (Bhutan); China (south China); Maha China (north China); Manasesa (Manchuria?); Nepal; Silahatta (perhaps, east Assam or

Indo-China); Gaur (perhaps, modern Faizabad); Kosala (modern Oudh—seat of the Solar Kings); Magadha (a country in the United Provinces); Kikata (Gaya province); Magadha (south Bihar); Utkala (Orissa); Sri-Kuntala (probably, a part of Gujarat); Hoona Desa (north of Marwar and south of Kashmir); Konkana (a coast strip, south of Bombay); Kekaya (in north-west India); Saurasena (south of Magadha and West of Vindhyas); Kuru Desa (south of Karnal and east of Panchala); Sinhala (said to be the best country in India—east of the Indian Desert and south of Kamagiri); Pulandhri (east of Silahatta, perhaps Lusai Hills); Kachchha Desa (Kachar: north of the Bay and east of Garo Hills, Sanskrit Ganesa Giri); Matsya Desa (country of fish—north of Pulinda and east of Cachar, probably Sylhet, Mymensingh and parts of Rajsahi Division); Madra (between Virata and Pandya); Sauvira (a sea-board tract between Sindh and Gujarat. But the *Sakti-Sangama Tantra* finds its locality between Mathura and River Gandaki); Nata (perhaps, British Baroda State); Barbara (a large tract from Haridwar to Sapta Sringa Hill); Saindhava (Sindh, the work state that the hilly tracts in the coast from Sindh to Mecca are known by); Pushkararanya (modern Mukran or Mekran Coast); Kaleswar (?); Traipura (British Central Province); and Swetagiri (Sikkim).

The ancient countries of India according to the astronomical work entitled *Jyotistatvam:*

(i) In the middle

Sarasvata (a part of the Punjab); Matsya (Jaipur); Surasena and Mathara (Mathura districts); Panchala (a long narrow strip on either side of the Ganges: the northern half is now called Rohilkhanda); Salva (a part of Punjab); Mandavya (?); Kurukshetra (Karnal); Gajahwa (ancient Hastinapur on the Ganges); Maru (the desert, probably Sindhu and West Rajputana); Naimisha (a large forest tract near ancient Hastinapur); the Vindhyas; Pandyaghosha (a part of Punjab); Yamuna (Delhi); Kasi (Benaras); Oudh; Prayaga (Allahabad); Gaya; and Videha (north Bihar).

(ii) In the east

Magadha (south Bihar); Sona (a country on the river Sona); Varendra (north Bengal); Rarhaka (the Gangetic delta); Burdwan; Tamalipta

(Midnapur); Pragjyotisha (Assam); Udayadri (Hill Tippera and the Chittagong division).

(iii) In the south-east

Anga (east Bihar); Banga (north-west Bengal); Upa-Banga (east Bengal); Traipura (Teori in the Central Provinces); Koshala; Kalinga (northern part of the British Madras Presidency); Odra (Orissa); Andhra; Kishkindhya (Bellary district); Bidarbha (Berar); and Savara (a forest tract).

(iv) In the south

Avanti; Mahendra; Malaya (Malabar); Rishya-Mikaka (part of Hyderabad); Chitrakuta (Bundelkhand); Maharanya (?); Kanchi (Chola); Sinhala (not Ceylon); Konkana; Kavery (south India); Tamraparni (Ceylon); Lanka and Trikutaka are small islands to the north-west of Ceylon.

(v) In the south-west

Dravira; Anarta (Kathiawar); Maharashtra (British Bombay); Raivata (a part of Gujarat); Javana; Pahnava; Sindha (Sindh); and Persia.

(vi) In the west

Haihaya (countries around the mouth of the Nerbuda); Tadri (?); *Mlechchha* Vasa, (probably, on the right bank of the Indus); Saka (perhaps, modern *Seistan*).

(vii) In the north-west

Gujarat, Nata (probably, the Baroda State) and Jalandhara.

(viii) In the north

China; Nepala; Hoona; Kekaya; Mandara (?); Gandhara (Kandahar); Himavan (the Himalayan States); Krauncha (?); Gandhamadana (now Belurtag); Malwa (?); Kailas; Madra; Kashmir; *Mlechchha;* Khasa; Balhika (Bulkh); Kirata (a part of Tibet); and Darada (Dardistan).

(ix) In the north-east

Svarna-Bhauma (Golden Chersonese); Ganga-Dvara (a part of trans-Gangetic Peninsula); Tankana (?); and Brahmapura (Burma).

The *Matsya Purana* also gives a list of the ancient Indian countries. The curious reader will obtain much profit and pleasure from a study of General Cunningham's *Ancient Geography of India*.

Hindu knowledge of and communication with all countries between India and the Arctic Ocean will appear from the *Ramayana, Kishkindhya Book, canto 43, verses 53–58;* the *Mahabharata, Book I, Chapter 120, shlokas 1–20;* the *Vayu Purana, Chapter 45, shlokas 11–16, 42;* the *Chhandogya* Upanishad, *pp. 358–60, pp. 171–81;* the *Vayu Purana, Chapter 39, shlokas 76–81;* Bhaskara's *Siddhanta Siromani;* Charaka's medical work; the *Vishnu Purana* and other works.

While the political relations of the Hindus with the north became gradually weaker, the trade relations with Central Asia, the Caspian Sea, Black Sea, and the Mediterranean Sea continued. A Hindu colony is extant at Astrakhan on the Volga. The Hindu fire-temple of Baku, on the western shore of the Caspian Sea, is well known. From the close of the third century BC onward, the Buddhist preachers carried the Indian wisdom, arts and religion to the different countries of the world. They not only gave, but also brought back much knowledge of new things from abroad. Hindus have preserved records, however brief, of all foreign invasions.

TRAVELS AND VOYAGES OF THE ANCIENT HINDUS

Latin, Greek and works of other nations furnish ample proof of Hindus going abroad on commerce and for other purposes.

Hindu writings also corroborate this. Hindus, Buddhists and Jains lived in large numbers in Arabia, Syria and other parts of Asia Minor. Lucian tells us that at Nineveh he once saw a great many travellers who had come there only for the sake of worshipping images. He further tells us that to that Sacred City, Hindus came every day in large numbers because they regarded that city as a place of pilgrimage. The truth of this statement is also confirmed by the Puranas where Nineveh is called Haripuri, Greek *Haliopolis* (City of God). The Indian name of Nineveh clearly shows what the Hindus once thought of it. The pilgrims who went beyond the Hinglez Sea in Col. Wilford's time, and reported that about 224 temples of Bhavani could be seen there even then. This place is about eight miles from Sindh. Few ascetics had the courage to travel on the road to that important historical place because it was rough and difficult. It was then a forsaken place. No one lived there. On the banks of the Euphrates, there stood two Hindu temples. Two images of Vishnu, called Kalynarob and Govindarob, were worshipped there. Many other Hindu idols with broken noses and ears told the tale of the influence of Brahmanical culture and worship on the ancient religion of that land. Baharam and Astrakhan, Cairo and Moscow were the centres of trade in ancient times; Indian merchants flocked to those cities every year to earn money.

Some of the Hindu families permanently resided in those cities. In the same way, Baku and Kongo also held a great many well-to-do Hindu families. Travellers to those regions reported that they were famous there for their honesty and learning. Numerous books on astrology written by them are extant. But before speaking of these learned men, something should be said about the great astronomer, Yavanacharya. He was born of a Brahman family in Arabia and was educated in the University of Alexandria. He was the author of several treatises on astrology. It is said that in those days, there were in Arabia a great many Brahmans well-versed in Sanskrit and Yavanacharya must have learned Sanskrit from one of them. Dr Buchanan, when he was in India, saw several tribes of Jains who insisted that they came originally from Mecca or Arabia and that they were expelled by either Muhammad or his successors.

A Hindu treatise on horses calls Arabia, *Arba*, noted for its steeds. The long strip on the Red Sea was called by the Hindus *Makkesa Desa*. The Hindus there set up an image of Siva called Makkesa (Lord of Mecca). After the rise of Islam, the Hindu temples were pulled down and the great stone image of Siva was placed at the entrance to the Great Mosque containing the tomb of Muhammad to keep shoes on.

Some Hindu families embraced Islam. Some came back to India. Some Brahman families still remained at Mecca, without changing their faith. It is said that their children are known as Hussaini Brahmans who dress like Muhammadans but wear a sacred thread and worship in their own way.

There are twenty-three famous astrologers and of them five were born in Mecca. Though they are called *Javanas*, they do not seem to be so from their names—Chetta, Cautta, Romaka, Hillaja, and Dishana. Ebn Dissan was born in Edessus. He gives the date of Muhammad's birth as AD 638. The catalogue of Raghunath makes O'mar and Dissan one and the same. Romaka is well known. K'Herbelot asserts that astrologer Cangha wrote a book which was translated into Arabic and as he was a Hindu, the Arabs called him Cancah-al-Hindi. Col. Wilford holds that in the first century AD, Hindu astrologers were held in high esteem and repute at Rome and none but the richest men could afford to employ them (*Asiatic Res, Vol X, p. 104*).

Hindu Rajas sent letters and ambassadors to ancient Persia. Zonarus, an author, says that when hostilities broke out between the Assyrians and the Median king Kykius about 620 BC, a Hindu raja agreed to arbitrate between them and wrote a letter to the king of Media.

Another Hindu raja sent several ambassadors and some coins to the Persian emperor, Cyrus (sixth century BC).

When Xerxes, the Persian emperor, invaded Greece about 480 BC, Hindu soldiers, clad in their white cotton garments and equipped with cane bows and iron-tipped arrows went to Greece with him. Hindu soldiers fought with Alexander, on the side of the Persian monarch, Darius, in the fourth century BC.

A Hindu raja had requested Antiochus, the king of Syria, to send him some wine, some dried figs and a learned Greek. The Syrian king in reply said, 'I can send you plenty of wine and figs, but no Greek scholar is for sale'.

HINDU GODS IN SYRIA

There was at Heliopolis (Sanskrit Haripuri, native Nineveh) in Syria the image of a goddess. Hindus worshipped her with the offer of various rich presents. Near the goddess, were two other gods, one mounted on a bull and the other on a lion. These were Siva and Parvati. Thus, there is no doubt that Hindu gods were worshipped there by the Hindu colonists.

HINDUS IN ARMENIA

It is recorded that some Hindus had gone to Armenia, who settled there and erected brass gods for worship, some time before Christ. A war ensued between them and the new Christians, and the Hindus were defeated. Nearly 1,039 men died on the battlefields on both sides.

The events of this battle were inscribed on their tombstones in three languages. The Christians demolished the Hindu temples. Six Brahmans, who wanted to stop it, were killed. St. Gregory thus forcibly converted 5,050 Hindus in one day to Christianity. Some Brahman families took a vow not to change their faith. Thereupon, a Christian king imprisoned them and shaved their heads.

Pheodu Elean sailed for India in 430 BC. He was taken prisoner by the Hindus and was afterwards sold to the Persians. From Persia he returned to Athens. There, he became a disciple of Socrates and was believed to have founded the Elean School.

In 24 BC, Porus, a Hindu king of Pandya, twice sent ambassadorial missions to Augustus, the Roman Emperor, as a gesture of friendship. The first mission succeeded in meeting with the emperor in Spain. The second mission found the emperor in the island of Samos. While coming back, some of them died on the way. With the ambassadors, there were some Brahmans and officers of the Indian king. The learned historian Nicholas of Damascus in Syria, talked with three of them. He writes that the Hindu king had sent a letter written in Greek, with the ambassadors. The following is its purport: 'I am lord over 600 kings. I seek your friendship; I am ready to help you in all reasonable matters'. Eight officers placed the presents before Augustus. Among its unusual contents, there were several very large uterus-born snakes, a 10-cubit long egg-born snake, a 3-cubit long river tortoise and a partridge larger than a vulture. One of the Brahmans, an astrologer and sooth-sayer, began to live at the court of Augustus. He afterwards killed himself in a fire. On his tombstone, it is written thus: 'Here lies a Hindu Brahman named Zermanochagus, i.e. Sramanacharya of Bergosa, i.e. Berygaza, now Broach in Gujarat. According to the custom of his country, he has immolated himself in fire' (Strabo, Dio Plutarchs and Niaal Damascin).

This shows that the early Hindus studied Greek. Garga, an astronomer of the first century BC calls the Greeks barbarians. Yet, he does not hesitate to say that Greek astronomy is worthy of study. Hindus knew the Greeks well and called them *Yawanas* (not to be confounded with the name *Javana* applied to the Turks). Hindu and Buddhist preachers had visited Greece and brought home new lessons on geometry, architecture, astronomy and astrology.

Hindus called Italy *Patachchara*—the country of volcanoes. Rome was known as *Romaka Pattan*. Though the Romans never ruled India, yet her trade and other relations with India were very close. Hindu rajas used to send presents and ambassadors to Rome.

To congratulate Trajan on his conquests, several Hindu rajas sent him ambassadors. When Aurelian had conquered Tadmore, some Hindu kings sent him presents and ambassadors who were present during his triumphal entry into Rome. In the first century AD, Indian astrologers were employed by the Roman emperors at Rome for astrological forecasts and fortune-telling. There are ample historical proofs of the Hindus going to the Roman Empire from the first century BC to the sixth century AD.

In his *Life of Isidorus*, Damascius mentions Severus, a Roman by nationality but born in Africa. He was a great philosopher and resided at the court of Emperor Anthemius. After the death of Anthemius in AD 473, he went to Alexandria. Here, he received a great many Brahmans and showed them every nook and corner of that singular city (*Photii Bibliotheca, p. 1040* and *Suidas V Severus*).

In AD 103, a few Indian kings and a king of Ceylon sent ambassadors to Claudius with complaints against the Parthian kings. There were Indian ambassadors at the courts of the following Roman Emperors: Antonius Pius, Diocletian, Heraclius, Maximian, Theodosius, Justinian. (*Auc. Universal History, vol. XVIII, p. 78*)

Hindu soldiers served in the Roman army. An Indian contingent was placed at Cirencester in England by the Roman governor of Britain. Before 189 BC Hindu servants, both male and female, were available in Greece and Rome. Indian muslin, ornaments and unguents were in high demand with the Romans. Neither law nor the wise counsels of Roman orators could prevail against the use of those foreign goods. This Roman lust for Indian luxuries, according to Gibbon, was one of the reasons that led to the decline and fall of the Roman Empire.

Several Romans sought shelter in India at different times. In AD 529 Almondar, the king of Hemiarites attacked Syria. The Roman governor of that province fled and came to India for his protection.

From the *Periplus* and the *Justinian Code*, we learn much about the imports and exports of those times (*Strabo II, p. 516*).

Some of the Greek traders wished to settle at Callian (Kalyan) near Bombay. But they were refused permission by the Indian kings. The Peutingerian Tables show that in India, Muziris was a Roman settlement and there was a garrison of 1,200 men there for the protection of trade. Some Jews settled in the Malabar coast. Several Arabian colonies also settled in Malabar, west Ceylon and Chittagong, long before the birth of Muhammad.

Many cities of Arabia and Persia were partially inhabited by Hindus. Some of the learned Hindu astrologers flourished and wrote their books there. In the *Romaka Siddhanta*, Bhaskara is represented as having been educated in the city of Rome. There are still Hindu settlements in Colchis, a country between the Caspian and the Black Seas.

The Buddhist missionaries visited and preached in almost all the countries of Europe. To them we owe the name of Skandanabha, or Scandinavia. The Rig Vedic *Hariyupia* seems to imply a part of east Europe. That may have given rise to *Europa*, finally *Europe*. The Rig Vedic *Roosam* is Russia in Europe or more properly Lithuania, where Aryan colonies lived and spoke a tongue akin to Sanskrit.

HINDU SHIPWRECK IN THE BALTIC SEA

About 60 BC, some bold Hindu navigators sailed to the Baltic Sea in Europe. When shipwrecked, they landed on the shores of Germany. The king of Serbia received them and handed them over to the Roman Consul (*Pliny's Nat. History II, 67*).

No objection to its authenticity has as yet been heard. Still, the point is, 'How could the Hindu sailors go to the Baltic Sea?' Were they carried round from India direct to the north of Europe by a current of the ocean?

This seems hardly possible, though such an argument had been most forcibly advanced in the discussions about the possibility of a north-west passage to India as mentioned in Hakluyt's *Voyages*. India held frequent commercial intercourse with China. I think, Hindu merchants from China sailed to the Baltic Sea through the Bering Strait and the Arctic Ocean. There is another explanation of this voyage. The north-east shores of the Black Sea still bear trace of Hindu occupancy (Eliot's *History, p. 510*). From this region, Hindu merchants may have sailed to the Baltic through the Mediterranean, Gibraltar, Bay of Biscay, English Channel, and the North Sea. Whatever might have been the route, the voyage was indeed, glorious for our Hindu Columbus or Vasco da Gama. The *Mahabharata* speaks of the earth as composed of islands, of which forty-nine are big. How could the writer make such statements, if not based on facts?

Modern scholars have proved satisfactorily that emigrations to the West of expatriate Indians took place early (Elliot's *History, I, Appendix, p. 507*).

Mr Pococke tries to prove that Greece itself was an Indian colony. Though Hindu tradition also says something of the kind, yet the point is still open to grave doubt. However, there are clear proofs of an Indo-Hellenic intercourse from the earliest times. We have already spoken of the Indian colonies on the shores of the Black Sea. Indian mercenaries served in the ranks of Persian and European armies. Indian scholars and merchants lived in the Persian courts and with the legendry Harun-al-Rashid of happy memory. Itinerant Hindu ascetics also travelled over a considerable part of the then known world, converting distant shrines into places of Hindu pilgrimage.

HINDUS IN AFRICA

Hindu knowledge of Africa as a continent is meagre. However, it appears that Hindus were well acquainted with some parts of North Africa. There is proof that ancient Egypt had social, political and commercial relations with ancient India. There are records of Hindus going to Carthage to trade. Before 252 BC, the Roman General, Metelus Celer, and the Carthaginian General, Asdrubal, fought fiercely on the island of Sicily, where the Carthaginians suffered heavily. Some Indian elephants and their riders on the Carthaginian side were killed and some captured by the Romans.

This shows that Hindu mahouts used to go to Africa and Europe where they settled. Pliny also states that the Carthaginians, while trading with Hindus, obtained plenty of precious rubies. Hindu voyage and battle appear from the Egyptian writing, too. Nonus, an Egyptian poet, says in his poem that Hindus are much accustomed to navigation and are brave in sea-fights. Professor Wilson also says that in the first few centuries of the Christian era, there was intercourse between India and Egypt via Hindu and Arab merchants. It is well known that Hindus had settled in the *Zokatara Diw*, i.e Socotra, (Sanskrit *Sokatra-dwipa*—Island of Safety) to the east of Africa. Again, when Alexandria became the chief port of Oriental commerce, it was frequented by Indian merchants, some of whom actually settled there.

Buddhist missionaries preached their new gospel in Syria, Palestine, Egypt, and other countries. Buddhists under different names lived in those countries (Pliny's *Natural History, V. p. 15*). Buddhism later on influenced the Gnostic heresies that rent the early Church and begot those classes described by Kingsley as 'a strange brood of theoretic monsters begotten by effete Greek philosophy on Egyptian symbolism, Chaldee astrology, Parsee dualism, and Brahmanic spiritualism'. (*Hypatia, Preface, p. XIII*).

The edicts of Asoka also tells us that he had sent missionaries and ambassadors to the dominions of the Seleucides and the Ptolemies in the third century BC. These emigrations certainly helped the diffusion of Indian ideas over the western world.

The points given above refer chiefly to the Mauryan period and the Puranic age. But there are abundant proofs of India's intercourse with the West from the earliest times. Indo-Egyptian relations: (i) political under Osiris, Isis and Sesotris; (ii) commercial; Egypt obtained various dyes, precious stones, and wood from India; porcelainwares from far-off China. The question of racial unity of the early Hindus, the Egyptians and the Greeks is still a moot point. But Sir William Jones, Dr Royle, Professor Heeren, Elphinstone, Tod, Pococke and others show several points of similarity and close relationship between those peoples. Hindu *Salmali-dwipa* is perhaps Africa, *Suryyarika* (sunburnt land) is perhaps *Sahara* or North Arica. Egypt is our *Misra Desa* (country of mixed people, so-called because people from different parts resided there for trade). Hindus still call Egypt *Misar*. The Egyptian Manes (first king, solar) sounds like Hindu Manu, the first solar king of India. There is still a statue of Manes in Egypt. Indian Manu's date is about 2800 BC; two or three Egyptologists give a similar date to Manes. Egyptian pyramid is Hindu *parimatha*. The bull-bannered Isis is Sanskrit *Isa*, Osiris is Sanskrit *Iswara*, River Nile is Sanskrit *Nila* (Blue River), Tripoli is Tripuri.

Manu and his son Priyavrata of the Vairaja dynasty in Bithoor are said to have possessed lands in Africa, too. It is said that there was a Hindu colony in Ethiopia. Homer mentions the righteous East Ethiopians and West Ethiopians. *The Historians' History of the World* (London) says, 'The Egyptians were essentially Orientals and they had four castes like the Hindus. The Egyptian style of architecture resembled that of ancient India to some extent'.

INDO-ASSYRIAN RELATIONS

The descriptions of the cuneiform inscriptions tally with the Rig Vedic accounts given of Vritra, Bala, and their allies, *Panis*, an Aryan people. But these people, though Aryan, were not Hindus. They were driven out from the north by the Deva-Aryans, (*Rig Veda I, 80, 1* and *2; III, 33, 7; IX, 63, 24.*). The Assyrian queen Semiramis had attacked India with a fleet of 400 sails, 3,00,000 foot soldiers and 20,000 horses. But being wounded in the battle, she fell back (2000 BC). The Assyrians had their gold, silver, stones, teakwood, sandalwood, apes, peacocks, muslin, and silk from India. Hindus most probably derived their knowledge of the solar zodiac from the Assyrians.

INDO-PHOENICIAN RELATIONS

The Phoenicians were an Aryan people, but not Hindus. Their own ancient works are mostly lost and fragmentary. The *Rig Veda* mentions a people called *Pani*, Latin *Poeni* = Phoenicians, i.e a trading people. They were a clan of the Asuras whose chiefs, Vritra and Vala fought with the *Devas*. The Asuras and the *Panis* were defeated and ousted from the North. Vritra and his brother Vala with their followers conquered ancient Persia and Turkey. The *Panis* followed them and finally settled on the Levant Sea. Their new colony was called *Pani-Desa*, Latin *Finides*, later Phoenicia. Its extent was 200 miles by 45 miles; in some parts, 150 miles by 35 miles. This colonisation took place perhaps around 2800 BC. Their capital, Tyre, was built in 2750 BC. The Phoenicians are described by the classical writers of Europe as faithless, treacherous and deceitful—a description quite in unison with the Vedic account (*Rig Veda 1, 35, 5; III, 51, 14; VII, 6, 3*).

Ancient Asia Minor contained numerous Aryan colonies. The Mitani branch of the Aryans became very powerful around 1500 BC. A plate of the fifteenth century BC, recovered from an old underground temple, at Boghozkioii, Asia Minor, shows the invocation of various Vedic deities such as Indra, Varuna and Nasatya. The Phoenicians first reached India in the fourteenth or the middle of the thirteenth century BC. Their trade empire extended from Great Britain to Ceylon. The people of *Ur* took teakwood from India to build their palaces. These merchants not only carried eastern commodities but also Oriental art and culture to the western world.

INDO-HELLENIC INTERCOURSE

Alexander the Great was not the first Greek to come in contact with the Hindus. An Indo-Hellenic intercourse existed from the earliest times. Striking resemblance between the Hindus and the Greeks in mythology, manners and customs, philosophy, medicine, and drama may lead some to suppose that the Greeks are Hindu in origin. The early accounts of the Greeks are lost. But they are an Aryan people of kindred stock. Their ancestors and ours, lived in Central Asia under the same roof, speaking the same tongue and worshipping the same gods. From the Aryan tongue which was an older form of classical Sanskrit, have come Sanskrit and the other tongues of the Indo-European family. Several eminent scholars say that Hindus were the last to leave the northern home, for Sanskrit has the largest vocabulary.

The Hindus and the Greeks were the two gifted Aryan nations of the ancient world. If India boasts of greater originality, Greece can claim a more perfect culture, a more practical, rational and comprehensive knowledge of things in general. Greece obtained her Indian ideas through the Phoenicians, the Persian courts, Buddhist preachings and other sources. On the other hand, India had her knowledge of excellent architecture, astronomy and astrology from the West. Aryabhatta and Varahamihira adopted the Greek zodiac and its divisions with the names slightly orientalised. Jewish relations with India were chiefly commercial. Solon (tenth century BC) took his building material from India. The Parsis were once one people with the Hindus. The courts of the Persian emperors were the meeting places of the Indians, Greeks and others. Indian lore reached Europe through Persia. From China to Egypt and Greece, there were constant intercourse and exchange of ideas. EB Wowell, editing Elphinstone's *History of India*, nineth edition, says in a note:

'We are too apt to look on the ancient world as a scene of stagnation. There were travellers and circulation of ideas. Spread of Buddhism shows how men's minds were awake to new ideas. Then, why should the tradition of the Eastern origin of much of early Greek philosophy be incredible or even importable?' Speaking of the Hindu *Aranyakas* and the Upanishadas composed between 2000 and 1400 BC, the same editor observes: 'No Hindu works have probably exercised a wider influence on the world. These forlorn guesses at truth are constantly spoken of as Eastern Philosophy. Familiar ideas occur in the Phoedrus, Empedocles or Pythagoras, in the neo-Platonism of the Alexandrian and also in the Gnostic schools. Plautinus alone tried to free Greek philosophy from Hindu influence. The Cabala of the Jews and the Sufism of the Muhammadans seem to be derived from the same source.'

This foreign intercourse of the Hindus appears from several lawbooks of India. Manu has excluded all Brahmans who had lived in foreign lands, from being invited to *sraddha* ceremonies. Almost all the ancient law-givers of India have prescribed certain penances (*prayaschitta*) for the purification of all Hindus who returned home after living in foreign countries for some years.

Though some ancient writers have shown aversion to foreign travels, luckily, Hindus showed little deference to those injunctions and made extensive travels and voyages to foreign lands. Hindu navigation and maritime activity appear from the earliest times down to AD 1832 when the Indian sailors made a voyage from India to Great Britain up to the River Tweed.

It is needless to say that Hindus were good shipbuilders. A work called the *Nishpada Yanoddesa* gives the construction of various vessels and boats. That work also takes the accounts of previous writers on the subject such as Bhoja and others. Strabo says plainly that Hindus used ships in battles. There were doubtless, Hindu shipwrights; Megasthenes found shipbuilding as a distinct profession of the Hindu class. The *Ramayana* also alludes to sea-fights of the Hindus. Manu's *Code* also sanctions sea-fights of the Hindu kings. Sir John Malcolm, writing on the ships of the Deccan and Ceylon says: 'Those ships fully served all the modern requirements. The European shipbuilders have not improved much. Shipbuilding was exactly so, even in ancient India'.

Various reasons almost killed our Hindu shipbuilding. Chittagong was the only port of India where some shipbuilding was done in early 20th century. India contributed a good part to the marine service of the world in the shape of *Lascars* and *Sharangs*, chiefly recruited from the Chittagong Division.

Though we no more possess our own Hindu ships, yet our Hindu merchants now go to the different parts of the world in British or foreign vessels. Perhaps, it was so in the most ancient times, too. It does not appear that there was much Hindu navigation and maritime activity on the Western waters. The Phoenician, the Arabian and the Greek vessels frequented India for trade. Most probably, Hindus travelled to the West in those foreign vessels.

To the east of India, however, Hindu conquest, commerce and colonisation were always very great and almost without a rival. Hindu traditions and foreigners' accounts equally show this.

The *Sutra*-author Baudhayana who flourished not later than the sixth century BC says that sea-voyage is good, for north India but bad for south India.

In the most ancient times, Bengal rose to the height of glory. Bengal is an old civilised country. When the Aryans were in the Punjab, even then Bengal was powerful and civilised. The Aryans, jealous of those Dravidian Bengalis, abused them as 'irreligious noseless birds'.

Before Buddha, Bengalis went to Ceylon with 700 followers and conquered it. Again, in the nineth century AD, Bengalis attained great political success in India. But the real glory of Bengal lies in the arts, commerce, agriculture, and colonisation. The glories of ancient Bengal may be found in Burma, Cambodia, Anam, Malaya Peninsula, Siam, Java, Tibet, Mongolia, and even China.

HINDU VOYAGE

Rig Veda I, 56, 2: 'As merchants desirous of wealth surround the sea, so do the priests surround Indra.'

Rig Veda I, 116, 3 and 5 mentions the first foreign invasion of India. Sayana adds the following note to the text: 'Rajarshi Tugra was a favourite with the two Asvin brothers. Being much harassed by the enemies of a foreign land, he sent his prince Bhujyu with a strong army to conquer them. The ship went to the middle of the sea and was driven by winds and wrecked. Then, Bhujyu sent a message to the Asvins for help. The Asvins rescued him with the soldiers in their own ships and brought him home to his father safely in three days and nights.'

Vasista, for a pleasure trip, once went out on a voyage: 'When I and Varuna both boarded the ship, she was far out on the sea and made good progress; then the vessel tossed about and we were pleased with the tossings. The great Varuna made Vasista board the ship on an auspicious day. Vasista also prayed to that mighty mass of waters. Thus passed away day and night' (*R.V. III, 88, 3* and *4*). Thus, we see that our Vedic seers also made sea voyages, for pleasure, experience and wisdom.

Manu in his *Code* VIII, 157 and 406, refers to sea voyage. But he excludes a Brahman sea-goer, from being invited to a *sraddha* ceremony. The law-givers Gautama, Sankha and Likhita ruled neither for nor against a voyage. Parasara (fifteenth century BC), however, sanctions a sea voyage in his *Code* XII, 62 and 63.

Yajnavalkya (fourteenth century BC) refers to it in his *Code* II, 39. The *Vishnu Purana*, Book II, discusses the earth surrounded by the seas and the oceantides. Chapter 3 describes the Hoonas and the Persians.

The *Vayu Purana*, Chapter 41, describes the earth with its continents; Chapter 45 mentions Balhika (Bulkh), Gandhara (Kandahar), Yavana (perhaps, a country on the right bank of the Indus), Saka (Seistan), Ramata (?), Barbara (a northern country beyond the confines of India proper) and Palhava (perhaps a part of Persia, Kaseruka). These are all northern countries. Next, it mentions Brahmottara (Burma), Malada (Malay Peninsula) and other eastern countries. Chapter 49 also mentions some lands inhabited by *mlechchhas*.

The *Garuda Purana*, Part I, Chapter 68, discusses corals and pearls. Chapter 69 discusses the pearls born of oysters and describes the pearls of the Palk Strait and of the Persian Gulf. Chapter 72 mentions the precious blue stones found on the seacoast of Ceylon. Chapters 77 and 79, describe various stones of Yavana, China and other lands. Chapter 80 mentions the bidruma, a stone of Romaka (Rome).

The *Varaha Purana*, Chapter 171 says Gokarna, a merchant of Muttra, landed on an island on the other side of the ocean after a four-month long voyage and returned home after a long time.

The *Markandeya Purana*, Chapters 57, 58 mention Kamboja, Barbara, China, Lanka, Ceylon, Syamaka (Siam), and other lands.

The *Padma Purana, Swarga* Part, Chapter III, mentions Yavana, Kamboja, Huna, Parasika, and other races.

The Bengalis are a mixed people of Mongols—Tibeto-Urmans, Dravidians and the Aryans. The Dravidians were a very smart people—brave, seafaring and active. The Dravidian chiefs of Bengal often held the sacrificial horses of the proud Aryan kings of the Indian midland. The Aryans spitefully called them bad names. Their great port was Tamalika, now Tamluk (literally port of the Dravidians). For the word Tamil is a corruption of *Dravira* (Dravida = Dravir = Davil = Damil = finally, *Tamil*).

The two prominent ports of north India were Broach in the west and Tamluk in the east. Tamluk was famous in the times of Buddha, in the days of Asoka. Vessels set sail from here to Ceylon, eastern archipelago, islands of the Pacific, China and Japan. Later, we hear of the following ports: Madura, Kalinganagar, Tamluk, and Ganganagar. The Aryan port near the mouth of the Ganges was known as Ganganagar. Formerly, the Ganges reached the sea in five branches. The Hugli is perhaps the western-most branch. The main stream of the Ganges is now known as the Padma. Again, formerly the Ganges flowed eastward to the Bay of Bengal only a few miles east of modern Dacca. The stream near Dacca is still called the *Buri Ganga*, i.e the old Ganges. Owing to earthquakes and consequent upheaval of the soil, the Ganges and the Brahmaputra have left their old beds and now send their waters through new channels—the Padma and the Jamuna. I think that Ganganagar has gradually developed into the modern city of Dacca.

Formerly, Dacca was not a town, but a country. It then comprised a considerable part of the modern Dacca and Mymensingh districts. The earliest name was *Dawaka* or *Davka*. As for the annual fair, mentioned by all foreigners, which was held at the port Ganganagar, we think it was at first removed to an island called Suvarnagram, now Sonargao. Thence it shifted southward till at last it is held, since the past fifty years, on an island near Munsiganj, in the district of Dacca.

Tamluk continued to be the port. The Buddhist work, *Dasa-Bhumisvara*, mentions it. In AD 414, Fa-hian returned home in a Hindu ship that sailed from here. The *Dasakumara Charita*, written in the sixth century AD by Dandi mentions it. In AD 1276, some Buddhist monks of Tamluk went to Penang and reformed Buddhism there. About 1495, Rama Chandra, Kavi-Bharati went to Ceylon from there.

Research reveals that colonies and kingdoms were founded in Burma, Cambodia and Annam from Magadha. The inscriptions found in the

French territories of Cambodia and Annam state that there were Brahmanic kingdoms and Saivism there in the fourth and the fifth centuries AD. In Annandale's report on Burma, 1913, it is stated that there is clear evidence of the existence of a Hindu kingdom in Pagan. Dr Annandale says that the Brahmans once held great sway over the Malkayan peninsula.

Here the Brahmans were called 'Pra'. The Pras have left ample evidence of their influence. It is not definitely known from where these colonists had come. All say, 'from Magadha'. As Bengalis were a seafaring people, it is likely that some of those colonies were founded by them also.

Sir WW Hunter says the following in his Orissa, pp. 314–15: 'The ruin of Tamluk as a seat of maritime commerce, affords an explanation of how the Bengalis ceased to be a seagoing people. In the Buddhist era, they sent warlike fleets to the east and to the west and colonised the islands of the Archipelago. Even Manu, in his inland centre of Brahmanic culture for the far north-west, while forbidding such voyages, betrays the fact of their existence. He makes a difference in the hire of river-boats and seagoing ships and admits that the advice of merchants experienced in making voyages on the sea and in observing different countries may be of use in fixing the rate of interest. But such voyages ... became alike hateful to the Brahmans and impracticable to an adealtaic people whose harbours were left high and dry by the land-making rivers and the receding sea. Religious prejudices combined with the changes of nature to make the Bengalis unenterprising upon the ocean.'

HINDU CIVILISATION IN CENTRAL ASIA

Religion, wisdom and civilisation of India spread to different parts of Asia—Tibet, Central Asia, China, Mongolia, Japan, Burma, Siam, Cambodia, Java, Sumatra, all contain the ruins and relics of Hindu civilisation. In Central Asia, many towns, villages, temples, monasteries are under the sands of the Gobi. We are indebted to Dr Stein and others for their exploration and discovery of many images, pictures and books. Dr Sylvain Lovi has written a paper on the Hindu civilisation in Central Asia. He especially notes the ancient Kucha kingdom and capital. Central Asia is a meeting-place of Hindus, Parsis, Turks, Tibetans, Buddhists,

Jews and Christians. The Kucha kingdom was in the heart of the Chinese Turkistan. At first it was peopled by the Aryans speaking an Aryan tongue. In the first few centuries of the Christian era, they adopted Buddhism and its civilisation. Sanskrit works were translated into the Kuchian tongue. Gradually, original Kucha literature and grammar were developed. Many works on Hindu astronomy and medicine were written; some portions of them are now in Petrograd; while others are preserved in the Japanese capital. The Buddhism prevailing generally was of the Hinayana school; the Mahayana school also was known. Tantric Buddhism also prevailed. The Kucha literature consists of stories and plays. Dr Lovi compares them to our *Yatra*.

Dr Lovi says that though recently published, the Kucha literature was ancient and substantial as seen from government and private documents which have been found. King Bharata of the Vairaja dynasty had conquered eight islands of the Indian Ocean (*Bhagavata, Book V, Chapter 19* and *Vayu Prana*).

Thirteen islands of the ocean were conquered by Pururava of the lunar dynasty (*Mahabharata* and elsewhere), Haihaya Arjuna had conquered eighteen islands of the sea (*Agni Purana; Sabdamala; Mahabharata* and other Puranas).

Java was colonised in AD 78. Sumatra was colonised in 75 BC. The first Buddhists from Gujarat and Sindh reached Ceylon; thence they went to Sumatra in the fourth century AD. Hindu supremacy in west Sumatra lasted till the fifteenth century AD. Then Islam made progress there. The remains of the capital are still extant in west Sumatra. The Hindu kingdom called *Mayapahita* of the island of Java, was most powerful till the fifteenth century AD. The great temple of Buddha (*Boro Bodor*) is said to be one of the greatest of world's architecture. A Hindu ship is illustrated in that temple (seventh century AD). Hindus still live in the island of Bali. Some of the islands of the Pacific Ocean contain extensive remains of Aryan civilisation (Gregory's *Geography*).

INDO-CHINESE RELATIONS

We cannot say when and how China got its present name. Many suppose that its Tsin or Tsan Dynasty (249–206 BC) gave the name. But the name China appears much earlier. The Tsin people ruled in the west of China from the tenth century BC. From them, the name may have spread to the country gradually. The Indo-Aryans called it Bhadraswa Varsha. This name is retained in almost all the Puranas. The name China first appears in the *Manu Samhita*, X, 44–44; *Mahabharata, Anusasana Book*, Chapter 33, shloka 21 and Chapter 36, shloka 18. Manu mentions them as denationalised Kshatriyas; a small band of Hindu warriors went to the north, conquered a land, mixed with the Mongols and formed the Tsin people. According to Manu and other later works, China is a northern country. In the *Mahabharata*, the Chinese are spoken of as allies of Bhagadatta of Assam. These Chinese even fought in the battle of Kurukshetra against the Pandavas. The same epic gives a list of presents sent by the Chinese to Yudhisthira. After the exile of Rama, Vasista the sage is said to have lived in China for some years (fifteenth century BC). Doubtless, China was one of the earliest seats of civilisation. Various Chinese articles, art objects and ideas found their way to the Western world through the mediation of India. India held intercourse with China both by land and sea.

Although our own information regarding the Indo-Chinese intercourse is meagre, the Chinese accounts of it are extensive, valuable and accurate. The Chinese authors give a regular account of the Indo-Chinese trade from 100 BC to AD 1700. The Chinese–Buddhist travellers of India (no less than some fifty) throw an interesting sidelight on Indian history. We have had some important political information from the Chinese source alone.

From ancient times, Indian merchants carried on trade with China under a peculiar system known as the *embassy system*. These expeditions were purely commercial and not political in any way. Merchants from different provinces of India sailed for China with various Indian goods, birds and beasts, reached the Chinese court, made rich presents and got the emperor's permission to trade in China. The Lord of the Celestial Empire would look upon the presents as tributes from Indian kings and the merchants. The following Indian articles were imported into China: various kinds of animals, horses, beautiful birds, artistic products in metal, diamonds, cotton fabrics, precious stones, gold, iron, lead, perfumes, incense, sugar cane, sweets, fruits, and gold ornaments set with precious stones.

In the pre-Chirstian era, Indian wisdom was no doubt carried to China by the Indian merchants. But that produced no lasting impression.

In the first few centuries of the Christian era, however, India gave to China something new—Buddhism. By AD 400, Buddhism was generally accepted by the Chinese. India now exported to China the following new things: the branches of the Bodhi tree at Gaya, Buddhist images and relics, religious books written on palm leaves.

Following Fa-hian's return from India to China (AD 414), there was an increase in the commercial intercourse between the two countries. Dr J Edkins, in his *Chinese Buddhism* (pp. 92–94) says: 'Many embassies came from the countries lying between India and China during the time of Sung-Wen-li. Their chief object was to congratulate the ruling emperor on the spread of Buddhism in his dominions and to pave the way for more frequent intercourse on the ground of identity of religion. The letter of an Indian monarch, preserved in the history of the dynasty, expresses his admiration of Emperor Wen-li in glowing language. He adds that though separated by a wide sea, it was his wish to have embassies passing and repassing between the two countries. Ceylon also sent an embassy and a letter to Wen-li.'

The Chinese historian Ma-touan-lin of the thirteenth century AD has noted the above facts in his great encyclopaedia.

In sixth century AD, Indo-Chinese maritime intercourse was very brisk on account of the general spread of Buddhism in China. In the early years of this century, three thousand Indian monks and ten thousand Indian families are said to have settled in a single Chinese province.

Chinese histories state that from the first to the sixth century AD, India carried on trade by sea with Syria, the Roman Empire and Parthia, in all kinds of precious things—coral, amber, gold, pearls, turmeric, and storax (Dr F Hirth's *China and the Roman Orient, p. 47*).

This Indo-Chinese intercourse received a setback in the seventh century AD. Ma-touan-lin states that Yangti, the first emperor of the Sui dynasty (AD 605), sent Fei-tou to summon the Tibetans, Indians and other people to pay homage to him as vassals. Many princes responded to this, but the Indian kings alone refused to enter into such a subsidiary alliance. The emperor was highly enraged at this.

With the accession, however, of the *Tang* dynasty in AD 626, the troubles were over and the Indo-Chinese intercourse revived.

In AD 641, Harshavardhan Siladitya, hearing of the glories of China and its then emperor Tait-soung, from the Chinese Indian traveller Yuan Chwang, sent some ambassadors and a letter to the Chinese emperor.

In reply, the Chinese emperor sent an officer under Li-I whom Siladitya received at the head of his ministers and again offered as present some micalaminae, perfumes and a tree called *Bodhi-druma*—the Tree of Intelligence (Pauthier, *p. 52*).

The mission sent by the Chinese emperor in return for this embassy of Harshavardhana reached Magadha in AD 648, when the later had died, and his throne had been unsurped by his minister Arjunaswa. The usurper gave the mission a hostile reception and plundered its property. Wang-hiuen-tse, who was in charge of the mission, fled to Tibet and came down with a Tibetan army, reinforced by an army of 7,000 horsemen from Nepal and inflicted a disastrous defeat on Arjunaswa. Kumar Varma, King of eastern India, also helped this Chinese expedition of Wang-hiuen-tse. (M Sylvain Levi, *J.A. 1900, p. 297;* also LA Waddell's 'Tibetan Invasion of India in AD 647 and its Results' in *The Imperial and Asiatic Quarterly Review, January 1911, pp. 37–65*).

In the same century, different parts of India sent out commercial expeditions to China in AD 667, 668, 672 and 690–92 (Ma-touan-lin; Pauthier, *p. 53*; Sylvain Levi, *J.A., 900, p. 297*; Julien, p. III).

During these years, Indian religion, learning, wisdom, preachers, scholars, and settlers went to China and spread their influence.

INDO-CHINESE RELATIONS (AD 700–1000)

Commerical and Religious

The commercial intercourse between India and China was very brisk for half a century from AD 701–750. North India now sent out commercial expeditions to China. A few went from west India, some went from southern India; while the largest number were from the kingdom of central India—Magadha. Matouan-lin in his encyclopaedia says: 'During the period AD 713–742, there arrived three times, several ambassadors from central India and one time an ambassador from southern India. They offered a bird of five colours which could speak.' At this period, the Tibetans by land and the Arabs by sea, interfered with the Indian trade with China. The Indians asked for military aid from the Chinese emperor against them but to no avail. The Tibetans at this time were very powerful and no mean rivals to the Chinese. They often obstructed the passage of caravans through their kingdom. The Arabs were a far greater enemy to Indian trade. Though not so powerful, they had already begun to fight with the Indians for supremacy over the eastern sea, so long enjoyed by India in the seaborne trade.

The following two centuries (AD 750 to 950) were a time of trouble for China, when civil dissensions and foreign invasions made her vulnerable. In AD 763, the Tibetans attacked China and the emperor fled his capital. The invaders easily captured and sacked it; and so hard-pressed were the Chinese at this period that in AD 787, Emperor Tetsung, on the advice of his ministers, applied to the princes of India and other foreign kings to join in a league against the Tibetans.

Such anarchy prevailed in China till AD 964 when the powerful Sunga dynasty came to the throne. As the Chinese government could not give sufficient protection to the foreign merchants visiting the ports of the country, Indian trade with China suffered during this period. Captain F Brinkley, in his *China: Its History, Arts and Literature*, vol. X, p. 142, says: 'Towards the end of the nineth century, when the empire lapsed into a state of anarchy preceding the fall of the Tang rulers, the various factories established by foreign traders had to be closed with the exception of Canton and throughout the greater part of the tenth century, merchants from overseas encountered many obstacles owing to the unsettled state of the coast.'

The absence of commercial embassies from India was, according to Chinese authors, due to China having lost possession of Holong which was perhaps, a place on the route from the Annam coast through Yunnan by which 'embassies' formerly passed to the Chinese Capital.

The Indo-Chinese intercourse was no doubt much disturbed during the two centuries. Yet, it did not come to a standstill altogether. The German scholar Professor C Lassen holds that up to the beginning of the tenth century AD Indo-Chinese trade was very brisk. He says, 'Under the reign of the mighty dynasty of Tang (AD 620–907), a very lively trade was carried on between China, India and the western countries, in which the Arabs also took part'. (*Indian Archaeology, Vol. IV, p. 884*).

The century from AD 950–1050, opens a new epoch. The very powerful Sunga dynasty is established in China; peace is restored. Indian trade is revived. The Chinese history of this period frequently refers to the arrival of Buddhist priests from India with manuscripts and relics. The history of the Sunga dynasty speaks of the arrival at the Chinese court of the Indian Sramana Samanta of western India with a large party of companions belonging to sixteen families or classes. Pian-i-tian and Ma-touna-lin also allude to similar facts. About AD 976, Manju Sri, a distinguished Indian Buddhist priest, the son of a king of eastern India, highly revered by the emperor and the people of China, went away from the court, displeased at the conduct of the Chinese monks.

From AD 996 to 1036, many Indian Buddhist priests came to the Chinese court with various articles, especially Buddhist books for the emperor.

Thus, we see that during the latter half of the tenth century, our Indo-Chinese intercourse was again very lively. Many Indian embassies went out to China carrying birds, horses, images, relics, Buddhist Sanskrit manuscripts on palm leaves, and Buddhist priests. On the other hand, a large number of Chinese pilgrims and students came out to India to be educated in the Buddhist scriptures and for the collection and collation of Buddhist manuscripts.

In the eleventh century AD, Indian embassies went to China mainly from the country of the Cholas who, about this time, held paramount sway over almost the whole of southern India and possessed a powerful navy with which they conquered the islands around India and established their supremacy over the Indian seas. These Cholas were a branch of the great Tamil race (Dravidians) of south India which had, from very ancient times, carried on a very active trade by sea with the east and the west. The Cholas, with their capital at Kanchipuram, had formed a very mighty kingdom extending from Orissa over the greater part of the Deccan and the south, including even Ceylon.

Of the Chola commercial expeditions to China, Dr H Hirth gives the following account: 'In the Sung-shih (*History of the Sung Dynasty*) period the names of two kings are mentioned who sent embassies with tribute from this country (Chu-lien) to China, viz., in AD 1033 'Shi-li-lo-cho-in-to-lo-ceo-lo' which probably stands for Sri Rajendra Chola; and again in AD 1077, 'Ti-wa-ko-lo' which probably stands for Deva Kola or Deva Kara. The last-named king made a good bargain with his colleague on the dragon throne, since the embassy, consisting of seventy-two men were given 81,800 strings of copper, i.e. about as many dollars, in return for the article of tribute comprising glassware, camphor, brocades, rhinoceros horns, ivory, incense, rosewater, put chuk, asafoetida, borax and cloves. This so-called embassy was probably like most of the missions to the coast of China; no better than a trading expedition on joint account, the seventy-two ambassadors being the shareholdes of their supercargoes' (*J.R.A.S., 1896, pp. 490–93*).

The Chola king of the Chinese historians is our Rajendra Choladeva I, surnamed Gangali Konda who reigned from AD 1018 to 1035. 'Ti-wa-ka-lo' is evidently Deva-kola, i.e. Kulottanga Chola Deva who ruled from AD 1070 to 1118. The earliest Chola embassy to China was in AD 1015 when Rajaraja the Great was the reigning Chola king (VA Smith's *E.H.L., 2nd edition, pp. 419–22*). The Cholas, great mariners from very ancient times, gave their name to the eastern coast, still known as the Chola *mandalam* or the Coromandel Coast. Their power reached its zenith under the aforesaid kings. They were practically lords over all tracts south of the Vindhyas. The inscriptions of the three great Chola kings show their victories on the sea obtained by their powerful navy. The strips on the Bay of Bengal, the islands around India including Ceylon, once knew the supremacy of the Cholas. The inscriptions on the walls of the magnificent temple at Tanjore built by the great Rajaraja show his conquests of 'Ira mandalam (Ceylon) and of twelve thousand islands of the sea' (*South Indian Inscriptions* by Dr E Hultzsh, *Vol. II, p. 72, no. 6*). This large number of unspecified islands perhaps mean the Laccadives and Maldives (Smith's *Early History of India*, p. 420). Before this, his fleet had destroyed the ships at Salai, i.e. the fleets of the Cheras.

The powerful navy of his son Rajendra Chola Deva conquered the whole Iramandalam (Ceylon) on the transparent sea, many ancient islands whose old and great guard was the sea which resounds with conchs (*South Indian Inscriptions, Vol IV, p. 6, No. 3*). And also 'his fleet crossing the Bay of Bengal attacked and captured Kadaram or Kidaram, the ancient capital of the kingdom of Prome or Pegu; and also the seaports of Takkolam and Matama or Martaban on the same coast. The annexation of the Nicobar (Nakkavaram, our ancient Nagabara) and Andaman islands followed on the conquest of Pegu' (VA Smith's *E.H.L.*, 2nd *edition, p. 420*).

About his victories in Burma, the inscriptions tell us that Rajendra Chola Deva 'sent many ships in the midst of the rolling sea and caught Samgrama-Vijayottunga Varman, the king of Kadaram, along with his elephants. In the fighting that took place the king had rightfully acquired a large heap of treasures.' (*South Indian Inscriptions* by Dr EA Hultzsch, *vol. II, part II, p. 108*).

Two granite pillars, still extant, were set up by the Cholas at Pegu to commemorate their victories. Taw Sein Kwo, Superintendent of Archaeological Burvey, Surma, remarks as follows in his Report of March 1907, p. 19: 'A little to the north-east of the Shwehmawdow pagoda, is a small hill, fabled to have been the resting-place of two *hansa* birds when the region around Pegu was under the sea. At the foot of the hill are two octagonal pillars of fine granite. The length of one is about eleven feet and that of the other is about five. They bear no inscriptions, but tradition has it that they were erected by the *kala* or Indians, who subsequently claimed the country as their own by virtue of occupation and they were driven out by a Talaing prince. This is confirmed in a way, by the history of the Chola dynasty of southern India. It is related that between AD 1025 and 1027, a prince of that line, Rajendra Chola I by name, crossed the sea and overran Kidaram (Sanskrit *Katah*) which may be identified with the ancient Talaing kingdom of Ramanna Desa, now called Pegu (Is *Ramanna* a corruption of *Ramanaka*, one of the attached islands of Asia?). In order to commemorate his conquest of a foreign land, he erected these 'Pillars of Victory' in accordance with a well-known Indian custom.'

On the extensive maritime trade of the Cholas, VA Smith says the following: 'Ancient Tamil literature and the Greek and Roman authors prove that in the first two centuries of the Christian era, the ports on the Coromandel or Chola coast enjoyed the benefits of active commerce with both the west and east. The Chola fleets did not confine themselves to coasting voyages, but boldly crossed the Bay of Bengal to the mouth of the Ganges, the Irrawaddy and the Indian Ocean to the islands of the Malay archipelago. All kinds of goods imported into Kerala or Malabar from Egypt found a ready market in the Chola territory; on the other hand, the western ports drew a large part of the supplies of merchandise from the bazaars of the eastern coast, which produced great quantities of cotton goods. The principal Chola port was Kaviripaddinam (Sanskrit, Kavery Pattana) situated at the northern mouth of the Kavery (Cauvery) river. This once wealthy city, in which the king maintained a magnificent palace and foreign merchants found residence agreeable and profitable, has vanished and its site lies buried under deep sand-drifts' (*The Early History of India, pp. 415–16*).

Smith makes the Malaya archipelago the eastern most point where the Chola maritime activity stops. But Chinese history clearly shows that their vessels carried their burdens to the Chinese coast as well.

Kanaka Sabhai Pillay shows, on the authority of an ancient Tamil work entitled *Perumpada-arrup-padai*, that around the Coromandel Coast, there were high light-houses built of brick and mortar which exhibited blazing lights at night to guide ships to the ports (*The Tamils 1800 Years Ago, p. 27*).

All these facats are sufficient proof of our Indo-Chinese relations.

Our eastern intercourse and maritime enterprise will appear from another source. About the beginning of the Christian era, the Andhras, a powerful people of south India, had established their supremacy over numerous places on the sea. This is proved by the figures of ships on their coins. VA Smith in his *Early History of India*, second edition, p. 201, notes: 'Some pieces bearing the figure of a ship probably should be referred to this reign (of *Yajna Sri*) and suggest the inference that Yajna Sri's power was not confined to land.'

Indian ships, during the Andhra period were also very large in size. Dr Sewell says in the *Imperial Gazettes of India*, new edition, Vol. II, p. 324: 'Pliny (Vol. VI) states that the Indian vessels trading with Ceylon were so large as to be able to cary 3,000 amphorae. On the east coast, the coins of the Andhra dynasty (roughly 200 BC to AD 250) confirm this, many of them bearing the device of a two-masted ship, evidently of large size.'

The Hindus of the remote ages possessed great naval power by which communication must have been maintained with the coast of Arabia, Persia as well as the Australian archipelago. The cosmography of the Puranas and some of the texts of Manu offer abundant evidence of an intercourse between the countries from the Oxus to the Ganges. The Hindu names of towns at the estuaries of the Gambia and Senegal appear in the *Tomba kunda*, Sanskrit *Tamra kunda* and other *kundas*.

Marsden and Sir W Jones discovered that the Malayan language dominated throughout the archipelago, 'extending from Madagascar to the Eastern Islands—a space of 200 degrees longitude—is indebted to Sanskrit for a considerable number of its words and close communication existed long, long before the conversion of Islam.' (*Asiatic Researches, vol. IV, p. 226, second edition*). 'Researches have proved that those countries were colonised by the Surjyas whose mythology and heroic history are depicted in the edifices and maintained in their writings. Ceylon was the first Hindu colony. Rama possessed great naval means inherited from Sagara (the Sa-king) 20 generations upwards' (Tod's *Rajasthan, vol. II, pp. 180–85*).

Hindu merchants and Buddhist preachers had visited Japan also. The Japanese do not call their land 'Japan' which seems to have originated from Hindu 'Javangaka', one of the eighteen islands conquered by the mighty emperor Arjuna of the lunar Haihaya race (fifteenth century BC). In the *Ramayana, Kishkindha Book*, canto 40, Valmiki also speaks of an island named 'Java' composed of seven islands. Whatever be its origin, it is certain that India had intercourse with Japan. Hundreds of Bengalis went there to preach Buddhism. The sign-boards of the temples in Japan are still written in Trihuti-Bengali characters. The 'Ainus' of Japan are an Aryan colony. Gregory in his *Geography* has given a wood-cut representation of them. Now, the question is, where were they from?

Some of the islands of the Pacific Ocean contain extensive remains of the Aryan civilisation.

INDO-AMERICAN INTERCOURSE

Favoured by nature with some of her choicest blessings, India was looked upon as a paradise on earth by the people of Europe. Poets sang of the riches of India and merchants and travellers carried away tales of a true 'Land of Cockaigne', overflowing with milk and honey. It was a country rich in pearls and diamonds, where the very rivers ran gold and where nature, decked in all her splendour presented an enchanting sight. Indian wisdom too, like the Indian riches, passed into a proverb among the ancients, bringing over men like Pythagoras and others to drink at this fountain of human knowledge.

For several centuries, our Indo-European trade was much disturbed by the opposition of the Saracens. However, when the Crusades were over, Europe became eager to revive trade with the East. But the routes were still uncertain and attended with great difficulties and dangers. This was when Venice and Genoa were the masters of the eastern trade.

Many reasons led the little state of Portugal to make maritime explorations. Prince Henry, the navigator, was a great patron of explorations. India was a dreamland, even in Portugal. Henry died before India could be found. King John of Portugal was equally ardent in encouraging explorations. At this time, Columbus, a native of Genoa in Italy, applied to King John to help him to discover India which he thought lay beyond the Atlantic. King John turned him away as a visionary. Columbus next applied to Spain. King Ferdinand and his Queen Isabella, then joint-sovereigns of Spain, entertained his application and fitted out a fleet for him. Now Portugal and Spain both strove hard to find India. Columbus sought India, but found a new world instead. Amerigo Vespucci, however, reached the main continent and published its first account, hence the name, *America*. About the same time, Vasco da Gama, a member of the royal household of Portugal discovered the sea-route of India, doubling the Cape of Good Hope (AD 1498). These discoveries soon brought about a revolution in the progress of mankind.

The year AD 1500 is a turning-point in the history of the world. The first distribution of the Aryan races took place long, long ago, from Central Asia. The second distribution of the Aryan races happened in AD 1500. This time, the centre of distribution was chiefly Europe. Before Columbus, America had been visited by the Phoenicians, the Icelanders and the Norwegian sailors. But nearly all knowledge of it was lost. America, being some 3,000 miles distant from Europe, its discovery was no doubt, a great wonder to the people of Europe. Though so far, yet the earliest bold navigators of Europe had explored America.

The southern half of North America and the northern half of South America had been the most civilized parts. But the American civilisation was of a quite different kind.

Hindu intercourse with America is still perhaps a startling news to many. But what I have said in this chapter and elsewhere, suggests the inference that bold Hindu mariners had earlier circumnavigated the earth, visiting foreign lands in every continent. The *Pushkara-dwipa*. (continent of fine lakes) and *Kusa-dwipa* (continent of grass, prairies) probably name the two Americas, North and South.

The following proofs may be cited:

(i) The Puranists say that the sun never set on the dominions of Priyavrata, mighty monarch of the Vairaja Dynasty of Bithoor (twenty-nineth century BC). The succession of days and nights had convinced our remote ancestors of the roundness of the earth.

(ii) Gokarna, the merchant of Mathura, had landed on an island on the other side of the ocean after a four-month Voyage (*Varaha Purana*).

(iii) From the earliest times, Hindus have sailed to China, Japan, and the islets of the Pacific Ocean (mentioned as 'the 12,000 Islands,' on the inscription of Rajaraja the Great). America was not far from there.

(iv) Hindu knowledge of the roundness of the earth, her vastness, her seven continents and seven oceans, forty-nine big islands, ocean-currents, and submarine volcanoes abounding in the Pacific leave no room to doubt the Hindu knowledge of and intercourse with America. We must not, however, suppose from these that the Hindus and the Americans are one people. Some suppose that there were Hindu colonies in Mexico, Peru and Bolivia. If they did ever exist there, they were small and were soon absorbed in the native population.

The Hindu word *patala* (antipodes) is sometimes applied to America. But it more often signifies a lower region. Thus, the Lower Indus and the Lower Ganges have been called *Patala* from the early classical days. Some blind patriotic Hindu writers have filled America with Hindu colonists, mistaking the word *Patala* for America.

Some Hindu writers, nay even Pococke, fill the ancient world with Hindus. Sir W Jones also shared a belief of that nature. But scholars, after careful examination of the subject, have given the right verdict that Hindus have no racial unity with any other nation of the world except the Parsis. Of course, small and numberless Hindu colonies had penetrated into foreign lands in early times but they have mostly been long absorbed. This foreign colonisation of Hindus appears also from a statement of Krishna to Yudhisthira (fourteenth century BC):

> The famous dynasties and other subordinate Kshatriyas of the world declare themselves, with noble pride, as the descendants of the lunar and the solar dynasties. These two have given rise to a hundred lines. The dynasties of Yayati and the Bhojas are highly meritorious and are very widespread; now they have filled all quarters of the globe. (*Mahabharata, Court Book, Chapter 14*).

The following points will show Hindu influence on the American civilisation:

- When the Europeans first founded colonies in America, they saw Hindu customs, and manners current there. India's connection with America had broken long, long before its modern discovery (Baron Humboldt).
- 'Hindu connection of America is still found in many things.... The ancestors of the Peruvians were once in connection with Indians' (Pococke).
- On the early American imitation of Hindu architecture, Hardy says: 'The ancient buildings of Chicane in Central America resemble the steeples of Indian temples.' Skier says: 'The Buddhist temples of south India and the Indian Archipelago were imitated in many buildings of Central America in design and materials.'
- 'Old temples, forts, bridges and tanks show an imitation of the Hindu style in every respect' (Dr Jarfew).
- Gods and goddesses were made after Indian idols and were duly worshipped. Prescott's *Conquest of Mexico* and Helps' *Spanish Occupation of America* give many examples of Hindu influence there.
- In Mexico, a human god with an elephant's head was worshipped. 'It presents some remarkable and apparently not accidental resemblance with the Hindu Ganesh' (Baron Humboldt).
- Recently, a stone image (possibly of Krishna or Buddha) has been unearthed. The American scholars think that it was carried there by the Aryans of Central Asia.
- 'It is very remarkable that Peruvians whose Inkas boasted of the same solar descent styled their greatest festival *Ram Sita;* whence we may suppose that South America was peopled by the same race who imported, into the furthest parts of Asia, the rites and fabulous history of *Rama*' (Sir W. Jones).

TWO

1

RISE OF NEW DYNASTIES AND KINGDOMS

Of the numerous clans or tribes that came into being after the Regeneration, the Daityas and the *danavas* were the oldest. At first they were pious. So, they soon rose to power and conquered lands; many of them performed the horse-sacrifice. All of them could move in the air in their aeroplanes. All were gallant fighters, invincible, truthful, followers of the Vedic religion and well-read. Even in their most palmy days, they knew no pride, were free givers and merciful. But in time their nature entirely changed for the worse. They grew quite wild in every respect. Irreligion, anger, malice filled them. In the meantime, the devas were rising to eminence. Then, a civil war ensued for the possession of *swarga*—the best lands of the north (*Mahabharata, Peace Book*).

A most sanguinary war raged for thirty-two years. The devas eventually conquered the Daityas and occupied the coveted lands. At that time, a large number of Vedic Brahmans conquered lands in India and fought against the devas; for they were ousted from their northern homes by the devas. The 88,000 Brahmans now made common cause with the Daityas and repeatedly attacked the devas. But they were mostly defeated and killed by the latter (*Mahabharata, Peace Book, Chapter 23*).

This was the first of a series of sharp conflicts between the priests and the warriors, for supremacy. The Brahmans lost their northern homes.

COMING OF FRESH ARYAN COLONIES IN INDIA

The deva–asura war, lasting thirty-two years, is described in all the Vedas. The devas, *manushyas* and *pitris* (of Mongolia) were on the one side; asuras, *rakshasas* and *pisachas* were on the other (*Black Yajur Veda, pp. 121–22*). The devas were small in number, the Daityas were many (*p. 133*). In the battles, the devas, being defeated, submitted to the Daityas and became their subjects (*p. 144*). The Daityas conquered three countries of the devas and colonised them (*Padma Purana, Creation Book, Chapter 30, shloka 12*). The Daityas and the *danavas* then lived happily in *Swarga*, i.e. Central Asia.

The victors, then jealous and afraid of the conquered devas, resolved to oust them from Central Asia. So, they began to harass and persecute them in all possible ways. The *Panis*, the mercantile branch of the asuras stole the cows of Angiras and hid them in caves. Indra went there, opened the doors of the caves and delivered the cows and gave them to the owners. Atri was seized, and confined in a machine-house (*Yantra griha*) of hundred doors, in order to be burnt alive. Indra saved him (*R.V.I, 51.3*). Atri was again saved from a similar fate by the two Asvin brothers (*R.V.I, 116. 8*). The same two Asvin brothers saved Manu, Sayu, Atri, Trita, Rebha, Bandana, Kanva, and others (*R.V.I, 112. 16; I, 150.17*). The devas now deemed it expedient to quit their homes. Brahma had already withdrawn to his new colony in north Siberia whither many seers, sages, Sadhyas, the Rudras, and others followed him. Some went eastward to Burma. A large band marched southward under Vishnu, Indra and others (*R.V.I, 9.6; I, 17.8; I, 21.6; I, 90.3; V, 81.3; VI, 49.13; VII, 91.1*) Thus Manu, son to Vivaswan, came to India, safely led by his uncle Vishnu (*R.V. VII, 46.13*). The *Yajur Veda (Krishna)* is certainly mistaken in stating that Manu came to India for sacrificial purposes. The *Rig Veda* plainly states that the tyranny of the Daityas forced Manu of come to Prithvi, i.e. the kingdom of Prithu, through Afghanistan. The *Satapatha Brahmana* has magnified this descent of Manu from the northern mountains on the Indian plains into the legend of the 'deluge'. How absurd is the connection of Manu with this tale of the deluge will appear from chronology. All traditions place Manu later than Hiranyaksha and Hiranyakasipu by a generation or two. These two tyrants are connected with the third and the fourth incarnations. How could then Manu, later in birth, be connected with the first incarnation?

With heavy hearts and tearful eyes, our pilgrim fathers left their dearest northern homes. They chanted the following *samas*, as they marched southward:

(1) 'Indra, Pushan, Tarkshya, Arishtanemi, and Vrihaspati, be propitious to us' (*R.V.I, 89. 6*).
(2) 'Lo! The wind blows fair; Oh how gently the rivers run! The trees also, be favourable to us on the way; so that we may not suffer from hunger' (*R.V.I, 90.6*).
(3) 'Our nights and dawns on the way be sweet. India where we are going, be genial to us and the *Swarga* we are leaving, be also sweet to us. Big trees on our way be sweet; the sunrays be sweet and let our cows give us ample milk. The Sun, Varuna, Aryama, Indra, and Vishnu, please do us good' (*R.V.I, 90.7–9*).
(4) 'Let the sun, the Great Eye of the world rise for our benefit: the four quarters, the firm mountains and the rivers do us good' (*R.V. VII, 35.8*).

Then Manu and others, ignorant of the route said: 'O Agni, take us through a good route, so that going there, we may have peace and prosperity. O Agni, deliver us from this terrible danger safely. Let us have vast lands and large towns in the country where we are going to, so that our children may live happily there'. (*R.V.I, 189.I.2*). Agnideva, Lord of Tibet, came down to India as a guide to these Indian colonists (Siva was the next chief of Tibet). Indra was their leader (*R.V. VI, 21.12; 47.7–8; 47.20*). Indra and Pushan led them; but unluckily, they lost their way and came to a land of robbers (*VI, 54.1*). Then asking experienced men, they again found a good and safe way and resumed their southward march on horseback. These Aryans led the horses by the nose and not by bridles put on their mouths (*R.V. V, 61.2–4*). At last, Manu came to India through Afghanistan (*R.V. IX, 65.16*). They arrived on the Sutlej (*III, 33.3*). Then afraid of the waves, Manu said, 'O Agnideva, please get us a large boat with a strong rudder and strong oars in which our heroes—the followers of Indra—our carriages and our tents may be ferried safely'. (*I, 140.12*). They safely crossed the river Indus. The route from Mongolia to India is well-depicted in the *White Yajur Veda, VIII,*

25 and 60 thus: 'Vishnu, the chief leader, conducted them first to the south-west corner of Tibet, near the source of the Ganges where he made a halt for some time. Thence he came down to a part of Afghanistan where eleven of the chiefs settled; Varuna became their king' (*R. V.*). Here in Suvastu (Swat Valley) they made another halt. Thence Vishnu brought the remaining eleven chiefs to India (*R.V.I, 139.11*). Even after the coming of Manu, many other Aryans, persecuted by the Daityas came out to India in different bands (*R.V.I, 159.4*). The *Vayu Purana, Last Book*, Chapter 39, shloka 28 states that *bhutas, pisachas, nagas*, and devas, came to India from north. The *bhutas* settled in *Bhutasthan*, now Bhutan; the *pisachas* settled in Pandya, Kekaya, Balhika, Salya, Nepal, and Kuntala; the *nagas* settled in the Naga Hills and in north-east India; the devas colonised *Aryavarta*. Some learned men think that Asia was peopled by races going out of Central Asia (Macmillan).

Before Manu came to India, there had been only a few Aryan kingdoms in north India. But there were numerous Daitya kingdoms. There was one large and very powerful Daitya kingdom along the Indus in the Punjab under Bali, often referred to as emperor. To enter India proper, the northern immigrants had to fight Bali first. But they were not strong enough to attack Bali. So Vishnu thought of a manoeuvre. On the Sutlej or Beas, they lived for sometime and gathered sufficient strength there. Then one day, Vishnu, a dwarf in size, went to Bali and humbly asked of him a little land to live in. King Bali granted him this. Vishnu thus obtained a footing in Bali's kingdom. This poor beginning gradually turned into a pretty fair colony filled by new settlers. After several years, Vishnu strengthened his army, fought Bali, defeated him and forced him to flee. Hindu tradition followed him to *Patala*, i.e. Bengal where he conquered a new land. Some Hindus affirm that Bali went to South America where he conquered a new land called after him Bali-Bhumi, now Bolivia. But tradition preserved in the *Mahabharata* and the Puranas gives the following: 'The large State of Bali, grandson to Prahlada, lay on the Upper Indus. Bali was very powerful but tyrannical. Many Aryan settlers, sages and seers lived in the State. Bali is described as the earliest Indian emperor, though of the Daitya branch of the Aryans. When Vishnu was preparing for a conflict, the Aryan settlers requested him to rid the land of his tyranny. Certainly they promised him help. Bali was duped, defeated and driven out from his realm. This deceitful victory of dwarf Vishnu is magnified as the divine work of his fifth incarnation. Bali fled to Bengal with his faithful followers. Here, he acquired some land and built a small capital on the Ganges. His queen, Sudeshna was childless. One day when the queen, with her maids, went to bathe in the Ganges, she saw a bright and beaming young sage in a raft near the ghat. This young blind sage was floated down the Ganges on a wooden raft with some provisions, by his rebellious wife and son. Bali, knowing his sad story, took him to his palace and requested him humbly to make his queen pregnant. The blind sage Dirghatama, much pleased with the treatment of Bali and his queen, agreed to the proposal. By him, the queen bore five distinguished sons one after another—all very pious, powerful and learned. These sons are said to have conquered most lands of far east India. Their kingdoms were called Anga (east Bihar), Banga (west Bengal), Kalinga (seaboard tract from Orissa to the Godavari), Sumha (Midnapur and the adjoining tracts) and Pundra (north Bengal). Their dynasties were probably short-lived and weak, being supplanted by Dravidians and other Aryan scions' (*Harivansa, Harivansa Book, Chapter 32, verses 32–42*).

The first Aryan colony in India was on the Indus (*R.V. VIII, 24. 27*). Vishnu knew well that without hard fighting, he could not obtain lands for his colonists in India.

Vishnu and Indra thus conquered Sapta-sindhu, i.e. the land of the seven branches of the Indus, Brahmavarta, Brahmarshi desa, the province of Oudh and other tracts of north India. 'Having killed many dark-skinned natives of India, Indra and Vishnu gave the lands to their white-skinned kith and kin'. (*R.V.I, 100. 18*).

Indra, slayer of Vritra and victor of Samvarapura killed and drove the dark-skinned robbers of India and set up Manu and others in India and Afghanistan. A sage praised Indra thus: 'Indra killed Pipur, Mrigaya, Susuvansa—the generals; subdued Rijisva, son to Vidatha, pierced the stone-built cities of *Samvara* and killed 50,000 dark-skinned soldiers—all noseless robbers'. (*R.V. IV, 16. 13 and V, 29.10*). Indra was up and doing, as it were, for Manu. Having defeated the enemies, he made Arsasana, the robber chief eat humble pie (*R.V. II, 20.6*), also (*R.V.I, 130, 8*). Thus, Indra brought the natives under the control of the Aryans (*R.V. V., 34.6*). After these wars, Indra and Vishnu performed two sacrifices on the plain of Kurukshetra (now Karnal). These Indo-Aryans now called themselves Arya, i.e. 'excellent lords' and the dark, conquered natives as Sudras. Needless to say, the Sudras were often oppressed, while the 'whitemen' were favoured. One sage asked all to be impartial (*Atharva Veda IV, p. 540*). As a mark of distinction, the Aryans now began to wear a thread or chain over their shoulder.

Having settled Manu and others in India, Indra and Vishnu again left for the north, raised a fresh army and regained *Swarga (White Yajur Veda II, pp. 33, 51 and 99*). The cries of victory of the devas filled the skies (*White Yajur Veda, p. 261*). The asuras were expelled from the twenty-one deva settlements in Central Asia (*ibid, p. 148*).

The Indians, for several generations, remembered their northern homes and relations (*R.V. I. 159, 4; I, 139. 11; III, 54.9; Viii, 27.10; VIII, 72, 7–8; I, 164.9; V, 41.19*). Charaka also, in his *Samhita, Chapter I, 15–9* alludes to the northern home. India was now called mother country, and Central Asia, fatherland (*Atharva Veda II, p. 726; R.V.I., 164.33; X, 138.6; I, 89.4; VI, 70.6; V, 43.2; IV, 1.10; VI, 5.5*).

We have described the devas as men, *Swarga* as Central Asia and so forth. Hindu readers, wedded to the theological notions of these, will certainly laugh at our historical delineation. The following, taken from our own writings, will convince them of the truth: The learned Aryans of the north were called devas (*Satapatha Brahmana*). They were kulins in the true sense of the word. Eminent Indian kings used to go to heaven (i.e. north) and devas also would come to India on occasion. Indra often asked the aid of the brave Indian kings to kill his enemies. The merchants of India used to send traders and merchandise to Indra in heaven through the several passes called deva-*yanas* (*Atharva Veda II, p. 424*). These passes were often impassable for floods and snow; so the merchants applied to Indra to make the communication with the north easier and safer.

By 2800 BC, innumerable kingdoms, both large and small and owned by the different sections of both Aryans and the non-Aryans came into being in north India. The *Rig Veda* has recognised even a few powerful Sudra kings (*R.V. I.V., 30*). Of the states, the so-called solar and the lunar kingdoms were generally the most powerful. Our history for the next 2000 years (2800 to 800 BC) will mainly give the events of the solar and the lunar dynasties of north India. No dynasty ruled so long; no dynasty ever remained pure and bright so long; and no dynasty ever threw out a hundred branches in the country and abroad.

2

THE SOLAR AND THE LUNAR DYNASTIES

Marichi, the eldest of the 'Seven Seers' begot Kasyapa, so called from his favourite drink, *kasya*. Kasyapa is said to have conquered the land, now called Kashmir (i.e. Kasyapa-meru) from an asura king, Jalodbhava by name. He married a daughter of Daksha, king of Kanakhala, the capital of a small state near Haridwar, and gave her twelve sons, called Adityas from their mother Aditi. Of them, Indra, Varuna, Vivaswan and Vishnu became the most distinguished. We have already said that Brahma, Indra, Vasista, Janaka were patronymics. Owing to the political disturbance, the first Brahma left his Central Asiatic abode and founded a new colony in north Siberia, the new capital being Siddhapuri (now, Sidrov). Indra became the Raja of the deva branch of the Aryans; his queen was Sachi, the daughter of Puloma, the king of the *Danava* branch of the Aryans. He had three sons and one daughter. Princess Jayanti was married to Rishabha Deva (of the Vairaja dynasty), the founder of Jainism. Vishnu was a dwarf. Though youngest, he was the ablest and the most qualified of the twelve brothers. Lakshmi chose him for her lord. Vivaswan was not a hero, but a poet, astronomer and a great medical expert. He had three wives and several children, of whom Manu, Yama and the two Asvin brothers, were the most noted. Yama got a small state to the north of the lake Mansarowar. The Asvin brothers were great physicians. Manu's mother Suvarchasa was one of the sixteen satis (chaste wives) of ancient India. We have seen how Manu, through the grace of his uncles Indra and Vishnu, had got a very large kingdom in north India.

We call the dynasties solar and lunar, because they are generally referred to as such. Historically, we should call them Vaivasvata and Sauma. The Sanskrit epics and several Puranas give the king-lists of the two dynasties. But it is strange that no two works entirely agree. In my list I have put in names recognised in the Vedas or other reliable works. I trust it will, at least, give an approximation to the truth. The chronology, however, is very uncertain. Fifty-eight rulers from Manu to Rama ruled some 1,350 years, an average of about twenty-three years per reign. Absolutely nothing is known about the length of each individual reign. Conjecture alone can lend charm to satisfy our curiosity a little. Our solar king-list runs as follows: 1 Manu, 2 Ikshvaku, 3 Bikukshi, 4 Paranjaya, 5 Anena, 6 Prithu, 7 Visvagaswa, 8 Ardra, 9 Yuvanaswa I, 10 Sravasta, 11 Vrihadaswa, 12 Kuvalaswa, 13 Driraswa, 14 Haryaswa, 15 Nikumbhaswa, 16 Sanhataswa (alias, Krisasva), 17 Prasenajit, 18 Yuvanaswa (No 2), 19 Mandhata, 20 Purukutsa, 21 Trasaddasyu, 22 Prisbadaswa, 23 Tridhanwa, 24 Tryaruna, 25 Satyavrata (*Trisanku*), 26 Harischandra, 27 Rohitaswa, 28 Champa, 29 Sudeva, 30 Vijayanandana, 31 Bharuka, 32 Vrika, 33 Vahuka, 34 Sagara, 35 Ansuman, 36 Dilipa I, 37 Bhagiratha, 38 Srutasena, 39 Nabhaga, 40 Amvarisha, 41 Sindhu-dwipa, 42 Ayutaswa, 43 Rituparna, 44 Sarvakama, 45 Sudasa, 46 Kalmashapada, 47 Asmaka, 48 Mulaka, 49 Anaranya, 50 Satyarata, 51 Viswa-saha, 52 Duliduha, 53 Ilavila, 54 Dilipa II, 55 Raghu, 56 Ajapala, 57 Dasaratha, 58 Ramachandra.

MANU

(*R.V.X, 63.1* and elsewhere, perhaps 2800–2790 BC)

We have already shown that Manu did not come down to India for penitence or after the so-called 'deluge'. Like Babar, he was forced to leave Central Asia. At the supplication of Manu and others, Indra and Vishnu, aided by others led the northern colonists towards the south, conquered vast tracts in Afghanistan and north India, established eleven kingdoms in the west and eleven in India. To the lot of Manu, fell a pretty large kingdom. Manu knew no fighting; like his father, he was a great lover of learning, religion and peace. He began to rule about 2800 BC He selected an excellent site for his capital, built it on the Sarayu and called it Ayodhya—the 'Invincible City'. It was well-guarded with a moat, wall and weapons. 'It had eight parts, nine gates, and an iron treasury and all the pomp and pride of heaven' (*Atharva Veda, II, 31, p. 742*). The *Satapatha Brahmana* (*I, 4.1*) states that the river Sadanira (Gandaki) formed the eastern boundary of Manu's realm of 'ample size'. Probably, at the instruction of Indra and Vishnu, Manu performed an 'Imperial Sacrifice' on the river Sarayu.

In the *Mahabharata* and elsewhere, Manu is called the law-giver. Possibly this is true. Manu is the first king of Oudh and the law-giver Manu is one of earliest of the twenty Hindu law-givers. Manu united in him the crown and the cowl. He had to organise his first state composed of different races living near a hostile population. So, it is highly probable that he had drafted the Dharma-Sastras (code), now lost and not yet recovered. 'The Dharma Sastras of Manu was held in high honour in the Sutra period, as the metrical Code of Manu is held in honour in the present-day' (RC Dutt).

The Code of Manu: Foreign Opinions

(1) A work of legislators.

(2) A manual compiled in the Sutra period to enable young learners to learn their duties as students, householders and citizens (M Muller).

(3) Date.

- (i) Hindu: Millions of years and the work of seven Manus?
- (ii) Sir W Jones: 1200 BC.
- (iii) Elphinstone: 900 BC.
- (iv) EB Cowell: 300 BC. In the present form.
- (v) Dr Buhler: second century BC.
- (vi) My view: twenty-eighth century BC.

(4) The very great antiquity of Manu.

Proof:

- (i) Hindu traditions know only two Manus—the first founded the Vairaja dynasty of Bithoor (thirtieth century BC) and the second is the first solar king of Oudh, 2800 BC. No list of sages and seers or kings given in the Vedic works or the epics, gives a sage named Manu. The *Mahabharata*, the lexicographer Amara Singha and others make the solar king, Manu, the well known law-giver.

(ii) Each of the law-givers must be and really was such that society might accept his laws with due deference for his birth, learning, penance, good conduct, varied experience, keen insight, and a thorough study of human nature, country, climate, and age. The solar Manu alone was one such individual.

(iii) Manu gives laws for the protection of widows: and knows nothing of the practice of Sati. A law-giver of 1200 BC or later, must have noticed this.

(iv) The *Rig Veda* and Manu's *Code* (*Chapter VIII,* 22) mention several powerful Sudra kingdoms overwhelmed with atheists. By 1200 BC atheism had almost died out in India.

(v) The differences of religion and manners from those of present times.

(vi) Frequent quotations in old authors—two prose quotations from Manu are found in the Code of Gautama, author of *Hindu Logic* and priest to the Janakas of North Bihar (fifteenth century BC).

(vii) His townships still exist.

(viii) The great mass of the work does faithfully represent the spirit and character of the most ancient Hindu world.

(ix) Manu's laws retained some of the Aryan laws and customs of the north; some of the Dravidian laws and some ideal laws for the gradual perfection of society.

(x) The *Code* shows that Manu had brought sufficient light of the renaissance. The caste system had already begun at Prithudaka, now Pehoa, in Bithoor. He fully approved of it and introduced it into his *Code* for immediate gain and to bring society to better order.

(xi) He strongly enforced the Vedic religion, because the atheists were very powerful and numerous then.

(xii) Of the twenty great Hindu law-givers, six belonged to the deva class of the north: Atri was the second of the Seven Seers. Vishnu was uncle to Manu. Angiras was the third of the Seven Seers. Usanas or Sukra was a poet, priest of the Daityas, astronomer, and a writer of *Niti-Sastra* (worldly wisdom). Yama was a hero, physician and step-brother to Manu. Vrihaspati was the spiritual guide to the devas and the rishis. He quoted some of their laws in his *Code*.

(xiii) His theory of creation from primal waters was borrowed from the *Rig Veda*.

(xiv) He repeatedly urged all to imitate the lofty morals and the pure manners and customs of the Brahmans of Bithoor. By 1200 BC, Bithoor fell from its pristine glory.

(xv) Manu knew nothing of the Deccan. Even his *Aryavarta* was small. By 1200 BC or later, *Aryavarta* comprised the whole of north India and the Aryans pushed up to Ceylon and founded small states in the Deccan. Agastya, Parasurama, Rama, Sarabhanga and others spread Hindu civilisation to the south. Doubtless, the present *Code* contains much that is original.

A code is never the work of a single age. All the Indian writings, except the Vedas, are later growths and not originals. 'Manu's code contains some of the earliest and rudest laws, with improvements of the most enlightened times' (Elphinstone's *History of India, 9*th *edition, p. 13*).

Like the early British rulers of India, Manu had also adopted the policy of conservation and reform. He retained the indigenous laws of the Dravidians, and introduced the good laws of the Aryans of the north and of the model state of Bithoor, with which perhaps, he had combined his own ideas of a perfect commonwealth. He framed laws for the organisation of his own state, for the guidance of his successors and other rulers and for general use. His code has formed the backbone of the Hindu nation. His code had so elevated the early Hindu character that it was praised and admired by all.

Like Babar, Manu was not a soldier of fortune. Not being a fighter himself, he relied upon several able and reliable ministers selected from the warrior caste. His counsellors and judges were mostly taken from the Brahmans. The army was placed under a commander-in-chief. Possibly, he had a prime minister to conduct the general administration. His war minister was also his ambassador.

His large kingdom was partitioned into military divisions, each having a body of troops commanded by an approved officer. The internal administration was carried on by a chain of civil officers composed of lords of one village or town; 10, 100, 1,000 villages or towns. All these officers were appointed by the crown. Each was to report all offences and disturbances to his immediate superior. The lord of one *grama* (village) was paid the provisions and other articles to which the king was entitled. The lord of two villages would get 10 ploughs of land; the lord of 100 villages was to have the land of a small village; that of a 1,000 villages, the revenues of a large town. These officers had superintendents or inspectors over them. They had to check the abuses of the distinct officers. Revenue was paid in grain or other agricultural produce. As to the owner of the land, Manu says in his *Code*, Chapter VIII, 39 and 243, that 'the king is the lord paramount of the soil.' Elphinstone thinks that the king owned a part and the village communities held the rest in common (Elphinstone: *History of India, 9th edition, p. 67*).

Manu had established courts of justice at the capital and at the important places of the provinces. The sources of state-income were the land-revenue, taxation, state mines, half of all precious minerals found in the earth, estates without heirs, unclaimed properties, twenty per cent of the profit on all sales, court-fees, and forests.

The rules on foreign policy and war clearly show that India even at that early date was divided into unequal and independent states.

The army was probably maintained by grant of lands or assignments.

Manu, like the patriarchs of all the nations of old, appears to be connected with the tale of a wonderful 'deluge'. The *Satapatha Brahmana* first gives the tale. But the Vedas know it not. We do not think it true in any way.

By his chief queen, Sraddha Devi, Manu had ten children, of whom Princess Ila was the eldest. He had fifty other sons by his other wives. They quarrelled and ruined themselves. Manu's was probably a short rule. Before his death, he had partitioned his state among his six children. Three of his sons took to religion and refused royalty. One son took to commerce, the remaining six inherited the property. We see here that the idea of the indivisibility of the Raj did not yet originate. Even the daughter got a fair share. By partition, Princess Ila, the eldest child, got the Doab, i.e. the land between the rivers Ganges and the Jamuna. Ikshvaku, the eldest son got the kingdom of Kosala lying between the rivers Ganges and the Gandaki. This was called Madhyadesa, i.e. midland of north India.

His second son, Narishyat got a tract in the north near the Himalayas. It is said that his children were afterwards known as Saka Kshatriyas, i.e. Scythians. The third son, Koshtu got the Varshaka Kshetra, probably a part of Karnal. The kingdom of Nabhaga cannot be identified now. Saryati got a state in Gujarat. His son, Anrita conquered Kathiawar and built the capital Kusasthali, afterwards known as Dwaraka.

The *Rig Veda*, I, 116. 3 and 5, records the first foreign invasion of India about 2800 BC or a little later. Sayana gives the story thus. The royal sage Tugra was a great favourite with the two Asvin brothers. Being much harassed by the enemies of a different land, he sent his son, Bhujyu with a strong army to conquer them. The ship went to the middle of the sea and was driven away by high winds and wrecked. Then, Bhujyu sent a prayer to the Asvins for rescue. The Asvins rescued him with the soldiers and brought him home safely to his father in three days and nights. The enemies were either the Assyrians or the Egyptians; in all probability, the former. For, we know that Indra had concluded a treaty with Vritra, the great Assyrian monarch (*Mahabharata, Effort Book, chapters 11–13*). Indra treacherously broke the terms, afterwards attacked Vritra and killed him and his brother Vala (Bel). The Assyrians roused by the murder of their kings, perhaps invaded India repeatedly to avenge the slaughter of Vritra by Indra (*vide R.V.I. 80. 2; III 33. 7; I. 90 I; IX, 63. 24*). In the *Zend Avesta*, Indra is called Verathraghna. The Indo-Assyrian relations of those times will partially appear from the following:

'If now we compare the Indian narrative with the records of the Cuneiform inscriptions, there can scarcely remain a doubt that the Vala of the *Rig Veda,* was the Belus or Bel of the inscriptions; that the lofty capital of Vala, in the *Rig Veda*, was the lofty citadel of Bel in the inscription: that the asuras, *Panis* of the Veda, were identical with Phinides of classical history or mythology; that the river crossed by Sarama was the Euphrates. We find that the Aryans who emigrated to India were once familiar with the lofty citadel of Bel and must have lived not very far from the Euphrates'. (Dr KM Banerji's *Aryan Witness, p. 62*).

RISE OF THE LUNAR DYNASTY

About 2790 or 2788 BC, Princess Ila began to rule in her capital at Pratistjama, near modern Allahabad. She was the first Indian woman to sit on a throne. It is said that in male dress and under the male name of Sudyumna, she ably managed her state for several years.

She was not married. She would sit on the throne in the open court and conduct all state affairs with the aid of her ministers. She was fair in form, pure in character and fond of hunting. One fine spring, mounted on her favourite Sindh horse and followed by a large retinue, she had gone hunting to the north of the Himalayas. One day, she entered a fair hermitage called the Kumara Bana and met Buddha there. Charmed by his exceptional beauty, she asked him to marry her. Buddha, although on penance, agreed. A gandharva marriage was performed. Ila brought down Buddha to her capital and thenceforward both ruled as joint-sovereigns.

The great sage Atri was the second of the Saptarshi brothers. He begot Soma, honoured in the *Rig Veda* with the title of Raja. He was very powerful. His state was in Mongolia, Rig Vedic *Mangar.* His land yielded abundant crops. Having subdued all the chiefs of Central Asia and north-west India, he performed an imperial sacrifice under the leadership of his father Atri. This afterwards led to the devasura war. The foulest deed that brought an eternal stain on Soma, was his stealing Taradevi, wife of Vrihaspati, priest to the devas. Vrihaspati fought with Soma for his wife, but was defeated. At last, with the aid of Indra and others, Vrihastpati recovered her. Tara bore a son by Soma. And, this son was Buddha who married Ila. He was called Buddha, i.e. wise, for he was noted for wisdom from his youth. He was very handsome in person. He studied various sciences, especially medicine. It is said that he first introduced the Hasti Sastra, i.e. a treatise on elephant. Soma also means the moon. The Puranists have therefore called his line lunar. Though historically wrong, the idea is not altogether void of poetry. The moon derives her light from the sun. Ila also derived her life and light from the sun (Vivaswan).

The king-list of the lunar dynasty is shown thus: 1 Ila, 2 Buddha and Ila, 3 Pururava, 4 Ayu, 5 Nahusha, 6 Yayati, 7 Puru, 8 Janamejaya, 9 Prachinvan, 10 Pravira, 11 Manasyu, 12 Charupada, 13 Sudyu, 14 Bahugava, 15 Sanyati, 16 Ahanyati, 17 Raudrasva, 18 Riteyu, 19 Rantinara, 20 Sumati, 21 Aiti, 22 Dushyanta, 23 Bharata, 24 Bitatha, 25 Manyu, 26 Vrihat-Kshetra, 27 Hasti, 28 Ajamira, 29 Riksha I, 30 Samvarana, 31 Kuru, 32 Janhu, 33 Suratha, 34 Biduratha, 35 Sarva-bhauma, 36 Jayatsena, 37 Radhika, 38 Ajutayu, 39 Akrodhana, 40 Devatithi, 41 Riksha II, 42 Dilipa, 43 Pratipa, 44 Santanu,

45 Vichitra-Virya, 46 Bhishma (Regent), 47 Pandu, 48 Dhritarashtra (Regent) and Bhishma (Protector), 49 Yudhisthira and Duryodhana, 50 Duryodhana. Then came the Pandu dynasty with Yudhisthira as the first ruler (1388–1373 BC).

Of the so-called solar and the lunar dynasties, the former was the most predominant from Manu to Rama. The latter boasts of several prominent figures. Besides, eight different dynasties, all noted in history, sprang from it.

IKSHVAKU

(perhaps, 2790–2750 BC)

After a short rule of ten or twelve years, Manu passed into religious retirement. His eldest son Ikshvaku succeeded him about 2790 BC. He is recognised in the *Rig Veda* and his dynasty is called the Aikshaka. He was tall, of golden complexion, sweet in temper and strong in brain, body and mind. He received his lessons from the noted sages and his father. He is called the first regular king of Oudh. He ruled wisely and well. He was very great and pious and performed many sacrifices. He had ten sons and one daughter. Five of his sons took to religion; one son turned a merchant. One son, Sakuni, went to the north and founded his line there. Bikukshi was the crown-prince. Though his reign was probably long, we hear of no fresh conquests except that he assisted two of his sons in founding new kingdoms. Certainly, he strove hard for the thorough organisation of his first state. Prince Nimi founded a small state afterwards called Mithila or Videha (north Bihar). Prince Visala is said to have built Visalapuri, afterwards Vaisali and now Bihar. Prince Dandaka built a kingdom south of the Vindhyas, perhaps between modern Nagpur and Nasik. He took to his kingdom many Aryan settlers from the north, whom he gave lands and wealth. This was, no doubt, the first Aryan state in the Deccan. Prince Dandaka employed a sage named Sukra as his priest. All was well for some years. Then, one day, Dandaka went to his priest's house, but Sukra was not in. Dandaka saw the priest's daughter who had not yet attained puberty. Charmed by her beauty, he seized her; but she asked him to wait till the return of her father and then marry her with his consent. Unfortunately, Dandaka paid no heed to her words, forcibly raped her and then returned to his capital

Madhumanta. Great was the wrath of Sukra when he learnt of this. He cursed Dandaka would perish with his people. It is said that a terrible volcanic eruption soon followed and rendered the fertile valley into an arid waste by the ceaseless downpour of burning ashes for days together (*Ramayana VII, 92–94 Cantos*). The awful calamity reminds us of the dreadful catastrophe connected with the origin of the Dead Sea. The neighbouring country where the sages had already repaired, leaving the sinful kingdom of Dandaka became afterwards known as Janasthana. Thus ended the first Aryan state of the south, afterwards called the Dandaka Forest. Some identify it with the later Dhanakataka.

The *Old Testament* and several Hindu works speak of a universal 'deluge'. Other Hindu works make it an untimely 'deluge' of a minor kind. We have disbelieved the tale of the universal 'deluge'. But several contemporary events attract our attention. The ruin of Prince Dandaka's realm by volcanic eruption; the rising of the sea-bed and forming the coast-strips now known as Bombay, Konkan and Malabar; the sinking of the Indo-African continent, our ancient *Plaksha-dwipa* and a high rising of the Arabian Sea are known to the Hindus as an untimely 'deluge'. Probably, all these were the effects of a violent volcanic eruption!

The crown-prince Bikukshi also gave the king some trouble. One day, to perform a *sraddha* ceremony, the king ordered Prince Bikukshi to procure meat. The prince hunted many animals. Hungry and thirsty, he however ate a hare in the wood and brought the rest to Ikshvaku. The royal priests discovered that the meat was rendered impure by the Prince's eating a hare and rejected it. This foul act of the Prince earned him the opprobrious title of *Sasada* (hare-eater). Ikshvaku was so annoyed at the Prince's act that he disinherited him. He died after a long and prosperous reign (2750 BC).

BIKUKSHI

(*Mahabharata* and *Puranas*, perhaps 2750–2730 BC).

On the death of Ikshvaku, the royal priest, the ministers and the leading people crowned Bikukshi king. He was called *rajarshi*, i.e. saintly king. He ruled his kingdom on righteous principles. Being of a religious bent of mind, he resembled his grandfather Manu. He begot fifteen sons, the eldest of whom, Paranjaya (literally victor) was a great hero. The Prince was very carefully trained.

PARANJAYA

(*Mahabharata* and *Puranas*; perhaps 2730–2700 BC)

On the retirement of Bikukshi, the crown-prince Paranjaya succeeded him to the throne. His queen Manonmathini, daughter of Bharga Deva, was a beauty. He had several sons and two daughters. Princess Taravati was married to Chandrasekhara, prince of Karavirapura on the River Drishadvati in Bithoor. Prince Chandrasekhara was the great-grandson of Daksha of Kanakhala near Haridwar. The other princess is said to have been a queen of Yayati of the lunar line. Paranjaya was ambitious and very fond of glory. His renown as a great warrior had reached even the north. For, at this time, the devas, defeated by the asuras, applied to him for aid. It is said that he agreed but demanded that he would fight for them, if their king Indra should carry him to the field on his shoulder. Of course, the devas could not yield to such a disgrace. However, at their entreaty, he agreed to fight from the hump of a big bull of the devas, called Indra. Paranjaya led the combined army against the asuras (Assyrians?) whom he defeated decisively. The victory earned him the title of *Kakustha* (i.e. Victor of the Bull). His Indian exploits are almost forgotten. For distinction, the solar line is often called the 'Line of Kakustha'. Paranjaya was followed by two peaceful kings (nos. 5 and 6) whose reigns were by no means eventful. They may have ruled till 2660 BC.

The Lunar Dynasty: The first several kings of the lunar dynasty, recognised in the *Rig Veda*, deserve special notice here. By Ila, Buddha had four sons, Pururava, Utkala, Gaya, and Vimala. The eldest Pururava came to the throne perhaps about 2758 BC. The other three princes are said to have founded their kingdoms in the Deccan. According to one account, Utkala acquired Orissa; Prince Gaya won the Gaya province and built the capital named after him.

PURURAVA

(perhaps, 2758–2748 BC, *R.V.X, 95. 18*)

He was an accomplished king. He was brave, learned, liberal, and given to the performance of various sacrifices. In his time he was unrivalled in prowess and fame. It is said that he had established his supremacy over thirteen islands of the ocean. His help was sought even by the devas of the north. He defeated the asuras for Indra who honoured the valiant Indian monarch with half his seat. While there, Urvasi, the fairest dancing girl of Indra's court was one day stolen by some robbers. Pururava, however rescued her by his valour. Now Urvasi became passionately enamoured of the young accomplished king. The devas allowed her to marry Pururava, as the latter also agreed. In several hymns of the *Rig Veda* Urvasi has herself narrated her love (*R.V.X, 95*) He begot in her several sons of whom Prince Ayu was the eldest. The later life of Pururava was rather unhappy. His power begot his pride; he fell out with the ministers and the sages and stole their wealth and jewels. Many tried to influence him for the better, but in vain. Power and greed made him mad and blind. To the great relief of all, he soon fell ill and died. Prince Ayu succeeded him. He is recognised in the *Rig Veda*. He was warlike like his father. In *R.V.I.*, 53. 8–10, it is stated that at his time twenty kings with 60,099 soldiers fought against a young, valiant monarch named Susruva who, however, with the aid of Indra, defeated them and subdued Kutsa, Atithigva and Ayu. We find no other mention of Ayu, By his queen Prabha he had five sons of whom Nahusha was the eldest. The third prince Raji was the most powerful. He is described as the very lion of the lunar dynasty. With his aid, Indra retrieved the fallen glories of the devas. He therefore called Raji a father.

NAHUSHA

(perhaps, 2730–2700 BC)

Nahusha succeeded his father to the throne. He was very clever, heroic and just. For the first several years he ruled his people wisely and well. Having defeated many kings, he performed an imperial sacrifice and gave away much wealth and lands to the Brahmans, sages and seers. So strong was his government that the *dasyus* (non-Aryan kings) could not make the least disturbance in the land. Later on, Nahusha grew very wicked and unpopular. He forced the sages to pay him tribute for the extensive estates they owned. His audacious presumption reached its climax when he forced even the seers to bear his palanquin. Fortune raised him to the most exalted place before his fall. Indraship at that time fell vacant. The devas and the seers elected Nahusha Indra. In this new sphere, he proved himself worthy but his insolence did not lessen. He insulted the devas and seers; one day, he even asked Indrani to be his wife. In the meantime, the missing Indra suddenly made his appearance. Nahusha was then unceremoniously driven out from the deva throne (*Mahabharata, Effort Book*). Probably, he did not live long after this. Of his six sons, the eldest Yati refused royalty, and turned an anchorite. So, the second son Yayati was placed on the throne. It is said that he had brought the dramatic art to India from the north.

YAYATI

(perhaps, 2700–2650 BC *R.V.X, 63. I*).

Yayati has been called the 'jewel of the lunar dynasty'. He was very powerful, popular and good. He organised a very strong army. We are told he had subdued almost all the kings of India in seven days. His accomplishments were highly admired even by the devas, who asked him to perform various sacrifices. Like his father, he also performed an imperial sacrifice. But unlike him, he was at first very modest, considerate and merciful. He had two chief queens, Devayani and Sarmistha, whose marriages form an interesting little episode. Sarmistha was the daughter of King Vrishaparvan and Devayani was daughter of Sukra, priest to Vrisahaparvan.

One day, these two girls were bathing together in a tank. Devayani rose out of the water first and by mistake, wore the clothes of Sarmistha. This act so annoyed and wounded the vanity of the princess that she hurled her into a blind well. Poor Devayani wept and groaned there alone in the wilderness. Luckily, Yayati came to that part of the wood while coming back from hunting, in quest of water. Out of compassion he raised her from the well and afterwards married her at her own request. The cruel act of Sarmistha much enraged Sukara who told Vrishaparvan everything. The king, to punish Sarmistha, ordered her to go as a maidservant with Devayani, when the latter was married to Yayati. After some time, Sarmistha also was married to Yayati. Later on, Yayati honoured her much. Devayani was a Brahman girl. Princesses were sometimes married to sages, but the sages seldom gave their daughters in marriage to kings. Such marriages were, no doubt, allowed in society, though not encouraged.

Here, we cannot but note on point in particular: our remote ancestors, the Aryans of those time, were not altogether civilised. We have already said that Soma stole his priest's wife, even fought to retain her. Prince Dandaka raped his priest's daughter. Prince Nimi insulted his priest because he had come late to perform his sacrifice. Here, Sarmistha cast their priest's daughter into a well! Vena and Nahusha were mad tyrants. We shall see later that such slights resulted in a long and deplorable war between the Brahmans and the Kshatriyas. Yayati was an overlord; late in life, he grew very insolent and overbearing. He often insulted the Brahmans, seers and others.

By his two queens he had five sons and several daughters. Yayati also married a daughter of the solar king Paranjaya. Perhaps she was childless (*Brahma Purana*). Devayani presented him Yadu and Turvasu and Sarmistha, Druhyu, Anu and Puru. Yadu was the eldest and Puru the youngest prince. All but Puru, were very disobedient to their father. Impatient of his long reign, perhaps not less than fifty years, the eldest prince, Yadu, revolted against his father. Princes Druhyu, Anu and Turvasu followed Yadu who proclaimed himself emperor and began to rule from a new capital on the Ganges. He summoned the vassal kings to pay him homage and insulted and punished many who refused to do so. He even thought of imprisoning his old father. But Yayati promptly put down the rebellion and pardoned the princes. He now thought of retirement. But before going, he set aside the four elder princes from the throne and declared the youngest and most obedient son, Puru, as his heir, On the coronation day, the leading Brahmans, sages and others came and asked Yayati why he was going to enthrone Puru to the exclusion of the four elder princes. Yayati spoke of their insubordination and they were satisfied. He gave Puru the large kingdom and four minor kingdoms to the four other sons, under Puru. Thus, Puru got the Doab and other parts of the empire. Turvasu got the south-eastern part. Druhyu got the western part. Yadu got a small kingdom in the Deccan; Anu was placed in the north. They were all under Puru. Having made these arrangements, Yayati repaired to the Bhrindatunga Hill where he lived with his queens for some years (*Mahabharata, Book I, Chapter 89*; also Dhritarashtra's counsels to Duryodhana before the War).

The good counsels of Yayati to his son Puru, at the time of coronation are well worth quoting here:

'All the lands that lie between the Ganges and the Jamuna are thine. My son, the peaceful is superior to the angry; the patient to the impatient, man to lower animals and the learned to the unlettered. Never take revenge; don't tyrannise over others; don't speak harshly to others; don't subdue your enemies by low means. Never displease others by your words. Bear patiently all malice, all abuse; be merciful, friendly, charitable, and affable to all. Honour the respectable. Always give, but never beg.'

Five distinguished dynasties sprang up from the five heroic sons of Yayati, all of whom are honoured in the *Rig Veda* for their valour and munificent donations to the seers. Puru's was the main line, Yadu's was the Yadava line, later famous in the Deccan and western India. Krishna was born of it. Druhyu's was the famous Bhoja clan of central India and Malwa. The children of Turvasu, living in the west, in the land of Raja Varuna, became known as Yawanas. They probably marched westward, reached Egypt and finally settled in Greece. The Greeks also claim to be the sons of Ourunos. Their language, mythology, custom clearly show their affinity with Indians. Hindu tradition abandons Anu and notes that he went to the west and became the king of a *mlechcha desa*. Puru was a good ruler and perhaps reigned till 2600 BC.

About this time, a mighty and generous king named Sudasa ruled in north-west India. His father was Atithigva (alias Pijavana or Divodasa) and grandfather, Devabana (*R.V.I, 51.6; I, 112, 14; I, 130.7*) They were non-Aryan kings, though we do not know their line. It is said that with Indra's help, Sudasa succeeded in conquering many countries. The *Aitareya Brahmana* states that Raja Sudasa conquered the whole of India. The *Rig Veda* calls him the greatest hero of the age. His glories evoked the jealousy of other mighty kinds. Under the leadership of Anu and Druhyu, an army of 6,666 men took the field against Sudasa, but he signally defeated them (*R.V. VII, 18*). At one time, Sudasa defeated ten independent kings who had come against him with a large combined army. The action is known as 'The Battle of the Ten Tribes'. Raja Sudasa killed over 60,000 soldiers in it (*R.V. VII, 18*).

Sudasa was a very great patron of learning, religion and good works. His patronage to Vasista, Visvamitra and their children are thankfully mentioned in the *Rig Veda* (these sages should not be confounded with the later sages of the same names). On one occasion, Sudasa gave to

Tritsu (title, Vasista) 200 cows, two cars, four horses, and many gold ornaments. Other poets and learned men also always received many benefits at his hands. Vasista has amply praised Sudasa (*R. V. VII, 22–23*). To encourage learning and religious deeds, his purse was always open. He was ever kind to the poor and very hospitable to guests and strangers.

The *Rig Veda* makes repeated mention of many worthy kings and emperors of the period. Of them, some were busy with conquests, some with grand sacrifices, some became rajrishis by pious deeds; some became famous by good administration. Such scrambling for overlordship continued for centuries.

VISVAGASWA

(*Mahabharata*; 2660–2620 BC)

The sixth solar king—Prithu—was a good ruler and was succeeded by his son Visvagaswa, said to have been very powerful, heroic, magnanimous, and endowed with all other princely qualities. His cavalry, the finest in the land, never came back defeated. His conquests, sacrifices and gifts were numerous (*Mahabharata, Anukramanika*). He was succeeded by his son Ardra (perhaps in 2620 BC), a mere blank name. Probably, he was very mild and peaceful. The nineth king, Yuvanaswa, I, is also mentioned in the *Mahabharata, Anukramanika* as very brave, generous and accomplished. He married his princess Kaveri to Janhu, born of the line of Amavasu, second son of Pururava. He reigned perhaps till 2590 BC. His son and successor, Sravasta built the city of Sravasti (2580 BC) in north Oudh, which afterwards became so famous in connection with both Hindu and Buddhist history (sixth century BC). The ruins of Sravasti are still extant in Gaur (now Gonda district). Sravasta was succeeded by his son Vrihadaswa, perhaps in 2560 BC. A very strong cavalry formed the best part of his army. It is said that he was an 'invincible Raja'. He was very mighty, quick and pious. He reigned long, till about 2525 BC. Desirous of retirement, he installed Prince Kuvalasva on the throne. At that time the great sage Uttanka appeared and requested him to stay and rid the land of the oppression of the mighty Daitya king, Dhundu. Vrihadaswa begged to be excused and ordered Kuvalasva to check Dhundu. The Daityas were cousins to the deva Aryans. Yet, there was great political enmity between the two houses. One line of the Daityas had attained great power and eminence in the Indian desert. Dhundu was the present king of the desert. He was a great hero and his army was very large and strong. Usually he hated the Brahmans, the sages and other Aryan kings.

In bravery and other princely qualities, Kuvalasva far surpassed his father. He had many sons, all of whom were learned and powerful. He was good, pious and heroic. His power of endurance was extraordinary. He was very quick in moving his army. After necessary preparation, he declared war upon Dhundu and invaded his desert kingdom. He led the main part of the army, his sons acting as assistants. A terrible fight ensued and raged long. Loss of lives on both sides was very great. After a good deal of strenuous exertions, Dhundu was killed by a fire-weapon. The victory earned Kuvalasva great fame and the glorious title of 'Dhundumara'. (Date perhaps, 2524 or 2523 BC). Kuvalasva ruled till 2500 BC (*Mahabharata*).

3

STATE OF THE COUNTRY: 3000–2500 BC

THE VEDIC AGE

The date of the Vedic age is not yet certain. Formerly, it was supposed to be from 2780 BC to 1820 BC. But the most recent theory on the point is that it extended from 4500 BC to 2500 BC. In India, we are concerned with its duration from 3000 BC to 2500 BC. During these five centuries, the Aryan settlers, colonists, adventurers, and 'Pilgrim Fathers' had got an almost secure footing in north India up to as far east as Mithila or north Bihar, and probably a little beyond the Vindhyas. Whatever be the claims of our ancestors, it is almost certain that their small states were like so many islands in the sea of Dravidians, Turks and other non-Aryans. These Dravidians were no mean rivals. If the Aryans were 'lordly lions' the Dravidians were 'terrible tigers'. It is also likely that the Aryans learned much from the Dravidians. Hostilities over, the non-Aryans submitted themselves to a higher civilisation and a nobler religion and were slowly coming under the influence and power of the Indo-Aryans. They formed the mass of the new community.

Below is given a sketch of the state of the country during the five centuries touching on several points of our early national life in India.

POLITICAL CONDITION

At first there was great political unrest. The Aryans faced constant dangers from unfriendly natives as also from foreign invades, such as Osiris and Isis of Egypt and the Assyrians. To the friendly natives, the Aryans were merciful and granted them Aryan franchise.

Even then the Indo-Aryans quarrelled among themselves and with the other powers of the land. Of course, there were times when the quarrels may have been justified. But a wise people evade quarrels to seek higher benefits in the common interest.

RELIGION

During this period, the Indo-Aryans appear to have been very bold and free in their religious thoughts. There were at least four different religions prevalent among them, viz., the Vedic religion, Brahmanism, Materialism or Atheism and Jainism.

THE VEDIC RELIGION AND BRAHAMANISM

The early rishis or psalmists sought *satyam*—truth; *sivam*—the sublime and *sundaram*—the beautiful. Religion dwelt more in their hearts, less in rites. They had great trust in their gods and in themselves. This was, no doubt, a great source of their inspiration, and prosperity in life. These great seers were generally averse to animal slaughter even for sacrifice. They prayed for the prosperity and progress of the country and people (*R.V. IV* and *X*).

With the deva-Aryans, the simple and good religion of the rishis became very grand. 'Sacrifice' was an addition. The devas sanctioned the slaughter of horse, cow, buffalo for various sacrifices. These religious differences led to a rupture between the rishis and the devas. We have seen that the rishis were ousted from the north. Acquiring lands in India, the rishis even waged a war against the devas but were mostly killed. The descendants of the devas founded kingdoms in India. In the new Indian homes, in the provinces of upper India, Punjab and the midlands, the Vedic religion, both Arsha (of the rishis) and Daiva (of the devas) came down and prevailed. The devas employed a class of learned men skilled in rites and rituals who became known as the Vedic priests, whose descendants still exist in India.

Our rishis should not be confounded with these Vedic priests who soon became very influential. The rishis aimed at moral beatitude—a highly reasoned existence—while the Vedic priests aimed at excellent performance of Vedic rites that were calculated to give eternal bliss. Backed by the kings, the Vedic priests grew very important and powerful, while the rishis lived aloof, worshipping in their own way. Good kings honoured them with gifts, free lands, reverence, and safety. Yet, there were wicked and powerful kings who dishonoured them, forced them to pay for their estates, whipped and kicked them even. The Vedic religion declined not under the rishis but under the priests, as we shall see later on.

Religion prevailed in society. Most of the people were pious, truthful and moderate. From the simple and sincere nature-worship rose thought-idolatry; thence henotheism, then monotheism. There was perfect toleration and catholic ideas prevailed.

Of the different doctrines of the period, the Vedic religion was the oldest. But it assumed two different forms, viz., Arsha and Daiva, professed by the rishis and the devas. The former was philosophical, while the latter popular.

The *Rig Veda* bears clear traces of polytheism, henotheism and monotheism.

The Vedic religion was simple and patriarchal. The Aryans in India were a conquering race, full of self-assertion, vigour, strong love of action, and a capacity for active enjoyment. They knew no 'discontent with present life' which tormented the later Hindus so much. They never left the world in disgust, but ever lived in homes and hearth, amidst pleasures and mirth, now worshipping, now fighting and now ploughing. Even the rishis were not a distinct class but good householders like us, owning estates, fighting battles, tending cattle, teaching pupils, and instructing people and the kings, framing laws, writing books and discovering new truths. The first Indo-Aryans were still far removed from the 'contemplative and passive Hindus' of later times.

They had no rigid caste, no priest, no temple, no idols, no offerings, no idea of an incarnation, no triad, no hero-worship. They worshipped the beneficent, cheerful and beautiful gods of nature such as Indra, Agni,

Varuna, and Nasatya. It was a religion of sacrifice consisting in the libation of *soma* juice mixed with milk. They prayed for health, wealth, prosperity, good offspring, good cattle, and the ruin of their enemies.

The worship of Indra was peculiar to India but never known in the north nor to the other Aryan nations of the world; while Dyaus (Greek, Zeus; Latin, Jupiter; A.S. Tiu; German, Zio), Mitra, Agni, Varuna, and some others were the common gods of the northern Aryans.

The Rig Vedic hymns knew no wicked divinities, no mean and harmful practices and give evidence of an exalted and comprehensive morality and grave duties.

Ordinarily, each householder was himself the priest, the warrior and the cultivator. Kings and rich men employed priests for grand sacrifices; again when a whole village would perform some common worship, priests were engaged and paid.

The religion of the *Rig Veda* has been called a progressive religion. For it travels from the simple childlike worship and admiration of the ruddy dawn, to the deep and sublime attempt to grasp the mysteries of creation and its great creator.

The Rig Vedic Aryans were conscious of sins and believed that God, sincerely prayed to, might take away all sins. The notions of a future life are no doubt indicated, but the doctrine of a future life, the transmigration of soul, cycle of rebirths, and torments of numberless hells are not yet distinct. Atonement for sins, the *sraddha* ceremony for the dead were well-known.

RISE OF MATERIALISM OR ATHEISM

Some tribes of the northern Aryans appear to have been quite antagonistic to the Vedic religion. They were atheists and did not believe in gods, soul, religious rites or the next world. With them, the attainment of materialistic happiness was the *summon bonum* of life. They believed in the eternity of matter. 'Eat, drink and be merry; for nothing remains after death'—was their cry. Though they had no practical religion, yet probably they had good morals which they admitted as the essential laws of matter.

Of the Daitya Aryans, Hiranyakasipu and Aswagriva, two powerful monarches were staunch atheists. The former is notorious for the persecution of his eldest prince Prahlada, who was devoted to the Vedic religion. Aswagriva, a sworn enemy of the Vedic faith, tried to efface all Vedic traces from the world. It is said that he once stole the Veda and often harassed the performance of sacrifice. From that time, memorisation of the Vedic hymns became a necessity. Later on, Vrihaspati, priest to the devas, turned Atheism to a political purpose. It is said that he had attacked Gayatri (the holiest Rig Vedic hyman personified) on the head and fractured it: the meaning is plain. He first formulated these atheistical views into something like a philosophy (*Vishnu Purana: Matsya Purana*).

These atheists grew numerous and powerful. In India, they were not allowed to live in the Aryan states; so they generally lived in the Sudra kingdoms. On the other hand, Brahmans were not allowed to live in the Sudra states 'overwhelmed with atheists'. These atheists were powerful in the court of Janaka of north Bihar. The spread of Sankhya philosophy soon weakened the force of their arguments. The sect, however, continued long. We hear of six other human Buddhas before Sakya Muni. But we do not know when and where they lived and taught and what success they had gained.

RISE OF JAINISM

Like Brahmanism, Jainism also is a very ancient religion of India. The Vedas do not know this new creed, but the *Mahabharata, Agni* and other Puranas mention it: 'Owing to the diversity of religions such as Aryan, Jain and *mlechcha*, people become doubtful', (*Mahabharata, Peace Book, Chapter 258*).

A Jina is a spiritual conqueror. His religion is Jainism. Rishabha Deva was a king of the Vairaja dynasty in Bithoor (twenty-nineth century BC). He had married Jayanti, daughter of Indra, the Raja of the deva-Aryans. He ruled for some time, then suddenly grew disgusted with the world, left the Raj to his eldest Prince Bharata and practised severe penance for some time. He became siddha, i.e. successful. Then he came back from the mountains and declared himself as Jina, spiritual conqueror. His tenets were: salvation is possible without the idea of a God; eternity of matter—creation is eternal and self-sown; moral self-culture; perfect preservation of all life. It is said that he himself had initiated King Vena of the same Vairaja dynasty. Probably, he was influenced by the Sankhya creed of Kapila.

His disciples became known as Jainas. The Vedas allowed the slaughter of animals only for sacrificial purposes, but Jainism allowed no sacrifice, no harm to any living thing. The Jainas lived on hills or in forests far away from human dwelling, almost in a state of nature. They would eat only those ripe fruits that fell from trees of themselves, would make fire with dry logs. It is evident that the religion was not at first meant for the masses. Probably in other respects, the founder agreed with the rishis. Another distinctive feature of Jainism is that 'nothing can be predicted with certainty'. Hence, Jainism has been sometimes called *Syatbada*.

Jainism is still a living religion, being professed by over five million Indians. They have ever held an intermediate position between the Hindus and the Buddhists. They agree with the caste system. This exists in full force in the south and west India; it is dormant in the north-east. Besides, they have numerous divisions of their own avoiding inter-marriage and other intercourse.

No doubt, they deny the scriptural character of the Vedas, yet they allow them great authority in all points agreeing with their religion. They have great objections to bloody sacrifices and loss of life which burnt offerings cause. They admit all the Hindu gods, worship some of them, but consider them inferior to their saints (arhats). Jainas have some opinions peculiar to them, e.g. worship of them Tirthankaras, twenty-four for the past, twenty-four for the present and twenty-four in future. Rishabha Deva or Adinatha is the first Jina of the present. Parsvanatha (eighth century BC) and Vardhamana Mahavira (sixth century BC) are the twenty-third and twenty-fourth Tirthankaras of reformers. They give no preference to the greater gods of the Hindus. They have sixty-four Indras and twenty-two Devis.

They have no all castes. They wear very large loose white mantles; their heads are bare, hair and beard clipped; they carry a black rod and a brush for sweeping away animals. They live on alms and never bathe.

They agree with the Buddhists in denying the existence or at least the activity and providence of God; in believing in the eternity of matter; in the worship of deified saints; in their scrupulous care of animal life; in their having no hereditary priesthood; in disclaiming the divine authority of the Vedas and in having no sacrifice and no respect for fire; in considering a state of impassive abstraction as supreme felicity and in all the doctrines which they hold in common with the Hindus.

We have seen that our early rishis had protested against the grand sacrifices, especially the slaughter of animals introduced by the devas. The result was that a bitter strife ensued between the rishis and the devas, in which the rishis were driven out of the north. *Ma hinsyah sarva-bhutani* is a lesson of the *Rig Veda*, meaning, 'Do not harm anything'. The bloody sacrifice came to India with the new settlers and gradually tended towards so much barbarity that even human sacrifice was deemed highly meritorious and was actually performed. The rishis spoke against it; Kapila disapproved of it and Rishabha Deva preached against it. Though the *Agni Purana* has branded Rishabha Deva as pashanda (wicked heretic), yet we find the names of Kapila, Rishabha Deva and Buddha on the list of the twenty-two *avtaras* (*Bhagavata*).

LITERATURE

The Rig Veda

'Originally the *Rig Veda* had over a lakh of hymns,' says It-Ching, the Chinese Indian traveller (AD 671–699). According to the *Charana Vyuha*, a work of Vyasa on the Vedas, it had originally 10,580 hymns. Now, there remain only 1,017 hymns. The rest have fallen into disuse. Of the twenty-one branches, only five, viz., the Sakala, Vaskala, Asvalayna, Sankhayana and Manduka were main ones. Now, only the Sakala branch is extant, containing 1,017 hymns. These Vedic lyrics mostly sing the praise of various gods. Therefore, it is rightly called a Book of Psalms. It is the most important and the oldest of the Vedas. Professor Max Müeller says in the *Origin and Growth of Religion:*

'One thing is certain; there is nothing more ancient and primitive, not only in India but in the whole Aryan world, than the hymns of the *Rig Veda.*'

There are, however, reasons to believe that some portions of Book X of the *Rig Veda* were a much later addition. It discerns many new things, viz., cosmogony, philosophy, wedding, burial rites, spells, and incantations. Its relation to the other Vedas is close. The other Vedas borrowed largely from it. The fixity of the Rig Vedic text dates from a period not later than 1000 BC (AA MacDonell).

The first arrangement and classification of the Vedas was by Atharvan (perhaps 2900 BC or later), and the second, by Vyasa almost about 1400 BC, some years before the *Mahabharata War* (1389 BC). This date of the fixity of the Vedic text cannot be much earlier, as the praise of Dasaratha, Rama and Santanu is recorded. Rama ruled about 1450 or 1460 BC.

Language, Accent and Metres

'The language in which the Vedas were composed, is an older form of classical Sanskrit. The text of the four Vedas and of two *Brahmanas* has been preserved in an accented form. The Vedic accent was a musical one, depending on the pitch of the voice like that in ancient Greek. It later gave place to stress accent. The Rig Vedic hymns consist of stanzas ranging in numbers from three to fifty-eight but usually in ten or twelve. Various metres are used. The metre Gayatri embraces nearly ¼ and Trishtubh, 2/5 of all the stanzas. The literary, as well as metrical skill with which the hymns of the *Rig Veda* are composed, is considerable' (AA MacDonell, *I.G.I., Vol. II, p. 210*).

Its Authors

Hindus in general believe that God revealed the Vedas to some chosen rishis. As 'divine revelation' does not come within the domain of history, we need not discuss the point here at all. We are indebted for these lyrical hymns to many enlightened seers.

The eight rishis from whom we the Brahmans of India claim descent composed many good hymns. 'Six of the ten Books (II to VII) are homogeneous in arrangement, while each of them is the work of a different family of seers. The first, eight and the tenth Books agree in being made up of a number of groups, based on identity of authorship' (*I.G.I. Vol. II, p. 209*).

One point deserves special mention here: so great was the appreciation of merits in those times that hymns composed by persons other than the highborn seers were cordially welcome by the seers. For instance, one Vedic writer says (*R.V. IX, 112*); 'My father is a physician, my mother grinds corn in a mill; but see, I compose a Vedic hymn!'

Again, (*R.V.X*) Kavasa Ailusa was a non-Aryan convert (Sudra) but he became a *rishi* and composed Vedic hymns. The female Vedic writers are briefly noted below:

(1) Vak Devi

Daughter of *Rishi* Ambhrina. Composed the eight riks of 125 Sukta, Book X, *Rig Veda*. These riks are known as *Devi-Sukta*. In the ancient Vedic times, the custom of reading the *Devi-Sukta* on some special occasions was in vogue. In modern times the *Chandi* (recounting of the deeds of Durga) by Markandeya, has supplanted the *Devi-Sukta*, only as an echo of the latter. In the above-mentioned eight hymns, Vak Devi has fully expressed her ideas of monotheism and chastity. It was really she and not Sankaracharya (b. AD 788), who had first expounded the monotheistic view of God.

(2) Biswavara

Of the Atri clan. Composers of six hymns (*R.V.V., Anuvak 2, Sukta 28*). These display the extremely tender ideas, beauty and sweet affections of female hearts.

(3) Aditi

Wife of the great sage Kasyapa and daughter of King Daksha and mother of the twelve Aditya brothers of the deva-Aryans. Composed five hymns of *R.V.X*, 153 Sukta; also the fifth, sixth and the seventh hymns of *R.V.*, IV, 18 Sukta.

(4) Apala

Of the Atri clan. Composed, like Biswavara, the eight hymns of *R.V.* VIII, 91 Sukta.

(5) Yami

Wrote the first, third, fifth, seventh, and eleventh hymns of R.V., 10 Sukta and also the five hymns of 154th Sukta.

(6) Urvashi

Described her love and marriage with Pururava, a lunar king, in seven hymns of the 95th Sukta, Book X, *Rig Veda*.

(7) Lopamudra

Princess of Vidarbha and wife of the great sage Agastya. Composed the first two hymns of the 179th Sukta of Book I of the *Rig Veda*.

(8) Romasa

Queen of Bhava-Yavya and mother of King Svanaya. Composed the seventh hymn of 126th Sukta, Book I, *Rig Veda*. (Hemendra N Sinha in *Sanjibani*, February 10–11–1911).

ITS RELIGION

The religious character of the Vedic literature is very prominent. From beginning to end, the Vedic literature bears an exclusively religious stamp. The primary doctrine of the Vedas is the unity of God. 'There is in truth,' say repeated texts, 'but one Deity—the Supreme Spirit—the Lord of the Universe, whose work is the universe.' Thus, the Indo-Aryans no more worshipped nature nor her powers personified, but the great god. The natural agencies were mere 'aids'.

The Vedas no doubt mention Brahma, Vishnu and Siva—the three chief manifestations of the divinity and most other gods, but there is no hero-worship. The triad enjoy no pre-eminence nor special adoration. There is no mention of incarnation. There seem to have been no images and no visible types of objects of worship. The practical part of the religion stressed the ritual and the moral. An Aryan's second birth through his investiture with the sacred thread, makes him a *dwija* (twice-born). Gayatri, the most holy verse of the Vedas is enjoined to be repeated either as devotion or expiation and which, joined to universal benevolence, may raise one to beatitude without the aid of any other religious exercise. Mr Colebrooke explains the Gayatri thus: 'Let us meditate the adorable light of the Divine Ruler; may it guide our intellect.'

Gods are worshipped by burnt offerings of melted butter and libations of the *soma* juice. Slaughter of animals, only for sacrificial purpose, is allowed. Offerings of perfumes and flowers are not alluded to. Idols are mentioned and are desired to be respected; but their general adoration is disapproved of. The daily religious duties of an Aryan are said to be studying the Vedas; making oblations to the fire in honour of the deities; giving rice to living creatures; and receiving guests with honour (HP Sastri; *H.H.W., Vol. II, p. 529; I.G.I., Vol. 2 p. 207*).

The Vedas

A repository of learning, the Rig-Vedic hymns not only deal with religious speculations, but also with the various branches of secular lore. They contain orthography, codes of law and ritual, grammar, philosophy, prosody, astronomy, philology, medicine, music, science of war, anatomy, geometry, and arithmetic. The entire Hindu learning is simply a gradual refinement of the most ancient Vedic lore. The Vedic literature first gives the specimens of poetry and prose. There are numberless poems of considerable merit and beauty. As regards thoughts and ideas, Professor AD Macdonell observes; 'It (*R.V.*) represents an earlier stage of thought than is to be met with in any other literature' (*I.G.I., Vol. II, p. 210*). The Vedic fables and parables gave rise to many didactic works of the kind. Some twelve hymns contain dialogues referring to past events. The learned Professor rightly holds that these formed the sources of dharma and epic poetry of later times. There are more than thirty non-religious hymns in the *Rig Veda.* Of these, some twelve are magical, consisting of spells directed against disease: here is the probable origin of the future Tantras. Law and ritual furnished models of all future codes or institutes. 'Manu's code was derived from the Vedas to which it refers in every page.'

Date and Period

'The chronology of the Vedic period is purely conjectural' (Professor AA Macdonell). Indeed, it is difficult to ascertain the exact date. Some scholars place the Vedic period between 2780 BC and 1820 BC. But the most recent theory on the subject is that the period of Vedic civilisation extended from about 2500 BC to 1500 BC. Professor HP Sastri says that the collection of hymns now extant, was dated 3500 BC. This is compilation. The composition of the various hymns, therefore, must be of much greater antiquity.

The Vedic poets kept an era of their own called the *Gavam Ayana* (cow's era). Reckoning the years in terms of intercalary days occurring once in every *yuga* or cycle of four years, they counted on the whole,

460 intercalary days or 'cows' as they termed it, in the course of 1840 years. This gives the length of the Vedic period. The mention of the kings Dasaratha, Ramachandra, Santanu and the rivers Ganges and the Jamuna and other incidents of the period, bring down the Vedic period almost to the middle of the fifteenth century BC. Vyasa arranged and classified the hymns for the second time about 3240 BC. Hence, we may be pretty sure that the early Vedic hymns were composed in old Sanskrit before 3300 BC. The new hymns went on being composed from 3300 BC to 1400 BC at the latest, in Medieval Sanskrit.

We may divide the entire Vedic period into three distinct parts:

(i) From 4500 BC to 3300 BC: Hymns composed in old Sanskrit in the cold northern home. Simple prayers for long life, good rain and good progeny; the idea of one Supreme Being was not yet distinct.

(ii) 3300 BC to 1400 BC: First collection of the Rig-Vedic hymns by Brahma. First classification of the Vedas as *Trayi* by Atharva. Worship of fire and sacrifice introduced; rise of priesthood; performance of grand sacrifices; henotheism; monotheism; discovery of 'Brahma'; rise of Brahmanism. Second classification of the four Vedas by Vyasa. *Atharva Veda* recognised. Hymns composed in medieval Sanskrit. New colonies and settlements in India. Non-Aryan opposition. Aryan prayer for the destruction of the foes. Vedic text fixed forever (1400 BC).

(iii) 1400 BC to 700 BC: No new hymns composed. Politics more prevalent than religion. Vedic Sanskrit dies. Prakrit gradually more powerful; Panini (perhaps 800 BC); end of ancient dynasties; end of Vedic influence; lifeless Vedic rites; cruelties. It is already stated that moral excellence leads to eternal bliss. How can such moral excellence be attained? The *Rig Veda* proposes three means viz.,—action, i.e. performance of sacrifice; wisdom; and faith.

Order of Creation

Gods—Inferior deities: representatives of elements as Indra, Agni, Varuna, Prithivi. Heavenly bodies; such as the Sun, Moon, Jupiter. Abstruse ideas; as Gods of Justice and Piety, Good and Evil Genii.

Nearly all the higher gods of the *Rig Veda* are personifications of natural phenomena, such as the sun, dawn, fire, wind, and rain. These gods are almost exclusively beneficent beings who grant long life and prosperity. The oldest god was *Dyaus pitri*, Greek Zeus Pater, Latin Jupiter. Next was Varuna, Greek Uranos, the great upholder of physical and moral order. The hymns addressed to him are more ethical and devout in tone than any others. They form the most exalted portion of the Veda, having sublimity of thought and diction. He is now a mere god of water. Next rank the solar deities, five in number—Mitra (friend) signifies the sun's beneficent agency, later on, he is invoked with Varuna as Mitravaruna; surya (the sun) is described as the eye of the gods beholding the deeds of man and as riding in a car drawn by seven steeds (i.e. seven rays of the sun); Savitri, the stimulator represents the quickening power of the sun, to him is addressed the Gayatri, the most famous stanza of the *Rig Veda* ('May we attain the excellent glory of Savitri the god, that he may stimulate our thoughts'); Vishnu typifies the course of the sun through the three divisions of the universe; and Aditya refers to the twelve different suns of the year.

Agni is the personification of the sacrificial fire. Goddesses hold a subordinate position. Usha (dawn) is the most charming and graceful creation of the rishis. She is celebrated in some twenty hymns which are the most poetical in the *Rig Veda*.

Life, Death and Social Elements

In the *Rig Veda* there are references to death and future life. The body is frail but the soul is imperishable. The soul is separable from the body not only after death, but even during unconsciousness. Notions of reward and punishment after death are clearly shown. Of secular hymns, there are some twenty. They deal with social customs, the generosity of patrons, ethical questions, riddles, and cosmogonic speculations—the most noteworthy being the long wedding hymn (*X, 85*). Five hymns deal with funeral rites: burial is occasionally practised but cremation is the usual manner of disposing of the dead. Widow-burning is of very great antiquity; at first confined only to the military chiefs. In medieval India, this cruel custom spread to all classes.

A remarkable poem of much beauty shows the antiquity of gambling. Three of the secular poems are of a didactic character; six or seven hymns treat of the question of the origin of the world. The 'Song of Creation' (*X, 129*), a poem of great literary merit, is noteworthy for its 'theory of evolution' (AA MacDonell's paper in *I.G.I., Vol. II, pp. 210–20*).

The remarks of EB Cowell on the *Rig Veda,* appended to Elphinstone's *History of India*, 9th edition, pp. 271–75, are entitled to our respect. So, we quote them here:

> The Rig-Vedic hymns alone are the earliest authority for the social and religious institutions of the Hindus. The *Rig Veda* contains 1017 hymns with eleven supurious ones. These hymns are far remote from our modern sentiment and sympathy. They represent an early stage of the worship of the great powers of nature personified and as such, possess deep interest for the history of human thought before Homer and Hesiod. Its religion is ultimate monotheism through polytheism. There are occasional moral ideas as spiritual hopes and desires, but the general strain is possibly earthly—prayer for the end of sickness and foes, and good offspring and cattle.

The poetry of the *Rig Veda* is deficient in simplicity and natural pathos or sublimity. Its language and style are singularly artificial. Many hymns are not intelligible; obscure constructions, startling ellipses are abundant. There are occasional fine outbursts of poetry. For example, the hymns to dawn. There are few grand similes and metaphors. Later Sanskrit poetry gives intense love and appreciation of all the varieties of natural scenery, delicate delineation of human character. But these are wanting in the *Rig Veda*.

The *Rig Veda* possesses an undying interest as the oldest monument of gentile thought and we can undoubtedly trace there the first outlines, concepts of which afterwards branched out in widely different directions in the ancient world.

The Value of the Rig Veda

It gives the picture of the earliest form of civilisation. It throws a flood of light on the origin and growth of the myth and religions of the Aryan nations of the world.

To the historian of man, it explains how the mind of man in its infancy worships what is bright and beaming in nature, what is powerful and striking. These brighter and pleasanter aspects of nature made the deepest impression and evoked songs of gratitude, praise and worship. Further, it shows us how the mind is led from nature to nature's god—*Brahman*, the Supreme Being.

To the historian of the Aryans, its value is still greater. For, it is their oldest work. It gives a picture of the oldest civilisation of the Aryans. It sheds light on much that is dark and dim in the religious and myths of the Aryan peoples all over the world.

To the Hindus, the *Rig Veda* is of considerable value. It explains the whole system of the later Hinduism; it shows the germs of all the later mythology; it enlightens the history of the Hindu mind from its earliest stage to the latest times. It further shows the gradual changes of historical and social mattes.

The Lessons of the Rig Veda

The *Rig Veda* teaches us many useful and great lessons; never harm anything; always protect thyself—for, existence is the first law of nature; never sleep in the day-time; monotheism—this appears from the latest hymns of the *Rig Veda*, the idea was certainly borrowed from the discovery of *Brahman* by Narayana in the thirtieth century BC; unity of matter; unity of force; theory of evolution; theory of sound—sound is eternal, sound is God, everything is from sound (the idea is reflected in the Greek *Logos* and the Christian Bible, probably borrowed from the neo-Platonic school of Alexandria); theory of the elements—the rishis say that all objects originate from a combination of five elements and die from their dissolution; forms vary but substance ever remains the same (the elements are—earth, water, heat, gas, and ether. These English words do not give the exact meanings of the originals. By electrolysis, modern scientists prove the common water—a gross thing—as a compound of hydrogen and oxygen. But the elementary water is a root-liquid, so subtle, so fine that its existence is almost inconceivable. And so of the other elements); high morals—truth, hospitality to strangers, self-control, benevolence are well inculcated; optimistic view of life—the *Rig Veda* knows no pessimism, no discontent with the present life, no self-torture, no wicked divinities, no harmful practices; plain living and high thinking; and aim at reasoned existence.

Hindu law books were called Dharma-Sastras in the Vedic and the epic ages; Dharma-*Sutras* in the rationalistic age of Samhitas in the

Puranic age. The last name means 'a compilation of old and new material'. To a careful reader, the present metrical Code of Manu presents latent traces of five different things, viz., the Aryan laws of the north, the laws of Bithoor, the Dravidian laws, his own ideas and the later additions and alterations. We may carefully hunt out from Manu's Code the laws that relate to the most ancient times. The *Rig Veda*, the Code of Manu and the historical chapters of the Puranas, have a great bearing on the state of the country in the Vedic age. Again, Hindus are the most conservative people in the world. 'With but slight changes, they are still the same people as they were, thousands of years back.' So, we may rely on Manu in writing this chapter.

THE SYSTEM OF ADMINISTRATION

A constitutional limited monarchy seems to have been the earliest form of government in India. A king is, no doubt, given unlimited power, glory and divinity, but he is subject to control arising from the name of the divinity, influence of the leading people and fear of mutiny and revolt. As for instance, the wicked king Vena of the Vairaja dynasty was killed, Trisanku of the solar line was dethroned and banished. The great monarch Rama Chandra was compelled to banish his beloved wife Sita by the clamour of his people. In the *Little Toy Cart* (first century AD) the king is dethroned for tyranny by a cowherd.

The Duties of the King

He is to act in his own realm with justice, chastise foreign foes with vigour, behave without duplicity to his friends and with leniency to the Brahmans from whom he is to learn respectfully lessons of modesty and composure, justice, policy, metaphysics, and theology. From the people, he must learn agriculture, commerce and other particulars.

He must be a man of excellent character. He shall constantly take care of his subjects, keep off all thieves, protect all beings, punish those who stray from the path of duty. He should not injure trees that bear flowers and fruits, unless it be to extend cultivation. He must guard against the falsification of measures and weights of things necessary for households. He should not take for his own use, property belonging to his subjects.

The Habits of the King

He must rise early; perform sacrifice; hold court in a decent and splendid hall; dismiss his subjects with kind looks and words. His council is to be held in a secret place without listeners. Then he should take manly exercises and bath; dine in his private apartments. This time and midnight are to be allotted to the regulation of his family appointments and other business of a personal nature. Next come relaxation, review of troops, religious duties at sunset, receiving the reports of his emissaries, supper, music. Next, he shall retire to rest. 'This picture is quite rational and pleasing' (Elphinstone).

Capital

The king is directed to build his capital in a fertile part, difficult of access and unfit to support invading armies. His fortress is to be well-garrisoned and provisioned: his palace is to be in the centre, defensible, well-furnished and brilliant, surrounded with water and trees. His queen must be noted for birth and beauty. Let him employ a chaplin to perform the rites of the royal house. In front of the palace there shall be an 'Assembly House' with doors on the north and the south to command look, both in and out. Fires shall burn constantly and oblations offered in these fires. The state guests, at least those who are learned in the sacred lore, should be put up in the Hall.

Rooms, a couch, meat and drink, should be given to them according to their good qualities. A table with dice should also be provided. Dancing, singing and music are allowed in the house of the king's servants.

The king must have strong guards to look after his person. Precautions should be taken about food, reception of emissaries. Female attendants should be searched. He must be always on his guard against plots of his enemies.

The king was the executive head. His ministers managed the departments generally. The treasury and the country were under the king himself. Police and army kept order. The king and his kinsmen were ever alive to all calls of distress and dangers from unfriendly natives or other foes. The king had to attend court every day. He would not leave the palace except on chase, worship or war. Presents, sowing of dissensions, negotiation and force of arms were the arts to be employed against enemies.

WAR AND ARMS

We have already said that even at that early age there were different Aryan kingdoms—Turanian states, Sudra states, Dravidian dominions, and the Nishada territories, i.e. Tibeto-Burman states. These states, while unequal, were independent, powerful and civilised. So, there was a great need of a foreign department and each state had one. This military department was conducted by the war minister or ambassador. Under the Aryan policy of dealing with an enemy, the king was strictly enjoined to fight hard, even alone. Spies were employed in foreign politics and in war. The rules of war were simple. The plan of a campaign was like that of the Greeks or early Romans. The army was composed of cavalry, infantry, elephants, and chariots.

The king must show example of valour to his troops, encourage them with short but animated speeches. Prize property goes to the person who took it. General prizes should be distributed amongst troops.

The laws of war were honourable and just. No unequal combat or slaughter was allowed. Other prohibitions were still more generous. The settlement of a conquered land was conducted on equally liberal principles—an assurance of immediate security was proclaimed. The religion and laws of the country were to be maintained and respected. If confident of trust, a prince of the old royal family was to be placed on the throne and was to hold his kingdom as a dependence on the conqueror. Such were the war laws of our remote ancestors who then lived not very far from the Assyrians whose monarchs boasted that they had covered the city walls with the skins of the conquered flayed alive! The Hindu army was generally maintained by grant of lands or assignments. The monarchy descended undivided to one son, probably to him whom his father regarded most worthy. Primogeniture was not always maintained. The other princes were given large estates or minor kingdoms.

Bow, arrow, sword, shield, helmet, armour, target, and fire-arms were used in the war. The *Rig Veda* I, 140. 10; 11, 39.4; IV, 53.2 refer to armours. *R.V.*, II, 34.3 refers to golden helmets. *R.V.* IV, 39.4 refers to armour for the shoulders or arms, perhaps a shield. A javelin (rishti) is compared to the lightning in *R.V.*, V, 52.6; V, 54.II. Also, sword or battle-axe is so compared. Bows, arrows and quivers are mentioned in *R.V.*, V, 57.2. Three thousand warriors are spoken of in VI, 27.6. Feathered sharp-pointed shining shafts are described in VI, 46. II. Sharp-edged swords are mentioned in VI, 47.10. War chariots and war drums are mentioned in VI, 47.26; VI, 47.29. In the *Rig Veda*, VI, 75, we have a spirited account of the arms and accoutrements of war. IV, 2.8 refers to horses with golden caparisons. We have spirited accounts of the war horse in VI, 46. 13–14. The war horses were so highly prized in the battle that we find their worship under the name of *dadhikra*. The *Rig Veda*, IV, 38 gives us a spirited account of the respect paid to this noble helper.

The *Rig Veda* I, 100. 18; I, 103.3; I, 104. 3–4; I, 130.8; I, 133, 2–5; I, 174.7–8; I, 182.4; II, 20.6–7; IV, 38. 5–8; IV, 28.4; IV, 30.15; V, 70.3; VI, 18.3; VI, 25.2; VI, 47.20; V, 29.10; VIII, 96.13–15; X, 22.8 describes the Indo-Aryan wars with the natives.

The *Rig Veda*, X, 173, refers to the coronation of kings which gradually developed into pompous ceremonies. The *Rig Veda*, VI, 47, contains an address to the war-drum on the eve of battle *R.V.*, X, 49.7 gives the triumph of Indra over the natives.

ADMINISTRATION OF JUSTICE

Justice is administered by the king in person, helped by counsellors or assessors. He is expected to take a more active part in criminal than in civil cases. In distant courts, king's representative fills his place. The king is allowed five per cent on all debts admitted by the defendants and ten per cent on all denied and proved. This fee perhaps goes to the judges. The king is to observe the look, gestures mode of speech of the parties and witnesses, local usages, peculiar laws of classes, rules of families and customs of traders, and also the precedents of former judges.

The king or his officers are not to encourage litigation, yet show no slackness to take up any suit duly constituted. A king must afford protection to the people from whom he receives revenue; he must not decide cases without consulting the persons learned in the law; nor disturb any transaction once settled legally. In trials, he is to stick to the established practice.

Criminal Law

The criminal laws of the age appear to have been rude and unfair, but not generally bloody, like those of Draco. Torture was never employed either against criminals or their witnesses. Punishments, though not so severe, were however quite disproportionate to the offence. Adultery was not only regarded as a crime and sin, but also as an offence of a heinous nature. So, it was discouraged. Capital punishment was for murder committed intentionally. Small thefts were punished by fines; thefts of greater value, with cutting off the hand. If caught with the stolen goods, the punishment was capital. The receiver of stolen goods and those who harboured criminals, were punished severely. Robbery was punished with the amputation of the limb; for violent robbery, there was capital punishment. Death was the punishment for forging royal edicts. False evidence was regarded as a mortal sin; nay, later on, it even involved the loss of caste. So, it was utterly discouraged. The literature of no nation contained more earnest injunctions to speak the truth. Truth, Sanskrit *satya*, literally means the very existence, being derived from root *as*, 'to be'. Fine was the punishment for defamation, abusive language, ordinary assaults. If any bone was broken by assault, banishment was the punishment. The right of self-defence was allowed against an incendiary, a poisoner, a slayer, a robber, a forcible seizer of land, and a stealer of wife. Suitable fines were imposed for rash driving and defilement of highways. Ministers taking bribes had their property confiscated.

Fines were extended to doctors for want of skill, breaking idols, frauds in goods. Goldsmith's fraud was met with being cut into pieces by a razor. The rules of police were harsh and arbitrary. Gamestes, public dancers and singers, revilers of scriptures, open heretics, persons not doing their prescribed duties, wine vendors were to be instantly banished from the town. Crimes against agriculture and trade were justly punished with the greatest severity, as in India, these two are the chief means of human subsistence. Suicide was highly discouraged: laws prohibited even funeral rites for such cases.

The prerogative of mercy could be exercised by the king alone.

As for the cruelty of these laws, it may be observed that practice differed from the theory. The civilised and sensible Aryan judges of learning, age, experience, pure descent, clever reasoning, exercised the laws intelligently. They enforced the laws with severity only in cases of refractory and very harmful criminals. Moreover, the laws were aimed at establishing Aryan supremacy over the natives. In civilised Great Britain, up to AD 1808, death was the punishment for stealing only five shillings. That year, the number of such deaths ran over several thousands. So, the House of Commons submitted a Bill for the repeal of the Act to the House of Lords. But the latter rejected the Bill. After repeated efforts, the Act was repealed in 1812. Is it reasonable to believe that the Indo-Aryans whose war-laws were so humane, were barbarous and unfair in their criminal laws without a noble motive? The motive was the good of the society. 'Fields and gardens, unweeded, seldom thrive.' The great and silent moral force that lies behind such seemingly severe laws, is what has made the Hindus, the Greeks and the British people great and good.

Civil Law

The civil laws of the early Hindus were superior, rational and mature for so early an age. Trial was held in the open court. Oath against false evidence was administered in the strongest terms for witnesses and even parties. The law of evidence was like that of England. White lies and necessary lies were made light of. Appeals to ordeal were admitted. There were eighteen different kinds of disputes. Principal titles of law imply an advanced stage of culture and civilisation. Money-lending was in vogue. Interest was allowed from two per cent to five per cent. Interest was half on pledge and nil if the pledge was serviceable to the creditor. There were rules regarding interest on money lent for a sea voyage and on similar risk by land. Rishis occasionally lamented their state of indebtedness (*R.S., IV, 24.9*).

The boundaries of village were marked by natural objects. Lands were leased as now. Provisions were made for undisturbed agriculture. Laws about the right of way were fair. Evidence in disputes regarding immovable property consisted of documents, possession and witnesses. The property of minors and widows was administered by the king as long as necessary.

The Law of Inheritance

To leave a male issue was regarded as a religious duty by the early Hindus. This had led to the strange custom of appointing childless widows and even unmarried daughters to raise the child. A widow was allowed to bear a son by her brother-in-law or by a kinsman or even by a caste-fellow. Exogamy was allowed. Some of the sons were heirs while others only members of the family. The following were the different kinds of sons—*Aurasha*, a legitimate son; *Jaraja*, a son begotten by the wife; *Dattaka*, an adopted son; *Kritrima*, a son made; *Gudhaja*, a son born secretly, and *Apaviddha*, a son abandoned. These might inherit the estate, while *Kanina*, the son of an unmarried damsel; *Sahodha,* the son of a pregnant bride; *Paunarbhava*, the son of a twice-married woman; *Putrika-putra*, the son of an appointed daughter; *Swayamdatta*, a son self-given; and *Krita*, a son bought, belonged to the family. A brotherless maiden was given a male name, a practice still prevalent in Kashmir. The second marriage of a woman was allowed in case of insanity, impotency, loss of caste, death of her husband before consummation. Her children could inherit. The father might distribute his wealth among his sons (*R.V., I, 114*). No will is ever alluded to. In joint families, after the father, the eldest brother was to feed and protect all. The following were excluded from inheritance—eunuchs, outcastes, those born deaf and dumb or blind, one losing a limb, the insane and idiots. These must be maintained by the heirs. The sons of such excluded persons, however, were capable of inheriting.

Ordinarily, the sons would inherit the property of a person. In default of a son, the daughter's son, was the heir (*R.V., III and VII*).

There were also laws for the partition of property among brothers. The law of primogeniture was never maintained in India. The shares were not equal; the eldest son got a little more than the others.

AGRICULTURE

The word Arya (Aryan)originated in Central Asia and meant 'cultivator', as distinguished from the Turanian, noted for their nomadic habits. These people were noted for their rapid journeys or the fastness of their horse. In India also, the old meaning of Aryan is found in R.V., I, 117.21. Also *Charshana* (*I, 3.7*) and *Krishti* (*I, 4.6*) meant cultivator. Here, the majority of the Indians were the *Nishadas* (hunters) who lived on games alone. The Sanskrit dictionary explains the word Aryan as *swami* = lord and *Vaisya* = cultivator. Needless to say that the first meaning of lord, noble or excellent people is derived from its true second meaning.

India is chiefly an agricultural country. Agriculture became the main industry of the Indo-Aryans. A hymn is addressed to the Lord of the Field (*R.V., IV, 57. I–10*). Another hymn is dedicated to agriculture (*R.V., X, 101. 3–7*).

The north-west parts of India enjoy little rain, as they lie beyond the monsoon area. So, irrigation was employed in cultivation. In the midland, the summer harvest got plenty of rain and flood; but the winter crops required irrigation. The fields were fed from rivers, brooks, ponds, lakes, and tanks through canals (*R.V.X, 68. I; and X, 99.4*). Water was raised out of the wells by means of well-wheels, called *ghati-chakra* or *araghatta* and used for fields and drinking (*R.V., X, 25.4 X, 93.13*).

With the Indo-Aryans, agriculture was a simple art. Their implements also were very simple: a plough (Sanskrit *phala*), a pair of oxen, buffaloes or horses, a hoe, a mattock, and sickle. The grain was trodden by the cattle. The fields were generally unenclosed. Agriculture required some special skill and industry. The cultivators had to eradicate weeds from the fields. Manure was used little except for sugar cane and some other crops. Some fields had to be fenced with mud-walls or prickly plants. Birds were frightened away from the corn by scare-crows, loud cries and throwing stones from slings. They understood the soil and season well; guarded against the following evils—excessive rain, drought, mice, locusts, parrots, and armies. Agriculture and agricultural produce were ever held sacred among the Hindus.

In the *Rig Veda*, allusions are made to the pasture. Pushan was the god of the shepherds. In a hymn to Pushan, recollection and songs of migrations in Central Asia are preserved (*I, 42. 1–10*).

One hymn refers to the practice of taking out cattle to the pasturage and bringing them back (*X, 19. 4–6*).

There are allusions to robbers, cattle-lifters and thieves who infested the outlying tracts of the country, around the villages and clearances, and who lived by disturbing peaceful industry.

Barley, wheat, rye, pulses, sesame, sugar cane, grapes, various succulent roots and fruits were chiefly cultivated. Vrihi (rice) was not yet known.

The Europeans and the Indo-Iranians come of the same Aryan stock. Yet, behold their difference now: they shine, we pine; they work, we dream. They plough the deep, play with the waves and extract all good things from the different parts of the earth, while we shrink from the *kalapani* (black waters of the sea) and nestle in narrow nooks to croak in spite. And, why so? Because Europe is by nature a very powerful continent, while India is probably on the whole a bad land for the Aryans to live in. Our poets and dreamers have described India as a veritable paradise on earth, flowing with milk, and honey shining with pearls and gold and ever blessed with good waters, good fruits and good grains. But more exact investigations reveal the fact that it is a country of countries, a land of strange extremes. It has at least six distinct regions, viz., Kashmir, called a *bhu-swarga*, i.e. earthly paradise; the rainless desert; the midland; the Himalayas; the over-humid Indo-Malayan region; and the Deccan. A curious blending of the natural forces is found in the Indians who are apparently alike but really different. So, the country as a whole has never known unity. Geologically speaking, the Deccan is the oldest part of the country, north India being a much later upheaval. India is however rich in soil, vegetable and mineral products, navigable rivers and long coastlines (seldom indented). These advantages have produced religion and philosophy, arts and industries, commerce and colonies ever admired by all while the natural defects have worked a world of woes for the people. Our ancestors had entered India not through choice or love, but under a painful necessity.

The prosperity of a country depends to a great extent on the judicious partition of lands amongst all classes of people. This idea gained in India from the earliest times. Lands were leased as at present.

Such is the climatic condition of India that occasional famines are inevitable. The earliest famine we have on record, occurred during the reign of King Prithu of the Vairaja Dynasty (twenty-nineth century BC). Though that good king fought hard, general distress and loss of lives were very great. From that time, Prithu gave a great impetus to cultivation. His example was followed in the other Aryan states. The horrors of this famine may have been particularly in Manu's mind when he often alluded to the times of distress.

NATIONALISM

In the Vedic age, a nation was formed by caste, creed, colour, and affinity of blood. The descendants of one great person formed a clan. Nationalism was personal and not territorial. This idea is still prevalent amongst all the Aryans of the world. A Brahman of India, wherever he be in the world, lives in his own way. So does an Englishman. This helps development and dispersion of the race. The first Aryan nationalism was hence originated in its clan. Many clans then formed a tribe and many tribes made a race or nation. The Indo-Aryans called Aryavarta their own, but yet territorial nationalism was not distinct. In time, when the aliens gradually came under the Aryan influence, then, through cohesion and coordination, a new nationality was formed. The Aryans had no feudalism. They had it from the Scythians, Huns and other native people.

The early Indo-Aryans of the Punjab had owned five lands (*Pancha Kshiti*) along the Indus (*R.V., I, 7.9; I, 76.3; VI, 46.7*). They were probably the *Pancha Krishti*, the 'five cultivating tribes' of the *Rig Veda, II, 2.10; IV, 38.10* and elsewhere. The 'five tribes' (*Pancha jana*) also appear from the *Rig Veda, VI, 11.4; VI, 51.11; VIII, 32.22; IX, 65.23* and elsewhere.

These five tribes of the Punjab and the other later tribes of the Aryans living in Aryavarta first formed the Indo-Aryan nation from which afterwards grew the great Hindu nation of India.

SOCIAL LIFE

The Caste System

The most distinctive feature of the Hindu society is its caste system. A stranger will naturally be inclined to ask, 'How early did it originate? Was it ever hereditary and bound by the same rigid rules?' And so forth. To answer these question, we must discuss these points. The Aryans of Central Asia knew no caste. The Indo-Aryans also in the first two centuries of their Indian life, knew it not. The only Rig-Vedic hymn that distinctly refers to the four castes is *X, 90.12* which is in fact a much later compostion. 'At first, there was no caste' (*Mahabharata, Peace Book*). Certain it is that the caste system as we have it now, or as appears from the Code of Manu did not exist in the Vedic age. Professor Max Müeller says: 'If then, with all the documents before us, we ask the question, does caste, as we find it in Manu and at the present day, form part of the most ancient religious teaching of the Vedas? We can answer with a decided No.' (*Chips from a German Workshop, Vol. II, p. 307, 1867*).

'There are no castes as yet, the people are still one united whole and bear but one name, that of *Visas*.' (Weber, *Sanskrit Literature, p. 38*). There is, however, evidence to show that caste in its most pliant and natural form, did exist in the Vedic age. The etymology of the four castes, gives the history of their origin.

In Central Asia, the word 'Brahmana' at first meant 'one expert in the religious rites'. Cf. *Mahabharata:* 'Mangah Brahmana-bhuyisthah' i.e. Mongolia had many Brahmanas. After the discovery of *Brahman* (the Supreme Being) by the Sage Narayana (see *ante*), the rishis and the devas became 'Brahmanas', i.e. knowers of *Brahman.*

From the counsels of Narada to Mandhata in the *Mahabharata*, it appears that formerly all were Brahmanas. (Cf. *Mahabharata, Wood Book, Ajagara Parva* and also *Padma Purana, Heaven Part, Chapter 25–27*). The earliest distinction that the Indo-Aryans had made between themselves and the natives, was one of varna (colour). The Indo-Aryans called themselves Svitnya, white and the natives Krishna-twach, dark (*R.V., I, 100.18*). Besides, there were possibly the Varna-sankaras, i.e. mingled colours.

Elphinstone rightly thinks that the caste system and other peculiarities rose from their situation without premeditation or design (*History of India,* 9th *ed, pp. 54–55*).

Some modern thinkers hold that the Indo-Aryans had started it to 'stop further mingling with the native blood' and to bring society to better order. Some call it a splendid organisation, citing its wonderful persistence as a proof, while others denounce it as pernicious.

All traditions point to its origin at Prithudaka (now, Pehoa, fourteen miles to the west of Thaneswar), capital of Prithu of happy memory, on the sacred River Saraswati (twenty-nineth century BC or beginning of the twenty-eighth century, *Mahabharata, Peace Book*).

Brahmavarta, modern Bithoor, was the scene of the earliest adventurers and a home of the most distinguished sages. The model institutions, lofty morals, pure manners, learning, and wisdom of Bithoor were so praiseworthy and attractive that even the devas of the north would often come down there to learn, nay with noble envy they even desired birth or life there. Out of high regard and admiration, Manu also in his *Code* (twenty-eighth century BC) had urged all to imitate the good morals and customs of the Brahmans of Bithoor.

Needless to say, Manu had organised his own kingdom of Kosala after Bithoor. Hence, we hear of pure manners of ancient Oudh and corrupt manners of the other Aryan states.

Thus we see, the Brahmans, i.e. all the worthy Aryans, especially of Bithoor were then looked upon with an eye of superiority and reverence. The Kshatriya and Visas grew out of the Brahmanas. Valmiki gives a very nice example: 'Fire was evolved out of waters, Kshatra from the Brahmana, and iron from the rock. These are powerful everywhere except their origin.' Kshatra or Kshatriya originally meant a saviour, a redresser of wrongs and is the same as the knight errant of early Europe. In India, the early Aryan settlers were often oppressed by the non-Aryan *dasyus* or *dasaa*. So, those warlike Aryans who would come with their kinsmen and companions to save the oppressed and punish the wrong-doers, were applauded with the glorious title of Kshatriya. It was at first a personal distinction and meant no king.

The class 'Vaisya' originated from *vis* or settlers (Sanskrit *Vispati*, Zend. *Vis-paiti* and Lith. *Wiez-patis* 'lord of the settlers'). Trade, cattle-rearing, cultivation, and money-lending became their noble profession. Even princes took to commerce.

Before 2800 BC, the Indo-Aryans lived in great political unrest. So, we find the same man as priest, warrior and cultivator. About 2800 BC, Indra, Vishnu and other new Aryan leaders had rid Aryavarta of all thorns and founded new states. Society now took a new turn. The same man was no more required to follow different pursuits in life. Experience made them wiser. They now adopted lifelong professions according to their taste and aptitude.

Now, some followed religion and studied exclusively: they became Brahmans. Some liked and followed religion, studies and war. They became Kshatriyas. Some liked trade and they became Vaisyas. The children of one and the same family might adopt one or other of those professions according to one's wish and aptitude. There were *professions* and not *castes* yet. There were inter-marriages and eating together.

The Brahmanas and the Kshatriyas were rather few; the Vaisyas formed the mass of the Aryan community. A good number of the freedom-loving Dravidians marched eastward to Bengal and thence to Kalinga and founded powerful kingdoms there. Few of those who had surrendered, were admitted by the Aryans as rishis and warriors. A good number became Vaisyas and the rest ranked as Sudras. The outcastes or fallen Aryans were also classed as Sudras. Thus, the Sudras were not originally a *race* but a lightless class.

The first three orders were dwija or 'twice-born', while the Sudras were regarded as 'once-born'. The first three orders were almost equally privileged. The Sudras were not allowed to study the Vedas or perform religious sacrifices. They were, however, at liberty to learn by listening to discourses, earn money by service, trade or industrial pursuits. The old and worthy of them were honoured and consulted. We even hear of powerful Sudra kingdoms.

Century after century, the professions based on taste and aptitude, gradually condensed into castes. It is not the Brahmans or the codes that have converted the professions into castes. Practice and experience wrought out the change. Modern science says that heredity, education and experience go to make a man successful in his profession.

Often, we hear of the despised Sudra. Was his condition a really degraded one? We have seen that the peaceful, inoffensive and dull Dravidian converts were generally called the Sudras. The *Rig Veda*, Manu and the Puranas record instances of Sudra kings. Certainly they were independent Dravidian rulers. It does not appear that the Sudras were a depressed class. Their merit was always appreciated. Generally, they served with the three superior classes. But they could live by handicrafts, masonry, painting, writing. EB Cowell adds the following important note: 'The position of a Sudra was infinitely preferable to that of a helot, the slave or the serf of the Greeks, the Romans and the feudal system. He was free; his services were optional and not agricultural, but domestic and personal and claimed adequate compensations. He could lay by wealth. He had the opportunity of rising to rank. He might study and even teach religious knowledge. Even a Brahman could get pure knowledge from a Sudra.' (Manu, *II, 238*). He might perform religious acts (Manu, *X, 128*; see Elphinstone's *History of India, pp. 121–31*; also *Vishnu Purana, p. 292* and Mill Wilson, *Note I, 194*).

Besides these four castes, there was a large class called the Nishadas (hunters). They are no more nomads, no more cruel hunters, but have long taken to peaceful and civilised life. Yet, it is curious to note that after so many anti-caste movements and religious revolutions, these pre-Dravidian races still form the lowest strata of Hindu society, and number over seventy per cent. They are regarded as untouchables.

As days wore on, the caste-rules became rigid, till they were declared hereditary at Benaras around 1200 BC. From the original four castes rose six, then thirty-six. Now castes are too numerous to be enumerated. The diversity has been due to intermarriage, Hinduisation and professions. In the course of several centuries, the system became established in the Indo-Gangetic Valley. It prevailed there long. The early Aryan tribes on the west of the Indus, the Aryan offshoots in the east and south India did not fully accept the system. So, they were often denounced by the law-givers of the middle country. Outside India, the Parsees and the Egyptians had adopted the four castes. Alexander and his generals found the caste system in Egypt (330 BC). Plato may have had a hint from the Hindus in making his 'divisions of labour.' The Chinese also have four division or groups of the people, though not exactly like our castes.

Prithudaka, Kanouj, Benaras, and Mithila were the chief centres of Brahmanical religion and culture. The Sarasvata Brahmans were the best in the Vedic age. Next came Kanouj. The Kanouj Brahmans are still regarded as the best in India.

The position of the Brahmans, though often assailed, was very high, as they were counsellors of the kings, teachers of the people, writers of extraordinary merit, and thinkers of very great truths.

What a grand example the Brahmans are to the world! Not only are the Brahmans a superior class of the Hindus, but they are also leaders of the nation. The Egyptians and the Assyrians are gone. The Aryans of western Asia and Europe have fallen from their old faith and customs. The Aryans in India alone still remain unchanged. The Brahmans have preserved the nation and its traditions. Invasions from without and rise of atheistical religions could do the nation no great harm. India has suffered politically only through the barbarous rivalry of her princes and not for any fault of the Brahmans.

The caste-system has not been a bar to outsiders coming within the Hindu pale. From a handful of Aryans has grown up the Hindu nation. From the Indo-Chinese frontier in the east to Ladakh in Kashmir, the slow process of HInduisation still goes on. The Greeks, Parthians, Scythians, Turks, Huns, and Kushans who had settled in India, became gradually absorbed in the Hindu population. Several centuries before

Christ, the sages of Abu (Rajputana) initiated new warriors known as the Agni-kula, i.e. fire-clan, to fight their enemies. These were the Chauhans and others. Akbar sought to Hinduise the Moguls, but did not succeed. He himself lived almost as a Hindu.

Food and Drink

Wheat, barley, milk, honey, roots, fruits, and animal flesh were the chief foods. They knew no rice yet. The fried barely (Rig-Vedic *dhana*) was used as food and offered to the gods. Various cakes were prepared from those grains, used as food and offered to the gods. *Pakti* (prepared cakes), *purodasa* (bread), *apupa* (pudding), and *karambha* were also used (*R.V., III, 52.I; IV, 24.7*).

Animal food was largely used. We find frequent allusions to the sacrifice and cooking of cows, buffaloes and bulls (*R.V., I, 61, 12; II, 7.5; V, 29.7–8; VI, 17.11; VI, 16.47; VI, 28.4; X, 27.2; X, 28.3*).

The *Rig Veda* X, 89. 14 mentions slaughter houses where cows were killed. In the *Rig Veda*, the cow is declared *aghnya*, i.e. not to be killed. Yet, in practice, the use of beef was general. In X, 91.41 there is an allusion to the sacrifice of bulls, horses and rams. The sacrifice of horse was extremely rare. The customs was brought from Central Asia, but in India, horse flesh as a food, soon fell into disuse. Later on, horse sacrifice was performed on rare occasions by emperors.

The *Rig Veda* (*I, 162.2–11, 13–18–20*) gives an account of the horse sacrifice. The carving, roasting, boiling of the horse for worship and food gradually developed into the 'imperial horse sacrifice'! In the Vedic age, all rites and institutions rose from simple natural beginnings.

Meat is prohibited in modern *sraddha* ceremony. But then, all sorts of flesh, especially beef, were a great delicacy with the best Brahmans. There was no prohibition against eating with other classes or taking of food cooked by them. Even the food cooked by a Sudra was acceptable to the gods and the seers.

The Indo-Aryans not only used the fermented *soma* juice but also liquors made from molasses and grapes. They were much addicted to drinking. They even worshipped soma. About one-fourth of Book IX, *Rig Veda* is dedicated to the praise of soma. The Indo-Aryans were more addicted than the Parsees whom they ridiculed as asura, i.e. people without wine.

Haoma (soma) of course, was known to the Iranians. The *Zend Avesta* has many allusions to this hateful custom of the Indians. The Indra puja of the Indo-Aryans was mainly a bacchanalian feast. This chiefly led to the Indo-Iranian separation. The process of preparing the soma drink is described in the *Rig Veda*, IX, 66.2–13; IX, 108.3; IX, 110.8; IX, 113.9.

Dress, Ornaments, Manners

In Central Asia, the Aryans certainly used very warm clothing made of wool and fur. In India, wool, fur, bark, i.e. fibres of plants, cotton, silk, fine threads from insects, were used for making dresses. The women wore an under-garment called *nibi*, over which they wore a cloth. The use of bodice was common. Women even then wore a veil. The use of coloured clothes seems to have been general. We cannot say why the rishis discouraged the use of blue and deep red clothes, especially by women. Clothes had fine borders called *tusha*. Their ends were called *dasa*. Besides ordinary cotton clothes (*dhutis*), they had fine saris. Though the upper part of the body was covered with half the cloth, yet *drapi* (a sewed cloak) and tarnya (a fine coat) were used. Warf was tantu, woof was *beman* and loom was called *tasara*. The embroidered cloth of women was called pesas and was only used by women while dancing (*R.V., I, 92.4–5*). The dancing of gentlewomen had long fallen into disuse. So, in Bengal, *nati* meant a harlot. Modern *pesakar* (prostitute) may be the Vedic pesakari, a woman who would use the poetry of the needle on cloth used in dance.

Wool (Sanskrit, *urna*) was much used. An uncoloured woollen sheet was called *pandwa*; that sewed was called *samulaya*; that with sewed margin was called *sich*.

The modern shawl is perhaps derived from the Vedic samulaya. Samula was a woollen shirt. The avi, wool of the sheep and ajina, wool of the goat made the chief warm clothing. Ajina afterwards meant a goat's skin, a deer skin, even a tiger's skin. The sheep of Gandhar were noted for their plenteous wool.

In the Aryan community, both men and women had head-dress, in some provinces at least (*Aitareya* and *Satapatha Brahmana*). Indrani also had a head-dress (*Atharva Veda, XV, 2.13*). The *Yajur Veda* states that kings, while performing sacrifices, used a head-dress. In performing religious rites, cloves that were sewed, burnt, moth or rat-eaten, another's, old, and tattered were forbidden to be used.

There were different dresses for different seasons. In winter, all used a shirt or coat called nishara. Nichola was a fancy female dress. Ironing (vahni saucha vastra) was known. An embroidered cloth was called rukma-patta. Pandu kamvala or karu-patta is our English carpet; kantha was a kind of quilt then. Kutha was a rich hanging for the elephant. Patamandapa was tent or camp. Masahari, mosquito-curtain was not known. A medicated fume was used to drive away pests. Tents were used by the kings while out on hunt. Kanda-pata, a tent, was used by the ladies. Vitana (awning), very dear to the Aryans, was used in feasts, ceremonies.

The washerman was called managa and the dyer, rajaka. Bapta (from baptri), English barber, used kshura (razor) made of good iron. The rishis and their wives prayed for plenty of hair on their heads (*Atharva Veda, VI, 136.37*). They took special care for the luxuriant growth and dressing of the hair. Both men and women used to have long hair. The men of the Vasista family were especially noted for their long hair. The *Satapatha Brahmana*, V, 1. 2. 14 states that it is not fair for men to wear long hair, as that gives an air of softness and effeminacy. Sikha (a tuft of hair on the crown) was not possibly known, for the word first occurs in the *Satapatha Brahmana*.

Usually, the hair of the women was well combed and put in braids. Only during the days of impurity caused by a relation's death, or the absence of their husbands, women were to leave their hair loose and flowing.

Even some men had braids. Kaparda (a braid) was worn by Vasista, Rudra and Pushan, when a long and loose braid was called pulasti. Almost all had such pulastis. Unmarried girls had four minor braids put together in coils. Loose hair tied into a knot, was called opasa (*R.V.* and *A.V.*)

The parting of the hair was called siman. After nicely dressing the hair, the women put on flowers on the head. An ornament named Kurira was used to hold the braid tight. The thorns of porcupine also were used for the same purpose.

A looking-glass called prakasa was in common use. Professor Macdonell has explained this Rig-Vedic prakasa as a highly glazed metal used for a mirror. We think, kacha (glass) was known, as early Egypt supplied it everywhere.

The Indo-Aryans used various kinds of shoes of thick soles made from the hides of various animals. Even the hide of boar was used to make shoes (*Satapatha Brahmana*). Wooden shoes were also used. There is no allusion to the use of shoes by the women in the Vedic age.

A leafed umbrella called chhatra was in use. Ornaments appear to have been numerous in the Vedic age. Their shapes cannot be imagined now. There were flowers for the head, ornaments for the braid. Some ornaments were used by both men and women such as, earrings and finger-rings, etc. Nyochani is our modern nose-ring. Mani, what was it and where was it worn? We have references to anji (?); srak, necklace; rukma, a golden breastplate or perhaps our modern hasuli; khadi, bracelets and anklets—(Rig Veda *V, 53.4; V, 54.11*). Khadi has corrupted into our kharu. Nishka is described as an ornaments in the *Rig Veda* IV, 37.4; V. 19.3. and I, 126.2. The gold coins *nishka* were stringed together and worn as a necklace. In India, pieces of coins are still used as ornament round the neck. The Rig-Vedic mani is a diamond. This could be bored, stringed and worn about the neck as a lace called mani-griva. Vimukta is the Vedic name for the later mukta (pearl). Like the mani, its use also was among the rich. Various ornaments were made from sankha (conch shell). Srinka was a beautiful necklace called hara. A lace of pearls was called a mukta-vali. The rajas used to wear diamond earrings. Rich ladies had gold earrings set with diamond and beryl (vaidurya). Some of the gems and jewels were known and used. A bridegroom also used ornaments and perfumes (*Rig Veda V, 60.4*). Sandalwood, saffron, red-dye and musk were used.

The manners of the Rig-Vedic Hindus were civilised if not refined. The position of women was high and honourable. There were different forms of salutation and civility to persons of all classes and relations. There was great respect for parents and aged, for learning and moral conduct, for wealth and rank.

Domestic Life

The Indo-Aryans mostly lived in joint-families (*Rig Veda I, 114*). The husband and wife were called dampati, i.e. lords of the house. The position of women was very high and honourable. They assisted at the sacrifices at home, ordered the necessary ingredients, prepared them with pestle and mortar, extracted the *soma* juice and strained it. Wives joined their lords and performed the sacrifices together, offered oblations, hoped to go to heaven together (*Rig Veda I, 131.3; V, 43.15; VIII, 31.5–9*). The cultured women called rishis composed hymns and performed sacrifices like men. There was no seclusion for them, they were on an equal footing with men. There is mention of veiled wives and brides. Women exercised their influence on society. The had legitimate spheres of action. They were expert in housekeeping, weaving, training their children, and cooking. They were devoted to their husbands, religion, learning, and domestic duties (*Rig Veda I, 124.4*). Chastity and thrift were regarded as the chief domestic virtues. We have occasional references to women gone astray (*II, 29.1*). We hear of maidens who had no brothers to watch over their morals, of faithless wives (*IV, 55; X, 34.4*). The wife of a ruined gambler became the object of other men's lust (X, 34.4).

Hindu parents were generally very affectionate. It appears that the women had some rites, ceremonies and vows peculiar to them, such as the worship of the goddess Sasthi. The majority of women, though ignorant of letters, were good wives, wise mothers, obedient daughters, model sisters, and clever mistresses. Girls were generally taught at home.

Marriage

The marriage ceremony signified a holy union, sacred bond—the taking of a helpmate to perform the sacred duties of life. Early marriage was unknown except perhaps in the cases of good girls taken from the non-Aryans and that also, to prevent premarital unchastity. *Rig Veda, X, 85. 21–27* and *40–47* allude to marriage after puberty.

The girls seem to have had some voice in the selection of their husbands, though such selections were often very unhappy. There is reference to swayamvara (self-choice of a husband) probably in the cases of most accomplished princesses (*X, 27.12*). Parents generally controlled the marriages of children. Some young men took to religion and never married. Even some girls took the vow of celibacy, devoted themselves to religion, lived in the father's house, claimed and had a share in the property! (II, 17.7). Princess Brinda, daughter of a king named Kedara, by his queen Trailokya Mohini, lived in a wood near Mathura, ever unmarried but ever devoted to religion. She had guards and attendants with her. Her penance-grove afterwards became known as *Brindabana*, held sacred even to this day. These tracts on the Jamuna, as meeting grounds for peaceful ascetics and the cattle, were known to the Rig-Vedic seers (*V, 52.17*). The very hill Govardhana means a nurse of cattle.

Marriage was always desired with worthy bridegrooms. Ornaments, dress and wealth had to be given as dowry (*R.V., IX, 46.2; X, 39.14*). A bridegroom also used ornaments and perfumes (*V, 60.4*). Marriage fee (modern *pana*) and rich dowry were in use. King Svanaya married his ten daughters to Kakshivan and gave him as dowry (*V, 125. I*). In marriage, there were sports, amusements, song, dance, music, and feast (*R.V., III, 51.7* and *Kaushitaki Brahmana*). Fancy dresses of bride and bridegroom were in use. Bigamy and polygamy were common in kings and rich men. Of course, domestic quarrels arose from that (*X, 145; X, 159*). Polyandry was rare. The ten Pracheta brothers are said to have had a common wife. Instances of misogamist and fighting women were also rare. There were some hymns and rites about conception and childbirth (*V. 78. 7–9; X, 162; X, 183; X, 184*).

The remarriage of widows was a prevalent custom (X, 18.8). The words didhishu, husband of a widow; parapurva, a woman married a second time; paunarbhava, son of a woman by her second husband—also show this clearly. The second marriage of a woman was allowed when her husband left her for asceticism before consummation, when he turned mad, was banished for ever, fell from religion or became impotent. However, such marriages were inferior alternatives, seldom resorted to by higher classes.

The higher classes could take 'good wives' from inferior ranks and not vice versa. Intercourse with women of upper classes was severely punished. Their offspring was degraded far below the rank of either of its parents.

Marriage was allowed in *sagotra*, i.e. kinsmen—a thing so revolting to our modern notion. Usually, girls, younger in age, were married to men older in age; occasionally, the reverse was the case.

Perpetuity of the line being regarded as a norm of nature, women were allowed to bear the child of their brother-in-law or kinsfolk. Occasionally, on the failure of a male child, a person could take a second wife or more. A barren wife could be abandoned in the tenth year; one bearing daughters only in the 12th and one, all of whose children died, in the 15th. Abandonment was not divorce. The wife was still maintained in the family with all the honours. Tuning a good wife out of the house for no reason brought a great stigma on the family.

Considering the small number of the Indo-Aryans, the early legislators allowed exorgamy, i.e. marriage outside the clan. So, they recognised the following eight kinds of marriage:

(i) *Brahma* marriage—The father pours out a libation of water and gives his daughter to a suitor, a student.
(ii) *Daiva* marriage—The father decks his daughter with ornaments and gives her to an officiating priest, when sacrifice is being performed.
(iii) *Arsha* marriage—The father gives his daughter for a cow or bull.
(iv) *Prajapatya* marriage—The father gives away his daughter to the suitor, saying, 'Fulfil ye the law conjointly'.
(v) *Gandharva* marriage—A lover takes a loving damsel. This custom was prevalent in the country of Gandhara.
(vi) *Kshatra* marriage—A bridegroom forcibly takes a damsel, destroying her relatives by strength of arms.
(vii) *Manusha* or Asura marriage—A suitor buys a damsel from her father.
(viii) *Paisacha* marriage—Simply a form of rape, when the suitor embraces a woman deprived of her consciousness.

Of these, the *Brahma* marriage is the most approved form of Aryan marriage. In it, the wife brings a dowry to her husband. The bride enters a new family free and is on a basis of equality with the man. She brings him what she has. Thus, from the very beginning, she occupies a high and respected position in her husband's house.

The eight different kinds of marriage were allowed to maintain the pristine purity of the Indo-Aryan blood; to provide Aryan husbands for Aryan women, fewer than the males and rendered still fewer by the hot Indian climate and also by the practice of exposing superfluous female children during migrations, mentioned in the *Yajur Veda* and in a *Brahmana* work; to admit the non-Aryans into the Aryan pale by free admission, by inter-marriage and by the system of concubinage.

There are examples to show that princesses married sages and seers and the daughters of rishis also married kings. For instance, Devahuti married the sage Kardama; Sukanya, daughter of Saryati, granddaughter of Manu, married Chyavana. Again, Degayani daughter to Sukra, married the lunar king, Yayati. Kritivi married Aunha. Sasvati, daughter to Angiras married the saintly king, Asanga. It is needless to multiply examples.

The people of the age were generally happy, honest, simple, and truthful. All things were much larger in size than they are now. There was gold in every family. People lived to a good old age. 'Satayur-bai purushash' (the age of man is hundred years) says *Rig Veda*. This led to the popular belief that people in that age lived 400 years. There was another reason for this belief. Then a year had four seasons; three months made a season. Time was calculated according to seasons. The idea of a year, lunar or solar was gradually developed—100 x 4 = 400. In the far remote patriarchal age, a man lived 400 seasons which in ancient belief came to be called 400 years.

The law of inheritance, already discussed, appears from *R. V.*, III, 31. 1–2. The Law of Adoption from VII, 4. 7–8. Belief in future happiness is given in X, 14. 7.19. The *Rig Veda*, X, 18. 10–12 refers to burial. Cremation of the dead appears from X, 16.I.

Rite of Sati

We next come to the rite of sati. The word sati means a chaste wife. Professor Macdonell thinks it of very high antiquity, originating with the military chiefs at first and spreading to other classes afterwards. Another thinker explains it as a safeguard against wives taken from non-Aryan sources, going back to their original practices, when widowed. The *Rig Veda* knows it not. Its supposed reference in X, 18.7 arises from a wrong interpretation. Manu does not mention it.

The practice of sati does not necessarily imply the cremation of a widow with her deceased lord. I think its origin may be traced to the following fact; King Daksha ruled at Kanakhala, near modern Haridwar (twenty-nineth century BC). One of his daughters was married to Rudra. She was exceptionally devoted to her lord. On one occasion, Daksha was present in an assembly of the deva-Aryans of the north. Here, all but Rudra rose to greet him. Daksha keenly felt the insult from his own son-in-law. Some time after, Daksha began a sacrifice to which he invited all the devas but Rudra. The daughter, highly aggrieved, came to her father's house to ask why her father had shunned her lord. In reply,

Daksha blamed Rudra so severely that she was cut to the quick and died soon thereafter. Now, they all call her a true sati. After cremation, her relics were preserved and distributed. Here occurs the first instance of a sati in the very lifetime of her lord. The next instance was in the twenty-nineth century BC and concerned Archi, queen of Prithu of the Vairaja dynasty of Bithoor (*R. V., X, 14. 8*). A true sati may die when her lord is seriously ill or gone. They may be burnt together or separately. It should be borne in mind that death, however bold, makes no sati. Death may happen from shock, despair of nervous weakness. A true sati was marked for the lifelong devotion to her lord. She might not die with her lord; yet very great was her glory, honour and prospect of heavenly bliss. The instances of true satis, though rare, have been known in British rule also. In the Vedic age, the practice of sati was rare. It gradually developed into the later cruel custom nay, a barbarous practice. In modern times, women led by blind glory, committed wilful suicides in the name of sati, on the funeral pyres of their husbands. The British government has done a great service to humanity and civilisation by suppressing the sati rite.

The *sraddha* or the funeral ceremony is an ancient custom. In it, the bereaved fed a small number of learned men versed in the Vedas distinguished by learning and virtue and free from all evil. How unlike our modern practice! The *Vrishot-Sarga*, i.e. 'dedication of the bull' in this ceremony is a Vedic rite. This was meant for excellent cattle breeding.

Domestic Rites and Ceremonies

These are historically important as they give the manners and customs of our remote ancestors and also as they are still performed by us to a great extent.

Marriage

With the Hindus, marriage has never been a contract or a love-knot, but 'taking a helpmate for the performance of religious duties for the good of this world and the next'. In the modern times, the bride's party has to find a suitable youngman, but formerly, the bridegroom had to send messengers to the house of the girl's father, reciting verse X, 85.23 of the *Rig Veda*. The actual ceremony consisted in the following: 'The bridegroom holds the bride by the hand and leads her three times round a fire, reciting some verses as 'Come, let us marry. Let us beget offspring. Loving, bright, with genial mind, may we live a hundred autumns.'

Ceremonies during pregnancy of wife:

Garbhadhana was performed to secure conception. The *pumsavaṇa* was performed to determine the male sex of the child. *Garbha-rákshana* secured the child in the womb from harm. The *simantonnyana* consisted in the husband affectionately parting his wife's hair with certain rites.

Birth of child

Jata-karman is a birth ceremony. *Medha-jananam* is the production of intelligence and *ayushya*, rite for prolonging life. On this occasion, the parents give the child a secret name, known to them alone. On the tenth day when the mother gets up from childbed, a name for general use is given.

First feeding of the child with solid food

This, the well-known *anna-prasana*, is still observed. This rite is performed when the child is six months old. In olden times, a greater variety of food was allowed, such as goat's flesh, flesh of partridge, boiled rice with ghee, etc.

Tonsure of the child's head (Chuda-karana)

In the first or third year, the child's head was shaved with certain *mantras*, leaving some hair on the crown.

Cutting of the beard (Godana-karma or Kesanta)

Performed on the sixteenth or eighteenth year of the boy.

Initiation (Upanayana)

This important ceremony gave the true life to a 'twice-born' boy. Here began his study of the Veda and performance of sacrifices. With the assumption of a sacred thread or a gold chain, his first lesson in the Veda begins (*R.V., III, 62.10*). As the boys no more perform sacrifice nor study the Veda, this rite has become quite meaningless now. The thread now shows the caste mark only. In Bengal, Vaisyas who form the bulk of the high-caste Hindus, have even long lost this thread.

The Building of the house

A homeless student, after finishing his studies, had to build a house, followed by a ceremony and the utterence of the hymns of the *Rig Veda* (*VII, 54.55*) to Vastospati, the lord of dwelling-houses, as well as to other gods.

Funeral ceremony

The relations of the dead carried his sacred fires and sacrificial vessels and aged men and women carried the dead body to the burning ground. The widow, first placed near the dead body, was afterwards helped to depart with verse X, 18.8 of the *Rig Veda*. After cremation, the bones were collected in an urn and buried in a pit.

The Sraddha

Unlike modern practice, only Brahmans endowed with learning, moral character and correct conduct were invited. To them the oblations were given. The Brahmans represented the manes. Gifts of perfumes, garlands, incense, lights, and clothes were then offered to the Brahmans. With permission of the Brahmans, food prepared for panda-pitri-yajna was smeared with ghee and sacrificed in the fire or in the hands of the Brahmans, with other food. When the Brahmans were satiated, the sacrificer recited the verse I, 82.2 of the *Rig Veda*. 'They have eaten, they have enjoyed themselves.'

Parvan

This rite was observed on the new and full moon days and consisted of fasting as well as in offering cooked oblations to the gods.

Sravani

This rite was observed on the full moon day in the month of *Sravana*, to propitiate serpents. The rite has been replaced by the modern Manasa puja.

Aswayuji

This rite was performed on the full moon day of the *Asvina* month (October), followed by a sacrifice to Sita, the goddess of the field furrow.

Possibly, this ancient rite of the worship of Sita and her consort Indra—the rain-god, has been replaced by our Lakshmi puja on the full moon night of the autumnal harvest.

Agrahayani

Adoration was offered to the New Year.

Ashtaka

A relic of this ancient rite survives in our modern *pausha parvan* when rice is harvested, wheat and barley thrive and when cakes, flesh, vegetables are not only acceptable to the season gods but are also highly gratifying to men. We now take simple vegetables and cakes, but our remote ancestors relished beef in the *Pausha Ashtaka*.

Chaitri

It was performed on the full moon day of *Chaitra*, the last month of the year. The sacrifices were offered to Rudra and the constellations propitiated.

'The healthy joyousness which attended ancient Hindu ceremonies, has certainly lost nothing in the course of a long, long time.'

LEARNING AND PHILOSOPHY

Though the rishis and the Vedic priests had brought a good deal of learning to their Indian homes, yet it is certain that for a century or two, learners from the Indus Valley, Afghanistan, Kashmir, Punjab, and the Indian midland went to the north for higher education, instructions on the performance of sacrifices, attending learned discussions and councils. We have seen that two Aryan women, Pathyasvasti and Sarasvati, went to the north, became learned and came back with titles. Afterwards, the rishis and the priests gave higher education to their pupils in different branches of learning. Numberless residential institutions sprang up. The most glorious thing of ancient India was its compulsory higher education. Every Aryan in Indian was socially bound to study the Vedas. The defaulters were not only denounced and despised but were also classed as Sudras. The states and richmen gave munificent subventions to teachers. Princes generally supported students financially. The poor students rendered personal service to their preceptors. Girls were generally taught at home. Women and Sudras learned by listening to Puranic lessons.

Like other subjects, philosophy also attained considerable progress in the twenty-nineth century BC. Kapila and Patanjali were the two great philosophers of the age. Before we note Kapila and his work *Sankhya*, we better indicate his probable source of inspiration. The following should be read in connection with it: 'Six or seven hymns of the *Rig Veda* treat of the question of the origin of the world.... Two of these cosmogonic hymns advance the theory that the waters produced the first germs of things. Two others again explain the origin of the world philosophically, as the evolution of the *existent* (*sat*) from *non-existent (asat)*. One of the latter (*X, 129*), a poem of great literary merit, is noteworthy for the daring speculations to which it gives utterance at so remote an age. The only piece of sustained speculation in the *Rig Veda*, it is the starting point of the natural philosophy which assumed shape in later times as the evolutionary Sankhya system. It will always retain a general interest as the earliest specimen of Aryan philosophic thought. With the theory of the 'Song of Creation' that after the non-existent had developed into the existent, first came water whence intelligence was evolved by heat, the cosmogonic accounts of the *Brahmanas* are in substantial agreement. Always requiring the agency of the creator, Prajapati, these treatises sometimes place him first, sometimes the waters. This fundamental contradiction due to mixing up the *theory of creation* with that of *evolution*, is removed later in the Sankhya system. The cosmogonic hymns of the *Rig Veda* are the precursors not only of the Indian philosophy, but also of the Puranas, one of the main objects of which is to describe the origin of the world (Macdonell, *I.G.I. [1909], Vol. II, pp. 218–19*).

Kapila was the son of the great sage Kardama, one of the twenty-one great progenitors sent by Brahma to regenerate. His mother was Princess Devahuti who had willingly shunned royal pleasures to live in a hermitage, preferring ascetic life. She was a very learned and wise woman. To her we owe several hymns of the *Rig Veda*. Kapila, worthy son of these worthy parents, published about 2800 BC or a little earlier, his famous and important philosophy, the *Sankhya*. Kapila's wife was the fair Srimati, a model of faithful wives, but never blessed with a child (*Vishnu Purana, Book II, Chapter 1*).

The chief points of Kapila's philosophy are:

(i) He calls his philosophy *Sankhya*, i.e. ascertainment of truth, which he explains in twenty-two concise sayings, now lost.

(ii) He speaks of twenty-five *tattvas*, i.e. philosophic truths, viz., nature, soul, intellect (ego or consciousness), mind, the five subtle elements, the five grosser elements, the five senses of perception, the five organs of action.

(iii) His idea of God is transcendental: hence his philosophy is often called agnostic or atheistic. Probably, he really means that God is something beyond our comprehension.

(iv) He gives the theory of evolution.

(v) He speaks of the three *gunas*, i.e. properties of matter, such as goodness, passion and darkness. These *gunas* have made the creation diversified.

(vi) He explains the process of creation through the combination of *prakriti* and *purusha* (primordial matter and spirit or soul).

(vii) In philosophical reasoning, it holds very high position. Davies in his *Hindu Philosophy* observes: 'The philosophy of Kapila is the first recorded system of philosophy in the world; earliest attempt on record to give an answer from reason alone to the mysterious questions which arise in every thoughtful mind about the origin of the world, the nature and relations of man and his future destiny.'

(viii) Kapila finds fault with the Vedic sacrifice and the slaughter of animals. *Viveka* (pure wisdom) according to him, is the key to *nirvana* (salvation).

(ix) He admits immortality of the soul; law of karma; fourteen orders of beings, eight above and five below man; intellectual creation; eternity of matter.

(x) He says '*tri-tapas*' (three miseries) plague all. They are—bodily and mental; natural and extrinsic; divine or supernatural. The end of this philosophy is to end these miseries—to give humanity a relief from the suffering and pain, the common lot of all.

Kapila taught Asuri and Borhu his philosophy. But its wide spread was due to the exertions of Panchasikha, disciple of Asuri. The *lokayatas* (materialists) prevailed in the court of Janadeva of Mithila. Panchasikha preached there the doctrine of Sankhya, defeated the atheists and established the Sankhya tenets. (*Mahabharata, Peace Book, Chapter 210*).

Panchasikha elaborated the text of Kapila's *Sankhya* in many parts, which long remained the sole book of *Sankhya* before all. After the great Buddhist flood was over, Isvara Krishna, not later than the fifth century AD, made a *karika* of it in a new form which is still current.

Kapila's philosophy became at once highly popular. The Vedas, the institutes, the Puranas, the Sanskrit epics, the other philosophies, Buddhism, and other systems are highly influenced by it.

On the evolution theory of the Sankhya, Professor AA Macdonell observes: 'From the original substance, the world is described as developing through certain evolutionary stages. The diversity of material products is explained by the combination, in varying proportions, of the three inherent *gunas* or constituents of that substance. At the end of a cosmic period, all things are dissolved into primordial matter. The alternations of evolution, existence and dissolution form a series of cycles, which has neither beginning nor end.' (*I.G.I., Vol. II, p. 216*).

Pythagoras was the first to introduce the truths of Kapila's philosophy into East Europe (sixth century BC).

RC Dutt observes: 'It shows no ordinary philosophic acumen in Kapila to have declared that the *manas* (mental activity), *ahankara* (consciousness) and even *buddhi* (the intellect) were material in their origin. More than this, Kapila declares that the subtle elements and the gross elements proceed from *consciousness*. Kapila herein seems to anticipate the philosophy of Berkelay, Hume and Mill, that objects are but permanent possibilities of sensations and agrees with Kant that we have no knowledge of an external world except as by the action of our faculties, it is represented to the soul, and take as granted the objective reality of our sense perceptions.' (RC Dutt's *Ancient India, Vol. 2, Book III, Chapter X, p. 141*).

'The latest German philosophy, the system of Schopenhauer (1819) and Von Hartmann (1869) is a reproduction of the philosophic system of Kapila in its materialistic part, presented in a more elaborate form, but on the same fundamental lines. In this respect, the human intellect has gone over the same ground ... but on a more important question it has taken a step in retreat. Kapila recognised fully the existence of a soul in man, forming indeed his proper nature—the absolute ego of

Fichte—distinct from matter and immortal; but our latest philosophy, both here and in Germany, can see in man only a highly developed physical organisation. 'All external things, says Kapila, 'were formed that the soul might know itself and be free.' 'The study of psychology is vain,' says Schopenhauer, 'for there is no Psyche.' (Davies' *Hindu Philosophy, Preface*).

Kapila's was a *pure* philosophy, not *religious* philosophy and as such, though admirable, it was not acceptable to the people. For, we have already shown from the words of Dr Thibaut that with the Vedic Aryans, religion and philosophy were inseparably connected. Kapila gave no idea of a popular God. But the appreciative Aryan mind did not slight Kapila. Patanjali (not the grammarian) soon followed and supplied the defect to Kapila. He accepted the views of Kapila and added thereto a Supreme Being, who could be approached by *yoga*—meditation. His *Yoga-Sutra*, hardly a philosophy, contains 194 aphorisms in four parts. The first part in 51 short rules, called *samadhi pada* concerns meditation. The second of 55 rules, called *sadhana pada* deals with exercise and practices necessary for the concentration of mind. The third of 55 rules called *bibhuti pada* treats of the powers of yoga. The fourth of 33 aphorisms called *kaivalya pada* is about the abstraction of the soul from all worldly attachment by which beatitude is obtained. The Vedic seers sought God outside; Narayana inside. Patanjali's inward search was complete.

THE VEDA, KAPILA AND PATANJALI ON CREATION

Modern science says that different forces of nature are but one. So, heat, light, electricity, magnetism may be changed into one another. The *Rig Veda* also gives a similar idea.

Gravity, gravitation, heat, light, electricity, magnetism, and power of thinking are but expressions of one force called *prana*. In the *Rig Veda, prana* means 'vibration'. When the great end or dissolution comes, these forces revert to their primordial state in very subtle form generally called *adi prana* (ether). In that state, it is almost inactive. Then again 'emanation and expansion' begins, called *srishti*, not covered by the English word 'creation.' The Rig-Vedic expression *anidavatam* explains that truth.

All that is in the world has come through the vibration of *akasa* (ether). Emanation and expansions; preservation, contraction and dissolution. Thirty Kalpas—fifteen sukla (lighted), fifteen dark, fourteen Manus in one white Kalpa. The middle, i.e. seventh (as ours) is the most vigorous and prosperous; gradual contraction from the eighth Manu; dissolution (?) with the fourteen. The seventh Kalpa is the brightest.

From the subtle proceeds the gross, gradually. The forces revert to *prana*, and gross forms to *akasa*. These two finally revert to *mahad*, i.e. an all-pervading and attributeless Brahma or force or energy.

Mind is a very subtle thing behind this gross body. Mind is not soul: soul is German 'self.' Soul is the true man of Man within—immortal, unchangeable. Like the Veda and Kapila, Patanjali also speaks of the evolution theory—'By the gradually developing property of Nature, one class is changed into a higher stage and the process continues for ever and ever. 'Hindus say that' all objects, all species are but derived from one genus. They differ only in their gradual development.'

Patanjali says, as the farmer feeds his fields, so a very great power feeds us from within. This body is the great obstacle. The more this body attains greater structural excellence, the more power does it express. *Tama* (darkness) yields to *raja* (passion) and *raja* change into *satwa* (goodness). For a superior life, for superior moral excellence, we Hindus are so careful in eating and drinking.

According to the secure Hindu traditions, I have placed Kapila in the twenty-nineth century BC. His very high antiquity will appear from the following: Chanakya, in his *Art of Government*, mentions the Sankhya, Yoga and the Lokayata (Atheistic) Schools (300 BC). Aswaghosha, in his *Life of Buddha* admitted the Sankhya origin of Buddhism. Buddha's Hindu preceptors were both Sankhya origin of Buddhism. Buddha's Hindu preceptors were both Sankhya scholars. This makes Kapila of the seventh or eighth century BC. Dr Rhys David is disposed to place Kapila some time between 1200 and 1000 BC. The Janaka dynasty of Mithila (north Bihar) came to an end before 1200 BC. Janaveda was one of its early rulers. Atheists prevailed in his court. Asuri, Borhu and Panchasikha spread the Sankhya system everywhere in India. The proud Brahmans of Brahmavarta were rather slow to recognise the merits of Kapila, but the Aryan kings, ever noted for their strong commonsense and appreciation, hailed Kapila's system of 'reason' with joy. Soon, the doctrine was established in the court of Janadeva. The

Mahabharata mentions Panchasikha but no Asuri. A Jain commentator has quoted a couplet of Asuri. Three or four sayings of Panchasikha are found in the *Yoga-Bhashya*.

In the *Bhagavata Purana*, Kapila is the fifth of the twenty-two *avatars*, i.e. incarnations of the deity. Many called him *adi vidwan*, i.e. the first wise man. He is called a *paramarshi* in the *Svetasvatara* Upanishad. The six schools of Hindu philosophy fall into three groups, viz., Sankhya and Yoga (twenty-nineth century BC); Logic and Atomic Theory (fifteenth century BC); Prior Mimansa and Vedanta (fourteenth century BC). We know the dates of Gautama, Uluka, Vyasa and Jaimini almost definitely, being fifteenth and the fourteenth centuries BC. All traditions place the first two much earlier. Manu accepted the views of Kapila. Rishabha Deva, founder of Jainism, echoed the views of Kapila when he denied the existence, or at least, the activity and province of God.

Geneology connects Kapila with the Vairaja Dynasty through his mother's side (see ante).

The grammarian Patanjali of the second century BC was a native of Gonarda in east India. Where as the philosopher Patanjali of the twenty-nineth or twenty-eighth century BC was a native of Kashmir or Central Asia, as a legend tells us that 'he fell from heaven into the palm.' Yoga, an abstraction of mind was well-known then. Vivaswan, father to Manu, was well-exercised in Yoga. He gave the knowledge of it to Manu and Manu to his son Ikshvaku (*Gita, II*). Vyasa—the 'arranger'—is said to have written a commentary on Patanjali's yoga system.

Law-Books

During the period under review, Atri, Angiras, Usanas or Sukra, Vrihaspati, Vishnu, Yama, Daksha, and Manu gave laws. The present works that go by their names, are quite unworthy of being connected with these revered rishis of old. Yet, to preserve tradition, to help future discovery and to make reference clear, I retain the names of these early law-givers in the right places. Each of them is a versatile genius.

The laws were made to organise society most perfectly, to regulate the daily actions of all. Truth, morality and other virtues are strictly enjoined. Originally, the law-books were composed in prose, but now they are mostly in verse.

The law-givers are said to have been numerous. But of them, twenty are held chief. Their very great antiquity can seldom be maintained from their present works that are, like the Sanskrit epics, later growths. Yet, we must preserve their ancient chronology according to tradition.

Manu is the prince of the Indian law-givers. He is regarded as the oldest and the most authoritative. His Code is rendered into many languages of Europe. His original prose Code is lost. The second edition, still in prose and made after the compilation of the Vedas, was called *Vriddha* or *Vrihat* Manu. Influenced by the different parts of the present metrical Code, different scholars have assigned different dates to its last compilation. Sir William Jones gives the date as 1250 BC Elphinstone and Cowell 900 BC, Professor Wilson, 800 BC (some parts; complete in the present form, by 200 BC); Dr Hunter 500 BC; Dr Buhler, second century BC; some even AD 200.

According to tradition, I have placed him in the twenty-eighth century BC. I have already shown his very great antiquity. For the further information of my readers, I may say that Manu is quoted in other Codes. He is even mentioned by name in some. Gautama (1500 BC) had quoted him. Parasara (fifteenth century BC), father to Vyasa, quotes him in I, 13–15. Yajnavalkya (1350 BC) quotes him in I, 5. Vasista (fourteenth century BC) has also quoted him. But the name of none appears in Manu. The views of Atri, Bhrigu, Gautama, and Saunaka are found in Manu. Either these sages were more ancient than Manu (and we have reason to believe so) or they are later insertions.

Manu does not mention the *Ramayana* and the *Mahabharata*, but is often quoted in them. He does not mention the rite of sati. Manu does not treat of the subject of philosophy except incidentally in his first chapter. Philosophy has occupied too great an attention of the later Hindus. Manu's Code, Chapter I gives the views of Manu and probably the state of opinion as it stood in his time. His account of creation—an allegorical idea—derives from primal waters (*ambha a-praketah*). He regards the creations as formed from the substance of the creator. In some points, he agrees with Kapila. Monotheism prevails in Manu (*Chapter XII, 85*).

Nature of God, the soul, creation and other subjects physical and metaphysical are very lightly dealt with in Manu. This shows that the present six schools of philosophy did not exist then.

It appears that the precepts of Manu on various duties and information were long known orally. In the sutra period, a sage named Bhrigu, first collected them and published them as *Manava Dharma Sutra* (*M. S., Book I,* last shloka). It was afterwards converted into the present Metrical Code. It has 12 Books and 2,704 shlokas and deals with all questions of human interest.

'The effect of the religion of Manu on morals, is indeed, very good. Distinction between right and wrong is well shown. False evidence is highly denounced. There are numerous injunctions to justice, truth and virtue. He extols honest poverty and decries unfair opulence. Manu's Code is not deficient in generous maxims or in elevated sentiments. Brahmanic morality leands towards innocence, tranquillity and not to *active virtue*' (Elphinstone, *p. 48*).

The Code of Parasara (fifteenth century BC) opens with a list of the most ancient law-givers whom we recognise from early traditions. They are Vasista—the progenitor (twenty-nineth century BC), Manu (twenty-eighth century BC), Kasyapa (twenty-nineth century BC), grandfather to Manu.

Astronomy

Garga was an astronomer, as was Gautama (not the logician), though both were of twenty-nineth century BC. Usanas was son to Bhriguy and priest to the Daitya branch of the Aryans. The father and the son were both law-givers. Usanas gave his laws to Saunaka and other sages (twenty-nineth century BC). Atri was second of the 'seven seers.' He was priest to five distinghished families. Vishnu was uncle of Manu and a very learned man. He was heroic and had conducted the northern colonists to India. Samvarta was a renowned priest and brother to Vrihaspati. Daksha was a Prajapati (progenitor) and king of Kanakhala, near Haridwar. Angiras was the third of the seven seers, a very learned man and a priest. Prachetas—ten brothers—were noted for their learning and penance.

Below is a list of the most ancient law-gives, astronomers and medical experts. The readers will see from it the state of learning and also how the same persons excelled in different branches:

I. Law-givers	*II. Astronomers*	*III. Medical Experts*
1. Atri	1. Brahma	1. Brahma
2. Angiras	2. Marichi	2. Rudra
3. Vasista	3. Atri	3. Vivaswan (Surya)
4. Kasyapa	4. Angiras	4. Daksha
5. Daksha	5. Pulastya	5. The two Asvin brothers
6. Vishnu	6. Vasista	6. Yama (a son to Surya)
7. Samarta	7. Kasyapa	7. Indra
8. Garga	8. Garga	8. Dhanvantari
9. Gautama	9. Narada	9. Buddha
10. Usanas	10. Vrihaspati	10. Chyavana
11. Manu	11. Vivaswan (Surya)	11. Atreya
12. Harita	12. Soma	12. Agnivesa
13. Prachetas	13. Bhrigu	13. Bhera or Bhela
	14. Parasara	14. Jatukarna
	15. Manu	15. Parasara
	16. Chyavana	16. Kshirapani or Ksharapani
	17. Harita	
	18. Bharadvaja	

In a previous chapter, we have spoken of the observations on astronomy made after 3000 BC. The lunar zodiac was fixed, the solstitial points marked and other phenomena carefully observed and noted. Those ancient works have not come down to us in its pure form. They have been repeatedly recast. An astronomer named Varahamihira wrote a revised edition of *Brahma Siddhanta* about AD 80. In the *Pancha-Siddhantika* or Varahamihira of the sixth century AD, the *Brahma Siddhanta* was superseded by the famous work of Brahmagupta, called the *Brahma-Sphuta-Siddhanta*. Marichi to Vasista were five of the seven seers. Their works are totally lost to us. Kasyapa, Garga, Narada, Vrihaspati, Soma, Bhrigu, Chyavana also are known as astronomers, but their works and observations are not preserved. Vrihaspati, Soma, and Bhrigu probably discovered the planets Jupiter, Moon and Venus. Vivaswan, son to Kasyapa and father to Manu, is noted for his work known as the *Surya Siddhanta*. Though recast times without number, yet it contains much that is original and old. Its present form is supposed to be of the fifth or the sixth century AD. Manu certainly inherited the knowledge of his father. In his *Code* he speaks of Vrihaspati (Jupiter) and other planets. The ancient work of Vasista was revised by Vishnu Chandra, says Brahmagupta. The modern work *Vasista-Siddhanta* is certainly quite different from the ancient one. The modern *Naradi Samhita* is a quite different work from the ancient *Narada Siddhanta*. Manu is quoted in the Garga Samhita (first century BC) as an authority on astrology. Varahamihira also has quoted Manu. Kasyapa, father to Vivaswan, son to Marichi and conqueror of Kashmir, excelled in astronomy. As a high authority in astronomy, he was often quoted by the astronomers of the later ages. It is gratifying to note that four successive generations, viz., Marichi, Kasyapa, Vivaswan, and Manu had devoted themselves to studies and investigations on astronomy.

Parasara is considered to be the most ancient of Hindu astronomers (Professor Weber). His name is connected with the Vedic calendar. This Parasara was perhaps of the twenty-nineth century BC. We have another Parasara of the fifteenth century BC. The modern work called the *Parasara Tantra*, is probably of the second century BC though it contains much that is old.

Medicine

From the *Bhava-Prakasa*, a well-known medical work and a discourse in the *Mahabharata*, it appears that various diseases prevailed in India among the early settlers. The hot and damp climate of India was indeed trying to the Indo-Aryans. It is said that Brahma had written a very voluminous work on medicine. Rudra, a practical physician was called the 'Lord of the Physicians.' Brahma taught his knowledge to Daksha, one of the twelve sons of the great sage Bhrigu and king of Kanakhala, and Vivaswan, father to Manu. Vivaswan wrote a work of his own, afterwards called the *Bhaskara Samhita*. Manu had no taste for medicine, but his three half-brothers, viz., the two Asvins and Yama studied medicine with Vivaswan and Daksha. Indra, the raja of the deva-Aryans, learnt the medical science from the two Asvins. From Indra, the science came down to India. The sage Atreya, seeing the Indians afflicted with various diseases, resolved to study medicine and so went to Indra in heaven. Indra most carefully taught him the science. The sage, highly proficient, came back to India, wrote a treatise of his own and set up a medical school. Six of his disciples became most distinguished. They were Agnivesa, Bhera, Jatukarna, Parasara, Kshirapani and Harita. To the great delight of the preceptor, these disciples also afterwards wrote excellent works on medicine.

Moved with compassion for the prevalence of disease in India, the sages and seers thought of some means of cure. So, they held a council on the Himavat. The following were present: Bharadvaja, Angiras, Garga, Marichi, Bhrigu, Bhargava (Sukra), Pulastya, Agasti, Asita, Vasista, Parasara, Harita, Gautama, Sankhya, Maitreya, Chyavana, Jamadagni, Gargya, Kasyapa, Narada, Bamadeva, Markandeya, Kapisthala, Sandilya, Kaundinya, Sakuneya, Saunaka, Asvalayana, Sankriti, Visvamitra, Parikshita, Devala, Galava, Dhaumya, Kapya, Katyayana, Kankayana, Vaijavapa, Kusika, Vadarayani, Hiranyaksha, Lokakshi, Saraloma, Gobhila, Vaikhanasa, and Valakhilla. After a general discussion, they sent Bharadvaja to Indra to be taught the entire medical science. He studied, came back, cured many and spread the knowledge.

The names, of Charaka and Susruta stand foremost in the Hindu medical literature. Both of them belonged to the epic age. They were not original authors but the best compilers. The works of the six noted disciples of Atreya Punarvasu were so excellent that they attracted the notice and admiration not only of their preceptor and the Indian seers, but also of the devas of the north. Charaka's original work had preserved much of them along with his own knowledge. What Charaka lacked were made up by the learned Drirhavala, a writer of Panchanada, i.e. the Punjab. The present work of Charaka was finally recast in the court of Kanishka.

Divodasa, a king of Benaras about 1500 BC, became highly proficient in medical science. So, they called him a *Dhanvantari*. He excelled in surgery. Susruta, a son of the great sage Visvamitra, learnt the subject from him. The knowledge of the preceptor and the disciple was recorded in the work known as *Susruta-Samhita*. The present work was recast by the Buddhist Nagarjuna.

Gautama wrote a work called the *Kumara-Bhritya*, i.e. treatment of the infants.

They discovered that the work of *pliha* (spleen) and *yakrit* (lever) in the body is to make blood. The Vedas spoke of 360 bones in the body, but Susruta proved 300 bones satisfactorily. As to the embryo in the womb, Saunaka, Kritavirya, Parasara, Markandeya, Gautama (son to Subhuti), and others held that the different limbs of the body grow one after another. But Dhanvantari, physician to the devas, gave the wisest view, for he said, 'All the limbs of the body grow simultaneously.'

The eight divisions of the medical science, coming down from Brahma, show the progress of the subject from the earliest times.

Punarvasu, son to Atri, and Dhanvantari were contemporaries. Besides the specialists, the rishis also in general, cultivated medicine. The sage Medhatithi cured king Asanga of his impotency and obtained much wealth from the raja (*R.V., VIII, I. 30–33*).

The frequent use of numbers in the *Rig Veda* clearly shows their knowledge of the science of numbers. The decimal notation was known to them from the earliest times. There are reasons to believe that the Indo-Aryans knew the rudiments of geometry, mensuration and trigonometry. A scanty knowledge of anatomy was obtained from the dissection of the beasts for food or for sacrifice. Dyeing, goldsmith's work and preparation of medicines, etc., show that the science of chemistry was far in advance.

Arts and Architecture

The Rig-Vedic Hindus knew the use of various metals such as gold, silver and iron, etc. There were goldsmiths, blacksmiths, potters, carpenters, sawers, barbers, sailors, washermen, dyers, physicians, weavers, and priests.

These various professions show the civilised life, though with not high refinement. The arts of life, though yet simple, were not rude. Gold, silver, gems, ornaments were in all families. The various grains, spices, perfumes, and other products show a highly cultivated country.

Many arts were carried to a high state of excellence. Women excelled in weaving (*R.V., II, 3.6; II, 38.4; VI, 9.2*). Weaving and bleaching of sheep's wool appears from X, 26. 6.

Blest in their northern 'land of promise', the early Aryans hated India as a 'land of vice.' But now they called India their *mother country* and the northern home in Central Asia their *fatherland*. The Aryans, a very brainy people, came here to a land of rich soil, large navigable rivers, ample mineral wealth, and various building material. So, they early cultivated the various arts of civilised life. Cotton-weaving was their oldest industry in India. Cotton cloth is the most remarkable of Indian manufactures—its beauty and delicacy, fineness of texture are not yet approached in any other country. Silk-manufacturing also was excellent and very ancient. Gold and silver brocade were original manufactures of India. Cotton fabrics were called in Greece *Sindon*—evidently from India or Sindh.

Mechanical professions were generally hereditary from the earliest times. So, the various arts thrived. 'Simplicity of life and permanence of employment are here (in India) combined with a high degree of excellence in design and honesty of execution.... The brilliancy and permanency of many of their dyes are not yet equalled in Europe.' (Elphinstone).

'In delicacy of texture, in purity and fastness of colour, in grace of design, Indian cloths still hold their own against the world.' (*Brittanica Encyclopedia,* 9th *ed, vol. XXI, p. 761*).

Dr Royle microscopically traced *indigo* (literally, the blue dye of India) in some of the mummy cloths of ancient Egypt.

The various industries were weaving, embroidery, carpet-making, jewellers' work, iron-work, copper-work, pottery, sculpture, painting, carving on stone, wood and ivory. The following abounded in India—gold, silver, iron, coal, rock-salt, copper, lead, antimony, saltpeter, mineral oil, lime-stone, precious stones, and pearl-fisheries.

Hindu taste for minute ornaments fitted them to excel in goldsmith's work. *Rig Veda*, VI, 3.4 refers to goldsmith's melting metal. The descriptions of various gold ornaments, iron utensils and implements of agriculture and war abound in the *Rig Veda*. Part II, 34.3 refers to golden helmets; IV, 2.8 describes horses with golden caparisons. In IV, 37.4; V, 19.3 and elsewhere, *nishka* (ornament) is described.

'In purity of ore and in antiquity of working, the iron-deposits of India perhaps rank first in the world.' (*ibid., p. 764*).

Rig Veda, V, 9.5 refers to the work of an iron-smith. 'Hindus enjoyed high reputation for jewels; but their taste is bad and setting rather rude. Their way of working at all trades is simple and their tools few and portable' (Elphinstone). Skin-vessels for curds are mentioned in VI, 48.18. Iron-vessels are mentioned in V, 30.15. One Hindu writer states that paper was manufactured from cotton in India from the earliest times (*Dawn Magazine*, Vol. XII, 1909, May and June).

Carpentry was well-known. There are frequent allusions to the construction of carts and chariots in *R.V.*, III, 53.19; IV, 2.14; IV, 16.20. Elephants, horses, and chariots were familiar as conveyances for men, as were cattle, camels and wagons for goods (*R.V., IV, 4.1*).

The *Rig Veda*, VII, 3.7; VII, 15.14; VII, 95.1 allude to iron towns which some explain as strong forts. We have also allusions to a hundred stone-built towns in IV, 30.20 and elsewhere. The Rig-Vedic Hindus used stone as a building material, for it was cheap, durable and strong against enemies. Such stone architecture prevailed in the Aryan colonies founded in the rocky region. In many Hindu towns, often structures and walls were of rock. Architecture was doubtless carried to some degree of excellence. The *Rig Veda* contains many allusions to mansions of a thousand pillars (*II, 41.5; V, 62.6*).

The Sanskrit words for a town or city shed some light on their condition. *Durga,* literally a well-guarded place or fort not easy to access *Nagara*, originally a hill-guarded place, a stronghold, from *naga*, a hill. *Pura* or *Puri* originally meant a protected or guarded place, from the root *pri*, to guard.

The arts of sculpture and painting were still in its infancy. There is no distinct allusion to any of these in the *Rig Veda*. Considerable progress was made in music. Dancing was a very popular pastime with both the sexes. Perfumes, incense and garlands were in use. Every village had washermen, dyers, and barbers. In *R.V.*, I, 164.44, the clearance of jungle by fire is described as the shaving of the earth.

Visvakarman, the deva architect, had brought about a revolution in the field of arts. No wonder that the children of the devas in India too would excel in various arts.

The Rig-Vedic Hindus knew earthwork. There were beautiful villages, towns, palaces, brick, stone and mud-built houses, leafed cottages, rest-houses, forts, roads and streets, fine steps for ascent on hills, fine cars drawn by ponies, boats, ships, other conveyances, fine clothes and turbans.

In Manu's *Code*, cities are seldom alluded to. This shows the very high antiquity of the law-giver. The only great cities were probably the capitals. Gardens, bowers and terraces, construction of ponds, tanks, wells and artificial lakes for irrigation and drinking, and orchards by wealthy men for the public benefit are here perhaps first enjoined (*Chapter IV, p. 226*).

Cows, buffaloes, sheep, goats, dogs, cats, and horses were domestic animals even in the Vedic age. Some were used as beasts of burden. The mother and the cow have received universal veneration from the Indians from the earliest times.

The Rig-Vedic feasts were held for religious, harvesting, and ceremonial occasions. The festivities, of course, helped political organisation, development of literature, culture of religion and development of arts and industries.

The learned Aryans spoke almost classical Sanskrit and composed hymns in it. The masses perhaps used a loose form of Sanskrit.

Trade and Commerce

The trade of the Rig Vedic Hindus was both inland and foreign. We have already noted many products and objects of luxury of ancient India. Their plenty shows that there was open trade between the different parts of India and Central Asia and West Asia.

'The earliest *Rig Veda* knew ocean' (*Imp. Gaz. of India, New ed, Vol. II, p. 220*). The Aryans used to go abroad by land and sea for commerce and conquest. The words *sindhu, samudra* and *arnava* in the *Rig Veda*, mean sea. The words *nau* (ship), *navika* (sailor), *navi* (navy or fleet), *san-yatra* (voyage to a foreign land), *pani* (trader) belong to the earlier Sanskrit. The *Rig Veda* mentions *sataritra nau*, 'a sea-going vessel of hundred oars.'

The *Rig Veda* knows no prohibition against voyages, while it has distinct allusions to voyages.

(i) 'As merchants, desirous of wealth surround the sea, so do the priests surround India.' (*Rig Veda, I, 56.2*).
(ii) The shipwreck of Prince Bhujyu and his deliverance by the two Asvins (*R.V., I, 116.3* and *5*).
(iii) Varuna is said to know the paths of the birds through the sky and the paths of the ships over the sea (*R.V., I, 25.7*).
(iv) People who desire to acquire wealth, pray to the sea before undertaking a voyage (*R.V., IV, 55.6*).
(v) For a pleasure-trip, Vasista once went out on a voyage with Varuna (*VII, 88.3–4*).
(vi) Manu also refers to sea-voyage (*VIII, 156-157; VIII, 406*).

This shows that the Hindus navigated the ocean early. In Chapter XI, Book I, I have shown that the Hindu maritime enterprise was not confirmed to the coasts alone.

An intercourse with the Mediterranean, doubtless took place at a very early period, both by land and sea.

(vii) The early kings of the Vairaja dynasty are said to have foreign dominions. Eight islands of the Indian Ocean once formed a part of Bharata's kingdom (twenty-nineth century BC—*Mahabharata, Puranas* and *Sabdamala*).

(viii) Pururava, son to Ila and Buddha (*R.V., X, 95.18*) of the twenty-eighth century BC is said to have occupied thirteen islands of the sea.

(ix) A son of Manu and two sons of Ikshvaku left royalty and gladly took to commerce (twenty-eighth century BC).

We have shown already that the two Aryan brothers, Vritra and Bala, and their allies—the *Panis*, were ousted from Central Asia, by the devas under Indra. They founded their states in Persia and Turkey (twenty-nineth century BC). The *Panis* finally settled on the Levant Sea, about 2800 BC. Tyre was built in 2750 BC. In India, Manu and others began to rule about 2800 BC.

Though the Aryans and the Rig-Vedic Hindus possessed commercial instincts, an enterprising spirit and good vessels, yet it does not appear that they ever took an active part in the western trade. No foreign account, nor any Indian tradition supports it. But east of Ceylon the entire fields of commerce belonged to the Hindus from the earliest times. The West gave gold and a few things that the Aryan-Hindus valued most.

The Chaldeans appear to have been the earliest to carry on a brisk trade with India. They brought to India many things from the West and took eastern commodities, including the porcelain, to their own people, to the Egyptians and to the Aryan colonists of western Asia. By 2500 BC the Egyptians themselves came out to trade.

'Under the name of Punt, the ancient Egyptians understood a distant country, washed by the great sea, full of valleys and hills, rich in ebony and other valuable goods, incense, balsam, precious metals and stones, rich also in animals; for, there are camels, leopards, cheetas, panthers, dog-headed apes and long-tailed monkeys. Winged creatures with strange feathers flew up to the boughs of wonderful trees, specially of the incense tree and the coconut-tree .' (*Historians' History of the World*, vol. I, p. 108). The learned editor thinks, it is Somaliland and not India. Any Indian traveller of the West will at once recognise India from the said description. That Punt was a province of India, appears from the following: 'It is said in the Egyptian history that the Egyptians went to the valley of the Nile from a holy country called Punt. From the hieroglyphics in the walls of the temple of Queen Husli-top at Dar-el-Babari, it appears that Punt was a province of India.'

'Under Saukh-Ka-Ra, the first Ophir Voyage to Punt (perhaps, Sindh) and Ophir (Sanskrit *Sauvira*) was accomplished under the leadership and guidance of Hannu.'

'In those ancient times, the road lay from Coptos to the harbour Leukos Limen (now, Kosseir) on the Red Sea, the great highway and commercial route of the merchants of all countries, who carried on a trade in the wondrous products of Arabia and India, the bridge of nations which once connected Asia and Europe.' (*Historians' History of the World, vol. I, p. 109*).

'Already in the reign of King Sau-Ka-Ra, 2500 BC, the Egyptians had some knowledge of the coast of Yemen and of the Hadramaut on the opposite side of the sea which lay in sight of Punt and of the sacred country,' (*ibid., p. 109*).

'Asia already supplied Egypt with slaves, perfumes, cedarwood, cedar essence, enamelled precious stones, lapis-lazuli, and the embroidered and dyed stuffs of which Chaldea retained the monopoly until the times of the Romans.' (*ibid., vol. I, p. 113*).

In the earliest *Rig Veda*, gold, copper and iron are often mentioned but not silver. Gold was in very high demand with the early Aryans. Bactria and the central Asiatic deserts where these was an abundance of gold, formerly supplied the Aryans with that metal. But now it became rare. New search for gold prompted the Aryans to look for it abroad. The Aryans used gold as ornaments, as gifts to rishis, as barter, and as medicine. They asked and earned foreign gold in exchange for their wood, wool, precious stones, dyes, carpets, ebony, and ivory.

The Rig-Vedic Indians traded from the Indus to the Malayan Archipelago. This eastern and western trade of India produced five advantages, viz., influx of immense gold and pearls, introduction of many foreign plants, flowers, fruits, silk, camphor, catechu and spices; colonisation; political conquest; and spread of civilisation.

CURRENCY OF MONEY

It appears that the Vedic Hindus, like the later Phoenicians, used money as the basis of their commercial intercourse with foreign nations. *Zend Avesta* and Homer mention other objects of barter (ox, cow) but no money. They currency of a gold coin called *nishka* was in India from 3000 BC, if not earlier. The Vedas, the epics and other works satisfactorily prove this. The fixed weight of a *nishka* was 32 ratis, i.e. one-third of a *tola*. The *nishkas* of lesser weights were also current in different times and in different localities.

Loans and usury were well-known in the Vedic age. Rishis sometimes regretted their state of indebtedness.

The *Rig Veda, IV, 24.9* has the following: 'One sells a large quantity for a small price, and then goes to the buyer, denies the sale and asks for a higher price. But he cannot demand more on the ground that he has given a large quantity. Whether the price was adequate or not, the price fixed at the time of sale must hold good.' Does it not show the existence of current money?

In the *Rig Veda,* rishis often thankfully acknowledged the gift of *nishkas* (*R.V., I,125; v, 272.2; VIII, I. 30-33*). Professor HH Wilson, in his note on V, 27.2 says: 'It is not improbable, however, that pieces of money are intended; for if we may trust Arrian, the Hindus had coined money before Alexander.'

The editor of *Historians' History of the World,* vol. II, p.340, notes: 'India only adopted such a use of money in a very small way in intercourse with foreigners.'

Ancient coins with *Brahmi lipi* on, prove that from very ancient times, coins with the figures of elephants and bulls were cast in the mould. Professor Rapson says: 'In any case, the act of casting coins must be very ancient in India. There is no question here of borrowing from a Greek source.' (*J.R.A.S, 1900, p. 182*).

ARYAN IMMIGRATION

I have already said that the Aryans had originally come probably from the north-west of Europe, several thousand years before Christ. They lived in Central Asia among the Turanians for several centuries. Then about 3000 BC or earlier, some of them went to West Asia, some to Persia and Turkey under Vritra and his brother Vala, some to Europe on the shores of the Mediterranean Sea. Some remained at home and gradually mixed with the Turanians. Hindus were the last to leave Central Asia, for they possessed the largest vocabulary. Later on, from the Indus Valley, the Aryans spread over the Iranian tableland, India, Ceylon, and the Malayan Archipelago. Even about 3000 BC, there were several Aryan kingdoms in east Europe. Rinanchaya, friendly to Indra and the devas, was king of Roosam, probably Lithuania, where the language is still less remote from Sanskrit (*R.V., V, 30*). The sons of Barasikha (Warwick?) ruled the different parts of Hariyupia (probably, east Europe). They were powerful but wicked. It is said that Abhyavarti, called a Samrat (emperor), son to Chayamana, descendent of Prithu, had marched against them and defeated them, and conquered eastern and western parts of Europe (*R.V., VI, 27.5–8*). This Prithu was probably son to Vena (*R.V., X*). Some 2250 years ago, Alexander led an expedition and came conquering as far as the Punjab in India. In the twenty-eighth BC, Abyavarti, a great hero of the same Punjab, went out with an expedition to east Europe which he conquered after a strenuous war. The geography of the *Rig Veda* thus comprised a very wide area. Frok Kikata, the province of Gaya in east India (*R.V., III, 53.14*) to the Euphrates and to Russia and Hariyupia in the far north-west, every region is known to the *Rig Veda*. Yet, the rishis never mentioned the Vindhyas nor any river of the Deccan.

In course of our present history, we shall again meet with many of our long-parted Aryan cousins in India, no more as colonists, but as conquerors, rulers and traders. From the earliest time, India has sustained many recorded and unrecorded foreign attacks and defeats. India has passed through many foreign rules. At last, God has placed her under the British, perhaps the greatest nation of modern times. In the eighteenth century last, there was a scrambling for suzerainty in Indian between the Hindu, Muhammadan and the Christian powers. But God's choice fell upon the English, the fittest of the contenders.

Greece was noted for wisdom and art, Rome for martial spirits and cartage for commerce. But now England alone is noted for all these and more. Like the magnificent banyan tree from a common seedling, the British power shines in the world in full grandeur! From AD 449 onward, in some 1500 years, the English have attained a glory and civilisation, never known in the history of mankind. Regions Caesar never knew are now under the British sway! The British Empire is now the largest, the greatest, the richest and the most populous in the world.

There is not a finer race than the English. Their rural feelings, manly exercises, ruling capacities, business instincts, aesthetic culture, inventive genius, keen insight, active habits, simplicity of life, and respect for merits are indeed marvelous.

Their rule in India is now based on righteous principles. Under them, India at last knows peace, safety, prosperity, various comforts of life, perfect toleration, and common interests. In ruling India, they have very wisely and rightly adopted the policy of conservation and reform. Six centuries of Muhammadan rule (AD 1200 to 1800) gave us very few persons of genius. But only a century's British rule has brought ample life, light and vigour to the Indians. All classes of people are now on the fair way to progress. Lord SP Sinha, Sir JC Bose, Sir PC Roy, Sir Asutosh Mukherji, Sir T Madhav Rao, Dr Bhandarkar, Dr Bhau Daji, Rabindranath Tagore, Sir Saler Jung, Sir K Shesadri Ayer, Dr Rajendra Lal Mitra, Dr Bhagwanlal Indraji, Dr Suhrawarthy, Dr Paranjpe, RC Dutt, Kesav-chandra Sen, Raja Rammohan Roy and many, many other luminaries are the product of the British rule in India.

Astronomer Ganga of the first century BC had called the Greeks barbarians. The greatest hero of the world, the most carefully taught pupil of Aristotle—I mean Alexander the Great—could not win a single line of praise, nay, even notice from the Hindus, Buddhists or the Jains to whom he appeared as an evil genius, *dasyu*—a mighty robber at best! Our orthodox Hindus often call the British rulers *mlechchhas*, i.e. impure barbarians. But they should know that the British people come of the same Aryan stock as we do. From the following comparison of English and Sanskrit, it will appear that English is essentially Rig-Vedic Sanskrit in disguise.

I. God—Persian *Khuda*, Sanskrit *Gudha*, 'the concealed one.' Sun—*Sunu* or *Syuna* or *Syona*. Moon—from *Mana*, the measuring star.

Time is calculated from the course of the moon. Star—*Stara*. Sky—from root *sku* to cover.

II. Father—*pitri*. Mother—*matri*. Brother—*bhratri*. Sister—*sasri*. Nephew—*napta*. Son—*sunu*. Daughter—*dogdhri* or *duhitri*. Foal—*putra* (our corrupt *pola*). Filly—*putri*. Boy—*bala*. Girl—*gauri*. Bride—*brita*. Man—*manu*. Woman—weaving man, and wife—from root *way* to weave. Widow—*widhawa*.

III. King—*Janaka* (father of the tribe). Queen—*jani*. Minister—*mantrin*. Kith and kin—*jnati*. Aristocracy—*Arya* (noble class). Baron—*Barenya*. Palace—*prasada*. Porter—*pratihara*. City—*chitti*. Town—*puri*. Family—*dhama*. Home—*sarma*. Door—*Dwar*.

IV. Beast—*pacu*. Latin—pecus. Lion—Rajan (King). Originally, the word was *pacurajan* = king of the beasts. Cf. Leon, Leo, Roy, Rollo. Tiger—from root *tij* to be fierce (Skeat). Elephant—*El*. article, Ephant—*ibha*. Cf. *ivory*. Horse—root *hres*, to neigh. Camel—Kramela, Ass—from a confusion with *Aswa* (horse) to which family it belongs. Bull—*bali*. Ox—*ukshna*. Calf—*kalabha*. Cow, Ancient Sanskrit—*go*. Ape—*kapi*. Dog—*dansaka* (the biter). Originally the word was *mriga dansaka*, i.e. the biting beast. Wolf—*ulkamukhi*. Otter—*udra*. Cat—*khattasa* (a species of cat). Jackal—*srigala*. Persian *shagal*. Bitch—*bitchari*. Hound—*swan*. Bear—*bhallu*. Boar—*bhudara* or *baraha*. Sow—*sukari*. Hog—*sukara*. Mouse—*musha*. Rat—root *rad*, to gnaw. Horn—*sringa*. Hoof—*sapha*. Milk—*dugdha*. Teat—root *dhet*, to drink. Yoke—*yuga*. Plough—*phala*. Acre—*ajra*.

V. Gold—*harid*. Persian *zarad*. Silver—*subhra* (white metal). Iron—*ayas*. Zinc—*yasoda*. Sulphur—*sulvari*. Rice—Latin *oryza*—Sanskrit *vrihi*. Wheat—*sveta* (the white crop.) Mead—*madhu*. Sugar—*sarkara*. Oil—*taila*. Drone—*druna*. Meat—*meda*. Fish—*pisita*. Egg—*anda*. Young—*yuwan*.

VI. Foot—*pada*. Knee—*janu*. Thigh—*sakthi*. Navel—*nabhi*. Breast—*uras*. Heart—*hrid*. Spleen—*pliha*. Hand—*hasta*. Nail—*nakha*. Shoulder—*sirodhara*. Mouth—*mukha*. Lip—from root *lap*, to speak. Nose—*nas*. Tooth—*danta*. Eye, axe, axle—*akshi*. Ear—*sravana*, root *sru*, to hear. Brow—*bhru*. Head—Latin *caput*, Sanskrit *kapala*.

VII. Bird—*vi, vis*. Latin *avis*. Cuckoo—*kokila*. Crow—*kaka*. Cock—*kukkuta*. Goose—*hansa*. Owl—*ulu*.

VIII. Wood—*edha*. Tree—*dru* or *taru*. Bark—*balka*. Root—root *ruh*, to grow. Box—*barksha*. Stick—*yasti*. Flower—*fulla*. Fruit—*phala*. Jute—*jautha*. Hemp—*sana*. Rose—*rasa*.

IX. Right—*ritam*. Rite—*riti*. Ceremony—*karman*. Fire—*pavaka:* root *pu*, to purify. Water—*uda*. Vapour—*vashpa*. Fume—*dhuma*. Dirt—*dhula*. Mud—*mrid*. Earth—*era*. Orange—Orange—*naranga*. Wind, winter, winter, weather—Sanskrit *wata*. Rain—*rinjasana*. Hail—*sila*. Snow—root *snih*, to fall in shower. Light—root *luch*, to shine.

X. Day—*diwa*. Night—*nisa* or *noctum*. Year—Latin annum, *hayanam*. Morning—*purvanah*. Evening—*apahna*.

XI. One—*eka*. Two—Persian *do*, Sanskrit *dwi*. Three—*tri*. Four—*chatur*. Five—Latin *penta*—*panchan*. Six—*shas*. Seven—*saptan*. Eight—*ashta*. Nine—*nawan*. Ten—*dasan*.

XII. He—*sa*. She—*sa*. It—*idam*. That—*tat*. They—*te*. You—*yushmad*. You (plural)—*yuyam*. I—*aham*. We—*wayam*.

XIII. Adjectives. Young—*yuwan*. Old—*vriddha*. Mew—*nu*. Great—*guru*. Low—*laghu*. Tiny—*tanu*. Bad—*badya* (blameable), Persian *bad*. Soft—*santa*. Red, ruddy, ruby, rufus—*rudhira* (blood). Right—*riju*. Better—*bhadra-tara*. Warm from—*gharma*, heat. White—*sveta*. Yellow—*harid*—Green. Sweet—*swadu*.

XIV. Serpent—*sarpa*. Sanke—*naga*. Creeper—root *sri*, to crawl. Reptile—from *srip*. Vermin, worm—*krimi*.

XV. Verbs. Eat—*AD*. Go—*ga*. Come—*gam*. Sleep—*swap*. Sit—*sad* (sid). Flow—*plu*. Feed—*pa*. Fart—*pard*. Ask—*ish*. Pray—*prachchh*. Dream—*dra*. Flee—*paray*. Be—*bhu*. Fall—*pat*. Fry—*bhrasj*. Do—*dha*. Bear—*bhri*. Move—*muv*. Run—*ri*. Speak—*vach*. Say—*sans*. Stand—*stha*.

4

SOLAR DYNASTY

Ten solar kings (seven to sixteen) paid great attention to cavalry. Kuvalaswa was succeeded by his eldest son Drirhaswa who was heroic, popular and peaceful. He probably had a long reign. He was succeeded by Haryaswa I—a mere blank name. His son and successor was Nikumbhaswa, whose exploits and sacrifices reduced the treasury. Nikumbha was succeeded by his son Sanhataswa (also known as Krisaswa). But for his wise reduction of the cavalry and curtailment of expenditure the state could not have been saved. He had two sons and one daughter. He ruled perhaps till 2400 BC. It appears that Princess Haimavati was his eldest child. The *Siva* and the *Brahma Puranas* made her the next successor. But the majority of the authorities omit her. We therefore, pass on to the next king, who is called Prasenajit (2400 BC). He was brave, warlike and a great conqueror. He is also noted for his gifts of numberless milch cows (*Mahabharata, Peace Book, Chapter 233*). His queen, Gauri bore him a very pious and heroic son, Yuvanaswa by name. This king was a lamb at home and a lion in the chase. Having subdued many kings, he performed a horse sacrifice with great pomp. His gifts were free to all deserving persons (*ibid*).

Being long childless, he left the reign to the ministers and went to the forest, with his queen, to practise penance for a worthy son. The sage Bhargava and his disciples, pleased with the piety of the king, performed a special sacrifice for him and gave the queen consecrated food and a nostrum to remove her barrenness. Soon, the queen had hopes of an heir. The son born of her, was the renowned Mandhata. From childhood, he received very careful tending and training. He was stately, fair in complexion and strong-built. It is said that he learned archery, the Vedas and the military science very easily. He was crowned at sixteen.

MANDHATA

(R.V., IV, 42.8-9; VIII, 39–40; I, 112: 2460 to 2300)

It appears that Mandhata was the title meaning the 'Indian Indra'. The *Rig Veda* gives his name as Durgaha and a *Purana* calls him Suvindu. But everywhere he is described by his title of *Mandhata*, a fully deserving one. Tradition makes him the greatest emperor of India. It is said that he was great as a man, as a conqueror, as a ruler and a patron of arts, industries and learning. On the assumption of royalty, he first organised a very powerful army which soon became a million strong. With this mighty force, he conquered the whole of Indian, Ceylon and other islands of the Indian Ocean. The most distinguished Indian kings whom he had defeated, were Janamejaya, Angara, Marutta, Sudhanva, Gaya, Puru, Vrihadratha of Anga, Asita, Rama, and others (*Mahabharata, Peace Book, Chapter 29*). About this time, the ancient Afghans grew very powerful and turbulent. They often invaded north India and harassed the people. Mandhata defeated them and conquered Gandhara. He was a just and vigorous ruler. It is said that under him, the land was rid of robbers. Unluckily, as the consequence of a long drought, a famine broke out in north-west India.

However, he combated it successfully. The pious filed of Kurukshetra (Karnal) was the site of his numberless sacrifices. Here, he performed his imperial and horse sacarifices with great pomp. He gave numberless cows and goldfish to Brahmans. To relieve the famine-stricken people, it is said, he raised hills of boiled rice and curry, excavated tanks of ghee, curd, honey, and milk. The *Rig Veda* has honoured him in *VIII, 39–40; I, 112* and elsewhere. His chief queen was Vindumati, daughter of King Sasavindu. He had three sons and fifty daughters. The princesses were all married to the sage Saubhari. Prince Gaura—his grandson on the daughter's side—built a kingdom with Gaur as capital (perhaps, now

Faizabad). About this time, ancient Mathura (Muttra) was the seat of mighty Daitya kingdom. One day when Mandhata, with an army, was coming back through that state, the Daityas attacked him. The old emperor with his army perished to a man. Thus ended the glorious career of the greatest Indian monarch after a long reign of some sixty years.

When Yuvanaswa II, father to Mandhata was ruling at Oudh, Marutta, a scion of the solar dynasty (not of Oudh) attained great political eminence in north India. He was son to King Avikshita, descended from Nedishta—a son of Manu. He is described as one of the five great emperors of ancient India. He had conquered all and performed an imperial sacrifice. During the latter part of his reign, a twelve-year drought prevailed in the western half of north India. A terrible famine followed. Miseries and loss of lives were very great. Event the seers who lived on the sacred river Sarasvati, fled to other countries for food. Only one young sage remained there, living on fish. He also remembered the Vedas. The large and noble heart of Marutta ached and wept for the people. He, with the ministers, spared no pains to relieve the distressed. Marutta of happy memory is still a favourite play on our Indian stage. We have seen that Marutta was defeated by Mandhata. Prince Visala of Marutta's line built Vaisali.

PURUKUTSA

(R.V., IV. 42.8–9)

About 2300 BC Purukutsa succeeded his father on the throne. Though he was brave and resolute, he lacked the tact and skill of a consummate general. The Gandharvas (ancient Afghans) rose in rebellion. He speedily led an expedition against them and was successful in putting it down. The Afghans gathered strength and again raised the standard of rebellion. Nay, they even dreamed of conquering north India. Purukutsa again marched against them at the head of a strong and large army. But unluckily he was defeated and made captive. This is the only instance of a solar king's captivity in the enemy's hands. This earned the late king the opprobrious name of *Purukutsa*, i.e. one of much ill-repute. As the queen was then pregnant, the ministers and the people could not place any of his brothers on the throne. Prince Muchukunda was a very brave general. He repeatedly defeated the Gandharvas and delivered his brother

Purukutsa from their hands. He even helped the devas of the north against their enemies. In the meantime, the queen gave birth to a son. They declared the infant prince king. Prince Ambarisha and Muchukunda were regents. Purukutsa was set aside from the throne on account of his captivity. He was, however, given a small kingdom to rule on the north bank of the river Narmada.

TRASADDASYU

(R.V., I, 112,; IV, 42.8–9)

Purukutsa ruled for some five years only. Then his infant son, Trasaddasyu, was placed on the throne (2295 BC). During the king's minority, the ministers and his uncles conducted the state.

He grew up a valiant monarch. Early in life, he had determined to avenge his father's disgrace. So, he led several campaigns against the fierce Gandharvas and shattered their power. The very terror of his name was enough to keep off foreign enemies from attacking India for some time. Within India, there were still non-Aryan and Daitya and *danava* Aryan powers, inimical to the Aryans. But all of them kept quiet now. The kingdom of Oudh was highly prosperous under him. The *Mahabharata* calls him a royal saint; he was magnanimous and stately. He ruled some seventy years (2295 to 2225 BC). Towards the latter part of his reign, the great sage, Agastya came to him for some money to make ornaments for his wife. But knowing that the income and expenditure of the state of Oudh were equal, he refused the king's gift. Agastya next went to the *danava* king, Ilvala of central India, who enjoyed the reputation of immense wealth at that time. The great sage and his work in the Deccan deserve special notice here. He was the most distinguished sage of India in the twenty-second century BC. He and his brother Vasista, were sons to Mitra-Varuna and a prostitute Urvasi by name. His true name was Mana (*Virhad Samhita*). He is highly honoured in the *Rig Veda* and all other traditions. He had first built his hermitage in the Chhapra district (Bihar); but afterwards repaired to the Vindhya mountain. He spent his whole life to spread Hindu civilisation in the Deccan. With the aid of his brother and disciples, he was highly successful in his mission. The south bowed to the north, attracted by the latter's superior civilisation. The works of Agastya in the field of politics were not less important. About this time, the western coasts of south India were constantly oppressed by pirates. It is said that after the fall of Vritra, the great Assyrian monarch, the Assyrians of the Mekran coast, being afraid, took to the sea and began piracy.

The Indian coasts and merchantmen were often attacked and looted by these people known to the Hindus by the name of Kalakeyas. These men gradually settled in the islands. A large colony of them finally settled in the Malabar Coasts. Thus, centuries passed amidst the alternate state of peace and war. In the twenty-second century, fresh troubles arose. It would be wrong to suppose that the new northern mission was universally hailed in the south. There were small but powerful communities who allied with the Kalakeyas to strongly oppose the new mission. Hermitages were attacked, missionaries killed, cows stolen and much harm done. Agastya now applied to the kings, received their aid in men and money. Formed a strong army and navy by which the enemies were crushed and the sea-pirates hunted out and driven from the islands of the Arabian Sea. After a stay of some twenty-five or thirty years near the Vindhyas, Agastya left for still further south, on the same holy mission, and settled permanently somewhere beyond the Godavari and Krishna. His mission in the new sphere went on with full vigour. While Agastya was busy, civilising the southern most peninsula, a political disturbance arose in the north. It appears that some solar king of the north led an expedition for the political conquest of the Deccan. But the Dravidians of the Vindhyan states checked his course, and resolved to turn the table. They formed an alliance and invaded the north. The fight went on for some time. At last, the Dravidians had the better of it. The northerners sent an envoy to Agastya to intercede. The great sage came from the south and bade the Dravidian allies desist from further warfare. They obeyed him and stopped.

There is no evidence to show that Agastya had filled any part of the Deccan with the Aryan settlers. True, some solar and lunar princes had already penetrated into the south and built small kingdoms there; but they were mere drops in the ocean of the Dravidians. The only Aryan state that had attained importance and distinction was Vidarbha (now, Berar and its neighbourhood). Agastya married Princess Lopamudra of Vidarbha. She was one of the sixteen ideally chaste Hindu wives. Her only son was Idhmavaha (*Rig Veda* and the *Puranas*).

According to *Vishnu Purana (Book IV, 1–4)* the next king, number, twenty-two, was Anaranya, whom all other Puranas mark as number forty-nine. We have followed the majority. Prishadaswa is our next king. He is honoured in the *Mahabharata* as a worthy king, but nothing in particular is known. As the wars of Trasaddasyu had emptied the treasury, the king was therefore, compelled to reduce the army expenditure by minimising the cavalry. His reign was probably very short. The next king was Tridhanva, known in the *Rig Veda* as Trivrishna: 'He was a great patron of learning, protector of the good, wise brave, and wealthy.' (*R.V., V, 27*). His son Tryaruna was the next king. He was a great Vedic scholar. Like his father; he also was a patron of learning. The seer Atri says: 'The royal saint Tryaruna, son to Trivrishna, has attained great distinction by giving me a cart with two bullocks and ten thousand gold coins.' (*R.V., V, 27*). The *Satyayana Brahmana* gives the following story: 'Solar king Tryaruna and this priest Vrisa were once driving together in a carriage. On the way, the carriage suddenly ran over a young Brahman boy who was grievously hurt. A question arose as to who was guilty in the matter. The elders of the royal family declared the priest guilty. At this, priest Vrisa's wrath knew no bounds. However, he immediately treated the boy carefully and saved him from death. Vrisa then resigned his priesthood. But the Ikshvakus then fell at his feet, begged his pardon and propitiated him in various ways.' Tryaruna perhaps, ruled till 2200 BC.

SATYAVRATA 'TRISANKU'

(2200 BC to 2175 BC)

Having crowned Satyavrata, the pious king Tryaruna passed into religious retirement. Though son to a pious and learned father, before long, he showed himself very wild, by committing three great sins for which they called him *Trisanku* (i.e. a king of three great sins). His sins were: stealing another's wife; slaughter of a milch cow and eating its beef. All classes of people became highly disgusted with him for these acts. Almost all shunned him. Being dethroned, he left the capital and went to the forest. A terrible famine, caused by a long drought, was then raging in the land. During that dire calamity, Trisanku saved the starving Visvamitra and his family by his hunted meat (*Mahabharata, Peace Book*). Helpless and cast away, he asked the aid of Visvamitra, a very influential sage of the age. Visvamitra pardoned the young king on promise of correction. Trisanku agreed and turned over a new leaf. To atone for his sins, the king took up a long and great sacrifice. The priests declined to preside. Thereupon, Trisanku asked Visvamitra who came and began the sacrifice in right earnest. But very great opposition from the priests and the Brahmans obstructed its completion. No *rishi*, no Brahmans, no friend came to the sacrifice, as all regarded Trisanku as a chandala (hunter). The king, helpless, looked to Visvamitra who, roused by the opposition, exerted himself to the utmost and induced, by his superior learning and penance, many Brahmans and rishis to be present and accept the king's gifts. The sacrifice met with limited success. His queen was Satyaratha by whom he had the renowned son, Harischandra (*Harivansa, XII, 13–B*).

HARISCHANDRA

(Perhaps, 2175 to 2130 BC)

On the retirement of Trisanku, his son Harischandra ascended the throne. He was extremely handsome, pious and very warlike. Having subdued the kings of India, he had celebrated an imperial sacrifice with such pomp that it ever remained unsurpassed and was only equalled by that of Yudhisthira the Just (fourteenth century BC). It is said that Harischandra gave to all five times more than what they asked for. Of the long roll of ancient Hindu kings, only Marutta and Harischandra were deemed by the Indians as worthy rivals of Indra (*Mahabharata, Salya Book, Chapter 20*). The king had built a town called Harischandrapura or Saubhapura. It appears that fame had turned his head. He grew insolent and now dishonoured Brahmans, sages and even great seers. Ere long, he succumbed to plethora. It is said that he was cured of it by the offer of a human sacrifice (*Aitareya Brahmana*). The growing unpopularity of the emperor reached the ears of the illustrious sage Visvamitra who had saved his father Trisanku from disgrace. He now resolved to correct Harischandra. It so happened that one fine morning, the king, out hunting, was passing by the hermitage of Visvamitra, not far from the capital, where, implored by several girls tied by the great sage for having torn his flowers plants, he liberated them out of compassion. This immediately brought him into disfavour with the sage. As the king boasted of his large heart, Visvamitra asked a gift of him; the king agreed. The sage asked for his kingdom. The king gave it. As a gift to a Brahman is always to be made with *dakshina*, a suitable fee, the sage demanded it, but the king could not pay. The sage, with affected anger, pressed the king hard for the fee. At last, the king sold himself to a *doma* (funeral assistant) of Benaras and sold also his queen and the only prince to a Brahman of the same sacred place, to pay the fee. Shortly after, the ex-queen Saivya came to the burning ghat of Kasi to cremate her son Rohitasva, bitten by a snake while culling flowers for the Brahman master. The royal pair recognised each other. Visvamitra now appeared and revived the prince by a nostrum.

Admiring the king's extreme devotedness to virtue and truth, the sage returned his realm. The royal party then went back to Oudh amidst the rejoicing and applause of all. Harischandra ruled till the prince was of age. His memory is still cherished by millions of Hindus.

Visvamitra was connected with the royal family of Oudh. His grandfather Kusika, a lunar king of Kanouj, had married the daughter of king Purukutsa of Oudh (*Harivansa*). Visvamitra was duly crowned and ruled for a short time. But he was not at all heroic. He was often defeated by his enemies. On one occasion, when coming back from a hunting excursion, he invited himself to the hospitality of the distinguished sage, Vasista. The latter however, was not then at home. The soldiers of Visvamitra tore the flower-plants and branches of the fruit-trees to feed the horses, camels and elephants. Vasista, on return to his hermitage, grew very angry. An unpleasant affray ensued. Vasista's army, mostly composed of sturdy non-Aryans, soon routed the army of Visvamitra who smarting under the defeat, repaired to Kanouj. Being of a religious turn of mind, he abdicated in favour of his eldest prince and turned a recluse. Through penance, he soon grew to be a very powerful sage and ranked as a Brahman. His daughter, Sakuntala, was fostered by Kanva and married to Dushyanta. The *Rig Veda* gives the names as Tritsu and his title as Vasista. He was a high priest to all great monarches and a *kulapati* (chancellor) to a residential university. He fed and taught over 10,000 disciples in different parts of north India. The rivalry of Visvamitra with him is notorious.

ROHITASVA

(Perhaps, 2130 to 2100 BC)

Harischandra was succeeded by his son Rohitasva. He built Rohitasvapura, now *Rhotasgarh*. He appears to have had three sons (*Brahma Purana*). Haritaswa, the eldest prince, perhaps succeeded him but he died soon after. The next king was Champa who built Champapuri, perhaps near modern Bhagalpur in east Bihar. The next king was Sudeva, noted as a good ruler. His son and successor, Vijayanandana, was a very great hero. It is said that his army never knew defeat. His name and fame appear from the *Mahabharata*, the Puranas and elsewhere. The great Jain scholar, Hemchandra, has noted him as one of the sixty-three 'great men' of ancient India. He was succeeded by his son Bharuka. This king was averse to fighting and loved peace. He applied himself vigorously to improve the condition of his people. This good king was succeeded by his son Vrika, the terrible. About this time, the Haihayas, and the Talajanghas—two offshoots of the lunar dynasty, grew very powerful in central and south-west India. The power and prosperity of Kosala, became an eyesore to them. So, they resolved to ruin it. But Vrika baffled all their attempts to do so. This heroic king probably ruled till 2000 BC, when his son Bahuka (the *longi-manus*) succeeded him.

BAHUKA

(Perhaps, 2000 to 1995 BC)

Bahuka was no doubt, a worthy king. He knew the grave dangers Kosala now lay exposed to. So, he lost no time and gave himself up to mobilisation. The Haihayas and the Talajanghas again attacked oudh but were defeated. Now, they allied with the Yavanas, the Hunas, the Paradas, the Sakas, the Keralas, the Chinese (probably Nepalese or the people north of Himalayas), and the Cholas. The allies attacked Ayodhya. Bahuka fought hard bt could not prevail against the enormous odds. The 'invincible city' was conquered by the enemies. Bahuka, with his two queens withdrew to the hermitage of sage Aurva in the Himalayas. Queen Yadavi was then pregnant. Out of jealousy, the other queen poisoned her. But Aurva saved her by a medicinal drug. Bahuka died in the meantime. The pregnant queen wished to be a sati but was stayed by the sage in whose hermitage Prince Sagara (literally *sa* = with, *gara* = poison) was born. Aurva taught him the entire Vedas, various arms and fire-weapons. Sagara collected a strong army and attacked Ayodhya. The people of Kosala flocked to his standard. After a hard struggle, the Haihayas and the Talajanghas were beaten off. Oudh was regained. Aurva gave Sagara material assistance. His ancestors, of the Bhrigu clan, were priest to the Haihayas who had robbed them of their treasure for military purposes. This led to a battle in which most of the priests were killed. The mother of Aurga, then pregnant, fled to the Himalayas where Aurva was born. So, the great sage was a sworn enemy of the Haihayas.

About 2002 BC, Queen Semiramis of Assyria invaded India and conquered a part of it. The account is given by Diodorus who took it from Ctesias. The queen marched with a large army and fought with Sthavarapati, Greek *Stabrobates*, i.e. 'Lord of the Earth', apparently a king on the right bank of the Indus. She founded the city of Kophen on the River Kabul. This proves that at this time, the country on the right bank of the upper Indus was subjected and paid tribute to the Assyrians (*Historians' History of the World vol. II*).

SAGARA

(Perhaps, 1975 to 1925 BC)

Having regained the throne, Sagara thought of establishing the power and glory of Kosala once more. So, he collected a very strong and large army, attacked his father's enemies and crushed them in several battles. We are told that Sagara was going to annihilate the several non-Aryan powers that had allied with the Haihayas. But those, now helpless, applied to priest Vasista at whose intercession Sagara spared their lives and liberty, but punished them in other ways. He laid them all under an interdict. Thus, those people, though originally pure Kshatriyas, were now forced to turn impure.

After immense conquests in India and the southern sea, Sagara became an overlord. Then, desirous of performing a horse sacarifice, he let loose the horse with some princes and an army 60,000 storng.

Passing through various countries, the horse at last came to Bengal where it was stolen all of a sudden by a Dravidian chief and placed in the hermitage of a great sage named Kapila, who lived near the Ganges. The princes and the army, after a good deal of search came of Kapila, and finding the horse near him, rashly charged him with the theft of the sacrificial beast. It is said that the princes and the whole army fell victim to the wrath of Kapila, then shining like a perfect mass of splendour. In the strife that ensued with the Dravidian army, the solar army suffered terribly. When this nhappy news had reached Sagara, he forthwith sent his grandson Ansuman to Kapila. The young prince, under proper escort, came down to the great sage, tendered to him his grandfather's humble regard and propitiated him with prayers, defeated the foes and went back to Ayodhya with the horse. The sacrifice was duly performed with great pomp.

Sagara was very pious and popular, but not happy in his private life. His first life was spent in hard fighting. He had two queens, Kesini (princess of Vidarbha) and Sumati; but both of them were long childless. So, leaving the raj to the ministers, Sagara went to the sage Bhrigu in the Himalaya where he, with the queens, practised penance. Bhrigu then gave the queens a drug each, by which Kesini presented Sagara with a son. Sumati bore him several sons. The eldest prince—Asamanjas, born of Kesini, grew up a very wicked lad. He oppressed the citizens in various ways. If not sufficiently respected, he would even hurl boys, bound hand and foot, into the river. The citizens complained to Sagara. The old emperor banished Asamanjas from the realm. After exile, the prince reformed but he was not recalled. His son Ansuman was crowned. Then Sagara passed into religious retirement. He ruled over fifty years and left the raj in a highly prosperous condition (*Matsya Purana, Chapter 12;* see also *Vishnu Purana, Book IV; Padma Purana, Heaven Part, Chapter 15* and the Sanskrit epics).

The following two kings, numbers thirty-five and thirty-six, are almost blank names. As the realm was now without a thorn, Ansuman gave himself exclusively to religion. He is called a *rajarshi*, i.e. a royal sage. With him perhaps closed the twentieth century. Having installed his pious son Dilipa on the throne, about 1900 BC, Ansuman turned an ascetic. His son Silipa I, after a short peaceful reign of some ten or twelve years, withdrew to the Himalaya for lifelong penance.

BHAGIRATHA

(1890 to 1850 BC)

On the early retirement of his father, Bhagiratha ascended the throne. He was physically very weak in early life but by the benediction of the learned though deformed sage, Ashtavakra, his weakness was cured. His physique gradually became very strong. Tradition makes him one of the five great emperors of ancient India. He was very pious, wise, learned, brave and kind. It is said that after Mandhata, India had not witnessed a more powerful king than Bhagiratha to whom bowed all the kings of India. His overlordship was distinctly marked by the performance of an imperial sacrifice and a horse sacrifice, besides many minor sacrifices. He showed greatness in not taking any tribute from the subdued kings. His gifts were free and amounted to a million in the shape of slave girls, chariots, elephants, horse, cattle, goats, and sheep. Besides, he gave to all whatever they asked. As a king he was exceedingly popular. After a splendid reign of some forty years, he left the raj to his able ministers, repaired to the source of the Ganges, north of the Himalayas, where he practised penance along with his queen, with the object of having an offspring. There after some time, a prince was born to him to his great delight and that of his people. A popular legend gives this monarch the credit of bringing down the Ganges from the north to the Indian plains. This is wrong, for, the *Rig Veda* tells us that at the confluence of the Ganges and the Yamuna, Varuna, Soma and other mighty kings, even Brahma himself had performed various sacrifices. Hence the name Prayaga, i.e. an excellent place for sacrifice. The probable fact is that the sanctity of the Ganges originated with this emperor. The Indus and the Sarasvati were sacred to the Vedic Aryans. The Sarayu was holy to the people of Kosala. Now, Bhagiratha declared the Ganga as sacred to all.

Prince Srutasena, son to Bhagiratha, was placed on the throne by the sages, people and the ministers about 1835 BC. We know nothing of him. The next king, Nabhaga, was son and successor to Srutasena. It is said that in direct opposition to his father's wishes, he had married a fair Vaisya lass, which displeased his father so much that he disinherited him. He obeyed his father, left the palace and practised severe penance in a distant hermitage, accompanied by his wife. The king afterwards recalled him and duly crowned him. Nabhaga was a very powerful monarch. The *Mahabharata* tells us that he asserted his overlordship after having subdued many kings of India and performed an imperial sacrifice as a token of his suzerainty. He probably ruled till 1800 BC, when he left the raj to his worty son, Amvarisha.

AMVARISHA

(Perhaps, 1800 to 1775 BC)

Amvarisha proved a very valiant monarch. It appears that he had made fighting his sole business in life. It is said that in numberless battles, he fought no less than a million of soldiers. He had defeated many kings, and conquered many lands. Every conquest was followed by a sacrifice in which food, drink, music, sports, and amusements were arranged for the entertainment of all classes of people. He gave away to the Brahmans over a billion cows. His other gifts were so liberal and general that the great seers declared that nobody had ever witnessed nor would ever see their like in India. He had a very fair daughter, Srimati by name. For her, two eminent sages fought with him though without success. He was a Vaishnavite and a very popular ruler.

About this time, numerous Aryan colonies of the Indo-Germanic family were forming new settlements on the shores of the Mediterranean Sea. The *Rig Veda* states that Hariyupia (perhaps, east Europe) and Roosam (most probably, Lithuania in Russia) had been colonised by the Aryans before 3000 BC. About 1800 BC, India presents to us the following three distinct regions: (i) The Aryan region between the Himalayas and the Vindhyas and from east Afghanistan to Mithila and Benaras. This contained Aryavarta, Brahmavarta, Brahmarshidesa, and Madhyadesa, including the countries of east Afghanistan, Kashmir, Punjab, Karnal, Matsya, Surasena, Antarvedi (the Doab), Kosala, Mithila, and Kasi. (ii) The *Vahya desa*, i.e. half-Aryan region including Sindh, Sauvira, Kathiawar, Gujarat, Magadha, Anga (east Bihar), Banga Bengal); and (iii) the Deccan.

The Vedic civilisation was prevalent in the first, the Vratya-Aryan in the second and the Dravido-aryan in the third region. Of the '*Arya mlechchha*' countries, Magadha was the most prominent. When the Aryans were in the Punjab, even then Bengal was powerful and civilised. The Aryans, jealous of the Bengalis, abused them as 'noseless', irreligious and 'speechless birds'. The province of Gaya is called Kikata in the *R.V.*, III, 53.14; it is also mentioned in the *Yajur Veda* and the *Atharva Veda* (*V, 22.14* which states that fever prevailed there). The Aryans despised the east Indians for, they never milked the cow for a sacrifice nor lighted a fire for it (*R.V.*). The philologist Yaska called Kikata (Gaya) a 'home of the non-Aryans.' The *Atharva Veda*, Vratya Part XV. 2.1.4, and the *Tandya Brahmana*, XVII. 1–4, describe the corrupt manners of those people. It is said that the Magadhans used an Aryan tongue. Dr Beridell Kith thinks that a Prakrit dialect was current among them. Mithila was a chief centre of the Aryan-Vedic civilisation. Mithila gave light to the eastern provinces. In spite of many prohibitive laws, many Aryan priests, scholars and missionaries lived in Magadha, Anga, Banga and gradually spread the Aryan civilisation among the people (*Sankhyayana Aranyaka, VII. 13*). Yet, it is plain that the Vedic civilisation did not enslave the Magadhan culture. However, the suitable name of the Vindhyas (barrier) and the mention in the Vedas of rice, elephants, large tigers, and some peculiar plants, clearly indicate the eastward migration of the Aryans.

Another point deserves notice here. About this time, the Indo-Iranian separation took place. By this time, not only the Gangetic Aryans differed from the primitive Indo-Aryan tribes of the upper Indus in manners, customs and some religious rites, but the latter even differed from one another, especially about religious matters. Religious differences led one of those north-western Aryans to seek a new home in the Iranian tableland. These were the ancient Parsis who took from India their mythology, language and four castes. A plate discovered by the German scholar, Hugo Vinclaire states that 3300 years ago, i.e. in 1385 BC, in a treaty between two kings of Babylon, mention is made of their gods Mithra, Varuna, Indra. The Parsis maintained their religion and liberty till AD 641 when defeated by the Arabs, they embraced Islam. Some however, fled to the mountains, and some to Kabul. Again, when Kabul was defeated and converted by the Arabs in the seventh century AD, the Parsis fled from there and came to Bombay in India and have been since living with us for over a thousand years. Though very small in number—being hardly over a lakh—they are still an influential community. They are mostly given to trade. They serve India in various way. Chiefly through their exertions, our Indian products reach the foreign markets of the world. Dadabhai Naoroji, Sir Ratan Tata and several others of the sect, are ornaments of the empire.

After Amvarisha, the power of Kosala seems to have declined under the following thirteen kings. Sindhudwipa, son and successor of Amvarisha, though mighty, passed most of his life at the sacred capital of Prithudaka on the north bank of the Saraswati, where he is said to have attained great Brahmanhood. His son, Ayutaswa, succeeded him. Bhangasuri was perhaps his other name. He was mighty and good. His son, Rituparna or Ritupala, ruled in the middle of the eighteenth century BC. He had sheltered Nala, king of Nishadha (probably, Narwara in Rajputana) in his distress caused by the loss of his kingdom by a stake in gambling with his younger brother. His faithful queen, Damayanti, abandoned in the wood by her lord, arrived at her father's house after a good deal of trouble and sent men in different directions in search of Nala. At last, the scent of Nala was brought to her from Oudh by a Brahman messenger. Damayanti, with the approval of her mother but without the knowledge of her father, King Bhima of Vidarbha (Berar), proclaimed her intention of choosing a worthy husband. Young Rituparna wished to attend the marriage assembly. So, he ordered his charioteer, Vahuka (Nala in disguise), to be ready. Nala was much skilled in coachmanship and Rituparna in gambling. On the way, they learned each other's art. They arrived at Kundina, the capital of Berar. The king received Rituparna and asked the cause of his coming. Rituparna was surprised at this. In the meantime, Nala was recognised and reunited with Damayanti. Rituparna, pleased to learn the fact, soon left for his capital, begging leave of both Bhima and Nala. The latter soon regained his kingdom.

It is already noted that Sagara had almost crushed the powerful Haihayas of Mahishmati, now Chola Mahesvar, near the mouth of the river Narmada, in the twentieth century BC. The following two centuries found them very powerful again. In the eighteenth century BC, Arjuna, son to Kritaviraya, of that Haihaya clan was the greatest monarch in India. He was a Jain by religion. He is described as one of the five great emperors of ancient India. He is said to have conquered not only India, but also the following seventeen islands of the sea: Indra (perhaps then the Indus Delta), Chandra (?), Caseru (*Kutch*), Malaya (Maldives), Tamraku (Ceylon), Gabhastiman (Andaman), Naga (Nicobar), Saumya

(Sumatra), Baruna (Borneo), Gandharva (Java), Baraha (Bali), Kanka (Cocos), Kumuda (?), Sankha (Hong Kong), Bhadraraka (?), Javangaka (Japan) and Kumari (Kuerile?).

The century from 1750 to 1650 BC was one of great unrest and bloodshed arising from the great rivalry between the Jains and the Hindus; between the Brahmans and the warriors; between the Vasista and the Visvamitra families.

The sons of Arjuna were regular tyrants. Their oppression forced the Brahmans to fight. It is said that the Brahmans, aided by the Vaisyas and the Sudras, attacked the powerful Haihayas. But, for the want of an able general, the allies were defeated. The Brahmans now discovered their error, appointed a *senapati* (commander) worthy to lead the allies' army again against the Haihayas. This time, the Brahmans were victorious and the enemies signally defeated (*Mahabharata, Drona Book, Chapter 50*).

We have seen that the Brahmans in general were being slighted by the warriors. There were of course, several reasons for it. The Jinas were all princes. The warriors were not only fighters but also philosophers—religious instructors and composers of the Upanishadas. On the other hand, the Brahman intellect was growing poor. The versatile genius that had characterised the early Aryans, was now rare in the Brahmans of the Indo-Gangetic plain. True, they still clung to the Vedic religion, but they lacked the moral force, the true spirit of the earlier seers. The Brahmans now delighted in almost lifeless but pompous rites and rituals. Sacrifice (formerly, holy communication) now meant an offering of man, beast, birds, to gods.

The Haihayas, defeated by the Brahmans, kept quiet for some time. But erelong they again provoked the Brahmans who not only crushed them but also exterminated the entire Kshatriya race of India. The case was briefly this:

The sons of Arjuna went to the Himalayas on hunting excursions. There, one day, did they lot of harm to the hermitage of Jamadagni, grandson to sage a Aurva. An affray ensued with the result that the sacrificial cow of the sage was forcibly taken by the Haihayas to their capital. Jamadagni had married Princess Renuka of Vidarbha and had five sons by her. The great Brahman warrior, Parasurama, was their youngest son. Coming back home, the hero learnt everything and soon marched with an army, beat the Haihayas and brought back the cow. Before long, the Haihayas again came with an army to punish the young Brahman hero. But Parasurama and his brothers were not in. The Brahman army fought hard but in vain. Jamadagni was seized and brutally murdered. His wife, Renuka, also was struck and left half-dead. The whole hermitage was dismantled and upset. Parasurama came home the same day. Soon, he collected a very strong army, attacked the Haihayas and after several battles, crushed them. He next turned his victorious arms against the warrior class of India. His great object was to prune down the overweening pride of the Kshatriyas and to re-establish the supremacy of the Brahmans. He entered into a long war in which he fought twenty-one battles and killed all the worthy Kshatriyas of north India. He now gave Aryavarta to the Brahmans and went to the Deccan, built his hermitage on the Mahendra Parvata (Eastern Ghats) and spread Hindu civilisation there. It is said that he had filled Malabar, Konkan and other parts of the Bombay Presidency with Aryan settlers from north India. He never married and lived to a ripe old age. Kurukshetra was his favourite field of battle. He had performed an asvamedha and a bajapeya sacrifice (*Mahabharata, Peace Book, Chapters 48–49*). As soon as the great Brahmanic war was over, the non-Aryan chiefs, finding north India destitute of heroes, began to cause political disorders all over the country. The Brahmans, now helpless and anxious, thought of the means of saving the land. After search, they found the following survivors: some pious Kshatriyas of the Haihaya race; the son of Viduratha of the Paurava dynasty, saved by the people in the Rikshavan hill; the son of king Sudasa of Kosala, kindly saved by Parasara: he was brought up as a Sudra; Gopati, son of king Sibi, was saved in a wood, fed by milk alone; Vatsa, son of Pratarddana of Kasi, was saved in the pasture-ground amidst the calves, nourished by milk alone; a Brahman, living on the Ganges, had saved the son of Diviratha, grandson of Dadhi-vahana; sage Bhuri-bhuti had saved Prince Vrihadratha, father of Jarasandha, on the Gridhrakuta hill amidst the non-Aryan people; some powerful warriors of the Marutta dynasty had fled into the sea and saved themselves there.

Kasyapa, Parasara and others reinstated those princes to their several kingdoms. Besides, the holy and young sages were engaged to raise up children in the widowed queens of the warrior class. These new scions, duly grown up, saved the land *(Mahabharata, Peace Book, Chapter 48)*. Some suppose that after the destructive war, fresh Aryan colonies came from the north and settled in India. We find no proof of it.

Artiparni (also called Sarvakarma) succeeded his father Rituparna to the kingdom of Kosala. He was a good king and a great friend of the poor. He may have ruled long perhaps till 1600 BC. His son Sudasa, the next king of Oudh, proved a very wicked tyrant. He was most probably killed by Parasurama about 1570 BC. Through fear of the young Brahman hero, the queen of Sudasa had given birth to a prince in the priest's house. Parasara brought up the prince as a Sudra child. Hence he was called Sarvakarma.

Sarvakarma came to the throne perhaps not later than 1560 BC. He hated the Brahmans from his heart of hearts. Due to constant thoughts of revenge, his reason began to give way. One day, while coming back from the chase, through a narrow path in the woods, he met priest Saktri, eldest son of Vasista, whom he kicked and whipped for not making way to him. This act earned him the opprobrious title of *Kalmasapada*, i.e. 'a king of sinful foot.' Before long, the king almost became mad, left the raj and wandered in the forests wildly. His queen, Madayanti, the model of a faithful wife, followed him wherever he went. The king did not recover soon. One day in the woods, driven by hunger, he is said to have forcibly seized a Brahman while in embrace. Despite the entreaties of his wife, he killed the Brahman and sucked his blood. The distressed Brahmani cursed him to die in an embrace. After 12 years, the king came to himself and returned to his capital. One day, when he was about to mate, the queen reminded him of the curse. As she was childless, the king permitted her to have a child by Vasista. She conceived, but did not deliver even after due time. Vasista came and struck the womb with a piece of stone. This helped the delivery soon. The prince born after being hit with a stone, was called Asmaka from *asman*, stone. The prince, was crowned, perhaps in 1530 BC. He had built a town called Paudanya. At this time, Amavasu, son of Raubhya and grandson of Visvamitra went to Parasurama and told him of his vow. Angry at the Kshatriya revival of north India, he again came to the north and killed the warriors. His attack on Ayodhya was so sudden that the young prince, Asmaka, was saved only by a large number of naked women placed at different parts of the city. Bieng saved by women, the prince was called *Narikavacha*. After the war, he remained as the only *mula* (root) of the warrior class; therefore his crown-name was Mulaka. He and the following kings, till number fifty-three, were not so brave. The sixteenth century closed with Ilavila.

The kingdom of Kosala again ranked as the first power in India under the following five kings, viz., Dilipa to Ramachandra—numbers fifty-four to fifty-eight. Dilipa, eleven, son to Ilabila and grandson to Duliduha, both mentioned in the *Mahabharata* as worthy kings, came to the throne about 1500 BC. He was unrivalled in archery, stately in person, fair in complexion and an accomplished statesman. He was a very wise, good and just ruler. He was very merciful to the feudatory chiefs. He made some fresh conquests. His kingdom was highly prosperous. It is said that famine, theft, premature death were rare in his reign. His queen, Sudakshina, princess of Magadha was long childless. He went to his priests, who gave his queen consecrated milk with a drug, swallowing which she soon conceived. The son born of her became the famous king—Raghu. Dilipa performed numerous sacrifices. Having crowned Raghu, Dilipa and his queen, passed into religious retirement (*Raghuvansa* and *Mahabharata*).

RAGHU

(Sanskrit epics, *Raghuvansa* and *Puranas*). Perhaps, 1482 BC

Raghu was a very good and warlike king. Kalidasa, in his *Raghuvansa*, canto IV, describes the extensive conquests of Raghu in India and outside. Now, the question is, are they true or imaginary? Some regard them as imaginary and a magnified account of Samudragupta's Indian conquests. I cannot say how far this idea can be maintained. Many reasons incline us to place Kalidasa in the first century AD. Considerations of astronomy have led some recent scholars of Europe to place the great poet not beyond the third century AD. The history of the solar dynasty was current in Kalidasa's time which was the source of his inspiration. Beyond controversy, Raghu was a colossal figure. Raghu's line, Raghu's children and the like expressions abound in the Sanskrit epics and elsewhere.

Below is given an outline of Raghu's conquests. From Oudh, Raghu marched down, in fine winter, to Suhma (a small country between Orissa and Bengal), conquering several kings on the way. The Suhman kings yielded easily. Next, he attacked Bengal. The Bengalis opposed him bravely in their war-vessels, but were defeated by him. He erected pillars of victory on the islands of the Ganges. This shows how powerful Bengal was in those remote times. Certainly, these Bengalis were then mostly Dravidians. Next, by an elephant-bridge, he crossed the river Kapisa and attacked Orissa which was easily won. He next attacked Kalinga and conquered it after a hard struggle. Having released and reinstated the Kalinga king, he marched south, doubled the cape and then turned northward. The kings of Pandya, Kerala, Malabar, Western Ghats, Konkan, and other chiefs of the western coast of India, being subdued, paid him much wealth. From the Indus he went to conquer Persia. After a very fierce fighting, the Persians surrendered. Thence, he came to ancient Afghanistan where his army drank much grapewine. Thence turning to the north, he arrived on the western bank of the Indus. There, he defeated the Huna kings after severe fighting. The Kambojas yielded and paid him wealth and fine horses. Thence he went to the Himalayas where he defeated seven different wild tribes. Then passing through Tibet, he reached the easternmost India, crossed the Lauhitya, i.e. river Brahmaputra and came upon Pragjyotis (Assam). The king of Kamarupa yielded easily and gave him his best elephants as presents. Thence, he returned to Ayodhya. He next performed the *Visvajit* sacrifice and gave away all his belongings to the Brahmans and the poor. His son was Aja who married the fair Indumati, the Bhoja princess of Vidarbha. Shortly after, having crowned Aja, Raghu turned an anchorite. But Aja begged Raghu not to go to the forest. So, Raghu built a cottage in the suburb where he used to give instructions to Aja and the ministers. After some years, Raghu died in peace. Being an ascetic, he was interred and not cremated. Aja was a sensitive, kind-hearted and beneficent ruler. He was a patron of learning. By Indumati, he had a very worthy son in Prince Dasaratha.

When the prince had reached his youth, Aja left the raj to him and began to live with the queen in a garden outside the town. Here one day, the queen suddenly fell ill and died. Now, the sorrows of Aja knew no bounds. He almost went mad. In this distempered state, he lived for seven or eight years more. Then one day, his dead body was found floating on the Sarayu. As a king, Dasaratha was heroic, truthful, popular, and merciful. The kingdom was highly prosperous under him.

The seers honoured him in the *Rig Veda*. Leaving Kosala well-guarded under his eight ministers, Dasaratha was out on his Indian conquests, in which he was fully triumphant. Of course, conquests in those days simply meant temporary subjugation of kings, payment of tributes and presents, and attendance upon the imperial victor when performing sacrifices. Having conquered Sindhu, Sauvira, Saurashtra, Matsya, Kasi, Kosala, Magadha, Anga, Banga, and some states of the Deccan including the flourishing Dravira (*Ramayana, Oudh Book, canto 10, verses 37–38*), Dasaratha performed a horse sacrifice with great éclat on the tract between the Sarayu and the Tamasa. He gave princess Santa, his only child, by an inferior queen, to his friend Lomapada, king of Anga (east Bihar). Santa was married to sage Rishyasringa who performed a special sacrifice for a male child of Dasaratha. Indeed, Dasaratha obtained four sons by his three queens, Kausalya of south Kosala (south-east of Hastinapur), Kaikeyi of Kekaya (north-west India) and Sumitra of Magadha. The princes received very careful training at the hands of competent sages. They all married in the royal family of Mithila (north Bihar). Rama, the eldest prince had to win the fair Sita, daughter of Siradhvaja Janaka by his queen Susatya, after a clear test of his strength, in the shape of breaking Shiva's adamantine bow, long preserved in the house of the Janakas. Dasaratha, now old, was going to crown Rama, then a heroic lad of some thirty springs, when Kaikeyi stepped in and asked the throne for her own son Bharata and the exile of Rama for fourteen years. On hearing this, the old king fainted. But Rama, learning that his father had promised his step-mother two boons on a previous occasion, cheerfully bowed to his awful destiny and left Ayodhya the same day with his wife Sita and half-brother Lakshmana, amidst loud wailings of all. The old king succumbed to grief on the sixth night. Bharata, then living with his grandfather in Kekaya, knew nothing of these unhappy incidents at home. The priests and the ministers soon brought him to Ayodhya. Having learnt all, Bharata became angry and child his mother for her wickedness. He then set out with the leading men to bring Rama back. But Rama would not come back and desired Bharata to rule for the benefit of the people. Saintly Bharata ruled Kosala as the regent, refusing all royal honours and placing the shoes of Rama on the throne, from a village called Nandigrama, only two miles from Ayodhya (*Ramayana, Lanka Book, canto 127, verse 29*). Rama passed ten happy years in the virgin forests near Chitrakuta in Bundelkhand. Thence, he shifted further south and lived on the Godavari. About this time, Ravana, a powerful Hindu Tamil King, ruled Lanka, capital of ancient Ceylon. The southern most parts of India also formed a part of his dominions. Ravana gave these Indian tracts to his sister Surpanakha, a young widow, under the protection of his grandfather, Malyavan. Hearing of the banished princes, Surpanakha one day came to Rama, with only a few attendants and asked him to go over to her capital and live with her. Rama refused, as he was with his wife. Then she turned to Lakshmana, who also begged to be excused on account of his being a married man. Hearing her passionate entreaties of Lakshmana, Sita laughed. Surpanakha, now indignant, was going to attack Sita, when Lakshmana stopped her and smote her nose and ears with his sharp sword. Overcome with disgrace, she went back to her grandfather who at once sent an army 14,000 strong, to punish Rama. The exiled hero faced the enemy bravely, fought like a lion and killed the Tamil generals Khara and Dushana. The rest took fright and fled. Alarmed at this, Ravana speedily landed on the continent with a powerful force.

Here, Maricha, an old enemy of Rama and son to Taraka, whom Rama had killed for Visvamitra, met Ravana and urged him to steal away Sita, as that would serve the double purpose of revenge and ruining Rama. Sita was stolen by Ravana, taken to Lanka and imprisoned in a garden. Rama marched southward in quest of his wife. On the way, he killed Biradha, Kavandha and other Tamil chiefs who had tried to oppose him. He arrived at Kishkindhya, now Bellary district, north of Mysore. Here he allied with Sugriva, killed his brother Bali and made him king. As soon as the rains were over, a search was made, Sita was found and then preparations were made for the Lanka war that happened in the fourteenth year of the exile. Bharata sent men and money. Pratardana, king of Benaras, an ally of Oudh, came to aid Rama in his distress. Sugriva and Prince Angada collected a powerful army in the south. Hanuman, an accomplished prince whose ancestors had come from the north and settled in the Deccan, became dedicated to Rama's cause. Nala, an expert engineer, built a wooden bridge for Rama across the strait. Huge pieces of rock were carried from quarries with the help of machines, to secure the posts in the sea (*Ramayana, Lanka Book, canto 22, shloka 56*). Bibhishana, brother to Ravana, requested him to make friends with Rama and return Sita, but he was ignored. Bibhishana now allied with Rama. The combined army crossed the strait in four days. All negotiations having failed, war began and lasted about three months. Prince Angada was the commander of Rama's force. Rama killed Ravana and declared Bibhishana the king of Ceylon. After a short stay in fair Lanka, Rama came back to Kishkindhya and thence proceeded direct to Ayodhya, his exile having expired in the meantime. In fourteen years, Rama had punished many refractory Dravidian chiefs and spread Aryan civilisation in the Deccan. On his return, Rama, Sita and the party were most cordially welcomed by Bharata, the priests, the ministers, and the leading merchants. He was soon crowned king amidst the rejoicings of all. Old Vasista, who had lived several years in the Chinese capital, came back to coronate Rama. Like Dasaratha, Rama also devoted his whole attention to the good of the kingdom. He was rather dark in complexion but bright in all princely qualities.

The following are the chief events of his reign:

(i) Abandonment of his wife, to obey the clamour of his people, who suspected Sita's character in the house of Ravana.

(ii) Conquest of Mathura. Oppressed by the tyranny of King Lavana, son to King Madhu—a powerful Daitya king, the Brahmans of the state complained to Rama who forthwith sent Satrughna with a strong army. Madhupur was invaded; the fight went on for several days. Lavana was killed by Satrughna, who occupied the capital, repaired and renewed it under the name of Mathura and lived there 12 years (*Ramayana, VIII. 73 to 85 cantos; Vishnu Purana IV. 4; Varaha Purana 157 to 161 Chapters*).

(iii) Conquest of Gandhara. Yudhajit, king of Kekaya, had sent a messenger to Rama complaining that the Gandharas often oppressed his people. Rama, before long, sent Bharata with a powerful force. After a long fight, the kingdom of Gandhara, lying on both sides of the Indus, was conquered.

(iv) Horse-sacrifice. After many conquests, Rama celebrated a horse-sacrifice with a golden image of his wife Sita by his side. Valmiki had compassionately housed the banished Sita and taught her twin sons—Kusa and Lava, a considerable part of the lyrical epic, the

Ramayana, composed in five books (now II to VI) and 12,000 shlokas (see *Mahabibhasha*). Instructed by the sage, the two princes, then in their teens and in hermit-garb, came to the capital and recited different parts in the sacrificial fair. All were spellbound by the recitation. By these means, Valmiki sought to induce Rama and the people to accept Sita. With the consent of Rama, Sita was brought before all. But Rama declined, as some people still objected. Upon this, Sita—that 'queen of the queens of miseries'—dropped down dead. Her twin sons Kusa and Lava, however, were accepted.

(v) Foundation of Lucknow. In compliment to his brother Lakshmana who had shared all his troubles and toils, Rama built the city of Lakshmanavati, destined to be the capital of Oudh long afterwards.

(vi) Partition. The four royal brothers had two sons each, amongst whom Rama had partitioned his empire thus: Ram's son Kusa was placed at Kusavati near the foot of the Vindhyas, and Lava was made king of north Kosala, capital Sravasti; Bharata's sons were given the Gandhara kingdom, Taksha's capital was Taksasila (Greek *Taxila*) and Pushkara's capital was Pushkaravati (Greek *Peukelaotis* or *Peucolaitis*), some eighteen miles from Peshawar (*Ramayana VIII. 114*); Lakshamana's sons Angada got Karupada (?), capital Angada, and Chandraketu got Malladesa, capital Chandrakanta (these two States were in the Terai. Buddha died in the land of the Mallas); Satrughna's sons Satrughati got Vidisa, now Bhilsa in central India and Suvahu got Mathura.

The solar occupation of these outlying countries was short-lived.

(vii) The empire. The pretty large empire of Rama comprised the two Kosalas, Mathura, central India, north-west frontier provinces and east Afghanistan, and some other tracts. The friendly states: Anga, Banga, Matsya (Jaipur), Srigaverapur (north of Allahabad), Kasi, Sindh, Sauvira, Saurashtra, the Deccan Peninsula, Kosala, Kishkindhya, Sinhala (Ceylon).

Distracted with grief for the loss of his beloved wife, most affectionate mother and the dearest brother Lakshmana, one day in a frantic mood, Rama drowned himself in the river Sarayu. He probably ruled till 1420 or 1415 BC. All traditions, both secular and sacred, extol him as an extraordinary man. He was an ideal ruler and an ideal husband. He is still worshipped as an incarnation of God. Rama was the last great and good ruler of ancient India. Soon after his death a bloody and barbarous age followed, which resulted in serious political disturbances.

After the death of Rama, the eight princes met at Ayodhya and with one voice, crowned the eldest Prince Kusa, king. Fifty-eight kings followed Rama on the throne but the glory of Kosala gradually declined. The Sṛavasti line alone was powerful for some time afterwards.

5

ASCENDANCY OF THE LUNAR DYNASTY

The first twenty-six kings of the lunar dynasty had ruled from their capital at Pratisthana near Allahabad. The twenty-seventh king Hasti removed the capital to Hastinapur on the Upper Ganges, some forty miles down Haridwar (perhaps, 2060 or 2050 BC). The solar kings reigned supreme in Kosala from 2800 to 1400 BC. Their only notable colony was Videha or Mithila (north Bihar). The lunar kings, though not as bright as the solar, were yet powerful and important. Their eight dynasties ruled in different parts of India. Some of their chiefs bore imperial sway. The main line, that of the Kurus, was supreme in the Doab (land between the Ganges and the Jamuna). Matsyas ruled around Jaipur. Panchalas were dominant about Kanauj. Yadavas were powerful about Mathura and Kathiawar; the Haihayas were supreme on the Narmada, near its mouth. The Varhadratha dynasty of Magadha lasted from 1400 to 780 BC. The Kasis were powerful around Benaras. Prince Vrihadratha of Chedi (Central Province) had defeated and killed the Daitya king Rishabha or Magadha and built his capital at Giribraja guarded by five hills (about 1450 BC). His son, Jarasandha, was the greatest monarch in India towards the close of the fifteenth century BC. After the Parasurama war, great anarchy prevailed in India for at least half a century. Then, by the efforts of the sages, peace was restored. But the fourteenth century again witnessed India in great turmoil, the like of which is rarely known in the history of the world. In east India, in Magadha, Jarasandha was the prince of the tyrants. He intended to offer hundred kings as sacrifice and he had already seized eighty-six kings. In north India, at Hastinapur, Duryodhana was trying his best, by various plots, to exterminate his rivals, the five Pandava brothers. In west India, at Mathura, the tyrant Kansa having imprisoned his father Ugrasena, usurped the throne and oppressed his own tribesmen—the Yadavas. In south India, in Chedi, Sisupala, another wicked tyrant, was a general of Jarasandha. The kings of Bengal, King Naraka and his son Bhagadatta of Kamrup, King Vana of upper Assam were vassals of Jarasandha. India thus groaned under the tyrants. But for the timely interference of the Yadava prince, Krishna, we cannot say what would be the condition of India. This greatest spirit of the age clearly saw the terribly barbarous state of things and immediately thought of a radical cure. With the aid of his heroic brother, Balarama, Krishna slew Kansa, his own maternal uncle and son-in-law to Jarasandha.

At this, Jarasandha invaded Mathura eighteen times. But the powerful Yadavas bravely held their own. The grand confederacy of powerful kings who had followed Jarasandha in his invasion of Mathura, is given in the Harivansa: The king of Karusha (in north-west India), Dantavakra (?), the king of Chedi (central provinces), king of Kalinga (upper Madras), king of Pundra (Deccan), king of Kishika (Deccan), and Sankriti, Bhishmaka, Rukmi, Venudara, Srutastha, Kratha, and Ansuman were kings of central India. The kings of Anga, Banga, Kosala, Kasi, Dasarna (in the Punjab), Sumha (Burdwan), Videha, Madra (between Ravi and Jhelum), Trigarta (Jalandhar), Salva, Darada, Yavana, Bhagadatta, king of Assam, Saivya king of Saubira, powerful Pandya, Suvala king of Gandhar (Candahar), mighty Nagnajit, Goinarda king of Kashmir, Duryodhana of Hastinapur, and Chekitana, king of Bulkh made up the rest. (*Harivansa, chapters 90–91*).

Ugrasena was again placed on the throne. The Magadha king now allied with another mighty tyrant Kalayavana by name. The Yadavas now left Mathura, withdrew to the Kathiawar Peninsula and made Dwaraka their capital. Krishna next slew Naraka, king of Kamarup and defeated his ally, King Vana of upper Assam. The state of north India was no better. After the good king Shantanu, honoured in the *Rig Veda*, troubles arose in the royal family of Hastinapur as to succession. Prince Dhritarashtra, being born blind, could not inherit the family dominions. His brother Pandu succeeded. After a splendid reign, Pandu withdrew to the north, with his two queens, as he had no son. There, by permission of Pandu, the queens bore five sons by rishis. Dhritarashtra had hundred sons and one daughter by his queen Gandhari, princess of Gandhara. After several years, the rishis sent the five Pandu princes to Hastinapur where Bhisma, the regent received them. But the Kuru brothers (sons to the blind king) strongly opposed them, as the Pandavas were deemed illegitimate scions. From that time, the Kurus hated the Pandus, and plotted many times to kill them. To secure peace, Dhritarashtra wisely gave half the kingdom to the Pandavas. Yudhisthira, the eldest Pandava prince, then built his new capital at Indraprastha, near modern Delhi on the Yamuna. The large Khandava forest reclaimed by the Pandus, was formerly owned by a Turkish chief who, losing his state, turned an enemy of the Pandavas. Krishna, related to the Pandavas, became their counsellor. Yudhisthira was a timid prince, but his four other brothers were very great heroes. Krishna begged on Yudhishthira to aim at overlordship. After hesitation, Yudhishtira agreed. The first step was to overthrow Jarasandha, the mightiest tyrant of Magadha. As the Pandavas dared not fight the Magadha king openly, wily Krishna took heroic Bhima and Arjuna with him, went to Giribraja in guise of Brahmans, met Jarasandha in his palace and challenged him to a duel with Bhim, in which Jarasandha was killed. His son Sahadeva submitted and Krishna placed him on the throne as an ally of the Pandavas. Krishna at once liberated the eighty-six kings imprisoned in jail for the purpose of sacrifice. They all vowed allegiance to the Pandavas and then went to their several kingdoms. The Pandavas then made preparations for conquest.

THE CONQUESTS OF THE PANDAVA PRINCES (1405 BC)

Arjuna to the north went with a strong army and first defeated the kings of Kulinda, then of Anarta and Kalakuta; next he defeated King Sumandala; with him he next invaded Scythia and fought very bravely with its kings who were defeated. King Prativindhya was next defeated. Accompanied by those kings, he next invaded Pragjyotishadesa (Assam): fierce fight then ensued with Bhagadatta and his allies, the Kiratas (hill-tribes), the Chinese and the chiefs on the Bay of Bengal, an arm of which then ran far into the interior. King Bhagadatta submitted after eight days' fight. He next conquered Antargiri, Vahirgiri and Upagiri (the hill tracts). He next conquered the various hill chiefs and collected from them much wealth and gold. He next fought King Vrihanta of the hilly country Uluka, who submitted after fierce fighting. With Vrihanta, he next attacked and defeated King Senavindu; next Modapur, Bamadeva, Sudama, Sukula, and north Uluka were conquered. He next encamped at Devaprastha, capital of Senavindhu, collected an army and then marched against King Visvagaswa and defeated the hill-chiefs on the way; he next subdued the seven non-Aryan tribes called Utsava-Sanketas. Thereafter the warriors of Kashmir were subdued. King Lohita with ten minor kings were subdued. Trigarta (Jalandhar), Daru, Kokanada were then conquered. He next took the fair Abhisari town. He defeated Rochamana of Uraga; he next occupied Sinhapura; he invaded and conquered the Sumhas and the Sumalas. He subsequently reduced the Valhikas, the Daradas, the Kambojas and other nomads of the north-west. Loha, west Kamboja and north Rishika made common cause, but he defeated them all. In the north-west, he received many excellent horses. He conquered the Nishkutagiri and the Himalayas; reached the Sveta Parvat, crossed it and then invaded the Kimpurusha Varsha (east Tibet); he next conquered Hataka (perhaps, a part of Tibet), then he visited the Mansarowar and other lakes, received many good steeds. He finally reached south Siberia and conquered it. A part of western China was also conquered. Then he returned to Indraprastha (Delhi).

To the east went Prince Bhima with a powerful army and conquered the Panchalas, the Gandakas and the Videhas. Sudharma, king of Dasarna fought hard but was defeated. Pleased with his bravery, Bhima made Sudharma his general. He next defeated Fochamana, king of Asvamedha. He next conquered the entire east India and then turned southward and subdued kings Sukumara and Sumitra of Pulindanagar. He next marched against Sisupala (of Chedi) who received him cordially and tendered his submission. Bhima stayed there for thirteen days. He next conquered Sreniman of the Kumara kingdom and king Vrihadvala of south Kosala. He next subdued Dirghayajna (alias Urukriya) of Ayodhya, Gopala Kaksha, north Kosala, and the Malla chiefs. Next, he conquered the sub-Himalayan tracts (Terai), Bhallata and the Suktimat hill. He next defeated Suvahu, king of Kasi. King Kratha of Suparsva, the Matsyas, the Maladas, the Madadhara hill and Somadheya,

Vatsabhumi, King Bharga, the king of the Nishadas, Maniman, the Bhagavan hill, south Malla, the Sarmakas, the Varmakas, King Janaka of Videha were successively conquered. The Sakas and the Barbaras he won by manoeuvre. He next conquered the seven kings of the Kiratas near the Mahendra hill (Eastern Ghats). Then he conquered Sumha (Burdwan) and Prasumha (Midnapur). Then he marched against Magadha and defeated Danda, Dandadhara and other kings. He next went to Giribraja where King Sahadeva yielded easily, to Anga (East Bihar) where King Karna fought fiercely but was subdued. Next, he fought with other hill chiefs, killed the chief of Modagiri (Mongyr or Rajmahal). Vasudeva, king of Pundra (north Bengal) and Mahaujas, king of Kausikikachchha (perhaps Hugli district) were both defeated, after fierce fights. He then came upon Banga (West Bengal) and successively defeated Samudrasena, Chandrasena, the kings of Tamralipta, Karvata and Sumha (Burdwan according to commentator Nilakantha) and other hill chiefs and non-Aryans. Having collected immense wealth from the conquered tracts, he marched against the Lauhitya desa, i.e. lower Assam, conquered it and other seaboard tracts peopled by the non-Aryans. They all gave him jewels, sandalwood, saffron, muslin, rugs, gems, pearls, gold, silver, and ruby. It is said that the non-Aryans had almost covered Bhima with various presents. Thence, Bhima returned to Indraprashta. The hill states of Manipur and Tripura (then called *Nagaloka*, i.e. land of the Tibeto-Burmans) had already been brought under Aryan influence. Arjuna married two princesses of those two royal houses. It may be noted here that an arm of the Bay of Bengal then extended to the Cachar district and the Ganges fell into the Bay, east of Dacca. That large Ganga, over ten miles in breadth near the mouth, has now shrunk into a very tiny stream called the Buri Ganga (old Ganges) on which the historic city of Dacca now stands.

To the south started Sahadeva the youngest Pandava prince with a large army, and conquered the Susrasenas, the Matsya king, Dantavakra, Rajakumara and Sumitra, west Matsya, Patachchara (literally land of volcano, perhaps refers to ancient Mewar), the land of the Nishadas (Bhils and Meenas), Gosringa hill, and Raja Sreniman. Raja Kuntibhoja yielded easily, for he was maternal uncle to the Pandavas. On the river Chambal, he had a terrible fight with Prince Jambhaka whom he defeated. Then he pushed on southward and conquered Seka and

Aparaseka and received from them gems and wealth. Next, he marched to the countries on the Narmada, followed by them. There, he fought with the large army of kings Vinda and Anuvinda of Avanti, whom he defeated. At Bhojakatapur, he had a fierce fight with King Bhishmaka, who was subdued. Next, he defeated the kings of Kosala and Venwata, the Kantarakas and the kings of eastern Kosala. Then were defeated the Natakeyas, the Heramwakas and Marudhas. Munjagrama was taken by him by force. Next, the Nachina and Arbuka chiefs and other chiefs of the woods, were subdued. The king of Vatapipura (Badami) was defeated. The Pulindas, being defeated submitted to him. Then he pushed on to the further south. After one day's battle, the king of Pandya was defeated. In Kishkindhya (Bellary), Mainda and Dvivida fought him for seven days and then submitted to him with the offer of many valued presents. Next he attacked Mahismati town whose king, Niladwaja, fought very hard. In the action, his army was much reduced and even his own life was at stake. Niladwaja at length submitted. Thence Sahadeva proceeded further south: the king of Traipura (Teoari) and Akriti, king of Saurashtra were defeated. He then encamped there and sent ambassadors to get submission. Rukmi yielded and paid much wealth. Next, he conquered Surparaka, Talakata and Dandaka (near Nasik, according to St. Martin, *Dhankakata*). He then defeated the non-Aryan islanders of the Arabian Sea, the Nishadas (hunter), the Purushadas, the dark-skinned mixed Dravidians, the entire Kola hill, Surabhipattan, Tamradwipa, Ramaka hill, and the Timingila king; he sent generals to receive the submission of Kerakas, who lived in the woods, olf Sanjayanti city, of Pashanda and Karahataka. Moreover, Pandya, Dravida, Udra-Kerala, Andhra, Talavana, Kalinga, Atavipuri (a town) and Yavanashta (a town), he subdued by ambassadors. Next, he went to the sea coast and sent an ambassador to Bibhishana (king of Lanka) who acknowledged the Pandava supremacy and gave various gems, sandalwood, ornaments, precious cloths, and jewels. Then he returned to Indraprastha.

To the west went Prince Nakula, with a large army. Starting from Khandavaprastha, he first attacked the Rohitaka hill where he fought hard with the Mayurakas. Next, he conquered the entire desert and the fertile and rich countries called Sairishaka and Mahettha. He next attacked King Akrosa, who submitted after a stubborn resistance. He conquered the countries called Dasarna, Sibi, Trigarta, Ambastha, Malwa, Panchakarpata and the people called the Madhyamikas and the Batadhana Brahmans. Returning thence, he defeated the Utsavasanketas of Pushkararanya (Mukran Coast?). He then came to the Indus and conquered the numerous chiefs there. The Sudras and the Abhiras on the Sarasvati, the fish-eaters and the hill-tribes, entire Panchanada, the Amar hill (Mer Koh?), north Jyotisha and the cities of Divyakata and Dwarapala were taken by him by force. Next, the Ramathas, the Harahoonas and other kings of the west were all reduced to submission. From there, he sent an ambassador to Krishna, who with the Yadavas, submitted. He next reached Sakala (Sealkot?), capital of the Madras, where King Salya—his maternal uncle—was won by affection. Next, he conquered the fierce *mlechchhas* of the sea and also the Palhavas, Barbaras, the Kiratas, the Yavanas, and the Sakas. It is said that 10,000 camels bore with difficulty the heavy load of presents which he placed before Yudhisthira.

The conquest over, the Pandavas began an imperial sacrifice attended with great pomp. The following powerful kings and nobles were present: Dhritarashtra, Bhishma, Duryodhana and his brothers; King Suvala and his son Sakuni of Gandhara (Kandahar); the great hero Karna of Anga (east Bihar); heroic Salya; Valhika; Somadatta. Bhuri of the Kuru dynasty; Bhurisrava, Sala, Aswatthama, Kripa, Drona (the Preceptor), Jayadratha king ofr Sindh, Drupada with his sons, Salwa, the mighty King Bhagadatta of Assam with his powerful allies living on the Bay of Bengal, numerous hill kings, Raja Vrihadvala, Vasudeva of Pundra, Samudrasena, king of Bengal; the kings of Kalinga, Akarsha and Kuntala; the kings of Malawa; the Andhrakas; the Draviras; the Sinhalese; the kings of Kashmir; Kuntibhoja, Gauravahana, the kings of Balhika (Bulkh); King Virata, with his two sons of Matsya (Jaipur); the mighty king Mavella; Sisupala with his son, of the Central Province; the Yadavas of west India; the kings of the Central Provinces.

THE LIST OF PRESENTS

(i) The Kamboja king sent many fine furs embroidered with gold laces, skins, 300 horses of different colours, and 300 camels.

(ii) The Brahmans and the Sudras sent a legion of bullocks, besides numberless gold pitchers filled with ghee.

(iii) The Sudras of the coasts sent many fair maidservants, deer-skins and Gandhara horses.
(iv) The Bairamas, the Paradas, the Abhiras and the Kitabas sent various kinds of gems, deer, goats, sheep, cattle, camels, honey, and various rugs and blankets.
(v) Bhagadatta from Assam sent horses, ornaments, fine ivory-handled swords.
(vi) People from the shores of the Oxus gave 10,000 asses, gold and silver.
(vii) The Ekaipodos sent fine wild horses and gold.
(viii) The Chinese, the Sakas, the Odras, the Barbaras, the Harahoonas sent miscellaneous things.
(ix) Tangana and the Para Tangana kings sent gold.

The following kings, summoned, came to wait upon Yudhisthira during his imperial sacrifice: the kings of Anga, Banga, Paundra (north Bengal), Odra (Orissa), Chola (Coromandal Coast), Dravira (a part of the Deccan), Andhraka (in the Deccan), islands of the sea, the lowlands of east Bengal, Pattana, Sinhala (a province in the Deccan), Barbara (?), Indian *mlechchha* desas (perhaps outlying states), Lanka, western states, the seaboard tract, viz., Palhava, Darada Kirata, Yavana, Saka, Harhoona, China, Tushara (Tochari), the Indus Valley, Jagara (?), Ramatha, Munda, the female-kingdom (?), Tangana, Kekaya, Malwa (in the north-west), Kashmir.

On the auspicious moment, the sacrifice began. With the approval of the elders, Yudhisthira showed Krishna some special marks of honour connected with the sacrifical rite. This exasperated Sisupala, the Chedi king, who left the camp and plotted with his allies to disturb the sacrifice. Sisupala was a sworn enemy of Krishna. A terrible confusion followed for a short time. Krishna then rose up and recounted the wicked deeds of Sisupala before all: 'Sisupala is cruel-hearted. Without the least cause, he is an enemy of the Yadavas. During our absence in Assam, he attacked Dwaraka and burnt it down. At the time of king Bhoja's excursion in the Raivatak Hills, Sisupala had killed many of his followers and imprisoned the rest. He had stolen the horse to disturb the horse sacrifice of Vasudeva. He stole the wife of saintly Akrura, while she was going from Dwaraka to the Sauvira kingdom. He stole Bhadra, princess of

Visala, betrothed to his maternal uncle. He insulted me times without number. He even insulted Rukmini, my wife.' With this, Krishna hurled his special weapon, the quoit-shaped charka at Sisupala with so much force that it severed the head of the Chedi-king instantly. Everything was silenced soon. The sacrifice was duly performed. In pomp, gifts and feasts, it equalled that of King Harischandra of old time but surpassed those of Rantideva, Nabhaga, Mandhata, Manu, Prithu (son of Vena), Bhagiratha, Yayati, and Nahusha (1405 or 1409 BC).

The Kauravas (sons of Dhritarashtra) could not accept the good fortune of the Pandavas, their rivals. So, they plotted anew to ruin the Pandavas. Gambling in those days was a prevalent vice. The Kauravas challenged Yudhisthira to gambling. The Pandava king agreed and played at dice, staking successively his raj, person, nay courting banishment. But he lost all. Now, Yudhisthira was to live in exile for twelve years and one year more in an incognito state. During the period of exile, the Pandavas visited different parts of India and in the thirteenth year, they lived in the house of King Virata of Matsya (Jaipur) in disguise. On the expiry of their term of exile, the Pandavas came back and demanded their kingdom. But the Kauravas would not give them even an inch of ground without fight. The well-wishers of both parties tried their best for an amicable settlement, but in vain. So, a war was inevitable. Preparations went on on both sides. Almost all the princes of India and outside joined one party or the other. This *Mahabharata war* took place in November and December, 1389 BC. Both sides met on the vast plains of Kurukshetra (Karnal) near Delhi. Through the noble self-sacrifice of Bhishma, the counsel of Krishna, and the bravery of Arjuna, the Pandavas, after a destructive war lasting eighteen days, won the day. Only five Pandavas, and three Kauravas survived. Leaving a friendly Kaurava as viceroy at Indraprastha, the Pandavas went to Hastinapur, where Yudhisthira the Just was persuaded by all to take up the reins of government. He agreed to rule only for the benefit of the people, till his grandson Parikshit was of age.

6

THE PANDAVA DYNASTY
(1388 TO 700 BC)

Shortly after Yudhisthira ascended the throne, Hastinapur was invaded by a non-Aryan chief named Krisna from the northern mountains. The Pandavas in their shattered condition could not prevail against him. At last, Prince Vrishaketu, the heroic son of Karna, defeated and brought him before Yudhisthira as a captive. The Pandava emperor spared his life and the sermons of Krishna turned him into an ascetic. 'Having got the kingdom, Yudhisthira ordered the people of the four castes to live after their own models and gave away thousands of gold *nishkas*. Restoring peace and order in the realm, he made over the charge of administration to Dhritarashtra, Queen Gandhari and Vidura.' (*Mahabharata, Peace Book, Chapter 45*). But the blind king, his queen, Kunti—mother to the Pandavas, and minister Vidura, disgusted with the world, withdrew to woods where they soon died in a conflagration. Soon after, Krishna, the principal figure of the Yadavas, then master of west India from Mathura to Dwaraka, was killed by a hunter. Erelong, another sad incident followed. The powerful Yadavas of 18,000 heroes, mostly given to excessive drinking, destroyed themselves in an inglorious war following a petty quarrel. After that, a sudden rising of the western sea flooded a considerable part of the peninsula. Dwaraka was engulfed. The Yadavas mostly scattered in different directions. The chief of Jaisalmer (Rajputana) claims direct descent from Krishna. Long, long after, the Yadavas built an empire in the Deccan.

It seems probable that after the Great War, fresh Aryan immigrants came to India from the north. In one case at least we have a proof of it. Prince Samva, son to Krishna had brought a pretty large colony of Sakali Brahmans from Central Asia to conduct the worship in his famous Sun-Temple at Multan, originally Mulasthana Sambapura, mentioned by Y Chwang as Mooltambura.

Having crowned Parikshit—grandson to Arjuna—Yudhisthira, with his brothers and wife went to the Himalayas for eternal peace. Parikshit came to the throne about 1370 BC. He was endowed with all the princely qualities. The kingdom was highly prosperous under him. He was very fond of hunting excursions. It is said that he died by snakebite at the age of 60. The 'snakebite' meant death at the hands of the Turks. To cover the disgrace, later writers invented the tale of the snakebite. The Turks had already occupied Kashmir and came down on the plains in large numbers. Parikshit went to fight them out, but was killed in action. Krishna, who had attacked Hastinapura in 1388 BC from the north, was most probably a Turk. This is not a mere assumption but a facat confirmed by the *Mahabharata, Rajatarngini* and the *Satapatha Brahmana.* Gonarda, king of Kashmir went with Jarasandha to attack Mathura. There he was killed by Balarama, brother to Krishna. Damodara, son to Gonarda, burned with revenge. Krishna and the Yadavas were present at the marriage assembly at Gandhar. There, Damodara with his army, attacked Krishna and party. But he was treacherously murdered by wily Krishna, who declared his pregnant wife Yasomati, queen of Kashmir. Prince Gonarda II was born. During his minority, the war took place. The Turks wrested Kashmir from this Gonarda. Kalhana says that 35 rulers followed Gonarda II, whose names he could not recover. These were Turks. The *Mahabharata, Wood Book, Chapter 82, verse 90* calls Kasahmir Takshaka Naga Bhavana, i.e. country of the Turks. His infant son, Janamejaya, was then placed on the throne by the priests and the ministers. He married fair Vapustoma, princess of Kasi. He began to rule from 1321 BC. His was an eventful long reign. About 1300 BC, King Sesostris (Ramases II of Egypt) is said to have invaded India and penetrated it as far as the Ganges. It was perhaps a passing storm. His government was involved in a war which may be called the Turkish War. The Turks of ancient times were known to the Hindus as *Takshakas* or *Nagas* i.e. snake-people. We have seen that the Indian Turkish chief, being ousted from his kingdom by the Pandu brothers had fought against them. Now the Turkish colonists of India and the Turks of the north allied and made war upon Janamejaya, who also rose equal to the occasion, defeated them signally and forced them to enter into tributary engagements with him at Taxila. This has been woven into the fine legend of Janamejaya's 'snake sacrifice' at Taxila. The Turks were driven to Kashmir. Other non-Aryan risings and invasions were put down. After great conquests, he performed a horse sacrifice. This is mentioned in the *Satapatha Brahmana*. He could not be a party to the Great War, as is wrongly supposed by some. The rest of his life was spent in peace and prosperity. The illustrious sage Vyasa published his epic entitled the *Bharata Samhita* during this imperial sacrifice. Sukadeva, son to Vyasa, was a minister of this king. He probably ruled till the middle of the thirteenth century BC. The political history of India for the following five or six centuries, is wrapped in darkness. We only possess the bare king-lists of different dynasties. After the great wars, the country at last enjoyed peace. Before 1200 BC, Hastinapur being eroded by the Ganges, the capital was removed to Kausambi (now, Kosam), some 30 miles west of Allahabad.

The Gangetic kingdoms continued. In the Punjab and the Indus Valley, many principalities came into being. Of them, Kashmir was the most important. Many clans had merged into tribes and many tribes had merged into nations.

The long period (1200 to 700 BC) witnessed the decline and the fall of the Indo-Aryans, due perhaps to the following causes: long-continued struggles with the non-Aryans; their fight among themselves; their fight with the later Aryan immigrants; the enervating climate and the fertility of their new abode on the Ganges and Jamuna, which were more conducive to religious contemplation and peaceful courses than to martial excitement and military life; gradual adoption of non-Aryan customs; and priestly domination.

7

THE EPIC AGE OF INDIA: *2500 TO 1300 BC*

GENERAL FEATURES

It was an age of priestly supremacy and unquestioning obedience on the part of the people (Max Müeller). The land of the Indus and the simple fervency of worshipping the natural phenomena were forgotten. The midland of north India was now the scene of general activity: great importance was given to solemn rites and pompous ceremonies.

It was an age of keen rivalry—an age of proud self-assertion and fiery valour. There were wars between the Hindus and the Jains; between the Brahmans and the Kshatriyas; between the Kurus and the Pandavas; between the Aryans and the non-Aryans; between the Hindus and the Turks; between the Vasista and the Visvamitra families.

It was an age of light and darkness, peace and unrest, progress and decline, prosperity and adversity caused by two long and terrible famines. The states of Kosala, Kasi and Videha were seats of excellent learning, culture, religion, philosophy, morals and manners, while Hastinapura, Indraprastha, Mathura, Magadha, Assam, Bengal, and Central Province were the homes of tyrants with corrupt morals.

The Brahmans of the age fought hard for their supremacy. But they did very little for the nation. If we exclude the rishis, the rest would appear as a set of 'blockheads', busy with mere rites and rituals, legends and tales. On the other hand, we find the Kshatriyas supreme in every field. The shone in noble and original thoughts and golden deeds but never in 'barbaric pearls and gold'. Rama, Krishna, Visvamitra, Ajatasatru of Kasi, the Janakas of Videha are only too well know. The new school of true wisdom in the Upanishadas, was started by the Kshatriyas alone.

It was, moreover, an age of migration and mission-work, spread of Hindu influence and culture in the east and south.

EXTENT OF THE HINDU WORLD

The epic age presents to us India in four different regions according to the nature and degree of Hindu civilisation and influence as prevalent there. These are:

(1) The *Sapta-Sindhavas*, i.e. land of the Indus comprising Kashmir, east Afghanistan (Gandhar) and the Punjab—now cast into shade.
(2) The *Madhya-Desa* (Midland) comprising the Gangetic heptarchy, viz., Kurukshetra (Karnal), Matsya (Jaipur), Panchala, Surasena, Kasi, Kosala, and Videha (north Bihar). This was now regarded as the home of the model Aryan civilisation.
(3) The *Vahya-Desa*, i.e. external countries, so called because they lay outside the Midland. These lands, though sporadically elevated by Aryan rulers, priests and missionaries, were yet generally notorious for their corrupt morals, manners and food. Even the Aryan offshoots who ruled there, did not fully accept the caste rules and follow Aryan ceremonials but adopted the local customs. So they were denounced as *Arya mlechchhas*, i.e. denationalised Aryans. These countries were Sindhu (Sindh), Sauvira (Sophir = Ophir), Anarta (Kathiawar), Saurashtra (Gujarat), Magadha (south Bihar), Banga (Bengal), Pundraka (Rajashi and the northern half of Dacca division), Kamarupa (Assam), Manipur, Nagaloka (Tripura), Odra or Utkala (Orissa), Kalinga (Upper Madras), Chedi (Central Provinces), Bidarbha (Berar), Bhoja, Vidisa (Bhilsa), Dravida, Andhraka, Pandya, Kerala, Malaya-Vara, Konkan Gomanta (Goa), Maheya (Mahe), Dasarna, and Avanti.

(4) The Native Deccan, containing Dravidian states. Besides, there were other tracts peopled by less civilised men ridiculed by the Brahmans as *Sattas, Banaras* (Ba = almost, and *nara* = man).

Taking account of the sacred books alone (the Vedas, the *Brahmanas*, the Upanishadas, some early scholars confined the Hindu activity of the age within the Gangetic Valley mainly. The other parts of India were dimly known to them. The so-called *revealed literature*, being chiefly religious, only referred to these countries incidentally. We cannot slight the secular works, viz., the Sanskrit epics, *Harivansa*, the Puranas, to ascertain the sphere of early Hindu domination. Century after century, the Hindus pushed on till 1400 BC when numberless Hindu and other powerful states sprang up all over India. Yet, doubtless, there was a good deal of darkness, low morals, corrupt manners, and nomadic living.

The Census of 1911 shows that even in these advanced days, there were about seventy-one per cent 'untouchables' in the Hindu society. In former times, these were certain nomadic hunters living on roots, fruits, worms, birds, beasts and reptiles. They had long learnt agriculture and the peaceful life. Mere hunting, in Indian plains, has now perhaps become as rare as Dodo in Madagascar.

Our rishis were the pioneers of civilisation. They travelled much all over India, selected suitable sites for their herimatages on hilltops, by tidal rivers or in some lovely and lively lap of nature. There, they lived with their families, cattle, pupils, and army, spreading love and light on the natives around, teaching them better style, moral and manners. Agastya, Parasurama, Sarabhanga and other leading sages and their adherents had spread Hindu civilisation in south India long before 1400 BC. The Aryans had not come to a land of mere barbarism and darkness.

The Dravidians before them, had a far advanced civilisation: Their 'hundred cities', roads, forts, arms, armies, and boats are well proven by the *Rig Veda*. A modern theory of several eminent western philosogists proves the same: 'It does not appear that the Dravidian tongues of the Deccan had any radical connection with Sanskrit or any other language of the north. In ancient times, many civilised peoples of the West such as the Egyptians and the Arabians traded with the Deccan by sea. Close intimacy with those civilised foreign peoples, is the root of the Dravidian tongue. On the one hand, the Aryans from the north, crossing the Himalayas, had spread the light of civilisation in north India; that is the origin of Sanskritic tongues in India. On the other hand, the Deccan was illumined by the light of civilisation brought by the rich and cultured merchants of the West. The Dravidian civilisation was anterior to the Aryan. The Deccan was civilised before Aryavarta (north India). That early light gave dignity and importance to Tamil and other Dravidian tongues of the south. Light came from Egypt to the Deccan. From that began the cultural excellence of the language and literature of the south. An analysis and examination of the Dravidian alphabets and phraseology also confirm that conclusion. The alphabets of the south want many letters and do not look well. So, they betray the imperfect skill of a primitive people. Hence, the originality of the Dravidian tongue, and its connection with the languages of Egypt, Arabia are entitled to our best credit.'

The proud Sanskrit-speaking Aryans of the Midland hated and ridiculed the still inimical and powerful Dravidians of east and south India (*R.V., V, 29.10*) as *a-vrata* (without ceremony), *a-nasah*, 'without a good language' (Sayana). Commenting on it, Professor Wilson says: 'Alluding possibly to the uncultivated dialect of the barbarous tribes.'

Hinduisation of the south began from the twenty-second century BC first. The south gradually bowed to the superior Aryan creed and culture. But the work went on generally very slowly. The early adventurous and exiled princes of the north, who founded new states in east and south India, soon became rather Dravidianised. So, they were denounced as *Vratyas*, fallen or denationalised. It is manifest from these that there had been numberless states in India, owned by different peoples, before 1400 BC. The conquests of the epic age as given in epics, are not 'airy nothings to which poetic fancy gave a local habitation and a name.' Nor, are they interpolations of a much later age. The population of east and south India was mostly native. Bidarbha (Berar) and its adjoining parts and Maharashtra alone could boast of a little Aryan element. It was only in the sixth or fifth century BC that Aryan settlers went to the south in large numbers.

Next, we must show the existence of the kingdoms of the epic age by reference to our ancient secular lore.

1. Kurukshetra

A tract between the rivers Sarasvati, now Sarsuti (lost in the Rajputana desert) and Drishadvati (Caggar). The royal sage, Kuru, born of the lunar king, Samvarana by his queen, Tapati, performed many sacrifices on this field. Hence it was so called (*Mahabharata, Salya Book, Chapter 53*). It is now called Karnal. Hastinapur, built by king Hasti, four generations later, was the capital. It was perhaps 65 miles to the north-west of Delhi and 40 miles down Haridwar (Tod's *Rajasthan, vol. I, Chapter IV*). Two other cities were Indraprastha, now Inderpat, south of Delhi, near which is about the Purana Qila, and Thanesvar, Sanskrit Sthanviswara (*Mahabharata, Wood Book, Chapter 83*). Hastinapur was cut away by the Ganges before 1200 BC. It was somewhere near modern Thanesvar. Prithudaka, now Pehoa, 14 miles from Thanesvar, was the capital of Prithu on the Sarasvati. The caste system first began here.

2. Matsya

Now, Jaipur State in Rajputana. Virata was its king about 1400 BC Cunningham's boundary: North—Jhunjhun to Cot-Casim, 70 miles; east—Jhunjhun to Ajmer, 120 miles; south—Ajmer to Bana and confluence of Chambal, 150 miles; west—Chambal confluence to Cot-Kasim, 150 miles. Its capital was Viratnagar, 41 miles north of Jaipur and 105 miles south-west of Delhi. The town was surrounded by hills abounding with ores of copper. The people were very brave. Yuan Chwang (seventh century AD) had been to Viratnagar, 2½ miles in circumference. He found the citizens very brave and spirited.

3. Panchala

The lunar king, Haryasva had five sons—all experts in affairs of state. Their kingdom became known as Panchala, i.e. state of the five. It was a long strip on both sides of the Ganges. The northern part is now called Rohilkhand and the southern part, Etawa and other district. Ahichchatra was its most ancient capital. Its king, Sumada, submitted to Rama when the latter's horse had reached his capital.

About 1400 BC, Drupada, son to King Prishata, was the lord of Panchala. His former classmate Drona—a poor Brahman, but a master of military science, once saw him and asked his assistance. The proud Drupada turned him away. Drona next became the military teacher to the Kuru and Pandava princes of Hastinapur. The princes became very proficient. At the bidding of Drona, the princes attacked Drupada, defeated him and brought him to Drona as captive. Drona took the northern part and returned the southern part to Drupada who built a new capital at Kampilla on the Ganges, the site of which is now between Budaon and Farukkabad. Kanoul, Sanskrit *Kanya Kubja*, was an important city of the Panchalas.

King Kusa, nineth generation downward from Pururava of the lunar dynasty, had four sons who built four towns after them: Kushamba built Kausambi now Kosam, thirty miles to the north-west of Allahabad. Hastinapur being eroded (1220–1200 BC), the Pandava capital was removed to Kausambi (*Vishnu Purana, IV. 21*). Kusanabha built Mahodaya, also called Gadhipura; Kausa, Kusasthala and Kanyakubja. His *kanyas* (daughters) were *kubja*, hunch-backed. So, the city was called *Kanyakubja*, modern Kanouj. Amurtarajas built Dharmaranya, not yet identified. Basu, the aeronaut (upari-chara) built Basumati, formerly Kusagrapura, afterwards Giribraja, then Rajagriha—capital of Magadha (*Ramayana 1, 32*). Giribraja was guarded by five hills. It was rich in cattle, well watered, safe and beautified with edifices (*Mahabharata, Court Book*). Giribraja is now the old Rajgir. Nepal formed a part of Panchala of old.

4. Sura-sena

Literally, 'home of brave soldiers', formerly comprised Mathura district, Bharatpur, Kshiraguli, Dholpur, and the northern part of Gwalior state. The circumference of the kingdom was 833 miles, or some say, 1,000 miles. The state was noted for its brave people, cotton and gold. We hear of Mathura from 1500 BC (*Ramayana, 73 to 85 cantos, Vishnu Purana, IV. 4; Varaha Purana, 157* to *161 Chapters*). Kansa was the tyrant of Mathura about 1400 BC.

5. Kasi

Originally, the town between the rivers Baruna and Asi, was called *Rishi* Pattana, i.e. 'city of the seers'. Afterwards, King Kasi or Kasyapa of the lunar dynasty founded a state about 600 miles in circumference.

Cunningham's boundary: North—river Gomati; west—Gomati to Allahabad: Ton to Bilhari; south—Bilhari to Sonhat; east—river Karmanasa and Ganges.

The *Rig Veda, Satapatha Brahmana, Vrihadaranyaka Upanishada*, Sanskrit epics extol its glories. Further reference: *Ramayana,* Oudh Book, canto 10, shloka 37; I, 13.23; VII, 48.15. Benaras was its capital (*Ramayana, VIII, 69.19 Vishnu Purana, V. 34*).

6. Kosala

Mentioned in the *Brahmana* works. The *Satapatha Bhahmana (1.4.1)* gives the river Gandaka as dividing Kosala and Videha. Its capital was Ayodhya (*Atharva* Veda, *II, 41. p. 742*).

Further reference: *Ramayana*, VII, canto 144, *Vayu Purana*, chapter 88, *Mahabharata, Court Book*, Chapter 30. There was another Kosala in the Deccan (*Mahabharata, Court Book, Chapter 31*), probably modern Gondawana. Ancient Lakshmanawati is now Lucknow. Srasvasti, to the north of Oudh, was another important town. Its ruins are in Gonda.

Videha or Mithila, later Trihut, is modern Darbhanga and Muzaffarpur districts in north Bihar. It was another seat of the solar kings. Title of the kings was Janaka. Its capital was Baijayanta (according to *Ramayana*), Mithilanagari, or Janakapura. The *Brahmana* and Upanishada extol the glories of its kings. In learning and wisdom, Janaka ranked as a Brahman.

Visala—another son of Ikshvaku built Visalapuri, later Vaisali on the east bank of Gandaka, now called Bisara or Besarah or Besar, 20 miles north of Patna. Benaras to Vaisali—153 miles (Y Chwang).

The other half-Aryan states of low or mixed people:

1. North India

(a) Kashmir (*Mahabharata, Wood Book, Chapter 82, shloka 90*). Said to have been under the Turks (*Mahabharata, Court Book*, shloka 27; *Harivansa, Chapters 90-91*).
(b) Kekaya (*Ramayana*): Capital Giribraja, now Girijak, by the side of Gandhara.
(c) Gandhara or Gandharav (*R.V., I, 126; Mahabharata; Ramayana; Harivansa, Chapters 90 and 91*).
(d) Madra, Salva, south Kuru, Trigarta (Jalandhar), Darada (Dardistan), Balhika (Bulkh), Yavana (to the west of the Indus), Prasthala (Beluchistan?).

(e) Sindhu (Sindh): Reference in *R.V.*, I.. 126; The *Brahmana* works; the Sanskrit epics; also, *Harivansa*, Chapters 90 and 91.

(f) Anarta (Kathiawar), founded by Prince Anarta, son to Saryati, son to Manu. His capital was Kusasthali. According to *Vishnu Purana*, some Dravidians under their leader Punyajana had attacked and sacked Kusasthali. A new city was built near it, called Dwaraka. The peninsula afterwards became the home of the lunar Yadava princes (*Mahabharata*).

(g) Saurastra (Good Kingdom); Afterwards Lata, then Gujarat (Sanskrit epics, *Harivansa* and the Puranas). Maru Desa (*Mahabharata*), Indian desert comprising modern Marwar, Bikanir and Jaisalmer.

(h) Magadha (south Bihar): 833 miles in circumference mentioned in the Rig-Vedic *Aitareya Aranyaka* (*II, I. 1*). The people of Banga, Bagadh and Cherapada are weak and accustomed to bad food. Then it was the kingdom of Rishabha, a Daitya Aryan. The latter was defeated and killed and the Varhadratha dynasty was established. Jarasandha was the greatest monarch of India here in 1400 BC (*Mahabharata, Ramayana, Oudh Book, canto 10, shlokas 37–38*). Kikata (Gaya province) is mentioned in the *Rig Veda* III, 53.14. Capital Gayapuri, an ancient sacred place. Dr Hunter and General Cunningham wrongly think that Gaya was at first a Buddhist and afterwards, a Hindu sacred place. The great antiquity of its sanctity appears from *Ramayana*, Oudh Book, 107 canto, 11–14; *Mahabharata*, Wood Book, Chapter 84; *ibid.*, chapter 87; *ibid.*, Anusasan Book, Chapter 22; *ibid.*, Wood Book, Chapter 97; Drona Book, Chapter 66 and *Harivansa, Vayu Purana.*

(i) Anga (east Bihar): Circumference 667 miles. Its capital was Champa on a hill near the Ganges, now Pathar Fhata, 50 miles from Mongyr and twenty-four miles from Bhagalpur. Malini, Lomadapur, Karnapur were the other names of the capital.

The kingdom was founded by Prince Anga, sixth generation downward from Dhruva of Svayambhuva Manu's line (*Vishnu Purana*).

According to *Mahabharata* and *Harivansa*, Prince Anga, son to Bali, founded it. In the fifteenth century BC, Lomapada, friend to Dasaratha, was its king. About 1400 BC. Duryodhana gave it to Karna.

(j) Banga (Bengal): Reference in the *Aitareya Aranyaka* II, I.I.; *Mahabharata* I, 104-5; *Harivansa, Harivansa Book,* Chapter 32, shlokas 32-42; *Mahabharata,* Wood Book; *Ramayana,* Oudh Book, canto 10, 37-38 shlokas; *ManuSamhita,* Chapter 10; *Vishnu Purana,* IV, Chapter 18; *Garuda Purana,* I, 144. 71; *Mahabharata,* Court Book, shlokas 16, 17 and 24.

Modagiri—Mongyr or Rajmahal. Pundra—north Bengal. Kausiki-Kachchha—Hugli? Sumha—Burdwan. Prasumha—Medinipur. Karvata?

(k) Tamralipta: Its circumference was 250 to 300 miles (Y Chwang). Its capital was on the sea. The state was rather a peninsula, on the west side of river Hugli. Tamalika was the port. Jamini, in his *Mahabharata* says that the Peacock dynasty was the oldest here. The first king was Mayuradhvaja, his queen was Kumudvati. When the horse of Yudhisthira had reached Tamralipta, Prince Tamradhvaja arrested it. A fierce fight ensued: the Pandavas being defeated, they made friends with him. The last king of the dynasty named Nishanka Narayana died childless.

A chief, Kala Bhaumika by name and a fisherman by caste, next occupied the throne. His dynasty lasted some time. After them came a Kayastha dynasty.

The Kshatriya heroes of Tamralipta were all killed by the arrows of Parasurama (*Mahabharata, Drona Book, Chapter* 70). In the days of *Ramayana,* Tamralipta was probably a part of Kalinga. Tamralipta is repeatedly mentioned in the *Mahabharata.* Its king was defeated by Bhima. In the war, its raja fought against the Pandavas. The kings here are called *mlechchhas,* i.e. corrupt in morals and manners. Jaimini calls Tomluk by the name of Ratnagarh, *Mahavansa*—Tamralipti, Megasthenes—Taluctoe, Ptolemy—Tomalites. Certainly, these parts were mostly peopled by brave Dravidians.

Paundravardhana, literally nurse of Pod people, a fishermen class, was north Bengal. Its circumference was 667 miles. The people were very brave. The Pod people still exist.

The deltas of the Ganges and Brahmaputra were called the Anupa Desa, i.e. lowlands, later Samatata. This included the entire presidency division, Faridpur, Barisal, Noakhali, Tippera, and Vikrampur. Dacca and Mymensingh then formed a part of Paundravardhana or Kamarupa. Kamarupa appears to have been an ancient country with Pragjyotishpuri as the capital.

According to Puranas, about 1500 BC one Mahiranga was the first Aryan king here. Four kings of his dynasty followed him. Then we hear of tyrant Naraka about 1400 BC. The *Harivansa*, Chapter 121, gives the following note on Naraka: In boyhood, he was brought up by Rajarshi Janaka of Videha. This heroic Brahman lad of 16, established his power over Kamarupa. His friend Vana, son to Bali, was ruler of the upper Assam, with his capital at Sonitapur, now Tejpur. Vana was very wicked and tyrannical. Naraka also grew up so. Once Vasista went to see the goddess Kamekhya. But Naraka did not allow him to enter the city. Moreover, the sage was maltreated. Krishna attacked Kamarupa, fought with Naraka and killed him. Naraka had four sons. Krishna set up the eldest Bhagadatta on the throne and then returned to Dwaraka. Bhagadatta was heroic and his kingdom extended to Indo-China to the east and to the Bay of Bengal to the south. Bhagadatta was followed by Bajradatta, Dharmapala, Ratnapala, Kamapala, Prithvipala, Suvahu and others successively on the throne.

Before the imperial sacrifice of Yudhisthira, Vasudeva, king of Pundra (north Bengal) became very powerful and formed a league with the hunter chief Ekalavya, Jarasandha of Magadha, Naraka of Kamrupa, and Vana of Sonitapur (Tejur). When Naraka was killed, Vasudeva challenged Krishna. A great fight ensued in which the Pundra chief was killed. The king of Kasi, another ally, then fought with Krishna but perished with his whole family. Kasi was burnt down (*Harivansa*. Also, *Matsya Purana, Chapter* 207).

Reference: *Ramayana,* Kishkindhya Book, canto 42, verses 30–31. Bhagadatta fought with Arjuna, helped by the armies of Kirata (hill tribes), China, where the Tsan or Tsin people, our Tibeto-Burman, from a part of Central Asia, had settled: and of the lowlands bordering on the Bay of Bengal. *Mahabharata*, Court Book, Chapter 26. Also, Asvamedha (horse sacrifice) Book, Chapter 57. *Ibid*., Bhishma Book, chapter 9.

The *Mahabharata* gives us a short geography of eastern India. We have already spoken of the *Anupa Desa*, i.e. Netherlands. The eastern most parts were also called *Patala*, i.e. lower province, as the lands here were almost on the sea-level, from which the later name of Samatata. Tripura and the hill tracts about Chittagong were called Naga-loka. An arm of the Bay of Bengal then extended up to Sylhet and Cachar. Manipur was not far from the Bay. Arjuna reached Manipur, going through the sea coast. Many ascetics lived on the Mahendra hill of Manipur. The two houses of Manipur and Tripura had already been brought under Aryan influence. Arjuna married two princesses of those two houses. Few princely houses in India can view with them in antiquity. The Princes of Tripura are noted as patrons of learning.

The same epic mentions the following hills: Sri, later Sripunja from which Cherapunji; Khasa, Khasia; Jayanti, Jaintia; Naga, Naga hills; Ganesa Giri is probably Garo hills.

2. *The Deccan*

Professor Wilson thinks that the civilisation of the south may possibly be extended even to ten centuries before Christ.

Dr Caldwell says: 'The Deccan had been civilised long before the Brahmanic influence spread over the south.'

The following, amongst others, were the states of the south before 1400 BC: Mekhala, Utkala (Orissa), Kalinga (upper part of Madras Presidency), Kosala, Chedi (Central Province), Dasarna (a Vindhyan state), Malwa, Avanti, Vidarbha (Berar), Bhoja (a part of central India), Konkon, Andhra, Dravira, Kishkindhya (Bellary District), Pandya, Kerala, Matsya, Kausika, Pundra, Chola, Ristithika Mahishaka, Vidisa (Bhilsa), Janasthan, south India and Lanka, Dandaka, Haihaya.

(a) Utkala (Orissa) is said to have been founded by Prince Utkala, a son of Ila, daughter to Manu, about 2750 BC. Manu (*Chapter 10, verse 44*) and Baudhayana call it a country of fallen Aryans. Ancient Orissa was sometimes separate and sometimes a part of Kalinga. Prince Odra, 13th generation downward from Yayati, the renowed lunar king, occupied it and gave his name from which rose Odra Desa, now Orissa (reference: *Ramayana, Kishkindhya Book, canto 41; Mahabharata, Drona Book, Chapter 4*).

(b) Kalinga (Upper Madras) said to have been founded by a son of Bali driven out by Indra and Vishnu from his kingdom on the upper Indus, about 2800 BC. Originally, it was Orissa and a part of Bengal

(*Harivansa, Chapter 32, verses 32–42; Mahabharata, I. 104; Vishnu Purana IV. 18*).

Reference: *Ramayana*, Oudh Book, canto 71; *ibid*., Kishkindhya Book, canto 41; *Mahabharata*, Wood Book, Chapter 144; *Harivansa*, Chapter 288, verse 35; *Manu Samhita*, Book X; *Baudhayana Sutra* I, I. 2.

The *Brahma Vaivarta Purana* makes another early mention of Kalinga where, about 2700 BC, a rich and powerful merchant named Biradha was king. His son was Drumina and grandson, Samadhi. This prince, left by his wife and children for extreme liberality, wandered and came to the river Pushpabhadra where he met Suratha, great-grandson of Buddha—the first king of the lunar dynasty, who had left his capital Kolanagari, being defeated and ousted by Nandi. Both, as friends, went to Pushkara, a sacred place, seven miles from Ajmer where they met the sage Medhasa at whose instance they worshipped the goddess Durga and by her grace, regained their kingdoms after a year.

Kalinga once reached the river Vaitarani of Orissa (*Mahabharata, Wood Book, Chapter 114*).

The circumference of this powerful state was 833 miles. Its ancient capital was Srikakola, corrupted into Chikakola, 20 miles south-west of Kalinga Patan, now Raj Mahendri (Cunningham).

In the Great War, the Kalinga king, Srutayu, fought with his two sons against the Pandavas and the three were killed by Bhima.

(c) Kosala, perhaps modern Gondowana, about 1,000 miles in circumference. Its capital was Chanda (Cunningham) or Bairgarh or Bhandaka (*J.R.A.S.*).
From Kalinga to Kosala (Kiasalo) was 317 miles (Y Chwang). Reference *Mahabharata*, Court Book, Chapter 31.

(d) Chedi (Central Province) is mentioned in the *Rig Veda*, VIII, 5. It was the kingdom of Tripura, a powerful Daitya Aryan killed by Rudra (Siva) in the twenty-nineth century BC. Its ancient capital Traipuri is now Teoari, six miles north-west of Jabalpur (Javalipattan). Sisupala, the tyrant of Chedi, was killed by Krishna.

(e) Dasarna was a country under the Vindhyas.

(f) Malwa is mentioned in the *Ramayana*, Kishkindhya Book, canto 41, verse 10. In the *Mahabharata*, Sanjaya describes to Dhritarashtra both Malwa and Avanti. Its capital was on river Avanti (Sipra). The circumference of the kingdom was about 1,000 miles.

(g) Vidarbha (Berar and its neighbourhood) was an ancient civilised state. Its capital was Kundinanagar. Lopamudra, wife of Agastya and a lady *rishi* of several Rig-Vedic hymns, was a princess of this land (twenty-second century BC). Damayanti also was born here.

(h) Bhoja, probably a state of central India. These Bhojas were an offshoot of Yadu dynasty. The mother of the Pandava princes was a Bhoja princess.

(i) Kerala. Ancient Kerala included Malabar, Canara and Konkan. Tradition asserts that the great Brahman hero, Parasurama, drove the pirates from the coast and colonized it with Aryans from the north (fifteenth century BC).

The language of Maharashtra is Aryan, not Dravidian.

(j) Andhra is mentioned in the *Aitareya Brahmana* work, in the *Mahabharata* and the *Sutra* works.

(k) South India and Lanka were under Ravana, a half-caste Aryan (1500 BC). Lanka, later Ceylon (Sinhala) was the ancient Tamravarna corrupted into Pali Tamraparni, foreign Taprobane.

(l) The Haihaya kingdom, with its capital at Mahismati, now Choli Mahesvar, was on the Narmada near its mouth.

Most of these southern states came into being after 2000 BC. So, the *Brahmana* works of the north knew very little of them. Some of those states were large, some small, some very small, not larger than a modern district. Some were civilised, some half-civilised, while others were barbarous. A considerable area was covered by jungles and forests peopled by wild men and beasts.

RELIGION

Europe has been always behind India in intellectual and religious freedom. While the history of Europe is marked by intolerance and abominable persecutions, India has always been noted for full spiritual liberty. India has produced all varieties of religion such as rationalism, theism, atheism, and materialism. Kapila's rational religion was confined to the wise alone. It was established in the court of Janadeva of Vedeha (north Bihar). Jainism was gaining ground. The rishis still worshipped the Supreme Being (*Brahman*) through the great powers of nature. They were in general, averse to animal sacrifice. They would offer *soma* juice and various grains. However, the children of the devas who had now become powerful kings in India, favoured animal sacrifice, gave great importance to sacrificial ceremonies, still worshipping the Vedic gods.

The *Mahabharata* has a fine discourse on the point. Once, about 1500 BC, the rishis and the devas quarrelled and asked the powerful Prince Vasu, a staunch Vishnuite and a friend of Indra, 'With what, either grains (*oshadhi*) or animal (*pasu*), are sacrifices to be performed?' In reply, Vasu said, 'By *beast*.' Hence, the seers cursed him, 'You have shown partiality to the devas, by not speaking according to the Shastras. So, go down to India and live there.' This Prince Vasu, son to Kritiraja, a lunar king, was a great favourite of Indra at whose instance, he came to India and occupied the Chedi kingdom. Indra gave him an air-car in which he could move with great skill. He was therefore, called *uparichara* (aeronaut). His son Prince Vrihadratha founded his dynasty in Magadha about 1450 BC.

True, gods were still worshipped and hymns uttered at sacrifices, but true veneration was shown to ceremonies. The Vedic priests allowed no departure from sacrifices, acts, movements given in the *brahmana* works. In place of simple and sincere worship, superstition gradually came in. Even penances were prescribed for mishaps (*Aitareya Brahmana, V* and *VII*).

Various were the sacrifices, from simple to highly elaborate, some lasting a year, some even ten or twelve years. Sacrifices were followed by gifts of cattle, gold, garments, and food to the Brahmanas and the poor.

The animals as victims are mentioned in the *Satapatha*, I, 2. 3. 7. 8. Even human sacrifice, though very rare, did exist in the epic age.

Sacrifices were of over a thousand kinds. Of them, twenty-one were chief, viz., seven havih sacrifices, seven soma sacrifices and seven paka sacrifices (Gautama).

The seven havih sacrifices were: setting up the sacred fire; daily oblation; full and new moon sacrifice; harvest sacrifice; four-monthly sacrifice; animal sacrifice; and an expiation for over-indulgence in *soma* juice. It is needless to enter into the details of other ceremonials.

There is evidence to show that new gods also were coming into oui pantheon. Arjuna (Indra) is mentioned in the *Satapatha Brahmana*. Rudra (Siva) is mentioned in the *White Yajur Veda*, Chapter XVI. The *Kaushitaki Brahmana* and also the *Satapatha Brahmana (II, 6. 2. 9)* give great importance to Isana or Mahadeva (Siva). Supremacy of Vishnu among the gods, is found in the *Satapatha Brahmana,* XIV. I. I. There was no worship of Krishna yet. He is mentioned simply as the son of Devaki and a pupil of Ghiora Angirasa in *Chhandogya* Upanishada, III. 17.6.

King Priyavrata of Bithoor had started the worship of the goddess Shashthi. The worship of Durga had been started by sage Medhasa at Pushkara, near Ajmer. Sacrifices to Kadsha and Parvati are found in *Satapatha Brahmana*. II. 4. 4. 6. Uma Haimavatik explained to Indra the nature of *Brahman* (*Kena Upanishad*). Victory of the gods over the Asuras (*Aitareya Brahmana*), VI, 15; (*Satapatha Brahmana*), I. 2.5. The *Mundakopanishada* mentions Kali and other goddesses. Krishna had started the worship of Sarasvati, the goddess of learning. Goddess Sri is invoked in *Taittiriya Aranyaka*. Professor EB Cowell holds that the hints of these goddesses are found in the *Rig Veda*. The worship of sun was set up by Samb at Multan.

In this epic age, we find mention of temples, idols and their worship. The Pandavas prostrated themselves before the gods in the temple (*Mahabharata*).

Atheism and materialism also were in full force. Charvaka was its great preacher and philosopher. This Charvaka should be distinguished from another Charvaka mentioned in the *Mahabharata*.

Theists and atheists all aimed at salvation and all held that 'true wisdom' alone can lead to that. Different thinkers show different ways to the attainment of that wisdom. We possess no regular work on early atheism. Madhvacharya, in his *Sarva-Darsana-Sangraha* has given us a distorted picture of the atheistic tenets then current or known. The teachings of Charvaka were: do not practise painful austerities for the fancied bliss of the next world; practise *ahimsa*, i.e. entire harmlessness which is the highest religion; like the cowards, do not depend on divine grace and fate. Not luck, but pluck; depend on yourself, self-reliance is true bliss, self-reliance is salvation; there is no God, there is no next world; do not believe the Vedas nor the priests who are mere frauds and cheats; never do a thing withut reason; matter is eternal and composed of four elements (he denies the fifth, i.e. *byoma* or ether); only seeing (pratyaksha = perception) is believing.

The materialists were rather a sect of the atheists. They were sensualists and sought enjoyment only in life, leaving at death 'as many debts as possible'. Probably, they had a scientific scripture of eroticism.

Jainism and Buddhism were of later origin. Atheism was very old. It came to India from the north. Some of the asuras (literally people without wine) were staunch atheists. Atheism was an anti-Vedic creed. They were sound practical men, worshippers of right conduct of duty, 'the stern daughter of the voice of God'. The atheists preached against the corruptions of the Vedic rites, such as drinking, immoral practices, slaughter of animals, suicide as a sacrifice, human sacrifice and so forth. In ancient India, these atheists were supreme and very powerful. So subtle were their arguments that even many great pundits, being defeated, turned atheists, according to the custom of those days. In time, Hindus, Jains and Buddhists combated them successfully. Now they are extinct. The Jains and the Buddhists are not atheists, says Dr Rhys David.

Towards the latter part of this age, society became to priest-ridden, barbarous and debased that even rishis and warriors became skeptical.

The Upanishadas now established monoism.

LITERATURE

Sacred

The Vedas, the *Vedangas*, the *Brahmanas, Aranyakas* and the Upanishadas form the so-called *revealed* literature of the age.

The Rig Veda

Most of the hymns were composed in the Vedic age and first compiled by Agni Deva. New hymns were composed till some time before 1400 BC, forthey mention Devapi, Santanu, Dasaratha, Rama, and others. They were finally arranged about 1400 BC. The other Vedas also were compiled in the epic age.

The hymns of the *Rig Veda* mention different classes of priests who performed different duties at the sacrifices. The Adhvaryus were entrusted with the material performance of sacrifice. They measured the altar, built the altar, prepared the vessels, fetched wood, water, and immolated animals.

The Udgatris sang or chanted hymns. The Hotris recited hymns. The Brahmans presided at sacrifices over all the rest.

The Adhvaryus and the Udgatris required special training and manuals. The *Rig Veda* has the name Yajur and Saman. The formulas and chants, collected and compiled later on, are the *Yajur* and the *Sama Vedas*, as we have now. Surya Deva, the younger brother to Brahma had at first compiled a portion of the *Sama Veda*. Dr Stevenson and Professor Bentley have shown that *Sama Veda* is mostly a selection from the *Rig Veda* hymns, set to music for a specil purpose.

The Yajur Veda

The more ancient *Black Yajur Veda* is called *Taittiriya Samhita*. Tittiri probably compiled or promulgated it in its present shape. In the Anukramani of the Atreya recension of this Veda, we are told that this Veda was handed down by Vaisampayana to Yaska Paingi, by Paingi to Tittiri, by Tittiri to Ukha and Ukha to Atreya. This shows that the existing oldest recension of *Yajur Veda* was into the first recension. The *White Yajur Veda*, also called Vajasaneyi Samhita was probably compiled and promulgated by Yajnavalkya, priest to Janaka after 1350 BC.

The arrangement of the two *Yajur Vedas* differs. In the *Black Yajur Veda*, the sacrificial formulas are followed by dogmatic explanation and by accounts of ceremonials belonging to them. In the *White Yajur Veda*, only the formulas are given in the book, while the explanation and ritual are given separately in the *Satapatha Brahmana*. Yajnavalkya was the promulgator of this new school. Its contents show that it was not the composition of one man or of one age.

Of its forty chapters, the first 18 are cited in full and explained in due order in the first nine books of the *Satapatha Brahmana*. The formulas of these eighteen chapters are found in the old *Black Yajur Veda*. These eighteen are perhaps the work of Yajnavalkya. The next seven chapters are probably later additions. The remaining fifteen are still later additions and are plainly called Parisishta (khila), i.e. supplement.

The Atharva Veda

Though composed early, it was, however, recognised after the epic age. Some *Brahmana* works alluded to the growth of a class of literature called Atharvan Girasas. The mention of three, and three Vedas only, appears from *Aitareya Brahmana*, V 32; *Satapatha Brahmana* IV, 6. 7; *Aitareya Aranyaka*, III. 2. 3; *Vrihad-Aranyaka Upanishada* I, 5; *Chhandogya Upanishada* III and VIII. This last work classes *Atharva Veda* with *itihasa*. The *Brahmanas* and the Upanishadas of the *Atharva Veda* alone recognise it uniformly. So, the *Gopatha Brahmana* pleads its necessity. Professor Whitney says wrongly that modern works are connected with Atharvan and Angiras—half-mythical names of ancient and venerated Indian families, for recognition.

Jayanta (seventh century AD) in his famous commentary on Hindu logic, discusses among other things, the great antiquity of the *Atharva Veda*.

Chanakya in his *Artha Shastra*, the *Taittriya Brahmana* (last *prapathaka, Chapter 18*), the *Satapatha Brahmana* (*kanda 11, prapathaka 4*) and other works distinctly alludes to three Vedas only. Next, he cites authorities in favour of it: *Satapatha Brahmana* (*XIII, 3. 7*); the *Chhandogya* Upanishada, *VII. 6;* also III, 3; Bhattacharya, an ancient authority; the *Taittiriya Upanishada*; *Taittiriya Brahmana;* the *Yajur Veda;* Patanjali in his *Great Commentary* (150 BC); the *Gopatha Brahmana*; Manu and other ancient law-givers.

The *Atharva Veda* has 20 books and 6,000 verses. One-sixth of it is in prose. One-sixth of Book X is taken from the *Rig Veda*. The 19th book is a supplement to the previous 18. The 20th is composed of extracts from the *Rig Veda*. It chiefly consists of formulas intended to protect men against baneful influences of divine powers, diseases, harmful animals, and curses of enemies. It is full of incantations for long life, wealth, recovery from illness; invocations for good luck in journey and gaming. These resemble hymns in the *Rig Veda*. Professor Weber points out that in the *Rig Veda*, they are apparently additions. The special feature of this Veda is its *Brahma-Vidya*, i.e. knowledge of the Supreme Being. Sayana supports it and says that the other three Vedas give the bliss of heaven, but the *Atharvan* combines both world and God.

The Brahmana Literature (c. 2500 to 2000 BC)

The *Brahmana* works—the Talmud of the Hindus—give details of the ceremonies, their origin and meaning, with curious legends, divine and human.

'The Brahmanas are theological prose works held to be divinely revealed and to form part of the canon. Their purpot is to supply a dogmatic exposition of the sacrificial ceremonial. Their contents, generally uninteresting, are yet of considerable importance, both as regards the history of Indian institutions, and as the oldest body of Indo-European prose, of a generally free, vigorous simple form, affording valuable glimpses backward at the primitive condition of unfettered Indo-European talk.' (Professor Whitney).

'In the Brahmana works, Hindus have shown how far human intellect can rise in thoughts.' (Professor Weber).

'Their contents, wearisome in the extreme, however, give a few gleams of beautiful thoughts. Their scientific value may be great, but they possess no interest for general readers. The Brahmanical intellect is here debased by a meaningless ritual.' (Professor EB Cowell).

The *Rig Veda* has two *Brahmanas*, viz., the *Aitareya* by Mahidasa, son to Itara, one of the many wives of a *rishi;* and the *Kaushitaki* by sage Kausitaka. These two agree in many respects. Only the last ten chapters of *Aitareya* are not found in the *Kaushitaki*, which probably belong to a later age.

The *Sama Vedą* has Tandya or *Pancha-Vinsa Brahmana, Sadvinsa Brahmana*, the *Mantra Brahmana*, and the Upanishada. These works, in forty chapters, form the *Brahmanas* of the *Sama Veda*.

The *Black Yajur Veda* has only *Taittiriya Brahmana*. The *White Yajur Veda* has the voluminous *Satapatha Brahmana*. It is the work of many and not of Yajnavalkya alone. Its first nine books are the oldest in sixty chapters called the *Shasthipatha* in the time of Patanjali, second century BC (Weber). The remaining five books in forty chapters, are of a later date.

The opinions of Yajnavalkya are authoritative in the first five books, while those of Sandilya, in the next four Books. Sanjiviputra reconciled the two schools and finally adjusted the first nine books. Five more were added at a later age.

The *Atharva Veda* has the *Gopatha Brahmana*, a comparatively recent work. Its contents are a medley derived from different sources.

The Aranyakas and the Upanishadas (2000 to 1400 BC)

The Aranyakas

These philosophical works, closely connected with the Vedas and the *Brahmanas*, relate to the forest and are meant to be read by those who have retired from the world and become ascetics. They are supplements to the *Brahmana* works. They are the depositories of bold speculations.

The *Rig Veda* has *Aitareya Aranyaka* by Mahidasa and Kaushitaki by sage Kausitaka. The *Black Yajur Veda* has *Taittiriya Aranyaka*. The last book of the *Satapatha Brahmana* is called its *Aranyaka*. The *Sama* and *Atharva Vedas* have no *Aranyakas*.

The Upanishadas

Upanishada literally means 'sitting near the preceptor' for spiritual wisdom. Hence, a book of that kind: from *Upani*, near and *sad*, to sit. Another meaning is, 'thorough destruction of ignorance', from *Upani*, entire and *sad* to destroy.

These philosophical works are of purely speculative nature and are the first attempts at a systematic treatment of metaphysical questions.

There is a total of 1,194 of these works. Of them, some 150 are old and important. The rest are modern and enter into sectarian views. The best and most ancient are ten. They are short treatises forming part of the *Aranyakas* or detached works composed in the latter part of the epic age. They are in dialogues, generally in prose, occasionally in prose and verse, or in verse alone. The authors are poets. They breathe a freedom of thought only found in the Rig-Vedic hymns themselves.

The Karma *Kanda* or the ceremonial portion of the Vedas is meant for purifying the mind and preparing it for sublime truths. The Upanishadas deal with the *Jnana-Kanda* (wisdom) and are parent of the Vedanta philosophy.

The *Aitareya* and *Kaushitaki* belong to the *Rig Veda*. The *Chhandogya* and *Talavakara*, called *Kena*, belong to the *Sama Veda*. The *Taittiriya* and *Katha* belong to the *Black Yajur Veda*. The Katha more properly belongs to the *Atharva Veda*. The *Vajasaneyi* (Isa) and the *Vrihad Aranyaka* belong to the *White Yajur Veda*. The *Mundaka* and *Prasna* belong to the *Atharva Veda* rich in Upanishadas, having no less than fifty-two. The *Mandukya* and *Prasna* are most important in the Vedanta School.

The question of moksha, i.e. liberation from the earthly encumbrances, appears to have attracted the serious attention of the Aryans. Of course, the notion of salvation has not been always the same. The *Rig Veda* says that action, wisdom and faith give salvation. By action, the early seers meant pious meditation and harmless sacrifice done by the offering of grains and *soma* juice. The deva-Aryans of the north gave great importance to ritual religion. Their animal sacrifice was an innovation. Strong opposition arose from several great thinkers. The rishis protested. Narayana discovered *Brahman*—the Supreme Being—the Highest Self—the Great Source of all. Vak Devi explained this monotheism in her famous *Devi-Sukta*. Uma Haimavati explained it to Indra and other devas. The rishis accepted it and introduced it into the later Vedic hymns. The authors of the *Atharva Veda* also devoted a chapter to it. Kapila blamed the animal sacrifice and gave a solution of his own, based on reason alone. Rishabha Deva, in his Jainism gave another solution; while the atheists showed a new path altogether.

The children of the deva-Aryans brought their ancestral religion to the north India plains, where they became powerful kings. For a century or two the ritual religion with animal sacrifice, might have been followed with the true spirit. But it declined gradually till at last both religion and politics became corrupt to the extreme before 1400 BC.

Luckily a reaction followed soon. In the field of politics, Krishna set to work in right earnest to establish a *dharma-rajya*, i.e. kingdom built on righteous principles. Sick of elaborate meaningless rites, some new thinkers earnestly enquired about the nature of the Supreme Being, creation, soul, and salvation. Such enquiries gave rise to the Upanishadas. In them we find an awakening from the dream of endless ceremonies, to grapple with the deepest problems of life and eternity. Though childish and fantastic, they are full of fine thoughts and deep meaning. The great teachers of this highest truth are not the Brahmans, but Kshatriyas with whom arose many great and noble thoughts in India. The Brahmans adopted this new idea and then secured the monopoly and became teachers.

The idea of a Supreme Being, a Universal Spirit, an all-prevading soul—is the keystone of the Upanishadas. Monotheism generally admits a God, creator as distinct from the created beings. The monotheism of Upanishadas recognises God as the Universal Being—all things emanated from Him, are part of Him, will mingle in Him and have no separate existence. This lesson Satyakama Javala learnt from nature. Yajnavalkya taught it to his wife Maitreyi. This idea is taught in the Upanishada, in a hundred similes, metaphors and legends. *Chhandogya Upanishada, IV, 14; VI; Kena Upanishada I; Isa Upanishada* 'He is all gods' (*Vrihad Aranayaka Upanishada, I. 4. 6* 'He is in all men' (*I. 4. 15*).

The idea of monoism is carried to its furthest limits. No dualism is recognised in the Upanishadas. In Kapila's *Sankhya*, nature is independent of purusha. In the Upanishadas it is not so. Here, everything is a manifestation of the Universal Being.

Upanishada attempts to solve the mystery of creation: From *non-existent* came *existent*; then the mundane egg; gradually the sun (*Chhandogya Upanishada, III, 19*). The *Chhandogya Upanishada* VI, 2 gives a different theory: 'At first there was only one without a second. He sent forth fire; then water and earth.'

Mahidasa's *Aitareya Aranyaka*, II, I. 1, derives creation from water, Prana and his companions made the world. Water is said to be the material cause of creation. Cf. *R. V.*, X. 129; also the *Old Testament*. The *Vrihad Aranyaka Upanishada* states: 'In the beginning, there was Self alone. From Him came a male and a female and from them all.'

They discovered a harmony or unity in the creation: that was *Brahman*, Self, Purusha or Prana. What becomes of the soul after death? Good acts lead to future bliss, but true knowledge only leads to union with the Universal Being. The doctrine of the transmigration of soul is fully developed in the Upanishadas. Souls go to the moon and moon sends them back to be born again according to their deeds and merits. The soul passes into *Brahman* by superior moral excellence. Pravahana Jaivali taught the transmigration of soul. Souls come back, with rain, are born again as rice or corn. Persons eat food and beget children. Good actions lead to good birth (*Chhandogya Upanishada*).

Final emancipation of the soul and its reunion with *Brahman* is given below: 'He who knows it, after having become quiet, subdued, satisfied, patient, and collected, sees self in Self, sees all in Self. Evil does not overcome him, he overcomes all evil. Free from evil, from doubt, he becomes a true *Brahmana* and enters the Brahma world.' (*Chhandogya Upanishada, VIII, 14.1*).

This is beatitude. This is union with *Brahman*. Buddha's nirvana rose from it.

The value and influence of the Upanishadas

The Upanishadas give man a divine origin. They set aside the animal law, viz., 'Man is the enemy of man' and establish the spiritual law, viz., 'All men are but kindred expressions of the one Self.'

'No Hindu works have probably exercised a wider influence on the world. These forlorn guesses at truth are constantly spoken of as eastern philosophy. Familiar ideas abound in the Phoedrus, Empedocles or Pythagoras, in the neo-Platonism of the Alexandrian and also in the Gnostic Schools. Plotinus alone tried to free the Greek philosophy from Hindu influence. The Kabala of the Jews and the Sufism of the Muhammadans seem to be derived from the same source. We are too apt to look on the ancient world as a scene of stagnation. There were travellers and circulation of ideas. Then why should the tradition of the eastern origin of much of early Greek philosophy be incredible, or even improbable?' (Professor EB Cowell).

'It is impossible to read the Vedanta or the many fine compositions in illustration of it, without believing that Pythagoras and Plato derived their sublime theories from the same foundation with the sages of India.' (Sir William Jones).

Victor Cousin, the famous French historian of philosophy, says: 'When we read with attention the poetical and philosophical monuments of the East, abobe all, those of India which are beginning to spread in Europe, we discover there many a truth and truths so profound and which make such contrast with the meanness of the results at which European genius has sometimes stoped, that we are constrained to bend the knee before the philosophy of the East and to see in this cradle of the human race the native land of the highest philosophy.'

Freidrich Schlegel says: 'Even the loftiest philosophy of the Europeans, the idealism of reason, as it is set forth by the Greek philosophies, appears, in comparison with the abundant light and vigour of Oriental idealism, like a feeble Promethean spark in the flood of heavenly glory of the noon-day sun, faltering and feeble and ever ready to be extinguished. The divine origin of man is continually inculcated to stimulate his efforts to return, to animate him in the struggle and incite him to consider a reunion and recorporation with divinity as the one primary object of every action and exertion.'

The great German philosopher Schopenhauer (1819) says: 'From every sentence, deep, original and sublime thoughts arise and the whole is pervaded by a high and holy and earnest spirit. Indian air surrounds us and original thoughts of kindred spirits. In the whole world, there is no study except that of the originals, so beneficial and so elevating, as that of the Upanishadas. It has been the solace of my life; it will be the solace of my death.'

Professor Max Müeller says: 'If these words of Schopenhauer required any endorsement, I should willingly give it as the result of my own experience during a long life devoted to the study of many philosophies and many religions.'

Dr Matheson says: 'It is not too much to say that the mind of the West with all its undoubted impulses towards the progress of humanity, has never exhibited such an intense amount of intellectual force as is to be found in the religious speculations of India. These have been the cradle of all western speculations and wherever the European mind has risen into heights of philosophy, it has done so because the "Brahman" was the pioneer. There is no intellectual truth is no modern solution of that problem which will not be found anticipated in the East.'

In *Religion and Reality*, a recent philosophical work, JH Tucknell says: 'In our main conclusion we have long ago been anticipated by the religious philosophy of India. In the West, our philosophy has been surely but slowly moving to the same inevitable monistic goal. In Professor Ladd of Harvard we have a notable western thinker who, by a process of careful and consistent reasoning, concrete in character, has also arrived at the conclusion that the ultimate reality must be conceived of as an Absolute Self of which we are finite forms or appearances. But it is the crowning glory of the Vedanta that it so long ago announced, reiterated and emphasised this deep truth in a manner that does not permit us for a moment to forget it or explain it away. This great stroke of identity, this discernment of the ultimate unity of all things in 'Brahman' or the One Absolute Self seems to us to constitute the masterpiece and highest achievement of India's wonderful metaphysical and religious genius to which the West has yet to pay the full tribute which is its due.'

Sir John Woodroffe says: 'The uniqueness of India consists in her religion of eternity. Indian doctrine is not one-sided, but has a time-religion also. The glory of India is that of a high spirituality, a unique genius for grasping and expounding the realities behind the phenomenal world and the innermost meaning of life.'

The Doctrine of Karma (action) and Rebirth

In the earlier books of *Rig Veda*, there is little reference to a future life. But there are many hymns in Books I, IX, and X, which give an idea of it in plain words. There is, however, no idea of heaven and hell in the *Rig Veda*. According to Karma, i.e. action, one would, after death, enter a kingdom of light, bliss and delight or a world of darkness, dejection and sorrow. In the *Brahmana* works of the Vedas, mention in made of *Swarga*, i.e. heaven. The doctrine of karma (action), future life, nature, and transmigration of the soul are fully developed in the Upanishadas. The doctrine has a strong rational basis. Some allege that it has produced great evil effects on the Indian people, such as enfeeblement of will, absence of energy and disinclination for progress. This is hardly right, for India has produced many eminent men of action, letters and arts.

Philosophers Hume and Cudworth considered the reincarnation doctrine the most rational theory of immortality.

Professor William Knight holds that pre-existence has fewer difficulties to face than the rival hypotheses. Once practically the whole civilised world embraced it, as the greater number, nearly two-thirds of the earth's people now do. It has been known since the dawn of history; and held by both primitive peoples and the highly learned.

It appears since the spread of Christianity. It is said to have been held by the ancient Egyptians (though this is disputed), by some Greeks, notably by Expedocles, Pythagoras, Plato, the neo-Platonists, and was taught in the *Mysteries*. It was held by some of the Latins and by the Gauls, the Druids, and the followers of the Edda.

It was in primitive Christianity, as for example in Origen. The Christian Gospels assume it (vide *Reincarnation in the New Testament* by JM Pryse).

It appears sporadically again in Europe in the Middle Ages. Christianity and Islam resisted the belief in Europe and Asia. Yet, in Europe the doctrine has never entirely disappeared. Recently, it has gained a number of adherents—ED Walker's *Reincarnation;* Rev WR Alger's *A Critical History of the Doctrine of a Future Life;* the grand Italian philosopher Giordano Bruno burnt alive by the Church as a heretic; the German philosophers Schelling, Fichte (younger); Leibnitz, Schopenhauer and the great poets and writers Goethe, Harder, Lessing; the English Christian Platonist Dr Henry More and others; philosophers Cudworth and Hume; the French and English scientists Flammarion, Figueir, Brewster, and the modern Christian theologians Julius Müller, Dorner, Ernesti, Ruckert Edward Beecher. It is held by a large number of poets; Professor McTaggart has an Essay on *Pre-Existence.* Sir John Woodroffe's *Is India Civilized?*, (*second edn., pp. 255–60*) also deserves mention. The Jains and Buddhists adopted and preached it.

The karma doctrine is not fatalistic. According to it, man is a little *Brahma* spheroid, i.e. microcosm. He is master of his destiny amidst unfortunate conditions due to his previous actions.

Nishkama karma, selfless action, leads to liberation. The doctrine of karma reconciles man to his lot. It is not selfish. It has full room for social service and philanthropy. He who serves another serves Self. 'To do good to others is the highest religion.'

The Vedanta gives profoundly based reason for all charity and brotherhood.

The Brahmans also framed new laws of phonetics, ceremonials, grammar, etymology, metre, and astronomy, to make the Vedic study easier. The works were lost or replaced by later manuals.

SECULAR LITERATURE

Brahma, Vivaswan and Sukra were the secular poets of the Vedic age. Valmiki was the first secular poet of India. He was born of the noted Bhrigu clan to which Sukra belonged. His father was Valmika and his name was Ratnakara, literally 'a mine of gems'. Having neglected education early, he began life as a robber, hunting game and looting travellers. Once two travellers awakened him to the nature and extent of his crimes. He now grew penitent, turned over a new leaf and took to an honourable course of life. His poetic genius burst forth with the change. About 1430 BC he wrote his lyrical epic, the *Ramayana.* The epic, as we have it now, is complete in seven books and some 25,000 verses. But the *Mahabibhasa* tells us that the poet wrote it in five Books (II to VI) and 12,000 verses. Book VII was added much later. Book I was added after Book VII. Besides, there are many interpolations. Books I and VII also are very old; for a verse from Book VII was quoted in the *Sama-Grihya-Parisishta.* The canto on Sita's ordeal was thrown into the War Book, after the composition of Bok VII. This interpolation also is old, for it (Sita's entry into fire) is mentioned in Bana's *Harshacharita.*

Valmiki, a contemporary poet, wrote his epic in the lifetime of Rama, its hero. This appears from a saying of Narada. It also tallies with the last book. The antiquity of *Adi Kanda*, i.e. Book I appears from Bana's *Kadambari.* Styles of different poets are perceived from a careful reading of the poem. At first, the poem ran from Oudh Book to War Book. The *Mahabibhasha* gives only the stealing of Sita, her deliverance and the Return of Rama to Oudh. It does not mention the first and the last books.

The epic begins from the Oudh Book and leaves all else, viz., Rama's statement before Bharadvaja, Sita's description of her story to Ravana, Lakshamana's description of Rama's life to Hanuman, Hanuman's account to Sita about Rama, Rama's going to the hermitage of Visvamitra, breaking of Siva's bow and marriage of the princes.

Several great wars, two terrible famines, general ignorance of the Brahmans, oppression of the tyrants, made India most pitiable towards the close of the fifteenth century BC. Prince Krishna righted the politics of India. *Rishi* Krishna now worked hard to preserve the ancient Hindu learning and thoughts.

Krishna (called thus for his black complexion), Dvaipayana (island-born), Veda-Vyasa (arranger of the Vedas) or more popularly called Vyasa, the colossal figure of Sanskrit learning, was a versatile genius like his father Parasara. He collected the scattered and almost forgotten Vedic hymns and arranged the Vedas, composed the Vedanta philosophy, compiled the Puranas and history, wrote a *History of the Great War,* and gave a law-book. Born of a woman of fisherman class, he was trained as a seer from his youth. He was ugly in appearance, but very comely in learning, wisdom and religion. It is said that he was at first a staunch Shaivite but late in life, he turned a Vishnuite. Having quarrelled with the Shaivites of Benaras, he tried to build a Kasi of his own on the eastern side of the Ganges. But he found no adherents. He had a residence in Kashmir, where he composed most of his works. His son, the free-souled Sukadeva was a minister of King Janamejaya in whose reign, his epic the *Bharata Samhita* was first published.

Like the *Ramayana*, the *Mahabharata* also has grown. Vyasa first wrote the outline of his epic in 8,800 verses (*Mahabharata, Introduction, I. 81*). Again, in *Mahabharata*, I. 101, he is said to have composed the *Bharata Samhita* in 24,000 verses. This original epic has undergone repeated revisions for sectarian and caste purposes. The book in its present form, was put together by Sauti, who received it from Vyasa through another person. Twenty-four thousand verses out of 100,000 are alleged to be the work of the original poet (*Oriental Magazine, vol. iii, p. 133*). By careful reckoning, several scholars have found that 24,000 verses still form the historical groundwork of the epic. Vyasa was an eye-witness to the exploits which he recorded. Certainly, there are things in the present book which could not be known to the first poet. As Krishna is deified, doubtless some parts were of later date (Preface to the *Vishnu Purana, p. IX*). Further, its claims to very high antiquity (fourteenth century BC) are disproved by the advanced stage of the language used in most parts. Professor Max Müeller holds that the two epics have been recast in modern Sanskrit—a view hardly tenable.

The great epic is mentioned as *Bharata* and *Mahabharata* in the *Grihya Sutra* of Asvalayana. The leading names of the poem are mentioned in Panini's grammar (800 BC). The word *Yavana* mentioned in the poem, does not imply the Greeks of the fourth century BC, but a people who lived in a part of Afghanistan, where Raja Varuna had been ruler in the twenty-nineth century BC (*Rig Veda*). These Yavanas, as children of Varuna, may have been the ancestors of the Greeks, according to a Hindu tradition.

The epic was familiar to the Hindus at least two or three centuries before Christ (*Oriental Magazine, vol. III, p. 133*). Patanjali also mentions it in his *Great Commentary* (140 BC). The earliest direct mention of epic poetry in India is made by Dion Chrysostom, (AD 80).

The Vedas, the Upanishadas and the philosophies were the favourite studies of the learned class. The epics and the Puranas were adapted for lightless women and the Sudras.

The *Mahabharata* in its present form was compiled perhaps, in the fifth century BC.

> All except Colebrooke are enthusiastic in their praise of the two epics. Nor, is this admiration confined to critics alone. Even Dean Milman and Schlegel vie with Wilson and Jones in their applause for the simplicity and originality of the composition, the sublimity, grace and pathos of particular passages, the natural dignity of the actors, the holy purity of manners and the inexhaustible fertility of imagination in the authors.
>
> The story of Nala and Damayanti (an episode) is a model of beautiful simplicity. The *Bhagavat Gita*—Song Celestial—a work of a much later age—is admired for the clearness and beauty of the language and illustrations. It deserves high praise for the skill with which it is adapted to the original epic and for the tenderness and elegance of the narrative by means of which it is introduced. (Elphinstone).

To the early foreign scholars, the epics appeared as 'utterly valueless' as histories, but sober modern critics rightly call them 'semi-historical romances.' They are valuable as records of the manners and civilisation of ancient times. They now rank as popular Hindu scriptures and exercise boundless influence on the Indians.

The *Ramayana* is prior to the *Mahabharata* on the following grounds:

(i) Tradition makes Valmiki *adi kavi*, i.e. the first secular poet of India.
(ii) The language of Valmiki approaches nearer than any other Sanskrit poem the early form used in the Vedas.
(iii) An epitome of it is introduced into the *Mahabharata*.
(iv) The names of the sages and seers mentioned in the *Ramayana* are found in the other, but not vice versa. Even the name of Valmiki occurs in the *Mahabharata*.
(v) The *Ramayana* knows nothing of Vyasa, the Puranas and the Battle of Kurukshetra.

(vi) *The Mahabharata* speaks of Vyasa and the four Vedas. The *Ramayana* never mentions the four Vedas. It gives *Trayi*, i.e. three Vedas. It makes repeated mention of the six *Vedangas*, Sruti, Smriti (law-books) but never the four Vedas.

(vii) The four Vedas, the Sankhya, the Nyaya (Logic), Upanishada, itihasa (history), *Vedangas*, Nataka (drama), stories, etc., are in the *Mahabharata*, but not in the *Ramayana*.

(viii) The *Ramayana* holds the systems of karma (action) and yoga (abstraction of mind), but knows no *jnana* (wisdom) and *bhakti* (faith).

(ix) Valmiki was the contemporary of Rama and Vyasa of the Pandavas whose exploits they sang. At the end of the Lanka war, Rama had placed Prince Bibhishana on the throne of Lanka. The same Bibhishana tendered his submission to the Pandava prince out on conquest of the Deccan. Again, Kripa and Kripi, grandchildren of Satananda, priest to the marriage of Rama and Sita, were fostered by King Shantanu of Hastinapura. Kripi was married to Drona, the military preceptor to the Kuru and the Pandu princes. This shows that Rama had preceded the Pandavas by some four or five short generations. We have already said that the kingdoms of Kasi, Kosala and Videha were noted for ther pure manners, lofty morals, high learning, and good religion while, Kurukshetra, Matsya, Panchalka were marked for their fiery valour, bold self-assertion, overbearing manners, and rather corrupt morals.

Vyasa also wrote the *Harivansa*, i.e. history of the dynasty of Krishna, a commentary on the Yoga philosophy of Patanjali. Jaimini, a disciple of Vyasa also wrote a *Mahabharata*, but now we possess only a portion of it. Kamandaka wrote his *Nitisara*, work on worldly wisdom, about 1400 BC.

LEARNING

No nation has valued learning and knowledge so much as the Hindus. Good works and religious rites lead to happier states of life and due reward, but true knowledge—pure wisdom—alone leads to final union with God. Every Aryan was socially bound to study the Vedas, to perform daily sacrifices. The defaulters were not only denounced and despised but were also classed as Sudras. The seats of learning were four, viz., royal courts, parishads, private schools of sages and seers, and the sylvan seats of learning and sanctity.

Learned men from distant towns and villages were invited to the royal courts, honoured and rewarded. They held discussions with the learned priests of the courts or other learned men, not only on rites and ceremonies, but on the mind, soul, the future world, nature of the gods, the fathers, different orders of beings, nature of *Brahman*, whose manifestation is all. Many of the *Brahmana* works and Upanishadas were probably composed there.

Learned Brahmans retired to forests where they taught higher wisdom and much of the boldest speculations. Those teachings are known as the *Aranyakas*.

A parishad was an academy of letters or a university. Young men learnt there (*Vrihada Aranyaka Upanishada, VI. 2*). Svetaketu went to the parishad of the Panchals for his education.

A parishad consisted of twenty-one Brahmans well-versed in philosophy, theology and law. Parasara (fifteenth century BC) says that even four or three learned Brahmans in a village may form a parishad.

Kashmir, Prithudaka, Taxila, Kanouj, Benaras, Oudh, and Mithila had grand parishads as they were great centres of learning.

Our sages and seers also maintained numberless private schools where pupils of different classes and countries would live for education. All studentship was then residential.

Every Aryan boy was sent to school early where all were educated together. Finishing studies after twelve years or longer, and making suitable presents, they would return home, marry and settle as householders.

As a householder, he would light a sacred fire under an auspicious constellation to offer libations, perform other duties, rites, offer hospitality to strangers, receive and honour guests.

The *Taittiriya Upanishada*, I. 2 sets forth his duties as follows: 'Say what is true; do thy duty; do not neglect the study of the Vedas. After having brought to thy teacher the proper reward, do not cut off the lives of children. Do not swerve from the truth. Do not swerve from duties. Do not neglect what is useful. Do not neglect greatness. Do not neglect the learning and teaching of the Vedas. Do not neglect the works (sacrifice) due to the gods and fathers. Let thy mother, father and the teacher be to thee like unto a god. Whatever actions are blameless, those should be regarded, not others; whatever good works have been performed by us, those should be observed by thee.'

Subjects of Learning

Even in those early times, various subjects were taught.

In the *Chhandogya Upanishad*, VIII. I. 2, Narada says to Santakumara thus: 'Sir, I know the four Vedas, *Itihasa-Purana* (history and theogony), the Veda of the Vedas (grammar), the *Pitrya* (rules for sacrifice for the ancestors), the *rasi* (arithmetic), the *daiva* (science of portents), the *nidhi* (science of time), the *vako-vakya* (logic), the *ekayana* (ethics), the *deva-vidya* (etymology), the *brahma vidya* (pronounciation, prosody, etc.), the *bhuta vidya* (science of demons), the *kshatra vidya* (science of weapons), the *nakshatra vidya* (astronomy), the *sarpa-deva-jnan vidya* (science of serpents and of genii)—all these I know, Sir.'

The *Vrihad Aranyaka Upanishada*, III. 4. 10 states that the four Vedas, *Itihasa-Purana* (historty and theogony), *vidya* (knowledge), Upanishadas, shlokas (verses), *sutras* (prose rules), *anu-vyakhyana* (glosses), and *vyakhyanas* (commentaries)—have all been breathed forth from Brahma.

The *Satapatha Brahmana*, XI, mentions the four Vedas, the *anu-Sasanas*, the *vidyas*, the *vako-vakyas*, the *Itihasa-Puranas*, the *narasansis* and the *gathas*. The original works on these subjects are lost to us, being replaced later by good books on the subject.

Encouragement of Learning

An eminent French writer has called the Hindus 'an immortal people'. Indeed, religion and learning have preserved them still. Numberless hymns of the *Rig Veda* show the grateful *dana-stutis* (songs of gifts) or rishis in praise of their great patrons. In the epic age, the Ikshvakus of Kosala, the Janakas of Videha and the kings of Benaras were renowned patrons of learning. Besides, the Vaisyas (merchants) encouraged learning much.

Janaka of Videha had gathered round him the most learned men of his time, discussed with them, taught them holy truths about the Supreme

Being. Gautama wrote his Logic and Yajnavalkya, compossed his works at Mithila that gave light to the eastern provinces. It attracted even Fyez, brother to Abul Fazal, minister to Akbar, who, in the guise of a Hindu, learnt the entire Hindu lore from a Brahman to whom Akbar gave a large estate inherited by the present Maharaja of Darbhanga.

King Ajatasatru of Kasi (Benaras), himself a learned man and a most renowned patron of learning, once exclaimed in despair, 'Verily, all people run away from my kingdom saying "Janaka is our patron!"—(*Vrihad Aranyaka Upanishada, II, I. I*). A somewhat similar lament came from a Maharaja of Sirohi state. Rajputana, who spoke to his minister thus: 'Good Sir, learned men do not come to our courts these days, for we do not honour them. Bees do not come to the flowers that have no honey!'

PHILOSOPHY: CLOSE OF THE FIFTEENTH CENTURY BC

The Logical Schools

The twenty-nineth and twenty-eighth centuries BC had witnessed a great display of reasoning in religion and philosophy. The sharp edge of reasoning was blunted by the ritual religion of the epic age. After ten or twelve centuries, a reaction, an awakening, followed. The learned persons again thought of God, soul, creation, life, death, and other vital questions. Their 'guesses at truth' are found in the *Aranyakas* and the Upanishadas. By a process of close reasoning, these sublime truths were soon systematised into philosophies. Formerly, logic or *Viko-Vakya* was one of the subjects of learning. About 1425 BC, Gautama dignified it in his *Metaphysics of Logic*. He was priest to Siradvaja Janaka of Mithila and had married Ahalya, a princess of Benaras. His *Nyaya* School contains five chapters and 521 aphorisms. Pakshila Swami's commentary on *Nyaya* is said to be the oldest known.

The Jain scholar Hem Chandra says in his *Dictionary* that Pakshila Swami and Chanakya (fourth century BC) were the same.

About 1420 or 1415 BC, Uluka, another philosopher probably of east India, wrote his physics or philosophy of sensible objects. We do not know his parentage nor his home, but he was a Brahman of the Kasyapa gotra (clan). He is better known as *Kanada* (from *Kana*=atom and *ada*=expounder).

Gautama and Kanada, founders of the logical schools of Hindu philosophy, agree and differ. Yet each supplies the corrective to the other's defects.

Kanada's *Vaiseshika* (atomic theory) work has ten chapters and 370 sutras or aphorisms.

It knows no Buddhistic tenets and is mentioned in the *Mahabbharata;* therefore, Western scholars think that its date was at least 1100–1000 BC. From the likeness of classification, method, arrangement, and syllogism, Gautama is often compared to the Greek philosopher Aristotle (fourth century BC). But Gautama's syllogism is rather rude in form, having five propositions, of which two are evidently superfluous. Kanada speaks of six *padarthas* or predicaments, viz., substance, quality, action, community, particularity, and intimate relation. According to some, there is one more—privation.

Striking resemblance is found between Hindu logic and that of Aristotle. The subjects of both are the same—the senses, the elements, the soul and its different faculties, time, and space.

According to all Hindu schools, mind is the sixth and the internal sense; it is the same with Aristotle. The definitions of the subjects often differ and the general arrangement is entirely dissimilar.

Gautama's arrangement is more comprehensive and complete than Kanada's.

Gautama's sixteen subjects are: proof; that which is to be known and proved; doubt; motive; instance; demonstrated truth; syllogism; reasoning by reduction to absurdity; ascertainment; thesis or disquisition; controversy; objection; fallacy; perversion; futility; and confutation.

The subdivisions are more natural and systematic. Proof is of four kinds, viz., perception, inference, comparison, and affirmation.

The objects of proof are twelve, viz., soul, body, the organs of sensations, the objects of sense, intellect, mind, activity, fault, transmigration, fruit of deeds, pain or physical evil, and liberation.

All these are fully and minutely discussed. The immateriality, independent existence, eternity of the soul are asserted. God is considered as the supreme soul, the seat of eternal knowledge, the maker of all things.

The Atomic School of Kanada supposes a transient world composed of aggregations of eternal atoms. It is not clear whether their temporary arrangement depends on their natural affinities or on the creative power of God. Gautama admits God, but not His creative power. Kanada admits God rather indirectly.

The Vedic Schools of Philosophy

The bold speculations, the sceptical theories seemed to have sealed the fate of the Vedic rites. But the Hindus cannot do without the Vedas. So, Jaimini, the most prominent disciple of Vyasa wrote about 1400 BC a philosophy called *Purva Mimansa* in defence of the Vedic rites. He admits the authority of the Vedas but not their revelation. According to him, an intelligent performance of the Vedic rites leads to salvation. His work has twelve chapters. He admits 'Brahma', but never uses the word *Isvara* (God) in his book.

Jaimini asserts that the gods are not separate powers, but the *mantras*, i.e. hymns alone are gods. Professor EB Cowell observes: 'In the course of its critical investigations, *Purva Mimansa* discusses various philosophical doctrines. It appears to have been originally atheistical, the sacrifices and other ceremonies which it so zealousy upholds, being said to produce their fruit by an inherent law or fate. One of its most curious speculations is the doctrine of an eternal sound underlying all temporary sounds. This, by some, is identified with Brahma. The grammarians have naturally adopted this doctrine' (Elphinstone's *History of India*, p. 123).

Jaimini here adopts the *Sabda Brahma Bada*, i.e. the sound theory of creation as given in the *Rig Veda*, Book X. This vast world had its origin in *Vak*, i.e. sound. All perceptions and conceptions rose from sound. This sound is Veda: this sound is Vedic hymns. All gods are really sounds. The Vedas have adopted *nominalism:* all existence are names in sounds (*R.V.*). Vak Devi, daughter to Seer Abhrina, in her *Devi Sukta* in the *Rig Veda*, says: 'Sound is Brahma. Sound is the origin of all cretion.' In the Greek philosophy also, this visible creation of God is spoken of as *Logos*, speech or sound. St. John in his Gospel says: 'Oiriginally, there was sound; sound was in God and sound was God.' This truth was taken from the neo-Platonists. Thus, Jaimini defended the ritual religion (karma *kanda*) of the Vedas. His preceptor, the illustrious Vyasa, having collected and arranged the Vedas next wrote about 1400 BC or shortly thereafter, a philosophical view of the Vedic tenets. Colebrooke, misled by the mention of Jains and Buddhists, thinks that Vyasa's first book was written in the sixth century BC. Needless to say that these Jains and Buddhists were early sects. Six Buddhas had lived and preached before Gautama Buddha. We have noted Jainism already. The 22nd Jain Tirthankara (reformer) called Neminatha or Arishta-Nemi, an uncle to Krishna, preached his Jainism some time before 1400 BC.

Vyasa's work called the *Uttara Mimansa*, in 558 aphorisms, is also known as Vedanta which shows the highest flights of Hindu philosophy.

Though based on reasonable arguments, it professes to be founded on the authority of the Vedas and appeals for proofs to texts from those scriptures.

Main Principles of the Vedanta

Everything is from God, is in God and shall merge into God in the end. Individual souls are from His substance like sparks of fire. Soul is infinite, immortal, intelligent, sentient, true, capable of activity, but naturally reposing. The Supreme Being causes it to act. It is encased in a body. There is a subtle body and a gross body. The former follows soul in all its migrations. On death, it leaves the corporeal body, goes to the moon, is closed in an aqueous body, falls in rain, is absorbed in some vegetable and hence through nourishment, into an animal embryo. Finishing transmigrations according to deeds, it receives liberation and divine grace. The Vedanta denies the eternity of matter, attributes the existence of the universe to energy and volition of God.

The Vedanta has two schools: one says, 'All that exists, arises from God.' The other says, 'Nothing does exist except God.' This last view was brought in by Sankara in the ninth century AD.

The Sankhya and the Vedanta

The Sankhya maintains the eternity of matter: its principal branch denies the existence of God, while Vedanta derives all things from God and one sect denies the reality of matter. Though atheistic and materialistic, Sankhya does not differ very widely from that which derives all things from the spirit. Kapila says, 'Nature exhibits herself like an actress. Soul perceives all, not being affected, like a mirror which receives all images without itself undergoing any change. Mind, like the village headman, takes perception and finally to the king, i.e. soul.' (Wilson's *Sankhya*

Karika, p. 107, 117). Kapila admits the separate existence of souls and holds that intellect is employed in the evolution of matter; hence he denies any Supreme Being, material or spiritual, by whose volition the universe was produced. Patanjali, however, admits the existence of soul, but besides, a Supreme Soul called God, the Supreme Ruler.

There are altogether nineteen different schools of philosophy in India. Of them, some are atheistic and so, inconsistent with the religious doctrines of the Brahmans; others, though perfectly orthodox, advance opinions not stated in the Vedas.

Hindu philosophy appears to have been originally atheistic, though afterwards made to serve religion.

In India, philosophy is practical and inseparably connected with religion. In Europe, it is theoretical and speculative.

All schools agree in having one object, viz., deliverance from all corporeal encumbrances.

Hindu philosophy teaches, among other sublime truths, the following: 'The Universe in its ultimate ground, is *spirit*. What is material, is the expression of the eternal spirit in time and space. Man is essentially either that spirit or a part of it or akin to it. The universe is governed by a just law which is the very nature of its true expression. All life is sacred. Morality is the law of humanity which is the master of its destiny and reaps only what it has sown. The universe has a moral purpose and the social structure must be so ordered as to subserve it.

Hindu and Early Greek Philosophies

The relation of mind to matter, creation, fate and many similar subjects are mixed by the Hindus with questions now discussed in modern metaphysics, but were not known to the Greeks. The various doctrines, viz., the eternity of matter or its emanation from God; of the separate existence of God or His arising from the arrangements of nature; the supposed derivation of all souls from God and return to Him; the doctrine of atoms; the successive revolutions of worlds were likewise maintained by one or other of the Grecian schools. Do they speak of independent origin? Was each coincidence accidental? How could a whole system as the Pythagorean, be so similar to that of the Hindus?

Certainly, they show a common origin. Tradition also speaks of the eastern journeys of Pythagoras.

Pythagoras and Hindu Philosophy

The end of all philosophy, according to Pythagoras, is to free the mind from encumbrances which hinder its progress towards perfection; to raise it above the dominion of the passions and the influence of corporeal impressions so as to assimilate it to the divinity and qualify it to join the gods.

The soul is a portion of the divinity and returns after various transmigrations and successive intermediate states of purgation in the region of the dead to the eternal source from which it first proceeded. The mind is distinct from the soul, diffused through all things, the first principle of the universe, invisible, incorruptible, only to be comprehended by the mind. Intermediate between God and mankind are a host of aerial beings and exercising different influences on the affairs of the world.

The aversion of Pythagoras for animal food and his prohibition of it unless offered in sacrifices, his injunctions to his disciples not to kill or hurt plants, the long probation of his disciples and their mysterious initiation clearly show his direct imitation. Further coincidences are—affinity between God and light; the arbitrary importance assigned to the sphere of the moon as the limit of earthly changes. These doctrines of Pythagoras were quite distinct from the opinions of all the Grecian schools that existed in his time.

The ancient Egyptians are said to have had some of these tenets, common to Pythagoras and the Hindus. The only early authority is Herodotus (450 BC). He lived long after the Pythagorean philosophy had been universally diffused. If, however, these doctrines existed among the Egyptians, they were scattered opinions in the midst of an independent system. In India, they are the main principles on which the religion of the people is founded, to which all philosophy refers and on which every theory in physics and every maxim in mortality depends.

Colebrooke says Indian philosophy resembles that of the earlier, rather than of the later, Greeks. He infers that the Hindus were in this instance, the teachers and not the learners.

ASTRONOMY

In a previous chapter on Astronomy, I have noted that considerable progress was made in the subject in the Vedic age. This we know from the *Rig Veda*, the *Surya Siddhanta* and other traditions. In the Vedic age, the year was divided into twelve lunar months to which a thirteenth month was added to make it solar (*R.V., I. 25.8*). The six seasons, viz., Madhu, Madhava, Sukra, Suchi, Nabha, Nabhasya were connected with different gods (*R.V., II. 36*). The phases of the moon were observed and deified. *Raka* was the full moon. *Sinibali* was the day before the new moon. *Gungu* was the new moon (*R.V., II. 32*). The position of the moon with regard to the *nakshatras* is also alluded to in the *Rig Veda*, VIII, 3. 20. Some of the constellations of the lunar mansions are named in X, 85. 13.

The lunar zodiac was finally arranged towards the close of the Vedic age. For, twenty-eight lunar mansions are mentioned in the *Black Yajur Veda, Atharva Veda* and the *Taittiriya Brahmana*.

There has been a good deal of controversy in Europe and America as to the originality of the lunar zodiac. Colebrooke (1807) is in favour of its Hindu origin. French Biot (1860) describes the Chinese *Sieu* as original, from which Hindu *nakshatras* and Muhammadan *manazil* were borrowed. Professor Lassen adopted this view. Professor Weber is for the Hindu origin. He, however, conjectures that the Hindu system was probably taken from Babylon. But the Assyriologists, by repeated search, could find no lunar zodiac among the archives of old Babylonian learning. Professor Max Müeller says that the Babylonian learnng. Professor Max Müeller says that the Babylonian zodiac was solar. There was no lunar zodiac. Hindu Veda and *Brahmana* works clearly show the lunar zodiac as original in India (*India: What can It Teach us, p. 126, 1886*).

Hindus also observed the solstitial points to fix the dates of events. Bentley gives 1442 BC as the date of the formation of lunar mansions and 1181 BC as the date of the naming of months (*Hindu Astronomy, p. 3* and *10, 1824, London*). Needless to say that these conclusions are not reliable.

The solar zodiac, if borrowed at all, was borrowed from the Chaldeans, both by the Greeks and the Hindus RC Dutt says that considerable progress was made in the subject in the epic period; but I find no proof of it. No doubt, astronomy continued to be cultured as a science and there were professional astronomers called *Nakshatra-darsas* and *ganakas*, as we have now; (*Taittiriya Brahmana*, IV. 5; *White Yajur Veda*, XXX. 10. 20); yet certain it is that no new truths were discovered. For ten centuries at least (2500 to 1500 BC), the subject suffered terribly from Brahmanic obscuration.

Of course, sacrifices were regulated by the position of the moon. Sacrifices lasting a year, were regulated by the sun's annual course divided ino the *Uttarayana* (sun's northern progress) and *Dakshinayana* (sun's southern progress). The southern progress was regarded as bad. All sacrifices were performed in spring, i.e. April and May (*Aitareya Brahmana* IV). The months were now of thirty days. They marked the Vishuvat, Equator or the Central Day (Dr M Haug's *Introduction, pp. 46–47*).

With the awakening, we meet with the venerable Parasara (flourished in fifteenth century BC) who not only wrote on astronomy, but also on law and agriculture. We still possess a portion of his astronomy. He first observed the place of the Collures. Davis holds (*As. Res. vol. V, p. 288*) that the observation was made in 1391 BC (?). Another passage quoted from Parasara shows that the heliacal rising of Canopus took place in his time at a period which agrees with the date assigned to him on other grounds.

Our best and most learned work on astronomy is the *Surya-Siddhanta*, remodelled in the fifth or the sixth century AD. It was written by Vivaswan, father of Manu. It is known as a revelation from heaven received upwards of 21,64,900 years ago. Here also is employed the enigmatic mode of communicating knowledge. Priestly obfuscation of early authors has cast a veil over our sciences. Even astronomy has been made subject to extravagant chronology; all the epochs are thrown into confusion and uncertainty. No general view of the system has been given. Only the practical parts of sciences are made known. Even here, the original sources are carefully concealed and the results shown as revelations from God. There is no record of a regular series of observations. This was certainly a great bar to the progress of science. The art of making observations was taught to few.

The *Ramayana*, Kishkindhya Book, speaks of the sunless polar region and refers to the Aurora Borrealis. The minister Sanjaya, speaking to the blind king Dhritarashtra, says: 'The roundness of the earth is seen in the moon when the shadow of the former is cast upon the latter.' (*Mahabharata*). Yaska, explaining a hymn of *Rig Veda*, probably composed in the epic age, says: 'The moon is lighted by the sun.'

Astronomical forecasts were taken by the kings to avert or mitigate the evils of the coming year. The youngest Pandava prince, Sahadev studied astronomy carefully and wrote a book on it, now lost.

Vyasa is our next astronomer. He gives us the following descriptions of the nine chief planets of the Hindus.

Sun—Red as China-rose, son to Kaspaya, very bright, foe of darkness, destroyer of all sins and maker of day.

Moon—White as a divine conch or snow, born of the Sea of Milk (this shows the extreme humidity, cf. *Moist Star*) marked by spots, shining like a jewel in the crown of Siva the Destroyer and Reproducer. (This probably refers to the moon causing death when in an unfavourable position.)

Mars—Born of the earth, shining like a mass of splendour, full of heroic spirits, bearing the weapon called sakti in hand and red in colour. (This is regarded as the planet of war.)

Mercury—Rather black in colour, like the bud of a Priyangu flower. Extremely handsome, matchless in beauty, peaceful, endowed with all the qualities and son of the moon.

Jupiter—Preceptor to the devas and the seers, like the very sea of talents, golden in hue, lovely and lord of the three worlds.

Venus—White as snow, spiritual guide to the Daitya Aryans, expounder of all the sciences, very bright and son to Bhrigu.

Saturn—Deep blue in colour, son to the sun, elder brother to Yama, born of Chhaya, i.e. shade, and very slow in motion.

Rahu (Node)—Half in body, heroic, cause of eclipse to the sun and the moon, born of sinhika and very dreadful.

Ketu (Apside)—Having a colour like that of burning flesh, crooked in nature, fierce in form and tormentor of the stars and the planets (*Stava Panchaka*).

These last two are not regular planets.

Similes and metaphors abound in the Sanskrit epics, illustrating the swelling of the sea by the attraction of the moon.

OTHER SCIENCES

Law

Laws form the backbone of a society. To bring about the best possible unity and harmony amongst the heterogeneous communities of ancient

India, very wise and good laws were required and our great rishis gave them. We have ample proof to show that Hindu civilisation was advancing daily towards polish, perfection, purity, and sanctity. The *Vrihad Aranyaka Upanishada* I, 4. 14 gives a very noble definition of law. There were punishment of criminals and proper administration of law. The judicial procedure was still crude. The criminals were often tried by the ordeal of fire (*Chhandogya Upanishada, VI, 16*).

The chief law-givers of the age who flourished from 1600–1300 BC, were Sankha, Shathatapa, Likhita, Apastamba, Katyayana, Gautama, Parasara, Vyasa, and Yajnavalkya. Their great antiquity is still discernible in their present but spoiled law-books.

Lofty conceptions of justice appear in the *Mahabharata*, Peace Book, chapter 91, verses 14–27 and 32. The Brahman criminals had no preferential treatment. The law recognised the rights of the weak and the supreme need of absolute impartiality for the king: 'Protecting all men by works, body and deeds and never forgiving even his offending son himself form the great duty of the king. Neither mother, nor father, nor brother, nor wife, nor priest is unpunishable in the sight of that king who rules agreeably according to his duty.'

MEDICINE

The trying Indian climate was a gret friend of disease. Addressing fever, the *Atharva Veda*, V, 22.14 says: 'As people give servants or wealth, so do we give you to Gandhari, Mujavan, Anga, Magadha, and other countries.' Fever still prevails in many parts of India and the weekly human sacrifice to this terrible goddess is over 10,000. Many in these days ignorantly ascribe the prevalence of fever to the railway embankments. We think it is a natural evil in India. Intense heat followed by excessive rain, generally produces fever. According to our rishis, rubbing the body well with oil before bath, putting cow-dung plaster on the ground, occasional fasts, Tulsi plants (holy basil) and neem trees in the house, good food, thoughts, air, water not only prevent fever and other harmful influences of nature, but also give longevity. But it is a pity that these time-honoured wise practices are falling into disuse.

The Medical Experts of the Age:

	Name	*Works*
1.	Janaka, a king of Videha, perhaps 2500 BC.	*Vaidya-Sandeha-Bhanjanam*
2.	Agastya, the earliest civiliser of the Deccan, 20–22nd century BC.	*Vaidha Nirnaya Tantram*
3.	JAvala, a sage, perhaps 2000 BC.	*Tantra-Sarakam*
4.	Jajali, a sage, perhaps 1900 BC.	*Vedanga Saram*
5.	Paila, a sage, perhaps 1800 BC.	*Nidanam*
6.	Kavatha, a sage, perhaps eighteenth century BC.	*Sarva-dharam Tantram*
7.	Kasiraja, the second king of Benaras, perhaps seventeenth century BC.	*Chikitsya Kaumudi*
8.	Dhanvantari, the fourth king of Benaras, perhaps sixteenth century.	
9.	Divodasa, the seventh king of Benaras, son of Bhimaratha by queen Ganavati, fifteenth century BC.	*Chikitsya Darpanam*
10.	Susruta, a prince of Kanouj and son to Visvamitra came with 100 *rishi* boys to study medicine with Divodasa of Benaras. He became highly proficient, especially in surgery.	*The Brava Prakasa*

The *Susruta Samhita* as we have it now, was remodelled by the famous Buddhist Nagarjuna. The fact is confirmed also by the annotators Dalvana and Bagbhata. The original work is known as *Vriddha Susruta*. Nagarjuna preserved a little of the original poetical work. The sense of the rest he explained in prose. Susruta was probably the first to discover that spleen and lever make blood in the body. The Vedas speak of 360 bones in the body; but Susruta satisfactorily proved 300 bones.

The earliest physicians spoke of the origin of limbs of the embryo in the womb, one after anotehr. But Divodasa appears to give the wisest view on the point, in that he says that all the limbs of the body grow simultaneously.

11. Charaka—(not later than 1400 BC). His parentage and home are not known. His name is explained as a spy on the earth to asc rtain the state of health. He brought together the works written by the six disciples of Atreya and consulted other works and compiled his own. The defects of Charaka were afterwards made up by the learned Drirhavala, a writer of the Punjab. Charaka is mentioned in the *Mahabharata*.

The properties of beel were discussed and ascertained by both Susruta and Charaka who, however, declared it unsuitable to the Indian climate.

The most ancient medical works, mentioned in the *Brahma Vaivarta Purana*, Brahma Part, chapter 16, were all based on the *Bhaskara Samhita* of Vivaswan whose *Surya-Siddhanta* is a learned work on astronomy. Of the numerous early works, those of Charaka and Susruta alone have survived the test of time.

12. Nakula and Sahadeva, the two Pandava princes wrote, about 1380 BC, the *Vaidyaka Sarvasvam* and *Vyadhi-Sindhu-Vimardakam*, respectively. Great improvements were made in medicine and surgery. The culture of anatomy and botany formed a party of medical training then. Hindu knowledge of anatomy, obtained from the dissection of the sacrificial beasts, was meagre; our ancestors never excelled in this subject.

The *Mahabharata* tells us that before the War (1389 BC), both parties were busy procuring the best physicians, surgeons, medicines, surgical instruments for the treatment of the sick and the wounded soldiers.

In chemistry and other sciences, progress of those early Hindus was no less remarkable.

SOCIAL LIFE

Caste

The later caste-system is wholly unknown in the *Rig Veda*. Traces of the three 'twice-born' are indeed found. The word Brahman (priest), even Brahmana occurs. The *Rig Veda* is entirely silent as to the Sudras except in the ninetieth hymn of Book X. The other Vedas give the system fully developed. Sudras were subjugated people. Sudras of ancient India, Demos in the Greek states and colonies, the Plebs of Rome, the Perioeci and Helots of Sparta, and the Tyrrhenes of Etruria were all of the same class to their Aryan conquerors.

Caste was regularly formed in the epic age by hard and fast rules. But the system was still pliant. The simple origin of caste based on professions, was afterwards obscured by myths and legends. The true origin of caste appears from:

(i) The *Vayu Purana*—'There were no castes in the first age. Divisions arose gradually according to their works.'
(ii) *Ramayana*, Book VII, chapter 74—'In the Vedic age, the Brahmans alone practised austerities. In the epic age, Kshatriyas were born: then were established the four castes.'
(iii) *Mahabharata*, Peace Book, Chapter 188—'At first, all were Brahmans. Then those who were fond of sensual pleasures, fiery, irascible, daring, forgetful of sacred duties became Kshatriyas. Yellow men living by cows, agriculture and not practising religious performances, became Vaisyas. Black, twice-born men, impure, addicted to violence, lying, covetous, living by all kinds of works became Sudras.'

Sir John Woodroffe's remarks will not be out of place here: 'Indian caste arose naturally under the influences of the unifying forces of advancing civilisation to bring about the best possible kind of unity and concord among the heterogeneous communities.'

Sociology shows the existence of caste everywhere. The distinctions of rulers, warriors, merchants, and agriculturists rose from the inherent needs of society and its organisation. Classes and the castes in a practical sense exist in the West today. The notion that all men are equal in work, capacity or utility is unfounded.

The original castes were four. Now only two remain, viz., the Brahmans and the Sudras. Sudra castes have multiplied into professions—secular occupations. The 'untouchables' were considered unclean. There was prohibition of intermarriage and inter-dining. Subject to caste rules, there is still social association.

Many are of the opinion that classes will always exist, however much they may shift. Professor Giddings, the sociologist says: 'Classes do not become blended as societies grow older: they become more sharply defined. Any social reform that hopes for the blending of classes is foredoomed to failure.'

The main class-divisions in modern Europe and America are between the rich and the poor. The ideal Indian scheme of social order is based on religious and philosophical principles which are also the practical ideals of daily life.

In the epic age, caste was organised mostly in the Indo-Gangetic Valley. The Dravidian converts formed the bulk of the people, Vaisyas (merchants) one compact body, were entitled to religion and learning. To preserve traditions, to guide the kings and the people and to save the nation morally, the Brahmans were made the guardians of the treasury of religion and learning.

The caste-rules were gradually made rigid to prevent the small Aryan community from merging into the natives whose daughters they married or kept and whose corrupt manners, morals and food were creeping into the Aryan society.

We find another institution, viz., the four stages of life, well developed in this age. An ideal Brahman's life aimed at dharma (morality), artha (fair wealth), kama (moral desires lawfully realised), and moksha (salvation). No nation but the Hindus has so justly and logically balanced, harmonised and served the world and God in one whole. An ideal Hindu life was mapped out into four stages, viz., continent studentship, married householder, liberation, forest life, and mendicancy in which a person without anything of his own and going to his death, sought union with the great source of all. The first two were paths of lawful enjoyment serving God. In the last two, an entry was made on the path of renunciation and union with the spirit. This round of life, first adopted by the worthy high-caste Hindus, was gradually imitated by all. Only some great souls might seek *vairagya* (renunciation) at once.

A somewhat clear view of the state of society may be had from the following professions given in the *White Yajur Veda*, Chapters 16 and 30:

Thieves, horsemen, infantry, dancers, speakers, frequenters in assemblies, lewd men, sons of unmarried women, charioteers, chariot-makers, carpenters, potters, jewellers, cultivators, arrow-makers, bow-makers, dwarfs, crookedly formed men, blind and deaf persons, physicians, astronomers, elephant-keepers, wood-cutters, horse and cattle-keepers, servants, cooks, gate-keepers, painters, engravers, washermen, dyers, barbers, learned men, women of various kinds, tanners, fishermen, hunters, fowlers, goldsmiths, merchants, men with various diseases, wig-makers, poets, musicians, and other sorts. The were professions and not castes. Till 200 BC, the masses were Vaisyas, entitled to the full rights of the Aryans; Sudras alone were disallowed, for they had neither tradition nor aptitude.

That the caste-rules were not so rigid, appears from the *Aitareya Brahmana*, I. 16 and II. 17. None other than a Brahman could perform a sacrifice (*Aitareya Brahmana, VII. 29*). Persons born in one class might enter into another. Visvamitra, Debapi and Janaka became Brahmans (*Satapatha Brahmana, XI, 6.2.1*). Kavasha, son to Ilusha, was admitted as a *rishi* for his learning, purity and wisdom (*Aitareya Brahmana, II. 19*). Satyakama Javala became a Brahman by his truthfulness and learning (*Chhandogya Upanishada V. 4*). A Brahman imparts knowledge to a Sudra accepting presents and taking his daughter for his wife. (*Chhandogya Upanishada IV. 2*). The upper three classes could sacrifice, not the Sudra (*Satapatha Brahmana, III, 9*). The supremacy of the Brahmans was nominal (*Satapatha Brahmana, III. 2. I. 40*).

RC Dutt says that the sacred thread came to be used in the epic age. The thread was worn by the twice-born at the time of the sacrifice only. Now it is habitutally worn at all times. In the Vedic age, probably mekhala or a golden chain was worn.

Special Features of Social Life

(i) Caste was almost unknown in the Vedic age; it was developed in the epic age.
(ii) In the Vedic age, people were warrior-cultivators; in the epic age, cultured Hindus. Culture and progress went on through centuries. Hindus were now highly refined, developed minute rules to regulate their social and domestic duties.
(iii) Royal courts were now seats of learning. Learned men from all quarters were invited, honoured and rewarded.
(iv) Justice was administered by learned officers. Laws regulated every duty of life.

(v) Towns with strong walls, fine edifices, were many, with their judges, executive officers and police.

(vi) Agriculture was fostered; king's officers settled all disputes, looked to the collection of taxes and the safety and comfort of cultivators.

(vii) Arrangements were made for the education of all clases of people.

(viii) The *White Yajur Veda*, XXII, 22 has an excellent prayer for the wealth of the people and the country.

(ix) Wealth was in gold, silver and jewels; in cars, horses, cows, mules, slaves; in houses, fertile fields and in elephants and buffaloes (*Chhandogya Upanishada, V, 13, 17* and *19; VII, 24; Satapatha Brahmana, III. 48; Taittiri Upanishada, I. 5. 12*).

Besides gold and silver, other metals and objects are mentioned in the *White White Yajur Veda*, XVII, 13; *Chhandogya Upanishada* IV, 17.7—lavana (borax), tin, lead, iron, leather, wood and copper.

(x) Food consisted of various kinds of grain and meat of animals. The *Vrihad Aranyaka Upanishada* VI, III, 13 mentions ten kinds of seeds, viz., rice (*vrihi*), barley (*jawa*), sesamum (*tila*), kidney bean (*masas*), millet and panic seed (*anuprijangavas*), wheat (*godhuma*), lentils (*masura*), pulse (*khalvas*), vetches (*khalakulas*). The *White Yajur Veda* XVIII, 12 adds *mudga, nibara, syamakara.*

Grains were ground, sprinkled with curds, honey, clarified butter and made into cakes; milk and its various preparations have always been a favourite food in India. Animal food was much in use. Beef was still a delicacy. Bull, ox, miscarrying and barren cows were killed when a king or an honoured guest was received (*Aitareya Brahmana* I, 15). The *Brahmana* of the *Black Yajur Veda* states the kind of cattle to be killed.

In the Asvamedha sacrifice, more than 180 domestic animals are killed. The *Gopatha Brahmana* gives the portions to be taken by different persons. Beef was washed with *soma* juice. The *Satapatha Brahmana* IV, 5 gives a detailed account of the slaughter of a barren cow and its cooking. The *Satapatha Brahmana* IV, 5 gives a detailed account of the slaughter ofa barren cow and its cooking. The *Satapatha Brahmana* III, I. 2.21. discuses the propriety of eating beef. Mild objections are, however, raised in the *Rig Veda, Atharva Veda, Satapatha Brahmana*, to cow slaughter. Priests are desired not to eat beef. Yajnavalkya says:

'I for one, eat it, if that is tender.' He draws some difference between a vegetable diet and animal diet (*Vrihad A. Upa. VI, 4. 17–18*).

(xi) Towns were surrounded by walls, beautified by finest edifices and laid out in spacious streets; the palace stood in the middle and was frequented by chiefs, soldiers, saints, priests, learned men, and by people on special occasions. All loved, respected and worshipped the king. There was perfect loyalty. Ministers and officers were loyal. Kings had a very high regard for their queens. Householders had wealth in various things, kept fire, honoured guests, lived up to the laws of the land, offered sacrifices, honoured virtue, learning and knowledge.

Various were the manufacturers of civilised society. All followed professions from generation to generation. The people were not yet divided into numberless castes. Agriculturists lived round each town. Saints and learned men lived in forests.

(xii) Position of Women: Women knew not absolute seclusion; had an honoured place from the dawn of civilisation. Many beautiful sayings are found which give honour to woman, marriage and motherhood. They inherited and possessed property (*stridhana*). They are regarded as the earthly representatives of the Great Mother of all. There are repeated texts to show that 'no injury, no ill word should be used to her. She should be honoured always.' They took a share in sacrifices and duties, attended assemblies, openly frequented public thoroughfares, distinguished themselves in learning, wisdom, administration, politics, and battle prowess. They never mixed freely with men. They were held in very high honour (*V.A. Upanishad*). Cf. learned Maitreyi, Gargi Vachaknavi and others.

They were well trained in general matters and especially in domestic duties.

Early marriage was still unknown. There was a distinct sanction for the remarriage of widows. Men of one caste married widows of another. Even Brahmans took widows of other castes (*Atharva Veda, V, 17.8*).

Polygamy was common in kings and wealthy lords. In ancient times, it was almost universal among the rich of all nations. Polyandry was exceptionally rare. A prohibition against it is found in the *Aitareya Brahmana*, III. 23. Marriage in near blood was objected for third or fourth generation (*Satapatha Brahmana I, 8. 3. 6*). Women were faithful and affectionate to their lords. Female unchastity was rather rare. The *Satapatha Brahmana*, II, 5. 2. 20 alludes to a confession of sin of adultery. Women took great care of their hair and used fine dress, bright ornaments, gems, jewels, perfumes, and dyes.

(xiii) Ceremonies, customs. Coronation ceremony, the imperial ceremony and the horse sacrifice were the most imposing and ostentatious royal ceremonies of ancient India.

The coronation rite is described in the *Aitareya Brahmana*, VIII, 6–9; IX, 39; X, 27. The advice given to a king in this last, is worth quoting here: 'If thou shalt be a ruler, then from this day, judge the strong and the weak with equal justice; resolve on doing good incessantly to the public and protect the country from all calamities.'

The imperial sacrifice (Rajasuya) was performed by an overlord. In it, even the menial offices are done by the vassal kings.

The horse sacrifice was a means of expiation of sin and of assumption of the imperial title.

Funeral Ceremonies—Cremation of the dead and the burial of ashes was general in the Vedic age (*R.V., X 15.4; X, 16.1*). There was occasional burial also (*R.V., X. 18. II*). There was no burial in the epic age. There was cremation and the burial of ashes only (*White Yajur Veda*, Chapter 35). Bones were collected and buried near a stream and a mound raised as high as the knee and covered with grass. Relatives bathed, changed their clothes, and went home (*Aranyaka* of *Black Yajur Veda*).

The practice of sati was in progress. Gift of cakes was made to the manes (*White White Yajur Veda*, Chapter 2). Cakes, wool, thread or hair were offered to the fathers. Departed spirits received offerings from their living children and none when the line was extinct. So, desire for a male child is a part of Hinduism. Continuity of line is a norm of nature.

ADMINISTRATION

Many deny self-government in ancient India. But we have clear evidence in favour of it.

'In no country in the whole world has communal autonomy been so developed.' (MB St. Hilaire).

'It was self-government in its purity' (Professor M Williams).

The constitution of self-governing Indian villages in the most ancient Hindu rule, as described in old Sanskrit works, was found almost unchanged by the servants of the East India Company from whose official records, made from actual observation and enquiry, the following is taken: 'A village, geographically considered, is a tract of country comprising some hundreds or thousands of acres of arable and waste land; politically viewed, it resembles a corporation or township. Its proper establishment consists of officers and servants of the following descriptions. The *potail* (Sanskrit *gramapati,* headman) who has the general superintendence of the affairs of the village, settles the disputes of the inhabitants, attends to the police and performs the duty already described, of collecting the revenues within his village, a duty which his personal influence and minute acquaintance with the situation and concerns of the people renders him best qualified to discharge; the *curnum* who keeps the accounts of cultivation and registers everything concerned with it; the *talliar* and *totie*, the duty of the former appearing to consist in a wider and more enlarged sphere of action, in gaining information of crimes and offences and in escorting and protecting persons travelling from one village to another; the province of the latter appearing to be more immediately confined to the village, consisting among other duties, in guarding the crops and assisting in measuring them; the boundary-man who preserves the limits of the village or gives evidence respecting them in case of dispute; the superintendent of tank and water-courses distributes the water therefrom for the purpose of agriculture; the Brahman who performs the village worship; the schoolmaster who is seen teaching the children in the villages to read and write in the sand; the astrologer who proclaims the lucky or unpropitious periods for sowing and threshing; the smith and carpenter who manufacture the implements of agriculture and build the dwelling of the ryot; the potter; the washerman; the barber; the cow-keeper who looks after the cattle; the doctor; the dancing-girl who attends at rejoicings; the musician and the poet.'

'Under this simple form of municipal government, the people have lived from time immemorial. States after states, kingdoms after kingdoms, empires after empires rose and fell; but the townships remained entire.'

'It shows us at a glance how the great agricultural population of India tilled their lands and manufactured their commodities in their own self-contained little republics through thousands of years. Happy it were if the British rulers had preserved and fostered and reformed these ancient institutions and thus continued to rule the people through their organised assemblies.' (RC Dutt's *India Under Early British Rule pp*. 119–20).

Krishnaswami Aiyangar, in his *Ancient India*, gives a description of the rural self-rule in southern India under the Cholas, in the eleventh century AD.

The villages of those days were generally large. Over each village, there was a headman. A union of ten villages was under a Superintendent. A group of hundred villages was under a Subdivisional Officer. Over him was the District Officer who had the charge of 1,000 villages. The village was self-governed. The king, the chief executive head of the state, bestowed honours and dignities upon the state officers. An SDO would get the revenues of a rich and populous village as his pay (*Mahabharata, Peace Book, Chapter 87, shlokas 3–7*). A district officer used to get the net revenues of a small town, after public charges and the costs of administration. A minister of the crown was in charge of these district administrations. All crimes in the village were reported to the subdivisional officer through the proper channel (*ibid., shloka 5*). Every large town had its may or for looking after all matters relating to his jurisdiction (*ibid.*, 10). Drinking shops, public women, pimps, actors, gamblers, keepers of gambling houses were put down (*ibid., Chapter 88, 14–15*). There was perfect religious toleration but there were laws against vagrancy. India now swarms with beggars, numbering over five million, but then nobody—holy or unholy—was allowed to beg. Of course, the physically unfit were an exception to the law (*ibid., Peace Book, Chapter 88, shlokas 16, 17* and *24*).The kings were occasionally despotic, but generally they were bound to rule according to law or they would risk their thrones. Public opinion was a great power in the land (*Mahabharata, Chapter 89, verses 15–18*). Lofty conceptions of justice appear from the *Mahabharata. Peace Book*, Chapter 91, verses 14–27 and 32.

Trade, agriculture, cattle-rearing, and money-lending on which depends the happiness of the subjects, were under the special care of the state. Advance of seed-grain was made, taking only a fourth part of the produce (*Mahabharata, Peace Book, Chapter 88, 26–30; Chapter 89, 23–24*). The state provided irrigation works at public cost and gave *takavi* advances (*Mahabharata, Court Book, Chapter 5, 76–79*).

Taxes were light and reasonable. The king was merely a public trustee. Public funds were religiously spent to promote the prosperity of the people (*Mahabharata, Peace Book, Chapters 87* and *88*). Necessities of life were exempted from taxation (*ibid., Chapter 87, shloka 14*). Excise duties were moderate. When the country was threatened with invasion, special war taxes were imposed and war loans were raised (*ibid., Chapter 97, 30–35*). The beneficent results of these policies were the advancement of trade, increase of wealth and general prosperity. There were a good many millionaires and billionaires in the land who were wealthier than most of the kings.

The kings were the chief executive officers and ever devoted to the good of the people. Monarchies were constitutionally limited. The voice of the leading people could not be slighted. Generally, the kings were just and popular. Their first care was for agriculture and commerce. Agriculture was held so sacred that even the worst could not disturb it. There was a system of state-loans to the poor people. The state maintained police and army for protecting the life and property of the people. Every state consisted of the crown, the spiritual lords the temporal lords and the commons, still found in the native states. The order is the same in England also. The king was the sole owner of the crown-lands. The third was the feudal system. Every state had large funds for the encouragement of learning. Every state would demand not more than twenty per cent of the produce. People were exempted from the payment of revenues or rents during famines or on occasions of a prince's birth or coronation. Prisoners were set free on state occasions. Due provisions were made for the convenience of all foreigners. There were hospitals for men and beasts, rest-houses, good roads, various conveyances, *jala-yantras* (fountains), *yantra nauka* (machine-boats), and air-ships. There were counties, divisions, districts, subdivisions, *mandalas*, and villages. There were village units or unions, each representing a miniature republic, managed by *panchata*, i.e. panchayats, a council of five members, now revived by the British government. During a crisis, the unions would get aid from the superior stations. There were emperor (*samrats*) kings, viceroys (*uparajas*) and ambassadors (*dutas*). Every state had eight ministers to manage eight different departments. The king was the spring of all. The Aryans lived in a joint-family system. Husband and wife were *dampati,* 'rulers of the house'. There were exogamy and endogamy. Marriage was held sacred. It appears that the Indo-Aryans tried their best to maintain their pristine purity of blood on the one hand and to admit non-Aryans into the Hindu pale on the other. The *purdah* and infant marriage were unknown. 'The Sanskrit epics give good illustrations of war and art, painting and sculpture.' (P Brown in *Dacca Review, June 1915*). The rishis discouraged the use of blue (indigo) and deep-red clothes. The practice of wearing long hair by both men and women, became gradually rare with the men, as that gave an air of softness and effeminacy. Ornaments of gold were in common use. Diamond, pearls and precious stones were used by the richer classes. The military science was much improved. Coloured clothes were much in use.

TRADE

The magnificent sacrifices of the kings and gifts of gold clearly show the extent of India's foreign trade.

Gold currency appears from the *Mahabharata, Virata Book*, shlokas 43–44; Drona Book, Chapter 17, shloka 25; Asvamedha Book, Chapter 65, shloka 20, Court Book, Chapter 23, shloka 53.

The Indians of the age traded more in the east than in the west. The Egyptians, the Assyrians and the Arabs traded with India till 1300 BC when the Phoenicians arrived and became supreme.

The *Old Testament* speaks of the 'wondrous products of the East'. The *Ramayana*, Ayodhya Book, Chapter 82 states that priest Vasista asked Bharata's permission to accept presents from the foreign merchants living in the northern, western and southern provinces of India and from those living in the islands (about 1460 BC). Hindu commercial activity will appear from the following points:

- 'Damayanti joined a trding caravan going to sea.' (*Mahabharata,* episode of *Nala* and *Damyanti*).

- 'Gautama left home and made for the coast; on the way, he met a body of merchants going to sea. With them he proceeded towards the shore.' (*Mahabharata, Peace Book, Chapter 169*).
- The *Ramayana*, Kishkindhya Book, Canto 40, alludes to Japan (Java Dvipa) composed of seven islands and also to gold and silver islands.

Professor Wilson, carefully examining the list of presents mentioned in the Court Book, *Mahabharata* says that India during Yudhisthira's imperial sacrifice, had commercial relations with China. Exchange of goods cannot be ascertained now, but it is certain that China was famous for its silk (see also *As. Res., vol. IV, p. 226*; Tod's *Rajasthan II, p. 185*; Dr Royle's *Essay, pp. 127–37*).

THREE

1

RISE OF MAGADHA

THE PRADYOTA DYNASTY (779 TO 655 BC)

The eighth century BC is a turning-point in the history of ancient India for it witnessed 'the old order changed, yielding place to new'. The old dynasties gave place to new ones; Sanskrit bowed to Prakrit; spiritualistic civilisation to a materialistic one; the Vedic rites to philosophical speculations. Magadha (south Bihar) will now exercise her imperial sway over India and outside for over a thousand years.

Ripunjaya, the last king of the Varhadratha dynasty was a despot and a profligate. The ministers and the people were equally sick of him and his long reign of fifty years. At length, Sunaka, the prime minister, most probably a Brahman, killed his master and secured the throne for his own son, Pradyota, who began to rule about 779 BC. The Pradyota dynasty, a short one of five kings, ruled some 124 solar years. The usurper Pradyota ought to have been a good king, but he proved the reverse of it. He was a hypocrite and believed none; nobody believed him in turn. The nobles of the state, a powerful body, showed him no regard. The *Matsya Purana* does not even mention his name. He ruled some fifteen years. The second king Palaka was a better monarch. It is said that he did nothing unbecomming of a king. He was powerful and wise. The vassal kings were all submissive to him. He rule twenty-three years (764 to 741 BC). The third king Visakhayupa, a mere blank name, ruled some thirty-five years (741 to 706 BC).

The next king was Janaka who ruled some thirty years (706 to 676 BC). The last king was Nandivardhana who ruled twenty years. The last three kings departed from the wise policy of Palaka and were thorough despots. The country groaned under them. At last, the people, justly indignant, dethroned Nandivardhana and set up Sisunaga in his place. The Puranists call the kings of the Pradyota dynasty *varna sankara*, i.e. mingled colours. Before we pass on to the next dynasty, we shall note here some other important points.

Parsvanath (820 to 750 BC), the twenty-third Jain reformer, son of king Asvasena and queen Bamadevi of Nenaras and son-in-law to king Prasenajit of Oudh, refused royalty, lived as an ascetic and attained the pure wisdom at Benaras. Then the began to preach. His Jainism prevailed from Bengal to Gujarat. The districts of Maldah and Bogra were great centres of his faith. His converts were mostly from the depressed classes of the Hindus and non-Aryans. He died on the Sumheta or Parsanath hill in the Hazaribag district, at the age of seventy-two years before the death of Mahavira in 527 BC. In Rajputana, his adherents grew very powerful and oppressed the Hindus in many ways. The rishis applied to Hindu kings for help, but in vain. At last, they created new warriors on Mount Abu to fight out their enemies, the atheistic Jains. The new heroes, Hinduised certainly from some foreign source, most probably from the early Scythians or Takshaks (Turks), defeated the infidels and saved the Hindus. We are told that this happened at least before 600 BC. The new warriors, called the 'fire-born', were Pratiharas, the Pramaras, the Chalukyas or Solanki, and the Chauhans. Agnisala was the first great Chauhan. We shall see them become powerful later on.

THE SISUNAGA DYNASTY (655 TO 405 BC)

Sisunaga was formerly a vassal of the Turanian Vrijjians. He founded his dynasty of ten kings who ruled for some 250 years.

Sisunaga was powerful, ambitious, wise, and popular. He conquered the neighbouring kingdom of Kasi where he placed his own son as king *(Brahmanda Purana)*. To the north of the Ganges lay the Videhas who were growing very powerful. The bravery and power of Sisunaga saved Magadha from the grasp of the heroic Vrijjis of the north. The Aryans, who had entered Magadha and other kingdoms of east India, were sound practical men. They loved politics, they loved conquests. Theirs was a stern materialistic civilisation. Besides, Magadha was a very ancient kingdom. But her military spirits had cooled under the later worthless kings. In Sisunaga, they now found a worthy leader. Afraid of the powerful rivals of the north, Sisunaga and his people desisted from fresh conquers. He consolidated his power at home. He ruled till 615 BC. His son Kakavarna, so long king of Benaras under him, succeeded to the throne of Magadha. Giribraja continued to be the capital. Kakavarna was dark in complexion and not heroic like his father. It appears that the king of Sravasti wrested Benaras from his hands. Kakavarna ruled till 600 BC. The next king was Kshemadharman, a good monarch, devoted to the welfare of the people. He ruled till 570 BC. He was succeeded by the heroic Kshatraujas who ruled till 546 BC. Buddha was born (564 BC) in his reign. About this time, there were sixteen principal kingdoms in north India. The next king of Magadha was the renowned Bimbisara, also called Srenika. He ruled from 546 to 496 BC. The following points are noteworthy:

(i) To save Magadha from the powerful Lichchavis of Vaisali (now Besar, twenty-seven miles north-west of Patna), he removed the capital to Rajagriha (now Rajgir), which he built and fortified.

(ii) He conquered and annexed Anga (east Bihar). He was the real founder of the Magadhan power.

(iii) He was mild, humane, just and a very popular king. Jivaka, educated at Taxila, was his physician.

(iv) The solar line of Ayodhya was now weak, whereas the solar line of Sravasti was now very powerful, and held both north and south Kosala and had subjugated the kingdom of Kasi (perhaps about 563 BC). King Brahmadatta or Brahmadanta of Sravasti married his daughter Kshemaka to Bimbisara and gave the revenues of Kasi as dowry. Bimbisara also married princess Vasavi of the Lichchavi king of Vaisali, by whom he had the prince Ajatasatru. Brahmadatta passed into religious retirement and his worthy son Prasenajit succeeded him to the Kosala throne. Bimbisara also resigned his throne in favour of his prince Ajatasatru and passed into private life. The *Vayu Purana* gives him a reign of twenty-eight years. But the other Puranas and the *Mahawansa* assign to him a reign of some fifty years. We adopt the latter. It is said that at the instigation of a wicked plotter named Devadatta, a cousin and rebellious disciple of Buddha, Ajatasatru killed his good and aged father Bimbisara by starvation. The first queen, princess of Kosala, died of grief. Thereupon her brother, Prasenajit, stopped the revenue of Kasi. Ajatasatru, thus insulted, attacked Kosala. He was victorious in the first three battles. In the fourth, he was defeated, made prisoner and taken to the Kosala king in chains. He renounched his claim to the revenue of Kasi and begged hard for release by his uncle. A treaty was concluded and Prasenajit gave his daughter, princess Bajira in marriage to Ajatasatru, with the revenue of Kasi as her dowry. Ajatasatru returned to his capital. Three years after this, Prasenajit went to Ulumba in the Sakya kingdom. In the meantime, his son Biruddhaka revolted against him. Prasenajit fled and came down to Rajagriha to seek the shelter of his son-in-law, but died outside the town, tired and worn out. Prasenajit was a great friend of Buddha. His aunt Sumana, noted for her learning and piety, became a Buddhist nun.

Prasenajit had asked for the hand of a Sakya princess. The Sakya chiefs could not agree, as both the houses belonged to the same solar stock. Yet, afraid of displeasing Prasena, they sent him the daughter of a maidservant Vasavakshatriya by name. Biruddhaka was born of her. He gained the throne about 490 BC. To punish the Sakyas for their fraud, he attacked the Sakya kingdom about 485 BC. The Sakyas fought hard but were defeated and brutally massacred by the ruthless savage victor. The Sakya kingdom was annexed to Kosala. Shortly after, Biruddhaka and his chief minister died in a burning house. The last Sakya king Mahanama, losing all the relatives, drowned himself. Seventeen stupas commemorate the massacre of the Sakyas by Biruddhka at Sagarwah, near the Vanaganga river in Nepal.

(v) The Bengali conquest of Ceylon. Prince Vijaya, banished by his father for numerous misdeeds, took to the sea with 700 followers, arrived in Lanka and conquered it (543 BC). From the Sinha dynasty, the country got its new name of Sinhala.

(vi) Cyrus, the Persian emperor, invaded India (541 to 40 BC).

(vii) About 512 BC Darious, son of Hystaspes, the Persian monarch, conquered the right bank of the Indus, north of Kabul, which formed the 20th province of his vast empire. This Indian province was the richest and most populous in the empire and paid Darius in gold bars to the value of over a crore of rupees. Of course, the Indus then was more easterly in course. There were Indians in the Persian court and army. The Indian troops, in the Persian service, went to fight even in Europe. Cf. Herodotus, VII, 65; VIII, 13; IX, 91. The Persian empire was the brightest in the world till the middle of the fourth century BC. Certainly, there were Indo-Iranian relations in those times.

(viii) Ajatasatru came to the throne about 496 BC. He met Buddha, confessed his crimes, begged his pardon and was taken into the prophet's grace. He was at first a Hindu, then a partron of Devadatta's *Ajivaka* cult and after wards of Buddhistic learnings. Perhaps, he was never a sincere Buddhist like his father-in-law Prasenajit.

Expecting an invasion from Pradyota, king of Avanti and also from Vrijjians, he strengthened his army and built a strong fort near Patna with the help of his Brahman ministers Sunidha and Varshakara. He had already conquered the Lichchhavis of Vaisali, who were a branch of the ancient Vrijjis, a highly civilised people. Buddha died in the nineth year of his reign, i.e. in 487 BC. He claimed a share of Buddha's relics, built a stupa over it and helped the celebration of the first Buddhistic council before the Saptaparni Cave (487 BC) About 483 BC after the sad death of his brother-in-law Biruddhaka, Ajatasatru conquered Kosala and the Sakya kingdom. Now, Ajatasatru was the master of Magadha, Anga, Vaisali (north Bihar) Kapilavastu, and the Kosalas. It is said that for better government he changed his capital to Champapuri (nor Patharphata), twenty-four miles from modern Bhagalpur. His favourite idea of conquering Avanti ended with his death in 473 BC. The great Sanskrit dramatist Bhasa gives us a very curious historic sketch of the time in his play entitled the *Savpna Vasavadatta*. Udayana, king of Vatsa kingdom near Allahabad, had stolen Princess Vasavadatta, daughter of Pradyota, the mighty king of Avanti. Udayana was made prisoner by Pradyota. The shrewd minister of Udayana not only delivered his master but also married him to Vasavadatta. Again, Ajatasatru had conquered a part of the Vatsa kingdom of which Kausambi was the capital. Ajatasatru left his son Darsaka on the throne of Magadha. His daughter Padmavati was as yet unmarried.

Pradyota's intended invasion of Magadha was for the recovery of his son-in-law's lost kingdom from Ajatasatru. Now, the clever minister of Udayana thought of marrying his master to Princess Padmavati of Magadha and regaining the lost parts of the Raj. He succeeded. Darsaka gave back the province. Bhasa in Act I of his play twice mentions Pataliputra as a capital of Darsaka. This king probably ruled till 464 BC. Darsaka was succeeded by his son Udayasva who in 460 BC built Kusumapura—'the City of Gardens', now Bankipore. Pataliputra now rose to great importance *(Vayu Purana, Chapter 99)*. Udayasva probably ruled till 431 BC. The next king was Nandi Vardhana who perhaps ruled till 420 BC. The last king was Mahanandi, a foppish person. He ruled some fourteen years. These kings kept the kingdom intact; they neither faced any invasion nor sent out any expedition for fresh conquest. They lived in gorgeous palaces. Mahanandi died early from the effects of excessive indulgence. His weak son Pinjamakha succeeded him to the throne (406 BC). But the heroic Nanda, the first-born son of Mahanandi by a Sudra concubine, organised an army, attacked and captured Pataliputra, killed Pinjamakha and ascended the throne (405 BC). The *Mahavansa* IV calls the last four kings of the dynasty parricide kings.

THE NANDA DYNASTY (405 TO 313 BC)

Nanda was ambitious, powerful and avaricious. Like another Parasurama, he killed almost all the proud Kshatriyas of the time (*Vishnu Purana IV, 24.4)*. He was the first Kshatriya of a low birth to sit on a reputed Kshatriya throne. So, his usurpation was much disputed and opposed. The allies, all proud of their high birth, warmly espoused the opposition. Heroic Nanda also proved himself equal to the occasion. In different battles, he defeated and overthrew most of the sixteen great powers of north India, plundered their treasures and gathered vast wealth. It is said that after Yudhisthira, he was the first samrat (emperor) of India. He assumed the glorious title of mahapadma, i.e. the rich. With an enormous army he held the country under military subjection. The *Mahavansa* alludes to his avarice and Yuen Chwang speaks of his immense riches. The five stupas near Pataliputra were believed to have contained the vast treasures of Nanda Raja. All troubles over, Nanda directed his attention to the condition of his people. A pond of his construction was afterwards repaired by king Kharavela of Kalinga in 165 BC (Inscription of Hasti Guha, i.e. Elephant Cave, Udaygiri). By the power of arms, Nanda made himself lord over a considerable part of north India. Of the sixteen states, some were under his direct rule and some were allowed to rule as his vassals. The power of Magadha was at its height under Nanda Mahapadma. Pataliputra, the capital, was now magnificent, populous and an important centre of trade. Katyayana, critic of Panini, was a minister of Nanda. Besides eight legitimate sons, Nanda had a son named Chandragupta, by fair Mura, probably a Persian woman. Nanda ruled twenty-eight years. Then his eldest son Sumalya succeeded him (377 BC) The Nanda brothers kept the empire intact and reigned until 340 BC when the eighth Nanda brother Dasasiddhika and his sons were murdered by his wife's paramour Indradatta who put his own son by the queen on the throne. This king, of base origin, was Sudhanva or Ugradhanva (Greek Xandrames or Agrames). His realm is mentioned by the Greek writers as the kingdom of the Prasii, Sanskrit Prachya (i.e. eastern) or Gangarides, Sanskrit Gangarashtra. In point of power, population and prosperity, Magadha was now the brightest kingdom in India (*History of the World, vol. II)*.

According to the Greeks, Sudhanva Nanda was extremely unpopular for his wickedness and base origin. The state, however, was administered by Brahman ministers of whom Rakshasa, a quite selfless Brahman was the chief. A rough idea of the extent and power of the Nanda empire may be had from its military strength consisting of 20,000 horses, 200,000 foot soldiers, 20,00 chariots, three or four thousand elephants. One may be curious to ask here why the Persians did not conquer India. Of course, attempts were made, though not crowned with full success. Cyrus failed to substantiate his dream. Some thirty years later, Darius conquered some Indian tracts north of Kabul. Probably, the Persians did not take the conquest of India so seriously, as they were busy fighting with the Greeks; or, they may have sent expeditions to India, but the Hindus beat them back. The following nine centuries (from 330 BC to AD. 530) found India in the midst of great troubles. The first invaders were the Greeks. India was saved by her two great heroes, Chandragupta (fourth century BC) and Pushpamitra (second century BC) and Pushpa Mitra (second century BC). Yet, the Asiatic Greeks had conquered some parts of India and Indo-Greek relations existed for 400 years.

ALEXANDER THE GREAT IN INDIA (327–26 BC)

The people of Greece, a small peninsula in the south-east of Europe, were an excellent people noted for their bravery, learning, wisdom, and arts. They were Aryan colonists of the Mediterranean islands called the Ionians. Hindu tradition markes them of Hindu origin, being the descendants of Turvasu, a rebellious son of Yayati. It is said that these Yawanas gradually marched towards the west. Greek Ionian and Hindu Yawana is the same world. Hindus applied the same word Yawana to the Greek invaders and conquerors of India of the fourth century BC and later on. The word Javana (applied to the Turks or Muhammadans in general) is often wrongly confounded by scholars with Yawana (the Greeks).

We are sure of an Indo-Hellenic intercourse, at least in learning and trade before Alexander, who however, made it closer. Alexander (356 to 323 BC), son of Philip II and queen Olympias of Macedon, a province to the north of Greece proper, was the pupil of Aristotle. He became king at twenty (336 BC). In 335 BC he subdued the northern tribes of Macedon. In 334 BC, when he was barely twenty-two, he was out to conquer and Hellenise the world, with 30,000 foot soldiers, and 5,000 horses. Of these, only 7,000 were pure Greek soldiers. The Greeks hated to serve him, as they called Alexander a foreigner. So, many deserted on the way. Of them, Memnon became the admiral of Persia; but he died of cholera in 333 BC. This proved good for Alexander. Darius III (Codomanus) was then the Persian monarch. Alexander invaded Persia. After many battles, Darius, being defeated, fled towards India but was assassinated by Bessus, one of his faithful friends. Persia, Asia Minor and Egypt were conquered. The port of Alexandria was founded near the mouth of the Nile. The Carthaginian power was annihilated. In 330 BC. Alexander reached Ekbatana. He next went to Bactria and conquered it. Here, he married Roksana. In 332 BC he founded Alexandria, thirty miles north of Kabul. In April 327 BC, he crossed the Hindukush in ten days, with his army of fifty or sixty thousand soldiers and came down on the rich valley of Koh-i-Daman. Alexander now conquered the Aryans on the right bank of the Indus. He captured Push-Kalawati after a siege of thirty days and overpowered the Gandharians. After a strenuous opposition, the Asvakas (Greek *Assances)* were subjugated during the winter. He next attacked Massaga. Here, Alexander was wounded by an arrow. Unluckily, the king of Massaga was killed by a blow from a missile. Alexander then took the formidable fortress by storm. The queen of the late Chief and her infant son were captured. She afterwards bore a son to Alexander. He next captured the fort of Aornos near the Indus and appointed a faithful Hindu officer, Sasigupta by name, as governor.

In January, 326 BC Alexander crossed the Indus at Ohind (Udabhandapura), 16 miles above Attock (ancient *Aratta-wahika)* where a bridge of boats was built by the friendly Indian chiefs under the supervision of the Greek generals. At Ohind, Alexander received an embassy from Ambhi, son to his late ally, the king of Taxila. The kings of Taxila sought his aid against their enemies, the hill-king of Abhisares and Puru. The king of Kashmir sent his brother to tender his submission. Several minor kings came personally to pay him homage. The kings of the Punjab, instead of offering Alexander a combined resistance, easily yielded to him one after another. Only two kings opposed the Greek invader. One was king Hasti, defeated after a month's efforts and the other was king Puru said to be of Pandava origin, and ruler of the Doab between the Jhelum and the Chenab. His kingdom contained 300 towns and is now identified with the districts of Jhelum, Gujarat and Shikarpur. Alexander advanced to Vitasta (Jhelum) and met the army of Porus on the bank of the river (May, 326 BC). No other Indian king came to the frontier to repel the foreign foe. The hill chief of Abhisara, an ally of Puru, now left him and joined Alexander. The promised contingent of the Kashmir king did not yet arrive. The Greek writers have called the Hindu raja of Taxila a most useful ally for his 'liberal supplies' to the Macedonian army. Puru alone, with his two sons and an army 50,000 strong, gallantly stood to oppose the mightiest hero of the world. To the eternal glory of this valiant Indian monarch let it be said that when Alexander summoned him to submission, gave the proud answer that he would indeed come, not as a supplicant but at the head of an army ready for fighting. Alexander now prepared for a decisive battle. The river was in flood. Puru had drawn his army in battle-array on a dry land before a hill. Thinking that the cavalry—the mainstay of his army—could not face the huge elephants of Puru, Alexander thought of a device. Leaving the camp well guarded, he marched 16 miles to the north, forded the river near an island and reached the eastern bank, under the cover of a dark night. A son of Puru hurried up with an army to oppose but was routed. Then Puru marched with the bulk of his army towards the north-east on the Carri plain. The Hindus fought bravely for eight hours but were defeated. Arrian ascribes the Hindu defeat to the following causes:

(i) The Indian bows, though very powerful, were useless against the mobile Greek cavalry.
(ii) The ground was slippery.
(iii) The Greek horsemen were superior and more disciplined.

The army of Puru was annihilated, his two sons were killed and 'Porus himself, a magnificent giant, six and a half feet in height, fought to the last, but at last succumbed to nine wounds and was taken prisoner in a fainting condition.' Alexander, pleased with the gallantry and princely dignity of Puru, not only reinstated him but also augmented his kingdom by giving him some conquered tracts. Puru was not a fast friend of Alexander. To commemorate his victory, Alexander built two towns, Nikaia, on the battle-field (modern Sukhchainpur) and Boukephala (in memory of his favourite horse)—now called the town of Jhjelum. The victory spread the Greek fame far and near and roused native fear. The king of Kashmir now came personally to pay homage. The Asvakas then revolted and the Khattios helped by the Kshudrakas and Malavas offered stubborn resistance but all were put down. Many other princes tendered submission and promised allegiance to the invincible invader. The Agalassians were severely defeated. Alexander now felt a strong desire to conquer Magadha but his troops were quite unwilling to proceed further. His promises and threats to the army were in vain. Their reluctance was probably due to the following; the Macedonian army was almost shattered; the Magadhan army was very powerful, whose fame had reached even Egypt; the bravery of the mean of Puru had convinced them that other Indians were no mean rivals to them.

The wise counsels of Koinos, his trusted cavalry general, persuaded Alexander to stop from further conquests and to give order for retreat September, 326 BC). On the eastern bank of the Sutlej, he erected twelve big altars, each fifty cubits high, dedicated to the twelve great gods. It is said that Chandragupta and his successors long venerated the altar and offered sacrifice on them. In 325 BC , Alexander sailed up the Chenab to the Indus. The tribes of the Punjab and Indus were easily subdued. King Subhuti (Sophytes), lord of the Salf Range, yielded without resistance. Before leaving the Punjab, Alexander publicly appointed Puru to be king of the entire Doab between the Hydaspes and the Hyphases. These tracts, peopled by seven different nations had nearly 2,000 towns. In the meantime, a marriage reconciled Puru and Ambhi as friends. The small states on the lower Indus were easily seized. Alexander fortified the conquered tracts and established satrapies. In August, he returned to Persia through Gedrosia (Mukran coast) with 80,000 men. In September, Nearchus sailed for Persia with the fleet. At Babylon, Alexander lived and ruled for a short time. Here, he married the eldest daughter of Darius III. Eighty captains and 10,000 Greek soldiers took Persian women.

After Alexander's departure, Philipus, the Greek governor of the Punjab was murdered by mutinous mercenaries. Eudemus and Ambhi of Taxila were made temporary governors. At the age of thirty-two, Alexander died of fever at Babylon (11 June, 323 BC). He had stayed in India for nineteen months. In 323 BC there was one bright Greek domain from Macedonia to India, from Bactria to Egypt. Alexander's communication with the distant home and other parts of the empire was excellent. His expedition was an organised one and had historians, geographers, scientists and merchants. He encouraged caravan trade from India to the Levant. His merchants collected Indian products, perfumery to be shown in Europe. One object of Alexander's conquest was to spread Greek civilisation abroad. But we regret to note that he himself and his men were orientalised in Persia! In 321 BC Antipater appointed Peithon satrap of the upper Indus and Puru of the lower Indus. But erelong, Puru, held in high esteem by the Hindus, was murdered by Eudemus (320 BC). This crime roused the heroic subjects of Puru against the Greeks. In 327 BC Chandragupta expelled the Macedonian satraps from the land of the Indus. By 316 BC he was master of Afghanistan,

Beluchistan, Sindh, and the Punjab. No Indian work—Hindu, Buddhist or Jain—makes the least mention of Alexander. The Indians probably regarded Alexander as a mighty robber and his expedition and conquests as a political hurricane. Indian was not changed—India was not Hellenised. The Persian India of the north-west also was not Iranised much.

Of the numerous adventurers who had flocked to the camp of Alexander in the Punjab for their private ends, Chandragupta (Greek Sandra Coptos), an exile from the court of Magadha, was the foremost. He induced Alexander to conquer Magadha. His object was to be the king of Magadha under the Greeks. But he displeased Alexander by his haughtiness; so, he was forced to flee the Greek camp. It seems probable that before Chandragupta met Alexander, he had visited the Persian capital and the emperor Darius III to induce him to help him capture the throne of Magadha somehow, but in vain. Chandragupta was ambitious, bold, heroic, affable, handsome and very strong in brain, body and mind. The great kings favoured him not, but fortune soon took to him. In the Punjab, he had carefully learnt the Greek mode of fighting. Now, the death of Alexander, quarrels of his generals, murder of Puru, and the native revolts paved the way of his future success.

Having left the Greek camp, Chandragupta probably entered the army of the king of Taxila where he soon won his laurels. His burning ambition only awaited an opportunity and it presented itself before long. The people of the Punjab did not like the Greeks; they wanted a suitable leader; on the murder of Puru, the natives revolted. Chandragupta put himself at their head, drove away or destroyed most of the Greek garrisons one after another, and became master of the Punjab (315 BC). Next, he thought of Magadha—powerful Magadha which could not be conquered easily. He dreamed, he planned, he thought of a stratagem. Luckily, another opportunity occurred soon which helped him to rise. Satakara, being insulted by Rakshasa, applied to Maharaja Nanda for redress! But getting no relief from the emperor, he left Pataliputra, vowing vengeance and came to the Punjab in quest of Chandragupta whom he found at Taxila where he had already secured the friendship of Chanakya, a clear-headed politician of firm resolve, sound learning but of poor means. Satakara and Chandragupta plotted together for a great political move and gain of their ends by making Chanakya the cat's paw. One day, Satakara asked Chanakya to go with him to Pataliputra where he was a minister and where he might rise in fame and fortune. Chanakya agreed and went to Pataliputra, where, soon, through the machination of Satakara, he was greatly dishonoured by Nanda Raja in a feast in the royal house. At this, Chanakya took the vow of ruining the Nanda family.

'In the meantime, the Saka, Yawana, Kirata, Kamboja, Persian, Balhika, and Chandragupta's other soldiers and the force of the mountain-king (probably Nepal), besieged Pataliputra on all sides' in 315 BC *(Mudra Rakshasam, act II)*.

At Pataliputra some of the Nandas wre ruling conjointly. The later Sisunaga kings used both Rajagriha and Pataliputra as their capitals; but the Nandas made Pataliputra their sole capital. Rakshasa was their most faithful old Brahman minister. Satakara was the second minister.

Chankya's full name was Chanakya Vishnugupta Kautilya, which means Vishnugupta son of Chanakya, the Indian Bismarck. He was a clear-headed politician. At his instigation and through his machination, Chandragupta killed the Nandas in private, seized the throne, proclaimed himself king of Magadha and Chanakya his prime minister. But strong opposition came from Ugadhanva (Greek Agrames). Chandragupta, with the aid of the Nepal king, defeated Ugradhanva and secured the throne *(Asiatic Researches, vol. V)*. Rakshasa, highly aggrieved at the ruin of his masters, joined Malayaketu, a hill king and induced him to invade Pataliputra. Rakshasa succeeded in inducing the kings of Gandhara, Saka, Hoona, Khasa, Kashmir, Chedi, and even the Greek satraps to back Malayaketu with their armies by tempting them of a fair share of the splendid kingdom of Magadha. All marched towards Patna. Everywhere there was a great din of battle. Rakshasa planned other schemes for murdering Chandragupta. But Chanakya, by spies, learned of all the machinations of Rakshasa and set about to frustrate them. First, he caused a division between Malayaketu and Rakshasa, by a false letter, as if written by Rakshasa to Chandragupta and detected by Malayaketu.

Malayaketu got angry with Rakshasa and killed five of the allies. At this, the soldiers, terrified, field and so did the other allies. Malayaketu remained alone. Erelong, he was made prisoner by several chief officers sent by Chanakya. Rakshasa, thus defeated and sad, came back to Pataliputra and lived in private. Chanakya and Chandragupta went to him and after showing him great honour, offered him the prime ministership. Rakshasa was thus won over. Malayaketu was released and allowed to go back to his own kingdom in state. Now, Chandragupta was secure. Rakshasa died soon; and then Chanakya was again the prime minister (*Mudra Rakshasam*). His conquests of north India were completed by 313 BC. Sudhanva Nanda was probably slain. Chandragupta was formally crowned in 312 BC.

THE MAURYAN DYNASTY (312 TO 180 BC)

Chandragupta (312 to 288 BC)

Chandragupta was the founder of a new dynasty called the Mauryan dynasty after his mother Mura. The Nanda brothers had scornfully rejected her claim to queenship. Now Chandragupta, her successful son and the first universal monarch of India exalted her name, by naming the dynasty after her. Dr Spooner holds that Mura was a woman of Persian origin. But neither Indian tradition nor Greek records support the conjecture. Yet, after careful enquiry, I am now convinced that Mura was a Persian woman. Her name does not seem to be Indian and is probably connected with Persian Meru or Maur. The Puranists called the Indo-Parthians Morandas, the 'Morundoe' of Ptolemy. This Noor Jahan ('Light of the World'), probably daughter of some Persian merchant of Pataliputra, had caught the eye of Nanda Raja who, late in life, made her a partner of his royal bed. Had she been a fair but common sudra woman of India, she would not aspire to the rank of a queen. The mother of Nanda raja also was at first a pretty dancing maiden; but Mahanandi, the last king of the Sisunaga dynasty, took a fancy to her and made her a concubine. Nanda was born of her by the king.

The word Brishala applied to Chandragupta seems to be a Sanskritised form of Parasyala, i.e. Persian. In his first rise and success in the Punjab, Chandragupta was much helped also by the Persians who sympathised with him as one of their own and against the common enemy—the Greeks. Later on, he conquered Magadha mainly with the help of Persian soldiers.

The term sudra applied to Nanda, Chandragupta and others by some later Puranists, it highly objectionable, as neither law nor usage sanctioned it in ancient India. They were genuine Kshatriyas, though of a somewhat low order. This dynasty of ten kings ruled for 133 solar years.

According to the *Kumarika-Khanda, Agni Purana* and *Skanda Purana,* Chandragupta began to rule from 312 BC. This is also our proposed date. It is likely that his Indian conquests were complete before 312 BC. For, some Puranas state that he ruled twenty-four to twenty-five years peacefully. Chandragupta built Chandragupta Nagari on the river Krishna (Deccan). The author of the *Mudra-Rakshasam* and his annotator both belonged to that town. From this we infer that Chanadragupta conquered almost the whole of India. His empire extended from the Persian frontier and the Hindukush to the Bay of Bengal and from the foot of the Himalayas to the 13th degree north latitude. Only Kalinga, Chera, Chola, Pandya, and Kerala—all covered now by the Madras Presidency, were allowed to live free. The merit of these splendid achievements was mainly due to Chanakya, the Peshwa of the Mauryas. His prince Bindusara also bore a great part. Chandragupta founded the Maurya era, counted from 312 BC. Shortly after his ascension, both he and Chanakya made a pilgrimage to the Sukla Tirtha on the Narmada to atone for their sins *(Kumarika Khanda* and *Agni Purana).* On the death of Alexander in 323 BC, his generals fought for his vast empire. Seleucus, one of the generals, succeeded in making himself master of the central and western Asia (312 BC). The Seleukian and the Mauryan eras began almost at the same time. Now, Seleucus made a vigorous attempt to regain the Indian possessions. But in 305 BC, Chandragupta, after a successful campaign, forced him not only to abandon all thoughts of conquest in India but also to cede all territories east of Persia. Thus Afghanistan, Baluchistan, the Mekran coast, the Indus Valley, Sindh, and the Punjab became Chandragupta's. In 303 or 303 BC, Seleucus concluded a treaty with Chandragupta under the following unfavourable terms; Seleucus renounced all claims on India; ceded a considerable part of Ariana, west of the Indus; in exchange for 500 elephants, he surrendered his claim on Afghanistan, Baluchistan and the Mekran coast; gave a daughter in marriage to Chandragupta and placed an envoy in the court of Pataliputra. Thus was India saved from Greek rule. Chandragupta was one of the greatest monarchs of the world. We are indebted to Megasthenes, the first Greek ambassador in the Mauryan court, for a full and accurate account of Chandragupta and his administration. The following points are chiefly notable.

(i) Pataliputra: It was now the metropolis of India and a great emporium of trade. Numberless foreign vessels always lay on the Ganges. The city was nine miles long and one a half miles broad, defended by a strong wooden paliade having 64 gates and strengthened by 570 turrets. It was further guarded by a deep and wide moat fed by the waters of the Sone (Haranyavaha, Greek *Eranaboas).*

(ii) The palace of Chandragupta was chiefly built of wood overlaid with floriated gold leaves, and was unsurpassed in splendour.

(iii) Chandragupta: His favourite amusements were combats of animals, gladiatorial contests, various races and the chase. Generally, he lived in the inner palace protected by female guards, probably composed of Greek women. He gave audience to the people once a day when he received petitions and heard cases in person. A certain Persian influence was visible in some of his personal habits and style of architecture. He was a Hindu raja; there was perfect toleration under him. The caste system was well organised and all followed the hereditary professions assigned to them. He highly honoured the worthy Brahmans with whom he held an annual council to discuss the welfare of the state. Shiva was worshipped in the royal family.

(iv) Municipality: The capital was administered by a municipal body of thirty members divided into six committees of five members each: the first committee superintended the industrial arts; the second looked after the foreign residents and visitors; the third inspected the vital statistics; the fourth had the charge of trade and commerce; the fifth looked after the manufactures, and the sixth collected a tithe (one-tenth) on sale of goods. The whole body was responsible for the good administration of the city and had to keep in order markets, temples and other public works.

(v) Provincial Government: The provinces were governed by viceroys, generally relatives of the king, who constantly watched over them by means of 'news-writers' who acted as spies and reported to the King privately all that occurred in the country. Taxila, Ujjain, Bhilsa in central India were the viceregal seats.

(vi) Justice was very strict; criminals were punished with much severity.

(vii) The agricultural land was regarded as the property of the crown. Cultivators had to pay a tax to the government amounting to one-fourth of the gross produce of the fields on which great care was bestowed. Large sums at public costs were spent on irrigation works. There was a regular system of canals, tanks, wells, and lakes. A special department looked after the irrigation of the country.

(viii) The army: The military administration was excellent. The sate maintained a huge standing army of 30,000 horses, 600,000 soldiers, 9,000 elephants, besides chariots, in regular pay. The military department was supervised by a committee of thirty members divided into six boards of five members each. The first looked after the admiralty; the second looked after commissariat; the third after the infantry; the fourth after the cavalry; the fifth after the war-chariots; and the sixth after the elephants. There were regular arsenals and docks. Soldiers were highly paid.

(ix) Peace, progress and prosperity reigned everywhere in the empire. Great encouragement was given to learning, arts and industries. The roads were maintained in excellent order. Pillars serving as milestones and signposts were set up at intervals of half a *kos*—20-22½ English yards. A grand trunk road about 1,000 miles long connected the north-west frontier with Pataliputra. The Greek observer, testify to the high degree of civilisation of the first Mauryan empire. Chankya's *Artha Sastra* (art of government) also fully supports it.

(x) Success of Chandragupta: Chandragupta was about twenty-three when he met Alexander in 326 or 325 BC. He was crowned in 312 BC and ruled for twenty-four years. So in twenty-two or twenty-three years, he rose from a mere helpless exile to be the greatest emperor India has yet seen. His splendid achievements were. (1) The expulsion of the Macedonian garrisons. (2) The decisive repulse of Seleucus, the conqueror. (3) The subjugation of the largest empire yet known in India. (4) The formation of a gigantic army. (5) The thorough organisation of the civil government of a vast empire. (6) His power was so firmly established that no disputes or opposition arose to his son and grandson's peaceful succession. (7) His alliance was courted by the powerful Greek Kings. (8) The Greek princes made no attempt to renew the aggressions and were content to maintain friendly diplomacy and commercial relations with the Mauryans for three generations. (9) Chandragupta received from the sent to Seleucus various gifts (VA Smith). In everything, Chandragupta adopted and worked upon the ancient Hindu model. 'The little touches of foreign manners in his court and institutions, were Persian and not Greek.' Towards the latter part of Chandragupta's reign, Chanakya had a quarrel with him; so he left for the woods for penitential purposes. Chandragupta also retired to Mysore in 288 BC and was succeeded by his son Bindusara alias Amitraghata, (Greek, *Allitra Chades*—slayer of foes). Chinraipatan in Mysore was probably the town built by Chandragupta.

Bindusara

He made no fresh attempt at conquests. The friendly relations with the Greek powers of the West continued. Megasthenes and Deimachus were the Greek ambassadors in his father's court. Ptolemy Philadelphus of Egypt placed Dionysios in his Court. Fully secure, Bindusara now gave himself up to worldly pleasures. By his sixteen wives, he had hundred children, male and female. His marriage with the mother of Ashoka is curious. An astrologer had predicted her great fortune. So her father, a poor Brahman of Champapuri (near Bhagalpur) came to Bindusara at Pataliputra to make fair Subhadrangi his queen. Bindusara accepted her. But the other queens, jealour of her beauty and youth, put her out of the emperor's sight and employed her in the inner quarters as a female barber. Thus she spent her days most miserably. One day, Bindusara wanted a barber at an unusual hour. The chief queen, thinking that the king had forgotten her by that time, sent her to shave the king. Pleased with her work Bindusara asked her who she was. She stated her case, and the king remembered everything. From that time, she became his most favourite queen.

She bore him two sons: the first was Ashoka and the second, Vitasoka. Ashoka was ugly in form, dark in complexion and very unruly. So, his father did not like him much. The people gave him the name of

Chand, i.e. terrible. For training, he was handed over to the great astronomer Pingala Vatsa who, struck with the many auspicious signs on his person, predicted his great fortune and said that he would next inherit the crown. Prince Ashoka reached due age but his nature remained quite unchanged. He became so wild that Bindusara sent him to far off Taxila to put down a mutiny or be killed in the attempt. Ashoka was heroic and a man of great parts. He quelled the revolt and was cordially received by all. Bindusara, pleased with him, next sent him out to Ujjain as viceroy. Here he married fair Devi, daughter of a rich jeweller, by whom he had the son Mahendra and daughter Sanghamitra. Certainly this name was given her after initiation.

Bindusara supervised all state affairs but the real burden was borne by the able ministers, of whom Radhagupta was the chief. Susima, the eldest prince did not like to be under the control of Radhagupta and began to be independent and tyrannical. This offended Radhagupta who cleverly sent him to Taxila and brought Ashoka to Pataliputra. Shortly after, Bindusara fell ill. Susima being away in Taxila and Bindusara not willing to nominate Ashoka his heir, the ministers induced Bindusara not willing to nominate Ashoka his heir, the ministers induced Bindusara to appoint Ashoka his regent. But as soon as the emperor died, Ashoka was declared emperor. On hearing of Bindusara's death, Susima hastened to Pataliputra but on his way learned that he had been deprived of his father's throne. So, he rebelled and being aided by some of his brothers, invaded Pataliputra. But Ashoka, with the help of his able ministers, defeated them and made them prisoners. Then, to guard against future evils, Ashoka commanded the ministers to put them to death, but they refused. Thereupon he himself cut off their heads. However, the allegation that Ashoka put most of his brothers and sisters to death is baseless.

Ashoka

Thus secure, be began to rule with an iron hand (264 or 263 BC). He was at first a staunch Hindu saiva and used to feed 60,000 Brahmans every day with meat, drink and other palatables. The compaints of the people against Buddhistic conversion and the probable insinuations of the Brahmans led Ashoka to be a bitter persecutor of the Buddhists: he had the Bodhi tree cut down, an image of Buddha broken and the executioner Chanda employed to kill every Buddhist monk he would meet with. Owing to its abstract character, Buddhism was a failure in India. In three centuries, there were only a few thousand adherents, mostly monks. Now, the persecution of Ashoka seemed to threaten its very existence. But erelong the table was turned and Ashoka became a strenuous advocate of Buddhism. In 261 BC, Ashoka conquered Kalinga, a very powerful ancient kingdom lying on the Bay of Bengal between the Mahanadi and the Godavari.

(i) His empire

Ashoka's empire extended in the north-west to the Hindukush; in the east to the Persian frontier and the Mukran coast. Northwards, his dominions reached the foot of the Himalayas and appear to have comprised the districts around Srinagar (built by him) and the territory round Lalita Patan in Nepal, two and a half miles south-east of Kathmandu (also built by him). The whole of Bengal acknowledged his sway. Only the upper Assam and the Tamil kingdoms of Chera, Chola, Pandya, Satiya were independent. The Andhra kingdom between the Godavari and Krishna was a protected state. The hill tribes of the empire were probably semi-independent.

(ii) His administration

Pataliputra was the metropolis and the seat of the central government. The vast empire was divided into five parts: (1) Magadha and the adjoining tracts were ruled under the direct supervision of the emperor. (2) The north-west provinces comprising the Punjab, Kashmir, Gandhara, Afghanistan, Baluchistan and Sind, and the capital Taxila—the famous seat of Hindu learning—were ruled by a viceroy. (3) The western provinces of Rajputana, Malwa, Gujarat, and Kathiawar were ruled by the nephew (sister's son) of Ashoka from the capital Ujjain, a sacred seat of Hindu learning, religion and astronomy. (4) The eastern provinces with Kalinga were ruled by a viceroy from the capital Toshali in Orissa. (5) The Deccan was ruled by a viceroy from the capital Vidisa, now Bhilsa. The administration was probably, on the whole, a highly efficient none.

(iii) His family

Ashoka, a polygamist, had four queens, Padmavati, Asandhimitra, Pavishyaraksha, and Tishyaraksha. The mother of Mahendra was rather a concubine, daughter of a Vaisya jeweller of Ujjain. On the death of Asandhimitra, Ashoka, in his old age married a young dissolute woman, Tishyaraksha by name. She tried to induce Kunala, son of queen Padmavati, to approach her. But pious Kunala declined. This enraged her much. Ashoka once fell seriously ill. It is said that by Tishyaraksha's careful nursing the emperor came round. He promised her a boon. Now, as a reward, Ashoka allowed her to rule the empire for a week. Ashoka had sent Prince Kunala to put down a rebellion headed by Kunjarakarna of Taxila. Kunala suppressed the revolt but was blinded by Kunjarakarana at the command of Tishyaraksha. Kunala turned a bhikshu and with his wife Kanchanamala came to Pataliputra and passed the night in the elephant-stable. Ashoka discovered him in the morning, learnt of the machinations of Tishyaraksha and at the earnest request of Kunala, spared her life. Ashoka was generally kind and affectionate towards all. He made ample provisions for his surviving brothers and sisters.

(iv) His conversion and work of Buddhism

The bloodshed and the miseries of the Kalinga War moved Ashoka. He preferred the peaceful life of a Buddhist monk. In the tenth year of his reign i.e. in 253 BC, he was initiated by saint Upagupta, formerly of Mathura. His brother, wives, ministers, and the Brahmans tried their utmost to change his mind, but in vain. With Upagupta, he was out on a pilgrimage and visited Kapilavastu, Lumbini park (now Rumindei), Sarnath (Benaras), Bodh Gaya, Nepal, Kashmir, and other sacred placed. He honoured the previous Buddhas, distributed the relics of Buddha by building holy stupas everywhere. He erected 84,000 Buddhist chapels, mostly in Magadha, which gave it the new name of Vihara (country of monasteries). For the upkeep and propagation of Buddhism, Ashokavardhana now made it his official religion, created a special department of religion, appointed Buddhist officials, held councils and meetings, gave alms, maintained a large number of learned monks, set up edicts, tables, sent missionaries all over the empire and abroad, employed censors to look after the morale of the people. He was now called Dharmasoka (pious) and 'beloved of gods'. He was perfectly tolerant, and equally honoured the Brahman and the Buddhist *Sramanas*. In the 17th or 18th year of his reign, i.e. in 246 to 245 BC, the third great buddhistic council of 1,000 monks met for nine months at Pataliputra with Tishya as the president. Its object was the supression of heretics and false monks and the settlement of much disagreement about the sacred books. The rules of the order and the doctrines of the faith were solemnly revised and settled. The result was inscribed in an edict found at Bhabra. At the end of the council the following missionaries were sent:

(1) Madhyantika went to Kashmir and Gandhar.
(2) Madhadeva went to Mahisa Desa, i.e. countries south of the Godavari, including Mysore.
(3) Rakshita to Banavasi Desa (a part of Rajputana).
(4) Dharmarakshita went to Aparanta Desa (countries west of the Punjab).
(5) Mahadharamarakshita went to Maharashtra (not Bombay Presidency, but Burma and the Malaya Peninsula), Madhyima to the Himalayas.
(6) Maharakshita Bhadanta to Yonaloka, i.e. the Greek countries of Egypt, Asia Minior, Syria, Greece, and Macedon.
(7) Sena and Uttara to Suvarna Bhumi, i.e. Golden Chersonese up to Singapore.
(8) Mahendra and Sanghamitra to Ceylon.

(v) The results of the mission:

They were indeed very great.

(a) It turned the sectarian Buddhism into a world-religion. (b) It made Ashoka the emperor of a religious empire never known before. (c) It made Ashoka a great benefactor of mankind. (d) It brought about a closer touch of the Indians with the Greeks and other peoples. (e) Through it, Indian lore again found its way abroad. (f) Bhadanta introduced Greek sciences, arts, architecture, astronomy into India. (g) It paved the way for the future rise and success of Christianity. He spent crores of rupees in maintaining monasteries, monks and preachers and himself turned a monk before his death. It should be noted here that these efforts did not extinguish, drive away or eclipse Hinduism, even from Magadha. Hindus also were stirred and preached the Pauranic Hinduism in north India and the Deccan. Buddhistic converts were mostly from the low-case Hindus and from the non-Aryans.

(vi) His Works for the People

His principles of government and ethical system, meant for the progress of the people, were engraved on rocks, pillars and caves throughout the empire. They speak of perfect toleration and persuasion as the best means of converting others, and bringing about purity of life. He excavated tanks and wells, planted trees on the wayside, built rest-houses, fixed milestones on the roads, set up schools, established hospitals, for men and women; took measures for the civilisation of the aborigines and strictly prohibited the slaughter of animals. To serve as a model, he himself refrained from all cruel sports, abolished the royal hunt and forbade torture of prisoners. He aimed at being a true father to the people. He would hear their complaints at any time. He strictly enjoined all officials to work earnestly for the good of the people. He appointed censors to look after the ethical conduct of the people. He held periodical assemblies to settle disputes or other intricate points of law and custom and thereby encouraged arts and letters.

(vii) Foreign Relations

His relations with the five Greek powers of the West continued friendly as ever.

(viii) His Edicts

Of the 84,000 chapels, few exists. Of the edicts, fourteen are as yet discovered. 'Those edicts are engraven in different Prakrit dialects on pillars or rocks, whose wide distance from one another shows the great extent of Ashoka's empire. The pillars are at Delhi and Allahabad, the rocks at Kapur-da-giri near Peshawar; at Girnar in Gujarat and Dhauli in Orissa and at Bhabra on the road running south-west from Delhi to Jaipur' (Dr Rhys David, *Buddhism, pp. 222–23)*. They are of three kinds, religious, administrative and personal.

(ix) Architecture

With Ashoka, the architectural history of India begins. Some of his pillars still stand. The Sakasar pillar near Mirzapur, District Dacca, seems to be of Ashokan origin. His monuments at Bharhut, Sanchi, and Bodh Gaya were contemporary or a little later. Nothing remains of his magnificent palaces; but Fa Hien in AD 414 says, from the ruins of his buildings and a tower, that his palace was too admirable to have been the work of any mortal. The ancient Pataliputra lies buried under eighteen feet of the present East India Railway, Bankipur and Patna. Some remains of ancient Patna have been recently dug out by Dr Spooner.

(x) The Partition

After a long and prosperous reign, Ashoka passed into religious retirement in 227 BC and lived as a Buddhist monk on Songir (Sanskrit, Suvarnagiri), to practise religion. His vast empire was partitioned among his sons. Kunala got the Punjab, Afghanistan under the name of Dharma-Vardhana. Prince Jalauka got Kashmir. Prince Suyasas got the home provinces and ruled as emperor at Pataliputra. Other princes got the remaining dominions. Ashoka's waste of the imperial funds for church forced the ministers to remove him from power and place the eldest prince Suyasas on the throne. Prince Tibara by the queen Charuvaki, a favourite child of the old emperor, had predeceased Ashoka. The new emperor Suyasas also died soon. His son Dasaratha succeeded to the throne of Pataliputra. He is known from brief dedicatory inscriptions on the walls of cave-dwellings at the Nagarjuni Hills bestowed on the Ajivakas. The script, style and language of Dasaratha's records show that his date was not far from that of Ashoka. Two Puranas assign to him a short reign of eight years only. Jalauka is reputed to have been an active and vigorous king of Kashmir, who expelled certain foreigners and conquered the plains as far as Kanouj. He was hostile to Buddhism and as a devout Saiva, erected many temples placed at which can be identified.

Kunala, as the eldest prince and son to the chief queen Padmavati, was heir to the throne; but for his blindness, he was set aside. His son Samprati, not verified by any epigraphic record, got the western provinces and ruled at Ujjain. The Jains of western India praised him as an eminent partron of Jainism, who founded many monasteries even in non-Aryan countries. He was called the Jain Ashoka. His successors were Vrihaspati Vrishasena Pushyadharman—Pushyamitra (?)—*(Bombay Gazette, vol I, part I, p. 15, 1896).*

The connection of Ashoka with the ancient Khotan kingdom appears to have been close. It is said that Ashoka had banished some nobles of Taxila to the north of the Himalayas as a punishment for their complicity in the wrongful blinding of Kunala. One of the nobles was elected king who reigned till he was defeated by a Chinese rival.

Another tale states that the earliest ancestor of the Khotan royal family was Kunala, son of Ashoka. Probably, Ashoka's political jurisdiction extended into the basin of the Tarim.

(xi) Downfall of the Mauryas

Seven weak kings ruled after Ashoka, but the vast empire dwindled into a small state. Soon after the death of Ashoka, Kalinga and Andhra became free. Akbar built the Mogul Empire but Aurangzeb ruined it. Chandragupta built the Mauryan Empire but Ashoka sowed the seeds of its speedy fall. The causes were:

(a) Extreme religious fervour. In an empire of different castes, creeds and colours, Ashoka was not right in being a religious zealot nor was he right in spending vast sums of his people's money for one particular religion.

(b) Weakness of his successors.

(c) Revolts from within:

  (i) After the death of Ashoka, the pent-up Hindu discontent began to burst forth. Ashoka had dethroned the Brahmans from the supreme place in religion and politics, had obstructed their sacrifice that essentially needed the slaughter of animals, and had filled all high offices by Buddhists. The Hindus at last revolted, led by Pushya or Pushpa Mitra, a heroic Brahman young of Rohilkhand. Vrihadratha, the last Mauryan ruler of Pataliputra, recognised the Hindu claim and appointed Pushyamitra as the commander of the Imperial troops.

  (ii) The Andhras, probably an Aryan people formerly living in the delta between the Godavari and Krishna, now after Ashoka's death became free and spread their power to the sources of the Godavari and soon stretched right across the peninsula from the Bay of Bengal to the Arabian Sea.

(d) Invasion from without: Bactria (Sanskrit Balhika Desa), north of the Hindukush mountain, was a kingdom of Seleucus and his successors. About 250 BC, the Greeks there became free. In 206 BC, Antiochus, the Greek ruler of Syria crossed the Hindukush, reached Kabul, forced its Hindu king Subhagasena to pay him tribute and then returned home through Kandahar. The Greeks next wrested Afghanistan from the Mauryas. About 190 BC, the powerful Greek king Demetrios conquered Kapisa, Gandhar, the Punjab, Sindh, and some other tracts. Next, Eucratides and other Greeks founded several small kingdoms in India. Menander was the next great Greek conqueror. He annexed the Indus delta, Gujarat, parts of Rajputana and Oudh. About 180 or 179 BC he was marching upon Pataliputra, but general Pushyamitra advanced, checked his progress, and signally defeated him. Thus, the Greeks had conquered north-west India, western half of north India, western India, and the central province. The Puranas mention eight great Greek rulers of India. Some of them embraced Hinduism and were Vaishnavas. Their empire was however overturned by the Sakas. The Greeks became gradually absorbed in the Hindu population. The last Mauryan ruler of Pataliputra was murdered by Pushyamitra who usurped the throne and founded the Sunga dynasty (179 to 178 BC). The Mauryan dynasty continued to rule in Magadha till the seventh century AD. Minor Mauryan dynasties, connected with the main house, continued to rule in Konkan, Chitor and other parts of western India till the eighth century AD.

2

THE RATIONALISTIC AGE: *1300 TO 200 BC*

GENERAL FEATURES

The practical spirit of the age exhibited itself, in the Sutra literature, not claimed as revealed, but admitted to be human composition. Now all learning, science and religious teachings were reduced to concise practical manuals, to enable teachers and learners to teach and learn all things and duties easily, well, and for ever. Philosophy became practical and popular. Hindus expanded over the whole of India and Ceylon. India received a new light from the Persians and the Greeks.

In the seventh century BC began a very great change: the old order changed, yielding place to new. Magadha rose with its highly practical civilisation composed of Aryan and Dravidian cults and culture. Sanskrit yielded to Prakrit. The sixth century BC witnessed a revolution in religion.

EXTENT OF THE HINDU WORLD

Aryan conquests went on with full vigour till, by 200 BC, we find India mostly reclaimed, civilised and Hinduised. Early in this age, India falls into three circles regarded with different degrees of esteem.

The first circle contained Aryavarta—the north Indian midland, marked for spiritual pre-eminence and still regarded as the 'meet nurse' of the Indo-Aryans. The rule of conduct, which prevailed there, was authoritarian.

The second circle—home of the people of mixed origin—included south Punjab, Sindh, Gujarat, Malwa, south and east Bihar. The Punjab—the earliest home of the Indo-Aryans—was now backward in culture and religion of the Gangetic Hindus.

By 1200 BC, these countries had already become recognised as Hindu kingdoms, and Hindu civilisation and influence had gone beyond these lands to other less advanced countries.

The third circle included the land of the Arattas (Attock) in the Punjab, some countries of southern India, east and north Bengal and Kalinga—the eastern sea-board from Orissa to river Krishna. A person going to those countries had to atone for the sin committed, by a sacrifice (*Baudhayana, I.I.2.)*.

This was the extent of the Hindu world before 1200 BC. In the fifth century BC, Ceylon was conquered and colonised by an exiled prince of Bengal, who founded the Sinha dynasty at Anuradhapur, from which the island received the name of Sinhala. In the same century, a large number of Aryans had colonised southern India.

Baudhayana, probably a southerner and of thirteenth century BC, writes that portions of south India had not only been colonised but had also become the seat of powerful Hindu kingdoms and of distinct schools of laws and learning. Baudhayana had a high regard for Aryavarta, yet he takes care to mention the particular laws and customs of south India.

LITERATURE

Sacred. Of the numberous *Brahmana* and *Sutra* works only a small number have come down to us.

The *Charana Vyauha* speaks of five charanas of the *Rig Veda*, twenty-seven of the *Black Yajur Veda*, fifteen, of the *White Yajur Veda*, twelve of the *Sama Veda and* nine of the *Atharva Veda*.

The *Vedangas* or six different branches of subsidiary studies relating to the Vedas, gradually assumed the Sutra form. They are indicated below:

1. *Siksha* (phonetics) is the science of pronunciation. The works on the subject of the epic age were replaced by more scientific works of

the Sutra period, called *Prati-Sakhyas,* i.e. collections of phonetic rules applicable to each recension of each Veda.

Most of the *Prati-Sakhyas* are lost. We have only one for each Veda except the *Sama Veda.*

Saunaka is given the authorship of a *Prati-Sakhya* of the Sakala branch of the *Rig Veda*, which is doubted with reasoin by Dr Gold stucker. Katyayana (not the critic of Panini) is said to have composed the *Pratri Sakhya* of the *Madhyandina* recension of the *White Yajur Veda.* A *Prati-Sakhya* of the *Black Yajur Veda* and one of the *Atharva Veda*, still exist, but the names of their authors are not known.

2. The *Kalpa Sutra* is the collective name given to three classes of writings, the *Srauta Sutra,* the Dharma *Sutra* and the *Grihya Sutra.*

The *Srauta Sutras* give details of ceremonials relating to Vedic sacrifices, condensed into short treatises. The *Rig Veda* has two such books called *Asvalayana* and *Sankhayana.* The *Sama Veda* has three called *Masaka, Latyayana* and *Drahyayana.* The *Black Yajur Veda* has four, called *Baudhayana, Bharadvaja, Apastamba* and *Hiranya Kesin.* The *White Yajur Veda* has one called *Katyayana.* All these works are left entire.

The *Asvalayana Sutra* is divided into twelve chapters. Asvalayana was a pupil of the illustrious Saunaka (1300). The teacher and the pupil are said to have jointly written the last two books of the Aitareya Aranyaka. Dr H. Oldenberg thinks that the short and metrical fourth book of the work probably belongs to an ancient age, while the fifth or the last book, in genuine Sutra style was the work of Saunaka and Asvalayana.

This reveals the curious fact that the earliest Sutra works are connected with the last *Brahmana* works of the epic age.

After Parasara and Vyasa, Saunaka is another colossal figure in the field of ancient Hindu letters. He flourished around 1300 BC. He was priest to Janamejaya Parikshita in his famous horse sacrifice. Many of his pupils were distinguished scholars.

The *Sankhyayana Sutra* is divided into eighteen chapters. Professor Weber supposes that this Sutra belongs to western India, as the *Asvalayana* does to the eastern.

The *Masaka Sutra* is only a tabular enumeration of prayers relating to different ceremonies; the *Satyayana* gives the views of various teachers. These two are connected with the *Tandya* or *Panchavinsa Brahmana* of the *Sama* Veda. The *Drahyayana* and *Satyayana* are almost alike.

The Sutras of the *Black Yajur Veda* have been chronologically arranged as those of *Baudhayana* (perhaps thirteenth century BC), Bharadvaja (perhaps twelfth century BC), Apastamba (probably nineth century BC) and Hiranyakesin (perhaps eighth century BC). Dr Buhler has recovered the lost *Bharadvaja Sutra.*

Katyayana, son of Gobhila and a pupil of Saunaka wrote a *Srauta Sutra* of the *White Yajur Veda* in twenty-six chapters. He strictly followed *the Satapatha Brahmana* and the first eighteen chapters of the work correspond with the first nine books of the *Brahmana.* Both Latyayana and Katyayana allude to *Brahmabandhus* of Magadha, supposed by some to be the first Buddhists but really inferior Brahmans (according to annotator Karka) who had entered Magadha early and were denounced by the Brahmans of midland.

3. The *Dharma Sutra* present to use the manners, customs and the laws of the times. They aimed at making the Hindus good citizens, while the *Srauta Sutras* show us the Hindus as worshippers.

The ancient Dharma Sastras were condensed into concise Dharma Sutras of this age and transformed into the materical law-books of the *Pauranic* age. The original *Sastras* were in prose, somethimes in prose and verse and the later codes are in continuous verse. The *Dharma Sutras* implanted in the minds of all, especially young learners, their religious, social and legal duties.

Most of the *Dharma Sutras* are lost and not yet recovered. Manu's early Dharma Sastra was condensed into a Dharma Sutra with suitable additions and alternations called the *Old Manu* which is discernible even in the present code. Manu's Dharma Sutra is lost and not yet recovered. As references to Manu are frequent in the Sutra literature, it is doubless that the he held in high honour. Of the existing *Dharma Sutra*, Vasista belongs to the *Rig Veda*, Gautama to the *Sam Veda*, Baudhayana and Apastamba belong to the *Black Yajur Veda*. These works have been translated by Dr Buhler.

Gautam, author of *Hindu Logic*, florished in the fifteenth century. It is said that Vyasa had pointed out to him several mistakes of his logic.

Enraged at this, Gautama took a vow to see Vyasa's face again. With soft and humble words, Vyasa, however, propitiated the old logician who then pleased, looked at him with downcast eyes. This earned him the new name of *Akshapada*, from *akshi*, eyes and *pada*, foot. This Gautama wrote a Dharma Sastra, afterwards condensed and codified into the *Gautama Dharma Sutra*.

Vasistaa also wrote a Dharma Sastra, changed into a Dharma *Sutra* later on. Baudhayana indeed flourished in the early part of the Sutra period. He had transferred a whole chapter of Gautama's into his Sutra. The same chapter is found quoted in Vasista's Sutra also.

One Apastamba, the writer of a Dharma Sastra belonged to the epic age. The Sutrakara Apastamba probably flourished in the nineth century BC.

Dr Buhler, translating the *Dharma Sutra* of Apastamba states that Apastama was probably born or naturalised in the powerful Andhra kingdom of south India, with its capital near Amarabati, on the lower Krishna and founded his Sutra school there. His date is supposed to be the fourth century BC; Mr R.C. Dutt gives it as fifth century BC. Apastamba speaks of the six Vedangas, the prior mimansa and the vedanta philosophy, from which and other reasons we conclude that Apastamba lived in the nineth century BC or thereabout.

The *Grihya Sutras* give the rules necessary to fix the details of domestic rites and social ceremonies performed at marriage, at childbirth, at the child's first feeding, at his assuming studentship. We still practise those rites and ceremonies almost unaltered in names and styles.

The *Asvalayana* and *Sankhyana Grihya Sutras* belong to the *Rig Veda*. The *Paraskara Grihya Sutra* belongs to the *White Yajur Veda* along with the *Khadira* which is an abstract of *Gobila Grihya Sutra* of the *Sama Veda* translated by Dr H Oldenberg. Gobhila's work is edited by Pandit Satyavrata Samasrámin with excellent notes.

In most cases we have only fragments of the *Sutra* literature left. The entire *Kalpa Sutra* of Apastàmba, still extant, has thirty sections. The first twenty-four of these deal with Vedic sacrifices, the twenty-fifth gives the rules of interpretation, the twenty-sixth and twenty-seventh treat of the domestic rites, the twenty-eighth and twenty-nineth contain the *Dharma Sutras* (civic laws) and the thirtieth section—the *Sulva Sutra*, 'rules of cord' has the goemetrical principles applied to the construction of varying altars of the Vedic sacrifices. Dr Thibaut first published these to the western world. Dr Von Schrader had concluded long ago that Pythagoras learnt his mathematics also from India.

4. Vyakarana (grammar): The great fame a Panini eclipsed that of all other grammarians of the age. His *Ashtadhyayi*, i.e. a grammar in eight lectures, said to be the 'shortest and the fullest grammar in the world', was in fact an abridgement of the *Mahesa Grammar* and was meant to serve both secular (Bhasha) and sacred (Chhanda) literature. He was born at the village Salatura in the ancient kingdom of Gandhara, North-West Frontier Province of pre-partition India. He was the last of the Vedic grammarians. His father was Devala and mother Dakshi. It is said that while at school, he was very dull and so was turned out. Being highly aggrieved, he did not return home. But went to a part of the Lower Himalayas where he worshipped Siva for sometime with great devotion and acquired great brain-power. Afterwards, he not only compiled his grammar, but also wrote a poem, a work on *Siksha*, i.e. phonetics and a work on Gana in which he derived the entire language from a few roots. Being a man of the extreme north-west, he knew little of the Brahmanas, Aranyakas and the Upanishadas, composed mostly in the Gangetic Valley. Yuan Chwang found Panini's image worshipped and his grammar school thriving in the north-west.

A curious 'battle of books' was waged by scholars about the date of Panini whom Dr Goldstrucker and most of the scholars have placed before Buddha. Professor Max Muüeller and Dr Hoernle place him in the fourth century BC, relying on a statement in the *Katha-Sarit-Sagara* (*Book* IV, 20–21–22), which has the following: —'Panini, his critic Katyayana and other boys read in the school of preceptor Varsha at Pataliputra. Finding Panini dull, the preceptor's wife turned him out of the house; thus expelled, Panini, wounded, went back not to his house but to the Himalayas where he obtained great power through the grace of Siva and then composed many works' (vide also *Agni Purana*, chapter on phonetics).

We think that Panini flourished about 800 BC; his hostile critic Katyayana lived in the fifth or fourth century BC and his defender Patanjali lived in the second century BC.

We advance the following grounds in favour of our proposed date:

(i) Sanskrit was a spoken ground in favour of our proposed date.
(ii) As the last of the Vedic grammarians, he stood in a transition period when Chhandas (Vedas) and Bhasha (secular Sanskrit) were both current.
(iii) Some grammatical compounds, such as Dvigu and Bahuvrihi reveal the poastoral condition of society.
(iv) In Panini's time, Chhanda (Vedic Sanskrit) was in its last stage and Bhasha ceased to be spoken in its purity; some words were corrupted and new words used. The obsolete Chhanda, living Bhasha (literary and polished tongue) and Apabhransa, i.e. rude and uncultivated cant of Patanjali's time, show that Panini lived about the middle of the Sutra period.
(v) His general ignorance of the Gangetic Valley and its sacred literature.
(vi) His distinction between a native place and a place of residence in IV. 3.89 and 90, shows that a spirit of adventurous emigration and colonisation strongly prevailed.
(vii) The valley of the Indus was the scene of great activities in Panini's time, though some explorers had penetrated into the valley of the Sone in the east (IV. 1. 43).

The power and suzerainty of one Kshtriya prince is recognised (V. 1. 41). He speaks of Valhika and its many towns (IV. 2.117); of Sankala and Kapisi (IV.2.75 and 99); of the Punjab, Sindh, Paraskara (Thala Parkrara), and Kachchha (Kutch, an island) IV. 3.133 and IV. 3.10; of the Kurus and Madras of the Punjab; of the Bharatas of the east (IV. 2. 130–31 and II. 4.66); of colonies in Kamboja, Sauvira, Magadha, and Kosala (IV. I. 175; IV. I. 148–170–171); of Ushinara beyond Kampila (Kabul) home of excellent blankets. Kabul is called Kampila in the *Vajasaneyi Samhita,* XXIII. 18.

Foreign opinions on grammar and phonetics:

'It was in philosophy as well as in grammar that the speculative Hindu mind attained the highest pitch of its marvellous fertility.' (Professor Weber).

Professor Wilson, speaking of the *Yajurvedic Pratisakhyas* says, 'No nation but the Hindus, has been yet able to discover such a perfect system of phonetics'.

Mr Thompson, Principal, Agra College says, 'The creation of the consonants in Sanskrit is a unique example of human genius'.

Professor Macdonell holds, 'We (Europeans) are still far behind in making even our alphabet a perfect one.'

Professor Max Müeller says—'That an entire language is based on a few roots is a truth not known to Europe before the sixteenth century AD. In India, the Brahmans knew it long, long ago.'

5. *Nirukta:* The names of many writers on *Nirukta* (Vedic glossary) are found in Yaska (prior to Panini, according to Dr Goldstrucker and others) who, however made his work a philological one by adding useful notes, comments and explanations.
6. *Chhandas* (metre). The Vedas, the *Aranyakas*, and the Upanishadas have even whole chapters devoted to metre. But the first scientific treatment of the subject is met with in the Sutra literature. Some chapters are devoted to the metre of the *Rig Veda* at the end of the *Pratisakhya.* The *Nidana Sutra* in ten *propathakas* discusses the metre of the *Sama Veda.*
7. Jyotisha or astronomy also received a practical treatment in the period to convey a knowledge of the heavenly bodies necessary for fixing the time for sacrifices and to establish a sacred calendar. Astrology was coming into use.

Astronomy was used for religious purposes; medical discoveries, for learning men's fortune, and the vagaries of weather and the crops.

In a work of Baudhayana, we first come across mention of the solar zodiac. Colebrooke thinks that the Hindus took hints of this from the Greeks. We have discussed this in a previous chapter.

Another class of works called the *Anukramani* (index to the Vedas) belongs to this age. Saunaka wrote several *Anukramanis* of the *Rig Veda*, of which one is still extant. His *Vrihad devata* is a voluminous *Anukramani.* His pupil Katyayana's fuller works replaced the preceptor's. Katyayana's *Anukramani* of the *Rig Veda* gives the first words of each hymn, the number of verses, the name of the poet, the metre and the god.

The Jain sacred literature is yet little known. The Buddhist *Three Pitakas,* i.e. books on morals and rules of conduct were complied about 375 BC. Early Buddhism had no books on metaphysics.

SECULAR LITERATURE

The Sanskrit epics and the Puranas were explained to women, sudras and the Dvija-bandhus, i.e. the fallen Brahmans. So, these works grew up till they attained their present shape, probably in the fifth century BC.

Drama of great antiquity, was especially cultured in this period. Instructive episodes from the Puranas and the Sanskrit epics were enacted before the public on festive occasions. Two disciples of Buddha once performed a play before their preceptor. Panini has preserved the names of two early writers on poetics, Silali and Krisaswa. Many acts of Buddha's life were performed.

Chanakya's *Art of Government*, II. 27 mentions stage, actors, actresses. There is proof of dramatic performance in the Sita Vengra and Jogimara Cave Inscriptions in central India. The *mahabhashya* of Patanjali (150 to 140 BC) mentions the two plays, *Balibandha and Kansa-vadha.*

The hostile critic of Panini—I mean Katyayana—wrote his *Vartika* probably in the fifth or fourth century BC. This Katyayana Vararuchi, a Brahman and son of Somadatta, a native of Kausambi, became a minister of Nanda Raja and wrote a Pali grammar. Towards the close of the fourth century BC, Chanakya wrote his *Artha Sastra* (art of government) in three books and a *Niti Sastra* (a book of worldly wisdom). The books show high learning, vast experience, useful information, and sound business-like ideas. His statements are confirmed by Megasthenses. His brother Vatsyayana wrote, before 300 BC, his *Kama Sastra, a* Treatise on Fine Arts.

Hindu Poetics of Bharata was finally compiled before 200 BC Professor Cowell says that it proves the previous existence of many plays. Some of the *Jatakas,* i.e. birth stories of Buddha, were probably composed in the third century BC. The Gatha portion of the *Lalita Vistara*, a poem on Buddha was written before 200 BC.

TALES AND FABLES

A good deal of our secular literature of this age is lost, having been replaced by later works. Tales and fables did certainly exist in the period, that found their way abroad, along with religion and philosophy. The *Tales of Aesop* (sixth century BC) were compilied from them.

Elphinstone remarks, 'In both of these compositions, Hindus appear to have been the instructors of all the rest of manking'. The most ancient tales of Bidpai, i.e. Bidyapati, have been found almost unchanged in their Sanskrit form and to them almost all the fabulous tales of other countries have been clearly traced.

'The complicated scheme of story-telling, a table within tale, is also of their own invention. Hindu tales show no taste for description (like Arabian and Persian), but simplicity, spirit and interest' *(History of India,* 9th *edition, p.* 172).

LANGUAGE

We have said in a previous section that Sanskrit was made by the Deva Aryans (twenty-ninth century). Hence it is often called Deva Bhasha, i.e. tongue of the devas. This Sanskrit also admits of three stages, the old, middle and modern.

The original Aryan tongue, loose, and irregular, was called *Brahma Bhasha* or *Balhika Bhasha* (the older form of classical Sanskrit, according to Dr Macdonell) from which sonorous Sanskrit was evolved by the devas, had been brought to India by the rishis, who composed the entire revealed literature in that ancient tongue, as a departure from that was deemed heretical. That *Brahma Bhasha* also had passed through several stages. Till 1400 BC *Brahma Bhasha* was used in sacred texts and in all profane Sanskrit literature. Besides, there is evidence to show that there had been several Prakrits before 1400 BC. The *Ramayana* states that Rama had good knowledge of many plays containing Prakrit elements. Yudhisthira had built his new town of Indraprastha near modern Delhi and filled it with Brahmans, merchants versed in Sanskrit, Prakrit and other dialects.

Most of the hymns and prayers of the Vedas, are composed in rustic and irregular dialect; but the language, metre and style of a particular hymn in one of the Vedas furnish internal evidence that their composition in the present arrangement took place after Sanskrit had advanced from its ruggedness to the polished and sonorous language in which the mythological poems, sacred and profane, have been written (Colebrooke).

'From the Vedas to Manu, from Manu to the Puranas, the change is the same as from the fragments of Numa to the twleve lables and from those to the works of Ciero'—Sir William Jones.

The historians of Alexander used Indian names easily resolvable into Sanskrit. They do not allude to a sacred tongue distinct from that of the people. So, it seems that Sanskrit was spoken in the fourth century BC. But in the earliest Sanskrit dramas, women and uneducated people speak in Pali or Prakrit, while Sanskrit is reserved for the higher characters.

Professor Max Müeller says, 'It is from the Prakrit and not from the literary Sanskrit that the modern vernaculars of India branches off in course of time'. *(Science of Language, 2nd series, Section I).*

But Katyayana in his Pali grammar advances a contrary theory: 'Pali is the origin of all the Indian languages; Sanskrit and other dialects are derived from it.'

The Sinhalese call Pali Magadhi; being used in palli (village), it was called Pali, i.e. vulgar tongue, a loose and corrupt form of Sanskrit.

Palasa was a name of ancient Magadha. So, Palasi (=Palayi=Pali) was the tongue of Magadha. Buddhists hold that Magadhi is the original tongue. It is current all over. Formerly it was a spoken language. In the time of Buddha, it became written and assumed a literary dignity.

Prinsep, Muir, Wilson, Burnouf, Lassen and other scholars say, 'Pali is the eldest daughter of Sanskrit. From Pali, the other vernaculars of India are derived. The language of Ashoka used in the edicts, proves this. From the Himalaya to the Vindhyas, from the Indus to the Ganges, Ashoka used a language intelligible to all, with the slightest variations'.

Cunningham divides that tongue into three groups, viz., Punjabi (west Indian), Ujjaini (central Indian) and Magadhi (east Indian). But doubtless, these three are one and the same; only for pronunciation, *r* is changed into *l*.

Prinsep calls the Ashokan language a cross between Sanskrit and Pali. Wilson calls it distinctly Pali. Lassen agrees with Wilson, but adds, 'Pali is the eldest daughter of Sanskrit.' When Sanskrit ceased to be a spoken tongue, Pali first came to be used in north India. Muir also endorses that statement. The Buddhist works of the third century BC, collected from Ceylon, show the same Pali as was used by Ashoka in his declarations. In the Rationalistic Age, the Buddhist literature and Pali flourished side by side with the Sanskrit Sutra literature. Pali followed Sanskrit and not the Prakrit.

ALPHABETS

Brahmi was the earliest alphabet of the Deva-Aryans. It came to India and in time gave rise to three, viz., Sarada, Sriharsha and Kutila. The *Sama-vaya Sutra* of the Jains mentions eighteen alphabets. The *Nandi Sutra* of the Jains speaks of thirty-six and the *Lalita Vistara,* a magnified life of Buddha gives sixty-four different alphabets, as follows: Brahmi, Kharostri, Pushkara-sari, Anga, Banga, Magadhi, Mangalya, Manushya, Anguliya, Sakari, Brahmaballi, Dravir, Kinari, Dakshin, Ugra, Sankhya, Anuloma, Ardhadhanu, Darada, Khasya, China, Huna, Madhakshara, Vistara, Pushpa, Deva, Naga, Yaksha, Gandharva, Kinara, Mahoraga, Asura, Garura, Mrigachakra, Chakra, Vayumarut, Bhaumadeva, Antariksha, Uttarakuru, Aparagauradi, Purvavideha, Utkshepa, Nikshepa, Prakshepa, Sagara, Braja, Lekha-Pratilekha, Anudruta.

RELIGION—PHILOSPHY—LEARNING

Hinduism, Jainism, Buddhism, and Atheism were the chief religions of the Rationalistic Age.

Hinduism

Hinduism appears to have had then three forms—Vedic Hinduism, Philosophical Hinduism and Popular Hinduism.

The efforts of Krishna, Jaimini, Vyasa, and Yudhisthira had revived religion with its true spirit and elevated morals; but the impetus lasted a few centuries only. By 600 BC, the Vedic religion became a mere bundle of lifeless rites and tenets.

Thoughtful Hindus still paid a nominal regard to the Vedic religion but they were rather sick of the rites and sought pure wisdom. Thus, philosophical Hinduism was making rapid strides among the thoughtful people. The lightless masses followed Popular Hinduism which consisted of the minor Vedic rites, the worship of gods and goddesses such as Siva, Indra, Sun, Durga, Shashthi, Sarasvati, idol-worship, pilgrimage to sacred places introduced by Vyasa. The *Varnasrama* Dharma, i.e. the four castes with respective duties were well organised.

Prince Samba, a son of Krishna, being cured of his leprosy by worshipping the sun god, brought a colony of the Sakali Brahmans from beyond India to conduct the sun worship at Multan (Punjab). The sun temple became as holy as the temple of Jagannath (Lord of the World) at Puri (Orissa) in our own times. Yuan Chwang visited it in the seventh century AD as will appear from the following:

> At Mula Sambhura (probably Sanskrit Mulasthan Sambnapura), there are convents mostly in ruins and eight temples, one of which, that of the sun, is one of unusual splendour. The statue of the god is of pure gold and the temple from its first founding has never ceased to resound with continual music and it is always lighted up brilliantly at night.

As the country now enjoyed peace, the Brahmans became eager to Hinduise the anti-Aryan people of India and in this perhaps they succeeded a good deal. Vyasa's Puranas and the *Mahabharata*, written for women and sudras, were daily made popular amongst the masses. 'The Brahmans tried to gain power over the regulate with their precepts, the state and law and civil life in all its manifestations' *(Historian's History of the World)*.

Jainism

Neminatha, an uncle to Krishna and the twenty-second Tirthankara of the Jains, flourished sometime before 1400 BC. His reformed religion lasted some five centuries. Next came Parsvanatha (820 to 750 BC), the twenty-third Jain reformer, son of King Asvasena and Queen Bamadevi of Benaras and son-in-law of King Prasenajit of Oudh, who refused royalty, lived as an ascetic and attained pure wisdom at Benaras. Then he began to preach. His Jainism once prevailed from Bengal to Gujarat. The districts of Maldah and Bogra in north Bengal were great centres of his faith. His converts were mostly from the depressed classes. He died on the Sumheta or Paresnath hill in the Hazaribag district, at the age of 72 (–72 solar), 230 (= 223 solar years) before the death of Mahavira in 527 BC. In Rajputana, his adherents grew very powerful and oppressed the Hindus in many ways. There were, however, great and noble persons of the warrior caste who preached the religion of reason, good morals and universal love. The sixth century BC is marked by a great flourish of religion. Vardhamana Mahavira (597 to 527 BC) reformed Jainism. He was born of a royal family; his father was King Siddhartha of Pawana and mother Queen Trisala. He married Yasoda, princess of Samvira city, had a daughter called Priyadarsana, who married Jamalio, a disciple of his. He lost his parents at twenty-eight, lived for two years with his eldest brother Nandi-Vardhana, renounced the world at thirty, practised yoga for two years, then preached chiefly in the Gangetic Valley. He had even approached many wild people to preach but was scolded and persecuted. Next he went to Kausambi. Satanika was king there and much respected. Many adotped his doctrines. After twelve years' severe yoga, he became enlightened, had 11 chief Brahman converts and died at 72 = 70 (solar) at the capital of king Hastipala of Apapa-puri. His sect is called digambara (naked), now raktamvara, i.e. red-robed, as they wear a piece of red cloth. His main lessons are:

(i) The senses cannot be the seat of wisdom; (ii) The law of karma must be admitted; (iii) A being is a reality, not an illusion; (iv) The next world must be admitted; (v) Slaughter of animals is the greatest sin ; (vi) What cannot be cured must be endured; (vii) Wilful mortification of the body is improper; (viii) Truthfulness, sincerity and good conduct are essential. (ix) Stealing is the foulest deed. (x) Pure conjugal love. Due control of all earthly desires.

Buddhism

Buddha was the great Hindu reformer (564 to 487 BC). He came of the Sakya clan, a minor branch of the solar dynasty of Ayodhya. His father was Suddhodana, king of Kapilavastu in Nepalese Terai and his mother was Mayadevi, who died a week after his birth at Lumbini Park (*Sanskrit, Ramyabana*), now Rumin Dei. He was nursed by queen Gautami, his mother's sister and was therefore called Gautama. From his youth, he felt keenly for the suffering humanity. At nineteen, he married the fair Yasodhara. At twenty-nine, a son was born to him. Then disgusted with the world, he turned as ascetic, came down to a hill near Rajagriha and carefully studied the Hindu philosophy with two Brahmans there; he next went to a village near Gaya, sat under a tree for six years to realise all spiritual truths by personal thinking. Here, he discovered the true wisdom he sought and became Buddha, i.e. the Awakened.

He began to preach at Benaras. His reformed religion was: (i) Indirect belief in the immortality of the soul, law of karma (action) and transmigration of the soul; (ii) Rejection of all rites and rituals, of the caste system, of a popular idea of God; (iii) Culture of love, truth, charity, forgiveness, absolute purity in life, thought and speech; (iv) Regard for animal life in any form; (v) Following the Golden Mean between a gay life and an austere life. From these it is no paradox to say that Buddha himself was not a Buddhist. After some 2,400 years, i.e. from 2950 to 550 BC, he was the only Hindu who gave a correct exposition of our true religion. His tenets, his order of monks, his missionary spirit, his Nirvana were Hindu but not his. Only earnestness, vehemence and awakening was his—all new and all his own. Hindus have recognised him as an incarnation of their deity. At Sarnath (Benaras), his former five disciples were his first converts. In three months, the number rose to sixty. Afterwards, Kashyapa with his 500 disciples was converted. Bimbisara, though not initiated, shared his faith and made the gift of Venubana to the Buddhist Order. He next visited Kapilavastu and converted the royal family. His son Rahula, brother Ananda, brother-in-law Devadatta, Aniruddha were converted. He preached for forty-six years at Rajagriha, Kausambi, Sravasti, Vaisali, and Kusinagar. His friends; (i) Udayana, king of Kausambi and Ghoshira, a rich merchant; (ii) Bimbisara of Rajagriha, whose son Ajatasatru was at first a foe but afterwards a friend; (iii) King Prasenajit of Sravasti; the merchant Sudatta purchased Jetabana for Buddha; (iv) The Lichchavi king of Vaisali made him a gift of Mahavana. At the age of seventy-seven (solar), he died in the sal wood at Kusinagar. The Mallas of Kusinagar and his disciples cremated him decently. After that, his relics were distributed. His rebellious disciple and brother-in-law Devadatta founded the Ajivaka sect (a rigid Jain form). Fa-Hien saw his followers in the fifth century AD. Materialism also existed in those days. 'Buddism did not thrive in India owing to its abstractness and morbid views of life, as well as by the competition of Shaivism and Vishnuism. But in modified form, it has flourished in a greater part of Asia.' (*Historian's History of the World, vol. II*). Over one-third of the people of the world still profess Buddhism.

Dr Rhys David syas, 'Buddhism is the product of Hinduism. Gautam's whole training was Brahmanical. He probably deemed himself to be the most perfect exponent of the spirit as distinct from the letter of ancient faith.'

Is Buddha indebted for his lessons to the Brahmans or to the six previous Buddhas? Our answer is, certainly not. The *Rig Veda* VIII, 49,

2–3–4; the *Yajur Veda* XIX., 77; XXXVI, 188; I.5; the *Satapatha Brahmana* I., XIV. 4, and some verses of the *Atharva Veda* also contain the lessons of Buddha. Later on, Gautama and Vasistha give the same morals. Professor Oldenberg says in *J.A.S.B.* 1913, 'Buddha and the Old Buddhism are the true descendants of that Yajnavalkya whom the *Brihad Aranyaka* places before us.'

Yet, we must say that Buddha was in no way indebted to the former six Buddhas, if they had existed at all, nor to the Hindu moralists spoken above. Historically, Buddhism may be regarded as the happy combination of the inward tendency of the Upanishadic wisdom and the outward practicality of Magadha.

Buddha consciously set himself up not as the founder of a new religion, but as an ardent Hindu reformer. He believed to the last that he was proclaiming only the ancient and pure form of Hinduism corrupted at a later date. Hindu Saṅyasins—Bhikshus, *Sramanas*—in the last stage of life, followed the faith of renunciation and morality, knowing no castes, rites, attachment. Hindus aimed at the supreme bliss through different stages of life; while Buddha was eager to bring that bliss—Nirvana—within the reach of all at once. Hindus regarded the Old Buddhism as one of their sects.

Philosophy

The original works on Hindu philosophy are long lost, but they were given a Sutra form in the Rationalistic Age. So, they are still called *Sankhya Sutra*, *Yoga Sutra, Nyaya Sutra*, and *Brahma Sutra*. The abstract questions of matter and spirit and creation were dealt with, not as in the Upanishadas in guesses and vague speculations, but with marvellous acumen and relentless logic. Learned men still paid a nominal regard to the Vedic sacrifices, but it was only halfhearted. Hence, thoughtful men learned more towards wisdom than to ritual religion.

Learning

Learning, ever valued by the Indians, was in a sound and flourishing state. At Taxila, the then chief centre of learning , were taught the Vedas, the six Vedangas, philosophy, law, medicine, mathematics, military science, Puranas, history, magic, astronomy, prosody, philology. Provisions were made for a general diffusion of knowledge among all classes of people.

Subscriptions were raised by the rich to maintain orphanages. The two Sanskrit epics and the Puranas then composed in Pali (according to Mr Justice Pargiter), were explained to women and the lightless masses.

The culture of medical science was highly satisfactory. Jivaka, royal physician to Bimbisara, king of Magadha, had studied medicine with Professor Atreya at Taxila. At the close of his studies, he was required to study all the medicinal plants within fifteen miles of Taxila. The works of Susruta, Charaka (Greek, Xarch) and others were in general use. Susruta was well-versed in medicine, anatomy and surgery. He has given a detailed and accurate account of the number of nerves, bones, and sinews of each part of the body. W Harvey discovered the circulation of blood in the body in AD 1627 but Susruta had discovered it long ago. He says that 175 veins carry blood to the system. These veins rise from the liver and the spleen and spread to all parts of the body.

Surgery (Sanskrit, Salya) excelled in ancient India. The *Mahabharata, Effort Book*, tells us that both parties were busy collecting the ablest surgeons, surgical instruments, bandages, medicines against the coming war.

Susruta's eight-fold divisions of surgery leant from Divodasa, are Chhedana, cutting; Bhedana, piercing; Lekhya, stripping off the skin; Bedhya, drawing out impure blood; Eshya, probing; Ashrya, taking out stones from the body; Bisrava, bleeding by operation; Siwana, sewing. Susruta speaks of 127 different instruments and of fourteen different kinds of bandage. Various kinds of forceps, probes and speculum were used, (vide *Susruta, Sutra Part, Chapter VII* and *VIII*). The Buddhist missionaries called Sthavira-putra gave the Greek word therapeutics. English surgery and hospital probably originated from Sanskrit salya and swasthya-sala (a house for repairing health).

Hindu Learning Abroad: The Egyptians, Arabs, Assyrians, and the Jews took from India not only commodities and building material, but also Indian cult and culture. The Phoenicians gave a larger currency to them in the West.

Hindus and Egyptians: 'Of all ancient nations, the Egyptians are the ones whom the Hindus seem most to have resembled.' Elphinstone, p. 52.

The points of resemblance are set forth by Professor Heeren in his *Historical Research (Asiatic Nations)*, Volume III p. 411 to the end. Alexander and his generals noticed the caste system in Egypt (fourth century).

Hindus and Greeks: Elphinstone calls the early Hindus far superior to the Greeks (p. 52).

'Their internal institutions were less rude; their conduct towards their enemies more humane; their general learning was much more considerable, and in the knowledge of the being and nature of God, they (Hindus) were already in possession of a light which was but faintly perceived even by the loftiest intellects in the best days of Athens.' (p. 52–53).

'Hindu civilisation was original and peculiar. This early and independent civilisation was probably a misfortune to the Hindus. For they grew blind, learned to revere their own and were averse to novelties.' We cannot give our full assent to this remark. Progress depends on mutual interchange of ideas. Whenever the different parts of the world were brought together by commerce or politics, then each country gave and received light, life, cult, culture in any form. Hindu wisdom once influenced the Egyptian and the Assyrian empires. The Phoenicians took eastern culture to all lands. Indian wisdom and religion were carried over the world by the Persian Empire. The Greeks, the Romans, the Buddhists, the Hindus, the Arabs, and the English have taken and spread Indian religion and metaphysics at least in foreign lands. In return, India also had many useful lessons from aboard.

We are sure of an Indo-Hellenic intercourse, however weak and interrupted, long before Alexander. The Greeks first had the Indian wisdom from the Phoenicians. Homer, Thales, Anaximander give the first glimpses of India and the Indian thought. Von Schrader, Schlegel, Dr Enfield and others think that Pythagoras and others came out to India to learn. Dr Enfield and others think that Pythagoras and others came out to India to learn. Dr Macdonell belives in the historic possibility of the Greeks having been influenced by Indian thought through Persia (*History of Sanskrit Literature, p.* 422). Pythagoras had his doctrine of metempsychosis, asceticism, vegetarian principles, and mathematics, from India direct or from Indian philosophers in Persia (Macdonell). The large part played by numbers in his metaphysical system is a noticeable point. He had his lessons on geometry from the Hindus.

Geometry as a science originated with the early Hindus in their construction of various altars. They made considerable progress, at least in 800 BC. The *Srauta Sutras* of the *Yajur Veda* have *Sulva Sutras*, i.e. 'rules of the cord,' the earliest geometrical operations in India. The *Taittiriya Samhita* (V. 4.11) describes various altars. The Kalpa Sutras of Baudhayana and Apastamba have a chapter on geometry. Great skill is shown in the demonstration of various properties of triangles. The area is expressed in the terms of the three sides (unknown to Europe till published by Calvius in the sixteenth century AD). The ratio of the diameter to the circumstance is given and is confirmed by the most approval labours of Europeans. It was not known outside India until modern times.

The Chaturasra-Syena, a falcon-shaped altar built of square bricks, was the most ancient. The Vakra-paksha Vyasta-puchcha Syena is a falcon-shaped altar, with curved wings and outspread tail. The Kankachit is a heron-shaped altar with two feet. The Alajachit is very similar to it. Various Chitis (brick-built altars) are mentioned: some are curved, some are angular, some circular, and others tortoise-shaped.

Dr Thibaut says, 'Squares had to be found equal to two or more given squares or to the difference of two given squares; oblongs had to be turned into squares and squares into oblongs; triangles had to be constructed equal to given squares or oblongs; and so on. The last task, and not the least, was that of finding a circle, the area of which might equal as closely as possible that of a given square. (J.A.S.B. 1875, p. 227)

Pythagoras certainly leant the theorem, viz., 'the square of the hypotenuse is equal to the squares of the other two sides of a right-angled triangle,' from India where it was well-known at least two centuries before, as will appear from the two rules; (i) The square on the diagonal of a square, is twice as large as that square, and (ii) The square on the diagonal of an oblong is equal to the squares on both its sides.

Some important propositions are shown below:

1. To describe a circle equal to a given square—Draw half of the chords stretched in the diagonal from the centre towards the line due east; describe the circle together with the third part of the piece of the cord which will lie outside the square. [The result is approximately correct.]

2. To turn a circle into a square—Divide the diameter into eight equal parts and again one of these eight parts into 29 parts; of these 29 parts, remove 28 and moreover the sixth part of the one left part, less the eighth part of the sixth part, i.e. $\frac{7}{9}+\frac{I}{8\times 29}-\frac{I}{8\times 29\times 6}+\frac{I}{8\times 29\times 6\times 8}$ of the diameter of a circle is the side of a square, the area of which is equal to the area of the circle.
3. To find the value of a diagonal in number, in relation to the side of a square. Increase the measure by its third part, and this third part by its own fourth, less the thirty-fourth part of the fourth. If I represents the side, the diagonal will be $1+\frac{1}{3}+\frac{1}{3\times 4}-\frac{I}{3\times 4\times 34}=1{,}4142156$. The real value is $\sqrt{2}$ = 1.414213.

Hindu geometry of the age seems to have involved even Mensuration and Trigonometry.

As the Brahmans found out that they could express all geometrical truths by arithmetic and algebra and as they began to worship images in the next age, requiring no more altars for Vedic rites, they neglected Geometry; but the Greeks, borrowing the science from India, soon excelled in it. Hindus, however, shone in Rasi, science of numbers, by their long-discovered decimal notation of which the ancient Greeks and Romans were almost ignorant.

In the science of Grammar, Hindus are still unsurpassed in the world. The entire Sanskrit language was resolved into some 1,800 roots before 1000 BC.

Panini also gave a like resolution. Discovery of Sanskrit (AD 1780) has enabled the great European scholars to discover Philology. Bopp, Grimm Humboldt and others have reduced the Aryan tongues to the same roots into which Panini had resolved Sanskrit in the ninth century BC.

The chapter on Indo-Persian relations is still dark, though partially illuminated of late by Dr Spooner and others. Hindus and Parsis were once one people. There was intercourse between the two. Indian influences were found in ancient Persia. The sun worship in various forms was current there. A plate discovered by the German scholar Hugo Vinclaire states that 3,300 years ago, i.e. in 1385 BC, in a treaty between two kings of Babylon, mention is made of their gods Mithra, Varuna and Indira. North-West India was conquered by Darius in 512 BC. Even before this, Hindu learning, religion, wisdom had spread in Persia and thence to Europe. The Persians also came to India to settle, to trade, and to travel. The Persian Empire was the most powerful, brilliant and model to the world from 550 to 330 BC. Doubtless, Persian influence on India was great then. Indian wisdom was also reflected in the philosophy of Confucius of China (sixth century BC).

Kanada's Theory of Atoms (modern electrons or protyles) was published in Greece by Democratus about 440 BC and afterwards proved also by Epicurus. Dalton has published the same in modern Europe.

ADMINISTRATION

The Sutra works of Gautama (X), Vasista (*XIV*) and Apastamba (11.10.25), the Pali Works, Chanakya's *Artha Sastra* (art of government) and the Greek accounts of India, show the highly organised system of administration, at least in some kingdoms of India. Of course, the system continued, as it was in the epic age, with the change that the sturdy and warlike manners of the former were replaced by more luxurious, effeminate and sophisticated habits of the Rationalistic Age. Chanakya and Megasthenes give us a general account of the careful system of administration under the Hindu rulers of the age.

The city of Pataliputra was administered by six bodies of five members each. The first looked to the industrial arts; the second, to the entertainment and convenience of all foreigners, giving them lodgings, escorts on the way, medicine when sick, burial when dead, and sending their property to their relatives. The third looked to the vital statistics, registering all births and deaths; the fourth, to trade and commerce, examining weights and measures, seeing that the products were sold by public notice. On payment of a double tax, one might deal in more than one commodity. The fifth, looked to manufactured articles saleable by public notice. There was a fine for selling adulterated goods. The sixth collected a tenth of the price of the articles sold, still called dahatra (Sanskrit dasottara).

The military department also consisted of six bodies of five members each. The first looked to the admiralty. The second, to the bullock-trains carrying engines of war, food for the army, fodder for the cattle and other requisites. The third took care of the foot soldiers; the fourth of the horses; the fifth of the war-chariots; and the sixth of the elephants.

The department of agriculture and public works had the charge of agriculture, irrigation, forests, rural tracts, huntsmen, collection of taxes, superintending the occupations of wood-cutters, carpenters, blacksmiths and miners; constructing roads and setting up a pillar at every ten stadia, to show the by-roads, and distance.

The villages were little self-governing bodies. The account of Megasthenes regarding the personal habits and occupations of kings almost tallies with that of the kings of the epic and the Pauranik ages.

Speaking of the Hindu equipment for war, Arrain says that the foot soldiers each carried a bow of his own size; the shaft was about three yards long. There was nothing which could resist an Indian archer's shot. In their left hand, they carried bucklers of undressed ox-hide and of about their own height. Some were armed with javelins but wore a broad sword about three cubits long; this they used in close fight with great effect. The horsemen were equipped with two lances, with a shorter buckler; they used no saddles, no bits, but a circular piece of stitched raw ox-hide studded with pricks of iron or brass pointing inwards, not very sharp, round the extremity of the horse's mouth. A rich horseman used pricks made of ivory.

Baudhayana 1.10, 18.11; Vasista IX. 20; Apastamba 11.5, 10–11 show how humane were the laws of war among Hindus. Megasthenes also says the same, 'Hindus do not ravage the soil and reduce it to a waste. The peasants remain quite unmolested even in the worst war. They do not ravage an enemy's land with fire, nor cut down its trees.'

Under a strong government, Indians were peaceful and law-abiding. In courts of justice, criminal and civil laws were administrated and judicial trial held, by men of learning, birth, age, and reasoning. In doubtful cases, truth was ascertained by reasoning, document and like means. The Dharma *Sutras* strictly enjoin all to speak the truth. Gautama says, 'To give false evidence is a mortal sin which involves loss of caste' (XXI, 10). 'To speak the truth before the judge is more important than all duties' (XII, 31).

The oath administered to a witness was of the most solemn character (vide Vasista, XVI; Baudhayana I.10.19). On the speaking of truth, vide also Gautama, XI; Apastamba II.11.19.

Megasthenes states, 'Hindus seldom go to law; they make their pledges and deposits without witnesses; they hold truth in high esteem and a person who bears false witness in India suffers the dreadful penalty of the mutilation of his extremities.'

LAWS

Unjust distinction now pervaded the criminal laws of the age. For the same offence, different caste had different punishments; higher the caste, lesser the penalty (see Baudhayana, I.10.18–19).

The same indelible stain marks the penalty for adultery between castes and other minor offences (see Apastamaba, II, 10.27; Gautama, XII).

For a sudra, the laws were ten times more severe. And, why so? The *Mahabharata* pleads for a thorough impartiality, a lofty conception of justice, requiring a king not to pardon even his offending son. Now, soon after the Great War, why were the laws made so unjust and cruel, especially for the sudras? R. C. Dutt says that the Brahmans framed such laws only to emphasise their own superiority; in practice, the laws were rather just, being intelligently exercised by sensible kings, officers and judges. We think, such unequal and cruel laws in this age, said to be the best in India, were necessitated by the evils of the times. After the Great War, there was a revival of the non-Aryan powers. Turks, Turanians, Sudras were astir. They caused great political unrest in the land. Some Turanians, having pierced the Himalayas, came down on north India and seized Videha (north Bihar). Ther renowned Janaka dynasty came to an end about 1200 BC. Cunningham says that Brijis (Sanskrit Birajas), people without a king, from bi=without, and raja, a king, were composed of different tribes such as the Lichchavis of Vaisali, Vaidehas of Mithila and Tirabhuktis of Trihoot. The ancient state of Briji, extended from the Gandaki to Mahanadi, was 300 × 83 miles. In time, nine towns belonged to the eight tribes, viz., Vaisali, Kesaria, Janakapur, Navandgarh, Simroom, Saran, Dwarbanga, Purneach, Matihari. Of them, the Lichchavis and the Vrjjains were the most powerful.

There are many curious legends to tell us that the Brahmans were generally slighted. The Kshatriyas, in their own estimation at least, stood supreme. Society was once more in disorder. To reset it, the caste system was thoroughly organised and made hereditary at Benaras about 1200 BC.

Death or corporal punishment was probably the penalty for theft in some cases (Gautama, XII 45). The prerogative of mercy was reserved by the king. A spiritual guide, a priest, a learned householder or a prince could intercede for an offender, if not guilty of a capital crime (Apastamba, II, 10, 27,20).

The right of self-defence was allowed to a person attacked by an incendiary, poisoner, one ready to kill with a weapon in hand, a robber, one who takes away another's land or abducts another's wife (Vasista, III, 15 to 18).

Suicide was highly discouraged. No funeral rites were allowed to a suicide (Vasista, XXIII, 14).

Agrarian laws were strict, yet good and reasonable (Gautama, XIII, 14–17). Megasthenes tells us that he who caused an artisan to lose his eye or his hand, was punished with death.

Lands were leased; good arrangements were made for crops and trade; stray cattle were impounded (Apastamba, II, 11 28; Gautama, *XII*). Unenclosed fields were used by all for grazing cattle, obtaining firewood, culling flowers and getting fruits (Gautama, *XII*, 28).

Vasista gives some good provisions on the right of way and evidence in disputes regarding immoveable property (*XVI*, 10 to 15). Gautama, XII, 37–39 and Vasista, XVI, 16–18, give the law of acquiring property by usage. The following eight things used by another for ten years continuously, are lost to the owner; ancestral property, a purchased article, a pledge property given to a wife by her husband's family, a gift, property received for performing a sacrifice, the property of reunited co-parceners, and wages.

> Note:—A pledge, a boundary, property of minors, an open deposit, a sealed deposit, female salves, the property of minors, an open deposit, a sealed deposit, female salves, the property of king, and the wealth of a Srotriya are not lost being enjoyed by others. Animals, land and women are also not so lost to the owner.

Property entirely given up by its owner, goes to the king. The king shall administer the property of widows and minors (Vasista, XIV, 8–9).

The interest for loan of money on security was only fifteen per cent per annum and the principal could only be doubled. Articles and products such as gold, grain, flavouring substances, flowers, roots, fruits, wool, beasts of burden, could be lent without security at an enormous rate of interest which could be increased six or eight-fold.

Vasista, II, 51, Gautama, XII, 29 and 36, Manu, VIII, 140, Gautama, XII, 34–35, name six different kinds of interest, viz., compound, periodical, stipulated, corporal, daily, and the use of pledge.

Ordinarily, the heirs shall pay the debts of a deceased person. But the money due by a surety, a commercial debt, a fee due to the parents of the bride, immoral debts and fines shall not devolved on the sons of a debtor (*XII, 40–41*).

LAW OF INHERITANCE

Gautama names twelve different kinds of sons: 1. Aurasa (legitimate), 2. Kshetraja (bastard), 3. Datta (adopted), 4. Kritrima (made), 5. Gudhaja (secretly born), 6. Apabiddha (abandoned by the parents). These six, as kinsmen and heirs, can inherit. 7. Kanina (son of an unmarried daughter), 8. Sahodha (son of a pregnant bride), 9. Paunarbhava (son of a remarried woman), 10 Putrikaputra (son of an appointed daughter), 11. Swayamdatta (a self-given son), 12. Krita (purchased). These six are kinsmen, not heirs and cannot inherit, but are maintained as members of the family. Vasista regards Aurasa, Kshetraja, Putrikaputra, Paunarbhava, Kanina and Gudhaja sons as kinsmen and heirs; while Sahodha, Datta, Krita, Svayamdatta, Apaviddha, and Nishada (son of a Sudra) as kinsmen, and not heirs. They cannot inherit except when there is no legitimate heirs of the first six classes (XVII).

Baudhayana (II, 2 3), names twelve kinds of sons of whom the first seven, viz., Aurasa, Putrikaputra, Kshetraja, Datta, Kritrima, Gudhaja and the Apaviddha were entitled to inheritance. The next four, viz.,

Kanina, Paunarbhava, Svayamdatta, and Nishada (son by a twice-born father in a Sudra mother) were regarded as members of the family. The last, Parasava, (son of an Aryan father by a Sudra mother begotten through lust) was not even regarded as a member of the family.

The law-giver, Apastamba, who flourished in the tenth or nineth century BC protested against the recognition of such heirs and sons on the grounds that those ancient customs could not be allowed amongst sinful men of the age (ii, 6, 13; II, 10, 27). He recognised the Aurasa son alone as legitimate to follow the ancestral occupations and to inherit the estate. Yet, the ancient customs did not die out soon. Adoption is still in force.

Baudhayana (*c.* thirteenth century BC) was probably a southerner. He had high regard for the Gangetic Valley. Yet, he mentions some peculiar laws and customs of south India (I, 1, 2).

Five customs peculiar to the north were dealing in wool, drinking rum, selling animals that have teeth in the upper and the lower jaws, following the trade of arms, and going to sea.

The customs peculiar to the south were eating in the company of an uninitiated person, eating in the company of one's wife, eating stale food, and marrying the daughter of a maternal uncle or of a paternal aunt.

PARTITION OF PROPERTY

The law of primogeniture never obtained in India. In the joint families, the eldest son would inherit the estate and maintained the rest. Gautama, the earliest law-giver of the age, seems to have favoured partition, for, in partition there is an increase of spiritual merit (*XXVIII*, 4). He lays down that the eldest son shall get, as an additional share, a twentieth part of the estate, some animals and a carriage; the middle-most son shall get some poor animals and the youngest shall get sheep, grain, utensils, a house, a cart, and some animals; and then the remaining property is equally divided, or, Gautama also allows the eldest two shares and the remaining sons one share each; or they may take one kind of property by choice according to seniority; or the special shares may be adjusted according to their mothers (*XXVIII*, 5 to 17).

The property of un-reunited brothers, dying without issue, goes to the eldest brother; the property of a reunited co-parcener goes to the co-parcener; what a learned co-parcener has acquired by his own labour, may be withheld from his unlearned co-parceners and unlearned co-parceners should divide their acquisitions equally (*XXVIII*, 27, 31).

A Brahman's son by a Kshatriya wife, if the eldest, shares equally with a younger brother by a Brahman wife. The sons of a Kshatriya by a Vaisya wife, share equally. The son by a Sudra wife, if virtuous, is maintained, while even the son of a wife of equal, caste does not inherit, if he be living unrighteously (*XXVIII*, 35–40).

Vasista allows the eldest brother to have a double share and a little of the wine and horses; the middle-most gets utensils and furniture; the youngest takes the goats, sheep and house. If a Brahman has sons by Brahman, Kshatriya and Vaisya wives, the first gets three shares, the second two shares and the third, i.e. the son bh the Vaisya wife gets one share (*XVIII*, 42 to 50).

Baudhayana allows all the children to take equal shares, or the eldest son to take one-third in excess. The sons by wives of different castes, will take four, three, two, and one shares, according to the order of the castes (*II, 2.3, 2.10*).

Apastamba protests against such unequal division of property and declares that all the virtuous sons inherit, but he who spends money unrighteously, shall be disinherited though he be the eldest son (*II, 6–14, 1–15*). The nuptial presents and ornaments of a wife were inherited by her daughters (Gautama, Vasista, *XVII 46*, Baudhayana, *II, 2.3, 43*). Apastamba holds that on the failure of sons, the daughter may inherit (*II, 6, 14.4*).

CASTE

To keep off foreign influence, to save society from spiritual contamination, to maintain the pristine purity of blood, to minimise faults, and to bring society into better order, the caste system was thoroughly organised in this age with well-defined coccupations for each caste, by means of rigid and inviolable rules. Formerly, members of inferior castes might enter even the priestly caste by virtue, knowledge and religion (see *Aitareya Brahmana and Satapatha Brahmana*) but now caste was declared hereditary at Benaras at about 1200 BC. These stringent measures show that people in general were growing more sinful than ever. Even our protestant law-giver Apastamba admits it. Yet, we are sure that merit was not slighted in society for mere birth, nor faults in high births passed over. The seers and the legislators now took a rational view of caste. The worthies among the low castes were held in high esteem (see Manu), while the sinful unworthies of the twice-born classes were depressed, denounced and even classed as Sudras. Loss of caste was the penalty for disreputable or criminal life. The law-givers of the age also determined the caste of the offspring of a concubine and criminal intercourse with women of upper classes and of others dead to civil life.

R. C. Dutt here seems to be wrong in supposing that in this age Manu and other law-givers forgot or ignored the true historical origin of caste and sought a new fictitious theory, viz., 'the different castes were created by a sort of permutation and combination among the men and women of the few parent castes.'

Before the Rationalistic Age, the Indians were composed of seven classes, viz., Brahmans, Kshatriyas, Vaisyas, Sudras, Vratyas (not fully fallen Aryans) accepting the caste system, their priests called brahma or dvija bandhus and atheists, children of conclubines and low caste paramours and the Nishadas, i.e. untouchable hunters. The mass of the Aryans were Vaisyas and those Vaisyas were mostly Dravidian converts. They followed different professions according to their choice and these professions were generally herediatry. The Vratyas could become pure Aryans, again by performing some prescribed penances.

Elphinstone calls the Kayasthas (Cayets) pure Sudras. But by all traditions, they are Vratya-Kshatriyas, i.e. fallen warriors who turned back for their lives. The etymology of the word also shows this; Kaya=body, and Stha=one who stands or lives for. Hence, a timid fugitive, a cowardly runaway was ridiculed in society as Kayastha. This class came into society from the time of Parasurama. The proud and true Kshatriyas broke all social association with them. It is said that they lost asi (sword) and got *masi* (ink). By the appointment of Parasara (fifteenth century BC), they were given the profession of writing, i.e. all the clerical work of the raj.

Their number is now about nine million. Outside Bengal, they still have a sacred thread and follow some of the customs of the warrior class. In Bengal, they have long lost the sacred thread and rank as aristocratic Sudras.

Formerly, men of the first three classes could take wives from inferior ranks (only good girls), but not vice versa. Their offspring were regarded as kinsmen, if not heirs in all cases. They were maintained in the family. About the beginning of the third age, concubinage became unrestrained and the offspring often sinful. The children of criminal intercourse also had now grown to a number. The law-givers now set about to determine their castes and professions. Was this act a meddlesome interference of muddlesome brains? Was this a violent trespass on human rights? We do not think so. Our legislators were scrupulous, merciful and far-sighted. They considered blood and framed laws according to its nature and quality. They wanted to make all good and great and to make birth a mere outward stamp. No nation but the Hindus, has placed sociology on a more rational basis.

Dr William Miller of the Madras Christian College observes, 'The solidarity of man was more markedly recognized in Hinduism than in any other religion.'

Sir John Woodroffe says, 'if the merits of all peoples were balanced, India would appear high in the scale.'

Vasista XVIII names the new classes thus:

1. *Chandala*, born of a Sudra father and Brahman mother.
2. *Vaina*, born of a Sudra father and Kshatriya mother.
3. *Antyavasin*, born of a Sudra father and Vaisya mother.
4. *Ramaka* is the offspring of a Vaisya father and a Brahman mother.
5. *Paulkasa* is the son of a Vaisya father by a Kshatriya mother.
6. *Suta* is the son of a Kshatriya father by a Brahman mother.
7. *Ambashtha* is the son of a Brahman father by a Kshatriya mother.
8. *Ugrans* are children of Kshatriya fathers but Vaisya mothers.
9. *Nishadas* are offspring of Vaisya fathers and Sudra mothers.

Baudhayana, 1, 9, 16–17 names the new castes in a slightly different manner:

1. The son of wives of equal or of the next lower castes are savarnas, of equal castes.
2. The sons of wives of the first, second or third lower castes, are Ambashthas, Ugras and Nishadas, respectively.
3. The sons of Brahman fathers and of Kshatriya mothers are Brahmans; those of Brahman fathers and Vaisya mothers are

Ambashthas and those of Brahman fathers by Sudra mothers are Nishadas or Parasavas.

4. The sons of Kshatriya fathers and Vaisya mothers are Kshatriyas; those of Kshatriya fathers and Sudra mothers are Ugras; those of Vaisya fathers and Sudra mothers are Rathakaras; those of Sudra fathrs and Vaisya mothers are Magadhas; those of Sudra fathers of Kshatriya mothers are Kshattris; those of Sudra fathers and Brahman mothers are Chandalas; those of Vaisya fathers and Kshatriya mothers are Ayogavas, the sons of Vaisya fathers and Brahman mothers are Sutas; the sons of Ugra fathers and Brahman mothers are Sutas; the sons of Ugra fathers and Kshattri mothers are Svapakas; those of Vaidehaka fathers and Ambashtha mothers are vainas. Those of Nishada fathers and Sudra mothers are Paulkasas; those of Sudra fathers and Nishada mothers are Kukkutakas.

Those sprung by an intermixture of the castes are Vratyas (not to be confounded with the original Vratyas, i.e. denounced and denationalised Ayans).

Gautama, IV has the following list:

- The children of Brahman parents are Brahmaṇs.
  The sons of Kshatriyas by Brahman wives are Sudras; those of Vaisyas by Brahman wives, are Magadhas; those of Sudras by Brahman women are Chandalas.
- The sons of Brahmans in Kshatriya women are Murdhabhishiktas; those of Kshatriyas in the same are Kshatriyas; those of Vaisyas in the same are Dhivaras (firsherman); those of Sudras in the same are Paulkasas.
- A Vaisya woman bearning sons by a Brahman, is the mother of Bhrigya-Kanthas; the sons of a Vaisya by a Kshatriya, are called Mahishyas; the sons of a Vaisya by a Vaisya father, are of course, Vaisyas and the sons of a Vaisya by a Sudra are Vaidehas.
- A Sudra by a Brahman, bears Parasava; by a Kshatriya, Javana; by a Vaisya, Kasrana; and by a Sudra, Sudra.

Gautama, X. 5 prescribes the study of the Vedas, performance of sacrifices and gifts of alms for all twice-born Aryans. The Brahmans are further allowed to sacrifice for others, receive alms, follow agriculture and trade, if they do not work themselves.

Vasista in his *Dharma Sutra* Book III strongly protested against the growing abuses of the privileges of the Brahmans in being idlers, ignorant and hangers on in the following way, 'Brahmans who neither study nor teach nor keep sacred fires, become equal to Sudras. The king shall punish that village where Brahmans, ignorant and unobservant of holy duties, live by begging, for it feeds robbers. The sin that fools, perplexed by ignorance, declare as duty, shall fall, increased a hundred-fold, on those who propound it. A Brahman unlearned, is a wooden elephant. Drought or some other great evil will befall the lands where ignorant men eat the bread of the learned.'

The special occupations of Kshatriyas were governing, fighting, conquering, learning the management of chariots and bow, and standing firm in battle, never turing back (*Gautama,* X, 15–16).

The special employments of Vaisyas were trade, agriculture, tending cattle, lending money and labour for gain (*Gautama,* X, 49).

Sudras were to serve the three superior castes of labour for gain (*Gautama*, *X*, *42*). They might also trade, earn money by independent work, listen to religious discourses, and sacrifice with the help of priests. But as they had neither tradition nor aptitude, they were not allowed to study the Vedas or perform sacrifices themselves.

The seven castes of Megasthenes (300 BC) are virtually our four. His philosopher and councillors were the Brahmans engaged in religious study and in state-employment. His soldiers were the Kshatriyas; his overseers were only special officers and spies of the king; his husbandmen, shepherds and artisans were the Vaisyas; Sudras were engaged in cultivation, pasture and manufacture.

He further subdivides the philosophers into Brahmans, householders and *sramans* (ascetics).

The Brahmans as disciples: The children are under the care of one person after another, and as they advance in age, each succeeding master is more accomplished than his predecessor.

The philosophers dwell in groves near the city, and in simple style lie on beds of rushes or skins; abstain from animal food and sensual pleasures and spend their time listening to religious discourse and in imparting their knowledge to learners.

The Brahmans as householders: 'After living in this manner for 37 years, each person goes back to his own property, where he lives for the rest of his days in ease and security. Then they array themselves in fine muslin and wear a few trinkets of gold in their fingers and in their ears. They eat flesh, but not that of animals employed in labour. They abstain from hot and highly seasoned food. For numerous children they marry as many wives as they please. As they have no slaves, they have more need to have children around them to attend to their wants.'

The Brahmans as *sramanas* (ascetics): 'They live in the woods on leaves of trees and wild fruits and wear garments made from the bark of trees. Kings consult them by messengers about the causes of things and who, through them, worship and supplicate the deity.' The order of monks existed in India before Buddha, whose monks were called the Sakyaputriya *sramans*.

'By their knowledge of pharmacy, they (the Brahman physicians) can remove barrenness and make marriages fruitful and determine the sex of the offspring. They effect cures rather by regulating diet than by the use of medicines. The remedies most esteemed are ointments and plasters.'

'The philosophers, being exempted from all public duties, are neither the masters nor the servants of others. They are, however, engaged by private persons to offer the sacrifices due in one's lifetime and to celebrate the obsequies of the dead. They forewarn assembled multitudes about droughts and wet weather and also about propitious winds and diseases.'

The Brahmans not only formed a caste by themselves but were also leaders and guardians of the Hindu people. They taught the young, presided at sacrifices and funeral ceremonies, advised villagers and cultivators on weather and crops, prescribed medicines, advised kings in peace and war, kept the royal treasury and sat as judges in all cases. The educated classes asked their priestly advice and help in large ceremonies. The peasants consulted them on the prospects of the year.

Such a universally honoured and useful body of men are indeed rare in the world. From what height to what deep base have the Brahmans now fallen! That high discipline is gone; that high moral ideal is obscure!

AGRICULTURE

'Most of the people of India are tillers of the soil and live upon grain, only the hillmen eat the flesh of beasts of chase'—Nearchus quoted by Arrian.

India abounds with vast plains—highly fertile, beautiful and watered by a network of rivers. A considerable area is under irrigation. The land bears two crops a year. The country teems with animals of all sorts. The elephants are of a monstrous size.

Besides cereals, there grow, throughout India, much millet, much pulse of various sorts, rice, bosporum, many plants useful for food, other edible products for animals. Famine seldom visits India; there has never been a general scarcity of nourishing food. The country enjoys a double rainfall—that of winter and of summer—yielding two harvests annually. The fruits and the succulent roots of varied sweetness afford abundant sustenance for man.

Humane war-laws and wise usages prevent the occurance of famine. Even the worst war does no harm to the farmers, crops, cattle, fields, and trees. The Indian peasants are laborious, intelligent, frugal, and honest. Agriculture flourished under an efficient adminstration, fair and just laws and secure life and property (*Megasthenes*).

ARTS

There is little or no room to doubt that the Indians had carried the various manufactures and arts to a high state of excellence. The products of India were taken to the foreign markets, especially to Alexandria by the Phoenicians and others.

Megasthenes says, 'The Indians are well-skilled in the arts, as might be expected of men who inhale a pure air and drink the very finest water. The soil, too, has underground numerous veins of all sorts of metals, for its contains much gold and silver, and copper and iron in no small quantity, and even tin and other metals, which are employed in making articles of use and ornaments as well as the implements and accountrements of war.'

'In constrast to the general simplicity of their style they love finery and ornament. Their robes are worked in gold and ornamented with precious stones, and they wear also flowered garments made of the finest muslin. Attendants walking behind hold up umbrellas over them: for they have a high regard for beauty and avail themselves of every device to improve their books.'

Vasista in his Dharma *Sutra*, III, 49–63, speaks of objects of gold, silver and copper, of stones and gems and conch shells, pearls and of things made of bone, wood, leather, and cloth.

Bohn's Translation of Strabo, III, p. 117, describes a procession thus; 'In processions at their festivals, many elephants are adorned with gold and silver; numerous carriages drawn by four horses, by several pairs of oxen; then follows a body of attendants in full dress; bearing vessels of gold, large basins and goblets, orguia in breadth, tables, chairs, drinking cups and laverse of Indian copper, most of which are set with precious stones, such as emeralds, beryls and Indian carbuncles: garments embroidered and inter-woven with gold; wild beasts as buffaloes, panthers, tame lions and a multitude of birds of variegated plumage and of fine song.' This description reminds us of the famous Janmashtami procession of Dacca, held annually in August in honour of the birthday of Krishna.

A dhuti (an undergarment of cotton) chadar (a sheet, serving also the purpose of a head dress) and occasionally a cotton coat made up the general dress of the people. Gobhila's *Grihya Sutra* describes the dress. Fibres of plants, cotton, silk, and wool were the stuff of garments. Nepal, Kashmir, Gandhar Usinara were noted for their best blankets and other woollen stuff. Ceylon was noted for the rich hangings for elephants. Kantha, now rages formerly meant a kind of quit (*Panini, II 4, 20: IV 2. 142–143*). Carpet was in use (*Panini, IV, 2, 12*). A medicated fume was used for mosquito-curtain. *Pata-mandapa* (tends*)*, *Kanda-patas* (ladies' tents), *vitana* (awnings) were in use. The use of a bodice by the Indian women was not copied from the Greeks. Arrian quoting Nearchus, says, 'The Indians wear shoes made of white leather and these are elaborately trimmed, while the soles are variegated, and made of great thickness.' Vatsyayana's *Kama Sastra* (treatise on fine arts) mentions six cannons of painting.

ARCHITECTURE

Poetry, painting, music, sculpture, archietcture flourished in India from the earliest times. The Vedic ceremonies much helped their rise and development. Besides tradition, we have no instance of any kind in the first two ages. The Rationalistic Age, however, is rather rich in tradition and proofs alike.

The temple of gods is mentioned in the *Manava Gribya Sutra* (1, 7, 10). 'Let a daughter be married in a temple'. The *Sankhyayana Gribya Sutra (IV, 12, 15), (Panini, V, 3, 96–100).*

The Baithak of Jarasandha and the walls of old Rajagriha in Bihar, the ruins of which are still extant, were built before the fifth century BC (General Cunningham). Many of the Buddhist caves like those of Khandagiri and Udayagiri in Orissa were anterior to the time of Alexander (326 BC).

Near Chinraipatan in Mysore, there is a gigantic statue of a Jain Tirthankara cut out of a rock, height from 54 to 70 feet. I think this Chinraipatan is our Chandrapattana, i.e. city of Chandra who is no other than our Mauryan Chandragupta who had retired to Mysore to pass his last days as a Jain ascetic. The statue was cut by him or by his successors. The author of the play entitled the *Mudra Rakshasam* and its commentator both belonged to this city.

Fine Hindu temples and palaces, Buddhist topes, chapels, monasteries, decorated pillars, engraved figures, paintings on the walls, rock-cut caves and temples still show the high state of fine arts culture in the latter part of this age.

The Buddhist *Jataka* storties tell us that the rich in those days lived even in seven-storeyed buildings. *Sudha-karma* (white-wash), *lepa* (plaster and cement), *golambuja*, literally round lotus (cupola) corrupted into modern gambooj, *mangaleshtaka* (foundation-stone) were well-known then.

Scholars hold two theories regarding Indian achitecture. Some regard it as the product of original Hindu genius; others admit it, but add an influence of foreign models. Professor E.B. Havell has maintained the first.

Stone buildings were well-known to the Vedic Indians. But the art was gradually laid aside, as the country was found subject to terrible earthquakes, floods and intense heat. This we learn also from a Greek writer. Brick-built houses and wooden superstructure on brick plinths came into vogue. Hindus again adopted stone as a building material after 500 BC when they came into contact with the Persians and the Greeks, from whom they certainly got hints. Yet, the palace of Ashoka was a free stone structure.

The Magadhan style of architecture began with Ashoka, the master builder of India. It was outward-looking and material; like the Grecian architecture and sculpture, it exhibited human interest and human expressions. The genius of the Magadhan people lay at the root of this 'frank naturalism'.

Idols, idol-worship, painting, sculpture did exist in India before Ashoka who, however, made them very general, (J.R.A.S. 1911, pp. 1114–19; 1912, p. 1059; 1913, pp. 651–53). Patanjali (150 to 140 BC) in his Mahabhashya (defence of Panini) probably alludes to Ashoka making idol worship general. To popularise religion, Ashoka used to bring out a procession (see edict no. 4) which displaced various images. His popular religion aimed not so much at nirvana as at heaven. Ethical conduct and some rites in the shape of the worship of gods formed the chief parts of his religion.

The excellence of the artists of Ashoka's time may be seen from the well-executed animals on the capitals of his pillars. Four capitals of the pillar edicts of Ashoka, with figures of animals, have so far been discovered. They have three chief parts: at the bottom is the bell which resembles the bell of the pillars found in the ruins of Persepolis, the ancient capital of Persia. Over the bell is the abacus and over it, the figure of a beast. In the body of some abacus, are executed birds or beasts in relief; in some, creepers and flowers.

Of these, the one at village Loria Nandangarh (disrrict Champaran, Bihar) stands almost entire in the very spot where it was placed. This noble pillar is a glaring proof of what excellence, architecture had attained in the time of Ashoka. On it, a flock of swans is very finely represented in the abacus. On the top is carved out an excellent lion facing east and resting on its two hind legs. The lion of the pillar at the village Rampurua, district Champaran, was buried in the ground. It has been discovered, brought to Calcutta and placed at the entrance of the Calcutta Museum. The upper part of its face is broken. Though not lifelike, its limbs appear lively and spirited.

The capital of the Sarnath pillar is the best. In the body of the abacus are shown figures of elephants, bulls, horses, and lions. Four large lions leaning against one another, stand on the top. The lions, all natural and lively, exhibit a thorough lordly mien. Dr Marshall observes, 'Both pillar and lions are in an excellent state of preservation. They are masterpieces in point of both style and technicalities—the finest carvings indeed that India has yet produced, and unsurpassed. I venture to think if anything of their kind exists in the ancient world.'

The pillar of Sanchi (central India) has similar four lions, on the top. Their heads are now broken. General Cunningham writes, 'Their muscles and paws are quite natural and may be compared with the samples of the Grecian sculpture (*Architecture Report, 1904–5, p. 36*). 'Mr V A Smith holds that 'that Sarnath pillar must have been wrought by a foreigner (*Indain Architecture, p. 62*).' Was this foreigner a Persian or an Asiatic Greek? Nothing has as yet been found outside India, of the execution of lions like those of Sarnath or Sanchi. On the other hand, ancient coins with Brahmi lipi on them, prove that from very ancient times, coins with figures of elephants, bulls were cast in the mould (Rapson, *J.R.A.S. 1900, p. 182*).

SOCIAL LIFE

The Rationalistic Age—the best in India, was singularly rich in great thinkers and moral preachers. Manu, Gautama, Vasista, Baudhayana, Apastamba, the last two Jain reformers, Gautama the Buddha—all stressed morality as the essence of true religion. The moral elevation of the people was indeed very great. 'Probably in institutions and morality, India was at its height just before Alexander.' Those were the days of Hindu greatness. The effects of the religion of Manu on morals is indeed good. The distinction between right and wrong is well shown. Drinking of wine is held a crime of the first degree. False evidence is highly denounced. There are numerous injunctions to justice, truth and virtue. He extols honest poverty and decries unfair opulence. He inculcates generous maxims and elevated sentiments. Kindness to animals is held most meritorious. Killing a suppliant and injuring a benefactor are heinous offences. The state of women is high and honourable. The family must not be in want. Ornaments, apparels and good foods must be supplied at festivals and jubilees. He gives laws for the protection of widows. A wife is to be devoted to her husband.

Manu gives excellent precepts of politeness and self-denial on hospitality to guests. He gives rules for forms of salutation and civility to persons of all classes and relations, great respect for parents and age, for learning and moral conduct, for wealth and rank and immemorial custom. Learning is greatly honoured. All classes are recommended to cultivate it. Gautama, in his *Dharma Sutra* (*VIII, 24–250*) says, 'Virtue alone holds society together and smooths the path of progress. Compassion, forbearance, purity, gentleness, performance of good actions, freedom from avarice, anger, and covetousness are esteemed as the eight good qualities. He whose soul is void of these qualities, will not be united with *Brahman* nor shall he reach his heaven' The following are his commandments to a householder, 'He shall always speak the truth, shall conduct himself as becomes an Aryan, shall instruct virtuous men, shall follow the rules of purification, shall take pleasure in the Veda, shall never hurt any being, shall be gentle yet firm, ever restrain his senses and be liberal.'

Vasista in his *Sutra* Book VI preaches the same sweet sermon, 'The Vedas do not purify him who is deficient in good conduct. As the beauty of a wife causes no joy to a blind man, even so the Vedic studies and rites bring no blessing to him who is wanting in good conduct.'

All the moralists are equally earnest in detesting and repressing crimes, sins and immorality.

The sins that led to loss of caste, according to Gautama (xxi, 1–10) were murder, drinking wine, violation of a guru's bed, incest, theft, atheism, a persistent repetition of sinful acts, harbouring criminals, abandoning blameless friends, instigating others to such foul acts, associating with outcastes, giving false evidence, bringing false charges, and similar acts.

According to Vasista (I, 19–21), the violation of a guru's bed, the drinking of wine, murder, theft and spiritual or matrimcnial connection with outcastes were the five greatest of sins causing loss of caste.

The drinking of wine was most strictly prohibited. The penance was death; hot liquor was poured into the sinner's mouth till he was scalded to death (Gautama, XXIII.1; Baudhayana, II.1. 1, 18).

Vasista (XIII, 47–48) inculcates a high regard for teacher, preceptors, elders, fathr and especially the mother who is a thousand times more veneralble than the father.

Sacred learning and philosophy were open to women.

Polygamy, prevalent among the rich, was however discouraged. 'A householder shall not take a second wife, if his first wife is willing and able to perform her share of the religious duties and if she bears sons' (Apastamba, ii, 5, 11).

Banishment, insanity, impotency, renunciation, loss of caste or death of a husband were circumstances which allowed a (willing) woman to marry again (Vasista, XVII, 20) A husband might abandon his barren wife in the tenth year, one who bore daughters only in the 12th, one all of whose children died, in the 15th and a quarrelsome one, without delay (Manu and Baudhayana, II, 2, 4,6).

The abandoned wife was still a member of the family. The husband took a second wife only for a male child. Hindus never knew an unjust divorce.

'He who has unjustly forsaken his wife, shall put on an ass's skin, with the hair turned outside and beg in seven houses for six months saying, "give alms to him who forsook his wife".' (Apastamba, I, 10.28, 19).

Formerly twelve, or even fourteen forms of marriage were admitted; but in the Sutra period, Gautama and Baudhayana recognised eight forms, Vasista and Apastamba admitted only six, viz. Brahma, Daiva, Arsha, Gandharva, Kshatra (Rakshasa), and Manusha or Asuri.

Marriages among kinsmen were strictly prohibited in this age. Baudhayana allows a person to marry the daughter of a maternal uncle or a paternal aunt (I, 1.2, 4). Vasista prohibits marriage between a man and a woman of the same gotra (clan) or *pravara* (line) or who are related within four degrees on the mother's side or within six degrees on the father's (*VIII*, 1, 2). Apastamba prohibits marriage between men and women of the same gotra or who are related within six degrees on the mother's or father's side.

Girl marriages, almost unknown in the first two ages, gradually came into vogue in this third. The remarriage of widows except in the case of child widows, was generally discouraged.

The dead were burnt with some rites—the relations entered water, changed their dress and fasted or lived on poor food for three days. Sapinda relationship extended to the seventh generation. Brahman Sapinda remained impure for ten days after the death; a Kshatriya for eleven days; a Vaisya for twelve days and a Sudra for one month. On the failure of sons, Sapindas could offer the funeral oblation.

At the *Sraddha* (funeral sacrifice), the bereaved would feed a small number of Brahmans versed in the Vedas, noted for learning, virtue and purity. The minimum number, according to Gautama, was nine and according to Vasista, one (Gautama, XIV, 1–5, and 13; *XV, 7–9*. Vasista, *XI, 29; IV, 11–17*).

Early in this age, a man might have chosen one of the four orders, viz., that of a student, a householder, an ascetic, and a hermit (Vasista, VII, 3; Baudhayana, II, 10, 17, 2). But Apastamba says that 'if he lives in all these four, he will obtain salvation.' (II, 9, 21.2).

Thus, householders formed the bulk and the best of the four orders (Vasista, VIII, 15).

Gautama prescribed at least forty sacraments or sacred duties for the householder. These domestic ceremonies we have already noticed in a previous chapter, so it is needless to repeat them here.

Apastamba (II, 2.3, 4–9) gave directions for keeping Sudra cooks of cleanly habits, whose preparations were deemed fit even for religious rites.

The *Sutrakaras* gave many rules on food. Bad animals and birds were no more used as food. Beef, though still used as a food, was gradually falling into disuse, owing to the growing disinclination to kill animals except at sacrifices. This is apparent from an altered text of Manu pointed out by Dr Buhler. In his Dharma *Sutra*, Manu gave permission to slaughter animals in sacrifices (vide Vasista, IV, 5). This has been changed into an absolute prohibition to take animal life, in the present materical code.

In some rites, slaughter of animals formed a necessary part. The *sulagava* (roast beef), the *ekashtaka*, the *atiratra*, the *nirudha pasubandha* required the sacrifice of oxen. The *madhu-parka* (honey-meat) had to be accompanied with the sacrifice of a cow, in honour of the distinguished guest. The use of beef went out with the discontinuance of Vedic rites and was finally given up to respect Jain and Buddhistic appearls.

INDIAN LIFE AND CHARACTER

In the Rationalistic Age, Brahmanical supremacy had established a high order of civilisation in India.

(i) 'From the early excellence of the Brahmans in all these branches of learning, viz., the Vedas, their commentaries and other connected books, thelogy, logic, ethics, physical science, astronomy, it is probable that they had made considerable progress even when Manu's *Code* was formed.' The professions mentioned show the civilised life. The various grains, spices, perfumes and other productions show a highly cultivated country. The code, in general, presents the picture of a peaceful and flourishing community. Gold, germs, silks, ornaments are spoken of as being in all families (*Chapter V, 111–112; VII, 130*).

Elephants, horses and chariots are familiar as conveyances for men, as are cattle, camels, and wagons for goods. Gardens, bowers and terraces are mentioned. Construction of ponds and orchards by wealthy men fo the public benefit is here perhaps first enjoined (*Chapter IV, 226*).

Note: Manu's present metrical code, written probably in the second century BC, was complied from the older documents (1200 BC) which again were systematised and codified from still older traditions.

(ii) Homer (eleventh century BC) speaks of the Indians as 'pious Ethiopians of the East.'

(iii) High Bramanic discipline, wisdom and morality had induced even men like Empedocles, Pythagoras and others to come out to the East and drink at this very fountainhead. The teachings of Pythagoras are an exact photograph of the Indian life and lore (sixth century BC).

(iv) Skylax of Corianda in Asia Minor (sixth century BC), ordered by Darius, went by sea to explore the Indus and the coast of India. He returned home in thirty months. His encouraging report had induced Darius to conquer a portion of India (512 BC). His work is lost and lives in scattered references. He gives the fabulous stories about one-eyed men, about sleeping in their ears, and other wonderful stories.

(v) Herodotus was born 484 BC at Halikernasus in Asia Minor. This 'Father of History' gives the first definite acount, however 'meagre and vague and nebulous' it may be. The Indian province of Darius, the richest and the most populous, yielded him an annual tribute of 360 talents of gold-dust.

An Indian contingent served in the army of Xerxes, clad in cotton garments and armed with cane bows and iron-tipped cane-arrows.

Dog-sized gold-digging ants abounded in the gold districts near the source of the Indus (*Mahabharata, Court Book* also mentions this). India—a land of many rivers and many tongues—was the farthest part of the inhabited world, being bound on the east by sandy deserts. (The India of Darius and Herodotus did not go beyond the Indus). The people, mostly dark, were of three distinct classes. The first two were the north-western aborigines living on raw rish and flesh and the third class comprised the Hindu sages. Being struck by cotton, Herodotus speaks of it as 'wool growing on trees more beautiful and valuable than that produced from sheep.'

(vi) Ktesias, the Royal physician of Persia, wrote about 398 BC his *Indika*, preserved in an abridged form by Photius, a Byzantine of the nineth century AD, who was indebted to Skylax in some measures. Gredulous, he collected the fables current about India in the Persian court. His book is a medley of marvels and matter. He speaks of large four-footed birds called griffins guarding gold in the mountain; of snub-nosed pygmies skilled in archery but having hair and beards trailing to their feet; of the wars of the cranes and the pygmies; gold-faced men having large and shaggy garments and living up to 200 years; of the one-footed men noted for speed; of the fountain of liquid gold; of the fountain of water congealing to cheese, a dose of which would make a guilty person confess his crimes. Aristotle used his reports on Indian animals, in his book on zoology. Ktesias says that India has no swine, tame or wild; he mentions the unicorn ass, cups made from whose horn had the virtue of protecting men form some disease and from poison. There was a small bird whose dung first produced sleep and then death. The Indian jackal could imitate the human voice, had the strength of a lion and the swiftness of a horse.

His account of the cochineal plant, the worm and the dyes made from it, is right. He mentions the monkey, the parrot, the elephant, and the tiger (man-easter).

He praises the Indians for their sense of justice, their devotion to their king and their contempt of death. Their complexion was fair. They were free from headache, tooth-ache, ophthalmia and from mouth-sores or ulcers in any part of their body. They generally attained the age of 120 years before death. There were a people to the north who lived even 400 years.

Ktesias mentions the Indus and the Hyparkhos (Ganges?). He says that no rain ever fell in India. (This shows that the Greek knowledge of India before Megasthenes, was confined to the Punjab.)

(vii) The two Sanskrit epics probably compiled in their present shapes not later than the fifth century BC, give traditional pictures of our early civilisation.

(viii) Some of the Pali *Jataka* stories give us a picture of the civilisation in north India in the sixth and the fifth centuries BC. From them appear the manners, customs, rules of conduct in ancient India. They show India free from contaminating foreign influence. They show Hindu society in its entire purity and completeness. The rich lived in seven-storeyed buildings; merchants went to foreign lands on trade in large vessels having expert sailors, guides, pilot. The citizens would raise subscription to maintain orphanages and educate the orphans as 'free student'.

(ix) The discovery (1898) on the Nepal frontier at Piprawah of the Stupa about which the *Imperial Gazetteer of India,* New Edition, Volume II. p. 102, observes, 'The construction and contents of the Stupa offer valuable testimony concerning the state of civilisation in north India about 450 BC which is quite in accordance with the elicited from early literary sources.'

(x) The *Maha-vansa*, Chapter X. King Pandukabhaya of Ceylon of the fourth century BC and a follower of Brahmanism, conferred the following blessings on the people: (a) The institution of hospitals; (b) Complete city organisation—capital Anuradhapura had probably the oldest municipal corporation in the world (c) Able administration of the city; (d) Advancement in sanitary science; (e) Appointment of Mayors in the capital; (f) Demarcation of the limits of the city; (g) Conservancy; (h) Different crematoriums for different castes; (i) Supply of water reclaiming and deepening a large natural marsh; (j) Different *dharamashalas* (rest houses) for different people. Modern municipal corporations are still wanting in some of these.

It is often alleged that the ancient Hindus were deficient in altruistic feelings, in terms of building hospitals. The first hospital of Europe was in France (seventh century AD). But in India, there were hospitals for men, beasts and birds long before Buddha. There is a chapter on *Vrikshayur* Veda (medical treatment of trees and plants) in the *Agni Purana*. Manu, IV 226 enjoined all wealthy men to construct ponds and orchards for public benefit. The rich maintained orphanages. Construction of road, bridges, rest-houses have been prevalent in India from the earliest times. Hindu rajas ever looked to all foreign residents in India, regarding their comforts, health, safety, wealth (vide Chanakya and Megasthenes). Generous maxims, noble sentiments, self-denial, hospitality to strangers, giving shelter to those seeking refuge, public spirit were never foreign to Hindu character. Hindu traditions show this, foreign accounts prove this.

(xi) The records of the Greek historians and geographers of Alexander the Great: (a) Good points—Greek observation and critical faculty were not much improved; so, from them we have good accounts of what they saw in the Punjab. (b) Their defects—general credulity (even in Megasthenes). Writers, mostly soldiers, were illiterate and wanting in critical acumen. They collected only topographical information for the purpose of war. They wrote little of fauna, flora, religion, and social life. Their accounts of men are also not worth much. They had probably neither time nor inclination to study Indians patiently and well.

Their knowledge of India was only partial, being limited to the Punjab. So, their general remarks are occasionally wrong. The knowledge of Herodotus and Ktesias had stopped at the Indus; Alexander carried it to the Sutlej. Besides, he collected ample information, mainly from Chandragupta regarding the rich Gangetic Valley (Arrian, *Anab*, V. 25). Moreover, he heard of Taprobane (ancient *Tamra–Varna*), now Ceylon, a distant unknown island rich in elephants, cetaceous animals, and pearls (Strabo, XV, 15).

The *Stathmi* of Amyntas, a Macedonian, is a compilation of facts about India before Megasthenes. It said that Diognetius and Baeto took measurement of all tracts traversed by Alexander. The *stathmi* is based on them. The Greeks thought India was like a rhomboid. From the

Alexander Bridge to the sea, the distance was, 149 English miles. A Grand Trunk Road ran from the Indus to Pataliputra. Patna to sea = 689 British miles. Therefore, Indus to sea is 149 + 689 = 838 miles. From the mouth of the Ganges to Cape Comorin = 838 miles. Again, from Cape Comorin to the Indus is 2,183 British miles. These measurements the Greeks learnt from the Indians.

The *Mahabharata* describes India roughly as an equilateral triangle. Alexander Cunningham says that, 'the close agreement of these dimensions given by Alexander's informations with the actual size of the country, is very remarkable and shows that the Indians, even at that early date in their history had a very accurate knowledge of the form and extent of their native land.'

The Greek writers noticed the following: Self-choice of husband and wife, polygamy, practice of offer of virgins as a prize to the victors, penance and wisdom of the sages (Diodus, Sic. Xxi. 30). Alexander himself, struck by the wisdom and penance of the sages, sent to them one Sicritus who, however, found them above temptation and fear. One of the saints named Kalanos agreed to follow Alexander and went to Persia with him, where he fell ill and burnt himself to death. Another point had attracted the Greek notice: the sages often fasted and lived on a frugal and sparing diet, which led them to believe that the Indians lived without food (Elliot, vol. p. 10, note).

The country, i.e. North-East India was then divided into many independent States with no common interests, and no unity. The form of government was monarchical in some and republican and aristocratic in others. These latter two probably referred to the ancestors of the Sikhs, the Rajputs and the Marhattas (see Professor Heeren's *Historical Researches* [Asia], *vol* II. P. 202, 1846). Kingship was hereditary, the Brahmans were ministers and law-makers. The laws were not committed to writing (Strabo, XV, 60). Slavery was unknown and the people everywhere enjoyed peace and prosperity (Arrians's Indika, 10). Sober and diligent, truthful and peaceful, the Indians were good citizens and good farmers. They were noted for physical bravery above other Asiatics.

The Indians are praised for their skill in manufacturing and imitations of foreign objects. Seeing the Macedonians use sponge, they exactly imitated it by sewing hair, strings and threads into wool (Nearchus, quoted by Strabo, XV, 67).

Nearchus testifies to the existence of writing in India before Alexander. 'This we know from Nearchus himself who ascribes to the Indians the art of making paper from cotton. (Max Müeller's *History of Ancient Sanskrit Literature*) Yajnavalkya (fourteenth century BC) speaks of paper made of cotton. Strabo, XV, 67 states that the Indians wrote on smooth cloth very cleverly woven and well-pressed. Curtius, VIII, 9 says that the Indian, at the time of Alexander used the tender sides of barks for writing.

No fee in money was either given or taken in marriage. The women were remarkable for their chastity (Arrian's *Indika*, c. 27). The common people were robust, abstemious in habit, finely dressed in white muslin, clad in sandals and in cotton clothes, a part of which was twisted round the head (Curtius, VIII, 9). They wore precious stones as earrings and decked their wrists and arms with golden bracelets (*ibid*). Some had a great liking for ornaments and gaudy garments interwoven with gold (Strabo, XV, 69). They were also fond of dyeing their beards and hair which they loved to wear long (*ibid.* 71). Needless to say that this was an old practice of the Hindus.

The Brahmans much liked the study of philosophy and medicine and even women were versed in metaphysics (Strabo, XV, 34 and 66). The Brahmanic indifference to gold and grave had impressed the Greeks much (cf. the bold answer of Dandamis). The Sramans mentioned by the Greeks were probably not Buddhist but Hindu. As in politics, so in religion, the different sects of the Hindus never knew amity and unity. Women freely mixed with the Sramans, yet there was no violation of the laws of chastity. The Indians worshipped Zeus Ombrios (Indra), the Ganges and other deities.

The soil, chiefly alluvial, was greatly fertilised by the floods during the rains. The country was subject to occasional earthquakes. The rivers often changed their beds (Strabo, XV, 19 and 71). India then had good periodical rains, mines of gold and silver, mountains of fossil salt, dogs of rare strength and grace, beasts of uncommon size, singing birds, talking parrots, imitating apes, huge banian trees affording shelter to 400 horsemen, plenty of medicinal plants and fragrant herbs, sweet reeds, precious stones, garnets of every class and pearls—'the gifts of the sea'—which enriched the far distant Indians. (Arrian's *Indika*, c. 16; Curtius, VIII, 9; Strabo, XV, 21–22; Horace, *Epistle* 1.6).

(xii) Chanakya's *Artha Sastra* (art of government), Book II, Chapter IV and his brother Vatsyayana's *Kama Sutra* (treatise of fine arts), both were compiled about 312 BC.

(xiii) Megasthenes (300 BC): The ancient writers say almost nothing about Megasthenes. Only Arrian notes that he lived in the house of Sibyrtius, governor of Arachosia (countries round Kandahar). Phylarchos tells us that Chandragupta had sent Seleucus a very curious present. Seleucus also sent Megasthenes to Pataliputra as an ambassador, probably to strengthen the bonds of friendship. Chandragupta's ambassador lived in the court of Seleucus.

Sibyrtius had been governor of Arachosia and Gedrosia, now Mukran coast in 322 BC; again in 316 BC (Diodorus, XVIII, 3; XIX, 48).

In all likelihood, Megasthenes was not present in Alexander's Indian expedition. He came to Pataliputra by the Grand Trunk Road marked by milestones to indicate distance and the by-ways. At the Magadhan capital, he was most cordially received as a friend. He came to his embassy after 305 BC, probably the date of the treaty between Seleucus and Chandragupta. At Pataliputra he lived long, but not continuously, for he went back to his royal master several times to submit his reports (Arrian, V. 6.2). His work called *Ta Indika* was complied about 300 BC mostly from reports and partly from personal experiences. Probably his book had four parts, viz., India and its physical features; Indian manners and customs; Indian nations; and Indian history, gods, and religious institutions. He paid more attention to descriptions than to style and language. His work is lost, but is preserved in fragments by Strabo, Arrian, Diodorus, Pliny, and others.

Of the Greeks, only he and Daimachus were aware of India's correct shape, length and breadth. According to him its breadth = 16,000 stadia [Indus to Pataliputra = 10,000 stadia; thence to sea, according to sailors; 6,000 stadia]. Himalayas to Ceylon is 17,500 stadia but Megasthenes makes it 22,300 stadia—even this is correct in a way. He names fifteen effluents of the Indus, viz., Indos = Sindhu; Hydaspes = Vitasta; Akesenes = Asikni = Chandra bhaga; Hydraotis = Udrawati = Iravati; Hyphasis = Vipasa; Soanos = Suvana; Saranges = Saranga; Cophen = Kabul; Soastos = Suvana; Saranges = Saranga; Cophen = Kabul; Soastos = Suvastu (Swat); Garocas = Pankor ; Peykelaitis = Pushkalavati; Tutapas = Satadru.

Megasthenes alone has given a correct account of the Ganges. Its minimum breadth was eight miles = 66 stadia; average depth 100 to 120 feet. Certainly, the Ganges was very large then. He names fifty-eight rivers of India and nineteen effuents of the Ganges; Sonos = Sona, Eranaboas = Hiranyavaha, Kondokwatis = Gandakavati, Jomanes = Jamuna, Kommenases = Karmanasa, Panzalai = Panchala, Oxymagis = Ikshumati, Andromatis = Andhramati (Tamasa), Cossoanos (Sona)?

Kaukasos = Himalaya, Meros = Meru, Erenuesis = Benaras, Matha = Magadha, Omalis = Bimala, Derdai = Darada (home of the ant-dug gold), Prasioi = Prachya Desa, capital Palibothra = Pataliputra, Saurasenai = Surasena (Muttra District), Methora = Mathura = Mutta, Corisobora = Clisobora = Krishnapura (Agra?), Capitalia = Aravalli and Mount Abu, Pandoeum = Pandya, Taprobane = Tamravarna (Ceylon).

Megasthenes has given a rather complete sketch of India and the Indian life recorded from his own observations and the reports of the well-informed Brahman ministers whom he repeatedly cited as proofs. Though not free from some faults, and mistakes, his book, the best of its kind in that age, exercised great influence on the Greeks and the Romans, and on modern Europe (eighteenth century BC).

As the faithful picture of India of a special period, drawn by an impartial foreign observer, the value of *Ta Indika* is indeed very high.

Megasthenes says that in India, there are:

(a) 118 states, large and small; of them, eight are very powerful. The Prasii, i.e. Magadhas are the most powerful and the foremost nation in India. [This Magadha included also the land of the Kurus and Panchalas as Megasthenes says that the Jamuna flowed through the kingdom of Magadha]. Their capital is at Palibothra (ancient Patna), a flourishing city, nine by two miles, girded with a wooden wall with 64 gates, 570 bastions and a deep ditch in front.

Palibothra for Pataliputra, is not a Greek distortion, but an imitation of corrupt native pronunciation. All foreigners have adopted and used Indian names as they are spoken and not as they are written in classics.

Since 1876, several excavations at ancient Patna have discovered parts of a wooden wall, a long brick-wall, a line of palisades, a gate, two wooden pillars eight or nine feet high, a number of wells, several iron spearheads. Dr Wadell discovered near Kumrahar some relics of an Asoka pillar. At Bulandibag, he discovered the capital of the pillar.

The excavation of 1913 has discovered some remains of Ashoka's palace, some remains of the hall at Kumrahar resembling the hundred–pillared hall at Persepolis, the signs of flood and subsequent fire (probably, first century AD), the brick-built houses of the Gupta period, a *tri-ratna*, a piece of rock with 'bha', inscribed, the middle part of an image of a Bodhi sattva very large and entire, the head of an image of Buddha, a coin of Indra Mittra, two copper coins of Kanishka, a coin of Chandragupta Vikramaditya (AD 375 to 413), eighteen seals, several entire earthen pots found near the wooden gallery.

King Chandragupta of Magadha had a standing army of 6,00,000 soldiers 30,000 horses and 9,000 elephants which indicate the vastness of his resources.

The Calingoe, people of Kalinga, had the entire seaboard from the Ganges to the Krishna. Their capital Parthalis is probably Burdwan now. Its powerful king had 60,000 foot soldiers, 1,000 horses and 700 elephants.

A large island in the Ganges is called Madhya Kalinga which is probably the modern Presidency division and a greater part of the Faridpur district. Our classical *Nava Dwipa*, 'new island in the Ganges' still surviving in a district, perhaps favours this supposition. The king had 50,000 foot soldiers and 4,000 horses. The Mandu and the Malli, lived in the sub-Himalayan region. The people of Gangarashtra, called the Gangerides living near the mouth of the Ganges, were the men of East Bengal. The Ganges then fell into the Bay of Bengal a few miles east of Dacca. Several powerful tribes lived here under a king who had 50,000 foot soldiers 4,000 horses and 400 elephants.

The Andhras, the most powerful nation of the south, had numerous villages, 30 walled towns, 100,000 soldiers, 2,000 horses and 1,000 elephants.

The Isari, Cosyri and other tribes lived in the extreme north-west near Kashmir. The kingdom of Magadha then embraced all north India and touched the frontiers of the Punjab.

In Rajputana the Bhils, Meenas, Kanjars and other wild tribes lived in woods infested by ferocious tigers. However, there were good tribes who lived in the fertile tracts, on the hills of Chitor, and Aravalli. Several tribes lived enclosed by the capital (Mount Abu).

The Horatoe, i.e. the Saurashtras were people of Gujarat. Their capital on the coast was a noble emporium of trade and their king had 1,600 elephants, 150,000 foot soldiers and 5,000 horses.

The Pandoe, people of Pandya in the extreme south were the only race ruled by women. A lunar prince of the Pandu line had gone to the south from Dwaraka and founded a state there. Mathura, now Madura was the capital. The king had 300 towns and an army of 1,50,000 soldiers and 500 elephants. Pliny, VI 23.6 describes their wealth and grandeur.

The Asangoe lived in the country between the Indus and the Jamuna, backed by the desert. Their king had 30,000 soldiers, 800 horses and 300 elephants. Patala was a large triangular island in the Indus near its mouth. Taprobane, ancient Tamrabarna (copper-coloured) is Ceylon. Megasthenes says that a river separated it from the continent. The island had gold, precious stones, pearls, and huge elephants. Aelian, indebted to Megasthenes, says that Ceylon was full of hills, palm-groves and huts of reeds. The people used to carry their elephants in their ships to sell them to the kings of Kalinga.

(b) India abounds in many mountains, hills and vast fertile plains yielding two crops a year.

(c) Towns: The towns in India are reported to be so numerous that they cannot be counted. The towns on the tidal rivers and the sea-coast are mostly wooden. Owing to heavy rains, brick-built houses do not last long. Rivers run over the sides in flood. The towns on hills and high grounds are brick-built or mud-built. Pataliputra is the largest city in India (Arrian's *Indika*, X. see also Strabo, XV I, 35–36).

(d) Fauna and Flora: Megasthenes speaks of the Royal Bengal tigers; elephants and their hunts are described at length. Many monkeys, large dogs, antelopes, electric eel, serpents, winged scorpions, big snakes, oysters, pearl fishery, gold-digging ants, one-horned horses (rhinoceroses?). There are descriptions of ebony growing in Bengal, palm, willow, wild grapes, ivy, laurel, myrtle, box-tree and various marine plants. The variety and plenty of flowers and fruits excited the women of the Greeks (Diodorus, II, 36).

(e) Metals: There is plenty of gold, silver, copper, iron, tin and other metals. They are used for ornaments, utensils and weapons (Diodorus, II, 36). There are also fragrant stones (Strabo). Gold is obtained by mining, by the digging of ants, and by collecting from streams. Ceylon is rich in gold mines.

(f) Indian lifestyle: The Indians are fond of ornaments of gold and precious stones. They raise no stone to the dead whose virtues and fame alone are deemed to be fit as a memorial (*Arrian, Indika*, X). Indians are all free and do not even have slaves of other nations (Strabo, XV, 1.54). They are frugal and temperate in habits, especially in camp; they do not like crowds and are orderly, moderate and regardful of truth and virtue. Thefts are rare. In Chandragupta's camp of four lakh of men, theft of rupees thirty only a day is reported; they possess a strong sense of justice; they never lie, never quarrel. They have perfect mutual trust. They never go to law, never complain about their pledges and deposits, require neither witnesses nor seals; they generally leave their houses unlocked, unguarded. Writing is unknown (?); everything depends on *Smriti* (code, not memory). The Indians are frank, frugal and happy. Their wine is prepared from rice; but they do not drink wine except at sacrifice. Rice and curry make up their staple food. A simple dress (dhuti and chadar), leather shoes and an umbrella make the usual attire. Usury is never practised. Finery is in use. Scarcity of food grains is unknown. They live in wooden houses. The people are fond of gaudy dresses and attendants follow them with umbrellas. Polygamy is prevalent and wives are purchased from their parents in exchange for a yoke of oxen (Strabo, XV, 54).

The penal laws, seldom required to be exercised, are very severe. A false witness suffers mutilation of his extremes. One causing the loss of hand or eye to a workman is put to death (Strabo, XV, 54). Death is also the penalty for the non-payment of tithe on sales. The war laws are very humane and good. The people take physical exercise in several ways. One favourite method is passing smooth ebony rollers on the body.

The following are prohibited—suicide, intermarriage, interdining, change of profession or trade in many articles. Indians dine singly; at no time would they eat together. They decorate the crematoriums on which they raise earth-mounds which are not very high. They use muslin worked in flowers. They honour beauty and try every art to improve their looks. They do not respect age without wisdom (cf. Manu, II, 156). They do not wear a garland to sacrifice. Their sacrificial beasts are not cut in two, but strangled, for the beasts are then offered to the gods entire.

Megasthenes further observed the treatment of sick elephants, the seven castes of the people, the Brahmans, philosopher, Germani (Hindi *Sramans*, not Buddhist), different stages of life, Hindu and Greek gods alike, culture of philosophy, astrologers' council of spring declaring annual forecasts, magicians, flourishing agriculture, irrigation, the stalwart and robust people, survey of lands, military and municipal boards, expert physicians, the intelligence department, spies, prostitute-spies, royal hunt, female guards, paid Indian soldiers in the Persian army, royal marine department, shipwrights, five elements calendar, rain of copper dust, wonderful caves, various horses, musical instruments, workship of gods, temples, drains and drainage, the next world, Indian as the cradle-house of the Hindus, muslin, pearls, formations of land, constant change of the royal bed, female education, inheritance by sons, the practice of sati, and the Indian stories (Strabo, p. 711; Pliny, VII, 2, 14, *Chapter* 22; Solinus, Chapter 52).

As for his account of the marvellous, we cannot blame Megasthenes. From Homer downwards, all the Greek writers on India adopted many Indian fables and unreal beings. Dr Schwanbeck says that the Indians magnified the ugly features and the physical defects of the various non-Aryans. That is the root of the one-eyed, three-eyed, mouthless, noseless, dog-faced tribes.

The *Mahabharata*, Book I, Chapter 28; Court Book, Chapter 31, Shlokas, 66-67; Salya Book, Chapter 46, Court Book Chapters 31 and 52; Sleep Book, Chapter 8, verses 129–32; Court Book, Chapter 51, verses 17–18; also *Ramayana* and *Harivansa* describe such beings.

The probable truth is that the aborigines and the non-Aryans of most of ancient India had strange physical defects but intercourse with the Aryans has gradually improved their types and features. The Phoenicians took their accounts to Asia Minor where the Greeks first learnt them. Homer's use of Indian tales in his epics probably originated in this way.

(g) Religion: The Macedonians believed in the identity of Hindu and Greek gods. Siva was their Dionysios and Krishna,

Hercules. They further believed that their two great gods had come to India, conquered it and taught the people various arts. Euripides described it by imagination. Megasthenes also gives similar accounts. Dr Schwanbeck says that the age was extremely credulous. The workship of Siva and Vishnu was very old in India. The Greeks up to Megasthenes knew nothing of Buddhism. Megasthenes tried to study Hinduism minutely, but his account is meagre, 'The Brahmans are never swayed by weal and woe. They often discourse on death. They think that this life is but a stepping-stone to brighter life and light in future. They never teach their wives philosophy. They do not like the material world much. Like the Greeks they say that the world is created, destructible, round, and is composed of five elements; it is the work of one Maker. The earth is at the centre of the universe. Birth, soul and other points are the same as with the Greeks. Like Plato, they hold soul immortal.'

Megasthenes may have written a chapter on Indian literature, but it has vanished altogether. His successor Daimachus was ambassador under Bindusara. His work on India also it totally lost. The short accounts of Patroclus, Eratoshenes and others tell us nothing new. The Ashokan edicts II and XIII also tell us of ancient civilisation.

TRADE

During the period under review, Indian trade, both inland and foreign, was brisk. India's foreign trade consisted of the following branches: Indo-Babylonian, Indo-Ceylonic, Indo-Malayan, and Indo-Chinese. Besides the sea-routes, there were overland caravan routes from India to Central Asia, China and the Levant Sea. The Indian merchants carried on trade with Assyria and China under the so-called Embassy System: the black obelisk of Shalmanaswer II and the Chinese records show this. Indian merchants settled at Alexandria, then the chief market of the world. Indian trade with Egypt continued under thc Ptolemies. One Greek writer says that the Indians procured immense gold from abroad. Indian goods were also carried to the shores of the Black Sea and the Caspian Sea along the Oxus. The trade routes once covered Asia like a network.

(For a full description, see Professor Heeren's *Historical Researches* [*Asiatic Nations*], vol. II, *Appendix XIIII* and *IX*).

Yet, it must be borne in mind that the Hindu maritime activity in the West was not very great and it declined gradually. At first the Egyptians, the Assyrians and the Arabs were prominent. Then the Phoenicians, the Jews and the Greeks became supreme. Nearchus (fourth century BC), Agatharchides (second century BC) and others say that trade was entirely in the hands of the Arabs.

Phoenician Trade with Indian

The Phoenicians, Latin Phoeni, Rig-Vedic *Pani* (trader) were an Aryan tribe living originally to the north of India. In the Deva-Asura war, they had helped the Asuras (thirtieth century BC). These allies, at first triumphant, were finally defeated and driven out by Indra. The Asuras under their leaders Vritra and Bala, founded states in Ancient Persia and Turkey (Mesopotamia, Sanskrit Madhya-Bhumika or Vedika). The *Panis* settled in a tract on the Levant Sea (2800 BC) and built their city Tyre about 2750 BC. Our Indian Indra had driven and not destroyed them; but the Greek Indra, I mean, Alexander the Great, annihilated them in the fourth century BC.

The Phoenicians were traders and most enterprising navigators from the earliest times. 'They aimed at the empire of the sea and actually possessed it. (Dr Robertson's *History of America, Introduction*). Tyre became the crowing city whose merchants were princes, whose traffickers, the honourable of earth (Isaiah, XXIII, 8). This mart of nations (*ibid.* 3) had all sorts of rich articles from precious stones to 'purple and broidered work (Ezekiel, XXVII, 16)'.

The Pheonicians came out to India not later than the thirteenth century BC. The former commerce of Pheonicia had three branches, viz., Arabian–Indian, the Egyptian and the Assyrio–Babylonian. Of these, the first is most important. They came to India by the Red Sea route and also by the caravan route from the shores of the Persian Gulf to the Mediterranean coast of Syria. Several good harbours of the Arabian Gulf were seized by the Pheonicians from the Idumeans. But the distance from that Gulf of Tyre being very great, they afterwards occupied the nearest Mediterranean port called Rhinocolura. Thither were taken overland all the articles to be re-shipped to Tyre (Robertson's, *Disquistion, pp.* 7–8).

'Long before the Persians had made themselves masters of Babylon (561 BC), the Phoenicians had established themselves for pearl-fishery and the Indian trade on the isles of Tylos and Aradus, the modern Bahrein Islands in the Persian Gulf.' (Dr Royle's *Essay*, p. 122).

The twenty-seventh chapter of Ezekiel gives a list of the articles of Pheonician commerce brought from various countries. It is now difficult to ascertain whether those were purely Indian. It is probably that cinnamon, aloes, onyx, agate, gold, diamond, ebony, ivory, timber, tin, embroidered work, rich apparel, cardamom, nard and other spices used in odoriferous waters and unguents were imported from India.

Proof:

(i) The large counties to which the Pheonician trade extended beyond Dedan—'The Bahrein Island'—Dr Royle's Essay, p. 122—could be no other than India; if this is not sufficiently proved by the situation, it is beyond doubt, by the commodities mentioned. Ivory and ebony could only have been procured in Dedan from India, for, there were no elephants in Arabia, (*Historians' History of the World, vol. II, pp. 336–37*). Ivory, Sanskrit ibharada=elephant's tooth and ebony are ascribed to India by the classical authors, vide Megasthenes (Strabo, XV, 37). Theophrastus quoted by Mc-Crindle in his *India as Desribed by Classical Authors*, p. 46; Virgil's Georgics, 1, 57' India sends ivory' II, 116–17, 'India alone produces black ebony' (Horace's Odes, I. 31).

(ii) Sanskrit names in Latin and Greek. Indigo, literally the blue dye of India; *Oryza,* Sanskrit Vrihi, English rice; Karpasos; Carbasus, Herbrew Karpas, English Canvas = Sanskrit Karpasa (cotton); Sachchra, English sugar = Sanskrit Sarkara; Piper, English pepper = Sanskrit pippala; Zingibery, English ginger = Sanskrit Sringa-wera; Agallachun or lingum aguila = Sanskrit agura.

Sindon (cotton fabrics), i.e. cotton of India; Sandalum = Sanskrit Chandana, Nardus, English nard; Sanskrit nalada, Malobathra = Sanskrit Tmbula – patra. Kassiteros (Homer) = Sanskrit Kastira (tin). Beryl = Baidurya. Tamarind = Tamari-Hind = Sanskrit intiry. Aurum = Swarnam (gold) [vide Gotz quoted in the *Encyclopaedia Biblica, vol. IV, Art, Trade Commerce.*]

(iii) Homer's references to the skill of the Sidonian artists such as the 'silver vase' (II, XXIII, lines 865–70...Pope), the garment offered by Hecuba to Minerva as a propitiatory gift (II, VI, lines 358–67...Pope). Sir George Birdwood and others confidently state that these articles of luxury though latterly produced in Sidon, came originally from India. 'The twelve costly carpets of refulgent hue', 'the garments stiff of gold' (II, XXIV, lines 281–4...Pope)—had their originals in the Indian Kincobs and Sataranjis which have, from time immemorial, been articles of western trade. In his *Industrial Arts of India*, pp. 263–64, Sir George Birdwood says of the costly garments that 'they are photographic vignettes from any wealthy India's house and in copying them, one seems to breathe again the very odour of the costly spikenard with which they are usually wrapped up.'

The Pheonician influence on history is great. Their position was due to their circulation of the cultures of the eastern lands to western countries than to their own creations (*Historians' History of the World, vol. II, p. 353*). Indirectly America owes its discovery to Pheonicia (ibid., p. 356).

Jewish Trade with India

The fortune of the Phoenicians soon roused in the neighbouring Jews a spirit of emulation. The Jews had inland trades and the *Old Testament* in some passages refers to extensive caravan routes. Yet, the Jews were not very active before the days of David and Solomon.

Luckily, the Jews under David and Solomon were great friends of the Phoenicians under Hiram (980 to 917 BC). Close friendship, instead of base rivalry, of those two ancient peoples produced their combined commercial enterprise. David conquered Idumoea in 1040 BC (II. Samuel VIII. 14). Solomon founded a seaport at Ezion-Gaber (992 BC)—vide I Kings, IX, 26. Solomon took building material from India (997 BC). From Ezion-Gaber, the ships of Solomon sailed under the guidance of the mariners of Hiram for distant lands (I Kings, IX, 27). They brought back once in three years the gold of Ophir (India, Coptic so far, originally sauvira), a seaboard tract in west India. [I Kings. X II & 22], its almug trees (perhaps red sandalwood), ivory, ape (kapi), and peacocks.

The impetus given by Solomon lasted a century or more. The Jewish commercial spirit gradually cooled. The fleet of Jehoshaphat, fifth in descent from Solomon, which had started on a voyage to Tarshis, was destroyed. After this, Jewish foreign trade came to a halt altogether.

The Assyrian Commerce

'Babylon occupied a favourable position for peaceful commerce. A glance at the map shows that Mesopotamia occupies the very centre of the world of ancient civilisation. It was the connecting link between Persia and India on the one hand and Lydia, Syria and Egypt on the other. Even Chinese ideas were to some extent accessible through the mediation of India.' (*H.H.W. vol. I, p. 472*).

'The pictures on the black obelisk of Shalmansaser II show us such beasts as apes and elephants, being brought as tribute to the conqueror, confirming in the most unequivocal way the belief, based on Ktesias and Strabo that the Assyrians held commercial relations with India.' (*ibid, p.* 484). 'The muslin of Dacca was famous in Roman and even Assyrian times' (Lee–Warner's *Citizen of India*).

'The investigation, however, is involved in greater difficulties as we proceed towards the east beyond Persia; through a principal country to which they traded, i.e. Persian India—or the present Belurland and with the parts adjacent, whence the Babylonians imported many of their most highly prized commodities, afford a clear proof, of the direction and extent of this commerce. The first article which we may confidently assert the Babylonians to have obtained at least in part from these countries were precious stones used for seals were obtained in the mountains bordering on the sandy desert. The testimonies of modern travellers have proved that the account of this author is entitled to full credit; and that even at the present time, the lapis lazuli is found there in its greatest perfection and if it be added to this that what Ktesias relates of India undoubtedly refers for the most part to these northern countries, we must consider it probably that the stones. In question were found in the mountains of which we are speaking, while with regard to sapplire of the ancients, that is to say, our lapis lazuli I have no doubt that it is a native of the country.'

The passage of Ktesias to which we have referred contains some indications which, relatively to onyxes appear to refer to the Ghat mountains, since he speaks of a hot country not far from the sea.

'The circumstance of large quantities of onyxes coming out of these mountains at the present day, viz.—the mountains near Cambay and

Broach, the ancient Barygaza, must render this opinion so much the amore probably, as it was this very part of the Indian coast with which the ancients were most acquainted. And, their navigation from the Persian Gulf to these regions, as will be shown hereafter, admits of no doubt. This opinon, however, must not lead us to conclude that the commerce of Babylon was confined to those countries; for that they were acquainted with the above-mentioned northern districts is equally certain, hence also the Babylonians imported Indian dogs. The native country of these animals according to Ktesias, was that whence precious stones were obtained. And, this account of the regions has been confirmed by Marco Polo who mentions that the large dogs of these regions were even able to overcome lions.

'A third and no less certain class of productions which the Persians and Babylonians obtained from this part of the world were dyes and amongst them the cochineal or rather, Indian *lacca*. The most ancient, though not quite accurate description of this insect and of the tree upon which it settles, is also found in Ktesias. According to him, it is a native of the country near the sources of the Indus and produces a red, resembling cinnabar. The Indians themselves use it for the purpose of dyeing their garments to which it gives a colour even surpassing in beauty the dyes of the Persians.'

Strabo has presented for us from Eratothenes a knowledge of the roads by which the commodities of the Indian districts bordering the Persian empire, were conveyed to its principal cities and especially to Babylon.

'The natives of the countries bordering Little Tibet and others of the Northern Indians of Herodotus and Ktesias, formed the caravans which travelled into the gold desert and it was the same people from whom western Asia obtained ingredients for dyeing and also the finest wool.' (*Historians' History of the World, vol I, pp. 487–90*).

'From Babylon, the Indian wares were conveyed to the shores of the Mediterranean.' (*ibid.*, p. 490).

Egyptian trade with India under the Ptolemies

Alexander the Great had founded Alexandria at the mouth of the Nile in Africa. 'With its countless masts and joisy quays, its motley crowd of foreigners and hubbub of all dialects from India to Cadiz, its vast piles of merchandise lying unsheltered in that rainless air, Alexandria soon rose to be a mart of the world and successfully held its superiority for centuries to come.' (Kingsley's *Hypaia* V).

Having got Egypt as his share, Ptolemy the First, a General of Alexander, made Alexandria his seat of government. He had visited India with Alexander and knew the full advantages of a commercial intercourse with that rich land. So, he at once directed his attention to naval affairs. He built the famous lighthouse at Pharos on the mouth of the bay of Alexandria which was dangerous to navigation. Unluckily he died soon. His son and successor Ptolemy Philadelphus gave great impetus to Indian commerce. He sent an embassy headed by Dionysos to Ashoka, Emperor of Magadha, to open up trade with India. He maintained a well-furnished navy in the Red Sea and founded the seaports of Berenice and Myos Hormos on the Egyptian coast. For easy transport of goods, he began constructing a canal joining the Nile with the Red Sea, but it was never completed. Ships trading with India arrived at Myos Hormos from where all goods were taken on camels on the 12th to Coptus, a city on a canal of the Nile and thence to Alexandria by water in another twelve days. Owing to great heat, the caravans crossed the desert at night. There were resting places on the road (Pliny, Natural History, VI, 23; Vincent's Periplus, vol. I, p. 80). The seaborne trade continued to be conveyed along the coast from Bereince round the south coast of Arabia and Persia to the mouth of the Indus.

Besides the Red Sea route, there were at least three overland routes by which Indian goods were carried to foreign markets. One ran across Cenral Asia along the Oxus, the Caspian and the Black Seas. The second lay through the heart of Persia over to the neck of Asia Minor, while the third was through the Persian Gulf and the Euphrates to Damascus and Tadmore and thence to the ports of the Levant.

The trade along Tadmore (Palmyra) was a very ancient one. It rose to great opulence. As the only green spot in the desert and for its fine location, Tadmore rose even in the times of Solomon, its founder (I Kings, IX, 18; II Chronicle, VIII A) and her opulence lasted down to the date of its conquest by Aurelian. Professor Heeren thinks that the Persian Gulf was closed to Indian trade in the time of the Pyrthian Empire, the articles being then conveyed along the Red Sea to Myos Hormos and thence overland to Palmyra (*Historical Researches* [*Asia*], *vol. II. P. 409*). The route was reopened in the days of the Roman Empire

(Appain, V. 9, McCrindle, *Horace, Ep. I. 45*). The Black Sea trade also was an early one and rose very high under the Byzantine emperors.

COLONIES

Commerce took Hindu civilisation and colonists abroad. In 500 to 400 BC, the emigrations of the Aryans extended to the Deccan, Ceylon and other adjacent islands. The pearls and corals found in those places gave a new impetus to trade. 'The emigrations of expatriated Indians took place in very early times and towards the west.' (Elliot's *History. I Appendix*, p. 507). Traces of Indian occupancy are found in the north-eastern shores of the Euxine (*ibid.*, p. 510). Indians settled in Persia, Mesopotamia, Arabia, Alexandria, Carthage and elsewhere; missionaries, merchants, mercenaries, mahouts, Hindu sanyasins of old used to travel over a large part of the world. The Buddhist monks lived in Persia, Turkey, Syria, Palestine, Egypt, Greece, and other countries of Europe. The *Bimala Prabha* tells us that the saying of Buddha were translated into Persian and Roomba (Latin?).

India also received foreign colonies. The Persians settled in different parts of India (*Mahabharata* and Purana), the Jews in Malabar, the Arabians in Malabar, Ceylon and Chittagong. These emigrations much helped the diffusion of knowledge and the interchange of ideas.

Modern scholarship speaks of the Hindu source of Greek science. India was for a long time the teacher of Europe, both directly and indirectly, in medicine, mathematics, philosophy, and other branches of human knowledge. Alexander and his officers found India as the home of medical and aromatic plants and herbs and praised the excellence of Brahmanic philosophy. Indian medicine had largely influenced the Greek healing art before Alexander. The works of Hippocrates, the 'Father of Medicine', and a contemporary of Ktesias, show traces of a distinct influence of the Hindu pharmacopoeia. He prescribes the two kings of pepper—long and round—for nearly the same maladies for which they are still used by the Indian *kavirajas* (Dr Royle's *Essay, p.* 89). The motto on his sign-board, viz., 'Life is short, art is long, opportunity fleeting', is also a distinct echo of a well-known Sanskrit text. Probably, he never came to India; certainly he got his ideas about Indian medicine in Persia which had a direct intercourse for a long time with India and Greece.

In philosophy and metaphysics, the European thinkers still work on Hindu materials. Many have thought it highly possible that so long as philosophy was cultivated in Greece, India was often regarded as the ultimate and permanent source of the true wisdom, the knowledge of things divine. Even as late as Lucian's time (AD 150, that author concludes his evidently true history of Antiphilus and Demetrius by making the latter a cynical philosophere by profession, resign all his property to his friend and depart for India, there to end his life amongst the Brahmans (*Toxaris* 34, quoted in *'Gnostics and their Remains,' p. 54*).

The stiking resemblance between some systems of Hindu and Greek philosophy and mathematics has already been noted.

3

FIRST FOREIGN RULE IN INDIA

The *Vishnu Purana* states that after the Andhras (AD 236) there shall be seven Abhiras, ten Gardabhas, ten Gardabhas, sixteen Sakas, eight Yavanas, fourteen Tusharas, thirteen Mundas, eleven Hunas, eleven Pauras (ruling 300 years), and Kailakila Javanas (106 years); after this confusion, shall come the Gupta Dynasty of Magadha.

By the light of modern research, we can re-arrange this confused list in the following correct and chronological order: After the Mauryans, there shall be eight Yawanas, i.e. Indo-Greeks; thirteen Maurundas, i.e. Indo-Parthians (Morundoe of Ptolemy); sixteen Sakas or Indo-Scythians; the Andhras of the south, winning the eastern part of north India, and their branch called the Andhra Bhrityas, also called Abhiras—seven in all, in Western India; ten Gardabhas or Gardabhilas, i.e. Kadphises; fourteen Tusharas, i.e. Tocharis or Kushans; the Guptas of Magadha; the Hunas; the Pauravas of Kanouj, (AD) 500 to 800); the Kailakila Javanas or the early Mussalmans of Sindh and Multan.

After Dasaratha, grandson to Ashoka, five princes succeeded, namely, Sangata, Salisuka, Somasarman, Satadhanvan and Vrihadratha. Garga, an astronomer of the first century BC alludes to Salisuka in his work. Mentioning Salisuka (200 BC), the fourth successor of Ashoka, Garga adds: 'When the viciously valiant Greks, after reducing Saketa (Oudh), the Panchala (the country about Kanouj) and Mathura, will reach Kusuma-dhvaja, i.e. the royal residence of Pataliputra, then all the provinces will be in disorder. (Max Müeller's *India*, p. 298).'

The descendants of Ashoka retained only Magadha and the neighbouring home provinces. The Andhra protected state was probably the first to throw off the nominal yoke and soon grew into a powerful kingdom stretching right across India. Till 25 BC, their power was, however, confined to the Deccan. The last king of the Imperial Mauryan line—Vrihadratha, a weak prince, was treacherously murdered by his commander-in-chief Pushyamitra—the Indian Macbeth.

The descendants of Ashoka continued to rule—unrecorded —in Magadha for many centuries. The last of them, Purna Varman, was nearly contemporary with Yuan Chwang in the seventh century AD (Beal, *Records, II, 118, 174; Watters, II, 115*).

Minor Mauryan dynasties, connected with the Imperial line, ruled in Konkan, Chitor and other parts of India during the sixth, seventh and eighth centuries AD. They are often mentioned in inscriptions (*Fleet, Dynasties of the Canarese Districts, 2nd edition; Bombay Gazetteer, vol. I, Part II, 1896, pp. 282–84*).

Nanda, Chandragupta and Ashoka seem to me like Babar, Akbar and Aurangzeb. Ashoka little thought how his religious zeal verging on fanatics, his theocracy, and his partition undermined the strength of the empire. His death was welcome news to the Brahmans of north India, to the powerful Andhras of the south and to the enemies of India outside.

The Mauryan control up to the Hindukush became weak soon after Ashoka's death. The North-West Frontier, ever exposed to foreign attack, now became a tempting field to the Greek princes of Bactria, Parthia and the warlike races on the borders. India and Italy have suffered terribly for their 'unhappy gifts of beauty'. From 200 BC downward, we have had a succession of invaders from abroad.

THE INDO-GREEK DYNASTY: HINDU YAVANAS, 250 BC TO AD 60

After the death of Alexander (323 BC), his vast empire was seized by his generals. Antigonus seized the Asiatic possessions. Seleucus fought with him and wrested the countries of Asia and built a very powerful monarchy, comprising Asia Minor, Pheonicia, Persia, Afghanistan, Baluchistan, a part of India, and Bactria. We have seen that Chandragupta had driven out and destroyed the Greek garrisons and occupied as far as the Persian frontier. Seleucus Nicator, i.e. conqueror, could not recover these Indian possessions and made friends with Chandragupta. Seleucus was murdered in 280 BC. His son Antiochos Sotor died in a battle with the Gauls in 261 BC. The vast dominions of Seleucus now passed to his grandson Antiochos Theos (god), a drunken sensualist who was even worshipped as a god. This worthless king ruled for fifteen or sixteen years. Two grievous losses happened towards the close of his reign—the revolt of Bactria under Diodotos and that of the Partians under Arsakes.

Bactria, now Russiatic Turkistan, was our Balhika or Bakshu Desa, a home of the Aryans in Central Asia. It was a rich plain, watered by the Oxus and occupied by civilized people from time immemorial. This country of 1,000 towns was always regarded as the foremost satrapy and was reserved as an appendage for a prince of the royal blood. Alexander continued from Persia his royal favours to the Bactrians who readily received and assimilated the Greek civilisation. It was one of the most valuable possessions of Seleucus, his son and grandson.

Diodotos, a heroic Greek, became governor of Bactria about 256 BC; about 250 BC after successful revolt, he became king of Bactria and ruled the 1,000 towns from Bulkh, his capital. His dynasty lasted from 250 to 176 BC. Diodotos II succeeded his father Diodotos I in 245 BC and entered into an alliance with the Parthian King.

THE INDO-PARTHIANS (250 TO AD 60)

Hindus probably called them Maurunds—the Morundoe of Ptolemy. The Parthians, a race of rude and hardy nomadic horsemen, dwelt beyond the Persian deserts south-east of the Caspian Sea. Their country Chorasmisi (Khwarizm), Sogdioi (Samarkhand) and Arioi (Heart) formed the 16th satrapy of Darius. All the tribes supplied contingents to the host of Xerses (Herodotus, *iii, 93; 117; vii. 64–66)*.

Alexander and the early Seleukidoe formed Parthia and Hyrkania into a satrapy. The Parthians never adopted the Greek culture. Though subject to the Persian and the Macedonian masters, yet they retained their own habits. They were equally skilled in the management of the steeds and the use of the bow (Justin,. *XLI, Chpater 4)*.

The Parthian struggle—a national rising under Arsakes—lasted from 250 to 248 BC. The Parthian independence was however, established in

248 BC. The Arsakidan dynasty, founded in Persia, lasted for about 500 years (248 BC to AD 226). The success of the Greeks and the Parthians was made easy by the war of succession after Autiochos Theos.

Diodotos II was followed by Euthydemos of Magnesia and of a different family (230 BC). He gained the crown by a successful rebellion and engaged in a long continued war with Antiochus the Great of Syria (223 to 187 BC), resulting in a treaty (208 BC) granting independence to Bactria. In 206 BC, Antiochus crossed the Hindukush and forced the Hindu king Subhagasena of Kabul to surrender a considerable number of elephants and a large treasure. Leaving Androsthenes of Cyzicus to collect this war indemnity, Antiochus in person led his main force homeward by the Kandahar route (Polybius, XI, 34).

Demetrios, son of Euthydemos and son-in-law of Antiochus, repeated his father-in-law's exploits with still greater success and conquered a considerable portion of north India, including Kapisa, Kabul, the Punjab and Sindh (196 BC). Thus, the unsatiated ambition of Alexander and the vigorous but vain attempts of Seleucus began to be realised. Eukratides, finding Demetrios engaged in the far Indian wars, rebelled against Demetrios and made himself master of Bactria about 175 BC. He waged many wars with the surrounding states and tribes, with varying success but unvarying spirit. Demetrios lost Bactria, but long held his eastern conquests. Hence, he was called 'King of the Indians'. Vrihadratha, the last worthless Mauryan ruler of Pataliputra could not beat the Greeks back. On the contrary, he sent a large hoard in gold to buy off Demetrios. This only intensified the thirst of the Greeks. To prevent the Greeks from further encroachments, Vrihadratha again sent a large treasure to Demetrios in the frontier; but on the way, it was plundered by Pushyamitra, the young leader of the Hindus of north India, roused against the Mauryan rule. Vrihadratha was, however, wise enough to admit the Hindu claims and appointed Pushyamitra commander-in-chief of the imperial forces. The heroic Brahman soon checked the further advance of the Greeks. Vrihadratha showered honours and favours on him.

Secure at Bactria, Eukratides next turned against Demetrios in India. A severe struggle followed (160 to 156 BC) in which Eukratides became victorious. It is said that once shut up for five months in a fort, with only 300 men, he succeeded in repelling the attack of Demetrios whose force was 60,000 strong (Justin, XLI 6). But the hard won triumph was short-lived. On his home journey from India, he had his eldest son Appollodotos with him. This vile wretch murdered his father, drove the chariot through the blood and even refused the honour of burial to the corpse (156 BC). Thereafter Appollodotos became king of the Punjab. Heliokles, another son to Eukratides, succeeded in Bactria and ruled for a few years precariously.

Strato I, probably of the family of Eukratides, succeeded Appollodotos in the Punjab. Agathokles and Pantaleon's coins, specially Indian in character abound. They were contemporary with Euthydemos and Demetrios. Indian borderland was now parcelled amongst a crowd of Greek princelings.

THE SUNGA DYNASTY (178 TO 69) AND THE KANVA DYNASTY (69 BC TO 25 BC)

At the instigation of the Brahmans, Pushpa or Pushyamitra treacherously slew his master, imprisoned the minister, usurped the throne, proclaimed himself king and founded the Sunga or Mitra dynasty. Banabhatta, in his *Life of Harshavardhana* (seventh century AD) alludes to it thus: 'And reviewing the whole army under the pretext of showing him his forces, the mean General Pushyamitra crushed his master Vrihadratha Maurya who was weak of purpose'. (Dr Buhler's translation in the *Indian Antiquary*, II, 363).

Extent of the Kingdom

Pataliputra continued to be the capital of the Sungas. Perhaps all the central or home provinces accepted their authority. The kingdom extended to the south up to River Narmada.

Proof:

'The Queen of Agnimitra, son of Pushyamitra, had a brother Virasena by name, of inferior caste, who was placed by the king in command of a frontier fortress on the banks of the Mandakini, Narmada.' (Introduction to *Malavika Agnimitra*). Besides, it embraced Bihar, Tirhoot and the modern United Provinces of Agra and Oudh. The Punjab was probably long lost to the later Mauryas and the Sungas. Pushyamitra's rule was disturbed by two great invasions from the east and the west:

(i) Invasion from the west (158 BC): Mahamegha Vahana Kharavela Kshemaraja, a powerful Jain king of Kalinga, capital Kalinganagami (Bhuvanesvar?) tried, like Ashoka, to establish a religious kingdom about 160 BC, led an expedition towards the west and obtained alliance of the Rastrikas. In 158 BC he attacked Magadha, won some success and humbled his foe. But his temporary success affected only the eastern Bihar where numerous instances of Jain influence still exist. His inscriptions at the door of the Elephant Cave of Khandagiri, Orissa, was published by Dr Luders in *Epics of India, vol. X, pp. 160–61*; and desciphered by Dr Bhagwanlal Indraji. The kingdom of Kalinga was afterwards absorbed in the Andhra empire.

(ii) The Greek invasion from the west (155 to 53 BC): Menander, a relative of the Bactrian king, Eukratides and king of Kabul and the Punjab, wishing to play the part of a second Alexander, advanced with a formidable force, crossed the Hyphasis at which Alexander's advance was arrested and (Kathiawar) and Sigerdis, probably Sanskrit, Sagara Desa (seaboard tracts). The author of the Periplus (AD 77?) noted the currency of the coins of Appollodotos and Menander was compelled to retire from the Gangetic Valley, his rule must have continued long in the countries on the west coast. Menander conquered Mathura on the Jamuna, besieged Madhyamika (Mewar), invaded Saketa (Ayodhya) and threatened even Pataliputra. But Pushyamitra repulsed him after a severe struggle. Menander was obliged to retire to his own country. He retained his conquests in western India for some years more. India was not attacked again by a European before Vasco da Gama in AD 1502.

Madhyamika, literally central region, was a part of the ancient Sibi country. Its former capital was Nagari, eleven miles north of Chitor (Madhyamika = Madhya Pata = Medpaat = modern Mewar). The Mauryans ruled at Nagari and then at Chitor till AD 724 when Mahendraditya Bappa Rao seized it from the Moris and founded the present house of the Ranas of Mewar.

For reference, see Strabo XI, section XI, 1; XV, section ii, 3; the *Periplus*; Patanjali's grammar mentions the siege of Saketa, the city of Ayodhya; Ind. Ant., VII 226; Cunningham's Report *VI, 201; XIV, 146*; the astronomer Garga's *Sambita*.

Menander went back to his capital at Kabul where he devoted his energies to the quarrels with his neighbours on the frontier. He enjoyed high fame as a just ruler. When dead, he was honoured with magnificent obsequies. He was a convert to Buddhism. His name is immortalised in a famous dialogue entitled, The *Questions of Milinda* (Pali *Milinda Panha*), a most notable book in Buddhist literature. The form, Milindra occurs in the *Avdanakalpalata* of Kshemendra.

The latter Greek rulers of India were gradually being Hinduised and became worshippers of Hindu gods. The Greek pillar discovered at Bes, an old town in the Gwalior dominions, was erected by Heliodorus, a worshipper of Vishnu, during the rule of the Greek king Antial or Bhasa.

The crown-prince, Agnimitra ruled as a viceroy from the capital Vidisa (now, Bhilsa) on the Betwa (Sanskrit, Betravati), in Sindhia's dominions. Agnimitra in a local war with the raja of Vidarbha (Berar), completely defeated the raja who ceded half of his dominions. The River Barada (Warda) formed the boundary between the two states. Pushpamitra now old, claimed the honour of lord paramount of north India. The Brahmans, in their jubilation, urged Pushpamitra to celebrate the horse sacrifice. The horse was let loose under Vasumitra, his grandson. He had a collision with the Greeks on the Sindh (not the Indus) that formed the boundary between Bundelkhand and Rajwara. These Greeks were a part of Menander's army which had undertaken the siege of Madhyamika (Mewar). After a sharp conflict, the Greeks were completely routed by Vasumitra. The horse came back victorious from every direction. An imperial sacrifice and a horse sacrifice were magnificently performed by Pushpamitra under the guidance and presidentship of his Guru Patanjali, the noted commentator of Panini's grammar. Pushpamitra tried his best to revive the Brahmanical faith. His sacrifice was rather a Brahmanic victory over the Buddhists. Buddhist writers have branded Pushpamitra as a persecutor. It is alleged that he burnt monasteries and slew monks from Magadha to Jullundhar in Punjab. There may be some truth in it. The motive of Pushpamitra's persecution probably was that there was a widespread Buddhist and Jain conspiracy against him.

After a long and evenful reign, Pushpamitra died in 148 BC and was succeeded by Agnimitra, the viceroy of the south. He reigned but a few years and was succeeded by Sujyestha, perhaps a brother, who ruled seven years and was followed by Vasumitra, the guard of the horse. He was very brave, active and warlike. The next four reigns covered only seventeen years. It was a period of confusion during which palace revolutions were frequent. Sumitra, a son of Agnimitra, was inordinately devoted to the stage and was surprised in the midst of his favourite actors by one Mitradeva, who severed his head with a scimitar. The nineth king, Bhagavat had a reign of twenty-six years, barren of events. The tenth king Devabhuti was a man of licentious habits and lost his life while engaged in a discreditable intrigue. Thus ended the dynastry after 109 solar (112 lunar) years.

'In a frenzy of passion, the over-libidinous Sunga was at the instance of his minister, Vasudeva, reft of his life by a daughter of Devabhuti's slave-woman, disguised as his queen.' (Bana's *Harshacharita, Chapter* VI). Vasudeva founded the Kanva dynasty of four kings ruling only forty-five lunar (44 solar) years. The low figures show that the times were disturbed and succession effected by violent means. We know nothing of the Kanvas in particular. About 25 BC, the last Kanva—Susarman, was slain by an Andhra prince not yet known. The Sunga and the Kanva were two Brahmanic dynasties, ruling for 153 years. Their political importance was not very great, but Sanskrit, Brahmanism, and letters were revived to a marvellous extent, and the overweening spirit of the Buddhists was pruned down. So far only two inscriptions of the Sunga dynasty have been found (see Luder's *List, nos. 687, 688; Ep. Indica, vol. x, p. 65)*.

The jubilation of the Hindus following the splendid victories of their champion Pushpamitra, over the Greeks and Buddhism, was sadly crossed by appalling news of new enemies in the north-west of India. These were the Sakas or Scythaians of Central Asia. Some Aryans remained in their old home after the repeated dispersions. Their descendants, afterwards mingled with the Mongolians and the Turks, became known as the Schythians. They grew very powerful, and overturned the Greek rule of Bactria. Some of them invaded Europe.

About the middle of the second century BC, the Scythians were driven out from Central Asia by Yuechis, a people to the north-west of China. Now, the Scythians poured on India in overwhelming numbers. They were barbarians, notorious for their corrupt manners. The Puranas mention eighteen Indo-Scythian kings. They ruled in the north-western part of India for many years under the Persian title of Satraps (viceroys). The Scythians had certainly occupied and ruled a considerable part of India and their outlandish manners had filled the whole land with consternation. At last, the great Hindu champion, Vikramaditya of Ujjain, aided by the brave Malwans and other Hindu allies drove back the Scythians to the north-western parts of the country. The ancestors of Vikrama, Scythian in origin but now thorough Hindus, had entered and settled in India centuries ago. Before their occupation of Malwa, they probably lived in Anandapur near Udaipur (Mewar). At some opportune time, Gandharvasena seized the throne of Ujjain and ruled there in the first century BC. He was succeeded by his eldest son Sanku who ruled for a short time and then fell a victim to the ambition of his brother Vikrama who made some conquests and consolidated a pretty large kingdom. After some years, leaving the reigns of government to his younger brother, Bhartrihari—the noted poet—he himself went out in the guise of an ascetic, to study India and Indian politics. Several years after, Bhartihari, disgusted with the world through a family calamity, left the raj to the ministers and passed into religious retirement. Hearing this, Vikrama hastened to his capital, organised a powerful army, beat back the Scythians and the Parthians, made ample conquests in north India. His power in the south did not extend beyond the Narmada. As he was a great patron of Hindu learning and religion, scholars flocked to his court. His was the famous 'court of nine gems,' a happy product of the Brahmanical revival. An era, called the Malwan era, was reckoned from the birth of Vikrama (57 to 56 BC) whom the Hindus now called Vikramaditya—'a very sun in prowess'. Tradition asserts that he was killed by Salivahana, a prince of the south. He probably ruled till AD 15 or AD 20. He was succeeded by his son Madhavasena who married Sulochana, daughter of the king of an island of the Arabian Sea (*Padma Purana, Kriya yogasara part, Chapter 168*). The Rajatarangini also speaks of the 'two generation'. After the death of Sakari Vikram, the Scythians again appeared on the scene and wrested from Madhava the greater part of his dominions. Now, another Hindu hero came forward to repel the Scythians. He was the aforesaid Salivahana, the alleged slayer of Vikrama. Salivahana beat the Scythians back and assumed the title of Sakari or Sakaditya (foe of the Scythians). His era, counted from his death or coronation in AD 78 (cf. Badami Cave inscription), is known as Sakavda. One *Purana* calls hims a Scythian; another account makes hihm of Turkish origin. He is the same as Hala—king of the Andhra list. Hala is the Marathi corruption of Sanskrit Sala. His other name of Salivahana originated from Sala Satavahana. It appears that he was not a true Andhra king. He was neither a Dravidian nor a Buddhist. He was a staunch Hindu, a patron of learning. His capital was Paithan, Sanskrit Pratishthana on the Godavari. At first he knew not how to read or write; but to please his queen, a learned woman, he asked Sarva Varman, a pundit of his court, to make the Sanskrit grammar easier. The pundit wrote the *Kalapa* grammar and especially and himself wrote the poem *Sapta Satak* in ancient Marathi. The well-known story book called the *Vrihatkatha* was composed by one of his ministers. This great Hindu king defeated the Andhras and became supreme in the south and in parts of north India. As he occupied the Andhra throne, he is included in the Andhra king list.

THE ANDHRA DYNASTRY (220 BC TO AD 236)

The Andhra nation of the south has been supposed by some to be of the Dravidian people. In all probability, they were an Aryan people of the Daitya or *Danava* branch several of whose colonies had penetrated into India during the Deva-Asura war of the north (twenty-nineth century BC). This is an ancient Hindu tradition. The *Aitareya Brahmana* (perhaps 2000 BC) first speaks of the powerful Andhras occupying the deltas of the Godavari and Krishna. The *Mahabharata,* describing the conquests of the Pandavas in the Deccan, noticed the same powerful Andhras (1400 BC). Again, we have seen that the banks of the Godavari and Krishna were peopled by the Aryans early in the Rationalistic Age (1300 BC). The great empire of the Andhras rose to power, started new schools of science and learning several centuries before Christ. In the fourth century BC they are reputed to have possessed an army second only to that of Chandragupta. They had thirty horses and 1,000 elephants. Their capital then was at Srikakolam on the lower Krishna. Now, the large population—perhaps a mixed one—speaking Telugu, literally, tongue of Tri-Kalinga, corrupted into Telinga from which Telugu, represent the ancient Andhras. After three years of hard struggle, Ashoka conquered Kalinga (206 BC). It is probably that the Andhras entered into a subsidiary alliance with Ashoka about 256 BC and remained a protected people till 220 to 210 BC, when they became independent and soon conquered Nasik. About 160 BC they are described as 'lord of the west' and they sent a force to help their ally Kharavela of Kalinga. About 25 BC, they occupied Magadha. The name of the slayer of Susarman, the last Kanva is not known. The Andhra kings claim they belong to the Satavahana family; their general title is Satakarni. About AD 78, King Hala, Sanskrit Sala, our famous Salivahana came to the throne (Badami Cave inscription). The next kings form a distinct group. Numbers 21 to 23 have distinctive coinage and are known by a good number of inscriptions and coins. Vilivayakura is a break in the dynasty, perhaps due to the amibition of a junior branch that came to power about AD 84 or later. He ruled only for six months. Some rare coins are his sole memorial.

His successor Sivalakura ruled twenty-eight years, whose successor Vilivayakura II ruled about twenty-five years and was distinguished for successful warfare against his western neighbours—the Sakas, Palhavas and Yavanas of Malwa, Gujarat and Kathiawar.

The Sakas in north India settled at Taxila and Mathura and ruled the principalities for several generations as Satraps of Mithridates I (171 to 136 BC) and his sucessors—the early Persian kings, as their overlords. Another branch of the Sakas occupied Kathiawar and some neighbouring tracts.

The Pahlavas were either the Parthians of Persia or the Pallavas of the south whose capital was Kanchi (Kanchivaram).

The first powerful foreign foe was Bhumaka, a Scythian satrap (first and second century AD). He was followed by Nahapana the Kshaharata satrap. He wrested dominions from the Andhras. About AD 126 Vilivayakura II recovered the losses and utterly destroyed the power of Nahapana. A general disgust spread against the foreigners. The hostility of the Andhra monarch was stimulated by the disgust felt by all Hindus and especially by the followers of the orthodox Brahmanical system at the outlandish practices of foreign barbarians who ignored caste rules and treated with contempt the precepts of the holy Shastras. This disgust is vividly expressed in the long inscription (inscription number 17 of Karli, in the great Chaitya Cava, edited and translated by Buhler in A.S.W.I., IV 109) recorded in AD 144 by the queen mother Balasri of the Gautama family, in which she glorifies herself as the mother of the hero who destroyed the Sakas, Yavanas and Palhavas—properly expended the taxes levied in accordance with the sacred law and prevented the mixing of the four castes. After destroying Nahapana, the Andhra victor, Vilivayakura, made one Chashtana, a Saka (Ptolemy's *Tiastance*) viceroy of western India at Ujjain. This line of Satraps ruled western India till the close of the fourth century AD when the last of them was overthrown by Chandragupta II Vikramaditya. The viceroy Rudradaman, grandson of Chasthtana, had married his daughter Dakshamitra to Pulumayi II, son of Vilivayakura II (before AD 130). Four inscriptions at Bhuj, capital of Kutch, show that Rudradaman was reigning in AD 130; Pulumayi II (Ptolemy's *Siro,* i.e. *Sri Polemaios*) ruled from AD 138 to 170.

Rudradama, an ambitious and energetic viceroy, made war upon his own son-in-law and was successful till AD 145. Out of affection for his daughter, Rudra returned the territories conquered and detached for ever Kathiawar, Sind, Kachcha, Konkon and some adjoining tracts, from the Andhra dominions.

Pulumayi II (AD 138 to 170): His ascension marks a new epoch. His capital was transferred. The 'bow and arrow' type of coinage was given up. The western capital at Hippokoura (Ptolemy) probably modern Kolhapur, was removed to Paithan near modern Hyderabad. Pulumayi enjoyed a long reign over the dominions curbed by his father-in-law.

Siva Sri (AD 170 to 177) and Siva Skanda (AD 177 to 184) were perhaps brothers to Pulumayi II. Nothing in particular is known about them. Siva Sri struck some rude leaden coins in his eastern provinces.

Yajna Sri (AD 184 to 213). The Puranas speak of seven Abhira kings who are supposed by some to be the shepherd kings of the north of India, or more probably and greeks, or Scythians along the lower Indus. Traces of the name as Abiria occur in the Ptolemy and the Ahirs as a distinct race are still extant in Gujarat.

These Abhiras were not foreigners. The name Abhira originated from Andhra-bhritya (servants of the Andhras = Andhra = Andhra-birththa = And—bhira = Abhira and the final Ahir). The *Matsya Purana* states that seven Andhra kings sprang from the servants of the original dynasty. These were the Abhiras who held sway in western India. Professor Bhandarkar's notion regarding the two branches of the Andhras ruling eastern and western India, is quite right. Geographer Ptolemy (AD 150) notices them as Abiria. Pliny saw them powerful in the second century AD. 'Andhre Indi on the Ganges' appears in the Peutengerian tables. The Abhirs of Malwa were very powerful once. The seven Abhiras ruling in the west probably belonged to the second century AD.

Yajna Sri was the most powerful of the last seven Andhra kings. He ruled twenty-nine years. Keenly feeling the loss of Andhra dominions under Oulumayi II, he renewed the struggle with the satraps, made conquests and recovered at least some of the lost tracts. His rare silver coins imitating the satrap's coinage certainly prove this. The silver coins were issued for circulation in the conquered districts. Similar coins were minted by Chandragupta Vikramaditya which finally shattered the power of the Saka satraps.

Yajna Sri's numerous and varied rude bronze and leaden coins current in eastern provinces, prove his long reign. Some of his coins, bearing the figure of a ship suggest the inference that his power was not confined to land. About AD 208 Yajna Sri sent an envoy to China. The Andhras had established their supremacy over numerous places on the sea. The Indian ships, during the Andhra period were very large in size (Pliny, N.H.VI; see *ante, pp. 211–12*).

The last three kings, viz., Vijaya, Chandra Sri and Pulumayi II (AD 213–23) are mere names. A few leaden coins of Chandra Sri have been discovered. Research may discover the coins of the other two.

The Andhra occupation of Magadha and rule in north India is proved by the Puranas, by K Pillay's *The Tamils 1800 Years Ago* and the newly discovered ruins of the old town of Bhita. The duration of the imperial Andhra dynasty, according to the Puranas is 456 ½ years, i.e. 220 BC to AD 237 during which thirty or thirty-one kings ruled.

The decline and fall of the Andhras was probably due to their continued struggle against powerful foreigners at least for two centuries; coming of fresh hordes; general inactivity of the east Indians: all fights happened in the north-west and west India; lukewarm sympathy of the allies and feudatories most of whom formed republics and free states at the earliest opportunity (inscriptions and coins prove this). The Madrakas and the Yaudheyas formed powerful republics in the Punjab. Mathura, Kausambi, Kosal and Panchala had asserted independence.

The Andhra occupation of Magadha is perhaps the first occupation of north India by the Deccan. Tamil literature says that some Tamil kings boasted of their invading north India as far as the Ganges (in the first century BC). Most probably, the Andhras attacked Magadha with the help of their vassals, the Tamil kings. So, this may be regarded as the expedition of the south against north. Some have traced Tamil influence on Bengali literature, on the scenery of Bengal in the Ajanta Caves. It is not unreasonable to hold that this expedition is at the root of all these. The Kushan occupation of Magadha is AD 237 ended the Andhra rule there.

THE INDO-PARTHIANS

Of their two dynasties, one ruled in Archosia and Sistan and the other governed the kingdom of Taxila (west Punjab). Maues or Mauas or king Moga Maha-Kshatrapa (great king of kings) ruled at Taxila about 138 BC (annexed to Parthia by Mithridates I). The war with the nomads and the murder of Phraates II and Artabanus between 130 and 120 BC, made the Parthian hold on India very weak. Thus, Maues became almost independent in the Punjab. Soon after, Vonones, a Parthian, became king of Archosia and Sistan under the great king at Ctesiphon and ruled for twenty-five years. For some time, the Parthians suffered severely from the nomads. They again became vigorous under Mithridates II the Great (123 BC). Azes, the viceroy at Arachosia and Sistan, was removed to Taxila where he succeeded Maues about 90 BC and ruled it under Mithridates II. Azes I was succeeded in the Punjab first by his son Azilises and then by his grandson Azes II. Azes II was a powerful prince; enjoyed a long reign of some fifty years. About the Christian era, no part of India was included in the Parthian empire. So, it is likely that Azes I succeeded in becoming independent. Azilises and Azes II also enjoyed long reign and power. Azes II had Aspavarma and Zeionises as subordinate satraps in the Punjab.

About AD 20 Gondophares succeeded Azes II. He conquered Sind and Arachosia and ruled a wide dominion free from Parthian control. A recently discovered inscription shows that Gondophares was initiated into Christianity by St Thomas about AD 21. He died about AD 60. In the partition of his state, his brother's son Abdagases got west Punjab and Orthagnes got Arachosia and Sind. No successor of Abdagases is known; the other was followed by Pakores. About AD 90 to 95, the

Punjab was annexed by the Kushana king, Kadphises II. Probably, Arachosia and Sind also soon came to his hands. Petty Parthian chiefs continued to rule in the Indus deltas (Periphus). The Indus then had seven mouths of which only the central stream was navigable. The port Barbarikon was on it. The capital Minnargar (Mihir-nagar?) lay inland.

The last Indo-Greek ruler Hermaios (AD 30 to 50) succumbled to the Yueshchi chief, Kadphises I when that powerful Kushana added Kabul to his growing empire.

For some 200 years, the valley of River Kabul, the Swat valley, some districts to the north and north-west of Peshawar and east Punjab remained under the local Greek princes who, free or fettered under a Parthian overlord, no doubt, exercised the prerogative of coining silver and bronze money.

Many proofs exist to show that the Punjab and a greater part of the United Provinces were once Greek. The coins of at least 30 different Greek kings have been found in the Punjab and the United Provinces. The last date is AD 50. India's relation with the Greeks was fairly close for nearly 400 years.

'I will make all men *Hellenes*,' were the words of Alexander to Aristotle. The later Greek rule in Asia fulfilled to a large extent the plan of that great hero. 'The influence of the Hellenic art has been traced even as far east as Japan. In north India, the imprint of the Greek is most strikingly seen in those mounds of shattered sculptures near Peshawar which mark the site of the ancient country of Gandhara. A comprehensive collection of those carvings is in the archaeological section of the Indian Museum. They illustrate the overlapping of the civilisations of the East and West. Here, the Greek Corinthian capital is found combined with the Indian figure of Buddha, soldiers with classic arms and armour, but Indian draperies, Greek features but the figures clothed with Indian costumes and many other composite conceptions depicting an intermingling of eastern and western symbols and ideas. Greek influences was not confined to the north India alone. In the south, as far as Madras, it is traceable in the bas-reliefs of Amaravati. At Mathura the dynamic touch of the classic hand has left its distinctive mark' (Percy Brown).

The Scythian rule in India lasted from 150 BC to AD 390. They gradually became Hinduised.

KUSHANA RULE IN INDIA (AD 45 TO AD 290)

Their two dynasties in India were the Kadphises dynasty and the Tochari dynasty. Kadphises in local Prakrit was uttered as Gaddasbhes, which the Brahmans Sanskritised as Gardabha, Garddabhin or Garddabhilas. Col. Wilfored wrongly calls them 'descendants of Bahram Gor, king of Persia'. A strange tale is prevalent in north-west India: a Gandarbha marrying the daughter of a king of Dhar (*Asiatic Researches, vol. vi, 35; ix, p. 147*) was changed into an ass, Sanskrit *gardabha*. I hold that Gardabha is the Sanskritised form of Kadphises. The Sanskrit word gardabha means as ass. Hence though misnamed, the foreign dynasty was afterwards known as Ass dynasty. Old *Gadhai pysa* or ass money has been found in various parts of western India (J.A.S.B. Dec. 1835, p. 688). It was certainly the coinage of the Gardabha princes. In the Sanskrit drama entitled The Little *Toy Cart* of the first century AD, mention is made of *gaddahi, Sanskrit gardabhi* explained by commentators as a coin (Wilson, J.R.A.S., iii. 385). Of the ten Gardabha rulers of India, we know only two. Fourteen Hindu Tusharas were the Kushan Tocharis, four of whom we know so far.

According to the *Matsya Purana,* the Indo-Parthians (Hindu Maurundas, probably from Meru or Maur, in Persia) were of *milchchha* origin; the *Vayu Purana* calls them Arya-*mlechcha* (Barbarians of Ariana?).

The nomad Yueh-chi, a people of Turkish orgin, came down from north-west China, expelled the Scythians and the Greeks from Central Asia and Bactria and formed five principalities including Bamian, about 65 BC.

KADPHISES I (AD 45 TO AD 85)

About 100 years after this division, north of the Hindukush, Kadphises I, chief of the Kushana section of the horde, made himself master of the Yueh-chi people (AD 45). The Yueh-chis crossed the Hindukush and conquered Kabul, Bactria and Kashmir (AD 45 to 60). The empire of Kadphises extended from the frontiers of Persia to the Indus and included the kingdoms of Bukhara and Afghanistan. He died at the age of eighty, about AD 85, after a vigorous reign.

KADPHISES II (AD 85 TO AD 120 OR 125)

Hima or Wima, better known as Kadphises II succeeded his father in AD 85. He was as ambitious and enterprising as his father and devoted himself to the further extension of the Yueh-chi dominions. The following points are especially notable.

(i) The great Chinese advance (AD 73 to 102) under General Panchao who made the greatest westward extension ever attained by the Chinese.

Alarmed at the steady advance of China, he boldly asked a Chinese princess in marriage. His envoy was arrested by General Panchao who considered it an insult to his master. The envoy was sent home. Full of indignation, Kadphises II sent his viceroy, Si with 70,000 horses to attack the Chinese. The army, while crossing Tashkurghan Pass (14,000 ft high) suffered terribly and on reaching the plain, fell an easy prey to Panchao and was totally defeated. Kadphises was forced to pay tribute to China (AD 90).

(ii) Conquest of north-west India (AD 95): Kadphises next successfully attacked India. All north-west India as far as Benaras (except perhaps Sind) passed to him.

The Indian provinces were ruled by his military viceroys who issued a large number of coins known as those of the nameless king. These pieces, mostly copper, a few in base silver, are very common from the Kabul valley to Benaras and Gazipur on the Ganges as well as in Kutch and Kathiawar.

(iii) Indo-Roman trade: The Kushan conquest much helped the Indo-Roman trade. Kadphises I had struck coins in copper or bronze only, and imitated the coinage in latter years, of Augustus or Siberius (AD 14 to 34). There was an abundant flow of Roman gold into India under the early emperors, in payment for the silks, spices, gems, and dye stuff of the east. Perceiving the advantage, Kadphises II struck gold coins like those of Rome, not inferior in weight and worth. In the same period, south India also maintained an active trade with the Roman Empire but the local kings did not copy the imperial gold coin; so the Roman gold coins were imported there abundantly for currency purposes.

(iv) In AD 99 Kadphises II probably sent an ambassador to the Roman emperor Trajan to announce his conquest of north-west India.
(v) Intercourse with western Roman Empire. Trajan conquered Mesopotamia in AD 116.

This brought the Roman Empire within 600 miles of the Yueh-chi empire. Probably the Kushan rulers knew the name and fame of the Romans and were sensibly actuated by their examples.

Conningham gives a thirty-five to forty-year-long victorious reign to this monarch.

THE KUSHAN TOCHARI LINE (AD 120 TO 290)

Hinu Puranists called them Tusharas or Tukharas, simply a Sanskritic form of Kushan Tochari. The eight remaining kings of the Kadphises (Gardabha) line are not yet known. Probably they were not so prominent. Of the thirteen or fourteen Tushara kings, we know the names of four only, viz., Kanishka, Huvishka, Jushka, and Vasushka or Vasudeva.

KANISHKA (AD 120 TO 150)

Kanishka, son to Vasispa or Vajheshka (Arrah inscription) is supposed to have succeeded Kadphises II as a relative. The supposition is open to question. Eight kings, not yet known, succeeded Kadphises II, one after another and their rule was confined probably to the west and north-west. With Kanishka, probably a new branch, viz., Tochari (Hindu Tushara) began, to end after fourteen rulers. The name and fame of Kanishka is cherished by tradition not only in India, but also in Tibet, China and Mongolia. To the Buddhists he is known not less than Ashoka. However, we know very little of his authentic history. His date is still unsettled. More than twenty of the inscriptions of Kanishka and his successors, no doubt, bear dates, but they are recorded in such a way that they are open to various interpretations. There are eminent scholars who still place his accession somewhere between 58 BC and AD 278.

The coins both of Kadphises II and Kanishka frequently display in the field the same four-pronged symbol and agree accurately in weight and fineness, besides exhibiting a very close relationship in the obverse devices. Hence, the inference is plain that the two kings were very near in time to one another.

Conquests and extent of empire

Tradition, monuments and inscriptions of his time prove that Kanishka ruled north-west India and as far south as the Vindhyas and over upper and lower Sindh to the mouth of the Indus. In AD 120 to 125 he conquered Kashmir where he erected numerous monuments and founded Kanishkapur, now Kanishpur 74°28' E and 34°14' N. In AD 125 to 130, he conquered Kashgar, Yarkand and Khotan. He attacked Pataliputra, but was unsuccessful; however, he took from that city a Buddhist saint named Asvaghosha.

His capital was at Purushapura, now Peshawar, which guarded the main road from the Afghan hills to the Indian plains. Here, he erected a great tower which was one of the wonders of the world. The superstructure of carved wood rose in thirteen storeys to a height of at least 400 feet, surmounted by a mighty iron pinnacle. The tower was thrice burnt and as often rebuilt by pious kings.

A very magnificent monastery stood by its side. Faint traces of the sub-structures are still visible at the 'King's Mound' outside the town. The monastery flourished till the tenth century AD. It was finally demolished by Sultan Mahmud of Gazni and his successors.

His foreign wars

The four great empires of Asia then were the Chinese, Kushan, Parthian, and Roman. A Parthian king, probably Khusru or one of his rivals, had attacked him, but he beat him back.

Kadphises II had attempted the conquest of the Chinese Turkestan, but had failed (AD 90). Kanishka, secure in India and Kashmir, made better preparations and boldly wrested from the Chinese the extensive provinces of Kashgar, Yarkand and Khotan. Thus, he not only freed himself from the payment of tribute to China, but also exacted the surrender of hostages from a state tributary to China.

His religion

His conversion to Buddhism, like that of Ashoka, was due to remorse for the bloodshed during his wars. His coins show the change of his faith: the finest and perhaps the earliest pieces bear legends (Greek in both script and language) with effigies of the sun and moon under Greek names of Helios and Selene. On later issues, the Greek script is retained, but the language is old Persian and the gods are those of the Greeks, Persians and Indians. The rare coins with images of Buddha with his name in Greek letters are supposed to be the latest, but they are well-executed.

The deified Buddha was worshipped throughout Kanishka's vast empire. But Kanishka, even after his conversion (AD 135), worshipped both the old and the new gods, like Harsha bowing before Siva and Buddha.

The fourth and last Buddhist Council

Kanishka, puzzled by the conflicting doctrines of the various sects, suggested to his advisor, the venerable Parsva, that it would be well to obtain an authoritative exposition of the truth. Parsva made arrangements for a general assembly of theologians. All the learned men assembled belonged to the Hinayana school. The place of meeting was Kundalabana near Srinagar in Kashmir. Vasumitra was elected president and Asvaghosha vice-president. The members were 500 in number. The business of the Council was a thorough examination of theological literature from the most remote antiquity and elaborate commentaries on the three main divisions of the cannon. The meeting over, the commentaries were copied on sheets of copper which were deposited in a stupa built for the purpose by Kanishka. These precious records may still exist buried near Sringar. Kanishka renewed Ashoka's donation of the kingdom of Kashmir to the church and went home through the Baramula Pass.

HUVISHKA

Kanishka was probably succeeded by one Vasishka whose name appears in the inscriptions, though not yet verified by a coin. Next probably followed Huvishka or Hushka, a worthy Kushana whose parentage is not at all known. From the chronological data supplied by Pankuo and

Wi-lio, I am inclined to think that Huvishka flourished in the third century AD. It was he who had conquered Magadha from the Andhras somethime between AD 226 to 237. He retained the vast empire intact. His dominions included Kabul, Kashmir Mathura, Magadha. For all practical purposes, he was the lord paramount in north India. All memory of his long and eventful reign is lost. His coins, every associated with those of Kanishka, are more varied than Kanishka's and show the continuance of Greek influence.

Several of his gold coins show well-executed and characteristic portraits of the king who was a determined-looking man with strongly marked features, large deep-set eyes and aquiline nose. The Kushana power was perhaps at its height under him. Professor Ramesh Chandra Mazumdar conjectures from the finds of some coins that the Kushana power had spread from Magadha to Madras. This southern extension was effected either by Huvishka or Vashushka. At Mathura, he built a splendid Buddhist monastery after his name. Like Kanishka, he was a liberal patron of Buddhist religious endowments. Like Kanishka, he also had a great liking for a curious mixture of Greek, Indian and Persian gods. The types on his coins had Herakles, Sarapis, Skanda, Visakha, Pharro and many others, but no figure and name of Buddha. Probably he was becoming a Hindu. His Buddhist convictions were not deep-seated. His town Kushkapura in Kashmir, now the village Ushkur, where the ruins of an ancient stupa are visible, continued for centuries to be a place of importance. Yuan Chwang enjoyed the liberal hospitality of the Hushkapura monastery for several days (AD 631).

Huvishka was probably succeeded by one Jushka about whom we know very little. The next Kushana emperor was probably Vasushka or Vasushkadeva from whom originated our Indian Vasudeva. His thoroughly Indian name shows how soon these Turkish invaders had yielded to the influence of their environment. That Vasudeva was quite Hinduised is proven by his coins which show on the reverse, the figure of Siva attended by his bull Nandi and accompanied by the noose, a trident and other signs of Hindu iconography. His inscriptions, mostly found at Mathura, show a reign of some thirty-five years (Sanchi inscription). Vasudeva, in his prime of youth may have conquered the eastern seaboard as far south as Madras. The Kushanas held east India till AD. 280 or 290 when the Guptas overthrew them. Mathura was the Kushana capital.

There was probably a Kushana viceroy at Pataliputra who ruled the eastern provinces. The later coins of Vasudeva represent him as clad in Persian garb. This shows that he held Kabul and the Punjab under the Persian king—Spor I (Shahpur) who ruled from AD 238 to 269. The Kushanas were very powerful in east India till at least AD 260.

From the remains of a stupa at Mathura, we have the lion-capital covered with records in intrusive Kharoshṛi characters which establish in a temporary occupation of that part of India, just after the time of Huvishka, by a power from the north-west which was represented at Mathura by the governors Rajula-Rajuvala and his successor (J.R.A.S. 1894, 525; 1904, 703; 1905, 154).

The Andhras declined by AD 210 and remained till AD 300. The later Kushanas were supreme in east India till AD 290.

The Sassanian monarchs of Persia exercised considerable influence on Indian affairs. It is not at all known how the Persian influence was felt in the interior of India. For lack of any positive proof, we can only conjecture an unrecorded Persian invasion, conquest and rule in India. The Puranists probably call these Persians 'Pallavas' (Pehlvis). These Pallavas were perhaps some plundering tribes subject to Persian influence; or they might have been sent by a Persian monarch for a regular attack.

The Persian period in the Indian history, is still a forgotten chapter. Cyrus (541 to 40 BC) and Darius (512 BC) had close political connection with India. To defeat the persecuting Jains and the Jain non-Aryan chiefs, the Hindu rishis and Brahmans made new heroes at Mount Abu. These heroes are called Agnikula or fire dynasty. They were heroic, tall and fair; they were not true natives of the soil. The Brahmans, in spite of their best efforts, could not change their manners. I think these new heroes were fire and sun-worshipping Persians; thus called Agnikula (fire-born dynasty). Of the four lines sprung from the four heroes, the Pramara and Chauhana were the most famed and powerful. The Mauryan dynasty is said to have been a branch of the Pramaras for Mura, mother of Chandragupta was a daughter of the Pramara clan. Of course, these Persians gradually adopted Indian names, manners and religion; yet they long remembered their Persian origin. Thus, Persian rule and Persian influence continued long in India. The Parsis and their priests, the Magas, have been noticed in many Hindu works.

Coins show that the Punjab renewed the ancient relation with Persia in the third century AD. It is probably that after the death of Vasudeva, the last paramount power in north India, the vast Kushana empire broke up into pieces. Coins show that the Kushanas ruled in the Punjab and Kabul for a long time. The Kushana kings of Kabul were very powerful till the fifth century AD when they were overthrown by the White Huns.

At the commencement of the fourth century AD, a Kushana king of Kabul gave a daughter in marriage to Hormazd H, the Sassanian king of Persia. And, when Sapor II besieged Amida in AD 360, his victory over the Romans was wom with the help of Indian elephants and Kushana troops under the command of their aged king, Grumbates, who occupied the place of honour and was backed by the Sakas of Sistan.

INDIAN IN THE THIRD CENTURY AD

The Andhras were most powerful till AD 210 when they began to decline and lost their political supremacy in AD 237. The Kushanas, powerful in north-west India, seized Magadha from the Andhras in AD 237 and probably occupied the eastern seaboard as far south as Madras. They were most powerful till AD 260 and continued till AD 280 to 290 when they were defeated by the Guptas who rose to importance from the close of the century. The Lichchhavis held Nepal and the neighbouring tracts. The Brahman Varman dynasty was powerful in Assam. Different parts of Bengal were under powerful kings who ruled Samtata, Dawaka and Pundra. The Kalachuris or Chedis, sprung from the ancient Haihayas, were powerful in the Central Provinces. Their era began from AD 249. The Deccan was under different chiefs, after the Andhras. The Abhiras were powerful in Malwa; the Pramaras at Dhar; the Arjunayans in eastern Rajputna; the Sah satraps in Gujarat till AD 249; the Ballabbis, ancestors of the Ranas of Mewar, at Ballabhipura till the sixth century when they were ruined by the Persians. The Yaudheyas, the Madrakas and other dynasties gathered strength in the Punjab.

4

THE GUPTA DYNASTY
(AD 290 TO 535)

The Chinese history *Wi-lio*, written between AD 239 and 269 states that the Yeuh-chis, i.e. the Kushanas conquered Magadha and were collecting revenues from that province. (The French Journal *Toung Pao 1905, p. 551*). This shows that up to AD 260 at least, Magadha was under the Kushanas.

Maharaja Sri Gupta, the founder of the Gupta dynasty ruled from AD 275 to 300 (*Indian Antiquary, 1902, p. 258; Allen's Catalogue, p. XVI*. Hence, it may be inferred that the Guptas took Magadha from the Kushanas and not from the Sakas, as supposed by some. These Guptas were Vaisya Rajputs, orthodox Hindus and of the Vaishnava sect. Their ancestors most probably ruled in some tracts north of Pataliputra, as vassals of the Andhras and the Kushanas. They rose as the Kushanas declined and fell. At last, Sri Gupta, backed by the Hindus sick of foreign rule, wrested Magadha from the thirteenth Tushara monarch. The title of 'Maharaja' of Sri Gupta and his son, the mention of their names in the inscriptions of the later powerful Guptas and the success of Chandragupta I clearly show that Sri Gupta was not a petty chief. Sri Gupta is most probably a title. His real name is not yet known. The inscription only mentions Gupta. He became master of Magadha and assumed the glorious title of 'Maharaja'.

SRI GUPTA (AD 275 TO 300)

The real power of the Guptas probably began from AD 290. Certainly, Sri Gupta was a great hero. We know very little of his battles or rule. It is said that he built a temple for the Chinese Indian travellers and gave the revenues of twenty-four villages for its upkeep.

GHATOTKACHA GUPTA I (AD 300 TO 319)

After Sri Gupta, his son Ghatotkacha Gupta ascended the throne about AD 300. He made no conquest, but amassed a large hoard and strengthened the army.

CHANDRAGUPTA I (AD 320 TO 326)

After Ghatotkacha Gupta, his son Chandragupta came to the throne about February 26, AD 320. He was a great conqueror, like the Mauryan Chandragupta. He inherited the vast wealth hoarded by his ancestors.

The Lichchhivis of Nepal, then very powerful, owned almost all tracts northy of Magadha and even encroached on Magadha to crush the rising Gupta power. Forthwith, Chandragupta with a strong army, invaded Nepal and defeated the Lichchhivis. The victor was, however, induced to a treaty with the offer of Princess Kumara Devi and the districts beyond Nepal proper. This marriage made Chandragupta great in every way. His power and prestige increased much. Soon, he conquered the North-West Provinces, Allahabad, Oudh and other neighbouring tracts (*Brahmanda Purana, Upasanhara*). He now assumed the glorious title of 'Maharajadhiraja', i.e. sovereign of sovereigns. The Gupta era marked the formal coronation of Chandragupta in AD 320. He began to strike coins bearing his name, his wife's name, their figures and the name of the Lichchhivi clan.

Hindu writers have distinguished the two names of Nichchhavi and Nichchivi corrupted into Lichchhavi and Lichchhivi. The former signifies the people of Vaisali and the latter, those of Nepal. The Lichchhivi history is lost for the most part. They founded a kingdom in Nepal and an era running from AD 319. The male name of Kumara Devi plainly shows that the Nepal king had no son. So Chandragupta, as son-in-law, succeeded to the power formerly held by his wife's relations. The Guptas were thus no mean rival to the Mauryans ruling six centuries ago. Pataliputra was built and fortified to curb the encroaching Lichchhavis of Vaisali who afterwards seized Pataliputra from a weak successor of Pushyamitra. Chandragupta subdued them.

For six years Chandragupta ruled a most fertile and populous kingdom in the Gangetic Valley. During his short rule, he did much. Yet, in the midst of his glories and probably towards the close of his reign, he sustained a great defeat at the hands of Chandravarman, a very powerful king of Pushkaran, a part of Marwar in Rajputana. He did not live long enough to resent and redress the defeat. He had several queens and several sons. Before death, he nominated the crown-prince, Samudragupta, born of Kumara Devi, as his successor to the throne. This selection was quite right and welcome, as Samudragupta had demonstrated all the princely qualities early on.

SAMUDRAGUPTA, THE INDIAN NAPOLEON (AD 326 TO 375)

Afate the death of Chandragupta, his son and successor Samudragupta came to the throne early in life (AD 326). He was very wise and expert in peace and war. His bravery, courage and skill were extraordinary. His place is very high among the distinguished emperors of India.

The first twenty-five years of his reign were spent in peaceful consolidation of the kingdom, hoarding wealth and encouraging arts and industries. About AD 350, there were two great powers in north India: that of the Guptas under Samudragupta, and that of the western satraps under Rudrasena. The Deccan was broken up into minor states. Meghavarna was the king of Ceylon.

Some describe Samudragupta 'as an aggressively ambitious monarch'. Was he so? The probable fact is that many enemies rose to oppose and crush the infant Gupta power. So, Samudragupta exerted himself to the utmost to subdue all. In actual fact, he was not fond of the game of the grab. A greater part of his long reign was spent in military exploits. He remembered the defeat of his father by Chandravarman of Rajputana who was out on his Indian conquests about AD 325–26. The glories of Chandravarman are sung in the rock inscription of Susunia and the iron-pillar inscription of Mehrauli near Delhi.

Samudragupta had profound faith in Hinduism and an uncommon knowledge of the Brahmanical sciences. Yet, he was free from bigotry. At the probable instigation of the Brahmans, he vigorously carried on Hindu revival in religion and politics, already started by Pushyamitra in the second century BC.

His conquests (c. AD 357 to 58)

To cripple the enemies, to make the Gupta power and Hinduism supreme in India, Samudragupta organised a great campaign and conquered eleven powerful kings of the Deccan and nine of north India, besides many forest chiefs and frontier kings. His invasion of the southern kingdoms required great boldness in design and masterly powers of organisation and execution. After 700 years, the army of Magadha with the eagle standard was out on conquests. Marching from Pataliputra, he first attacked south Kosala, conquered its king Mahendra, and also conquered the states of Orissa and the wild parts of Central Provinces. Byaghraraja of Mahakantara submitted to him. Next, he conquered the valley of the Mahanadi; marching by the east coast road, he next attacked Svamidatta, king of Pishtapura, capital of Kalinga (now Pithapuram); conquered the hill forts of Mahendragiri and Kottura in Ganjam; King Mantaraja of Kollar (lake Kolair); the king of Vengi between Krishna and Godavari; Vishnugopa, the Pallava king of Kanchi (Kanchivaram). Thence he turned westward and conquered Nilaraja of Abimukta, Hastivarman of Kesi, and Ugrasena, king of Palakka, now Palghatcherry in the Nellore district. Next he conquered Kuvera in Devarashtra (Mahratta country) and Damana of Erandapalla (Khandesh) and Dhananjaya of Kusthalapura.

In north India, Achyuta, Nagasena, Rudradeva, Ganapati Naga of Nalapur(?), Nandi, Valavarman, Matila, Nagadatta, Chandra Varman, and other powerful kings were subdued.

His march of some three thousand miles through different and difficult countries must have taken him two years at least. Rich spoils, precious presents, submission but no permanent annexation of the southern states were the results of his splendid campaign.

His Inscription (AD 359 to 60)

Samudragupta's Allababad inscription, composed by the learned poet Harisena, not only describes his military exploits, but also gives the chief events of the time. Dr Buhler has proved that that the inscription was not made afterwards (*J.R.A.S. 1898, p. 386*). Its language and style prove it to have been of AD 360 or shortly before or after. It is now in the Allahabad Fort. Most probably it was placed there from some other place. Samudragupta's bloody conquests were engraved on the very stone pillar on which Ashoka had his moral sermons inscribed six centuries before.

This epigraphic record (undated) still entire, gives a detailed account of the events of the reign. It is also important for its Sanskrit composition partly in prose. It is further important as a linguistic and literary landmark.

The poet-laureate divided Samudragupta's expeditions into four classes, viz., that against the eleven kings of the Deccan; that against the kings of north India, nine, amongst others, are mentioned by name—that against barbarous chiefs of the forests and that against the frontier kings.

Now, there is no means of identifying the battlefields, as the places themselves and their names have undergone considerable change. The inscription states that the kings of Samatata, Dawaka, Kamarupa, Nepal, Kartripura, and other frontier fountries and those of Malwa Arjunayans, Yaudheyas, Madrakas, Abhirs, Prarjunas, Sankanikas, Sakas, and Kharparikas paid Samudragupta revenue and homage.

Were the frontier kingdoms under his direct rule included in his empire of outside it? Scholars differ. The point is not so clear. Doubtless, the frontier kings owned Samudragupta their overlord, paid him tribute and homage and carried out his imperial commands.

Note. Kartripura is now Kumaon, Almora, Garhwal, and Kanpa. Nepal like now, was almost independent. Samatata, literally *lands on the sea-level*, was littoral Bengal—all lowlands south of the Ganges and between the River Hugli and the Meghna. Formerly, the main stream of the Ganges flowed eastward south of Dacca and fell into the Bay of Bengal. The lower Brahmaputra was then large enough to be called an arm of the Bay. Dawaka or Davaka (Dhak-ka=Dacca), called a country in the *Bhuripayoga*, a Sanskrit dictionary, then comprised Dacca, Mymensingh and the eastern parts of the Rajsahi division. Kamarpura was Assam proper, Garo Hills, north-east Mymensingh, Sylhet and Cachar. The River Jamuna, now between the Rajsahi and Dacca divisions, did not exist a hundred years ago. The language of Dawaka was called 'Dhakki Prakrit'. The Kharaparikas were a heroic tribe of Jabbalpoire in the Central Provinces. Finds of many coins of the Gupta emperors at various places near Dacca and at Kotalipara (district Faridpur) seem to show that east Bengal also was under the direct rule of the Guptas.

Extent and boundary of his empire

Samudragupta's empire probably extended from the Brahmaputra to the Yamuna and Chambal and from the Himalayas to the Narmada. After Ashoka, no other emperor had such a large empire. Inscriptions tell us that the Kushanas of Gandhar and Kabul, the powerful kings of the Oxus, the kings of Ceylon and other distant islands were in political alliance with him. He maintained relations with the Saka satraps of western India.

All the kingdoms of the south were forced to acknowledge his paramountcy. The frontier kingdoms of Kartripura, Nepal, Assam, east Bengal, the free states of Rajputana and Malwa were attached to the empire by subsidiary alliance.

Embassies from Ceylon

The Buddhist king, Meghavarna of Ceylon sent two monks to do homage to Samudragupta and to visit Ashoka's monastery at Bodh Gaya. The monks received very little hospitality in India and returned home dispirited. Meghavarna resolved to found a monastery in India for the convenience of his own pilgrims. So, he sent a mission to Samudragupta, laden with the gems of Ceylon and other valuable gifts and requested permission to found a monastery on Indian soil. Samudragupta granted them permission. Meghavarna, receiving the imperial orders on a copper plate, erected a splendid convent to the north of the Bo tree. Yuan Chwang visited it in the seventh century AD, then occupied by a thousand Buddhist monks. The site is now marked by an extensive mound.

Horse sacrifice

To make his conquests ever memorable and to assert his paramount power, Samudragupta celebrated a horse sacrifice with great pomp. After

Pushpamitra, he was the only emperor to perform it. He made lavish donations of gold and silver to the Brahmans. His Asvamedh coins of gold with the figure of the horse and Yupa have been found at many places. It is said that such splendid conquests were unknown even to the most ancient Hindu kings.

His character

Samudragupta was not only an extraordinary hero, fighter and politician but also a great patron of many musicians, poets and other learned men. He could compose fine poems in elegant Sanskrit. So, they called him Kaviraja, a great poet. His gold coins also show his taste in music. The figure of Vinapani (goddess of learning) appears on these. In one, Samudragupta sits cross-legged, with scanty clothing ond playing on his favourite vina (harp). Often, would he listen to religious and other discussions in his court. He did for Hinduism what Ashoka had done for Buddhism. Though an orthodox Hindu, he was tolerant of the Buddhists, Jains and others. He was a great hero, poet, musician and a very learned man. Modern scholars have rightly called him the 'Indian Napoleon'. He was a great patron of fine arts. Hinduism, Sanskrit and the various sciences attained great perfection under him.

Before his death (date not yet certain), he nominated the heroic prince, Chandragupta, by his queen Datta Devi, heir to the throne.

CHANDRAGUPTA II ALIAS DEVAGUPTA VIKRAMADITYA (AD 375 TO 413)

On the death of Samudragupta, his son Chandragupta, named after his grandfather, succeeded to the throne, probably in AD 375 and ruled till AD 413. He is known in history as Chandragupta II. He fully inherited the martial spirit of his father. He not only kept the empire intact, but also conquered the kingdom of the Sakas or the western satraps (AD 395). The Gupta empire now extended from the Brahmaputra to the Indus Valley and to the Arabian Sea. He now assumed the glorious title of Sakari Vikramaditya. Kashmir seems to have been under his protection. He sent Pratapaditya, a relation, to rule there. He was a staunch but tolerant Vaishnavite.

At Mehrauli near Delhi, there is an iron pillar bearing an inscription which describes the conquests of a king named Chandra who is said to have defeated the allies in Bengal. Scholars have so long differed as to the date and personality of this king Chandra. Some think that this Chandra was Chandragupta II. Prinsep thought the pillar inscription of the third or fourth century AD. Dr Bhau Daji thought it post-Gupta. Dr Furgusson thought it of the time of Chandra Gupta I or II of the Guptas, from palaeographic consideration. Dr Fleet took it to be of Chandragupta I or of a brother of Mihirkula. Dr Hoernle thinks it of Chandragupta II and of AD 410. VA Smith makes 'Chandra' a king of north India, perhaps of Assam, or Chandragupta II, whose son Kumaragupta erected the iron pillar on the Vishnupadagiri near Mathura, afterwards removed to Delhi by Anangapala (*J.R.A.S., 1899*).

Recently, Professor Haraprasad Sastri of Calcutta has solved the point satisfactorily. The Susnia Inscription mentions a country called Pushkarana or Pokarana. Professor Sastri has seen in the *History of Marwar* by their poets and chroniclers that a part of that kingdom was formerly called Pokarana or Pushkarana. Several years ago, he discovered an inscription at Mandasor, Sanskrit Dasapura, in Malwa. With its help, he has now explained the Susunia Inscription. That inscription tells us that Naravarman, son of Sinhavarman, grandson of Jayavarman, reigned at Mandasor in 461 VS=AD 404. Now Kumaragupta I's vassal Bandhuvarman, king of Malwa, was born of Naravarman's line. Hence it is plain that Chandravarman, king of Pushkarana was the son to Sinhavarman, king of Malwa. Samudragupta conquered this Chandravarman who had, some years before Samudragupta, gone out of Rajputana to conquer the whole of India. When he had reached Bengal, the allies gave him battle and fought very bravely; but they were defeated. Most probably Ghatotkacha or Chandragupta I was defeated by this Chandra. Therefore, he described his conquests in the rock of Susunia Hill. Afterwards, Samudragupta defeated Chandravarman (vide Harisena's inscription) and placed his younger brother Naravarman on the throne.

Though a staunch Vaishnavite, yet Chandragupta II never persecuted or slighted the Buddhists and the Jains. Fa-Hien travelled in India (AD 399 to 414) during his rule. But he speaks little of politics. He collected Buddhist works and sayings, made images and pictures.

Chandragupta II ruled for forty years. He issued many coins bearing the figures of fighting soldiers and of Goddess Durga borne on the lion.

He had two queens; the first was Kuvera Devi who bore him Princess Prabhavati married to Rudrasena, son of Vakataka. Prabhavati bore Divakarasena. The second was Dhruva Devi who bore the crown-prince Kumaragupta I (*Indian Antiquary, 1912, pp. 214–15*).

His contemporaries were Harivarman of the Maukhari dynasty of Kanouj, who married Jayaswami, daughter to Jayagupta of the Gupta dynasty and Krishnagupta, ancestor of Maharajadhiraj Aditya Sena.

KUMARAGUPTA I MAHENDRADITYA (AD 413 TO 455)

On Chandragupta II's death, his son Kumaragupta I, born of the queen Dhruva Devi, became king (AD 413). Bamana's *Kavyalankara Sutra* refers to a prince named Chandraprakasa as born of Chandragupta. Professor HP Sastri infers from this that Chandragupta II had two sons, viz., Chandraprakasa and Valaditya. Valaditya befriended the Buddhists. On Chandragupta's death, a quarrel arose between the two brothers as to succession. Chandraprakasa was defeated; Valaditya was victorious and occupied the throne (*J.A.S.B., 1905*). But the point appears to have no historical basis. Some think that Chandraprakasa ascended the throne under the name of Kumaragupta. This also is absurd according to Bamana's statement. His inscriptions and coins show his long and able reign. He also performed a horse sacrifice. His copperplate inscription, dated AD 432 has been discovered at Dhanaidaha (dist. Rajsahi, Bengal). A gold coin with the figure of the horse, has been found at Maneswar near Dacca. On the coins of Kumaragupta I, there appear two females on two sides of the royal figure. Certainly they were his two queens. The first was Ananta Devi; the other's name is unknown.

NEW DANGERS TO THE EMPIRE AFTER AD 450

Kumaragupta was a great friend of the Buddhists. This highly incensed the Brahmans who made vigorous attempts to restore the descendants of Pushyamitra. The Mitras were at first very successful. But the heroic Prince Skandagupta defeated them in several battles and suppressed the revolt.

The Hunas, a brave Mongol people, marched westward from the steppes of Asia and divided themselves into two parties after AD 350.

One stream invaded Europe and under Attila the Hun, ruined the Roman Empire, early in the fifth century AD. The other stream called the White Hunas, conquered the Oxus Valley and Balkh. When Kumaragupta ascended the throne (AD 413), the Hunas slowly advanced towards India, attacked it and laid waste the Punjab, Kashmir, Kabul, Dardistan, and Khasa land. The Kushans of Gandhar fell to these powerful Hunas. Balhika and Kapisa also were subdued by them. Next they attacked the western frontier of the Gupta Empire. Kumaragupta was now old. In spite of his best efforts, Prince Skandagupta, then viceroy at Mathura, could not prevail against them. Mathura fell.

Sriharshagupta, son to Krishnagupta and Aditya Varman, son to Maukhari Hari Varman, were the contemporaries of Kumaragupta. Aditya Varman married Harshagupta, daughter to Sriharsha.

SKANDAGUPTA KUMARADITYA (AD 455 TO 480)

Kumaragupta was succeeded by his son Skandagupta, formerly viceroy of Mathura (AD 455). Skanda had already repelled several Huna attacks. Skanda, the brave general of the deva-Aryans of the north, had defeated the Asuras (twenty-nineth century BC). This Skanda, as general of the Gupta devas, first beat the new Asuras—the Hunas. He now assumed the title of *Vikramaditya*. About AD 470, the Hunas fell on the empire in overwhelming numbers. Though he fought hard, he could not prevail. His treasury was emptied. He even issued gold coins of seventy-three grains instead of 108 grains. His step-brother Puragupta revolted at home; his vassal kings were half-hearted. He was killed in the battle of Pratisthana (Allahabad) about AD 480. The western half of north India was lost to the Guptas. Skanda's infant son was Chandragupta III with the title Dwadasaditya. His son was Prakasaditya and his son was Ghatotkachagupta II.

A coin of Skandagupta has been found at Kotalipara (district Faridpur, Bengal).

PURAGUPTA VIKRAMADITYA I (AD 480–485 OR 490)

Paragupta probably usurped the throne and ruled the eastern half of north India. The few of his gold coins hitherto found, bear on the reverse,

Prakasaditya, which according to scholars, was his title. His mother Anata or Ananda Devi was perhaps daughter to the Maukhari king, Ananta Varman. He probably ruled from AD 480 to 490. About AD 480 his general, Bhattaraka, conquered Vallabhi and founded his own dynasty there. This Vallabhi should not be confounded with Ballabhipura founded by Bijayasena in the third century AD. The ruins of the latter still remain eleven miles to the north-west of Bhownagar in Kathiawar. About AD 478, the Guptas were bifurcated (the Bhitari coins). About AD 490, the Huna chief, Toramana, conquered Rajaputana and Malwa.

Some think Puragupta died in AD 485. The point is not yet settled. Allen says in the *Catalogue of Indian Coins (pp. Li–Liii)*: Puragupta's coins bear *Sri Vikramaditya* on the reverse. Hence, his title was perhaps Vikramaditya.

Paramartha's *Life of Vasuvandhu* tells us that Vikramaditya of Oudh had embraced Buddhism, being influenced by the precepts of Vasuvandhu for instruction. When Valaditya became king after his father, he invited Vasuvandhu to this court. Then, whose was the title *Prakasaditya*? That was perhaps the title of Skandagupta's son or heir. Absence of any other copper-plate grant or inscription has led scholars to place Puragupta after Skandagupta.

It is doubtful if all the coins with the figure of duelists or soldiers, generally ascribed to Chandragupta II, may be accepted as such; for their weight exceeds even 144 grains. Such heavy coins were not issued before Skandagupta's reign. On the reverse of these coins, between the feet of the royal figure, is written the word *bha*; such a sign is used by Skandagupta. The letters on the reverse are rather indistinct; the initial *para* and the final *aditya* are clear. So they are like the heavy coins of Skandagupta. In form and purity of gold, they do not belong to a much later period. Perhaps not after Narasimhagupta. On one side, below the royal hand, is written *Chandra*, i.e. Chandragupta; but on the reverse we have for *Srivikramaditya* or *Vikramaditya*, the title *Dwadasaditya*. Rapson read *Dwadasaditya*, yet hesitates to accept it as such (*Num. Chron. 1891, p. 57*). Certainly they do not belong to Chandragupta II. It was some King Chandragupta III. The St Petersburg Museum has coins of Ghatotkachagupta (Allen's *Catalogue of Indian Coins, p. 4, IV*). Hence the existence of Prakasaditya, Ghatotkacha and Chandragupta III, is apparent in the later Guptas. This leaves us room to suppose that during Skandagupta's absence on the Huna war in western India, his step-brother Puragupta revolted and built a new kingdom in east India. The Bhitari coins display the descendants of Puragupta. So, the above three kings were certainly descendants of Skandagupta. Most probably in the latter part of the fifth century AD, the Guptas bifurcated. New discoveries will prove that Puragupta's revolt happened before the death of Skandagupta in AD 485 according to Dr Hoernle (*J.A.S.B., 1889, p. 96*) VA Smith also accepts it (*E.H.I., 2nd f.d, p. 293*) as does Numismatology. Puragupta's queen was Vasta Devi.

NARASIMHAGUPTA VALADITYA (AD 485 TO 530)

Narsimhagupta Valaditya (AD 485–530) succeeded his father Puragupta. Paramartha states that like Skandagupta, he also honoured Vasuvandhu much and was highly inclined to Buddhism; he built a monastery and a floriated stupa at Nalanda. He was a great hero and was bent on driving out the Hunas. Abaout AD 510 or 515, Mihirakula, son to Toramana, became king of the Indian dominions of the Hunas, with Sakala in the Punjab as capital (*Indian Antiquary, 1889, p. 230*). Bamian (near Herat) was the headquarters. Balkh was their second capital. India was only a province of the Huna empire of forty countries from Persia to Khotan. Malwa was under a Huna prince. Vallabhi and other kingdoms must have been tributary to Mihirakula. About AD 528, Narasimhagupta, as the leader of a confederacy of Hindu princes, signally defeated and shattered the Huna power in east India. The Mandasor Inscription gives the date as before AD 533–34; Dr Hoernle, as AD *525* (*J.R.A.S., 1909, p. 131*). Mihirakula retired to Kashmir. Between AD 560 and 570; the Persians, allied with the Turks, overthrew the White Huna empire which was annexed by the Turks. Narasimha died about AD 530. His son Kumaragupta II, born of queen Mahalakshmi Devi, came to the throne and ruled till AD 550, as the last emperor of the Guptas (*Ind. Ant., 1890, p. 227*). The Gupta coins found at Kalight, Calcutta, mostly belong to Narasimha and Kumaragupta II. Some of these, with the word Vishnu, belonged to Vishnugupta Chandraditya, successor of Kumaragupta II.

FALL OF THE GUPTA EMPIRE: ITS CAUSES

The Hunas were no doubt driven out, but the Gupta Empire melted for ever. The causes were the Mitra War, the Huna War, family dissensions and the revolts of the vassal kings. Yasodharaman of Malwa threw off the Gupta yoke about AD 530 and in Gujarat, the Maitrake dynasty became free. Other provinces fell gradually.

5

YASODHARMAN VIKRAMADITYA AND HIS SUCCESSORS *(AD 500 TO 800)*

THE PAURAS, i.e. PAURAVAS OF THE PURANAS

Yasodharman began life as a common soldier under Skandagupta, displayed great valour in the Huna war, saved Skanda's life in several battles and soon rose to great power. Narasimhavaladitya succeeded in saving Magadha from Mihirkula and Yasodharman inflicted a crushing defeat on the Huna lord, made him captive and annihilated the Huna power (*Dr Fleet, Ind. Ant. 1889, p. 228*) at Korur, near Multan, Punjab (AD 528). Mihirakula sued for peace which Yasodharman granted. This is alluded to the poet's inscription as 'Mihirakula worshipped the royal feet of Yasodharman' (Fleet's *Gup. Ins., No.33*). The Mandasor Inscription makes Yasodharman, and Yuan Chwang, a century later, makes Valaditya, the victor of the last Huna war. The royal poets' account is more trustworthy for he was a witness to events, while Yuan Chwang recorded the confused tradition of the people. Dr Hoernle rejects Yuan Chwang's account on the grounds that Yuan Chwang placed Mihirakula and Valaditya some centuries previous to his own time and represented Valaditya as holding a position subject to the orders of Mihirakula. Yasodharman delivered west India from the Hunas who were ruined in Asia by the Turks, but the other section founded Hungary in east Europe. The surviving Hunas of India soon became Hinduised and absorbed in the people. Some of their minor lords became Rajputs and married Indian wives. After Valaditya Narasimhagupta's death. Yasodharman was without a rival. With perseverance and valour, he soon built an empire larger than the Guptas' or even Hunas'. His empire extended from the Brahmaputra to the Arabian Sea and from the Himalayas to Mahendragiri in Ganjam near Madras. The Gupta kings of north-west India and Magadha now begged his mercy. The Brahman kings of Assam, afraid of Buddhist Yasodharman, would offer sacrifice of animals at dead of night. In the Himalayas and in the desert, the Khasas and the Hunas quaked with fear. His pillar of victory was set up on Mt Mahendra in Ganjam on the eastern sea. Three inscriptions of Yasodharman have been found. The first pillar inscription of Mandasor (Sanskrit *Dasapura*, Malwa) was erected in AD 531, the second, in AD 533 (Fleet's *G.I. Nos 33 and 35*). Yasodharman conquered east India from the Gupta king Dharmaditya Maharajadhiraj Parama Bhattaraka (*Ind. Ant., 1910, p. 139; J.A.S.B, 1910, p. 429*) before AD 533. He was the last Indian champion to assume the title of *Vikramaditya*. The former era of Malwas was now converted into *Vikram-Samvat*. He probably ruled till AD 560. Kalhana gives us the following account: Hiranya, the third king of the sixth dynasty of Kashmir, died without a male child. Anarchy prevailed. So, about AD 558, they requested Vikramaditya of Ujjain to rule Kashmir. He, however, sent Matrigupta, a poet of his court to rule Kashmir. Were he Kalidasa, Kalhana would certainly name him. Matrigupta ruled well for four years and nine months. Then Pravarasena, a scion of the royal family, claimed the throne. Matrigupta abdicated gladly. Then Vikramaditya was gone. This happened about AD 562. Matrigupta turned an ascetic. Pravarasena was a great hero. He extended the kingdom up to Saurashtra (Gujarat). He also defeated Siladitya I, successor of Vikramaditya, and recovered the Kashmir throne taken by Vikramaditya to Ujjain. This Vikramaditya was certainly Yasodharman of Malwa, son to Mahendraditya by Queen Saumyadarsana. He is also called Bishmasila. He slew the *mlechchas*. Ujjain was his capital.

There was no emperor in India between AD 560 and 605. The following powers, however, were important: Kashmir held all tracts up to Gujarat; Siladitya I, successor of Yasodharman held Malwa and other neighbouring tracts; the Vardhan dynasty of Thaneswar (these Vardhans were the second branch of the *Pauras*, ancient Pauravas who ruled all lands about Kanouj: Dushyanta, husband of Sakuntala was a noted Paurava king of old); the Second Gupta and Maukhari dynasties held Magadha: Dharmaditya, Gopachandra and Samachara Deva held east India successively; the Chalukya empire in the Deccan.

In the beginning of the seventh century AD there were three empires in India, viz., those of the Vardhans of Thanesvar, of Sasanka in east India from Brahmaputra to Ganjam (Sasanka's copper-plate inscription of AD 629 to 30) and of the Chalukyas in the Deccan. About AD 570, Pushpabhuti founded the Vardhan dynasty of Thanesvar. His son Jaya Vardhan married a daughter of the Guptas. His son Prabhakara Vardhan founded a large kingdom in west India about AD 590 and assumed the title of Maharajadhiraj. He was heroic. The White Hunas again appeared in India. He went out with a strong army and beat them back. By his queen Toshavati, he had two sons, viz., Rajyavardhana and Harshavardhana and one daughter called Rajyasri, married to Prince Grahavarman of Kanouj. About AD 604, the Hunas again plundered the frontiers. Rajyavardhana went to fight them. Prabhakara died in AD 605. Then a scramble for the suzerainty of north India followed. Devagupta, Sasanka's governor of Malwa, marched with a large army towards Kanouj, occupied it, killed Graha Varman and imprisoned his widowed queen, Rajyasri, in chains.

Sasanka (AD 600 to 625) of Karna-Suvarna (north-west Bengal), often supposed to be a Gupta but most probably a scion of Gaur, aimed at an empire and occupied a considerable part of north India. His father was Mahasena and General of Yasodhavala. His title *Narendraditya* (literally, a very sun of a feudatory chief) shows that he was not a Gupta. The fall of the Guptas and other opportunities accounted for his attempt at building an empire. Both Devagupta and Sasanka were marching on Thanesvar from different directions. Rajyavardhana hurried home and with 10,000 horses, defeated Devagupta of Malwa and before he could deliver Rajyasri, came down to oppose Sasanka whose progress was checked. Rajyavardhana again went to drive out the Hunas, but died in the enemy's land while fighting (Harsha's Banskhera plate, *Ep. Ind., vol. IV*). Harsha then invaded the Gaurian empire of Sasanka with 5,000 elephants, 2,000 horses, 50,000 foot soldiers (Beal's *Bt. Rec., vol. I, p. 213*) but could do Sasanka no harm even by six years' fighting (*Ep. Ind., vol. VI, p. 143*). Madhavagupta of Pataliputra sought Harsha's friendship and help (*Apasada Ins*). Madhava was the root of Sasanka's ruin. The army of Thanesvar and that of Bhaskaravarman, Harsha's ally of Assam, drove Sasanka from Gaur-Banga to Mahendragiri in Ganjam where he was afterwards killed in a battle (AD 625) before the aid of Pulakesi arrived. The Chinese works of the time mention Bhaskaravarman as the lord of east India. The truth is that he helped Harsha in building his empire.

HARSHAVARDHANA (AD 606 TO 648)

The chief points of his reign are:

(i) The thirty-five years' war made him emperor of north India, from sea to sea.

(ii) About AD 620 he led an expedition against the Deccan, but being defeated by the Chalukya Emperor Pulakesi II, was forced to accept the Narmada river as his southern frontier.

(iii) The kings of Kamarupa (Assam), Vallabhi in Kathiawar and Nepal were his vassals. His son-in-law was king of Vallabhi. Kalinga was now almost depopulated. Pataliputra, mistress of India for over a thousand years, was almost decaying. Bhaskara belonged to the Brahmanic Varman dynasty of Kamarupa existing from 1500 BC downwards. Eastern-most India, least troubled by serious foreign attacks allowed the dynasty to run on unbroken for over two thousand years. A copper-plate inscription of Bhaskaravarman has been found at the villate Nidhanpur (dist. Sylhet, Assam). This gives the main line. Ratnapala's plate has been found at Tejpur and Indrapala's at Gauhati (Assam). The plate of Banamala has been found at Tejpur and that of Balavarman at Naogao (Assam). Brahman Mahiranga was the founder of the Varman dynasty of Kamarupa about 1500 BC. Several followed him. Then came Naraka in 1400 BC, then his son Bhagadatta, and then his son Bazradatta. Then follows a long gap. Bhaskara's plate gives the line from the Gupta period, as follows:

Pushyavarman, probably contemporary of Samudragupta (AD 326 to 375)—Samudravarman (Datta Devi)—Valavarman (Ratnavati)—Kalyanavarman (Gandharvavati)—Ganapativarman (Yajnavati)—

Mahendravarman (Subrata)—Narayanavarman (Devavati)—Mahabhutavarman (Bijnanavati)—Chandramukhavarman (Bhogavati)—Sthitavarman (Nayana Devi)—Susthitavarman or Mriganda (Syama Devi)—Supratisthitavarman— Bhaskaravarman.

(iv) Yuan Chwang's travels in India (AD 629 to 645).
(v) First appearance of the Muslims in India. AD 636. Osman sends a naval expedition to the Bombay Coast.
(vi) Beginning of the Harsha era (AD 606): His formal coronation in AD 612.
(vii) Removal of the capital from Thaneswar to Kanouj.
(viii) He was a great scholar and patron of learning: Banabhatta, a native of Bihar and a famous poet and novelist, was his court bard. He gave much wealth to a poet named Dhavaka. He equally worshipped Shiva and Buddha.
(ix) His quinquennial festival at Allahabad and his boundless charities to all.
(x) He founded charitable institutions for the poor and the sick: res thouses for travellers; set up schools and hospitals. He died in AD 648, leaving no successor. Arjuna Arunasva (i.e. one mounted on a red horse), the general of Harsha seized the empire. There was an attempt to dethrone the usurper. Bhaskaravarman sent aid to the Chinese ambassador for that purpose.

THE CHALUKYA EMPIRE IN THE DECCAN

The Chalukyas, a Kshatriya tribe of Oudh, came down and imposed their rule on the Dravidians of the south. After the fall of the Andhras, the Rathor family became powerful in Maharashta. Defeating these Rathors, the Chalukyas established their empire. Jayasimha was the first Chalukya king. His grandson Pulakesi I was the first emperor (about AD 550). Batapipura, now Badami, was his capital. He performed a horse-sacrifice. His grandson Pulakesi II, was the greatest emperor of the line. The Cheras, Cholas, Pandyas, Pallavas, Gujarat, Rajputana, Malwa—all felt the weight of his mighty arms. He defeated Harshavardhan. Khusru, king of Persia, sought his friendship and sent envoys to his court. A painting in the Ajanta caves depicts the reception of the Persian envoys.

He probably ruled from Nasik. In his last days, he was defeated and killed (in AD 642) by the Pallavas whom he had so often defeated. But his son Vikramaditya I regained power, signally defeating the Pallavas.

After Harsha's death (AD 648) India again became a medley of small states. Yuan Chwang gives the political state of India of the period—about AD 671 Adityasena, son of Madhava Gupta seized east India, claimed over-lordship and performed a horse-sacrifice. The Arabs conquered Persia in AD 642, Afghanistan in the eighth century AD; thence Islam religion went to Central Asia. India was conquered not by the Arabs, but by the northern Muhammadans. Repeated Arab expeditions against India failed. In AD 711, Muhammad, son of Qasim, invaded Sindh, fought at Alor, defeated the king, Dahir Despati and his queen and conquered Sindh and Multan. In AD 725, the invaders overthrew the Vallabhis of Kutch. Aboul AD 828, the Hindus regained Sindh from the Muhammadans (*H.H.W., vol. II*). Hindu Puranists call these early Muhammadan rulers of India *Kailakila Javanas*, who ruled for 106 years.

SUPREMACY OF THE RAJPUTS (AD 800 TO 1200)

A century's anarcy—AD 650 to 750—prevailed after Harsha. Yasovarman of Kanouj (d. 753) built an ephemeral empire. Lalitaditya of Kashmir defeated Yasovarman and other chiefs of India, and took away poet Bhavabhuti to Kashmir.

Amaraja, son to Yasovarman, was the next important king. He embraced Jainism. It is said that powerful Dharmapala of Bengal was his great enemy. Then rose the Rajputs all over India. They belonged to many castes including the Hinduised foreigners. Most of them were of pure descent. The Rajput states about AD 800 were in northern India: Kashmir, the Punjab, Sindh, Gujarat, Rajputana, Malwa, Delhi, Kanouj, Magadha, Bengal, and Assam; and in the Deccan—the Rathor leader Dantidurga defeated the Chalukyas and built empire of his own with Manyakheta (Malkhed) as capital. AD 977 to 1176 was the period of Muslim invasion from without and great feuds within. Harshdeva of Assam seized Bengal, Orissa, Kalinga, and Kosala (south).

6

THE PALA DYNASTY
(AD 780 TO 1080)

Great anarchy prevailed in Bengal about AD 750 caused by the repeated invasions of Yasovarman of Kanouj, Vatsaraja of Gurjat, Rathor Dhruva and Harshadeva of Kamarupa (Lama Taranath's *History of Buddhism; Indian Antiquary, vol. IV, p. 366*). For reasons of security, the people elected Gopala, son to heroic Bapyata, grandson to Dayita-Vishnu king of Gaur-Banga (Dharmapala's Khalimpur copper-plate inscription; Taranath's *History of Buddhism;* Cunningham's *Arch. Survey Reports, vol. XV, p. 148*).

With the Palas, the Bengalis entered the field of Indian politics, arts and architecture.

The Palas were Kshatriya Rajputs of the ancient solar race, professing Buddhism of almost the Hindu type.

GOPALA (AD 780 TO 795)

First of all, he put down the anarchy of Bengal, suppressed a local revolt, and made a gallant stand against the aggressive Indian monarchs. His kingdom extended to Samatata (Devapala's Monghyr Inscription). His queen was Dadda Devi, daughter to a king named Bhadra (according to Professor Keilhorn). Gopala built a Buddhist temple at Nalanda.

VA Smith in his *Early History of India* (*3rd edition, pp. 378* and *397 to 98*) makes Gopala come to the throne sometime between AD 730 and 740, which does not seem possible. According to Taranath, Gopala ruled forty-five years. Smith also accepts that. But no evidence shows it. According to Smith, Gopala died about AD 800; but there is evidence to show that Dharmapala, son to Gopala was on the throne before AD 800. Amaraja was Dharmapala's enemy.

The Khalimpur Inscription states that Gopala's grandfather was 'versed in all the sciences'. His father Bapayata was 'a great vanquisher of foes' and his fame reached the sea. Yasovarman defeated Gaur-Banga in AD 730. At this time, Dayita-Vishnu had displayed great valour (Stein's *Introduction to Raj-Tarangini, p. 49* and *Gaudo Vaha*).

DHARMAPALA (AD 795 TO 830)

Dharmapala, born of Queen Dadda Devi, succeeded Gopala about AD 795. Powerful even in his youth he was able to establish his supremacy over a greater part of north India.

The Buddhist scholar Haribhadra, annotator of *Ashta-Sahasrika Prajnaparamita*, flourished in his time. He calls Dharmapala a descendant of Rajbhatta (Introduction to *Rama Charita* by S Nandi). From this, some think him to be a descendant to the Khadga dynasty of Samatata, mentioned in the Asrafpur Inscription. By 'Rajabhatta', Professor Sastri means the 'descendant of a military officer of some king' (Introduction to *Rama Charita, p. 6*). The Rajputs all over India were staunch Hindus, but the Palas were Buddhists: the Khadga kings were Buddhists. Samatata was a home of Buddhism. So, it is probable that the Palas were scions of the Khadga line. From the fifteenth century BC to fourteenth century AD, Vikrampur in Samatata had been the seat of powerful dynasties. A descendant of the Khadga house may have seized Gaur at some opportune moment.

In their inscriptions, the Pala kings style them as 'Gauresvara of Gauradhipa', i.e. Lord of Gaur. In the Sagartal Inscription of Bhoja of the Pratihara clan, Dharmapala is called *Bangapati* and his soldiers are called *Bengas*, i.e. Bengalis. Therefore, Banga was a part of the Pala empire and most of the soldiers were good Bengalis. The Garuda Pillar

Inscription, Shloka 2, states: 'I have made Dharmapala the lord of eastern quarters, now master of all quarters.'

Taranath says, the Palas first conquered Banga (east Bengal) and then Magadha. The Pala kings were Bengalis. According to Taranath, Dharmapala first ruled Banga; then his power spread to Gaur and elsewhere. These lead us to surmise that Dharmapala was at first governor of Banga under his father.

The dates of Cunningham, Hoernle, Rajendralal now appear erroneous by the discovery of many new inscriptions. VA Smith has therefore given it to the close of eight century AD (*E.H.I., 3rd ed., p. 398*).

The inscriptions of Bhagalpur, Gwalior, and Amoghavarsha I prove that Dharmapala of Gaur-Banga, the Kanouj kings—Indrayudha and Chakrayudha, the Rathor king—Govinda III, and Gurjar king—Nagabhatta II were contemporaries (*Ep Indica, vol. IX, p. 26, note 4*).

According to Taranath, Dharmapala ruled for sixty-four years. RP Chanda makes it fifty. The Khalimpur Inscription was issued in his thirty-second year. So, he may have ruled for thirty-five years.

Dharmapala married Ranna Devi, daughter to the Rathor king, Paravala, granddaughter to Karkkaraja (Devapala's Monghyr Inscription). The Rathor king, Paravala, left Gujarat and migrated to the central province at Pathari. Here also he was harassed by the Gurjars. Paravala sought the aid and alliance of Dharmapala, the great rival of the Gurjar-Pratihars, by giving his daughter in marriage to Dharmapala.

According to Taranath, Dharmapala conquered Assam, Tirhoot and Gaur. So, his empire extended from the sea to Delhi. The Khalimpur copper-plate inscription states that Bhoja (Bundelkhand), Matsya (Jaipur), Madra, Kuru, Yadu (i.e. Punjab), Avanti (Malwa), Gandhar, almost the whole of Afghanistan, Yavana (Turkey), and Kira (Kangra valley) formed his dominions (*Ep. Indica, vol. IV, p. 246*). Kanouj was given to Chakrayudha. Dharmapala had conquered Kangra, Turashka, the Punjab, and Rajputana before he set up Chakrayudha on the Kanoun throne. Narayanapala's Bhagalpur Inscription makes this fact more distinct.

In the nineth century AD, Vatsaraja was at first supreme in north India. Then rose Dharmapala aided by Chakrayudha of Kanouj. Nagabhatta II inherited not only his father's state, but also his valour. He repeatedly defeated Dharmapala and his ally Chakrayudha. The

Sagartal Inscription makes Nagabhatta conqueror of Anarta (Kathiawar), Malwa, Kirata, Turashaka, Vatsa (Allahabad), and Matsya. Vatsaraja conquered almost the whole of India, but was finally defeated by Dhruvadharavarsha and driven to the desert. Great rivalry then followed between Nagabhatta II and Govinda III of the south. Dharmapala and Chakrayudha, being repeatedly defeated by Nagabhatta, begged shelter from Govinda III, when the latter arrived at the Himalayas in course of his conquests (Amoghavarsha's copper-plate inscription in the possession of Dr RK Bhandarkar). Govinda III heard Dharmapala's prayer and marched against Nagabhatta who was defeated and driven to the desert like his father. To prevent the incursions of the Gurjars and to confine them to the desert, Govinda III placed his nephew, Karkka, on the Gurjar throne (*Ind. Antiquary, vol. XII, p. 160*). Thus, Govinda III conquered a good part of north India.

Amoghavarsha I's Sirur and Nilgunda inscriptions tell us that his father Govinda III had defeated the Gaurians (*Ep. Indica, vol. VI, pp. 102–103*). No proof of any quarrel between Govinda and Dharmapala has been found as yet. Doubtless, Dharmapala had to bow down his head to Govinda III to subdue his great enemy Nagabhatta II. Amoghavarsha's inscription may have hinted at that. The Sagartal and Una copper-plate inscriptions both speak of Dharmapala's defeat. Vahukadhavala, a vassal king of Saurashtra under Nagabhatta II, aided his master in defeating Dharmapala (*Ep. Indica, vol. IX, pp.* 5 and 7).

On Rathor King Govinda III's return from north India to the Deccan, Dharmapala got the opportunity to establish his supreme power in north India. Dharmapal's younger brother, Vakpala was a great general. He conquered many lands for Dharmapala (Narayanapala's Bhagalpur Inscription).

Devapala's Monghyr Inscription gives the extent of Dharmapala's empire. Dharmapala sent the defeated kings home with ample rewards. In the central province, Paravala maintained his independence under the shelter of Dharmapala. Dharmapala's Khalimpur Inscription shows that he was exceedingly popular with all classes of people. Dharmapala knew that the people made his father king. So, it was his duty to make them happy in every way. The Khalimpur Inscription mentions 'Yavaraj Tribhubanapala'. Probably, he died in his father's lifetime or it was simply another of Devapala.

DEVAPALA (AD 830 TO 865)

He was the son of Queen Ranna Devi. Tribhuvanapala was probably the son by another queen. There is nothing to show that there was a dispute between the two brothers about succession.

Almost the whole of India, from the Himalayas to Ramesvaram; from the Bay of Bengal to the Arabian Sea belonged to Devapala without a rival (Monghyr inscription). Bhattagurava Misra's Dinajpur pillar inscription states that Devapala, under the guidance of his able minister Darbhapani, succeeded in conquering the entire tract between the Himalayas and the river Rewa; and the eastern sea to the western sea. Taranath says that Devapala conquered all north India (*Ind. Antiquary, vol. IV*).

Conquest of Orissa and Assam

Jayapala, nephew to Devapala, a great general, occupied Orissa without striking a blow. The name of the Orissa king is not known. The very terror of Jayapala's arms, made the Orissa king take to his heels, leaving his capital (Bhagalpur Inscription). Orissa and Kalinga were under Sasanka in the seventh; under Harsha of Gaur in the eighth and under the Palas in the nineth century AD.

Banamala, son of Harjjara, king of Assam, at the approach of Jayapala, tendered his submission and concluded a treaty with him. The Harjjara dynasty is proved by Banamala's Tejpur Inscription and Bala Varman's Naogaon Inscription.

The Bhagalpur and the Garuda pillar inscriptions distinctly mention Jayapala as the conqueror of Orissa and Assam.

The Kambojas and the Hunas

The Kambojas of the north-west Himalayas were very powerful at this time. They would often come down on the Indian plains and cause havoc. Devapala, therefore, marched with a large and strong army and defeated them. The Bangarh pillar inscription and another preserved in the garden of Dinajpur Raj show that the Kambojas conquered the Gaur kingdom in the tenth century AD coming from their Himalayasn, home. The Garuda pillar inscription states that Devapala humbled the pride of the Hunas who still remained in parts of India, especially in central India. The *Harsha Charita* describes Prabkakaravardhan as a 'Lion to the Huna deer'. Rajyavardhan fought out the Hunas in AD 605 (*Harsha Charita, V.P. 310*). Most probably, Devapala conquered the Hunas of Malwa. In the tenth century AD, these Hunas were great rivals to the rising Pramara dynasty of Malwa. Padmagupta's *Nava Sahasanka Charita* and the inscription of the Pramara kings tell us that he Pramara King Siyaka II, his son Utpala Manjaraja (974–995) and Sindhuraj fought hard with the Hunas.

King of Dravida and Gurjara

The Garuda pillar inscription tells us that under the guidance of the minister Kedara Misra, he was able to defeat the kings of Orissa, Dravida, Gurjara and rule for a long time, and empire that bordered the sea. The fifth shloka of the same points to Devapala's Vindhay expedition, attested further by Devapala's Monghyr Inscription. Hence, it is obvious that Devapala was in collision with the Rathor and the Gurjar kings at the same part of the Vindhyas, in which Devapala conquered both of them whose names are not given in the plate. Probably, Krishna II (about AD 877 to 913), the Rathor king of Malkhed was this Dravida king and Mihirabhoja was the Gurjara king; or Ramabhadra, son of Nagabhatta II, was defeated by Devapala. To avenge the defeat of Ramabhadra, his son Bhojadeva (Mihirabhoja), conquered Kanouj before AD 843; for he issued a copper-plate grant from Kanouj in AD 843 (*Ep. Ind., vol. V, p. 211*). Devapala fought hard with Bhojadeva for his empire, Bhojadeva'sGwalior Inscription is given in the *Ep. Indica, vol. IX, p. 95.* Bhojadeva defeated the Bengalis. Bhoja's Sagartal Inscription does not say that Bhojadeva defeated Devapala (*Annual Report*, A.S. of India, *1903–4, . 281*). However, Devapala could not prevail against the repeated attacks of the Gurjaras who under Mihirabhoja were able to occupy Kanouj before AD 843. This occupation was so long that in his history, Vatsaraj dynasty is called Mahodaya-Gurjjara-Pratihara Vansa.

Mihirabhoja conquered the Huna kingdom on the Punjab frontier, Saurashtra in south-west, Kanouj in north-east and in south-east, a tract at the source of the Narmada. So Devapala's empire soon lost several provinces.

The Ministers

Devapala's success was due to his own genius, to his able ministers, to the valour and skill of his nephew, Jayapala and to the practicality of the Gaurian people. Darbhapani was his first Prime Minister; he was much honoured by Devapala. These ministers were more like 'king-makers'. The Buddhist Pala kings honoured and feared the Brahman ministers. They were Bengali 'Peshwas'. Darbhapani's son, Somesvara, was probably a general of Devapala (Garuda pillar inscription). Kedara Misra, son to Somesvara, next became a very able Prime Minister. Three generations of ministers show Devapala's long reign. Devapala's Monghyr Inscription was executed in the thirty-third year of his regin. So perhaps, he ruled for thirty-three years.

His Religion

Devapala was a Buddhist, but was very catholic in spirit. He equally honoured the Buddhists and the Brahmans. Devapala was very generous and gave much to charity. So, he has been compared to Bali, Bhargava, Karna, Vikramaditya, and others.

VIGRAHAPALA ALIAS SURAPALA (AD 865 TO 870)

Devapala's crown-prince was Rajyapala (Monghyr Plate, lines 51–52) but he died in the lifetime of Devapala. So, General Jayapala's son, Vigrahapala I, alias Surapala, succeeded to the throne of Gaur-Banga (*Ep. Ind., vol. III, App. I, p. 17*). From the inscription of Narayanapala, Mahipala I, Vigrahapala III, and Madanapala, it appears that Jayapala begot a very powerful son Vigrahapala by name, who married the Haihaya princess, Lajja Devi, of exceptionally pure character. He inherited neither the genius nor the ambition of Dharmapala or Devapala. He probably did nothing worth mentioning. He ruled for five years when he left the reign to his son and turned an anchorite (Bhagalpur Inscription). Kedara Misra was his minister. Poet Sandhyakara calls Kedara a Vrihaspati and Vigrahapala an Indra.

NARAYANAPALA (AD 870 TO 925)

Born of Queen Lajja Devi, Narayanapala came to the throne of Vigrahapala. He ruled for fifty-five years. A brass image of Parvati was established by a merchant in the fifty-fourth year of his reign. His Bhagalpur Inscription was issued in the seventeenth year of his reign. Decline of the Pala power began from his father's time. Even in Devapala's time, Kanouj was occupied by the Gurjaras who later on, conquered Benaras and even advanced as far as Mudgagiri (Monghyr) where a great battle was fought in which Narayanapala was defeated. Bhojadeva's allies were Karkka of Mandapapura, Mandore in Marwar (Karkka's son Bakka's Jodhpur Inscription: *J.R.A.S., 1894, p. 7*); Sorha Deva's Kalha Inscription states that Gunambudhi Deva I, defeated Narayanapala (*Ep. Ind., vol. VII p. 89*). The Bhagalpur Inscription bestows on him ample praise for his strong sense of justice, charity and pure character.

RAJYAPALA (AD 925 TO 930)

Rajyapala succeeded his father Narayanapala on the throne of Gaur-Banga. He acquired high fame by excavating many large tanks and building many lofty temples. He married Bhagya Devi, daughter to the Rathor king Tunga Deva.

GOPALA II (AD 930 TO 945)

On Rajyapala's death, his son, born of Queen Bhagya Devi came to the throne. Of him, nothing glorious is recorded. It is said that he was able to recover a part of the lost kingdom.

VIGRAHAPALA II (AD 945 TO 975)

Soon after his ascension, Vigrahapala left Gaur and took shelter in Banga. The Khajuraho Inscription of the Chandela king Yasovarman, executed in AD 954, states that Yasovarman defeated the kings of Gaur, Kosala, Kashmir, Mithila, Malwa, Chedi, Kuru, and Gurjar. Certainly through fear of Yasovarman, Vigrahapala sought refuge in east Bengal, which is full of rivers. The Kambojas also occupied Gaur before AD 966 (*J.A.S.B. New Deries, vol. VII, p. 690*). Losing the kingdom, Vigrahapala wandered about here and there. He fled to Vikrampur from the Kambojas. The army, scattered, were moving in the hills of Tripura. A work called *Pancharaksha* written in the twenty-sixth year of his reign, has been found (*J.R.A.S., p. 151*).

MAHIPALA I (AD 975 TO 1026)

Mahipala inherited only Samatata (littoral Bengal); its capital was in Vikrampur. Here, he fathered a stong army and boldly fought and recovered his fathers' state. Doubtless, he spared no pains to retrieve the fallen glory of the former imperial house. But in his efforts, he lost south Rarha and Banga. For in AD 1023 Rajendra Chola found Ranasura in south Rarha and Govindachandra in east Bengal. His Baghasura Inscription was executed in the third year of his reign. He ruled fifty-two years (*Ind. Ant., vol. IV, p. 366*). Shortly after his ascension, the Turkish invasion of north-west India took place. Jayapala was on the Udabhandapur (Ohind) throne. Kashmir, Kanouj, Kalinjar gave Jayapala utmost aid, but in vain. Sultan Mahmud occupied the Punjab. Mahipala fighting his own enemies, could lend no help to the Hindu confederacy. The fall of the Palas was due to the conquest by the Kambojas, the revolt of the people under the leader Divya, and the rise of the Sena kings of Bengal.

DHARMAPALA (AD 795 TO 830)

Dharmapala conquered the eastern half of north India. In the nineth century, three powers struggled for the suzerainty of India—the Palas of east India, the Gurjars of Rajputana and the Rathors of the Deccan. Vatsa, the Gurjar king conquered almost the whole of India, but was afterwards defeated by the Rathor king Dhruva and driven to the desert. Govinda III, son to Dhruva, conquered the whole of north India (*Ind. Ant., vol. XII, p. 160*). Then Devapala (AD 830 to 65) claims to be the one absolute lord of India, Ceylon and other islands, Kambojas and the Hunas and a part of Tibet (Mongyr, Inscription). His Brahman minister Darbhapani and General Jaipal were his main props (*Ind. Ant., vol. IV*). About AD 992, Sabaktigin conquered as far as the Indus. His son Sultan Mahmud defeated Jaipal of Lahore at Peshawar (AD 1001). The kings of Bhatia, Multan and the combined army of Gwalior, Malwa, Kalinjar, Kanouj, Delhi, and Ajmer were defeated at Peshawar (AD 1008). He plundered the rich temples of Nagarkot, Thaneswar, Mathura and Somnath. His dealings with the Hindu kings were lenient. He conquered the Punjab in AD 1022.

About AD 973, the Chalukyas again became supreme with their capital at Kalyan. The Cholas of the east coast rose to importance. Rajaraja the Great (AD 985 to 1011) overthrew the Pallavas. He conquered Kalinga and Ceylon. As lord paramount, he ruled over the Madras Presidency, Ceylon and a large part of Mysore. His son Rajendra Choladeva (AD 1011 to 1025) spread his power over Orissa and Bengal and maintained a powerful navy. The Hoysala or Ballals occupied western Mysore and Malabar. Their capital was Dvarasamudra, now Halebid.

The house of Gazni, after 150 years, had been supplanted by that of Muhammad Ghori (AD 1186 to 1206) resolved to conquer north India, then held by numerous Rajput clans: Delhi and Ajmer were under Prithviraj at deadly enmity with the Rathors of Kanouj and the Baghilas of Gujarat. The effect of the quarrel was disastrous to both parties. In AD 1911, Muhammad was no doubt, defeated at Tirouri by Prithvi and his allies, but in AD 1193. Shahabuddin utterly routed the Rajput at Thanesvar, slew him and annexed his dominions. In AD 1194, defeat of Jayachandra, the Rathor king of Kanouj at Chandrawar near Etawa, Muslim occupation of Kanouj, Benaras and other tracts made the Rathors found the principality of Marwar. In 1195, Gwalior, was taken, and Gujarat invaded: its capital Anhalpattan was taken. In 1196, Kalinjar and Bihar were taken. In 1198–99, north-west Bengal (capital Gaur) was seized by Baktyer from Lakshmanasena who fled to Vikrampur where his descendants ruled 130 years more. Thus, by AD 1200, the whole of north India except Kashmir, Nepal, east Bengal, Orissa, and Assam were conquered by the Muhammadans. Malik Kafur, General of Alauddin, conquered a greater part of the Deccan by AD 1312, East Bengal fell in AD 1328, Orissa in AD 1565 and the powerful empire of Vijaynagar in AD 1565. Mysore, an offshoot of Vijaynagar, till Independence bore the crown and glory of our last brightest Hindu state of the south. The king was a descendant of Krishna who was worshipped as an *avatara* of the Supreme Being.

The Ahoms, a Tibeto-Burman people conquered north-east India in the thirteenth century. From them is the name Assam. They became Hinduised and ruled for centuries and had a regular history.

7

PAURANIC AGE
(200 BC TO AD 1200)

Some scholars have made much of Buddhism in India. They think that at one time (say, from 242 BC to BC 500), Buddhism had eclipsed Hinduism, that a great majority of the people had embraced Buddhism and that almost every thing was Buddhistic in style. It does not appear that there is much truth in it. Buddhism was, no doubt, prevalent in east India. In other parts of India, it was rather sporadic. The large province of Assam was entirely free from Buddhism. The provinces about Haridwar, Kanouj, Allahabad, Benaras had little Buddhism. Karnal, Jaipur, Panchala, furnish no proof as to the prevalence of Buddhism there. Even in Magadha and Bengal, Hinduism flourished side by side with Buddhism. The monks were regular Buddhists, but the laymen were mostly Buddhist Hindus, i.e. men who followed some Buddhist doctrines on the Hindu basis, having castes and Hindu manners. This is why they could be won back to Hinduism easily. There are some native Christians in south India, who still follow caste system and some other ancestral Hindu manners. In Bengal, the Vaishnavas worship their own god—Vishnu or Radhakrishna; yet they worship Durga and Kali. The Buddhist pilgrims of Ceylon and China of the fourth century AD did not notice Buddhism flourishing in India.

The editor of the *Historians' History of the World* is right in observing that owing to its abstraction and the rivalry of the Hindus,

Buddhism was a failure in India; in modified form, it has, however, prevailed in other parts of Asia.

RELIGION

(i) Vedic Religion

In spite of the Upanishadic doctrine of one Supreme Being with the universe as His emanation, the Vedic religion—the worship of the elemental gods by sacrifice in the fire and sincere and earnest prayers—continued till 200 BC, after which it became less and less gradually. The Khans of central Asia still worship the Vedic gods (*Historians' History of the World*). But the Hindus have almost forgotten the Vedic form of worship. An orthodox Hindu will, however, prefer to call his religion of today a veiled form of Vedic Hinduism.

Some learned Brahmans with Patanjali (150–140 BC) at their head, tried to revive the Vedic religion. Under their influence, Pushyamitra performed a grand Vedic rite. The Sungas, the Kanvas, and the Guptas partially revived Vedic Hinduism. The last great effort was made by Kumarilabhatta of Bihar. The great poet–dramatist Bhavabhuti also joined the movement. He wrote three great works that profess partiality for Vedic rites. But the Tantric schools opposed and frustrated the efforts. After more than ten centuries, Dayananda Sarasvati of Gujarat again took up the subject, established his Arya Samaj for the revival of Vedic religion and civilisation. The society has been doing good and useful work.

(ii) Pauranic Religion or Modern Hinduism

The Vedic gods now became inferior. The worship of the Supreme Being in his triple form—Brahma, Vishnu and Mahesh—came in (the *triad* is mentioned in the Rig Veda *I, 34.II; I, 45. 2; I, 139.11*) Their three-fold functions are creation, preservation, destruction, and reproduction. The trinity are not however, worshipped in their divine characters. Brahma, Vishnu and Mahesh or Siva are now semi-historical gods and worshiped as such. Their wives also are deified. Brahma's wife is Sarasvati (Savitri), Vishnu's Lakshmi and Siva's Durga or Parvati. Hints of goddesses are also found in the Vedas (Cowell).

(iii) Image-worship

Idols are mentioned in the Vedas and desired to be respected, but their general adoration is discouraged. The image-worship may be traced back as early as the fourteenth century BC. Of course, idolatry is not ennobling. Idols are not gods themselves; they are mere aids. They are made of either stone, metal, wood, straw, clay or paper.

Whence is the origin and idea of an image? Hirendra Nath Dutta of Calcutta gives a curious theory of it. He says that an image is formed by the vibration of ether or any other medium. Gods and goddesses, modes of tunes in music are represented on paper or clay as male or female figures. Dutta argues that when hymns are uttered with some set accents, images are formed in the air through the vibrations of ether. The particular images are formed of particular gods.

It is given in the acoustics that if a quantity of sand be spread on a glass or a metallic plate and the musical rod of the violin be passed over the sand, then various curious figures are seen, called *Chladni's Figures*. The images of our gods seem something like them. Now the question is, does vibration of ether produce such figures as are spoken of above? Mere analogy cannot do. It awaits scientific experiment. The worship of historic persons such as Rama and Krishna began after AD 1000.

(iv) A world of legends

Incarnations unknown to the Vedas and Manu, now gained ground and became objects of popular worship and adoration. Vishnu is said to have had ten incarnations (according to the *Bhagavata*, 22). The first was a fish that saved Manu, his family and the Veda in an ark from the deluge. This is probably a myth. The second was a tortoise that raised up the earth from sinking. Here, the tortoise is perhaps a celestial sphere; its back is the heavenly vault; Ananta is infinitude: Ananta Naga is the ecliptic: Mandara mount is the Pole. *Satapatha Brahmana* mentions the fish and the boar. The *Taittiriya Aranyaka* refers to the boar incarnation. A big boar killed Hiranyaksha, an enemy and pest of the Aryan community. Hiranyakasipu, another tyrant, was killed probably by a lion. The fifth was a Brahman dwarf called Vamana who duped, defeated and drove away the tyrant Bali. The sixth was Parasurama, the great Brahman hero who had humbled the imperious warriors of India and established the Brahman supremacy once more. The seventh was Rama, an ideal king, conqueror of Ceylon. The eighth was Balarama, brother to Krishna, both of whom had re-established a pious empire in India, after killing the tyrants. The nineth was Buddha. The tenth, Kalki, is yet to be born.

Krishna was deified before the fifth century BC. Megasthenes also refers to it. Deification of Krishna is found also in the *Great Commentary* of Patanjali (150 BC). But his general worship in a rather debased form began after AD 1000.

(v) Gods

Thirty-three gods are magnified into 330 million. Brahma, Vishnu, Siva, Indra, Jalakara (Varuna), Kartika, Ganesha, Visvakarman, Kuvera; Durga, Sashthi, Sarasvati, Lakshmi, Sitala, Manasa; Rama, Lakshmana, Hanuman, Krishna, Balarama.

Besides, large trees, great rivers and rocks are visible types of worship.

(vi) Heaven and Hell

The good and pious souls go to heaven and the wicked ones go to hell. Salvation—that final absorption in the universal soul by pious thoughts—is for the wise.

(vii) Pilgrimage, organised on a very large scale.
(viii) Pompous melas, pujas, processions, decorations; offering of flowers, fruits, perfumes, rice, sandal-juice, and incense.
(ix) Temples, priests, religious endowments in lands and money, rules of purity, caste, rules, vows, fastings form important parts of modern Hinduism.

With the rise of the Rajputs, temples multiplied. Indian towns are now crowded with temples on which the nation's wealth and energies are lavishly spent. Poetry, arts, architecture, sculpture, music have lent their aids. These have, at the same time, produced their evil effects. Worship has been transferred from the domestic hearth to temples; the 'twice-born' now seldom worship themselves at home; priests do their pujas. Priests have become idle and ignorant; a gradual blind veneration of images has come upon the people. Superstition has spread its web and ensnared the healthy and strong brain power of the nation.

(x) Sacrifices

Hindu kings and wealthy men still perform some sacrifices. Sacrifice to the fire in some minor yajnas, is still in vogue. Hindus lived in five sects, viz., Saivas, Saktas, Sauras, Ganapatys and Vaishnavas.

Brahma was little worshipped. 'The worship of Siva and Vishnu is very ancient in India' (Megasthenes). Alexander and his men found Saivism and the Pasupatas. Chandragupta and Ashoka were Saivites at first. It is said that Panini obtained his great brain power by worshipping Siva. Arjuna had obtained great military skill by worshipping this great god. He is now chiefly sought for wisdom. Everywhere in India, his linga (symbol of phallic energy) and not his image, is worshipped. Sankara (AD 788 to 820) popularised the worship of Siva throughout India.

A worshipper of Siva is a Saiva or Saivite. A worshipper of Sakti (literally goddess of power) in the form of Durga, Kali or any of Siva's consorts, is a Sakta. One who worships the Sun-god is a Saura. The Sun temple of Multan was noticed even by Alberuni (AD 1030). As the giver of health, the sun is worshipped by the Hindus to this day. The Saurav as a special sect, lived in the Punjab and west India. The Ganapatyas were worshippers of Ganesha. This sect is now probably rare. Ganesha is the giver of all good things. His red figure with an elephant's head is to be met with everywhere in India. He is worshipped first of all. For he destroys all harm and evil, and confers all blessings. The Vaishnavas worship Vishnu. Ancient Vaishnavism is long gone. Ramanujam and his disciple Ramananda preached a new Vaishnavism in which they asked their adherents to worship Rama as early Vishnu. Soon, another school preached a new tenet. Madhavacharya, Chaitanya and Ballabhacharya preached Vaishnavism in which Krishna was worshipped as Vishnu. Formerly, Puri had the temple of Purushothama, a name of Vishnu. Then Buddhism prevailed. The present temple of Jagannath (Lord of the World), a form of Krishna, was established in the twelfth ventury AD.

In this age, Hinduism had a face many new faiths. It has not only saved itself, but also has successfully withstood all foreign influences, nay even converted many foreigners. The Agnikula heroes were Hinduised Persians; some of the Indo-Greeks, Indo-Scythians, Indo-Parthians, Kadphises monarchs, Kushanas, Hunas, were Hinduised. The powerful Gurjars were Hinduised Hunas. The Rajputs of all ranks were devoted champions of Hinduism. The Sungas, the Kanvas, Vikramaditya, the Guptas, Kumarila, Sankara and the Rajputs made Hinduism supreme. Buddhism melted forever.

Christianity rose in the Deccan and made some progress. Ramanujam and Ramananda set up neo-Vaishnavism, a 'religion of redemption', and saved the lower classes from Christianity. From the fourteenth century AD, lower-class Hindus began to embrace Islam in large numbers. The later Hindu reformers took a stand against it.

Professor Wilson found eleven classes of Saivas, four classes of Saktas, nineteen classes of Vaishnavas, besides other miscellaneous sects.

(xi) Tantric Vedantism after AD 1000

'Hinduism, in its essentials is one of the most rational of religions. No country has placed greater reliance on reason than India has done. Indian thought touches the root of things. Here man is a little Brahma Spheroid, i.e. microcosm. Man as spirit is God. Man as mind and body, is the power of God. Man is this God and His power. As God's power, man and the Universe are real. The world is real, though it changes and does not last forever. The world is the experience of Siva in the form of all beings and His experience is never unreal. Siva and Jiva are one. So, give no needless pain to the body. Leave not the world. Leave ill thoughts, ill-doing. All beings are the kindred expressions of the one Mother-Self. Man is his own master. Never be virtuous beyond thy nature. Worship Dharma (virtue), Devata (gods) and Go-Mata (Cow). There is no religion higher than truth. Truth will conquer.' (Sir John Woodroffe).

BUDDHISM

We have already said that Buddha was a Hindu reformer and his religion was a form of reformed Hinduism. So, the Hindus regarded him as an incarnation of Vishnu. Buddhists gradually made Buddhism different from Hinduism. Before Ashoka, there had been two sects of the Buddhists. Ashoka resolved to revive the old Buddhism. About 300 BC the Brahmans had started the practical worship of the Vedic trinity in the shape of image-worship. To popularise religion, Ashoka used to bring out a procession referred to in the Rupnath Hill Edict, displaying various images. The popular religion of Ashoka aimed not so much at Nirvana, as at heaven. That included, besides the eight-fold path of ethical conduct, certain rites also.

The worship of gods formed a chief part of the rites established by Ashoka. Ashoka made image-worship general throughout India. Patanjali (150 BC) also hints at it. Ashoka's title 'Beloved of Gods', shows this. 'The gods that were not so long worshipped in *Jambu Dwipa* (India) are now being worshipped by the people.' (*J.R.A.S., 1911; 1912; 1913*). Buddha preached his creed by sweet sermons, by fables and parables; by preachers, ministers, missionaries; and finally by personal renunciation. It is often alleged that Buddhism was triumphant under Ashoka. We cannot accept the view without grave doubt.

NEO-BUDDHISM

In spite of the best efforts of Ashoka, Buddhism was not largely followed by the Indians. The very abstract nature of the religion and Hindu rivalry made it a failure. Erelong, another great champion rose to make it successful. He was the great scholar Nagarjuna of the second century AD. The Andhras were probably his first patrons. He showed a new way to all for salvation which he called *Mahayana*, i.e. the Excellent Way to Nirvana. Ashoka's school was called *Hinayana*, i.e. the Inferior Way.

The *Mahayana* school was largely of foreign origin; its development was the result of the complex interaction of Indian Zoroastrian, Christian Gnostic and Hellenic elements. In this neo-Buddhism, Buddha became a god, with his ears open to the prayer of the faithful and served by a hierarchy of Bodhisattvas and other beings acting as mediators between him and sinful men. This deified Buddha was worshipped throughout Kanishka's vast empire. But Kanishka, even after his conversion, worshipped both the old and the new gods like Harshavardhana bowing before Shiva and Buddha.

Causes of the decline and fall of Buddhism in India:

(a) Its abstractness and morbid view of life.
(b) Rivalry of the Hindus.
(c) Want of state-patronage.
(d) Want of selfless learned monks.
(e) Its later gross idolatry and tantric superstitions.

(f) Fiery preachings of Kumarila, Sankara and their disciples.
(g) Its early neglect of Sanskrit.

Hinduism, Jainism and Buddhism are the three chief religions of India. The last two never thrived much because they have few rites. A religion cannot stand without rites. A paddy grain sprouts in the ground, but not a rice grain, void of husk. Yet, rice is the essence of a paddy grain. A mere set of morals makes no religion. Jainism is a cross between the other two. Buddhism of Nepal was philosophical and scientific.

In ancient times, men were not hired to preach Hinduism. Those who did, were actuated by love and duty. Nor, did it try to thrust itself upon unwilling people or make their miseries or worldly ambitions its opportunity.

JAINISM

Jainism progressed in the sixth or seventh century AD, became conspicuous in the eighth or nineth and highly prosperous in the eleventh; but declined after the twelfth century AD. Its principal seats are in south India, Gujarat and west of Hindustan. It was never successful in the provinces on the Ganges. Dr Buchanon speaks of several persecutions by the Brahmans in the south of India (*vol. I, p. 81*). Jains are still numerous—over five million—especially in Gujarat, Rajputana and Canara. They are generally rich; many are bankers and possess a large portion of the commercial wealth of India.

They have sixty-four Indras and twenty-two devis. They give no preference to the greater gods of the Hindus. No doubt, they deny the scriptural character of the Vedas, yet they allow them great authority in all points agreeing with their religion. Their objections are to bloody sacrifices and loss of life which burnt offerings cause. They admit the whole of the Hindu gods, worship some of them, but consider them inferior to their saints. They have no veneration for relics, no monastic order: their priests, called Yatis, are of all castes. They wear very large loose white mantles; have their heads bare, hair and beard clipped; carry a black rod and a brush for sweeping away animals; live on alms; never bathe. According to the Digambara sect, women are not fit for salvation and the Sudras cannot worship the saints.

Jain temples are generally very large and handsome, often flat-roofed, with courts and colonnades, occasionally like Hindu temples; sometimes circular and surrounded by colossal statues of the Tirthankaras. The walls are painted with legends, mixed with those of the Hindus. Besides images, they have marble altars with figures of saints in relief; impressions of foot steps of saints in relief and those of holy men.

The finest specimens of Jain temples of the Hindu form are the noble remains on Mt Abu. Jain caves of Ellora, Nasik and other places are noticeable. A magnificent one lies near Ahmedabad. Jains have a gast learning like the Brahmans, but usually vary in chronology and geography. Their sacred language is Pali or Magadhi.

The two—Jainism and Buddhism—arose out of Brahmanism which is natural. Hinduism rose from the worship of the powers of nature to theism and declined into scepticism with the learned and human worship with the vulgar.

Buddhism was triumphant in India and Ceylon under Ashoka in the third century AD. It went to Tibet and Tartary early; to China in AD 65 where it was fully established about AD 310. Its decline in India was noticed by Fahien in the fifth century AD. He found it flourishing in lands between China and India, declining in the Punjab, languishing in the last stage in the Gangetic valley. Kapilavastu was ruined and deserted. Buddhism was not yet in Java. It was driven out of India by Kumarila and Sankara; but it was yet supreme in Hindustan in the eighth, prevailing at Benaras till eleventh and in the north of Gujarat till the twelfth century AD (Erskine, *Bombay Transc., vol. III, p. 533*, with Major Kennedy's note).

It is no more in the plains of India. It is still established in Ceylon, Chittagong, Burma, Tibet, Siam, countries between India and China, Russian Tartary, China, Korea, Japan and is followed by over half the mankind (Elphinstone).

CHRISTIANITY

The apostles of Christ spread his religion and morality in every land. It is likely that they also came to India so well-known in Palestine. St Thomas is indeed, mentioned in connection with India, by the apocryphal 'Acts of Apostles' written towards the close of the second century AD. *Origin*, however, states (third century AD) that 'Thomas received Parthia as his allotted portion.' The Syrian text of the *Acts of St Thomas* first mentions the connection of St Thomas with Gondopharnes or Gondophares, (Sanskrit Gandharvesa, i.e. lord of Gandhar). Gondophares was an Indo-Parthians of the north-western frontier during Gondophares, reign. The usual Catholic tradition is that St Thomas converted King Gondophares about AD 21 and then preached in south India on the Malabar and Coromandel coasts, founded several churches and at last died a martyr's death at Maliapur near Madras about AD 68.

'The coins of Gondophares are common in Kabul and Kandahar and in the western and southern Punjab.' (Cunningham quoted by Rae in his *Syrian Church in India, p. 53*). The coins and inscription of Gondoiphares, found at Takht-i-Bahai, north-east of Peshawar, confirm the date and conversion of this monarch.

As regards the mission and evangelisation of south India by St Thomas, opinions vary. Bishop Medlycott has tried to prove it. The Rev. G Milne Rae brushes it away, saying, 'Southern India received Christianity not from any of the ancient seats of the Church, but from the Nestorian Patriarchate on the banks of the Tigris.' Kennedy, has shown reason for believing that the Mailapur story was invented in the sixth century AD. VA Smith regards it as purely mythical, 'The historical church of the South is of Nestorian origin, dating from either the fifth or the sixth century AD.'

We think that the first planting of Christianity on the Indian soil did happen in the first century AD and that it was an established religion in south India about the second century AD we have proofs of it:

(a) Malliapur or Mailapur near Madras, was our ancient Hindu town called Mahilaropya, Ptolemy's *Mahilarpha* (AD 140 to 150). Early in the second century AD, a powerful Hindu king named Amarasakti ruled there. He had three wild princes. Nobody could make them learn. The renowned Pandit Vishnu Sharma—the Indian Froebel, however, made them proficient in various sciences (see Preface to the *Panchatantra*). This learned Brahman of eighty, in his reputed *Beasts' Tales* often railed at the Buddhist monks, Jain ascetics (Kshpanakas) and even unlettered begging Brahmans. In one tale, he makes a jackal say, 'Oh how shall I touch this fleshy string with my teeth on this Bhattarakabara, i.e. Sundary?' *Bhattaraka* or Dominica, was a Latin word for Sunday. Like *Dinara* from *Denarius* (a coin), it was coined from Latin. Eating or touching of fish or flesh on Sunday was not prohibited in ancient India. Hence, it is plain that Vishnu Sharma here sarcastically alluded to the earliest Christians of Malliapur, who observed Sunday, refrained from meat and drink and work; probably fasted and read the Bible and said prayers in the churches.

(b) Other Missionary efforts: Eusebios, Bishop of Caesarca, born AD 264 (McCrindle, *Ecclesiatical History V, 10*) tells us that Pantainos of Alexandria, being very eager to preach the Gospel of Christ to the eastern nations, set sail for Indi towards the close of the second century AD.

In Malabar he found a missionary named St Bartholomew who had already come there and preached the Hebrew Gospel of Mathew, a copy of which was shown to Pantainos.

In the sixth century AD, Kalyan was a great seat of Christian mission. Cosmas Ludikopleustes, i.e. the Indian Navigator, (AD 565) found in both Ceylon and south India many Christian churches established by missionaries from Persia. These were certainly offshoots of the Nestorian Church, settled in Persia.

Pilgrims occasionally came to the shrines of bothy St Thomas and St Bartholomew. Alfred the Great of England is said to have sent there in discharge of a vow, an ambassador named Sighelm, with some presents in AD 883. The English envoy took back from India many bright gems and aromatic juices. Some of these Indian presents might be seen even as late as the time of William Malmesbury (*Chronicle of the Kings of England, II, iv*).

Professor Max Müeller and several other scholars have clearly shown that Buddha himself figured as a Christian saint named Josaphat, who is said to have been an Indian prince converted to Christianity by Barlaam. The story of Josaphat and Barlaam was first written in Greek by St John of Damascus in the eighth century AD. It was done into Arabic and then into Latin and afterwards made popular in Europe in Troubadour poetry. In it, Josaphat (Bodhisattva) and Theudas the magician, employed to seduce the royal convert, was Devadatta, the enemy of Buddha (Max Müeller's *Chips from a German Workshop. IV, ed. 1875, pp. 177–89*).

Missionary activity of the Christians, however, begañ in India after the arrival of the Portuguese in the sixteenth century AD.

BUDDHISM AND CHRISTIANITY

The *historians' History of the World,* Vol. II, p. 170 says that 'the tenets of Christ were all of eastern origin'.

A similar view is held by many others. So, we show their points of likeness:

(i) The moral precepts and teachings of both are the same. Immediate relationship existed between India and Greece before Christ, in scientific, religious and literary ideas. Buddhist ideas and precepts penetrated into the Greek world before Christ (vide Ashoka's Girnar Inscription).
   - The Therapeuts in Egypt and the Essenes in Palestine were Buddhist sects (Dean Mansel).
   - 'Buddhism in Syria was a preparation, a fore-runner of Christianity.' (Professor Mahaffy).
   - Bunsen, Seydel and Lillie say that Christianity has sprung directly from Buddhism.

(ii) Christian legends, tales, traditions, forms, institutions, moral precepts are largely based on Buddhism.

(iii) A divine annunciation to the parents of both before birth.

(iv) Both were miraculously born. A star Pushya presided at the birth of both. Asita is the Simeon of the Buddhist story. Auspicious omens were seen at the birth of both.

(v) Temptation of both.

(vi) Both had twelve disciples, the same missionary spirit. Both gave the sublime precepts: the very phraseology of both was the same.

The utterances of Buddha in the Dhammapada were current as household words among the Essences. The young preacher Jesus went to John from whom he learnt most of the precepts and teachings of the Essences.

(vii) Trinity of both: Father, the son and the holy ghost; Buddha, Dharma and Sangha.
(viii) Both performed miracles. Both had used parables.
(ix) Gautama adopted the Hindu theory of Metamscychosis. Jewish *Gilgal* is the same and universally believed by the Jews. The doctrine of resurrection is the same as Hindu transmigration of souls.

Note: The ancient nations thought much in the same way.

(x) Monastic forms, rites and ceremonies are alike. (Even Doctor Rhys Davids admits them).
(xi) Architectural similarity (Doctor Fergusson).
(xii) 'The crozier, the mitre, dalmatic, the cope or pluvial, service with a double choir, psalmody, exorcisms, the censer swinging on five chains, benediction with the right hand on the head of the faithful, the chaplet, sacerdotal, celibacy, Lenten, retirement from the world, the worship of saints, fasts, processions, litanies, holy water, confessions, tonsure, relic-worship, the use of flowers, lights and images before shrines and altars, the sign of the cross, the trinity in unity, the worship of the Queen of heaven, the use of religious books in language unknown to the masses, the aureole or nimbus, the crown of saints, wings to angels, penance, flagellations, the flabellum or fan, popes, cardinals, bishops, abbots, presbyters, deacons, amulets, medicines, illuminated missals, baptism, the mass, requiems. All these are the points of likeness (Abbe Huc, Alfred Lillie, Balfour, Thomson).

Some hold that John the Baptist was an Essence himself. Pliny in his *Natural History (V, 17)* describes the Essences of Palestine. They spread the tenets of Buddha to the pious and thoughtful Jews. Christ learnt from John and other sources, the tenets of Buddha.

Some say that early Christianity was Essencism, that is, Buddhism as it prevailed in Palestine.

RC Dutt says that Christianity as a doctrine, is not indebted to Buddhism. Christ adopted the national monotheistic faith of the Jews, as Gautama had adopted the Hindu doctrine of karma, transmigration, and the final beatitude. The ethical and moral elements of Christ were certainly Buddhistic. Before Christianity, Mithra puja was current in Europe. Europe had the worship of Mithra from Persia and Persia had it from India.

HINDUISM AND CHRISTIANITY

Similarity between these two also, is no less striking. Both turn on Bhakti (faith) as the means of salvation. 'Action, wisdom AD faith are the three steps to salvation' say the Vedas.

The *Brahmana* works deal with rites, ceremonies, sacrifices that prepare, purify and ennoble the mind. The Upanishadas treat of pure wisdom. Sandilya's *Bhatri Sutra* treats of faith. Some scholars hold that Ramanuja, the philosopher reformer of the South, adopted the Christian doctrine of faith from the early Christians of southern India and introduced it into his neo-Vaishnavism. Hindus knew *Bhakti* (faith)long long before Christ (vide also Doctro Grierson's view on *Bhakti* in the *Imperial Gazette of India*). Doctor BN Seal also holds that Hindus took Bhakti from the Christians of southern India. We think that the success of the first Christian missions in southern India had encouraged Ramanuja, Ramananda, Madhvacharya, Chaitanya, and others to turn to the same faith, as a counteraction against Christian conversions.

Krishna (often called Krishta), the expounder of Bhakti in the Gita and Christ appear much alike in their life and teachings. It was predicted that Krishna was to be the founder of a kingdom of righteous principles; Christ was to be the founder of a religious kingdom. Like predictions occur in the Vedas and the Old Testament; Kansa is the Herod of the Hindus, Krishna is a cowherd; Christ is shepherd. Both make their sudden appearance before the public. Many accept them: both preach religion and lofty morality. Both had many enemies. Krishna's theory of yajna is Christ's self-sacrifice. Their great antiquity appears from the *Chhandogya Upanishad*, Panini's grammar. Both Hinduism and Christianity have trinity, transmigration of soul in common. The Jews had not the custom of eating the consecrated wafer or Eucharist, which the Christians adopted from the Persians who used to have *Havih-Sesha* (Eucharist) after the Mithra puja. This is Vedic 'ida' that is, consecrated purodasa, bread made from powdered rice or barley. It is still current in India.

Professor EB Cowell has shown how the Upanishadic monotheism early spread to different parts of the world. There were Hindu colonies in Syria, Palestine and other parts of western Asia. Hence it seems probable that Christ was indebted to both Hindus and Buddhists for his tenents.

MUHAMMADANISM

The Arabs, composed of independent tribes, were naturally trained to cope with extremes of fatigue and privation; were laborious and abstemious; had a keen eye, slender body, determined countenance, grave demeanour, and martial energy.

Muhammad born in AD 570 belonged to a tribe of Koreish, a priestly class of Mecca. Poor in youth, he accompanied his uncle's camels in a long trading journey. A rich marriage early raised him to independence.

Most of the Arabs of his time were sunk in idolatry, worship of stars and low morals. Some Jewish and Christian tribes then lived in Mecca. Hindus, Jains and Buddhists also then lived in Mecca and other cities of Arabia. Higher notions of faith and practice were introduced there. The Arab idolaters knew the Supreme Being and their other gods were subordinate. Yet, the influence of monotheism was limited.

Muhammad often contemplated in Mount Hira. A cousin of his wife's skilled in Jewish learning, translated into Arabic the Hebrew scriptures. Perhaps from that, Muhammad derived his idea of the unity of God. After intense meditation, he felt within that he was commissioned by God to restore pure belief and worship. Muhammad was now aged forty. After three or four years, he publicly announced his mission. For the next ten years, he endured every kind of insult and persecution. Toleration was ever unknown to the world outside India. Gradual progress of his religion and the death of his uncle Abu Taleb, induced the rulers of Mecca to aim at his life. So, he fled to Medina (AD 622), resolved to repel force by force. Here, throwing off his former mildness, he now grew bold and vigorous as a leader.

He was at first perfectly sincere in preaching. Before his flight to Medina, he disclaimed force as a means of conversion. He now declared that he was authorised to have recourse to arms in self-defence and that he was commanded by Heaven to use arms for the conversion or extermination of all unbelievers.

This new spirit was quite agreeable to the Arabs. He had only nine followers on his first military expedition, yet before his death (AD 632) he had brought all Arabia under his obedience. Soon, he began the attack on the dominions of the Roman Emperor.

The causes of his popularity were:

(i) A warlike spirit.
(ii) He was a reformer and conqueror.
(iii) His religion was founded on the sublime theology of the Old Testament.
(iv) Pure morality as compared with the contemporary practices of the Arabs.
(v) His law also prohibited retaliation.

Muhammad as Reformer and Conqueror

Conversion of the Arabs was perhaps sincere and general. 'To conquer in the cause of God or to die in asserting His unity and greatness'—was the wish of every Mussalman. Love of power, spoil, the thirst of Glory, and even hopes of Paradise only increased their absorbing passion.

(i) Arab Conquests

The Roman Empire was broken and dismembered. Christianity was degraded by corruption and weakened by sectarian feuds. Muhammad first attacked Syria. In AD 638, his successors subdued Syria and Egypt. Roman Africa was conquered in AD 647 to 700 and Spain in AD 713. Before AD 732, the Muhammadans had pushed their conquests in the heart of France where, however, they were defeated by Charles Martel in AD 732 between Poitiers and Tours. This saved Europe.

The second Tartar invasion of Europe: The Mongols were defeated by the Hungarians left there in the fifth century AD. Ottoman Turks captured the whole Byzantine Empire. Europe struggled hard against Asia for ten centuries. This hardening process made the Europeans great. The Arabs gave to Europe their great learning and culture. From AD 1500 the relation of East and West was reversed.

(ii) Persia

The proud Persian monarch tore the letter of Muhammad for submission to pieces. Persia was first invaded in AD 632. Her force was broken in the great battle of Cadesia in AD 636. The battle of Jallalla was fought in AD 637. After the battle of Nehawend (AD 642), the Persian government was entirely destroyed and her king fled to the Oxus. In AD 644 when the second Caliph Omar died, the whole of Persia was annexed to the Arab Empire. In AD 650, the Persians revolted against the Arab government. The exiled king tried his fortune once more but his attempt failed and he was cut off near the Oxus. The northern frontier of the Arabs now advanced to the Oxus, including Bulkh, and all the country north of the Hindukush. The conversion of Persians was as complete as its conquest.

(iii) Afghanistan

At the time of the Muslim invasion, Mukran was peopled by the Beloches, and the mountains of Sulaiman and Ghor, by the Afghans. Ghor, eastward to the Indus, was peopled by the Indians, and the upper country by the Persians. An Arab force from Merv first penetrated into Kabul in AD 664, and made converts of 12,000 persons (Brigg's *Ferishta, vol. I, p. 4)*. The prince of Kabul revolted, so there was a fresh invasion in AD 682 (*ante, p. 5*). The prince was made tributary, if not subject. On this occasion, the Arabs were drawn into a defile, defeated and made captive. However, they were ransomed. The Arab governor of Sistan soon amply avenged the disgrace. A greater part of Afghanistan was subdued by Abdur Rahman, governor of Khorasan. Hajjaj, governor of Basra was much displeased at these proceedings. So, Abdur raised the standard of rebellion, took Basra, occupied Cufa (capital) and threatened even Damascus, the residence of the Caliph. The struggle went on for six years, helped by the prince of Kabul. Abdur was finally driven to voluntary death. The Afghans or a part of them may have been converted early, but were conquered only in the time of Sultan Mahmud. West Afghanistan was early reduced by the Arabs. The Afghans were fire-worshippers.

The example of Persia spread Islam among powerful nations such as Tartars, Chinese, Malaya, Asiatic Islands—independent of their arms.

(iv) India

(a) The earliest Arab descendents on the Bombay coast and Sindh by sea, under Omar, were probably piratical expeditions to carry off Indian women whose beauty was much esteemed in Arabia (Pottinger, *p. 388*).

Several detachments sent through the South of Mukran failed because of the desert character of the country. In AD 664, at the time of their first expedition to Kabul, Mohalib and his army penetrated to Multan and brought back many prisoners from there. Probably, he meant to explore the intermediate country and that his report was not encouraging.

(b) The second Arab Invasion of India (AD 711). An Arab ship, being seized and looted by pirates at Dewal, a seaport near modern Karachi, Raja Dahir was called on for restitution. He declined compliance saying tht Dewal was not subject to his authority. The Mussalmans, not admitting his excuse, sent 1,000 foot soldiers and 300 horses to enforce the demand. The detachment perished like its predecessors. Hajjaj, the governor of Basra, then prepared a regular army of 6,000 men at Shiraz and made his nephew Muhammad ibn Qasim, aged only twenty, its commander. Provided with catapults and other engines of siege, he conducted the army safely to the walls of Dewal.

Dahir despati was lord of a pretty large kingdom extending probably from Kanauj to the mounts of Kalabagh, and from the mouth of the Indus to Kabul and Kandahar (Brigg's *Ferishta, vol. IV, p. 401*; Captain M'Murdo, *J.R.A.S. No. 1, p. 36*; Pottinger, *p. 386*; Captain Barnes, *vol. III, p. 76*). This Brahman dynasty was established in Sindh and Multan by his uncle named Kachchha about AD 632 (Sir H Eliot's *Arabs in Sindh*). His capital was Alor (near Bakkar), Sanskrit Visalapura, a town of very great antiquity. Qasim took temple after temple, place after place almost unopposed, till he came near Alor.

Dahir met him with an army 50,000 strong. The Hindu attack was terrible no doubt; but fortune favoured the Muslims. The raja's elephant being suddenly struck by a fire-ball, left the field with the master. The army without Dahir, fell out of ranks. The raja came back on a horse, rallied the soldiers and fought hard; but the day was lost. He fell fighting bravely in the midst of the Arabian cavalry.

Dahir's prince first fled to Brahmanabad and thence to Chitor. His heroic queen collected the army, gallantly defended the city, and held out long; but provisions failed; yet she was firm in her resolve not to surrender. The example of this widowed Brahman queen is unique in Hindu history. The Rajputs remained devoted to her to the last. The women and children were first sacrificed in flames. The men bathed, performed ceremonies, took leave of each other and of the world. The gates were then thrown open. The Rajputs rushed out sword in hand, fought hard and perished to a man.

The city was carried by an assault. All the men in arms were put to death and their families were reduced to bondage (Brigg's *Ferishta, vol. IV, p. 409.* Tod's *Rajasthan vol. I, p. 327*).

One more desperate stand was made by the Hindus at Ashcandra (Pottinger *p. 390;* M'Murdo, *J.R.A.S. No.1. p. 31*).

Multan next fell without resistance. Muslim success was unopposed. Every part of Dahir's state was occupied.

Here, I beg to draw my readers' attention to Kashmir, the so-called 'Paradise on Earth'. When Puru fought with Alexander, Kashmir stood aloof. Even the promised contingent arrived too late. When Dahir fought with Qasim, Kashmir had an extraordinary hero in the person of Lalitaditya who thoughty it wiser and more glorious to fight his own Hindu brothers of the plains than the Arabs—the common enemy of India! And yet, Kashmir is the only land in India, where the bulk of the people have become Muhammadans! Kashmir is now practically a Muhammadan state under a Hindu ruler.

A mixture of ferocity and moderation marked the early conquests of the Arabs. When a Muslim army approached a city, they would call upon the citizens either to become Mussalmans or subjects by paying tribute. In case of refusal, the city was attacked and conquered; all the fighting men killed and their families sold for slaves. The merchants, artisans and others were not molested in any way. The subjects were allowed all former privileges and free exercise of religion. A subject king was allowed to retain his state.

A fine instance of Arab toleration is on record. Failing to decide what to do with the conquered people, temples and lands of India, Qasim referred the point to Arabia and received the following answer: 'As the people of the towns in question have paid tribute, they are entitled to all privileges of subjects. They should be allowed to rebuild their temples and perform their rites; temples, lands and money of the Brahmans should be restored; and three per cent on the revenue which was allowed to them by the Hindu government shall be continued by the Mussalmans.'

Qasim was prudent and conciliating. He induced several of the Hindu rajas to join him in the war. He appointed Dahir's Prime Minister to the same office under him, as he would be best qualified to protect old rites and to maintain established institutions (*Tariki-Hind O Sindh*).

The Muslim writers assert that Qasim now thought of conquering India. Dahir's eldest son had fled to Chitor. Qasim attacked Mewar with 8,000 soldiers, augmented by Hindu soldiers recruited in Sindh; but he was repulsed and chased by General Bappa Rao (Mahendraditya) about AD 714 (*Tarikh*). He even planned a march to Kanouj. Amidst his projects, a sudden reverse befell him. Two princesses of Raja Dahir, among other female captives were sent to Walid, the sixth Caliph, who placed them in the harem. When the eldest princess was brought to the Caliph, she wept a flood of tears; she said that she had been already dishonoured by Qasim, while in Sindh.

Moved, the Caliph sent orders that Qasim should be sent to Damascus, 'sewed up in raw hide'. Qasim was taken so. The princess, overjoyed, said that Qasim was innocent, but that she had now avenged the death of her father and the ruin of her family (Brigg's *Ferishta, vol. IV, p. 410; Ayin Akbari, vol. II, p. 119;* Pottinger's *Travels, p. 389*).

Qasim died in AD 714, A.H. 96. The advance of Muslim arms ceased with the death of Qasim whose conquests were made over to his successor, Tamim. The caliphs continued to send governors to Sindh and to receive nominal submission. Caliph Mu'tamad gave Yakub ibn Laith the government of Sindh, Balkh, Tukristan, Sejestan, Kirman. Sindh was divided into Multan and Mansura: both attained a high degree of power and prosperity. Ibn Haukal states that even in the neighbouring states, the Musalmans were allowed special privileges as having mosques and living under their own laws. The Karmathian heretics appear to have spread in Sindh in the fourth century AD and to have upset the local governments in both Multan and Mansura. Mahmud drove them from both the states (Sir Henry Elliot's *Arabs in Sindh*).

Sir H Elliot, in Appendix iii, shows that the Arabs were compelled to leave the internal administration especially the finances, in the hand of the natives. The first conquerors received large tracts of lands free of tax while on military service; but the bulk of territory was held by the natives on heavy land-tax. There were many half-independent native chiefs. Land-tax and jizia were the chief sources of revenue. The annual revenue of Sindh is said to have been 11,500,000 dirrhums, equal to 150 lbs (pounds) of aloe wood. The courts of law were purely Muhammadan and the Quran the only law allowed. (vide Professor Dowson's edition of Sir H Elliot's Papers, in his *History of India As Told By Its Own Historian vol. II*).

The Arabs easily conquered and converted Persia. But why not India, though the latter afforded greater temptations by its proverbial riches and the inoffensive character of its people?

In Persia, the priests (the magis) were a most despised class. Religion and government were not combined. The Parsee religion had nothing inspiring and encouraging; to the Parsees, the new Arab religion of one God, 'the most powerful and the most merciful,' was like a triumph of a good principle. The overthrow of one king alone was enough for the complete conversion and conquest of Persia.

In India, on the other hand, there was a very powerful priesthood, highly revered by the people. Religion and government were inseparably connected; religion was interwoven with the laws and manners of the people exercising great influence on their thoughts. A horror of change gave all a passive courage. The division among the Hindus, the defeat of one raja was not conclusive; An invader had to fight hard for every inch of ground. There were other discouraging circumstances. Hence, the slow progress of Muhammadan religion in India. There was a change in the spirit of the Arab government; their chiefs were now political sovereigns but not ardent missionaries. From rude soldiers they had now become magnificent and luxurious princes. Omar burnt the library at Alexandria, while Al Mamun translated the Greek philosophers.

The place of Arabia in the history of the world is not mean. She can rightly boast of her superior position, sea-faring spirit, skilled navigation, early foreign trade, Muhammadanism, a vast empire, Harun-al-Rashid, and the spread of learning and culture.

The Muhammadan rulers of India began to settle in the country from the middle of the fourteenth century AD. They sought converts and gradually made many from the low caste Hindus. Muhammadans, form about one-fourth of the entire population of India. In East Bengal and Kashmir, Mussalmans are twice as many as the Hindus. In Bengal, Mussalmans in general follow the Hindu manners, but in Hindustan proper, Hindus still follow the Muhammadan manners.

PHILOSOPHY

In India, we have now altogether nineteen different schools of philosophy, both orthodox and heterodox. But the great Jain scholar Hemchandra calls the following six schools *Tarkikas*, that is the sceptics: the non-absolutist Jains, the absolutist Buddhists, the Hindu schools of logic, sankhya and atom; the atheistic sects, sects of Vrihaspati and Charvaka and the materialists. Hemchandra belonged to the thirteenth century AD. So, it is probable that the Hindu schools were made orthodox much later. Sankara is the root of modern culture. It is said that he added a chapter, the *Maya-bada*, that is, the theory of ignorance or illusion to the original Vedanta. Probably he gave publicity to it.

As Indian philosophy turns more or less on soul, its nature and destiny, we give the different views on it. The Charvakas regard the gross body as soul. Another sect of the atheists look upon the senses as soul. Other atheists regard life as soul. Another class regards mind as soul. The Buddhists regard intellect as soul. The Prabhakaras regard ignorance as soul. Bhatta regards pure consciouness as soul. Other Buddhists (later school) regard sunya (void) as soul. The original work of Kapila is lost. Some say that the *Tattv-Samasa* is now the oldest; some again consider *Sankhya Sutra* the oldest. Its commentary entitled the *Sankhya Pravachana* by Bijnana Bhikshu, annotated by Aniruddha, is now taught in schools and colleges. Next comes Iswara Krishna who wrote his *Sankhya Karika* before fifth century AD. It was done into Chinese about AD 550. Garudapada annotated it about AD. 700. Vachaspati Misra wrote his *Sankhya-tattva-kaumudi* in the twelfth century AD. Some say that modern *Sankhya Sutra* is based on that.

The commentaries of Vyasa and Bhoja (eleventh century AD) are most famous on Patanjala school. Mandana Misra of Mithila wrote his

Lilavati on logic (nineth century AD) Udayana of Mithila wrote his *Kusumanjali* on logic about AD 1200. Bengal gives preference to the study of logic. Here, the new school of logic is much current. On the Atomic School, we have Prasastapada's *Padartha-dharma-Sangraha* and Sankara Mishra's *Vaisesika Sutropaskara*. Savara Swami was the commentator of Jaimini's *Karma-Mimansa Sutra*. Kumarila (eighth century AD) wrote a commentary on it in his *Tantra-Sara-Vartika*.

Sankara (AD 788–820) popularised Vedanta in India. He was a non-dualist, while Ramanuja, Madhvacharya and others were dualists. Sankara denied all existence except God: The Supreme being and all beings are one and the same. Ramanuja and others admitted the reality of all beings and regarded them as derived from God.

Sadananda Yogindra wrote his *Vedantasara* about AD 900. The Vedanta is now the chief religion and philosophy in India. It is much appreciated in Europe and America also.

Isvara Krishna's *Sankhya-Karika* has been done into Latin by Lassen; into German by Windischmann and Lorinser; into French by Pauthier and Saint Hillaire; into English by Colebrooke, Max Müeller, M Williams and Davies.

South Indians now rule the religious and philosophical thoughts of all India. Even Chaitanya of Bengal was a disciple of the South.

LITERATURE

Sacred

Samhitas or Law-Books

The culture of philosophy and gradually made the learned sceptical. True wisdom vanished. All rites became corrupt and lifeless. Then the sages modernised the ancient Dharma *Sutras*, with new suitable laws and published them under the name of *Samhitas*. Upwards of hundred are quoted in modern commentaries and digests. The *Padma Purana* mentions thirty-six, Yajnavalkya twenty, and Parasara twenty law-books. The old books, gradually remodelled, assumed their present shape in the Pauranic age.

A review of the twenty law-books will not be out of place here.

1. Manu

The present metrical code in twelve books and 2,704 shlokas, was probably compiled in the third or second century BC. It deals with all questions of human interest. The attainment of spiritual wisdom and salvation, is its ultimate aim.

2. Atri

His code is in 391 shlokas. Four orders of life, rules of purity and atonement are described. It mentions rites, earth-work, six duties of Brahmans, worship of Gadadhara at Gaya, bathing in the Ganges, the practice of Sati. Sale of daughters is a great sin. Even the offspring of a daughter sold is unfit to perform the *sraddha* of the parents.

3. Vishnu

It is written in poetry, prose and aphorisms. Of its hundred chapters, the first was added much later. It is generally deemed of great antiquity. Doctor Jolly points out its resemblance with *Grihya Sutra* of the *Kathaka Kalpa Sutra*. The book was repeatedly recast and modified between fourth and eleventh centuries AD.

4. Harita

It was first in Sutra Form; then in the present metrical version in seven chapters and 194 shlokas. The superiority of the worship of Narasimha, a god, is maintained. This is regarded as another ancient work; it is often mentioned by Baudhayana, Vasista and Apastamba; extracts are found in the *Mitakshara* and the *Dayabhaga*.

5. Yajnavalkya

It is, in many respects, nearer to Manu. The author was priest to the renowned king Janaka of Mithila. Its three chapters run over 12,000 shlokas. Bijnanesvar Bhatta's *Mitakshara* and Jimutayahana's *Dayabhaga* (law of inheritance) were compiled from it. The latter is in force in Bengal, while the former in Hindusthan. Yajnavalkya prohibits the marriage of a high-caste person with a low-caste woman, formerly sanctioned by Manu.

6. Usanas

The code has nine chapters and 620 shlokas. Its present form is quite modern. It discusses the rules ofr purity, *sraddha*, propriety of food, and atonement. One who goes on a voyage, is not eligible to perform the *sraddha* ceremony. The glory of Trimurti (Triad) and Omkara is described. Five great sins are mentioned. The practice of sati and suicide of sinful men are spoken of. A Brahman is absolved from all sins by repeating his holy Gayatri ten thousand times.

7. Angiras

The present book in seventy-two shlokas, is modern. Atonement and the duties of women are set forth. The author discourages the use of blue clothes and even the indigo plantation. If a daughter betrothed to one, is married to another, she becomes a *punarbhu*, i.e. a remarried widow. Food cooked by her, is not acceptable.

8. Yama

Its present form—only in seventy-eight shlokas—is probably modern. It is quoted by Vasista. It treats of only laws, prohibitions and atonement. Washermen, cobblers, dancers, fishermen, butchers, and Bhillas are untouchable classes. It strictly prohibits study of the Vedas at sundown.

9. Apastamba

The modern metrical work is in ten chapters and 183 shlokas. It abounds in rules of atonement for the benefit of the depressed classes. It praises forgiveness above all and states that forgiveness alone can lead one to salvation. The views of Harita have been quoted.

10. Samvarta

It is in 227 shlokas, and deals with the duties of the four orders of life—food, atonement, charity, and drink. A Brahman is absolved from all sins by repeating the *Gayatri mantra* (the holy prayer) regularly for a month.

11. Katyayana

Katyayana is said to be Gobhila's son. His twenty-nine chapters in over 500 shlokas, completed his fathers' *Grihya Sutras*. Parts of the twelfth and the fourteenth chapters are written in prose. *Sraddha* and good manners engage several chapters. Worship of Ganesh Matrika are recommended. It approves the worship of pictures and idols. Ablution, *sraddha*, pinda (cakes to the manes), and rules on impurity are given. Cases when a younger brother can marry before his elder brother are indicated. It mentions Uma and Rama and Sita.

12. Vrihaspati

The present work, in eighty shlokas, is a modern one and is done into English by Dr Jolly. Charity is considered to be of great merit. Excavation of tanks, wells, ponds; laying out of gardens and orchards are also highly meritorious. The book further states that a Brahman's wrath ruins a family.

13. Parasara

The present work in twelve chapters and 599 shlokas is declared modern by scholars. Some say that he favoured the remarriage of widows; but as he speaks of a widows' pure austerities or the merits of sati, many doubt it. He recommends pilgrimage, a visit to Rameshvaram is meritorious. Living with bad characters or sinful men is strictly prohibited.

14. Vyasa

In four chapters and 241 shlokas it is thought to be among the more recent works. Some say that the word *mlechchha* mentioned in it, misleads scholars who regard it as modern. Daily duties, domestic ceremonies and merits of charity are its main topics. Probably, the book has many interpolations.

15. Sankha

It is in eighteen chapters and 314 shlokas. Parts of 11th and 12th chapters are in prose. Westerners consider it an ancient work. Duties of the four castes—forgiveness, truth, mastery over passions, and purity—are its main topics. The titles of the four castes are Sarma, Varma, Dhana, and Dasa. It enumerates the circumstances in which the twice-born Aryans fall from their ranks. High-caste people taking Sudra wives, or travelling in countries with people of impure manners, shall lose their caste. Next, it speaks of many sacred places, impurity, atonement and good and bad foods.

16. Likhita

The present work is modern and is in ninety-two shlokas. According to it, good works include excavation of tanks, the Agnihotra sacrifice, supply of water, living at Benaras, offerings of cakes to the manes at Gaya, and repeating the holy verse *Gayatri* 108 times.

17. Daksha

The work, comparatively modern, has seven chapters and 211 shlokas. It speaks of a householder's daily duties, purity, yoga or abstraction of mind, and of virtue as true happiness. Parasara's shloka on concremation is quoted in it.

18. Gautama

It has twenty-nine chapters, all in prose. The present work is written in imitation of the ancient *Gautama Sutra*. Initiation of a student, Vedic study, household duties, begetting children, royal duties, trial of cases, purity, *sraddha,* and atonement are his main points of teaching. In case of disputes, points should be settled by parishads or councils. Fulfilment of duties leads one to heaven.

19. Satatapa

The present work in six chapters and 231 shlokas is said to be the most recent. According to it, all human miseries are due to evil deeds. So, the author proposes suitable atonements. To expiate different sins, worship of different gods and goddesses is recommended. In the first two chapters are given the rules for the worship of Brahma, Vishnu, Yama, Vasudeva, Krishna, Asvini, Kuvera, Indra, Prachetas, and Sarasvati. Idols of gold and silver are to be given to Brahmans after worship.

20. Vasista

The present work in twenty-one chapters, is in prose and verse. The influence of Sutra literature is especially marked. Religion is at the root of salvation. Vedic rites are highly recommended. Good manners and pure conduct form a part of true religion. The book imitates Manu and often quotes Manu, Gautama and others. A daughter betrothed to one, may be married to another. He exhorts all not to learn the language of *mlechchhas.*

Note: The codes were made to organise society most perfectly. Even daily actions are well-regulated. Truth, morality and other virtues are strictly enjoined. The Brahmans consider the pious and the learned as supreme. Irreligious, ignorant and greedy Brahmans shall go to hell. A Brahman is strictly enjoined to be affectionate and impartial to all. All equally denounce drinking, theft, wrongful passion, and impurity. All the codes generally follow Manu—the prince of Indian law-giver.

Now Raghunandana's laws are current in Bengal and Sulapani's in west India. The *Nirnayasindhu* based on Manu and Yajnavalkya, are established in the Deccan. The *Mitakshara* of Bijnanabhikshu and the *Dayabhaga* of Jimutavahana are the more familiar works.

Puranas

They have been current from the most ancient times. Formerly, the subject was *Itihasapurana*, i.e. history and theogony. The historical chapters of the modern Puranas now represent the ancient *itihasa*, of course, in an abridged form. Vyasa (fourteenth century BC) was the first to collect the ancient Puranas which he called the *Purana Samhita* and which he gave to his disciple Romaharshana to preserve and spread.

Gradually thirty-six Puranas arose, eighteen principal and eighteen minor. Jains and Buddhists also have their Puranas. But we know very little of them yet.

Puranas are mostly written in verse. Prose Puranas also exist. The eighteen chief Hindu Puranas contain four lakh of shlokas. They have five characteristic topics, viz., cosmogony, regeneration, geneology, grand periods of Manu, and the history of modern nations.

Some portions of Puranas are spirited and poetical. Of the eighteen Puranas, six are given to Brahma viz., *Brahmanda* (12,000 shlokas), *Brahma Vaivarta* (18,000), *Markandeya* (9,000), *Bhavishya* (14,500), *Bamana*) (10,000), and *Brahma* (10,000). Six are given to Vishnu, viz., *Vishnu* (23,000), *Naradiya* (25,000), *Bhagavata* (18,000), *Garuda* (19,000), *Padma* (55,000), and *Varaha* (24,000). Six are given to Siva, viz., *Matsya* (14,000), *Kurma* (17,000), *Linga* (11,000), *Vayu* (24,000) *Skanda* (81,000), and *Agni* (15,400).

The Puranas now rank as the scriptures of the ordinary Hindus. They explain, by examples, all branches of human learning, viz., history, geography, law, medicine, grammar, philosophy, Veda, Vedangas, music, rhetoric, mathematics, astronomy, sacred places, worship of gods, priests, traditions, modern cults, sectarian beliefs, stories, fables, anecdotes, arms, weapons, war, village, towns, city, municipalities, metals, pearls, precious stones, dress, jewels, roads, trades, countries, continents, ships, duties of men and women, foods, religion, morals, virtues, vices, hell, trial, kingdom, subjects, learning, wisdom, and salvation.

The *Bhavishya Purana* notices the Magas (Parsee priests) who are silent worshippers of the Sun. The Puranas carry the Vedic religion and high philosophical truths to the common people in simple modern Sanskrit. Pargiter holds that the Puranas were rendered into Sanskrit from Pali or Prakrit.

Tantras

The Vedic religion essentially needed the slaughter of many animals. Powerful Buddhist kings almost stopped the slaughter of animals. Thus, Vedic rites gradually fell into disuse in India. Even beef and fish were given up as food. To revive Hinduism, the Brahmans created the Pauranic Hinduism and made it attractive in every possible way. Buddhists also tried hard to save their religion from extinction. The success of the Hindus inclined the later Buddhists to adopt the good parts of sacrifices. Here is the probable origin of the Tantras that resemble the Puranas in some respects. After the Hindu Rajput supremacy, the *Brahmana* portion of the Vedas was converted into the Tantras. Their number is sixty-four. Modern pujas, rites and ceremonies, all performed according to the Tantras, are semi-Vedic in nature and type.

Secular

Drama

As the most important of literary compositions, it gives a picture of real life and national interest.

Hindu drama rose to a high pitch of excellence. Sir William Jones and Professor HH Wilson have rendered many of the dramas. The long period from first century AD to AD 1800 produced only sixty Sanskrit plays. Why so few? Probably, the plays were only once acted on some festival in the great hall or inner court of a palace, with no chance of gaining popularity outside. Many are lost, being neglected by the learned. Brahmans lost the taste for drama. Professor EB Cowell says, 'We have only a few of the plays. The *Vikramorvasi* of Kalidasa refers to Bharata's *Natya-Sastra*. The long-lost *Poetics* of this Hindu Aristotle has been lately discovered by Dr Hall. Many plays must have been composed before a critic could have written so copiously on the theory.' Panini (*IV, 3. 110–11*) mentions Silali and Krisasva as two writers on *Poetics*. Patanjali (150 BC) refers to several plays.

We have no pure tragedy; yet the plays show a variety unsurpassed on any other stage. Besides the different classes of dramas farces, moralities, and interludes are almost unlimited. We have no satires; some of our plays exhibit that.

Some plays relate to the actions of heroes; some to the wars and loves of kings; some to the intrigues of ministers; while, others are strictly confined to the incidents of private life. A play, rendered by Dr Taylor of Bombay, is a lively humorous illustration of the tenets of the different schools of philosophy. The plays differ also in character. In some, there is no trace of supernatural agency or an allusion to religion. In others, nymphs of paradise are attached to earthly lovers. Gods and demons appear in others. Enchantments influence the fate of some. In one, almost the whole pantheon is brought on the stage to attest to the innocence of the heroine.

The acts range from one to ten. The unity of time, place and action is generally well observed. Plots are generally interesting. Dialogues are lively but prolonged. Women and inferior persons use Prakrit (vulgarised Sanskrit), while the higher and educated persons use classical Sanskrit. The tone of the actors is grave and declamatory. Their dresses are seen on ancient sculpture. Mimics and buffoons are still common.

Hindu strength and delight are in descriptions. Bhavabhuti's descriptions are full of grandeur and sublimity. There is no lack of the emotions of love and tenderness, nobler feelings of devoted attachment, generous disregard of selfish motives; but there are no traits of vigour, pride or independence, no ardent spirit, no patriotism.

'All the compositions of the Hindus show moral defects: voluptuous calm contemplation of the beauties of nature, but no exertion of energy or enjoyment of adventure.' (Elphinstone).

A few of our plays are historical.

The name of Bhasa, a great Sanskrit poet-dramatist was hardly known to the public. Only the Sanskrit reading persons and students knew of his fame from quotations by other authors. Recently, Ganapati Sastri, librarian to His Highness the Maharaja of Travancore, south India, has discovered thirteen long-lost plays, of which the *Sapna-Vasava-Dattam* is the longest.

He was the courtbard of Narayana, the third king of Kanva dynasty. So, his date is first century BC. Bhasa is mentioned by Kalidasa, Gunadhya in his *Vrihatkatha* (AD 78) and in the '*Little Toy-cart*'. The Sunga and the Kanva kings were great patrons of drama. Bhasa's parentage or home is not known. His popularity was immediate and immense. His works served as models to all subsequent dramatists of India. The plots of many later plays were his. The plot of his play *Avimaraka* was copied by Bhavabhuti in his *Malati and Madhava*. Many of his lines are quoted verbatim in the '*Little Toy-cart*'. His genius took the Indian world by storm. His language is simple and natural. His works lack only description of nature. The works of Saumilla are not yet found.

Kalidasa, the Shakespeare of India and a gem of the court of Vikramaditya, probably wrote his three dramas early in the first century AD. He excels in tenderness, delicacy and highly poetical descriptions. He was a versatile genius. It is said that he was a great fool in early life but through divine grace, he rose to great eminence afterwards. His parentage is not known. His home is believed by many to have been Kashmir or its neighbourhood. Kali is pre-eminently the goddess of Bengal. So his name, *servant of Kali* and his writings induce me to think of him as a Bengali. Early in life, he had, no doubt, suffered from the pangs of poverty and neglect. Vikramaditya may have found him while journeying in India and taken him to Ujjain. Kalidasa was a Saivite and very humble in spirit like his patron. He died at Mataram in Ceylon where he was probably recouping his health.

The beauties of his pastrol drama *Sakuntala* have long been admired. On its first appearance, it created a sensation throughout Europe and the most rapturous praise was bestowed upon it by men of taste. His *Vikramorvasi* (the Hero and the Nymph) is in a still more romantic strain. It is often compared in wildness of design to the *Tempest* or *Midsummer Night's Dream*. His *Malavika and Agnimitra* is an historical play describing the love of Prince Agnimitra of the Sanga dynasty (second century BC) for Malavika, the conquest of Pushyamitra and his horse sacrifice. His works show the superior order of his scholarship, his acquaintance with the important systems of philosophy—the Upanishadas and the Puranas, his close observation of society and its intricate problems, his delicate appreciation of the most refined feelings, his familiarity with the conflicting sentiments and emotions of the human heart, his keen perception of and deep sympathy with the beauties of nature, his constructive imagination of a superior order, his power of depicting all shades of character, the aptness of his similes that touch directly the heart and at once enlist the sympathy of the reader and his chaste diction, free from extravagance.

His felicity of expression, spontaneity and melody earned for him the epithet 'the favoured child of the Muse.'

The *Mrichchhakatika* (The Little Toy-cart') by Sudraka was written towards the close of the first century AD or early in the second century. It describes the corrupt social life of Ujjain.

The dramatic Muse was then silent for several centuries. About AD 600, Subandhu wrote his romantic play called the *Vasavadatta*. In the seventh century Dhavaka wrote *Nagananda* (Joy of the Serpents)—a Buddhist play and *Ratnavali*, a short play, which he published in the name of his patron Harshavardhana Siladitya from whom he obtained much wealth. Next comes Bhavabhuti who belonged to the late seventh and early eighth century. He was a native of the village Padmapura in Bidarbha (Berar). His father was Nilakantha, mother Jatukarni and grandfather Gopalabhatta. He belonged to the Udambara Brahman clan. His wonderful memory and vast erudition earned him the title of *Srikantha* (minerva-throated). He began life as the court bard of Bhojaraja of Dhara (now Dhar in Malwa) who flourished about AD 665. Next, he repaired to the court of Yasovarman, king of Kanouj. Here, his fame rose very high. About AD 700 Kumarila rose against Buddhism and preached for Vedic revival. Bhavabhuti joined the movement and even asked his patron to espouse the cause. His plays show his partiality for Vedic rites. His fame made the people of Ujjain invite him there. His plays were acted before the famous Shiva called Mahakala or Kala Priyanatha. Powerful Yasovarman was, however, conquered by Lalitaditya of Kashmir, who took Bhavabhuti with him there, where the dramatist probably passed his last days. He wrote *Viracharita* (Early Life of Rama), *Uttaracharita* (Later Life of Rama) and *Malati-Madhava*, a play of pure fiction.

Like Kalidasa, Bhavabhuti possesses the qualities of sublimity of description, a manly tone and a high and even martial spirit that is without parallel.

About AD 725 or 730 Adisura, a king of Gaur in Bengal, applied to the king of Kanouj, probably Yasovarman for five learned Brahmans to revive and reform Hinduism in the eastern parts. Bhattanarayan was one of the five sent. He wrote a spirited play entitled the *Beni-Sanhara*, i.e. 'Binding of the Braid of Draupadi.' To the same century belongs Visakhadatta's *Mudra Rakshasam* ('The Seal and the Minister Rakshasa'). Visakhadatta was son to Prithudatta and grandson to Vateswardatta, a feudatory chief. Visakha is said to have beenb a native of Chandragupta Nagari (Chinrai Patan?) on the River Krishna in Mysore, south India. Visakha was well skilled in statecraft and made a special study of stratagems and crooked policies with the result that the bent of his mind was mainly directed to business and not to sentiments. So, his poetry is business-like and vigorous, but wanting in sweetness, beauty and the tender emotions. The play describes the upset of the Nandas by Chandragupta with the help of Chanakya.

About AD 900 flourished Rajasekhara who wrote *Biddha Sala-Bhanjika* (The Carved Statue), *Bala-Ramayana* and the *Bala-Bharata* (the two Sanskrit epics for boys in the dramatic form) and the *Karpura Manjari* (Camphor Cluster, a play in Prakrit alone) and the *Prachanda Pandava*. In the tenth century AD, Kshemisvara wrote his *Chanda Kausika* (The Offended Visvamitra) under the patronage of King Mahipala of Kanouj. The subject is the correction of the proud king Harishchandra of Oudh by sage Visvamitra.

In the eleventh century was written the *Maha Nataka* (The Great Drama) under the patronage of Bhojadeva of Dhara (AD 1040). This dramatised *Ramayana* in fourteen Acts, ascribed to Hanuman, is really the product of different hands. Its first author was Madhu Sadana Misra. The second author was Damodara Misra who wrote it under Bhoja. About AD 1100 Krishna Misra wrote his *Prabodha Chandrodaya* (Rise of the Moon of True Knowledge). It is an allegorical play. Abstract ideas—like dramatis personae—are divided into two conflicting hosts. Virtues always triumph in the end.

Murari Misra's *Anargha-Raghava* is a *Ramayan* in dramatic form. Jayadeva's *Prasanna Raghava* is also a play of that kind (AD 1200).

Poetry

The *Lalita Vistara*, a long poem on Buddha, was written in part in the third or second century BC. Other parts were added after Christ. The first great Vikramaditya, a renowned patron of learning and a descendant of the Tomar line of the ancient lunar Yadava race, ruled at Ujjaini in the first century BC. During his travels, his brother Bhartrihari was regent. But finding his chief queen faithless, he left the kingdom, and retired into a cave where he passed the rest of his life with his faithful wife Pingala, writing poems and thinking of heaven. He wrote three poems, each of hundred stanzas, called *Sataka* (century). One is on love, the second on peace and the third on renunciation. He wrote towards the close of the first century BC. It is the terse and epigrammatic character of Bhartrihari's short poems which make them stand out among the works of the other Indian poets and the perfect art with which they are composed, make them worthy of being ranked among the masterpieces of Indian genius.

Vikramaditya was the earliest Hindu champion against the foreign Sakas. Religion, philosophy, science, astronomy, medicine, poetry, and drama gathered strength and life under him. Dr Hall's supposition that the 'idea of the *nine gems* of the court of Vikramaditya, is also modern' is quite wrong. It is proved by a verse in the *Jyotirvidabharana* by Kalidasa; by an inscription of Bodh Gaya dated 1015 Samvat (AD 948) which states: 'Vikrama was certainly a king renowned in the world. So in his court were nine learned men called *nava ratna*, i.e. nine gems.'

The nine gems were:

Dhanvantari, an expert physician mentioned also by Dandi (sixth century AD) in his *Dasakumara charita*.

Kshapanaka was a Jain sage (vide *Panchatantra*). His name was Siddha Sena Divakara. He belonged to the white-robed sect and followed Parsvanatha. He was disciple of Vriddhabadi Suri and received the name of Kumuda Chandra at the time of ordination. He was noted for his scholarship and spiritual eminence. It is said that he converted many learned Hindus of Ujjain, who were formerly devoted to Mahakala of that place. Jains believe that he was the spiritual guide to Vikramaditya (Vide *Kumarapalacharitra* and other works. It is further said that he converted Vikramaditya to Jainism, 470 years after the death of Mahavira (Klatt's Pattavali, *Indian Antiquary, vol. XI, 1882, p. 247*). The earliest Jain work on pure logic is his *Nyaavatara*, a metrical work in thirty-two stanzas (Professor Peterson's Fifth Report on the Search for Sanskrit Manuscripts, Bombay Circle). Chandragupta Suri wrote its commentary in AD 1102.

In India, logic is usually mixed up with metaphysics and religion. Kshapanaka distinguished logic from the cognate subjects. He is also the author of *Sammati Tarka Sutra*, a Prakrit work on philosophy containing an elaborate discussion on the principles of logic.

Amara Sinha—This lexicographer was a Buddhist. His *Amarakosha* is well-known and was done into Chinese in the sixth century AD. One Amara Sinha's vihara (monastery) is commemorated in an inscription found by Wilkins at Bodh Gaya and published in the first volume of the *Asiatic Researches*. Yuan Chwang says that this Amara Sinha was a Brahman worshipper of Maheshvara (Shiva), but warned by that deity in a dream, he had resolved to build a Buddhist convent near the Bo tree. Vikrama's Amara Sinha was a Buddhist so he could not possibly be the builder of the convent about AD 500.

Sanku—We know little of him. He was probably a poet or a great mathematician.

Betala Bhatta—He was a good poet. He is still known by his work entitled the *Niti-Pradipa* (Lamp of Wisdom).

Ghatakarpara—He was a noted poet. He often challenged Kalidasa to contest of wit in which he showed great skill in the composition of doggerels, quips, cranks, and puzzles. But Kalidasa could not be defeated. On one occasion, he gave Kalidasa a very difficult puzzle saying that if Kalidasa could solve it, then he would fetch the victor water in a pitcher, like a menial servant.

Of course, this was a form of humiliation. The puzzle was solved by the great poet; but it is not known if Ghatakarpara kept his word.

Kalidasa—The prince of Indian poets has written three immortal poems, viz., *Kumara Sambhava* (Birth of Hindu Mars), *Raghuvansam* (Dynasty of Raghu), and *Meghaduta* (the Cloud Messenger). The first two show how historical topics became so delightful by the talismanic touch of the poet's superior genius. The *Meghaduta* is an excellent example of purely descriptive poetry. Kalidasa also wrote a work on prosody and another work on astronomy.

The poems *Pushpa-Vana-Vilasa, Nalodoya* and *Ritu Sanhara* are also ascribed to Kalidasa. I think they came from the pen of a second Kalidasa.

Varahamihira—He was a renowned astronomer. Dr Bhau Daji shows that Varahamihira lived from AD 505 to 587. This has disturbed chronology and led some scholars to drag down Vikramaditya to the sixth century AD. We have already shown the existence of five Varahamihiras. The first lived in the first century BC; the second about AD 80; the third about AD 285; the fourth in the sixth century and the fifth in the sixteenth century AD. The first one was Mihira, son to Varaha, an astronomer of Ujjain. To avoid confusion, he was called Varahamihira, i.e. Varaha's son Mihira. Khana, a young and fair lass of Ceylon was very proficient in astronomy and general learning. For a suitable young man, her father was coming to India with her. The ship was wrecked near the coast. However, they reached the shore safely. She was married to Mihira. She lived happily for some time. Her father-in-law was the royal astronomer. It is said that Varaha could not answer the difficult questions on astronomy put to him in the court by his opponents. Khana, knowing this, often helped Varaha with her wonderful calculations and solutions. Varaha thus won the laurels for some time. The truth came out and Varaha was abashed. It is said that the barbarous father-in-law, out of spite, had cut out Khana's tongue in her sleep. She died soon after. Many of her wise sayings in vernacular are still current in all parts of India.

Vararuchi, a scholar, wrote a grammar on Prakrit called the *Prakrita-Prakasa.*

Vikrama's son and successor Madhava Sena was a rather weak king. He married Sulochana, daughter to Gunakara, king of Divanti. His capital was in an island in the Arabian Sea (*Padma Purana, Kriya-Yoga-Sara Part, chap. 5*).

Our next poet and patron of learning was Hala (17th king of the Andhra list) also, known as Sala, Sali-Vahana, Sala Satavahana (AD 78 to 83). His poem was the *Satta Sai*, i.e. Sapta Sati or 'Seven Centuries' written in a form of Pali.

Bharavai (literally, the very sun of poetic genius) flourished about AD 300. Certainly, he was a poet of north India. We neither know his home nor his parentage nor his patron. His *Kiratarjuniyam* (the Hunter-Chief and Arjuna) is a noble poem, full of sound sense.

The *Vaya Purana*, the earliest of the class, was composed in its present form about AD 300, the *Vishnu* about 350 and the *Matsya* about AD 450.

Samudragupta, *Kaviraja* was himself a good poet and a liberal patron of fine arts.

The Indian Muse was mute in the fifth century AD. In the sixth, Malwa was again her favourite haunt. Yasodharman Vikramaditya was a gret patron of letters. Matrigupta was his chief poet. He is probably the second Kalidasa of Indian tradition. Probably, he wrote the poems entitled the *Ratimanjari* (Blossom of Love), *Nalodaya* (Rise of Nala), *Pushpavanavilasa* (Sports of Cupid) and the *Ritusanhara* (Assemblage of Ṣeasons). Dr Bhao Daji believes him to be Kalidasa. I think people called him a Kalidasa, as a compliment. Certainly, he was a man of genius; otherwise Yasodharman would not have sent him out to rule Kashmir. He was a popular ruler and ruled there for about five years, then abdicated in favour of Pravarasena and came down to Benaras where he passed his life as an ascetic. Pravarasena built a bridge of boats on the Vitasta. There is a poem in Prakrit on the bridge. A commentary on the poem attributes it to Kalidasa.

That Yasodharman was a Vikramaditya will appear from the following:

Subandhu in his *Vasava-datta* speaks of Vikramaditya as departed not long ago.

Yuan Chwang speaks of a mighty king who had ruled an empire in India some sixty years before his time.

Kalhana speaks of him as Vikramaditya, though he does not forget the first great Vikrama of first century BC, for which he even assigns three centuries to King Ranaditya.

The *Satrunjaya Mahatmya* states that Vikramaditya ascended the throne in 466 Saka or AD 544 (Wilford, *Asiatic Researches, vol. IX, p. 156*, quoted by Dr Kern in his Vrihat Samhita). An inscription of AD 637 mentions both Kalidasa and Bharavi.

King Pravarasena of Kashmir, himself a good poet, wrote the *Setuvandha* or *Ravanavaha* in Prakrit, sixth century AD. Amaru wrote his *Amaru-Sataka* probably in the same century. The *Satrunjaya Mahatmya*, the earliest Jain work in Sanskrit verse, was written in the sixth century AD. The *Dipavansa* and *Mahavansa*, two historical poems of Ceylon, were composed in the fifth or sixth century AD. Bhoja I, a king of Dhara in Malwa and a renowned patron of learning, flourished about AD 575.

Harshvardhana Siladitya II also was a great patron of poets. Dr Macdonell gives AD 651 as the date of the death of poet Bhartrihari, the author of the three *Centuries*. We have placed him in the early first century AD. Bhartrihari, author of the *Bhattikavya* may have died about AD 651. The title *Bhattikavya* evidently shows that it was the work of a poet named Bhatti. Bhartrihari may have been his classical name and Bhatti his popular name. Whatever be the fact, certain it is that Bhartrihari, brother to Vikrama and author of the three *Centuries*, was a different person from the author of the *Bhattikavya*. The Yasodharman's Mandasor Inscription tells us that the panegyric was composed by a poet named Vatsabhatti. The general style of this author, especially the description of *Sarat* (autumn) as given in the inscription and in the *Bhattikavya, canto II*, would hardly incline one to question the identity of the two poets. We think, this Vatsabhatti, a Brahman, native of Ballabhi ruled by Sridharasena IV (vide colophon to *Bhattikavya*) was early in life, the poet laureate of Yasodharman and wrote his *Bhattikavya* later towards the close of the sixth century AD. This poet–grammarian of Kathiawar has not only described the exploits of Rama, but has illustrated Sanskrit grammar as well.

In the beginning of the seventh century AD, Sriharsha, son to Srihira and Mamalla Devi and nephew to Mammatabhatta, wrote his *Naishadhakavya* (Love of Nala and Damayanti), marked for its melodious expressions. Magha, son to Sridattaka, belonged to the second half of the seventh century AD (Professor AA Macdonell). His work is the well-known *Sisupalabadha*, a great poem noted for its strength of metaphor, sound sense and melodious phraseology. Bhoja II, patron of Bhababhuti and other poets flourished at Dhara about AD 665.

Bakpatiraja was the poet-laureate of King Yasovarman of Kanouj. He wrote his *Gaura Vaho* in Prakrit and other poems in AD 800. It is a very clever work. Each stanza at once describes a prince of the solar and a prince of the Pandu line, only by a different reading. However, it has little value as a poem. Sankara, the noted scholar, wrote several short poems of which the *Mohamudgara* (Club of Ignorance) is still popular (AD 815). Some ascribe the *Bhagavat Gita* to him. This is wrong. For, from an inscription of west India, of the second or third century AD, we have the eighteen books, a lakh of shlokas and other parts, as they are now, in the *Mahabharata*. The *Gita* was probably the Bible of some religious sects of yore, now no more extant. Sankara made its study popular throughout India.

India produced no good poet in the tenth century AD. In the eleventh century AD , Sandhyakara Nandi, son to Prajapati Nandi, a war minister, wrote his *Ramacharitam*, a long poem on the Pala dynasty of Bengal. He is often called the Valmiki of modern times.

No Indian king has shed so much lustre on Hindu literature as Bhojadeva of Dhar in Malwa. He was son to King Sindhu. He ruled from AD 1010 to 1042 when he was defeated by Somesvara II who ruled from AD 1043 to 1068–69. The great poet Vilhana in his historical poem, *Vikramarkadevacharita*, says that Bhoja, being defeated, fled to some safe nook, leaving Dhara (*I, 91–94* shlokas). To please the victor, Bhoja married his daughter Princess Bhanumati to Vikramarka, son to Somesvara II. Afterwards, Udayaditya, son of Bhoja, was able to retrieve the fallen glory to a great extent (Udaipur inscription).

Bhoja was himself a great poet, a great learned man and a great patron of learning. His title was Kaviraja. He defeated king Indraratha of Chedi, Toggala of Karnataka, Bhima of Lata (Gujarat), and fought hard against Sultan Mahmud for the defence of the Somnath temple. A staunch Saivite, he built many temples. His court was full of poets who came from different countries. He gave them much. It is said that there were several learned women in his court. Sita Devi was a good poet. Lila Devi, Bhoja's own chief queen, was very learned and a poet. An inscription of the time of Yadava Sinha tells us that Bhaskarabhatta, great grandfather of Bhaskaracharya, had obtained from Bhoja the title of *Vidyapati*. This Bhoja is credited with having introduced *Bhojavidya*, i.e. magic. In Bhoja's court, religion, philosophy, poetry, rhetorics, astronomy, and other sciences were discussed. Commentaries on all the sciences were written. The *Kamadhenu* was the chief of these.

Works by Bhoja

The *Saraswati-Kanthabharana*, the *Raja Martanda* (a commentary on the Yoga Philosophy), the *Raja-Mrigankakarana*, the *Viddajjana-Ballabha* (an astronomical work), the *Samarangana* (a work on architecture) and the *Sringara-Manjari-Katha* (a poem).

Works by the learned men of his court: *Aditya-Pratap-Siddhanta* (on astronomy), *Ayurveda Sarvasva* (a medical treatise), *Champu Ramayana*, *Charu-Charya* (a religious work), *Tattva-Prakasa* (a Saiva work), *Viddajjana Ballabha-Prasna Chintamani*, *Visranta Vidya Venoda* (medical), *Vyavahara Samuchchaya* (a law-book), *Sabdanusasana* (a grammar), *Salihotra* (medical treatment of beasts), *Siva-datta Ratna-Kalika*, *Samarangana Sutradhara*, *Siddhanta Sangraha*, and *Subhashita Prabhandha*.

Bhoja's authority has been quoted by Sulapani, Dasavala, Alladanatha, and law-giver Raghunandana of Bengal; in the *Bhava-Prakasa*, and Madhava's *Nidana*; in Kesavarka's *Astronomy*; by Kshirasvamil, Sayana and Mahipa, by Chittapa, Devesvara Vinayaka and other poets; by the philosopher Vachaspati Misra in the *Tattva-Kaumudi* (twelfth century AD). The *Life of Bhoja* has been written by Ballal Pandit. The work is a farrago of nonsense, by Padmagupta in his *Navasahasankacharita* (Padmagupta was the court bard of his father and grandfather); by Meru-unga Acharya in his *Prabandhachintamani* (AD 1300); by Rajaballabha; Vatsaraja; Ballabha; and by Subhasila (disciple of Sundara Muni).

Bilhana wrote his *Chaura-Panchasika* (the thief's fifty stanzas) during the latter half of the eleventh century AD. He was probably father or brother to Kalhana, who wrote his *Rajatarangini* (the Kashmir chronicle) in AD 1148 to 49. Somadeva of Kashmir (flourished AD 1125) wrote his *Kathasaritsagara* in 22,000 shlokas.

Lakshmana Sena (AD 1119 to 1199), the greatest of the Sena kings of Bengal, was a reputed conqueror and patron of learning. Halayudha was his Prime Minister. The five poets, viz., Umapati, Govardhana, Sarana, Dhogi, and Jayadeva were the *five gems* of his court. Jayadeva, a Vaisnavite, was a native of the village Kendu-Vilwa (dist. Birbhum, Bengal). He lived on the River Ajaya. His wife was Padmavati. His *Gita*

Govinda, a specimen of pure pastoral, is still popular all over India. After the Muslim conquest of north-west Bengal in AD 1199, old Lakshmana, Sena fled to Vikrampur and Jayadeva went to the court of the Orissa king.

One point deserves notice here. Bengal before Adisura (flourished in AD 725 or 730) was ever noted for bravery, trade, arts, industries, and agriculture. Adisura first gave impetus to religion and learning. The Pala kings were nominally Buddhist. Their able Brahman ministers were the Peshwas of Bengal. Hindu religion and learning were encouraged. The Sena kings were staunch Hindus and did much for Hinduism and learning. Bengal is indebted to Halayudha and his learned brothers for its present superior learning and civilised manners.

Mallinatha, the eminent scholiast, specially noted for his new method, vast erudition and serious research, was also a poet of no mean original genius (fourteenth century AD). He was born at Devapura, Deccan. His father was a famous professor of the Vedas. But Mallinatha was at first very dull; so he was called Peddabhatta. He was married in due time. But all of his wife's house jested and ridiculed him as a fool. At his wife's instance, he went to Benaras and studied with a learned man. Here, he repeated the word '*Siva*' many times a day with the result that his brain grew steady and powerful soon. Gradually, he studied all the sciences and became a profound scholar. Kolachala was his clan name and *Mahamahopadhyaya* was his title (*Katha Sangraha*, written in Canarese, Deccan.

His two sons were Pedda-Yarya and Kumara Swami. Mallinatha has mentioned several preceding annotators such as Dakshinavartanatha and others. He wrote in imitation of them. His poem was *Raghuviracharita*, now almost lost and unknown. Ganapati Sastri has succeeded in finding out only a few pages of his poem.

Chaturbhuja of Gaur was probably the last poet of India. He was a Varendra Brahman. As a result of the efforts of the Asiatic Society of Bengal, his poem, the *Haricharita* in thirteen cantos and 1,250 shlokas, was discovered in the Durbar library, Nepal in 1905. The date of its composition is AD 1493 when the Abyssinians were on the throne of Bengal. Hussain Shah is also described.

Sanskrit dictionaries, all in verse, show skill, though no poetry. Amara Sinha wrote his *Kosha* in the first century AD; Sasvata's

Anekartha-Samuchchaya was written probably in the fourth or fifth; The *Bhuri Prayoga* and *Sabda Chandrika*, in the sixth, Yadavaprakasa's *Vaijayanti* about AD 1050; Hemchandra's *Abhidhana Chintamani,* about AD 1150. Halayudha's *Abhidhana Ratna Mala,* about AD 1160 or 1170; Hemadri's *Chaturvarga Chintamani* about AD 1300.

Prose

The *Milindro Panho,* dialogue of Menander with Nagasena on Buddhism, in Pali, was written about 155 or 50 BC. The Buddhist Jataka stories are the oldest memoirs in the world. Professor Rhys Davis has shown that in India, many of those tales, in slightly altered forms, found their way in the *Vrihat-katha* of Gunadhya, a courtier of Salivahana (AD 78 to 83), in the *Vrihatkathamanjari* of Kshemendra Vyasadasa (AD 1037) and in the *Kathasaritsagara* of Somadeva (AD 1125), in the *Panchantantra* and *Hitopadesa* of Vishnu Sharma (second century AD.).

In Europe, they found their way in the fables of Aesop, in the tales and poems of Dan Chaucer and La Fontaine; and in the popular stories of the two Grimm Brothers.

The tales of Vishnu Sharma, the Indian Froebel, were done into Persian (AD 531 to 572); into Arabic in the eighth; into Greek by Symeon Seth about AD 1050; into Latin by Possinus; into Hebrew by Rabbi Joel (AD 1250); into Spanish in AD 1251; into German in the fifteenth century AD; then into all the languages of Europe, called the fables of Pilpay or Vidpai, i.e. *Vidyapati.*

In the second century AD Asvaghosha wrote his *Buddhacharita* (Life of Buddha) and Nagarjuna wrote his *Mahayana* (Excellent Way to Salvation), besides many other works.

In the sixth century AD, a great change came over our Sanskrit prose. Authors undertook more ambitious works and the style became ornate and artificial. Dandin wrote his *Dasakumaracharita* (Adventures of Ten Princes.) Banabhatta was a native of Bihar. His father was Chitrabhanu and mother Rajya Devi. He lost his father at fourteen. He came to the court of Harshavardhana where his genius found full play. About AD 630, he wrote a biography of his greater master entitled, *Harshacharita,* full of historic information. His *Kadambari* is a highly enchanting novel written in prose-poetry. The book was completed by his son Bhushana Bana. Subandhu's *Vasavadatta* is a short romance composed about

AD 600. To console Queen Suryavati of Kashmir, on the death of her grandson Harshadeva in AD 1125, Somadeva abridged Gunadhya's *Vrihatkatha* into the *Kathasaritsagara* in eighteen books and 124 chapters, which gives the entire folkore of India. Balala Sena, a powerful king of Bengal, wrote his *Danasagara* in the eleventh century.

Rhetorics: Bamana's *Kavyalankara sutra* (fifth century AD) and Dandin's *Kavyadarsa* (Mirror of Poetry) seem to be the earliest works on the subject (sixth century AD). Mammata Bhatta's Kavya Prakasa (Rules on Composition) was probably composed in the seventh or early in the eighth century AD. The *Sarasvatikanthabharana* was composed by Bhojadeva of Dhar (eleventh century AD) Visvanatha Kaviraja of east Bengal composed his *Sahitya Darpana* (Mirror of Composition) in AD 1450. Vidyadhara's *Ekavali* was probably written in the twelfth, the *Ujjala Nilamani* in the sixteenth; the *Alankara-Kaustubha*, the *Chandraloka*, the *Kavya Chandrika*, and the *Kuvalayananda* were perhaps written in the sixteenth and seventeenth centuries. 'The rhetoric of the Hindus in its analysis of the phenomena of taste and style is inferior to that of no other nation.' (Cowell, *p.166*, note).

Hindu learning reached its zenith in the Christian era. According to Hindu tradition, the most flourishing period of literature is that of Vikramaditya, a little before and after Christ. Good writers extend from the second century BC to the eighth century AD. Though works of merit—both in literature and science—continued to be composed for sometime even after the Muslim invasion, the Muses left our Indian lordly hall, practically after AD 700, when genius died and the age of commentary began.

About AD 700 Garudapada wrote a commentary on Isvara Krishna's *Sankhya Karika* and Kumarila in his Tantras*ara Vartika*, commented on Savara Swami's Karma *mimansa Sutra*. Sankara—the root of modern culture—wrote very able commentaries on the chief Upanishadas, the Vedanta and the Gita (AD 810–820). Sridhara Swami wrote his commentary on the *Vishnu Purana* and the Gita (nineth century AD). Medhatithi gave his valued notes on the *ManuSamhita about* AD 900.

Jimutavahana was the Prime Minister of Vijaya Sena, a most powerful king of the Sena dynasty of Bengal. He wrote a commentary of Yajnavalkya Samhita, called the *Dharmaratna* in AD 1005 of which the well-known *Dayabhaga* (Law of Inheritance) is a part.

Ramanujam, born AD 1017 wrote a commentary on the Gita and the Vedanta. Bijnanesvara wrote his Mitakshara about AD 1100. Kulluka gave notes on Manu about AD 1250.

Bhojadeva (eleventh century AD) wrote commentaries on the yoga, philosophy and many other works. Madhava and Sayana, two learned brothers, were ministers to Raja Ramachandra of the Vijayanagar kingdom, Deccan. Madhava wrote on philosophy and other works. Sayana, perhaps the greatest scholar of India, wrote his commentary on the *Rig Veda* and other works (fourteenth century AD).

Vatsyanan first wrote a commentary on Gautama's *Nyaya* (logic). Jain Devanandi wrote his *Patra-Pariksha,* a work on logic in which he criticised Gautama. Kunda Kundacharya wrote eighty-four works on different subjects. Udayana of Mithila wrote his *Kusumanjali* on logic in the twelfth century AD. Mallinatha, the prince of Indian commentators, annotated Kalidasa's *Raghu, Kumara* and the *Meghaduta*: the *tika* is called *Sanjivani.* Bharavi's *Kirata*: the *tika* is called *Ghantapatha. Megha'Sisupala-Badha*: the *tika* is called *Sarvankasha.*

Harsha's *Naishadha*: the *tika* is called Jivatu. Bhatti's *Bhattikavya*: the *tika* is called *Sarvapathina* (recently discovered). Vidyadhara's *Ekavali*: the *tika* is called *Tarala.* His *tika* on the *Tarkika Raksha* is called *Nishkantika.* The *Siddhanjana* and the *Svara Manjari Parimala* were annotated both by Mallinatha and his son Kumara Swami. The *Prasastapada Bhasya* on the atomic theory of Kanada, was also annotated by Mallinatha. From the tenth century AD, sprang vernacular literature. Rajput Rasas, Dhal and Sijhai contributed to political or biographical literature.

ARCHAEOLOGY

Its value in history as the most secure source of information, is indeed great. Moreover, it contributes much interest to general literature. With its help, much lost history has been recovered in the last seventy years. Its branches are architecture, epigraphy and numismatology.

Numberless are the ancient temples and tombs in India. Architecture gives no history, but shows the splendour and power of kings. Inscriptions are widespread and most reliable. The rock inscriptions, the edicts are unique in character. Sanskrit plays are described in rocks at

Ajmer and Dhar. Architectural arts are described in the inscriptions of Chitor Fort. Piligrims' notes are also found in the inscriptions.

Most of the inscriptions are signs of victory, donative grants or dedication of temples of gods.

Inscriptions of victory are generally in rock and stone. These *prasastis,* i.e. panegyrics often display good Sanskrit, metric skill, fine poetry, and authentic history. Donative grants are generally on copper-plates.

Inscriptions abound in the Deccan. Many thousands are yet to be found. But those of north India are more important. The southern inscriptions date only two thousand years ago. The north Indian inscriptions are more ancient.

Coins are various and many. The oldest is a quadrangular copper piece called *karshapana,* at first without letters. Then it bore the figure of animals. Next it bore a letter or two. Persian, Greek, Scythian, and other foreign coins are found in plenty. The Greek coins are most beautiful. Hence, many Indian kings stamped their own coins after the Greek model. Sanskrit, Nagari, Greek, Persian were used in them.

LANGUAGE

From 200 BC to AD 700, Sanskrit was in a full living state. It was not only the language of the learned, but also of the court and camp, of the writers, of coins and inscriptions, of the northern Buddhists, of the Jains. Even common people understood easy Sanskrit in towns and centres of learning.

Pali was still the sacred language of the Buddhists, and especially of the southern Buddhists. The lightless common people used different forms of Prakrit in different parts.

About the Christian era, four principal Prakrits were *Matharastri* spoken in the Bombay Presidency; *Sauraseni* spoken in the Mathura districts; *Paisachi* spoken probably in north-west India; and *Magadhi* in east India. All these four were born of Pali.

Bararuchi's *Prakrita-Lankesvara* and Visvanath's *Sahitya Darpana,* chapter VI, give the details and examples of eighteen languages as spoken in India before the rise of the vernaculars. These were Sanskrit, Prakrit, Udichi (northern dialect), Maharashtri, Magadhi, Misrarddha Magadhi (mixed half Magadhi), Sakabhiri (dialect of the Scythians and Abhirs),

Sravasti, Dravidian, Odrain (Oriya), Paschatya (western), Paschatya (eastern), Valhika, Rantika, Deccanese, Paisachi, Avanti, and Sauraseni.

The vernaculars came into being after the tenth century AD. Pali follows Sanskrit, but the Prakrits do not. The revival of Hinduism drove Pali away. Gradually, Prakrits became powerful. The Aryan vernaculars were Assamese, Bengali, Oriya, Hindi, Nepalese, Kashmiri, Punjabi, Sindhi, Gujarati, and Marathi. The Indo-Chinese tongues were used by the Tibeto-Burmans of the Himalayan states.

From *Dravidian* sprang up twelve languages of the south, viz., Tamil, Telugu, Canarese, Tulu, Malayalam, and Coorgi. These six were excellent while Tura, Kotal, Gond, Khond or Ku, Oraon, Maler or Rajmahali were not literary (Dr Caldwell).

Tamil, Telugu and Canarese are distinct from Sanskrit. Tamil is the most pure and often regarded as the source of Telugu and Canarese. Telugu is much mixed with Sanskrit words. Malayalam of Malabar is closely connected with Tamil.

All the northern vernaculars contain a little non-Sanskritic element. Professor EB Cowell thinks it as a relic of the aboriginal languages. This non-Sanskritic basis of the northern vernaculars saturated with Sanskrit, is hardly perceivable without close scrutiny. The non-Sanskritic tongues of the Deccan were probably of Turanian origin; the tongues of the hill-tribes also possibly belong to the same Turanian family.

The *Pandu-lupi Sangraha* (Collection of Manuscripts—a Sanskrit work) names six principal Prakrits and twenty-seven dialects of north India. The *Prakrita Chandrika* describes them as Maharashtri, Avanti, Sauraseni, Ardha-Magadhi, Valhiki, Magadhi. The dialects are Brachandra (?), Lata, Baidarbha, Upanagara, Nagara, Barbara, Avantya, Panchala, Malawa, Kaikaya, Gaura, Odra, Daiva, Paschatya, Pandya, Kountala, Sainhala, Kalinga, Prachya, Karnata, Kanchya, Dravida, Gourjjara, Abhira, Central, and Bairala.

'It is from the Prakrits and not from the literary Sanskrit that the modern vernaculars of India branched off in course of time.' (Max Müeller).

Katyayana in his Pali grammar starts a new theory. He says that Pali is the origin of all the Indian languages—Sanskrit and Prakrits. Prinsep, Muir, Wilson, Burnouf, Lessen, and other great scholars say that Pali is the eldest daughter of Sanskrit.

The *Vrihad* Dharma *Purana,* Part I, chap. 25, 11–13 verses state that there were fifty-six languages in India and also grammars in those for the education of children. The work seems to be modern.

India was never uniform in script. The *Lalita Vistara* speaks of sixty-four scripts, the Prakrita Lankesvara of eighteen, the *Samavaya Sutra* of the Jains of eighteen, the *Prajnapana Sutra* of eighteen, the *Nandi Sutra*, of thirty-six.

SCIENCES

Grammar

The science of grammar also betrays a spirit of revival in the period. Katyayana, a minister of Nanda (fifth to fourth century BC) had belittled Panini by his hostile criticism. So, it is not probable that Panini was much known or studied in the Indian plains. About 15 BC Patanjali, a native of Gonarda in east India, published his masterly work—the *Mahabhashya* (Great Commentary) written in full defence of Panini. In this curious battle of books, the learned public at once perceived how barbarously Katyayana had repressed the genius of Panini and now they declared Patanjali victor with the title of Churnikrit (Hammer). Panini and Patanjali now became popular. Patanjali's mother was Gonika. He was guru to Pushyamitra and fought hard for the revival of Vedic Hinduism. This Patanjali should be distinguished from the philosopher and the physician Patanjalis.

About AD 650 was written the *Kasikavritti* (Benaras Commentary) on Panini. Bhattoji Dikshit, son of Lakshmidhara of Benanras, perfected the entire grammatical studies in his monumental work called the *Siddhanta Kaumudi* in the seventeenth century AD. Bhattoji also wrote thirty-three other works.

About AD 480 Buddhist Chandra Gomina wrote a non-Paninian grammar. About the Christian era, Vararuchi, a gem of Vikramaditya's court, wrote a grammar on Prakrita, called the *Prahrita Prakasa.* His work on letter-writing, called the *Patra-Kaumudi* is also well-known.

Rebuked by his learned queen, Salivahana resovled to learn, somewhat late in life. But Sanskrit grammar puzzled him. To enable him to study Sanskrit easily, to cut a royal road to learning, Sarvavarman, a scholar of his court, wrote the Kalapa or Katantra grammar on an unscientific but easy method (AD 78).

Another excellent and popular grammar is the *Mugdhadodha* (Grammar Made Easy) by Bopadeva, son to Kesava Misra and disciple of Dhanesvara, both physicians. Bopadeva was a Marathi Brahman of the twelfth century AD. Besides this grammar, he wrote *Kavikalpadruma, Ramavyakarana, Kavyakamadhenu, Satashloka Chandrika* and edited the *Bhagavata* as we find it now.

Like Valmiki, Paninim, Kalidasa, Mallinatha and others, Bopadeva was at first very dull. He was turned out of school. On his way back home, he sat in a forest on a step, all gloomy and cast down. He noticed an erosion in a rock but could not make out its cause. Presently, some women came there for water and placed their full pitchers on the rock. Now, he understood how constant touch of the pitchers had worn out the rock. Thereafter, he persevered and shone in life.

Mathematics

The mathematical science was perfected in India in the fifth century AD. Professor Brajendra Nath Seal's *Positive Sciences of the Hindus* and Professor Benoy Kumar Sarkar's *Hindu Achievement in Exact Science* will show Hindu progress in the positive sciences. The cultural superiority of the West dates from the sixteenth century AD. Discovery of steam in the nineteenth, made Europe and America great.

Modern scholarship speaks of the Hindu source of the Greek sciences. The Saracens had their mathematics, chemistry and medicine from the Hindus. Pure mathematics was not only in advance of some of the systems of the Greeks, but also anticipated European discoveries of the sixteenth, seventeenth, and the eighteenth centuries.

Hankel says, 'It is remarkable to what extent Indian mathematics enters into the science of our time.' Mathematics, like other subjects in India, had its origin in religion.

Arithmetic (Patiganita)

The invention of the decimal notation gave our ancestors a great advantage over the Greeks in the science of numbers. A writer in the *Edinburgh Review,* vol. xviii, p. 211, contends that decimal notation is not a very old invention and says that if it had existed in India in the sixth century BC, Pythagoras would have imitated it.

We have seen that *rasi,* i.e. science of numbers was a distinct subject of learning in the epic age. The *Rig Veda* abounds in the use of numbers. The largest number in Hindu arithmetic is of eighteen digits. The philosophy of Pythagoras is not void of the use of numbers. Baha-ul-din, an Arab writer, calls the Hindus inventors of the decimal notation. Another proof appears from an introduction to an Arabic work on poetry. All the Arabic and Persian works call the Hindus inventors of the system. Hindu arithmetic reached Arabia in the eighth century and thence found its way into Europe.

The decimal notation was known to Aryabhatta in the fifth century AD Dr Morgan says, 'Indian arithmetic is that which we now use.' Bhaskara's arithmetic was called *Lilavati*.

Algebra (Bijaganita)

Cajori says, 'The Indians were the real inventors of Algebra'. From India, the science went to Arabia and thence to Europe. Colebrooke says that Muhammad-ibn-Musa first published Algebra among the Arabs. He had compiled his work from the Indian astronomical works, during the rule of Al-Mansur (AD 749 to 775).

Hindus mostly excelled the Greeks in Algebra. Discoveries of Algebra are found in the works of Brahmagupta (born AD 598) in whose time, the science was probably at its height. Colebrooke makes him a predecessor or contemporary of Diophantus, the first Greek writer on Algebra (about AD 360). Dr Bhau Daji (*J.R.A.S., New Series, vol. I, p.405*) gives the date of Aryabhatta as AD 476. I think like Varahamihiras, there were other Aryabhattas.

Hindus were superior to the Greeks in their perfection of Algebra. Aryabhatta is superior to Diophantus by his knowledge of the resolution of equations involving several unknown quantities and in the general method of resolving all indeterminate problems of at least the first degree. He and his successors (Sridharacharya and others) press hard upon the discoveries of algebraists who lived almost in our own time (Elphinstone, p. 142).

Aryabhatta is not the inventor of algebra among the Hindus. The science was in his time in such a state that it required the lapse of ages and many repeated efforts of invention to produce (*Edinburgh Review, vol. xxix, p.143*). It was in his time or fifth century AD at the latest that Indian algebra seems to have attained its highest perfection.

The *Edinburgh Review*, vol.xxi, p. 372 gives a striking history of a problem, 'to find x so that ax^2+b shall be a square number'. Diophantus first tried to solve it. Fermat extended it and sent it as a defiance to the English algebraists in the seventeenth century AD but it was only carried to its full extent by Euler who arrives exactly at the point attained before by Bhaskara in AD 1150.

Another solution given by Bhaskara in AD 1657. The general solution was unsuccessfully attempted by Euler and only performed by De la Grange in AD 1767, although it had been given by Brahmagupta in the seventh century AD.

Hindu superiority over the Greeks lies more in the excellence of method than in discoveries (Colebrooke's Indian Algebra quoted in *Edinburgh Review, vol XXIX p. 162*).

The Hindu process of Cuttaka was published in Europe by Brachet de Mezeriac about AD 1624 and is virtually the same as that explained by Euler (*ed. Rev., vol XXIX, p. 152*).

'The *Cuutaca* is a quantity such that a given number, being multiplied by it and the product added to or subtracted from a given quantity, the sum or difference will be divisble by a given divisor without remainder.' (EB Cowell).

'The application of algebra to astronomical investigations and geometrical demonstrations is also an invention of their own, and their manner of conducting it, is, even now, entitled to admiration.' (vide Colebrooke's views on *Hindū Algebra, p. XXII, 1817*).

Arabic writers translated Hindu algebra in the eighth century. Leonardo of Pisa took it to Europe.

Geometry and Mensuration

We have shown already that Geometry as a science originated in India in the construction of Vedic altars. Geometry is discussed in the Sulva Sutras of the *Taittiriya Samhita,* of Baudhayana, of Apastamba and was studied till the time of Bhaskara, twelfth century AD and beyond. Pythagoras learnt his geometry in India. Geometry is still used in India, though to a small extent, in measuring lands, in architectural designs and in making *Mandalas,* i.e. sacrificial fields with coloured powders.

Mensuration was known to the Hindus. The ratio of the diameter to the circumference is given in the *Surya Siddhanta*. The areas of triangles, circles, quadrilateral figures are discussed.

Altitudes of distant things were ascertained. The Puranas often speak of the heights of mountains and hills and also of the measure of their parts that lie below the surface of the ground. How this latter was ascertained seems to be a wonder.

Vachaspati (twelfth century AD) anticipated in a rudimentary manner the foundations of solid (co-ordinate) geometry (B N Seal). Disuse of Vedic altars and the help of algebra have made geometry a lost science in India.

Trignometry (Trikona-miti)

In some points the Hindus anticipated modern trigonometry devising the *sines*, Arabic corruption of Sanskrit *Sinjini* and versed Sines unknown to the Greeks who calculated by the help of the chords. Bhaskara (AD 114) had discovered 500 years before Newton, the principle of the Differential Calculus and its application to astronomical problems and computations. Bhaskara's *Goladhyaya* portion deals with spherical trigonometry (translated by Wilkinson).

The *Surya Siddhanta*—a very ancient work, but spoiled by later interpolations—contains a system of trigonometry which not only goes far beyond anything known to the Greeks, but also involves theorems which were not known or discovered in Europe till the sixteenth century AD. Such is that of Vieta pointed out by Professor Playfair, in his question sent to the Asiatic Society (*As. Res. Vol. IV, p. 152*). Professor Playfair has published a memoir on the Hindu Trignometry (trans. of the R.S. of Edinburgh, vol. IV) which is referred to by Professor Wallace with the following important observation of his own: 'However ancient therefore any book may be in which we meet with a system of trigonometry, we may be assured, it was not written in the infancy of science. We may, therefore, conclude that geometry must have been known in India long before the writing of the *Surya Siddhanta*.' There is also a rule for the computation of the *sines* involving a refinement first practised by Briggs in the beginning of the seventeenth century *(British India, vol. III, p. 403,* in the Edinburgh Cabinet Library). Professor Playfair speaks on Hindu trigonometry thus: 'It has the appearance, like many other things, in the science of those eastern nations of being drawn up by one who was more deeply versed in the subject than may be at first imagined and who knew more than he thought it necessary to communicate. It is probably a compendium formed by some ancient adept in geometry for the use of others who were mere practical calculators.'

In *Kinetics,* the Hindus analysed the concept of motion, gravity (ascribed to the attraction of the earth), acceleration, the law of motion, and the accelerated motion of falling bodies.

Some of their investigations were solid achievements in positive knowledge, as in material medica, therapeutics, anatomy, embryology, metallurgy, chemistry, physics, and descriptive zoology.

Hindus were pre-eminent in all these sciences besides metaphysics and religion.

ASTRONOMY

Hindu astronomy labours under the following defects: absence of a general theory; unequal refinement of the different portions now present; want of demonstrations and of recorded observations; crudeness of the instruments used; inaccuracy in observations; suspension of all progress at a certain point. In spite of these disadvantages, Hindus made great advances in astronomy.

Some of the most brilliant results in astronomy were attained by our ancestors in the Pauranic age.

Garga wrote his *Samhita* in the first centrury BC. He speaks of the Greek conquests in India; he calls the Greek 'viciously valiant barbarians.' Yet, he does not hesitate to say that the Greek astronomy is worth of study. This regard for the Greek astronomy from a hostile critic plainly shows subsequent Greek influence on Hindu astronomy. The Buddhist missionaries not only gave to the west Indian cult and culture but also brought back many useful lessons from Alexandria and Greece. Hindu kings imitated beautiful Greek coins, and sculptures illustrated in the Gandhara school. Except the work of Lagadha, all other astronomical works after Christ, betray a distinct Greek influence. The *Samvat* is a lunar, but the *Sakabda* is a solar year. Solar year was, no doubt, known to the Vedic rishis. But the lunar one was long in practice.

Indians brought it probably from Alexandria. Hindus never borrowed or copied a whole system from outside. They took hints—germs—that soon fructified into splendid things on the rich Indian soil. Knowledge of Greek astronomy certainly helped the Hindus in correcting and improving their own.

The first Varahamihira, son of Varaha, an astronomer of Ujjain wrote the *Vrihat Samhita* in the first century BC under the patronage of first Vikramaditya. The second Varahamihira (AD 80) gave a revised edition of *Brahma Siddhanta*, an ancient work. The work of Lagadha, probably of the second or third century AD, is free from any foreign influence. The third Varahamihira, author of the present *Vrihat Samhita*, lived in AD 285 (see *Vrihat Samhita, chapter I, verse 2; chapter III, verse* 2). But it is perhaps wrongly ascribed to the fourth Varahamihira (AD 505 to 587). This *Vrihat Samhita* is edited by Dr Kern. Its 106 chapters deal with various subjects: chapters 1 to 20 relate to the sun, moon, earth, and the planets; chapters 21 to 39 deal with rain, winds, earthquakes, meteros, rainbow, duststorm, thunderbolts; chapters 53 to 60 speak of various miscellaneous matters including portents, house-building, gardening, temples, images; chapters 61 to 78 treat of various animals, men and women; chapters 79 to 85 relate to precious stones and furniture; chapters 86 to 96 treat of various omens; chapters 97 to 106 treat various matters including marriages, the divisions of the zodiac. It is an encyclopaedic work of utmost value for general information and merit, as well as an astronomical work. Chapter 14 is a complete geography of India and names numerous provinces and towns of India. Chapters 41 to 42 give a vast number of commodities, vegetables and manufactures. Chapters 61 to 67 describe various animals. Chapters 79 to 85 state various articles—from a diamond to a toothbrush. Chapter 58 lays down rules for constructing various images, viz., Rama, Bali, Vishnu with eight, two or four hands, Baladeva, Subhadra, Samba with four faces, Indra, Siva, Bharani, Buddha, the gods of the Jains, the sun, the Linga, Yama, Varuna, Kuvera, Ganesa with his elephant head. Chapter 60 states that the Bhagavats worship Vishnu; the Magas worship the sun. The twice-born smearing their body with ashes, worship Siva. Matris are worshipped. The Brahmans worship Brahma. The Sakyas and the naked Jains(?) worship the calm-souled Buddha. The book also alludes to the perfect toleration of the age.

Utpala wrote a commentary of it in the tenth century AD. The *Surya Siddhanta* is said to have been first written by Vivaswan, father to Manu (twenty-ninth century BC). Vivaswan's dynasty is now called the *Surya Siddhanta*. The original work is lost. Being repeatedly recast, the book, still a learned one, has received its final reduction in the fifth century AD. The present book was written in the vernal equinox. The position of the vernal equinox is shown by Colebrooke (*As. Res., vol. II, p. 329, Note;* also by Sir William Jones, *As. Res., vol. II, p. 392*).

The *Surya Siddhanta* is an authority, along with Varahamihira.

Its fourteen chapters treat of mean and true places of the planets; of questions on time; of eclipses of the sun and moon; of the conjunctions of planets and stars; of the phases of the moon; of the positions of the moon's cusps; of the declination of the sun and moon; of cosmography; of the construction of astronomical instruments, and of the different kinds of time.

Aryabhatta was born at Pataliputra in AD 476. the Arabs called him Aryabhar. He was one of the earliest Hindu writers on algebra. His work called the *Aryabhattiya Siddhanta* consists of the *Gitikapada*, the *Ganitpada,* the *Kalakriyapada* and the *Golapada*. Its English translation is edited by Dr Kern. Aryabhatta in his work maintains: the theory of the revolution of the earth on its own axis; true cause of the solar and lunar eclipses. (Before him, Kalidasa, in his *Raghuvansa*, XIV, 40 refers to it: 'What in reality is only the shadow of the earth, is regarded by the people as an impurity of the pure moon.' Minister Sanjaya also speaks of the same in the *Mahabharata*); in *Golapada,* he gives us the twelve divisions of the solar zodiac; he gives the approximate length of the equator or circumference of the earth as thirty-three *yojanas,* of four *krosas* each. 1 *yojana* = 8 miles. Therefore, 3300 x 8 = 26,400 miles. This is not far of the mark.

The fourth Varahamihira (AD 505 to 587), was the son to Adityadasa of Ujjain, who was himself an astronomer. His work is the *Pancha Siddhantika,* a compilation of the five astronomical works, viz., Brahma, Saura, Vasista, Romaka, and Paulisa.

The second Varahamihira revised the *Brahma Siddhanta* about AD 80. The Saura, i.e. *Surya Siddhanta* in its present form, belongs to the fifth century AD. 'The ancient work of Vasista was revised by Vishnu Chandra,' so says Brahmagupta in AD 628. The present work is a modern one. Both Brahmagupta and Alberuni ascribe *Romaka Siddhanta* to Srisena. A spurious modern *Romaka Siddhanta* also exists, containing a horoscope of Jesus Christ, an account of the kingdom of Babar and the conquest of Sindh by Akbar.

Alberuni obtained a copy of *Pulisa Siddhanta*. He calls the author Pulisa a Greek, the Paulas Alexandrianus of Professor Weber, the author of an astrological work called the *Eisagoge*. Dr Kern doubts this, though he believes that Pulisa was a Greek. Srisena lived long at Rome and wrote his book there. So, he was often called Romaka Srisena. Pulisa was a Hindu, and not Greek, as is supposed. He too, lived abroad. Dr Kern holds that these five Siddhantikas were composed about AD 250. Kasyapa is often quoted as an authority in the astronomical work of the Pauranic age.

Brahmagupta (b. AD 598), like Aryabhatta was a Sakali Brahman of east India. He wrote his *Brahmasphutta Siddhanta in* AD 628, when he was only thirty. The book has twenty-one chapters: 1 to 10 contain an astronomical system showing the true place of the planets, the calculation of solar and lunar eclipses, the position of the moon's cusps, the conjunctions of planets and stars. The 12th and the 18th chapters are rendered by Colebrooke.

Great political convulsions followed in India after AD 650 and the consequent darkness for five centuries. *Bhaskaracharya* was born in AD 1114 at the village Vijjaravira in Maharashtra. His father was Mahesacharya and great grandfather, Bhaskarabhatta.

He came of a family of scholars. His wife was Lilavati. He lived on the Godavari. At thirty-six, he wrote his *Siddhanta Siromani* (AD 1150) that contains chapters on algebra, arithmetic, geography, spherical trigonometry, and astronomy. He was the evening star of farewell.

Colebrooke notes the following in connection with Hindu astronomy: regulation of time by the sun and moon; adjustment of calendar both civil and religious; careful observations of the luminaries; determination of the moon's synodical revolution; division of the lunar ecliptic into 27 or 28 parts and observation of the fixed star. They knew well the most splendid of the primary planets—the period of Jupiter is introduced by them in conjunction with those of the sun and the moon, two extraordinary points of the early Hindus—precession of the equinoxes (in it, they are more correct than Ptolemy) and diurnal revolutions of the earth on its axis (*Hindu Algebra, p. xxii).*

The Question of Originality

The following points are in favour of Hindu originality in astronomy.

(i) In the first part of their progress, all other nations were in still greater ignorance.

(ii) In the more advanced stages, not only is their mode of proceeding peculiar in themselves but is founded on principles unknown to other ancients. It shows a knowledge of discoveries not made even in Europe until recently. As far as their astronomical conclusions depend on those discoveries, they cannot have borrowed; moreover, persons who had such resources within themselves, must not have relied on others. Hindus probably took hints from the Greeks of Alexandria, but they never copied the doctrines of others. Hindu writers speak respectfully of the Greek astronomy. Their astronomy, with its apparatus of eccentrics and epicycles, resembles that of the Greeks. Hence, it is probable that the Hindus received from the Greeks that knowledge which enabled them to correct and improve their imperfect astronomy.

At regards the solar zodiac, Hindus may have taken the hint, not from the Greeks but from the Assyrians. Greeks invented the names and figures only gradually. Cleostratus (sixth century BC) added the ram and the archer. The balance was introduced in the time of the Ptolemis (see Letronne, *Journ. Des Savans, 1839*). In India, *Baudhayana* (long before the sixth century BC) in his *Sutra* first mentions these signs (Colebrooke's Essays, *vol. I, p. 202*).

Dr Bhau Daji in J.R.A.S., New Series, vol. 1, p. 409, quotes a couplet from Varahamihira (AD 285, not AD 505 to 587 as is supposed) giving all the Greek names in a corrupted form. Moreover, his work contains many Greek terms such as *heli* (helios), *jyamitra* for diameter, *hora, Kendra, lipta.* See also Dr Kern's Preface to his edition of the *Vrihat Samhita*. These do not prove that the Hindus borrowed the solar zodiac from the Greeks. The *Baudhayana Sutras,* the two Sanskrit epics and other ancient works make occasional mention of the signs, or some of them.

'Their astrology,' says Colebrooke, 'is almost entirely borrowed from the West'. This is perhaps the only instance where Colebrooke speaks rather rashly. Astrology, like astronomy, was early cultured in India. In the epic age, astrology is a subject of learning. We then hear of *ganakas,* i.e. astrologers. Astrology helped the discovery of new medicines, performance of sacrifice and other good works. The Brahmans counselled the householders and the peasants on annual forecasts. Out readers probably remember the council of Chandragupta (312 BC) held in spring every year for astrological purposes. Subhadrangi, mother of Ashoka, though a Brahman girl, was married to the Kshatriya Vindusara only because a Brahman had told her great fortune. It is needless to multiply examples. Manu is quoted in *Garga* (first century BC) as an authority on astrology.

Col. Wilford says that in the first century AD, Hindu astrologers were in high estimation and repute at Rome and none but the richest men could afford to employ them (*As. Res., vol. X, p 104*).

Yavanacharya was born of a Brahman family of Arabia and educated in the University of Alexandria. He wrote several treatises on astrology. Of our twenty-three astrologers, five, viz., Chetta, Cautta, Romaka, Hillaja, and Dishana were born at Mecca. They are Hindus, though generally called *Javanas*. Cangha was a Hindu astrologer. His Arabic translator calls him Cancah-al-Hindi (De Herbelot). The *Jatakas* (birth-registers) furnish materials afterwards worked into *kosthis* (horoscopes), which tell the entire fortune of a man's life. Palmistry is an important branch of astrology. Reading the lines, signs and figures on the palm and other parts of the body, they can clearly and correctly tell one's fortune. There are means of reading another's mind, tracing the missing articles, warding off the evil influence of enemies or bad planets.

Chanakya in his Art of Government or *Arthashastra* speaks of a kind of clock according to which they would ring bells to conduct office-work. He probably meant a sun dial. Another means is to find the hour of the day, stand in the sun, measure your shadow by your steps, double the steps and add 14 to it. Then divide 292 by the sum—the quotient is the time before or after noon. Suppose, your shadow measures 20 steps. Then 20 x 2 + 14 = 54. Therefore, 292/54 = 5. 16/27 dandas—a little over two hours. The time is then about 5. 1/2 dandas after sunrise; and if in the afternoon, it is so many dandas to sunset.

MEDICINE

Europe's Debt to India

The works of Hippocrates, 'the father of medicine,' show traces of a distinct influence of the Indian pharmacopoeia. Of course, he had his ideas in Persia (Royle's *Essay, p. 89*). Ktesias also wrote an account of the Indian plants. Alexander's writers described India as the land of medicinal and aromatic plants. The Brahmans paid great attention to medicine and philosophy.

Nearchus and Arrian say that the Brahmans could cure snake-bites and other generally incurable diseases.

Early Enquiries of Europe into Hindu Medicine and Works

Professor H H Wilson's brief notice in the Oriental Magazine (1823). The great traveller and scholar Csoma de Koras gave a sketch of Hindu medical opinions as rendered into Tibetan languages in *J.A.S.* 1835. Heyne and Ainslie collected much information on Hindu medicine. Dr Royle combined points from these previous works and added his own original researches in his *Antiquity of Hindu Medicine* (1837). Dr Wise published in 1845 a commentary on Hindu medicine. His *Review of the History of Medicine* was published in London in 1867.

Greek origin of medicine was now set aside and its Hindu origin established. Dr Royle shows, after an exhaustive inquiry that much of the *Materia Medica* of Dioscorides (first century AD) was taken from the more ancient Hindu *Materia Medica* (Essay, pp. 82–104). Professor Wilson's paper, read before the Ashmolean Society of Oxford, refers to the products of India noticed by Ktesias (fifth century BC). Theophrasus had much from Hindu medicine (third century BC). GREEK *Therapeutics* originated from the system of medicine of the Therapeuts, Sanskrit *Sthaviraputras*, Buddhist missionaries of Egypt and Alexandria. Aetius, an Alexandrine writer on surgery (fifth century AD)was acquainted with the medicines, diseases and practices of India.

Hindu Medical Science in Europe through the Arabs

Of the numerous sciences taught by the Arabs of Europe, the foremost was the science of medicine. 'They had acquired a great skill in the uses and properties of medicinal herbs, for to them (Arabs) had been early opened the oldest and at the same time one of the richest sources of knowledge—the medical system of the Indian physicans.' (Humboldt).

The Arabs themselves admit their debt. The author of the *Kitab-ul-fihrist* (tenth century AD) says that by order of the Caliphs Harun and Mansur, several Hindu works on medicine, *Materia Medica* and therapeutics were done into Arabic. *Susrud* (Susruta) was translated by Mankh, the Indian who had cured Harun-ar-Rashid of a severe illness and was appointed physician in charge of the royal hospital. Professor Max Müller has clearly shown that not only Susrut but also Charaka (Xarch, Scirak), the Nidana (Badan) and the *Ashtanga* (Asanbkar), a book on poison by Sanaka and several other works were translated into Arabic (Dr P C Roy's *History of Hindu Chemistry, vol.I*). Charaka is very often mentioned in the Latin translations of Serapion (Ibn Sarafyun), Avicenua (Ibn Sina) and Rhazes (Al Razi). *Deudar, Sanskrit davadaru* (not a modern discovery) was described long ago by Avicenna by its Sanskrit name *deiudar*. Serapion mentions the Indian *Triphala*, the decoction of the three species of myrobalan. The Europeans knew their ultimate indebtedness to the Indians. Dr Wise says, 'It is to the Hindus we owe the first system of medicine.'

Dhanvantari, a gem of Vikramaditya's court, (in the first centuries BC and AD) was a medical expert but his work is now lost. Hindu medical science made great progress after the Christian era. Patanjali was probably a great writer of the first century. Salihotra of the Punjab, another great physician about the Christian era, wrote especially on veterinary treatment.

The following is Professor Wilson's analysis of ancient Ayurveda:

(i) Salya, the art of extracting extraneous things like arrows or wood, with the treatment of inflammation and suppuration, the cure of all phlegmonoid tumours and abscesses.

(ii) Salakya, the treatment of external organic afflictions or diseases of the eyes, ears and nose. The word is from Salaka, a thin sharp instrument which must have been in use from ancient times.

(iii) *Kaya-chikitsya* is modern science of medicine. The *Salya* and *Salakya* together make up surgery.

(iv) *Bhuta Vidya* is the restoration of the faculties from a disorganised state supposed to be induced by demoniacal possessions.

(v) *Kumara Bhritya* is the care of infancy comprehending the management of infants and the treatment of disorders in mothers and nurses.
(vi) *Agada tantra* treats of the administration of antidotes.
(vii) *Rasayana* deals with the purification of blood.
(viii) *Bajikarana* professes to promote the increase of the human race.

Like the two Sanskrit epics, the two great medical works *Susruta* and *Charaka* have come down to us from the tenth or fifteenth century BC. They are mentioned in the *Mahabharata,* but not in the *Ramayana.* Even in their original form, they were but compilations from older documents. Like the epics, they have undergone many revisions. The present books, remodelled after Christ, contain much unworthy interpolations. Annotator Dalvana and Bagbhata say that the present *Susruta* was remodelled by the great Buddhist scholar Nagarjuna in the second century AD. Nagarjuna retained only a part of the poetical portion of old *Susruta* and explained the rest in his own prose.

The defects of *Charaka* are said to have been made up by Drihravala, a learned writer of the Punjab. *Susruta* treats of surgery and Charaka of medicine. Their fame spread abroad early.

Divisions of Susruta's work

(i) *Sutrasthana* treats of medicine; of elements of the body and various forms of disease; of the selection of surgical instruments and medicines and of the practice following surgical operations. Next comes a description of the humours and the surgical diseases, the removal of extraneous substances and the treatment of wounds and ulcers.
(ii) *Nidanasthana* treats of the symptoms and diagnoses of diseasis. The causes of rheumatism, piles, stone, fistula, leprosy, diabetes, and ascitas are spoken of. The symptoms of unnatural presentations in midwifery, internal abscesses, erysipelas, scrofula, hydrocele and diseases of the organs of generation and of the mouth are considered.
(iii) *Sarirasthana* or anatomy treats of the structure of the body. The soul and the elementary parts of the body, puberty, conception, growth of the body, bleeding, treatment of pregnancy and of infants are considered.

(iv) *Chikitsyasthana* describes the symptoms and treatment of diseases, wounds ulcers, inflammations, fractures, rheumatism, piles, stone, fistula in anoleprosy, diabetes, and dropsy. Extraction of the child from the uterus in unusual positions and other matters are described. The use of clysters, of errhines and of the smoke of medicinal substances, is also described.

(v) *Kalpasthan* treats of antidotes. The means of preparing and preserving food and drink and of distinguishing poisoned food are explained. The different mineral, vegetable and animal poisons and their antidotes are explained.

(vi) *Uttarasthana* treats of various local diseases and other diseases like fever, dysentery, consumption, tumour, diseases of the heart, jaundice, discharge of blood, fainting, intoxication, cough, hiccough, asthma, hoarseness of voice, worms, stertorous vomiting, cholera, dyspepsia, dysuria, madness, demoniacal possessions, epilepsy, and apoplexy.

Susruta's arrangements of drugs and plants:

This comprised of roots, barks, trees, leaves, flowers, fruits, seeds, acid, astringent vegetables, milky plants, gums, and resins. Susruta's botanical geography shows the sites and climates and seasons, when and where the plants grow; prescribes the weights and measures; gives direction for extracting juices from fresh vegetables, making powder out of well-dried plants, preparing infusions and decoctions of various kinds. Hindu physicians knew well the vast variety of vegetable medicines, and 1,300 different plants.

Besides assuaging and depuratory medicines, there were drastic and mild purgatives, emetics, diaphoretics, and baths. Acid poisons were used with arsenic and mercurial preparations and stimulants, sedatives, and narcotics.

On Susruta's surgery, Dr Royle says, 'It will, no doubt, excite one's surprise to find among the operations of these eminent surgeons, those of lithotomy and the extraction of the foetus *ex utero;* and that no less than 127 surgical instruments are described in their works.'

Surgery was divided into *chhedana* (scission), *behdana* (excision), *lekhana* (scarification and inoculation), *vyadhana* (puncturing), *eshyan* (probing), *aharya* (extraction of solid bodies), *visrava* (*extraction of fluids*), and *siwana* (sewing).

Professor Wilson classifies the surgical instruments, as *yantras* (implements), *sastras* (instruments), *kshara* (alkaline solutions or caustics), *agni* (actual cautery), *salaka* (pins), *sringa* (horns), *alabu* (gourds used for cupping) and *jalauka* or leeches. Besides these, we have threads, leaves, bandages, pledgets, heated metallic plates for erubescents, and a variety of astringent or emollient applications.

Instruments are desired and directed to be of metal, always bright, polished and sharp, sufficiently so to divide a hair longitudinally. Learners are directed to acquire skill in the instrument by making incisions on vegetables, fresh hides of animals and the vessels of dead animals.

Professor Wilson observes, 'The surgical operations were evidently bold and must have been hazardous; their being attempted at all is, however, most extraordinary unless their obliteration from the knowledge, not to say the practice, of later times, be considered as a still more remarkable circumstance. It would be an enquiry of some interest to trace the period and causes of the disappearance of surgery from amongst the Hindus.'

The causes are social and religious degeneracy and political disaster. Professor Madhusudan Gupta of Medical College, Calcutta, editing *Susruta* (Hindu Surgery) observed, 'Ancient Hindus had no prejudice against pursuit of medicine in a scientific way'. Brahmans are seldom physicians now. They have long neglected surgery and left it to the barbers. Hindu medicine and not surgery, has revived a little, of late years, under the British rule.

The names of so many diseases, the numerous and varied preparations of medicines, show the great progress of medical science. Hindu knowledge of medicines was very extensive. They gave early lessons to Europe. They have taught the benefit of smoking *dhutura* in asthma and the use of cowitch against worms. They knew the use of artificial limbs. Their use of acids, oxides and other chemical compounds as medicines was certainly very bold. They were the first nation to apply minerals internally. They not only gave mercury in that manner, but also arsenic and arsenious acid as remedies. They have long used cinnabar for fumigations by which they produce speedy and safe salivation.

They cut for the stone, couched the cataract and extracted the foetus from the womb. They were very successful in cataract; but the operations for the stone often proved fatal. Stone can be cured by medicinal drugs that dissolve the stones. They had long practised inoculation but still many died from smallpox.

Hindu physicians are very attentive to the pulse, to the state of the skin, of the tongue, eyes, and to the nature of evacuations. They form correct prognostics from the symptoms. They are not always judicious in their treatment. In fever, the patients are shut up in an artificially heated room, deprived of food and drink. They knew the use of blister (Elphinstone).

The following points are worth remembering:

(i) 'Always protect thyself: for, existence is the first law of Nature.' (Vedas).
(ii) 'On health, depends everything.' (Kalidasa).
(iii) Prevention is better than cure.
(iv) Food, drink, air, water, light, ground, clothing, etc., should be as good as possible.
(v) Purity, noble and good thoughts, virtuous energy are conducive to good health.
(vi) Envy is the cause, not the effect.
(vii) Constipation is the root of many diseases.
(viii) Many diseases are cured by diet alone. No disease can be cured, even by the best of medicines, without a suitable diet.

We usually ascribe our Hindu neglect of surgery to prejudice and political disaster. But the true cause seems to be the discovery of many new and wonderful medicinal drugs that could cure without surgical aid. As the invention of algebra led the Brahmans to neglect geometry: so the discovery of new medicines led to the neglect of surgery. It is well known that many of our Puranas and Tantras mention many excellent medicines, used to this day. The neglect of Hindu surgery thus began from the Tantric age, i.e. the tenth century AD. Many of our countrymen know how common medicines cure cases declared 'incurable, hopeless' by competent physicians.

At Bharatpur (Rajputna) I met a Muslim gentleman versed in both Hindu and Muhammadan medicine; he could cure blindness simply with a collyrium. At Radha Kundo (dist. Mathura) I saw a Hindu ascetic curing a cobbler of stone, simply with the juice of a few green leaves of a plant, mixed with a little sugar. I know of a lady who can cure sinus, tumour, carbuncle, gangrenous wounds, even ulcers by some leaves and roots. The best surgical aid failed to set right the unnatural position of the uterus of a girl. An old kaviraja of Calcutta gave her a drug swallowing which her uterus was set right. Now, she is the mother of several children.

In time, the true reason was forgotten and a prejudice arose to say that the use of steel is forbidden to the Brahmans.

Formerly, there were Hindu physicians in the Persian Court. Alexander kept Hindu physicians in his camp. Harun-ar-Rasid of Baghdad kept Hindu Saleh and Manka as his own physicians. The Arabs openly acknowledged their obligations to the Hindus (Dr Royle's *Essay p. 44*). Bagbhata, Madhava, Chakrapani (AD 1060), flourished under the Pala kings of Bengal and others wrote on medicine. Recently, His Highness the Thakur Sahib of Gondal, has written an able work on Hindu Medicine.

CHEMISTRY

Hindus knew *rasayana* (chemistry) and the preparation of chemical compounds. Their chemical skill is a fact more striking and more unexpected.

India abounds with materials from the earliest times. Hindus knew lime, charcoal, sulphur, sal ammonia, alum (abundant in Kutch), saltpetre, sulphate of soda, borax (abundant in Tibet) and rock-salt (in west India), alkalies, and acids. The Arabs borrowed those from India.

Dr Royle, in his Essay, pp. 43–44 describes the Hindu preparation of muriatic acid, medicinal use of metal, antimony, medicines prepared with quicksilver, arsenic and nine other metals. They knew oxides of copper, iron, tin, zinc, and lead; sulphurets of copper, zinc and iron; the diacetate of copper and the carbonates of lead and iron. Hindus applied numerous metallic substances internally (*p. 45*). They knew several chemical processes as solution, evaporation, calcinations, sublimation, and distillation. They knew the processes for making calomel and corrosive sublimate. They could prepare various *dravakas* (acids) such as sulphuric, nitric and muriatic. Chemistry lent great aid to various smiths and especially to medication. They knew *svarnikarana* (gilding), *raupyikarana* (silvering). They knew how to make gunpowder. Hindu magic derives considerable aid from chemistry. Curious readers will have much pleasure and profit from the study of Dr P C Ray's two volumes on Hindu chemistry.

ARTS

Music

Sir W Jones and Paterson call Hindu music systematic and refined. They have eighty-four modes of which thirty-six are in general use and each of these has a particular expression and the power of moving some particular sentiment or affection. They are named from the seasons of the year and the hours of the day and night: each possesses some quality appropriate to the time. Vina (harp), fiddles and drum are the musical instruments.

Indian music, like Indian medicine, went from India to Europe and has also influenced both Chinese and Japanese music. In India, music is generally regarded as a female quality.

Painting

We have seen that painting was a subject in the epic age. We have no specimens of our early painting. Vatsyayana (close of the fourth century BC) in his *Kamasutra* (work on fine arts) gives, among other things, the six canons of painting. The Chinese painter Hsich-Ho (AD 479 to 501) mentions it. Taj Kuchi first painted a fine picture of Buddha (AD 300). Both men and women indulged in the art. Coloured earth was in use.

The walls of houses were painted in water-colours and sometimes in oils. Their subjects were mythology, battles, wrestles, male and female figures, animals, trees, and buildings. Hindu paintings resemble those on the wall of Egyptian tombs. They have also pictures of small sizes—likenesses of individuals. Hindus have often beautifully illuminated manuscripts. Portraits are common in the dramas.

Sculpture (Bhaskara Vidya)

It has generally failed to attain excellence. There are numberless images. All caves and temples are covered with statues and reliefs. Some are bold and spirited and produce every fine specimens of grace in figures and attitude. Later examples betray a disregard for proportion and a want of skill in grouping.

ARCHITECTURE

Hindus attained great excellence in architecture, sculpture and painting. For these, they were not indebted to Greece, Egypt, Babylonia or Assyria. Dr Fergusson, speaking of the railings of Bharhut (200 BC) says, 'The art here displayed is purely indigenous. The figure sculpture was elaborated on the spot by the Indians and Indians only'. (*I and E Arch, p. 89*). The Gandhar style of north-west India bears a Greek stamp.

Architecture in stone before 200 BC was confined to city walls, gates, bridges , and embankments. Places, religious and civil edifices, if of stone, are all lost. Hindu and Jain edifices of stone after fifth century AD, abound in India. The Buddhist-Hindus were great builders.

Dr Fergusson's classification:

(i) *Lats* or monolithic pillars bearing inscriptions.
(ii) *Stupas* or topes.
(iii) *Railings* around topes.
(iv) *Chaityas* or churches.
(v) *Viharas* or monasteries.

Pillars

That of Allahabad bears the inscriptions of Ashoka, Samudragupta and Jehangir (AD 1605). Like most other pillars, it has lost its crowing ornament. The Tirhoot pillar has the figure of a lion on the top. That of Sankissa between Mathura and Kanouj, bears the mutilated figure of an elephant. The Karli pillar is surmounted by four lions. The two Erun pillars belong to the Gupta times.

The Iron Pillar of Delhi (twenty-two ft above ground and twenty inches underground) bears an undated inscription on it. Prinsep gives it to fourth or fifth and Dr Bhau Daji, to fifth or sixth century AD.

Dr Fergusson wonders at the Hindu skill in forging such huge iron bars at that age, unknown to Europe until recently. The temple at Konarak had similar long bars on the roof. It is still unrusted; the capital and inscription are as clear and sharp now as when put up, fourteen centuries ago. J C Allen thinks that the Iron Pillar probably belonged to ancient Indraprastha. The writing on it shows that it was called 'The Arm of Fame of Raja Dhavala who subdued a people that lived by the seven mouths of the Sindhu (Indus) and obtained with his own arm, undivided sovereignty on earth.' Iron Pillars exist also at Abu and Dhar. J Hoffmann has taken a photo of the Delhi pillars. Sir Robert Hadfield has made a chemical analysis of it. The pillars and beams were probably originally painted. The ancient Hindus were quite familiar with the use of iron and steel. The Vedic literature mentions *surmi,* sword and other weapons.

Many arms and implements have been discovered at Tirunelveli, south India. The south has been famous for its steel called wootz. Specimens of steel have been found in those ancient weapons and implements.

Stupas or Topes

They are erected to mark some sacred event or site or to preserve some relic of Buddha. The great topes of Sanchi and Bhilsa in central India are the most famous. The gateway, most elaborately sculptured, is thirty-three feet high. The Sarnath Tope, near Benaras, is a solidly built structure (sixth or seventh century AD).

Yuan Chwang saw the Jarasandha Baithak, a tope twenty-eight ft in diameter and twenty-one ft high (AD 500?) and the dagoba (Central tope) at Amaravati, now no more. The Gandhara country has numerous examples. The great Dagoba of Kanishka, over 470 feet high and seen by Fa-Hien and Yuan Chwang, has disappeared. In 1830, General Ventura and M Court first noticed the group of M Court first noticed the group of Manikyala in the Punjab, the most important of the Gandhara topes.

Railings and Gateways

The generally round topes, are richly ornamented. Those of Bodh Gaya (250 BC) and Bharhut (between Allahabad and Jabalpur), dated 200 BC, are the oldest. The Bharhut railings are the only monument in India with inscribed legends. Dr Fergusson calls the sculpture here thoroughly original. Representation of elephants, deer, monkeys, trees, hunman figures all truthful to nature, is unsurpassed in the world. For an honest, pre-Rephaelite kind of art, there is probably nothing better to be found anywhere. The railing round Sanchi tope in Bhopal has elaborate and profuse scrolls, discs and figures. The sculptures of the four gateways or *torans* form a perfect pictorial Bible of Buddhism, as it existed in India in the first century BC. The Amaravati railing was dated fourth or fifth century AD. Amaravati was the capital of the Andhra empire on the lower Krishna.

Chaityas

They were assembly halls or churches, mostly excavated. Some thirty are known to exist. Hindu and European temples have imposing and noble features outside, but not so the Buddhist. The frontage alone is ornamented.

Bombay Presidency—the cave district of India—has most of the Buddhist chaityas. The Saptaparni cave of Rajagriha in Bihar was originally a Hindu cave. There is a group of caves, sixteen miles to the north of Gaya. The Lomasa *Rishi* cave is the most interesting (third century BC). The hall is 33 ft x 19 ft.

> *Note*: The cave churches were of Hindu origin and not Buddhist. Five or six caves in the Western Ghats were excavated before Christ. The cave at Bhajan is the most ancient (third century BC). The Bedsor caves show great skill (first half of second century AD).

The Karli cave on the road between Poona and Bombay, is the largest and most perfect yet found in India (first century AD). It shows perfect architecture. The style is chaste and pure. The building resembles an early Christian church. The statues of Buddha appear in the later Ajanta caves (first to sixth century AD).

The hall of Visvakarma, cave of Ellora (AD 500?) is 85 ft by 43 ft. The façade looks like an oridinary two-storeyed house with verandahs richly sculptured.

The Kenheri cave on the Island of Salsette in the Bombay harbour was excavated early in the fifth century AD. It copies the Karli cave, but the style is very inferior.

Viharas or Monasteries

In Nalanda, south of Patna, successive kings built many stupas and towers. All trace of the superstructure, probably wooden, is lost.

Khandagiri and Udaigiri caves are in Orissa, twenty miles south of Cuttack. The Hasti Guha (Elephant cave) bears an inscription of Kharavela 158 AD. The Ganesa Guha and the Rajarani caves were excavated before Christ.

The Nasik group has three chief viharas, viz., of Nahapana (AD 100), of Gautamiputra (AD 300 to 400) and of Yaduyasri (AD 500). It has a colossal figure of Buddha.

The Ajanta Viharas (nos. 16 and 17) are the most interesting in India. They have fresco paintings with perfect distinctness (AD 500?). The decorations are chaste and correct in style and very effective. Dr Fergusson calls these curious paintings of ancient India 'invaluable treasures.' The Ajanta Vihara no. 17, is often wrongly called the Zodiac cave after the Buddhist Chakra or Wheel as the sign of the zodiac. At Ellora, there are many monasteries attached to the Visvakarma cave. There temples here, viz., the Do-tal, the Teen-tal and the Das-Avatar, show the gradual merging of Buddhist excavations into Hindu.

The temple of Kailash by the Hindus of south India (eighth or nineth century AD), makes Ellora one of the wonders of the world. Buddhist churches and monasteries are caves inside hills and rocks, while the Hindu masses cut fine edifices out of rocks. Such buildings stand out in bold relief. Greek influence modified the Gandhara monasteries.

Ceylon Architecture

Anuradhapura, capital of Ceylon for ten centuries (500 BC to AD 500), contains numerous ruins of ancient topes and other edifices. The large tope at Abhayagiri, 1100 ft in circumference and 244 ft high, was constructed in 88 BC. The Jetavana tope is dated AD 275.

The noblest monuments in Indian sculpture and architecture were constructed between third century BC and first century AD. The art, glorious for three or four centuries, however, showed no progress. Painting also attained its highest excellence in the fifth century AD. After AD 500, all arts declined. The sculpture of Hindu temple of seventh or eighth century AD, lost much of its higher aesthetic qualities. Size grew disproportionate, gods were shown with many heads, hands and eyes. There was however, no lack of ornamentation. Later Hindu works give no aesthetic grace.

Hindu and Jain Architecture (AD 500 to 1800)

Specimens of Hindu work are rare from the sixth to nineth century, except these of Orissa. Political convulsion in north India stunted architecture. Fresh works date from the nineth, with the Rajput revival. Hindu temples multiplied in north India, gradually increased in size and grandeur, but not in taste. This change was due to the new mode of worship. The beautiful and magnificent Rajput edifices were admired even by the first Muslim conquerors. Hindu architecture almost stopped in north India with the Muslim conquest. The south, never under the Muslims, has religious edifices of great size and magnificence till the nineteenth century AD. Jain architecture flourished from the nineth century in Rajputana and elsewhere. In north India, Jains borrowed the north Indian style, while in south India, they borrowed the Dravidian style.

North Indian style

Its features:

The outline of the high tower or *vimana* is curvilinear and surmounted by amalaka (a fruit). No trace of division into storeys is found. There are no pillars or plasters anywhere. The porch has a conical top with a series of cornices.

Orissa: Pure and profuse specimens of earliest architecture abound at Bhuvaneshvar in Orissa (dating from AD 500). Of several hundreds of temples, numerous specimens still remain; the most celebrated is the Great Temple built between AD 617 and 657. The buildings is not imposing, though the effect of the whole is marvellously beautiful. The sculpture is of a very high order and great beauty of design (Fergusson, *p. 422*).

Benaras: The modern temples, mostly built in the seventeenth century retain, in spite of modifications, the Orissa style of *vimana* and *amalaka*. The black pagoda of Konarak of which the porch alone now remains, was built in AD 850 or 873. Hindu pagodas show no majesty or symmetry.

The temple of Jagannath in Puri, built in AD 1174, shows not only a change in creed (from Saiva to Vaishnava) but also degeneracy in the spirit of Hinduism. The art declined here forever.

Bundelkhand in central India is rich in ancient Hindu temples. Khajuraho boasts of a group of nearly thirty temples of AD 950 to 1050. The Orissa style here is slightly modified.

Bhopal in central India has a temple built by a king of Malwa in AD 1060. The vimana is also exquisite in design. Carving is precise and delicate.

Rajputana: The ruins of Chitor contain the structure of Rana Kumbhya, a Jain king who erected the Jain temple of Sadri and the marble pillar of victory at Chitor. Mirabai was an orthodox Hindu and built two temples (AD 1418 to 1468) now in ruins. Mirabai's temple at Nathdwar in Mewar is still extant. I visited it in AD 1900. The style is that of Orissa.

Maharashtra: Specimens of ancient temples exist but they are neither rich nor numerous. A mixture of north Indian and Dravidian styles is found in their structures. The Gangetic valley is very poor in specimens. Temple architecture began there late, perhaps in the tenth century AD. The Muslim conquerors demolished old temples and built mosques and minars and effectively stopped all further progress. Hindu independence lingered in Rajputana, Malwa, Bundelkhand, Orissa, Bombay. So, there the old temples were left unharmed and later more temples were erected.

Kanouj was one of the most ancient cities in India, a cradle of Aryan civilisation and sometimes capital of the Guptas, the Vardhans and others. In AD 140 Ptolemy mentions it as Kanogiya. Its kingdom once extended from Kashmir to Assam and Nepal to the Narmada.

All traditions extol its splendour. Sultan Mahmud was struck with wonder when he attacked it in AD 1016. Ferishta describes it as 'a city which raised its head as high as heaven and which, in fortifications and architecture, could justly boast that it had no rival'.

Kanouj, Khajuraho, Mahoba and many other famous towns now in ruins, were the seats of mighty empires. Of these, the most celebrated were governed by the Rajputs, the only one whose dynasties still exist and who have preserved, though not independence, its institutions and customs.

Mansingh's seven-storeyed temple of Govindji at Brindaban was knocked down by Aurangzeb. The temple is partly restored by the British government.

Benaras temples have both Orissa and Saracenic styles.

Bengal: Stone-temples are rare. Brick temples of Siva are built like thatched roofs. Walls are occasionally covered with elaborate designs in terracotta. The modern temples of Siva are a departure from the original north Indian style.

Jain architecture was at first north Indian, but afterwards, Saracenic. Group-temples are peculiar to the Jains. They appear as a 'city of temples'. The temples of Palitana in Gujarat are such. Some are as old as eleventh century AD. They lack the grandeur of Hindu temples; but their general effect is superb. Jain group-temples at Girnar date from the tenth century onward. One is built by Tejpala and Vastupala.

The Somnath Temple of Siva was ruined by Sultan Mahmud. The famed temples of Abu are dedicated to Rishabha Deva: they were built entirely of white markble taken from 300 miles away. One is built by Vimala Shah about AD 1023; the other, by Tejpala and Vastu Pala in AD 1197 to 1247. The porch is supported on elegant pillars exquisitely carved and the inside of the dome is ornamented with elegant and exquisite designs unequalled in India.

The temple of Chandi-Siva, like the Taj, was built on the island of Java, centuries before the Taj. The art of Borobudor was derived from India.

In the nineth century AD, the Gaurian style of Varendra (north Bengal) became supreme under Dharmapala and Devapala. Architects Dhiman and his son Bitapala were authors of this new style.

'The Naga productions of Nagarjuna's time were rivalled by the creations of Dhiman and his son Bitapala, natives of Varendra (Bengal) who lived during the reigns of Dharmapala and Devapala.' (V A Smith's *History of Fine art in India, chapter IX, p. 305*). Specimens of this Gaurian style noted for its peculiar grace, grandeur and graphic representation of ideas and sentiments, are perhaps still extant in Bengal, Bihar, Kalinga, the Malayan archipelago, and elsewhere.

South Indian or Dravidian Style

It grew out of the Buddhist style of excavation. Its two kinds are rock-cut temples (earlier) and structural edifices (later).

The Dravidian Cheras or Cholas conquered northward in the eighth or nineth century AD. So, the temples at Ellora and of Kailas are of Dravidian design and construction. The monolithic character of these vast edifices, gives to them an air of solidity, strength and grandeur.

The structural temples are very modern in date. The southern builders continued till the Anglo-French war. The great pagoda of Tanjore (fourteenth century AD) was probably built by a king of

Conjeevaram. Its total height is 190 feet and general view is elegant and graceful.

The temple of Chillamvaram near the mouth of the Cauveri is most venerated and ancient (tenth or eleventh century AD). The most imposing buildings of it, the Great Gopuras, the Temple of Parvati and the Hall of Thousand Columns were built in the fifteenth, sixteenth and seventeenth centuries AD.

The great temple of Serigham was built in the eighteenth century. An imposing central structure is wanting in all south Indian temples. The Madura temple, a rectangle 750 ft by 840 ft with a hall of 1,000 columns, was built by Trimulla Nayaka in AD 1622 to 1657.

The temple of Ramesvaram on an island, shows all the beauty of Dravidian style in its greatest perfection (seventeenth century AD). 'Its immensity and picturesqueness produce an effect unsurpassed by any other temple in India and by very few elsewhere.' (Fergusson, *p. 358*).

The Great Temple of Conjeevaram is picturesque and vast. Vijayanagar, the last seat of Hindu learning and glory, and free till AD 1565, contains the largest ruins in all India. Similar ruins exist near Ahmedabad, Gujarat.

The temple of Vitopa in granite has an elegant and tasteful porch. The master-works of the Vijayanagar kings are to be seen at Tarputry, about hundred miles south-east of Vijaynagar. They are remarkable for better taste than anywhere else in this style (Fergusson, *p. 375*).

Chandragiri, like Chinraipatan in Mysore, probably owes its name to Mauryan Chandragupta. Chandragiri Hill has on it a group of fifteen temples containing the chief image of a Tirthankara.

In Canara, as in Nepal, most of the temples (Jain) are wooden. Even the stone buildings closely copy the wooden style. Southern Jains have erected colossal statues, not at all known to northern Jains. One of them at Sravana Belagola is a statue 70 ft 3 inches high, hewn of a solid hill. 'Nothing grander or more imposing exists anywhere out of Egypt and even there, no known statue surpasses it in height.' (Fergusson, *p. 268*). There are two other statues of this nature: one at Karkala 41 ft 5 inches high and the other at Yannur 35 ft high.

Deccan Style

The Chalukya or Deccan style prevails between the Vindhya range and the Krishna river. Mysore (ancient *Mahisades*) developed the Deccan style. The temples have a polygonal or star-shaped base; the walls rise perpendicular to some height and then the roof is pyramidal, tapering to a point. The works of the Ballala dynasty of Mysore and Carnatic, are dated from AD 1000 to 1310. Among their three remarkable groups, one is at Somnathpur built by Vinaditya Ballala (AD 1043). His temple is noted for elegance and elaboration. One is at Baillur, built by Vishnu Vardhana about AD 1114. the richness and variety of pattern in the twenty-eight windows are remarkable. The Hullabid group of temples are the Kayet Isvara Temple—built by Vijay, the fifth king. It is covered with sculptures of the very best class of Indian art. From the basement to the summit, the Great Double Temple of Halebid, in progress for eighty-six years, was magnificent, but not completed, being stopped by the Muslim conqueror in AD 1310.

The temples of Vijaynagar on the river Tungabhadra are of magnificent dimension. The general character of the buildings is strikingly original. The palaces retain their early Hindu character in part.

Tanks as reservoirs for water, are the greatest of the Hindu works. They are of two kinds. One is dug out of the earth; the other is formed by damming up the mouth of a valley, for purposes of bathing and irrigation.

Hindu embankments are magnificent stone works. Temples, shrines, tanks have occasional splendid flight of stone steps. Wells are very deep and broad: they are both round and square, with galleries and have broad flight of steps. Some of the Hindu bridges have posts of stone. Stone piers are connected by stone beams. Stone bridges are common in south India. An example of a gateway or *torana* is a highly wrought column of 120 ft high at Chitor. The finest example of it is at Barnagar, north of Gujarat. It is indeed among the richest specimens of Hindu art.

Resemblance between Hindu and Egyptian style consists in their massive character, both of buildings and the material, the quantity of sculpture on some edifices, the practice of building high towers at gateways, and columns. Special points of Egyptian style are the pyramids; the sides of buildings slope inwards till they reach the top to meet a flat roof with a deep and bold cornice. Pyramidal roofs to the walls before temples are general in India, but they are hollow within. Solid pyramids are unknown in India. The arabesques, the running patterns of plants and creepers in particular, are often of a elegance scarcely equalled in any other part of the world.

Elphinstone complains, 'Hindus display more richness and beauty in detail than greatness in the conception of the whole. The cave temples alone show boldness and grandeur of design.'

Dr Fergusson also says, 'Indian architecture displays a joyous exuberance of fancy and pure feeling but lacks pure refined intellectual power.' His second charge is the 'representation of profane things on religious edifices.'

In reply, I fully agree with RC Dutt in saying that specimens of arts of ancient India are still wanting; that there was no lack of pure intellect in the land of Kapila and Aryabhatta. But disinclination of upper classes for manual exertion was due to intense heat and the enervating climate of India. All had recourse to contemplation and intellectual pursuits. After the caste system, disinclination to physical exertion became a part of social rules for the upper castes. So, Brahmans and Kshatriays—the thinkers—never applied themselves to carving and sculpture. Intellect of a higher order was divorced forever from these fine arts. The artisians, however, were expert in decorative arts in all branches of industry. The wonderful edifices of India show more gigantic labour, minute and endless elaboration, but no lofty design of a creative mind. The high order of intellectual conception that marks the marbles of Greece and Rome, is absent in India where a Phoedias and a Michael Angelo were impossible.

The idea of religion in Europe is connected with the glory of God and the teachings of Christ, with the sermons in churches and the keeping of the Sabbath. To the Hindu, his whole life in all its minute acts, is a part of his religion. So, the Hindus sculptured their temples not only with the images of gods and goddesses but also with the representation of men and women; their wars, triumphs and processions, of aerial and imaginary beings, the Gandharvas, Apsaras, dancing girls, horses, snakes, birds, elephants, lions, trees, creepers—all being the kindred expressions of *Brahman*, the Great One.

Buddhist Nagnajit's work on architecture is lost. Hindu work entitled the *Rajaballava* by Sutradhara Mandana is still extant. There are fragments of other early works on architecture. Ram Raja's *Essay on Hindu Architecture* is published by the Oriental Translation Fund. In it, twelve different mouldings are described: the cyma, toro, cavetto are the same as the English. A few are peculiar. The forms, proportions of pedestals, base, shafts, capitals, and entablatures are given. He names sixty-four sorts of bases.

Jakhanacharya (twelfth century AD), a prince of the royal house of Mysore, was a good architect.

Lately, EB Havell, Dr A Coomaraswami and OC Ganguli have written on Indian architecture. Professor EB Havell in his *Indian Architecture* (1993) declares Indian architecture as extraordinary and as the product of original genius. Another view holds that Indian architecture was largely influenced by foreign models. Even some of the second group call Indian architecture extraordinary and most probably the work of original genius.

We think, imitation of foreign models to a certain extent is quite natural to a land so long under foreign rule. The three chief objects of Havell's work are—Muslim rule did not alter the old Hindu style of building; the old architecture of India, though neglected, has not yet left India; to build New Delhi, Hindu style should be revived and adopted.

'The Persian influence which flowed into India with the Moghuls, was largely a return wave of the Buddhist influences' (Havell's *I.A.P.,99*). Akbar's Fort at Agra contains more than 500 stone edifices in the fine styles of Bengal and Gujarat (*Arch. Survey of India, 1903–04)*.

Humayun's tomb is only one link in the evolution of the Taj and the remaining links must be sought for in India, not in Persia or Central Asia (Havell, *pp. 29–30*). The cupola of the Taj was built after the Buddist stupa. The Taj belongs to India, not to Islam. (*ibid., p. 21*)

'Hindus first knew architecture. From India, the knowledge found its way to other countries' (Dr Fergusson). 'It is indeed not improbable that our western steeples owe their origin to the imitation of Buddhist topes' (Professor Weber's *Indian Literature*).

Dr Hunter in his *Imp. Gaz. of India says,* 'English decorative art, in our own day, has borrowed largely from Indian forms and pattern.'

'That the natives of India, under favourable conditions, are capable of excellence both as architects and builders, the beauty and solidity of many of the historical monuments of the country fully testify and that they could compete withy European skill in the choice and composition of building material, may be proved by comparing an old terrace roof at Delhi or Lahore, with an Allahabad gun shed or many a recent barrack' (Report of Principal Lang, Roorki Coolege, 1870–71).

The beautiful 'city of Jaipur, built in AD 1728, was planned by a Bengali pandit named Vidyadhara. Dr Bhandarkar has dug out of the town of Bes (Gwalior State) two bits of genuine steel from beneath the Tham Baba Pillar' (140 BC) and a very old brick wall the mortar of which, according to Dr Mann, was 'far superior to any ever used by the Phoenicians and the Greeks'.

Industrial Arts

From the date of Greek and Roman civilisation to the eighteenth century AD, India was noted for its artisanship and industries. The 'wealth of Ormuz and of Ind' was proverbial. Pliny complained of the drain of gold from Rome to India. English experts speak of the unrivalled beauty and delicacy of the Indian cotton cloth, as 'the finest the earth produces.' Silk manufactures also are excellent and very ancient. The brilliancy and permanency of many of their dyes are not yet equalled in Europe. Gold and silver brocade are also original products of India. Hindu taste for minute ornaments fitted them to excel in goldsmith's work.

Travellers Pyrard, Jourdan, Roe, Bernier, Peter Mundy, Tavernier witnessed industrial, artistic and commercial activity of the seventeenth and eighteenth centuries.

LAWS

The Hindu kings were not autocrafts. Duties of kings and the subjects were well established. So, the time honoured laws were enforced intelligently. Yuan Chwang, in his long travels in India, did not find a single instance of oppression. People enjoyed self-government in all its purity. Communal autonomy was nowhere developed as well as in India.

Ancient India possessed a notable substantive law and procedure which in particular, has been found even superior to that which we possess today. Sir William Markby held that the English law of prescription should be remodelled on the lines of Hindu law. Sir Rasbehari Ghosh characterises the Hindu law of securities' as a model of good sense and logical consistency.' The Hindu spirit displayed itself politically in a form which was worthy of its other great achievements. Indians ever enjoy full spiritual liberty. 'Twenty-five thousand new laws have been enacted in ten years (1897 to 1907) for the restriction of their own liberties in the British Empire' (Justice Woodroffe of Calcutta High Court).

Manu's present code was remodelled about the third or the second century AD. It contains new suitable additions and also contradictory interpolations. The other law-books were remodelled more or less in the first few centuries of the Christian era.

The following are prohibited for the people of *Pauranic* age: sea-voyage, renunciation, taking Sudra or other inferior wives, long studentship and single life, having a child of the widow of the elder brother, use of meat in the *sraddha* ceremony, slaughter of beasts in honour of a distinguished guest, human and horse sacrifices. It is notable here that most of these prohibitions proved simply dead letters.

Change since Manu. Many laws are no more effective in entirety:

- No unequal marriage.
- Widow-marriage has stopped.
- The practice of sati in full progress.
- Profession-castes after the Muslim conquest.
- Extinction of many religious rites. Even Brahmans do not perform many.
- Kshatriyas and Vaishyas are now like Sudras, void of sacred learning.
- Except Brahmans, the three castes are now mixed, more or less. The Brahmans also have departed from the rules and practices of their ancestors. They do not follow the four stages of life except some. They go into service, trade, army, agriculture. In the south, Brahmans are still superior in occupations. Even in the Gangetic valley, Brahmans are no more held in high veneration.
- Loss of caste for trivial offences.
- End of the servile class: now all classes are free.
- No longer military divisions no longer exist: no courts of justice except at the capital (if any).

CASTE

Vaishyas still from one body: distinct profession-castes arose after the Muslim conquest. All the law-books speak of four castes. Sudras were not allowed Vedic study or the performance of grand religious rites. Before the *Pauranic* age, they had a position and influence: trade, agriculture, arts, industries were open to them. They were rich; they became useful members of society. There were Sudra kings, Sudra chiefs, Sudra ministers. Sudras had become Hindus. They were not despised. Their water was acceptable. They could follow different arts (Vishnu II). Yajnavalkya speaks of thirteen mixed castes formed by the union of men and women of different castes. Kayasthas—'fallen Kshatriyas'—were accountants and record-keepers of the royal courts. Vyasa and others hated them because they became grasping, greedy and degraded.

Vaidyas were Vaishyas, Devas (De), Nandis, Vardhanas, Palas, Dattas, Surs, Soms, Hresh, Kundus, Chandras, Chandas, Kars, Dhars, Senguptas, Das or Dattaguptas, Hazras, Rakshits, Palits, Gopas, Silas, Vaniks, Malakaras, Modakas, Barujas, conchmakers, weavers (Basukas=Basakas), potters. By foul acts and impurities, they had degraded themselves to the rank of mere Sudras. So, the law-givers hated them. Yajnavalkya had contempt for all honest trades and professions. Probably the men, not the professions were despised. Some of the law-books laud extravagantly the priestly caste.

Caste rules became more stringent after the Muslim conquest. Caste now forms a basis of Hinduism. Hindu castes are really moral classes, admitting of worthy promotions. Many faults have crept into our caste system. We should reform society, and not deform it. Formerly, the worthies of inferior castes were honourably admitted into higher ranks. Hindus were the first to discover the law of evolution in Nature (cf. Sankhya and Yoga philosophies). Why should we be blind to social evolution? Gold comes from obscure ore; fire is born of smoke. Then why should we not even accept water from our worthy Suvarna-Vaniks, Jogis, Sahas, Nama-Sudras? Luckily, Hindu society under the British rule, has been progressive. Slowly and sensibly, necessary changes are going on.

SOCIAL AND DOMESTIC LIFE AND STATUS OF WOMAN

The rules of social and domestic life continued as ever with the following restrictions. No intermarriage, interdining and exogamy (Yajnavalkya, *I, 56–57;* Vishnu *XXIV, 4;* Sankha, *iv, 6–9;* Vyasa, *II, 11*). The ancient eight forms of marriage were falling into disuse (Yajnavalkya, *I, 58–61;* Vishnu *XXIV, 18–32;* Sankha, *IV, 3;* Harita, IV, *2–3* recommended the first four only, viz., *Brahma, Daiva, Arsha* and the *Prajapatya*). Early marriage of girls was now insisted upon (Yajnavalkya, *I, 94;* Parasara, *VII, 6–9;* Yama, *22–24;* Sanvarta, *66–67;* Vyasa, *II,* 7). Remarriage of widows was still in use, though regarded with disfavour since Manu (Yajnavalkya, *I, 67;* Vishnu *XV, 7-8;* Parasara, *IV, 26;* Sankha, *XV, 13*). Of the 12 kinds of sons, the first four were, legitimate, begotten, adopted and made, according to Parasara *IV, 19*. In modern times, only two are recognised, viz., *aurasa,* legitimate and *dattaka* adopted.

Domestic virtues continue the same as ever.

Duties of a Wife

She will rise before her lord at early dawn, clean the house, sweep and clean the room of worship, clean all the utensils and implements of religious worship and put them in order, wash all the utensils of cooking and wipe the hearth, and having thus performed all the preliminary work of the day, will come and do obeisance to her father-in-law, mother-in-law and others; next, cook the food, feed the children, then her husband, next herself. She must not quarrel or use harsh language; must avoid extravagance, anger duplicity, pride, secpticism; serve her husband to the best of her ability. Obedience, gentleness and regard for their lords, are the most noted virtues. Hindus have ever understood and appreciated true womanhood.

Duties of a Man

Morning prayer, early bath, worshipping of gods and fire, study of the Veda, looking after household affairs, support of family and dependants; ablutions, prayer to the Sun, offerings to gods, manes, men, spirits, and all living creatures; then, meals, a little rest, then reading Puranas and *itihasa* (history), pious recreation. Again, inspection of worldly affairs; at sunset recite Gayatri or prayer to God; evening meals; looking after domestic affairs; a little Vedic study; rest. Charity to all living creatures and abnegation of self were the very ideal of a pious Hindu life. Some sacrifices were still performed.

Domestic ceremonies or Sanskaras of ten kinds were in vogue from the earliest times. Religion regulates Hindu life, not the beliefs alone.

Men of other creeds do not follow these (ct. the *Vratyas*). Hence, this is the origin of the two-fold basis of Hindustan. To be a true Hindu, 'are like a mirror or a grain of rice. *Dhanya,* a paddy grain when it sprouts, has no rice-grain void of husk. A mirror reflects things but cannot give tangibility. Hence, Hindustan has been ever *living*, Jainism lingering and Buddhism, *dead*.'

There were nineteen domestic ceremonies in the Rationalistic Age. Vyasa (*I, 13–16*) gives 16 fpr *Pauranic* age, viz., conception, security of conception, parting the wife's hair, child's first feeding with solid food, tonsure, piercing the ear, initiation, study of Veda, first clipping of the beard, holy bath, marriage, lighting the martial fire and lighting the three fires. Women and Sudras are allowed the first nine, but without *mantras*.

Sankha names sixteen places of pilgrimage, while Vishnu fifty, from Haridwar to Nilgiri. Brahma, Vishnu, Siva and various other gods are universally accepted.

Beliefs in the transmigration of souls, in different heavens and hells formed a part of religion. References to agriculture, commerce, arts, vices of towns given the state of society. Atri, 219, given a humane rule: 'A pair of bullocks are to work for three hours only.' Yajnavalkya speaks of woolen and cotton fabrics, of skillfully woven fabrics and of fabrics covered with wool, silken stuff, fibrous (*II, 182–83*). He mentions cultivation and manufacture of indigo, joint-stock companies for trade, gives laws against trade guilds raising the value of things unduly. For immediate sale, ten per cent of the profit is allowed on imports and five per cent on home-spun goods (*II, 254, 255, 257*). There were gambling houses in towns under royal guards (*II, 205*). The courtesans of the age, not so degraded creatures like modern harlots, possessed some virtues and received some consideration from the citizens. There were liquor shops for the low. Drinking was a great sin with gentlemen. Education of boys was as year (Yaj., *I 14–50; Vishnu, XXVIII to XXX*). Criminal and civil laws and administration continued as ever. War laws were still humane. Annexation is not recommended (Vishnu, *III, 47*). Laws of inheritance continued to be the same. Rate of interest was the same. For criminal trials ordeals by fire, water, poison are spoken: these were however falling into disuse. Cases were decided by oral and documentary evidence. There were stamps (lekhyas or patras), nirnayas (decree). Truth was held in high esteem (Vishnu, *VIII, 27–30*). Penalties for crimes were as severe as ever. The same inequality prevailed: Brahmans were exempted, while the Sudras were depressed.

Kings had guards, soldiers, learned courts; were luxurious, martial, active and were fond of war and hunting. A fool was a king's boon companion. The king had female guards; he had many wives in stately ladies and pretty maidens of low origin. Jealousies and discords were known in the harem. The chief queen was held in high honour and esteem; she was mistress of the household and sharer of the king's glory on every state occasion. We hear of women's inner apartments. They had a peaceful domestic life. No absolute seclusion is known even in this age. Women wore a veil up to their forehead. They were virtuous and modest. Ladies of the royal household were kept under strict seclusion.

Marriage was arranged by the parents. No courtship was known. Women wore bright garments and rich ornaments. The marriage ceremony was performed at a proper age. The custom of early marriage according to later Dharma Sastras, prevailed; yet it was not universal. The ceremony of marriage was as ever: stepping round the fire, offering of grain as sacrifice, and the utterance of some promises by the bride and the bridegroom were essential rites. Hindu parents usually take various precautions for the happiness of their daughters. Before selecting a suitable bridegroom, they see if the *gana,* i.e. classes of both, agree or not. All men belong to three *ganas*, viz., deva-*gana* (divine class or temperament), *nara-gana* (human class) and *rakshasa-gana* (demoniacal class or disposition). A married pair of like *ganas* has the best constancy. Deva and *Nara ganas* make a middling combination, Deva and *rakshasa* inferior, and *nara* and *rakshasa* are opposed, inimical. Death, or extreme sorrow or lifelong bitter quarrel gall the domestic bliss. A body or girl's *gana* is determined by the *rasi* (sign of the zodiac) and *nakshatra* (constellation) under which he or she is born.

Girls were educated: Women read Sanskrit. Music was often a female accomplishment. Princesses attained great skill in dancing, singing and other accomplishments. Painting was a virtue of both male and female. Nagara Swami was painter-laureate to Vikramaditya (*Katha Sarit Sagara, chapter 122*).

Poems and plays betray tender connubial love: regard and love of husbands and devotion of wives. Professor Wilson observes in his *Hindu Theatre (1871, vol. I, p. 77)*, 'The Hindu writers rarely disparaise their women: they almost invariably represent them as amiable and affectionate.'

Varahamihira, in his *Vrihat Samhita*, gives a very lofty ideal of the female sex. Hindus seldom show ungallant propensitites.

Domestic sorrows and troubles were not wanting. Poverty, loss of friends, contempt of relations, cruelty of husbands, bad temper of wives often made the house unquiet and life a burden. Family dissensions, ill-treatment of mother-in-law and sister-in-law towards a submission of wife, are mentioned in the *Katha Sarit Sagara, Pamchatantra.*

In India, great beauty, especially in women, has been ever regarded as an 'unhappy gift'. Damayanti, Sita, Savitri, Ahalya, Srimati, Tilottama were all 'Queens of Miseries'. So, the wise are directed not to ask a very fair wife (Devi *Purana*, chapter on the entrance to Nanda Kunda).

Courtesans then lived a more intellectual and elevated life. Ambrapali invited Buddha; Aspasia received Socreates in her house. Their courts had a gambling table, books, pictures and other means of recreation. They had pomp and splendour, relieved the needy and the unfortunate, lived in palaces, received a higher regard and attained great accomplishments.

Merchants and bankers were simple folk; they had branch firms all over India; traded in skills, jewels, and valuable goods; lent money to kings in need; practised charity and religion; beautified the towns with fine temples; supported priests, Brahmans and learning; encouraged all good public and relief works.

Skilful artists examined precious gems and jewels; some set rubies in gold; some worked gold ornaments on coloured threads; some string pearls, lapis lazuli; some pierced shells; and some cut corals. Perfumers dried the saffron bags, shook the musk bags, expressed the sandal juice, and compounded the essences.

These would go to the world, were appreciated by Harun-al-Rashid and astonished the great Charlemagne and his barons. The king's guards kept order in the gambling houses—1/5 or 1/10 of the winning was the king's dues (*Agni Purana*). Suvarna was a gold coin. A *Nishka* = 4 Suvarnas. Dinara was adopted from the Romans. *Nanaka* was another coin. *Rupika* (now rupee) a silver coin, mentioned by Chanakya in his *Art of Government*, was probably replaced by the later *tanka*. Low caste people frequented the grog shops. Drinking was common among courtiers and the profligate. Kalidasa speaks of 'ladies' lips scented with liquor.' Ladies of the royal household had their fair share (K S Sagara, *Chapter 110*). The mass of middle, industrial and agricultural classes abstained from drink. Other vices of large towns existed. Loose persons, cut-throats, robbers, thieves, courtiers, and courtesans were not rare. Wealthy men had many retainers, spacious courts, fine buildings, carriages, oxen, horses, elephants, jewellery, aviary, and menagerie. In the eighth court lived the owner of the house in profuse magnificence, with a lovely garden behind the house, which was a delight of the ladies. There were garden houses and villas in the suburbs far away from the city. They had domestic slaves, conveyance, covered litters drawn by oxen, horses, cars drawn by fine ponies.

LEARNING AND EDUCATION

Learning and education were widespread. Every means was adopted by Hindus, Jains and Buddhists for a general diffusion of knowledge. The Sanskrit epics and the Puranas were explained to the lightless masses. The dramatic performances, explanations of new good poems of Kalidasa and others, lent no little aid to the cause of education. Girls were generally taught at home or placed under good women preceptors. The following were prohibited to students: wine, meat, perfumery, garlands, sweetmeat, and women. Students were marked for diligence, self-control, application and obedience. Studentship was residential, education was sound and life useful, loyal and happy.

Taxila was the earliest and the greatest university. Afterwards, Kanouj, Benaras, Ujjain, Mithila, and Magadha became great seats of learning. Nagarjuna (second century AD) not only remodelled Susruta and improved Hindu Chemistry, but also founded a new university at Sridhanyakataka on the River Krishna in Vidarbha (Berar and Nagpur). Both Hindu and Buddhist learning was taught there. The Dapoong University of Tibet was founded on its model. The Buddhist monasteries at Rajagriha, Vaisali, Kapilavastu, Sravasti, Kausambi were great seats of learning. The Jeta-Vana of Sravasti and the Vidyodaya Parivena of Colombo, were the most famed of the monasteries. The next great university was of Nalanda, probably founded in the sixth or seventh century AD. Its famous library called the Ratnadadhi (Sea of Gems) was lodged in a nine-storeyed building. Yuan Chwang studied Buddhist and Sanskrit literature here. About 10,000 pupils of different countries used to read here. Their expenses were met by public charities. Learned Silabhadra, born at Bajrasana (now, Bajrajogini in Vikrampur, dist. Dacca) was the most renowned teacher here. Under the Palas, the Odantapur monastery grew into a university. During Mahipala's regin, 6,000 Buddhist monks and pupils studied there. The Pala library here is said to have been burnt by the Muhammdans.

The *Sakya Vihara* in Tibet was established under its Tartar rulers, on the model of the Odantapur Vihara.

The Vikramasila University was founded in the eighth or early nineth century by Dharmapala, on the Vikramasila hill on the north bank of the Ganges. One hundred and seven other minor monasteries surrounded it. All were walled around. The university had 108 teachers; for 400 years, this residential university was conducted most ably. Jagaddal and Tamluk also were great centres of learning. Besides the universities, there were lots of *tols* for Hindu pupils. Sacred and secular subjects were both taught and learnt.

In India, education divorced from religion, is poison to the people; while, education, subject to religion and morality, is the slave of their lamp. Hindus knew it well, and made their education most useful and successful.

Hindus as Teachers of Medieval Europe

We have already spoken of the Arabic literature and science as a source of European knowledge of India. The Arabs roused Europe from its dull torpor of the Middle Ages. Harun-al-Rashid of happy memory tried his best to make literature and science the permanent denizens of his empire. His son and successor Al Mamun's caliphate introduced the Augustan Age of Islām. Learned men were invited from different countries and paid princely sums for their labours. The best works of Greek, Syrian, Persian and Indian writers, were done into Arabic and spread over the Muslim world. In Spain, the University of Cordova was in no way inferior to Baghdad in literary fame. Muhammadan writers appeared everywhere, preserving and spreading knowledge. The large number of manuscripts on different subjects in the library of the Escorial at Madrid shows the universality of their literary tastes. The fame of their wisdom and learning attracted students from France and other countries of Europe to the Moorish universities of Spain. Hindu philosophy, medicine, literature, folkore, mathematics reached Europe through the Arabs. Arithmetic is called in the old European works, as the *Arithmetic of the Indians*. The nine figures, now known wrongly as 'Arabic numerals' were of Hindu invention and first introduced into Gaul by Gerbert, afterwards Pope Sylvester II who studied at the University of Seville about AD 1000. Bombelli, in a treatise on Algebra published in 1579, says that he and a lecturer at Rome had translated parts, of Diophantus (the earliest Greek writer on Algebra) and that they had found 'many Indian authors cited in the said work' (Hutton's Dictionary quoted by Strachey in his article *History of Algebra* in the *As. Res., XII, p.161*). Thus, Diophantus acknowledged his indebtedness to Hindu mathematicians. Arab writers say that Hindu algebra and astronomy were zealously studied by their countrymen at the court of the Caliphs. The first Arabic mathematician rendered a Hindu work in AD 733. Leonardo of Pisa first introduced Algebra into Europe (AD 1202). He learnt it at Bugia in Barbary where his father was a clerk in the custom house.

The early European works on Algebra followed the Arabic ones in mentioning the Indian sages uniformly in terms of high esteem. One more source of European knowledge about India is the Arab works on geography and travels in India by Sulaiman, Abu Syed, Idrisi, Ebn Haukal, Ibn Batuta, and others.

In medicine, philosophy and metaphysics, Europe is still working on the materials furnished by India. To Greece, India was a land of 'true wisdom and things divine'. Even Lucina (middle of second century AD) concludes his history of Antiphalus and Demetrius by making the latter—a cynical philosopher—give up all his property to his friend and depart for India, there to end his life amongst the Brahmans. There is a striking similarity between the neo-Platonist doctrines and the principles of the Sankhya philosophy. Both Plotinus (AD 204–269) and his renowned disciple Porphyry show strong proofs of their being influenced by Indian philosophy (Professor Macdonell's *History of Sanskrit Literature, p. 421*). Porphyry also speaks highly and sympathetically of the austerities and high moral principles actuating the Brahmans (*On Abstinence from Animal Food*).

European Accounts of India

(1) Strabo (d. AD 26): His geography is a comprehensive work (Mc Crindle). He was a great traveller, but never came to India. He speaks of the entire world, as then known. His Indian account forms a part of whole. He has preserved for us a good deal of the ancient accounts of India. Besides, he gives us a fair idea of the extent of Indian commerce of that time. He says that some 120 ships sailed in his time from Myos Hormos to India (*II, V, 12*). He also speaks of the Black Sea trade (XI, VII, 3). As he speaks of the one mouth of the Ganges, it is plain that he knew little of the eastern parts of India. He speaks of the embassy of Porus, a south Indian king, to Augustus Caesar (*XV, 73*).

(2) Pliny the Elder (first century AD): His *Natural History* contains numerous references to India, some of which are of singular value. With great pains, he gathered together all previous accounts of India to which he added his own discoveries. Yet, he was not free from credulity, so common in that age. He notes the following: many kingdoms of India; the voyages to India in his time; the land of satyrs; men with ears covering them all over; women conceiving at five and living only eight years; the curious animal *monoceros* having a stag's head, elephant's feet, boar's tail and horse's body; 4 cubits long lobsters and 300 ft long eels of the Ganges; Indian plants and trees; minerals and precious stones; ebonym indigo, pepper, ginger and their great demand in Rome. Indian minerals and precious stones were the best of the world; diamond and pearls, beryl, and opal, onyx and jasper, amethyst and carbuncle were held in great esteem by the Romans. India was the great producer of the most costly gems (*Nat. Hist.: VI, 17 VII, 2; VIII, 31; IX, 3; XII, 4; XXXV, 6; XII, 7; XXXVII 1; 6*). The demand for precious stones and gems, especially diamonds and pearls from India, was great and Roman ladies were mad after them.

Pliny is the first to give a regular account of *Tarprobane* (Ceylon), ancient *Tamrabarna*: the ancient Greeks called it *Antichthones* (another world). At the time of Alexander, the Greeks came to know clearly that it was an island. 'A river divides it from India: it is more productive of gold and pearls than India itself' (Megasthenes). Its Sanskrit name,

Ratnadwipa ('the island of gems') justifies it. Its distance from Pataliputra was supposed to have been twenty days' sail, while really it is seven days' sail. The intermediate sea was full of shallows. The sailors steered not by the stars, but by the flight of birds. Diodorus, a contemporary of Pliny, relates that a trader named Iamboulos was driven by a storm from near Arabia to veylon where he stayed for seven years. Iamboulos gives the following points about Ceylon—the perpetual verdure of the trees; the equality of day and night; size of the people and the flexibility of their joints; the length of their ears, broad and pendent; their attachment to the study of astronomy; their worship of the elements especially the sun and the moon; their cotton dress; the prevalence of polyandry (Vincent's *Periplus, pp. 20–24*).

Pliny further speaks of an embassy from a Ceylonese king to the emperor Claudius (AD 41 to 54) for friendship, under the guidance of a Roman freeman who was driven to a port in Ceylon by a storm from near Arabia. From this source, the Romans learnt that the island was rich in gold, silver, pearls, and precious stones, there were no slaves, no courts of law, no litigation. The king was chosen by the people and had thirty counsellors, none of whom could be condemned to death without the vote of the majority. The condemned person might appeal to the people. An unpopular king was condemned to disrespect forever: nobody would talk with him or look at him. The people were very fond of hunting and fishing. Coliachum was the nearest Indian point to Ceylon, being only four days' sail from Ceylon. A big inland lake fed two rivers that watered the whole island

(3) *The Periplus of the Erythrean Sea* (AD 77). *Periplus,* a book on commercial geography, was practically a guide book for mariners, stating trade routes, ports, articles of trade. This particular treatise, written by an experienced sailor, has two parts, the first describing the coast of Africa from Myos Hormos to Rhaphta on the mouth of the Red Sea; the other from Rhaphta to Ceylon sketching the entire seacoast.

The *Periplus* states that Scynthus (Indus) was the greatest river that fell into the sea; only one of its seven mouths was navigable; on the middle mouth lay the great port of Barbarike where ships were unloaded and re-cargoed. Trade was considerable. Here, silk threads, bedellium (a gum), spikenard, sapphires, indigo, cottons, emeralds, and costus (a spice) were exchanged for cloth, coral, glassware, money, wine, frankincense, and topazes (Vincent's *Periplus, II, p. 352*). Next crossing the Gulf of Eirinon (Kutch) the vessels came to the coast of Syrastrene (Kathiawar), rich in grains and cotton. The *Periplus* praises that country for the superior stature of its inhabitants (*ibid., p.356*). Then turning a cape, the ships reached the Gulf of Barygaza (Cambay?) called after a city, some thirty miles from the sea, on the north side of the Namnadios (Narmada). Barygaza, now Broach or Bharoach, ancient Bhrigukachchha, was the chief port of western India.

The mouth of the river was obstructed by the flat shore and many shoals and navigation was difficult by violent and frequent bores. The traders would come to Barygaza where a great fair was held in July. The imports were brass, tin, lead, sashes, white-glass, back-lead, gold and silver coins, wines, topazes, corals, and perfumes in small quantity. The exports were onyx stones (chiefly from Ougein, Ujjain—a great city and the capital of an extensive kingdom), porcelain, fine muslin, cotton in large quantity, spikenard, perfumes, ivory, ebony, myrrh, silk, pepper and precious stones like diamond. The coins of the Bactrian kings, Menander and Apollodotus, were met with at that place (Vincent's Periplus, *II pp. 363–65*).

The country beyond Barygaza was called *Dakinabades* (Sanskrit *Dakshinapath desa*, i.e. the Deccan), containing vast regions, mountains and deserts full of wild animals. In the interior were two great capitals, *Plithana* (Sanskrit Pratisthana) and *Tagara* (?), rather Nagara (not yet identified).

Note: The *Periplus* here fully confirms the Hidu tradions. Ujjain, in the first century BC and AD was the capital of a vast and powerful kingdom under the Sena dynasty.

Gandharva Sena, Vikrama Sena and Madhava Sena ruled there successively. Vikrama is better known as the first great *Vikramaditya* who, trying to conquer the Deccan, is said to have been defeated, or killed or forced to terms by the valiant Prince Salivahana who ascended the Andhra throne about AD 77 or 78. the Narmada was fixed as the boundary between the north and the south. Salivahana left the usual Andhra capital and built a newer one at Pratisthana (now, near modern Hyderabad, on the left bank of the Godavari). Tagara is rather Nagara, perhaps the capital of the Andhras. Salivahana is properly Sala-Satavahana (Sala= Hala, the seventeenth king of the Andhra list).

He is also called *Saka* or *Kumarapala.* Saka means the powerful. Hence his era is called *Sakabda.* The years 58, 57 or 56 BC is generally given as the initial point of the eara of Malwa or the so-called *Vikrama Samvat.* We doubt it. So, the Vikrama Samvat or the Malwan era probably began from AD 5 or 6 and Vikramaditya began to rule after AD 45.

From these southern capitals, goods were carried on wagons to Barygaza. Plithan sent a good deal of onyx stones and Tagara (Nagara), common cotton-cloth, muslin and other articles (Vincent's *Periplus II, p. 473*). The south-ward coast have several ports—Kallien, now Kalyan opposite to Bombay was one of them. The coast abounded with pirates whose chief hunt was the Khersonesus, the peninsula near Goa (*Gomanta* of the *Mahabharata*). Further south lay the three ports of Tyndis, Musiris and Nelkynda. Greek ships from Egypt often visited the prosperous port of Musiris. The imports were pepper, betel and other articles. The exports were chiefly fine silk, pearls, ivory, tortoise-shells, diamonds, rubies, and amethysts (*ibid. p. 415*). The 'Red Hill' here is still known to sailors as the 'Red Cliff' (Yule, quoted by McCrindle). Beyond this point, the Roman sailors learnt everything from reports and had probably no personal experience. The author of the *Periplus* next notices the following: the city of Colchos, in the sea below which pearl-fishery was carried on; Comar—a town in the Cape, having a convent for persons of both sexes who professed celibacy (*p. 441*); Palesimonda (Ceylon) noted for pearls, precious stones, fine linen and tortoise shells; Coromandel Coast—Masalia, a part of the seacoast was noted for the manufacture of very fine cloths and Argalau, an inland city, noted for its manufacture of muslin adorned with small pearls; a land of terrors and prodigies; the gangetic delta where there was a great commercial mart called Ganganagara. Its trade consisted in cloth of the most delicate texture and extreme beauty. Megasthenes referred to it; Chanakya called it 'the white and soft muslin of Banga'. Later on, it became known as the 'muslin of Dacca'. This Ganganagara is also mentioned by Ptolemy (AD 150). Beyond the Ganges was the golden country, the Aurea Chersonesus of Ptolemy.

Note: Of the scholars, Dr Taylor alone has discovered the right locality of Ganganagar. The place, still a rich one, is now known under its bilingual form of *Nagar Kasba* (four miles to the west of Munsiganj, dist. Dacca). It was once the capital of the ancient Hindu kingdom of Banga (East Bengal).

Banga is a forgotten kingdom now. But it has always borne an important part in Indian history. So, we must say a few words on it. In the twenty-nineth century BC Bali, an Aryan king of the north-west India on the Indus, being defeated and driven out by newer Aryans from the north under Vishnu, came down to *Patala,* i.e. lower province (now Bengal) where his five heroic sons, raised in his queen Sudeshna by the blind sage Dirghatama, occupied Anga (Bhagalpur division); Banga (Dacca division); Kalinga (Presidency division); Pundra (Rajasahi division or north Bengal), and Sumha (Burdwan division). As the Aryans pushed on southward, Orissa and a part of Bengal next became Kalinga; afterwards, the eastern seaboard also became Kalinga. These three were sometimes called Tri-Kalinga, when under one rule. Tri-Kalinga corrupted into Telingan or Tailanga. The fame of Banga reached even the Midland. The *Aitareya Brahmana* notices Banga—Bagadha—Cherapada, i.e. Coromandel coast. The *Ramayana* speaks of 'rich and powerful Banga.' The *Mahabharata* mentions Samudrasena and Chandrasena as the lords of Banga. Buddha came to Banga and lived here for seven days in the capital. Pradyota, king of Malwa (sixth century BC) speaks of powerful Banga king. Megasthenes describes its power. There is no knowing how many dynasties ruled in Banga from the earliest times till AD 1328. The Khadga, Chandra, Sur, Varman, Pala, and the Sena dynasties are the latest. About the Christian era, Banga was divided into two parts, viz., Samatata (deltaic part) and Davaka (a greater part of Dacca and Mymensingh districts and eastern parts of north Bengal).

The capitals of Banga, were always in Vikrampur. Parthalis (Sanskrit Prasthali?), Ganganagara, Vikrampur, Rampal were some of the capitals. The *Periplus* states that tej-patra (acasia leaves) grow in abundance in Kiradia (Chitagong division). They are conveyed from Ganganagar to Tamralipta and thence to Europe. A large fair is held annually on the border of this country. Chinese merchants come there and in exchange for their own goods, take *tej-patras* to China. The Greek word *sindon* (cotton fabrics) shows the land of their manufacture. The Latin sericum is from Sanskrit *Chinansukam* (muslin of China). Banga had silk and sericulture early from China.

Dr Taylor says, 'This fair is being held annually in a place near Munsiganj (Dacca) on the river, from the time of Hindu rule. It was formerly called Lakshmi or Laksha Bazar, as none but millionaires could live here by order of the king of Vikrampur. From Ganganagar, corals, chequered cloth, muslin and other fine things were exported to the different countries of the world.' Vikramaraja, an ally of king Ramapala, of Devagram (Dev-gà, now Debhag) built Vikrampur, later Edrakpur, now Munsiganj (Dacca). The Sen kings made Rampal in Vikrampur, their (chief) capital. Sonargao, Nadia and Gaur were their other capitals. The Sens, of the lunar race, came originally from the Carnatic in the Deccan. The Sens king list is—Virasena, Samantasena, Hemantasena, Bijyasena, Ballalsena, Lakshmanasena, Kesavasena, Narayana, Mudhusena, Danujamardana, Bhagavati or Vedasena, and Ballalasena II.

Vijayasena was lord of Gaur, Banga, Kamarupa, and Kalinga. He was unrivalled in east India. His fleet sailed from Vikrampur to Benaras.

Lakshmanasena (AD 1119 to 1119) again wrested Kamarupa from Trailokya Sinha. The Mog king Galaya (1133 to 1153) often attacked east Bengal. Lakshmana drove them out for ever. Kalinga revolted and became free. Lakshmana reconqured it. He conquered Benaras and Gaya and set up pillars of victory there. He conqured Mithila and introduced his era there. In 1146, Govinda Chandra Dev of Kanouj attacked Magadha and advanced as far as Mudgagiri. Lakshmana marched to the frontier and defeated Govinda. At eighty, being surprised by Bakhtiyar (AD 1199), Lakshmana fled to Vikrampur from Nadia. However, a greater part of Bengal gallantly opposed the Muslim power and remained free till AD 1328, when Paragal Khan conqured east Bengal from Ballalasena II. Repeated invasions of the Coch, Ahoms, Tipras, and the Mogs on the one way and the Turkish attacks from the north-west Bengal, at last ruined the last Hindu power of far east India. Islam Khan, the first governor of East Bengal, pulled down the buildings of Ramapala and built Dacca with the materials (AD 1330). Vikrampur fell, as Dacca rose. Vikrampur should be again raised to the status of a district at least.

Aelian's Indian Zoology

The works of Aelian (second century AD) have noticed many Indian animals. He speaks of Indian apes, dogs, tigers, elephants, sheep, goats, winged scorpions and snakes, parrots, cocks and various other beasts. Gladiatorial fights between men and men, beasts and beasts were common. He also notices, inter alia, the physical features of the land. 'The Ganges,' he says, 'has no tributary streams at the source but is enlarged on its march, by other rivers. There are islands in it larger than Lesbos and Kymos' (Aelian, *On the Peculiarities of Animals*, III, xii, McCrindle).

Ptolemy (AD 140 OR 150). His first scientific *Geography* long governed the world's ideas. He connected astronomical observations with mathematical calculations. He gave latitudes and longitudes of places. His work led Columbus to believe that India lay across the Atlantic.

India intra Gangem, i.e. Western India with Afghanistan and Beluchistan, and *India extra Gangem* embraces all south-east Asia to China. He describes the entire coast from the mouth of the Indus to the Gulf of Siam, nothing the most important towns with their latitudes and longitudes. The seven mouths of the Indus, Syrastra (Surat), Monoglosson (Mongrol) in Gujarat, Gulf of Barygaza, mouth of the Namados (Narmada) difficult of navigation owing to terrible bores, Ariake (Maharashtra), Soupara, a town (Solomon's Ophir?) and Byzantein, Sanskrit *Vijayanta,* modern Vijayadanga, the south entrance of the Vaghtan river in ratnagiri (McCrindle). He also describes a few towns—Muziris the great seaport; Bakarei a great emporium; Comar (Comorin) the cape town. Here he errs, placing Comar near Bombay. Next comes Kolkhoic Gulf (Manar) on which was Kolkhoi (Coel) an emporium of pearl trade; Cape Cory. Then comes the coast: the mouth of the Khaberos (Kaveri); seaboard of Maisolia (Maslipatum) noted for the manufacture of finer cotton-fabrics; Orissa coast; four rivers; Manada (Mahanadi); Koonarak (a town) is Konnagara. Ptolemy next describes the Gangetic delta. He mentions its five mouths. His Kambyson is Hugli river. His towns Polura and Tilogramon on the mouths, are probably Jelasor and Jessore. Next he speaks of mountain ranges and the rivers. His Mt Ouidion is Vindhya; Mt Sardonyx, the Satpura Hills, home of the sardonyx stones. His description of the Indus is full, but of the Ganges, meagre. The Diamouna (Yamuna) is given a prominent Place. His Namados is Narmada and Mophis, Mahi. He next describes the different countries and peoples of India classed after the river-basins, with the towns of each: Lobaka (Lavakot, i.e,=Lahore); Sagala — its ruins lie sixty miles from Lahore. Indabara (Indraprastha, i.e. ancient Delhi); Madura (Mathura in the Deccan); Prasiki (Eastern Province); Sambalaka is Sambal in Rohilkhand); Lpmagpra (Kanouj); Abiria is the land of the Abhir Kshatriyas, to the east of the Indus where it divides to form the delta; Syrastrene is Saurashtra, i.e. Gujarat; Barygaza (Bharoach); Ozene (Ujjayini); Nasika; Palimbathara (Pataliputra); Tamalites (Tamluk); the *Gangaridoi* (Gangarashtra) about the mouth of the Ganges with its capital Ganganagar, an important seat of commerce. Modogulla (Mudgol), Pounnata, whence came the beryl and Madura, the Pandya capital of southern India.

His ideas about the trans-Gangetic peninsula are meagre. Most of the places cannot be recognised now. His Pentapolis is probably Chittagong; Malay Peninsula is the Aurea Chersonese. He wrongly thought the Indian Ocean was like the Mediterranean, bound on all sides by land. His account of Ceylon is very accurate and full. Among other things, he notices the long tresses of its men, its produce of rice, honey, ginger, beryl, hyacinth, and mineral wealth. Elephants and tigers abounded. He speaks of the magnetic rock on the south coast of India often attracting ships with iron nails passing near it (Dr Ball's *Economic Geography of India, p. 37*).

Other Classical Writers of India:

(i) Dion Chrysostom (first century AD) refers to the Indian epic—the *Ramayana*.

(ii) Bardesanes (second century AD) Clemens Alexandirnus, Porphyry (third century AD), Stabois (sixth century AD) give curious information about the Brahmans. Alexandrinus refers to the Buddhistic worship of stupas (topes). Dionysios Periegetes (third century AD) in his *Universal Geography* gives some lines on India, done into English verse by Dr Nolan.

(iii) Appollonius of Tyana: His life, written by Philostrates (second century AD) contains many reference to India. He was a Pythagorean and came to India to mix with the Brahmans accompanied by Damis, a learned Assyrian. Their alleged travels are subject to grave suspicion.

(iv) Cosmas (middle of sixth century AD): He was at first a merchant of Alexandria and had visited many lands as far east as India: hence his surname *Indikopleustes* (the Indian Navigator). Afterwards he turned a monk and wrote the *Christian Topography*. He describes some Indian plants and animals and gives an account of Taprobane

(Ceylon), then under two kings. Her foreign trade was considerate: her ports were frequented by merchants from India, China, Persia, Ethiopia. The imports were silks, aloes, clove wood, sandal wood, pepper, copper, sesame wood, material for dress, musk or castor and horses from Persia, free of customs. The Persians had entered into the Indian trade. Cosmas found many Christian churches in Ceylon and southern India.

Indo-European intercourse suffered a good deal from the Saracenic opposition. After the crusades, Rabbi Benjamin of Tudella was the first of the mediaeval travellers to India. A translation of his travelogue is given in Pinkerton's *Collection of Voyages* (*vol. VIII, p. 1*). Sir George Bridwood's *Report on the Old Records of the Indian Office* (second edition) gives an account of the mediaeval travellers to the east. A complete list is given by Lord Curzon in his *Introduction* to *Persia.*

(v) Benjamin set out from Spain in AD 1160. He mentions an island called Nekrokis (Ormuz?) in the Persian Gulf, which had a great trade in Indian goods, especially in silk, purple manufactures, hemp, cotton, flax, cloth, and spices.

Benjamin most probably visited the west coast of India. For, he mentions a place growing immense quantities of pepper and noted for intense heat, where the people were mostly fire-worshippers who exposed their dead to the mercy of the elements. This description reminds us of Malabar noted for its pepper cultivation and the Parsee settlers. Benjamin here repeats the Hindu story of the birth of pearls: at a certain season of the year, there fell from the stars a kind of dew, a drop of which, when sucked in by an oyster, turns into a pearl. Indians believe that water flowing from the star Svati (Areturus) is transformed into pearls in oysters and in the skull of elephants.

(vi) Marco Polo (b. 1250, d. 1324), the *Mediaeval Herodotus*: His travelogue on different parts of Asia from 1271 to 1295, edited by Yule and revised by Cordier (1903), was one of the most famous books in the Middle Ages and created a thrilling interest among the learned men of Europe.

Shortly before his birth, his father and his uncle set out on their eastern travels from Venice, reached the court of Kublai Khan at Xanadu

(Shantu) where they were received with great kindness. After nineteen years of stay here they went back to Venice as envoys of the Khan to the Pope. After two years they set out again with young Marco Polo and came to Ormuz where many merchants brought spices, pearls, precious stones, cloths of gold and silver, elephants, tusks, and other precious things from India. During great heat, the people of Ormuz spent the whole day in water.

The Polos next went to Persia. Then traversing Kerman and Khorasan came to Badakshan where young Polo fell ill and had a long delay here. Polo recovered. They resumed their journey, ascended the Pamir tableland and at last reached the court of Kublai Khan, who loved the young Polo for his intelligent and keen observation. Young Polo here learnt the language of the Mongols. The Khan sent him on diplomatic missions to the neighbouring countries, which increased his knowledge of Asia. After a long residence at Xanadu, the Polos were eager to return home. But the Khan spared them not. The Khan next asked the Polos to safely escort a Mongol princess to Tabreez where she was meant as a bride for a Persian Khan.

The Polos readily agreed, and set out with the Princess in 1292. Travelling through China, the Chinese Sea, the Indian Ocean, the hardly Venetians, after two years of perils, at last safely delivered the bride. After this they returned home in 1295. Three years later, Polo was taken prisoner by the Genoese. In the prison cell, he dictated his travels to a fellow-prisoner named Rusticiano who wrote down the details and afterwards gave them to the public.

Marco Polo noted, among other things, the beauty of Kashmiri women, the notoriety of the men as magicians, the idolatry of the people and the excellent climate. Mission to Annam made Marco know Tibet and Bengal. He noticed the idolatry of the Bengalis, their trade in cotton, their simple food of rice, milk and flesh; the spices, sugar and ginger in their land. He further mentions its notoriety for a trade in eunuchs and slaves, both male and female (Marco Polo, *vol. I, p. 115*). He knew of the islands about India and southern India, during his home voyage. Java was supposed to be the largest island in the world (Marco Polo, *vol. II, p. 272*). Zeiland (Ceylon), the richest island in the world, had the best rubies, sapphires, topazes, and amethysts, plenty of rice, sesame oil, milk and wine trees: he mentioned the sepulcher of Adam or of

Sagomon Barcha (Sakya Muni Buddha). His fore-teeth and a dish were still shown as holy relics (ibid., *vol. II, pp. 317–318*). In India, he described the pearl-fishery of Malabar or the Coromandel Coast (*vol. II, p. 432*), where the people and the king were so many naked savages, yet shining with barbaric pearl and gold (*II, p. 338*). The criminal laws were very severe. Wives threw themselves on the funeral pyre of their husbands (*II, p 340*). The people were superstitious, and believed in sooth-sayers. They were pharisaical in their food and ablutions. They washed twice a day, never used the left hand while eating. Each drank from his own pot without touching the mouth. Drunkenness was detested. Animal food, except beef, was allowed. Only the Gauis ate beef, if the cow had died of itself. They were the descendants of those who had killed St Thomas. Some girls were dedicated for dancing in the temples. To escape from scorpions and fleas, men slept in cane litters high up in the room. The floors were plastered with cow-dung (II, pp. 340 and 346). The tomb of St Thomas was much frequented by both Christians and Saracens. Mutfili (now, Telingana) was then under a queen noted for her love of justice, peace and equity. She was of the Kakatgeya dynasty, with Warangal as her capital. The state had an abundance of diamonds.

Westward from Mutfili was Lar (Malabar?), a home of good many Brahmans who were honest merchants. They never told a lie for all the world and betrayed nobody's trust. They were known by their sacred thread and each had but one wife. They were versed in astrology; practised great moderation and enjoyed long life. They always chewed their *paan* leaves with lime and spices, which they thought good for their teeth and digestion. Some of their ascetics were stark naked: they lived austerely, venerated the cow, believed everything to have a soul, ate no green vegetables, never killed an animal. They highly valued chastity and would not admit a novice who had no self-control.

Cael, a great city, was ruled by a king who was very kind to merchants. In Coulam, 500 miles south-west from Malabar, there were pepper and indigo. Here, the people married their sisters and near relations. In Camari, apes were as large as men and Delai had a great quantity of spices (Marco Polo, *II, p. 386*). Pirates were many in Malabar and Gujarat. Gujarat had abundant cotton, the plants of which grew high and lasted twenty years. Cambay produced much indigo, buckgram and cotton, and Somnath was full of idolators and merchants.

(vii) Marino Sonuto: About AD 1300, this Venetian nobleman set upon his eastern travels. He gives a good account of western commerce with India. The Venetians and other nations of Italy controlled the European side and the Arabs (Moors) the Asiatic side. Goods reached Europe via the Persian Gulf and also the Red Sea.

(viii) Odorico de Pordenone came out on a pilgrimage to the shrine of St Thomas. From Ormuz, he came to Thana near Bombay (1321). Here or at Soupara, he gathered the bones of four missionaries, who had suffered martyrdom shortly before his coming. He speaks of the pepper cultivation of Malabar. From India he went to Sumatra in a Chinese junk. He then visited many other countries and described Tibet and its Grand Lama who was its Pope.

(ix) Sir John Maundeville, as English Knight: He is said to have travelled over a greater part of Asia (1322 to 1345) and written an account of the various countries he claimed to have seen. Some modern scholars hold that the book was really a compilation by a physician of Liege, Jehan de Bourgogne by name who wrote under the *nom de guerre* of Sir John Maundeville, Knight of St Albans in England.

(x) Nicolo Conti (AD 1417): A nobel Venetian travelled in the east for twenty-five years. He left an account of his travels.

(xi) Athanasius Niktin, This Russian gentleman started in 1468, descended the Volga, reached Hormuz, crossed the Indian Ocean to Moshkat, thence to Kuzart (Gujarat) and Kambat (Cambay)—a port of India, manufacturing damask, satin, blankets, indigo. Calicut produced pepper, colour plants, Muscat, cloves, cinnamon, aromatic plants, adrach (ginger), and other spices. He next visited Kulburga, Bidar, bechenagar (Vijayanagar). He was so dazzled by the magnificence of Bidar that he took it for the chief city in india. Vijayanagar was surrounded by three forts and ruled over by a Hindu king who had a large army and a palace built on a hill.

Chinese Accounts of India

The Chinese history of Suma-sien, Etoalin, Pankuo, Wi-lio and others, refer to India from 700 AD downwards. So far, some 45 Chinese Indian travellers are known. The earliest was Chi-tao-an, at the beginning of the fourth century AD. His work is lost.

Fa-Hien (AD 399 to 414) was born in the province of Sansi and became a monk at three. His real name was *Kunga* initiated name Fa-Hien and title Si (one dedicated to Buddha). He never married. He set out for India in AD 399 with several of his companions. After many troubles on the way, he reached India in seven months. His accounts are saturated with Buddhism. His work was done into French by Remusat (1836); into English, by Laidlay in Calcutta (1848). It contains 43 shorts chapters, entirely devoted to Buddhistic details.

Passing through Oigours, Khotan, Kabul, Udyana (Suwat valley), Gandhara, he reached India; he next visited Taxila, Mathura, Sankasya, Kanouj (where he saw the Ganges), Kosala, Sravasti, Kapilavastu, Vaisali, Magadha, Pataliputra, Nalanda, Rajagriha, Gridhrakuta, Gaya; next Benaras, the Deer Park of Sarnath, Kausambi. Then he gives a short chapter on the Deccan, visited some cave temples, probably those of Ellora. From Benaras, he next repaired to Pataliputra where he lived three years studying the language and precepts. Next, he went down the Ganges to Champa and Tamralipta where he passed two years, transcribing the sacred books, and depicting the images. From Tamluk, he sailed to Ceylon in a Bengali ship and lived there for two years. He found Buddhism highly flourishing there, collected several rare books, and paid honour to Buddha's tooth. On the homeward voyage, he visited Java where Hinduism flourished. From Java, he reached China in 82 days. It is notable point that Brahmans in large numbers would go out on sea voyage to Sumatra, Java, Bali, China as passengers and merchants, not afraid of the *Kalapani* (Black waters of the sea)! An Indian named Buddhabhadra, then living in China on mission work helped Fa-Hien much in rendering the Indian works into Chinese. Fa-Hien died at 86.

Hpeo-seng and Sony-Yun (AD 502) lived and travelled only in the Kabul valley and the north-west of India. Their account is very brief.

Yuan Chwang (AD 629 to 645). His work, called the *Siyu-Ki*, gives an account on 138 states of which he himself visited 110. His personal narratives are full and correct, but his statements based on the reports of the Buddhists, are often wrong.

His work is rendered into English by Jullien, in three volumes. Yuan Chwang was an ardent student of Buddhist philosophy. So, he set out for India, while aged only twenty-six, with the object of resolving various doubts and for collecting Buddhist works.

Yuan Chwang compares the shape of India to a half-moon with the diameter on the broad side to the north and the narrow end to the south (Cunningham, *Anc. Geography of India, vol. I*). His idea of the half-noon probably originated from the *Mahabharata's a-krishta dhanurakara,* i.e. shaped like a bow bent. Faki-lo-to says, 'India is broad in the north and narrow in the south.'

His travels. He starts from the north-west end of China, AD 629, passes through the land of the Ougours and Tartar tribes, the states of Okini and Kharashan and stops sixty days for now. Buddhism was prevalent more or less in those countries. He takes one week to cross Mt Ling-Chau (Musur Aola). Here, he loses several of his companions from hunger and cold and many of the beasts of burden. He noticed Buddhism flourishing in Central Asia. After much trouble and toil, he reached India by the Kabul road. The kingdom of Kapisa (now Cabulistan), was then under a Kshatriya king to whom ten others were subject. He found Buddhism prevalent in north-west India. At Peshawar, then under Kapisa, he beheld the ruins of Ashoka and Kanishka. Kashmir was under a Hindu king; Hinduism was prevalent there. At Thanesvar and Mathura, he found both Hinduism and Buddhism flourishing. He wondered at the huge skeletons of the Kashtriya heroes on the plains of Kurukshetra (Karnal). The kingdom of Kanouj was the most powerful and prosperous in India. Harshavardhana Siladitya II was its emperor to whom twenty other great kings bowed their heads. He was a Vaishya Rajput. Pulakesi II was his only great rival in Maharashtra. Harsha, a great patron of learning and religion, equally honoured Siva, Buddha and the Sun. In Oudh, Buddhism was still supreme. The state of Prayag (Allahabad) had little Buddhism. He found Buddhism declining in Avanti. He was sorry at the ruin of Kapilavastu. Brahmanism was well established at Benaras and other towns. Vaisali was in ruins and her convents deserted. In Magadha, fifty monasteries had only 10,000 monks. Besides, there were many Hindu temples. Pataliputra had fallen from her former glory. Its ruins extended over fourteen miles. Next he visited Bodh Gaya from where he was invited to Nalanda near Gaya. The residential university was maintained by Siladitya. Ten thousand Buddhist pupils of eighteen Buddhist sects studied religion, logic, philosophy, physics, mathematics, literature, and medicines here. The pupils resided in four-storeyed buildings. There were hundred lecture halls besides the professors' rooms in the middle. It was located in a garden. Silabhadra, the most distinguished scholar of the times, was the Principal. This learned professor, born of a Brahman Raj family of Vikrampur, east Bengal, was honoured by all for his profound learning, versatile genius, pure conduct and experience. Yuan Chwang was given a hearty reception at Nalanda. Here, he became the pupil of Silabhadra for five years and studied Panini's grammar, Tripitaka and all the Brahmanic sciences. From Nalanda, he went to Bengal, Deccan and central India. Assam under the Brahman Bhaskaravarman, had no Buddhism. Kumara Bhaskara was a friend of Harshavardhana. Tamralipta was a chief port.

Maharashtra was very powerful; here almost half the people were Buddhists. King Pulakesi was brave, generous, and popular. Harasavardhana made an unsuccessful attempt at defeating him.

Yuan Chwang gives curious details regarding the public buildings, the household furniture, dresses, manners, divisions of time and gives minute observations of the four castes. Vaishyas are merchants, Sudras are agricultural labourers. He also mentions numerous mixed castes. He is highly impressed with the truthfulness and honesty of the national character; praises the administration of justice and speaks of four modes of ordeal. He refers to the partition of the produce of the royal lands: the first is for the payment of the state expenses; the second is given as jagirs for the officers of state; the third is given to the learned men; the fourth is given to the Buddhist and Brahmanic sects. Taxes are light; every one has and tills hereditary land, 1/6 of the produce is paid as revenue to the king who advances seed. There are transit duties at the fords of rivers and on highways; there is no forced labour, but every one is obliged to pay reasonable wages. A small army is kept to guard the frontiers and the king's person. The rest is levied in time of need. Governors, ministers, magistrates all receive a certain portion of land to support them by its produce.

Next, he gives details on current literature: five sciences are prominent, viz., grammar, that of arts and trades, medicine, logic, metaphysics. Next he describes the four Vedas. Term of education lasted till the student's thirty years. There are eighteen different philosophical schools, but all are at strife; often very hot discussions ensue. There are special clerks to write down memorable sayings; others to write the narrative of events. The record of annals and royal edicts is called *Nilapita,* the 'Blue Collection'. India is divided into seventy big kingdoms. *The Brahmi lipi* is the writing of Brahma. The primitive text of a million shlokas was called *Vyakarnam* (Grammar)—a mnemonic treatise for the knowledge of sounds. Indra condensed it in 1,00,000 and Panini in 8,000 shlokas. 'They are only stepping-stones through a thousand years of fable' (E B Cowell). Yuan Chwang did actually study the Vedas.

Yuan Chwang found India prosperous. A judicious distribution of lands amongst all classes of people is at the root of a country's welfare. In this respect, England and India are singularly blest from the earliest times. But baneful changes have been brought into India by foreign rule.

Under the British rule, Bengal, Bihar and Orissa alone have the permanent settlement. Even in these parts, cultivators had no right in the lands they ploughed. The government of Lord Ripon first passed the Bengal Tenancy Act in 1885, by which the Bengal peasants have acquired a right (*jot sattva*) in their arable lands. The defects of the Act were remedied afterwards. It is a wonder that people have no right in their homestead lands! They are foreigners to their homes! They cannot excavate tanks and wells, cut down trees they plant, erect buildings unless they purchase *mirash* (an intermediate right) from the taluqdars or zamindars. I have heard complaints from many that these landowners do not grant *mirash* to their permanent settlers, even on the offer of heavy sums. What is this but veiled slavery? What is then tenancy? In all cases of the transference of rights, government gets a certain registration fee only. The settlers of homelands have no right; government gets no share in the sales of lands while the immediate owners—zamindars, or taluqdars or hawaldars—have at least double rights! The lion protects the people, but the lion's shares goes to the fox.

I-Tching (AD 671 to 695) also gives us an interesting account. Some pilgrims came to India in eighth century AD. Khinie visited India in AD 964 with 300 ascetics. But their accounts are of little interest.

Alberuni on India (AD 1030)

Alberuni (Abu Rihan), a learned scholar and mathematician, was born in Khiva, AD 973. Sultan Mahmud of Gazni conquered Khiva in 1017 and Alberuni was his prisoner. He came to India in the train of Sultan

Mahmud, studied Sanskrit and wrote an account of India, nothing on the merits and demerits of the Hindus and their civilisation.

> Mahmud utterly ruined the prosperity of India by his wonderful exploits; Hindus became like atoms of dust. Hence is the Hindu aversion for all Muslims. Hindu sciences have fled from our conquered tracts to Kashmir, Benaras and others places not yet conquered (Alberuni's *Enquiry into India, chapter I*).
>
> Hindus—isolated from other nations—are ignorant of the outside world: to them, all others are *mlechchhas*. They are haughty; their ancestors were not so narrow-minded as the present generation is. (*ibid.*).
>
> India is divided into many petty states. The chiefs are free but often at feud. Kashmir is free. Mahmud could not conquer it. Anangapala is at Delhi; Sindh is under Muslim chiefs; Somnath is under the Rajputs; Malwa is under a Rajput: Bhojadeva, patron of letters, rules at Dhara. Kanouj, capital of Madhyadesa, is under the Pala dynasty. Rajyapala is plundered by Mahmud. His capital is removed to Bari where Mahipala lived. Monghyr is their capital in Bengal. They are Buddhists (*ibid, chapter XVIII*).

Vaishyas—the mass of the people—were fast degenerating to the rank of Sudras (*ibid., chapter IX*). To them religious learning is disallowed; Brahmans teach the Vedas to Kshatriyas. Vaishyas and Sudras are not to hear it (*ibid., chapters XII and LXIV*). The eight *antyaja* castes below the Sudras are the fullers, shoemakers, jugglers, basket and shield-makers, sailors, fishermen, hunters, and weavers. Haris, Doms, and Chandalas are outside all castes (*ibid., chapter IX*).

Parents arrange early marriages of children. Gifts are made to wives (*stridhana*). There is no marriage of widows, nor marriage within the fifth degree no exogamy (*LXIX*). The practice of sati is in vogue (*LXIX*).

Festivals. The year begins in *Chaitra*, about the time of Holi. In *Baisakh* (April–May), the festival is *Gauri Trittiya;* women bathe, worship Gauri, light lamps, offer perfumes, and fast.

Sacrifices are made before ploughing fields. At vernal equinox, Brahmans are fed.

In *Jaistha* (May–June), the frirst fruits are offered for a favourable prognostic. The *Rupa Pancha* festival of women follows.

In *Asharvan,* (June–July), alms-giving and supplying of new vessels to the house is done. In *Sravana,* feasts are given to Brahmans. *Bhadra* is full of celebrations. The Dhruva *Griha* festival is for a pregnant woman to obtain healthy children. In the *Parvati* festival, a thread is offered to the priest. In *Asvina,* sugar cane is cut. In the *Mahanavami* festival, fruits are offered to Durga. *Kartika* is noted for *Diwali* when a great number of lamps are lighted. The Lakshmi .Puja happens after the Durga Puja. *Agrahayana* has a feast for women in honour of Gauri. *Pausha* is celebrated with a variety of dishes. *Magha* comes with a feast for women in honour of Gauri; it has other festivals also. In *Phalguna,* a feast is given to the Brahmans. *Sivaratri* is dedicated to Mahadeo or Siva (*ibid., chapter LXXVI*).

There are numberless idols and temples all over India; numerous pilgrims and devotees. The Sun Temple of Multan is famous. That of Vishnu is at Thanesvar; the wooden idol of Sarada in Kashmir. The Sivalinga of Somnath was destroyed by Mahmud (*ibid., chapter XI*). Pattan itself is a centre of maritime trade and a harbour for sea-faring people (*ibid., chapter LVIII*).

Benaras is the most sacred place; old men go there to die. The holy lakes of Pushkar, Thanesvar, Mathura, Kashmir, and Multan attract vast crowds (*ibid., chapter LXVI*).

Hindus have large and excellent excavated tanks with spacious flights of steps in holy places (*ibid., chapter LXVI*).

Of the Hindu gods, three, viz., Brahma, Vishnu and Siva are principal: they make a triad like the Christian Trinity. The three form one substance (*ibid., chapter VIII*). The wise Hindus believe God to be one Eternal Being. Gods are many only in vulgar belief (*ibid., chapter II*). Hindus believe in the transmigration of souls (*ibid., chapter V*). Marriage ceremony is described in chapter LXIX. A monument is raised where the dead body is burnt (*ibid., chapter LXXIII*). This practice is still found in east Bengal.

Written plaints are generally filed; oral complaints are also entertained. There are different kinds of oath. Decision of cases is made on testimony of witness. The criminal law is extremely mild like the spiriti of Christiantity. A Brahman is never punished with death. Theft is punished according to the value of the stolen property. A Brahman and a Kshatriya thief might be punished with the loss of a hand or foot. An adulterous woman is driven out and banished from the husband's house. Children inherit ancestral property. A daughter gets one-fourth of a share of a son; widows do not inherit, but are supported while they live. Heirs in direct lines inherit. Debt of the dead, devolves on the heir (LXX–LXXI–LXII).

Only Brahmans are exempted from all taxes. The king gets one-sixth of the produce of the fields. Labourers, artisans and trading classes also pay taxes on their income.

Literature: The Vedas are taught orally. Vyasa arranged the Vedas into four groups and taught each to his four disciples. The *Mahabharata* has 18 books, besides the *Harivansa*. The *Ramayana* is full of legends. There are eight grammarians including Panini. Sanskrit has various metres. There are 20 law-books called *Smriti* and 18 Puranas. Hindu astronomy is good. Aryabhatta, Varahamihira, Brahmagupta are great astronomers. They have five *Siddhantas*. Varahamihira (AD 505) is the greatest astronomer and an honest man of science. The following are notable—12 suns of the 12 months named from the lunar constellations, 12 signs of the solar zodiac. Mars, Mercury, Jupiter, Venus and Saturn are the planets (*ibid., chapter XIX*). The law of gravitation is known. Brahmagupta (AD 628) says, ' All heavy things fall to the ground by law of nature. It is the nature of the earth to attract and keep things.' Varahamihira says, 'The earth attracts that which is upon her' (*ibid., chapter XXVI*). Aryabhatta holds, 'The earth *revolves,* the heaven does not turn round as appear to our eyes' (*ibid., chapter XXVI*). Roundness of the earth is known. The circumference of the earth is stated to be 4,800 yojanas (*ibid., chapterXXXIX*). Hindus know the precession of the equinoxes (*ibid., chapter LVI*) and the helaical rising of Canopus. The wisest Hindu is not free from superstition. Their most advanced notions of astronomy are mixed up with silly conceptions and ancient myths.

Hindu geography is almost murdered. Chapter XXI of Alberuni's *Enquiry into India* is quoted from the *Matsya Purana.* The *Vayu Purana* gives a correct geography of India and its neighbourhood (*ibid., chapter XXIX*).

In arithmetical notation, no nation goes beyond the *thousand,* but the Hindus extend the names of the orders to 18th which is called *Paradha* (*ibid., chapter XVI*).

Various scripts are current. The *Siddhamatrika* is current in Kashmir and Benaras. The *Nagara* is used in Malwa. The *Ardha Nagara,* the *Marvari,* the *Sindhava,* the *Karnata,* the *Andhri,* the *Draviri,* the *Gauri* (Bengali) are current in those countries. The writing material are palm leaves, birch leaves in north and central India (*ibid., chapter XVI*).

The medical science is the monopoly of a few. There is much superstition even in it. Hindus also culture Rasayana (chemistry).

Alberuni gives a brief account of the Sankhya and other schools of Hindu philosophy and gives a meagre sketch of Buddhism. He makes no mention of Tantric religion or literature.

INDIAN LIFE AND CHARACTER

Want of unity, intense heat, enervating climate, narrow compass of public activity, spiritual aspirations are some of the causes that have led to the fall of the Hindu nation. The *Pauranic* age has been practically a period of Hindu struggle against foreigners. India has lost her former culture, cultivations, arts, industries, health, wealth but the character of her children has not yet undergone much change, as will appear from the following:

(i) 'They (Indians) are so honest as to neither require locks to their doors nor writing to bind their agreements.' (Strabo).
(ii) 'No Indian was ever known to tell an untruth.' (Arrian).
(iii) 'They are faithful to their promise' Faitu, the ambassador of Chinese emperor Yangte (AD 505?) to India.
(iv) 'With respect to the ordinary people, although they are naturally high-minded, yet they are upright and honourable. In money matters, they are without craft, and in administering justice, they are considerate. They dread the retribution of another state of existence and make light of the things of the present world. They are not deceitful or treacherous in their conduct and are faithful to their oaths and promises.' (Yuan Chwang).
(v) 'I have had before me hundreds of cases in which a man's property, liberty and life, has depended upon his telling a lie and he has refused to tell it.' (Col. Sleeman).
(vi) 'Judged by any truthful standard, the people of India are on a far higher level of morality than an Englishman.' (Sir Lepel Griffin).

(vii) 'Their whole social system postulates an exceptional integrity.' (W C Bennet).

(viii) 'I find among my acquaintances who have long resided in India that after travelling over Europe, they have reason to think more highly of the natives of India.' (Gen. F Briggs).

(ix) 'No set of people among the Hindus are so depraved as the dregs of our great towns. The mass of crime is less in India than in England.' (M Elphinstone).

(x) 'The morality among the higher classes of the Hindus was of a high standard and among the middle and lower classes, remarkably so. There is less of immorality than you would see in many countries in Europe.' (Sir GB Clark).

(xi) 'There is simply no comparison between Englishmen and Hindus with respect to the place occupied by family interests and family affection in their minds. The family in the old sense of the world, still exists in India. In England, it is a very different institution. The romance of Indian life is the romance not of the individual, but of the family.' (Dr W W Hunter).

(xii) 'In statesmanship, unhappily permitted to exist only in the feudatory states, there are few in Europe, Asia and America, to surpass the achievements of Sir Salar Jang the First, Sir T Madhav Rao, Sir K Sheshadri Ayer—to refer only to the departed.')*Prosperous British India)*.

(xiii) 'In education and manners, the Hindu shines far above the European. Without a knowledge of an alphabet the Hindu females are dutiful daughters, faithful wives, tender mothers, and intelligent housewives; such is the result of my own observations.' (Abbe F A Dubios).

COMMERCE AND COLONISATION

During the period under review, Indian commerce, both inland and foreign was brisk. It consisted of the following branches: the Indo-Babylonian; the Indo-Ceylonic; the Indo-Malayan; and the Indo-Chinese. Besides, there were caravan routes from India to Central Asia, China, Persia, and to the Levant. The Chinese writers have recorded a regular Indo-Chinese trade under the embassy system. Indian trade with Egypt continued. The Greeks and the Arabs were foremost in western trade. Before Christ, Alexandria was the chief market of the world. Indian goods were also carried to the shores of the Black Sea and the Caspian Sea across Central Asia along the Oxus. The trade routes once covered Asia like a network. The Romans conquered Egypt in 47 BC and caught the commercial spirit from there. About and after the Christian era, the Roman trade with India was very great. The luxuries of India were in great demand in Rome, in the Roman Empire and among the northern people. Indian perfumes, unguents, pearls, diamonds, ornaments, gems, silk, the muslin of Vikrampur, drove the Romans almost mad. Neither law nor wise counsels could prevail against the Roman craving for the voluptuous products of India. To the evil effects of his indulgence, Gibbon attributes the decline and fall of the Roman Empire. Rome perished in the fifth century AD. The merchants of Syria and Egypt scattered over the Empire the rich products of India. The lucky discovery of the monsoon, soon facilitated Rome's eastern trade. About AD 33, Happalus, a navigator was brought by the monsoon to Muziris in the Malabar Coast in forty days. Finds of Roman coins in and about Coimbatore district and Madurai prove the Roman trade. Southern India supplied Rome with spices, pepper, perfumes, ivory, fine muslin, precious stones, and beryl (Ptolemy, *p. 181*; Pliny, *Natural History, XXXVII, 5*). Roman trade gradually declined. Rome now asked for the articles of necessity and not of luxury. The trade at Alexandria suffered much at the hands of Caracalla. The Palmyrene trade was ruined by the destruction of Palmyra in AD 273. The powerful Sassanids of Persia now monopolised the Indian trade. Roman vessels were driven out of the Indian seas. Constantine weakened the empire by changing the seat of government (AD 330). Alaric seized Rome in AD 410. Attila ravaged her lands in 451. In 454, a huge wave of vandalism swept off her arts. She was again pillaged in 472 and in 476. Now Rome—that *Eternal City,* the mother of arts, civilisation and heroes—stood childless and crownless in her voiceless woe, like another Niobe, all tears.

Constantinople next became a centre of Indian trade which flew in not only through the Oxus and the Caspian, but also along the Red Sea and the Nile. The rise of Islam proved a wet blanket to Indo-European trade which was forced to resume its old and tedious route: goods were carried up the Indus; thence on camels to the banks of the Oxus; thence to the Caspian Sea; thence through Volga and Don, to the Black Sea whence ships carried them to Constantinople.

Rise of Venice and Genona. Venice had been formed in 452 AD on a crowded cluster of islets at the head of the Adriatic. She had begun trading with Alexandria and Constantinople. Genoa had a good position. Her people soon acquired an aptitude for navigation and commerce. She traded with the Levant before Venice. The Arabs having conquered Egypt and Syria, Constantinople became the chief mart. The antipathy between the Muslims and the Christians gradually obated. They now looked to the common interests of gain. Venice and Genoa, two bitter rivals, frequented the markets of Syria and Alexandria. The Crusades removed all barriers to the eastern trade. The Genoese now commanded the entire Black Sea trade. Taking the sanction of the Pope, Venice began to trade with the Muslims at Damascus and Alexandria. Indian goods through the Persian Gulf, passed to Damascus. Alexandria commanded the Red Sea traffic. This share in the wealth of Ormuz and of Ind, the priceless gems of the exhaustless East—made Venice a new Tyre and her people the richest in Europe. Her maritime glories remained intact till AD 1500—the time of the discovery of India by Vasco da Gama.

Commerce took Hindu civilisation and colonists abroad. Sumatra was colonised in 75 BC and Java in AD 78. Bali is still Hindu. The entire Malayan Peninsula was colonised and conqurered by the Hindus. At Loyang (China), 3,000 Buddhist monks and 10,000 Indian families lived to teach religion and arts to the Chinese. There were numberless Indian settlements in Persia, Arabia, West Asia, Socotra, Alexandria, Carthage, Astrakhan (on the Volga), Baku, and on the shores of the Black Sea. India also received many foreign colonies. The Parsis settled in different parts of India, the Jews in Malabar, Ceylon and Chittagong.

Here I come to the end of my short history. Turning to the civilised nations, I may say that the world is indebted to the ancient Hindus for its present store of love and civilisation. The eminent French scholar Creuzer says, 'If there is a country on earth which can justly claim the honour of having been the cradle of the human race or at least the scene of a primitive civilisation, the successive developments of which, carried into all parts of the ancient world and even beyond, the blessings of knowledge which is the second life of man—that country assuredly is India.'

To the Hindus I offer the wise counsel of Professor Max Müeller: 'A people that can feel no pride in the past, in its *history and literature,* loses the mainstay of its national character. When Germany was in the very depth of its political degradation, it turned to its ancient literature and drew hope for the future, from the study of the past.'

BIBLIOGRAPHY

I. RELIGION

1. H H Wilson, *The Religions of India.*
2. Kennedy, *Researches in the Hindu Mythology.*
3. Steele, *Summary of the Laws and Customs of Hindu Castes.*
4. Burnouf, *Buddhism Indian* (1844).
5. Rhys Davids, *Buddhist India,* (1903).
6. Cowell and Rouse (ed.), *The Jataka Tales*, 6 vols. (1895).
7. Edwin Arnold, *The Light of Asia.*
8. Paul Dahlke, *Buddhist Essays,* trans. Bhikshu Sila Cara. (1908).
9. H F Hall, *The Soul of a People* (1905).
10. Beal, *Records of a Buddhistic World.*
11. V A Smith, *Ashoka,* (Rulers of India Series)
12. Hodgson, *Essays on Buddhism.*
13. Alex Csoma Korosi, *Tibetan Buddhist Books* (vol. XX of the *Asiatic Researches*).
14. Rev. S Beal, *Buddhism in China.*
15. Bigandet, *Life of Gautama* (1868).
16. *The Sacred Teaching of the Three Treasures.*

Note: Most important portions of the Buddhist Scriptures, taken to Ceylon by Mahendra in 242 BC have been translated by Turnour, Fausboll, Childers, Oldenberg, Spence Hardy, Rhys Davids, Max Müller, Weber, and others.

II. PHILOSOPHY

1. Davis, *Hindu Philosophy*.
2. Max Müller, *Hindu Philosophy*.
3. Wilson, *Sankhya Karika*.
4. Ballantyne, *Sankhya Pravachana* or *Sutra*.
5. Davies, *Sankhya Karika*.
6. Fitz-Edward Hall, *Sankhya Sara*.
7. Rajendra Lal Mitra, *Yoga Sutra* or *Yoganusa Sana*.
8. Gough, *Hindu Logic*.
9. Dr Banerji, *Dialogues* on *Hindu Philosophy*.
10. Monier-Williams, *Indian Wisdom*.
11. Colebrooke, *Philosophy of the Hindus*.
12. Enfield, *History of Philosophy*.
13. Stanley, *History of Philosophy*.

III. LITERATURE

1. Rosen, *Rig Veda* (trans.).
2. Ludwig, *Rig Veda* (trans.).
3. H H Wilson, E B Cowell, W F Webster, *Rig Veda Samhita* (trans.).
4. Z A Ragozin, *Vedic India*.
5. Weber, *Indian Literature*.
6. Roth, *Indian Literature*.
7. Max Müeller, *Ancient Sanskrit Literature*.
8. Max Müeller, *Sacred Books of the East* (50 vols.)
9. Macdonell, *History of Sanskrit Literature* (1900).
10. Raja Rammohan Roy, *Chief Upanishadas* (trans.)
11. Max Müeller, *Chief Upanishadas* (trans.)
12. C V Vaidya, *Epic India* (*Ramayana* and *Mahabharata*).
13. T Wheeler, *Ramayana of Valmiki* (done into English prose).
14. M N Dutt, *Ramayana of Valmiki* (done into English prose).
15. R T Griffith, *Ramayana of Valmiki* (done into English verse).
16. R C Dutt, *Ramayana of Valmiki* (done into English verse).
17. R C Dutt, *Mahabharata* (done into English verse).
18. Pratap Chandra Roy, *Mahabharata* (done into prose), Calcutta 1893–1896.
19. Manmathanath Dutt, *Mahabharata* (done into prose).

20. T Wheeler, *Mahabharata* (done into prose).
21. F S Growse, *Ramayana of Tulsidasa* (done into English).
22. Dean Milan, *Nala and Damayanti* (trans.).
23. K T Telang, *Bhagavat Gita* (rendered by), Oxford.
24. Edwin Arnold, *Bhagavat Gita* (rendered by).
25. V G Tilak, *Bhagavat Gita* (rendered by).
26. A. Besant, *Bhagavat Gita* (rendered by).
27. C Wilkins, *Bhagavat Gita* (rendered by).
28. W Jones, *Institutes of Manu*.
29. Buhler, *Institutes of Manu*.
30. Dr Jolly, *Institutes of Vishnu*.
31. Upham, *Sacred and Historical Works of Ceylon*.
32. Turnour, *Mahawansa*.
33. Wilson, *Vishnu Purana*.
34. Wilson, *Theatre of the Hindus*.
35. Wilson's *Other Works*, 12. vols.
36. S M Mitra, *Anglo-Indian Studies*.
37. A B Keith, *The Vedic Akhyana and the Indian Drama*.
38. E P Horrwitz, *The Indian Theatre*.
39. M Bath's, *Review of Leri's Theatre*.
40. Pischel's *Home of the Puppet* (trans. By Mrs Vyvyan).
41. *Drama in Encyclopaedia Britannica*, 11th edition.
42. Muir, *Original Sanskrit Texts*.
43. Fraser, *The Goldern Bough*.
44. Miss Harrison, *Themis*.
45. *Annals of Oriental Literature*.

Note: Some *Brahmana* works have been edited in Europe.

IV. LANGUAGE

1. G A Grierson, *The Linguistic Survey of India and the Languages of India*.
2. John Beams, *The Languages of India*.
3. Cardwell, *Dravidian Languages*.
4. Max Müeller, *Science of Language*.
5. Sayce, *Science of Language*.
6. Goldstucker, *Panini*.
7. Ballantyne, *Laghu Kaumudi*.

V. ARCHAEOLOGY

1. *Archaeological Survey Reports.*
2. *Epigraphica Indica.*
3. *Corpus Inscriptionum Indicarum.*
4. Dr Burnell, *Palaeography of the Deccan.*
5. Taylor, *History of Alphabets.*
6. Keilhorn, *Epigraphy of North India.*
7. Fleet, *Catalogue of Gupta Inscriptions.*
8. Luther, *Epigraphy of Brahmi Inscriptions.*
9. L Rice, *Epigraphy.*
10. Cunningham, *Ashokan Edicts.*
11. Rapson, *Indian Coins.*
12. Cunningham, *Coins of Ancient and Mediaeval India.*
13. Von Sollett, *Coins of Greek and Scythian Kings of Bactria and India.*
14. V A Smith, *Gupta Coinage.*
15. Allen, *Catalogue of Gupta Coins.*

VI. JOURNALS

1. *Journal of the Asiatic Society*, Bengal.
2. *Journal of the Asiatic Society*, Ceylon Branch.
3. *Journal of the Royal Asiatic Society*, London.
4. *The Indian Antiquary,* Bombay.
5. *The Vedic Magazine,* Panjab.
6. Punjab Historical Society's Journal.
7. Colebrooke, *Asiatic Researches.*
8. Heeren, *Asiatic Researches.*
9. Sterling, *Asiatic Researches.*
10. Col. Wilford, *Asiatic Researches.*
11. Blaquire, *Asiatic Researches.*
12. Capt. Moore, *Asiatic Researches.*
13. Capt. Mahony, *Asiatic Researches.*
14. Davis, *Asiatic Researches.*
15. Bentley, *Asiatic Researches.*
16. W Jones, *Asiatic Researches.*
17. The Oriental Magazine.
18. Hodgson, *Transactions of the Royal Society.*

19. Ellis, *Transactions of the Royal Society.*
20. Davis, *Transactions of the Royal Soçiety.*
21. Knox, *Transactions of the Royal Society.*
22. Major de la Maine, *Transactions of the Royal Society.*
23. *The Edinburg Review*, vol. XXIX.
24. Bishop Heber, *Journal.*
25. Coat, *Bombay Transactions.*
26. Erskine, *Bombay Transactions.*
27. A Remusat, *Journal,* (1831).
28. Wilson, *Mackenzie Collection.*
29. Lassen's *Works.*
30. Wilson, *Collected Works,* (12 vols.).
31. *The Encyclopaedia Britannica,* (11th edition).
32. Wilson, *Oxford Lectures.*
33. Colebrooke, *Hindu Courts of Judicature.*
34. Colebrooke, *Digest.*
35. Works by *W. Jones.*
36. Cowell, *Tagore Law Lectures.*
37. Morley, *Digest.*
38. Max Müeller, *Lectures.*
39. Prinsep, *Useful Tables.*
40. De Guignes, *Memoirs.*
41. Growse, *Memoirs of Muttra.*
42. Colebrooke's *Essays.*
43. Prinsep's *Essays.*
44. Calcutta *Review.*

VII. ARTS

1. George Birdwood, *The Industrial Arts of India.*
2. W Jones and Paterson, *Hindu Music.*

VIII. ARCHITECTURE

1. Ram Raz, *Essay on Hindu Architecture.*
2. Works of the Daniells on Caves, Temples &c. of India.
3. Fergusson, *Eastern and Indian Architecture.*
4. V A Smith, *Architecture in India and Ceylon.*

5. E B Havell, *Hindu Architecture* (1913).
6. O C Ganguli and Coomarswami, *Architecture.*
7. Cunningham, *Indian Architecture.*

IX. HISTORY

1. Historians' *History of the World* (London).
2. *The Unrivalled History of the World* (America).
3. *The Imperial Gazetteer of India,* New Edition, 1909 London I–IV vols.
4. Thornton, *British Empire in India* (1859).
5. Thornton, *History of India.*
6. Elphinstone, *History of India.*
7. Havell, *Aryan Rule in India.*
8. Mc Crindle, *Ancient India as Described by Megasthenes and Arrian.*
9. Mc Crindle, *Ancient India as Described by Ktesias.*
10. Mc Crindle, *Ancient India as Described by Ptolemy.*
11. Mc Crindle, *Ancient India as Described by Classical Authors.*
12. Mc Crindle, *Ancient India as Described by Classical Authors.*
13. Robertson, *Disquisition on Ancient India* (1972).
14. Robertson, *History of America.*
15. Nolan, *British Empire in India and the East,* London, 1857.
16. Gibbon, *Decline and Fall of the Roman Empire.*
17. V A Smith, *Ashoka* (Rulers of India Series).
18. V A Smith, *Early History of India.*
19. V A Smith, *Early History of the Deccan.*
20. Heeren, *Historical Researches, Asiatic Nations.*
21. Max Müeller, *Chips from a German Workshop.*
22. The Old Testament.
23. The New Testament.
24. G M Rae, *Syrian Church in India* (1892).
25. Elliot, *History of India.*
26. Orme, *Indostan.*
27. Orme, *History of South India.*
28. George Birdwood's Report on the 'Old Records of the India Office'. London, 1891.
29. C W King, *Gnostics and their Remains.* London, 1857.
30. Mill, *History of British India.*
31. Fraser, *Hisotry of British India.*

32. History of Mysore.
33. Ward, *Hindoos.*
34. Col. Tod, *Annals and Antiquities of Rajasthan, 2 vols.*
35. John Malcolm, *Central India.*
36. Henry Maine, *Village Communities in the East and West.*
37. Buchanan's Journey through Mysore.
38. Wilson, *History of Kashmir.*
39. J C Dutt, *History of Kashmir.*
40. Stein, *History of Kashmir.*
41. Turner, *Tibbet.*
42. Hugh Murray, *British India.*
43. Buchanan, *Hindu Geneologies.*
44. Pope, *Iliad.*
45. V G Tilak, *Arctic Home in the Vedas.*
46. K M Banerji, *Aryan Witness.*
47. Pococke, *India in Greece.*
48. Herodotus.
49. Horace, *Odes.*
50. Horace, *Epistles* (Lonsdale and Lee's translation).
51. Arrian, *Anabasis.*
52. W W Hunter, *Brief History of the Indian People.*
53. W W Hunter, *Imperial Gazetteer of India. Calcutta.*
54. W W Hunter, *Indian Empire.*
55. Kingsley, *Hypatia.*
56. Pliny, *Natural History.*
57. Wright, *Celt Roman and Saxons.*
58. Max Müeller, *India and What it Can Teach Us.*
59. Virgil, *Georgics.*
60. Virgil, *AEneid.*
61. Thomas Brown, *Hydrotaphia.*
62. Chronicle of the Kings of England.
63. Ben Jonson, *Alchemist.*
64. *The Ecclesiastical History.*
65. M Taylor, *History of India.*
66. Vincent, *Periplus of the Erythrean Sea* (1800).
67. Vincent, *Commerce and Navigation of the Ancients.*
68. Arrian, *Indika.*
69. Marsden, *History of India.*
70. Marsden, *Marco Polo.*
71. Henry Yule, *Marco Polo revised by Cordier,* 1903.

72. Aelian, *Peculiarities of Animals.*
73. Mc Crindle, Porphyry: *'On Abstinence from Animal Food.'*
74. Pottinger, *Travels.*
75. Rules of India Series, 28 vols.
76. Allen, *History of the Punjab,* 1856.
77. Forbes, *Hindu Annals of Gujarat,* 1856.
78. C Bayley, *History of Gujarat.*
79. J Douglas, *Bombay and Western India,* 1893.
80. Bhandarkar, *History of Western India.*
81. Ranade, *Early History of the Deccan.*
82. A Lyall, *Asiatic Studies,* 1899.
83. Duff, *Chronology of India.*
84. Duff, *History of the Mahrattas,* 1893.
85. Col. Sleeman, *Rambles and Recollections,* 2 vols.
86. E A Gait, *History of Assam,* 1906.
87. W Lee-Warner, *Native States of India,* 1910.
88. *The Calcutta Review:* First 50 vols. 1873.
89. *Gazetters of India*—Provincial and District: Calcutta, Bombay and Madras.
90. H G Keene, *History of India,* New Ed, 2 vols. 1906.
91. Marshman, *History of India,* 3 vol. 1867.
92. Wheeler, *Short History of India,* 1899.
93. R C Dutt, *History of Civilisation in Ancient India.*
94. R C Dutt, *History of Ancient and Modern India.*
95. De La Fosse, *History of India.*
96. R W Frazer, *Literary History of India,* 1898.
97. Mrs Manning, *Ancient and Mediaeval India,* 1869.
98. *Bombay Gazette,* part I., vols. I, II.
99. L Rice, *Mysore and Coorg from the Inscriptions.*
100. Cunningham, *Ancient Geography of India.*
101. Blochmann and Jarrat, *Aini-i-Akbari.*
102. Brigg, *Ferishta.*
103. Stewart, *History of Bengal,* 18013.
104. Ghulam Hussain Khan, *Seir Mutaqherin,* 3 vols. 1789.
105. V Ball, *Tavernier's Travels.*
106. A Constable, *Bernier's Travels.*
107. D F Karaka, *History of the Parsis,* 2. vols. 1884.
108. R Sewell, *Vijayanagara:* A Forgotten Empire, 1900.
109. Lord Curzon, *Persia and the Persian Question* (Introduction).
110. Benoy Kumar Sarkar, *Hindu Positive Sciences.*

111. Brojendra Nath Seal, *The Positive Sciences of the Hindus.*
112. H P Sastri, *History of India.*
113. R D Banerji, *History of Bengal.*
114. R K Mukherji, *Hindu Ship-Building and Maritime Activity.*
115. H C Chakladar, *Indo-Chinese Relations* (Dawn magazine).
116. Justice Pargiter, *Dynasties of the Kali Yuga.*
117. John Woodroffe, *'Is India Civilized?'*
118. Hoernle, *History of India.*
119. J M Roy, *History of Dacca.*
120. P C Roy, *History of Hindu Chemistry,* 2 vols. 1902.
121. Ball, *Economic Geology of India.*
122. Playfair, *History of Hindu Astronomy.*
123. Cassini, *History of Hindu Astronomy.*
124. Bailly, *History of Hindu Astronomy.*
125. Bentley, *History of Hindu Astronomy.*
126. Prof Joges Chandra Roy, *History of Hindu Astronomy.*
127. Dr Royle's Essay on the Antiquity of Hindu Medicine.
128. Hindu Medical Science by HH The Thakur Sahib of Gondal. Macmillan & Co.
129. Burgess, *Surya Siddhanta.*
130. Strachey, *Bija Ganita.*
131. Colebrooke, *Indian Algebra.*
132. Kern, *Vrihad Samhita.*
133. R L Mitra, *Indo-Aryans.*
134. R L Mitra's other works.
135. *The Voyage and Travels of Sir John Maundeville.*1866; re-issue of Halliwell's edition.
136. P C Ghosh, *India as known to Ancient and Mediaeval Europe,* Calcutta. 1905.
137. Fa-Hian, *Travels in India.*
138. Yuan Chwang, *Siyuki.*
139. I T-ching, *Travels in India.*
140. Whitney, *Historical Researches.*
141. Alberuni, *Enquiry into India.*
142. Chanakya, *Art of Government.*
143. Stein, *Ancient Khotan.*
144. Taylor, *Origin of the Aryans.*
145. The Census Reports.
146. Schlegel, *History of Literature.*
147. Haug, *Essays on the Parsees.*

148. B Hamilton, *Hindustan*.
149. Bombay Sanskrit Series.
150. P K Roy's paper on 'Hindu and Greek Philosophy'.

INDEX